WORD
BIBLICAL
COMMENTARY

General Editors
David A. Hubbard
Glenn W. Barker

Old Testament Editor
John D. W. Watts

New Testament Editor
Ralph P. Martin

WORD
BIBLICAL
COMMENTARY

VOLUME 5

Numbers

PHILIP J. BUDD

THOMAS NELSON PUBLISHERS

Nashville

Word Biblical Commentary:
NUMBERS
Copyright © 1984 by Word, Incorporated

Library of Congress Cataloging in Publication Data
Main entry under title:

Word biblical commentary.

  Includes bibliographies.
  1. Bible—Commentaries—Collected works.
BS491.2.W67   220.7'7   81–71768
ISBN 0–8499–0204–5 (v. 5) AACR2

Printed in Colombia

4 5 6 7 8 9 QWG 9 8 7 6 5 4

To
Janet
with love and gratitude

Contents

Author's Preface

This commentary is a product of extended reflection on the problems associated with the origins, exegesis, and interpretation of the Pentateuch. It builds on earlier researches into priesthood, and into the murmuring motif as exhibited primarily in the books of Exodus and Numbers.

The commentary is, of course, far from definitive. Such a state is impossible in a situation where too many pieces of the jigsaw are missing, where too much remains tantalizingly unknown. Nor is it desirable in a situation where the Word of God has to be rediscovered by each generation. What can be reasonably claimed is that this book gathers together some of the relevant scholarly discussion pertaining to the book of Numbers, and that in certain respects it offers new ways of arranging the pieces, of looking at the background of the book, and at the possibilities of interpretation.

I am grateful to my parents, Harry and Mildred, who first introduced me to the Old Testament, and to teachers and examiners who over the years have offered help and encouragement, among them Professor Douglas Jones of Durham University who prompted my first attempts at research. I am also grateful to the editor, John Watts, for keeping my nose to the grindstone and to Word Books for the opportunity of putting my ideas into print. My wife Janet has provided the loving support and sympathy essential to any such enterprise.

PHILIP J. BUDD

Oxford, February 1983

Editorial Preface

The launching of the *Word Biblical Commentary* brings to fulfillment an enterprise of several years' planning. The publishers and the members of the editorial board met in 1977 to explore the possibility of a new commentary on the books of the Bible that would incorporate several distinctive features. Prospective readers of these volumes are entitled to know what such features were intended to be; whether the aims of the commentary have been fully achieved time alone will tell.

First, we have tried to cast a wide net to include as contributors a number of scholars from around the world who not only share our aims, but are in the main engaged in the ministry of teaching in university, college and seminary. They represent a rich diversity of denominational allegiance. The broad stance of our contributors can rightly be called evangelical, and this term is to be understood in its positive, historic sense of a commitment to scripture as divine revelation, and to the truth and power of the Christian gospel.

Then, the commentaries in our series are all commissioned and written for the purpose of inclusion in the *Word Biblical Commentary*. Unlike several of our distinguished counterparts in the field of commentary writing, there are no translated works, originally written in a non-English language. Also, our commentators were asked to prepare their own rendering of the original biblical text and to use those languages as the basis of their own comments and exegesis. What may be claimed as distinctive with this series is that it is based on the biblical languages, yet it seeks to make the technical and scholarly approach to a theological understanding of scripture understandable by—and useful to—the fledgling student, the working minister as well as to colleagues in the guild of professional scholars and teachers.

Finally, a word must be said about the format of the series. The layout in clearly defined sections has been consciously devised to assist readers at different levels. Those wishing to learn about the textual witnesses on which the translation is offered are invited to consult the section headed "Notes." If the readers' concern is with the state of modern scholarship on any given portion of scripture, then they should turn to the sections on "Bibliography" and "Form/Structure/Setting." For a clear exposition of the passage's meaning and its relevance to the ongoing biblical revelation, the "Comment" and concluding "Explanation" are designed expressly to meet that need. There is therefore something for everyone who may pick up and use these volumes.

If these aims come anywhere near realization, the intention of the editors will have been met, and the labor of our team of contributors rewarded.

General Editors: *David A. Hubbard*
Glenn W. Barker
Old Testament: *John D. W. Watts*
New Testament: *Ralph P. Martin*

Abbreviations

AASOR	Annual of the American Schools of Oriental Research
ADAJ	Annual of the Department of Antiquities of Jordan
AfO	*Archiv für Orientforschung*
AJSL	*American Journal of Semitic Languages and Literature*
AJT	*American Journal of Theology*
AOAT	Alte Orient und Altes Testament
ASTI	*Annual of the Swedish Theological Institute*
ATANT	Abhandlungen zur Theologie des Alten und Neuen Testaments
ATD	Das Alte Testament Deutsch
AusBR	*Australian Biblical Review*
BA	*Biblical Archeologist*
BASOR	*Bulletin of the American Schools of Oriental Research*
BBB	Bonner Biblische Beiträge
BDB	F. Brown, S. R. Driver, and C. A. Briggs. *Hebrew and English Lexicon of the Old Testament.* Oxford: Clarendon Press, 1966.
BHS	*Biblia Hebraica Stuttgartensia.* ed. K. Elliger & W. Rudolph. Stuttgart: Deutsche Bibelstiftung, 1967/77.
Bib	*Biblica*
BIES	*Bulletin of the Israel Exploration Society*
BK	*Bibel und Kirche*
BKAT	Biblische Kommentar: Altes Testament
BR	*Biblical Research*
BTB	*Biblical Theology Bulletin*
BWANT	Beiträge zur Wissenschaft zum Alten und Neuen Testament
BZ	*Biblische Zeitschrift*
BZAW	Beihefte zur ZAW
CBC/NEB	Cambridge Bible Commentary on the New English Bible
CBQ	*Catholic Biblical Quarterly*
EvT	*Evangelische Theologie*
ExpTim	*Expository Times*
FRLANT	Forschungen zur Religion und Literatur des Alten und Neuen Testaments

GKC	*Gesenius' Hebrew Grammar.* ed. E. Kautzsch. Tr. A. E. Cowley. Oxford: Clarenden Press, 1910.
HAT	Handbuch zum Alten Testament
HKAT	Handkommentar zum Alten Testament
HUCA	*Hebrew Union College Annual*
ICC	International Critical Commentary
IDB	*Interpreter's Dictionary of the Bible.* ed. G. A. Buttrick. Nashville/New York: Abingdon Press, 1962.
IDBSup	Supplementary volume to *IDB*, 1976.
IEJ	*Israel Exploration Journal*
Int	*Interpretation*
JAOS	*Journal of the American Oriental Society*
JB	*Jerusalem Bible*
JBL	*Journal of Biblical Literature*
JNES	*Journal of Near Eastern Studies*
JPOS	*Journal of the Palestine Oriental Society*
JQR	*Jewish Quarterly Review*
JSOT	*Journal for the Study of the Old Testament*
JSS	*Journal of Semitic Studies*
JTS	*Journal of Theological Studies*
KAT	Kommentar zum Alten Testament
KB	L. Koehler & W. Baumgartner. *Lexicon in Veteris Testamenti Libros.* Leiden: E. J. Brill, 1958.
KJV	*King James Version*
NCB	*New Century Bible*
NEB	*New English Bible*
OTL	Old Testament Library
OTS	*Oudtestamentische Studiën*
PEFQS	*Palestine Exploration Fund Quarterly Statement*
PEQ	*Palestine Exploration Quarterly*
RB	*Revue Biblique*
RevQ	*Revue de Qumran*
RSV	Revised Standard Version
RV	Revised Version
SB	Sources Bibliques
SCM	Student Christian Movement
SEÅ	Svensk exegetisk årsbok
Sem	*Semitica*
SJT	*Scottish Journal of Theology*
SOTSMS	Society for Old Testament Study Monograph Series

SPCK	Society for the Propagation of Christian Knowledge
TB	*Tyndale Bulletin*
TBT	*The Bible Today*
TLZ	*Theologische Literaturzeitung*
TPQ	*Theologische-Praktische Quartalschrift*
TZ	*Theologische Zeitschrift*
UF	*Ugaritische Forschungen*
VT	*Vetus Testamentum*
VTSup	*Vetus Testamentum Supplements*
WMANT	Wissenschaftliche Monographien zum Alten und Neuen Testaments
ZAW	*Zeitschrift für die alttestamentliche Wissenschaft*
ZDPV	*Zeitschrift des Deutschen Palästina-Vereins*
ZTK	*Zeitschrift für Theologie und Kirche*

Translations and Versions

Aq	Aquila
G	The Septuagint
MT	The Masoretic Text
Q	Qumran Literature
Syr	The Syriac (Peshitta)
Sam	The Samaritan Pentateuch
Sym	Symmachus
Tg	The Targums
	T^O Targum Onqelos
	T^J Targum Pseudo-Jonathan
	T^N Targum Neofiti I
Vet Lat	The Old Latin
Vg	The Vulgate

The version of the Septuagint used is *Septuaginta.* ed. A. Rahlfs. Stuttgart: Württembergische Bibelanstalt Stuttgart, 1935.

Biblical chapter and verse references relate to the MT, unless otherwise indicated.

Alternate numbering given with the Scripture translation is that of the English versions.

Main Bibliography

Commentaries and Analyses

Addis, W. E. *The Documents of the Hexateuch.* London: D. Nutt, 1892. **Bacon, B. W.** *The Triple Tradition of the Exodus.* Hartford: Student Publishing Co., 1894. **Baentsch, B.** *Exodus, Leviticus, Numeri.* HKAT 2. Göttingen: Vandenhoeck & Ruprecht, 1903. **Binns, L. E.** *The Book of Numbers.* London: Methuen, 1927. **Carpenter, J. E.** and **Harford-Battersby, G.** *The Hexateuch.* London: Longmans, Green, & Co., 1902. **Dillmann, A.** *Numeri, Deuteronomium, und Josua.* Leipzig: Hirzel, 1886. **Eissfeldt, O.** *Hexateuch-Synopse. Die Erzählung der fünf Bücher Mose und des Buches Josua mit dem Anfange des Richterbuches.* Darmstadt: Wissenschaftliche Buchgesellschaft, 1962. **Gray, G. B.** *A Critical and Exegetical Commentary on Numbers.* ICC. Edinburgh: T. & T. Clark, 1903. **Gressmann, H.** *Mose und seine Zeit. Kommentar zu den Mose-Sagen.* Göttingen: Vandenhoeck & Ruprecht, 1913. **Heinisch, P.** *Das Buch Numeri.* Bonn: Hanstein, 1936. **Holzinger, H.** *Numeri.* KHAT 4. Tübingen & Leipzig: Mohr, 1903. **Jones, K. E.** *The Book of Numbers.* Grand Rapids, Baker, 1972. **Kuenen, A.** *A Historico-Critical Enquiry into the Origin and Composition of the Hexateuch.* Tr. P. H. Wickstead. London: Macmillan, 1886. **McNeile, A. H.** *The Book of Numbers.* Cambridge: Cambridge University Press, 1911. **Morris, P. M. K.** and **Jones, E.** *A Critical Wordbook of Leviticus, Numbers, Deuteronomy.* The Computer Bible 8. Wooster, Ohio/Missoula, MT: Biblical Research Associates/Scholars Press, 1975. **Noth, M.** *Numbers. A Commentary.* OTL. Tr. J. D. Martin. London: SCM Press, 1968. **Paterson, J. A.** *The Book of Numbers.* Leipzig: Hinrichs'sche, 1900. **Rudolph, W.** "Zum Text des Buches Numeri." *ZAW* 52 (1934) 113–20. ———. *Der "Elohist" von Exodus bis Josua.* BZAW 68. Berlin: A. Töpelmann, 1938. **Simpson, C. A.** *The Early Traditions of Israel.* Oxford: B. H. Blackwell, 1948. **Snaith, N. H.** *Leviticus and Numbers.* NCB. London: Nelson, 1967. **Sturdy, J.** *Numbers.* CBC/NEB. Cambridge: Cambridge University Press, 1972. **Vaulx, J. de.** *Les Nombres.* SB. Paris: J. Gabalda, 1972. **Wellhausen, J.** *Die Composition des Hexateuchs und der historischen Bücher des Alten Testaments.* Berlin: Reimer, 1889. **Wenham, G. J.** *Numbers.* London: Tyndale Press, 1982.

Other Books and Articles

Coats, G. W. *Rebellion in the Wilderness.* Nashville: Abingdon Press, 1968. **Cross, F. M.** *Canaanite Myth and Hebrew Epic.* Cambridge MT: Harvard University Press, 1973. **Eerdmans, B. D.** "The Composition of Numbers." *OTS* 6 (1949) 101–216. **Eissfeldt, O.** *The Old Testament. An Introduction.* Tr. P. R. Ackroyd. Oxford: B. H. Blackwell, 1965. **Fohrer, G.** *Introduction to the Old Testament.* Tr. D. Green. London: SPCK, 1970. **Fritz, V.** *Israel in der Wüste. Traditionsgeschichtliche Untersuchung der Wüstenüberlieferung des Jahwisten.* Marburg: N. G. Elwert Verlag, 1970. **Gottwald, N. K.** *The Tribes of Yahweh. A Sociology of the Religion of Liberated Israel, 1250–1050 B.C.E.* London: SCM Press, 1980. **Hayes, J. H.** and **Miller, J. M.** (eds.) *Israelite and Judaean History.* OTL. London: SCM Press, 1977. **Hyatt, J. P.** *Exodus.* NCB. London: Oliphants, 1971. **Jenks, A. W.** *The Elohist and North Israelite Traditions.* Missoula, MT: Scholars Press, 1977. **Mowinckel, S.** *Tetrateuch-Pentateuch-Hexateuch. Die Berichte über die Landnahme in den drei altisraelitischen Geschichtswerken.* BZAW 90. Berlin: A. Töpelmann, 1964. **Noth, M.** *Exodus.* OTL. Tr. J. S. Bowden. London: SCM Press, 1962. ———. *A History of Pentateuchal Traditions.* Tr. B. W. Anderson. Englewood Cliffs, NJ: Prentice-Hall, 1972. **Sandys-Wunsch, J.** *The Purpose of the Book of Numbers in Relation to the Rest of the Pentateuch and Post-Exilic Judaism.* Oxford University: Dissertation, 1961. **Vaux, R. de.** *Ancient Israel. Its Life and Institutions.* Tr. J. McHugh. London: Darton, Longman, & Todd, 1961. **Vink, J. G.** "The Date and Origin of the Priestly Code in the Old Testament." *The Priestly Code and Seven Other Studies.* Ed. P. A. H. de Boer. Leiden: E. J. Brill, 1969.

Introduction

Contents

The title of the book comes from the Septuagint and Vulgate, and probably refers in the first instance to the census with which it begins (1:20–46). There are other calculations in the book which give the title a degree of appropriateness—some further censuses in 3:15–31; 26:5–51, enumerations of offerings in 7:10–83; 28–29, and of booty in 31:32–52. The Hebrew title is "In the Wilderness" and is perhaps to be preferred. There are three important geographical references which help both to shape the structure of the book, and also serve to move Israel from Sinai to the borders of Canaan. These are the wilderness of Sinai (1:1), the wilderness of Paran (10:12), and the plains of Moab (22:1; 36:13). The fact that the book contains law and history of the wilderness period, pre-dating the occupation of the land, is very important to the author/editor. One of his chief concerns is to establish principles of attitude and behavior which are a precondition of possession and enjoyment of the land. His work is on the whole well ordered, and falls into three major sections:

A. Constituting the community at Sinai (1:1–9:14)
B. The journey—its setbacks and success (9:15–25:18)
C. Final preparations for settlement (26:1–35:34)

The final chapter (36:1–13) appears to be an appendix, supplementing the information of 27:1–11.

A. *Constituting the Community at Sinai* (1:1–9:14)
The section begins with an exploration of the dimensions of the community (1:1–46), and proceeds to a description of its character as a priestly theocracy (2:1–34). The inner structure of the priestly hierarchy, already hinted at in 1:47–54, is analyzed in detail in 3:1–4:49. Some of the rights and responsibilities of the sons of Aaron in the community are set out in 5:1–6:27. An indication of the commitment of the community to the theocracy is evident in 7:1–88. In 7:89–8:26 the Levitical order is purified for its newly defined sphere of service within the community, and further information about the observation of Passover, the community's foundational rite, follows in 9:1–14.

B. *The Journey—Its Setbacks and Success* (9:15–25:18)
This section begins with discussion of the means of guidance—the cloud and the trumpets (9:15–10:10)—and then describes the order of movement and the departure from Sinai (10:11–36). It next explores various issues associated with the principle of Mosaic leadership and authority (11:1–12:16), as a preliminary to the account of three major setbacks experienced during the course of the journey. The first is the sin of the community in failing to

believe the faithful spies (13:1–14:45). In the material following there is a renewed commitment to the land, and additional stress on the need for obedience (15:1–41). The second setback is the sin of the Levites, and its aftermath (16:1–17:28). This is followed by a renewed commitment to the Levitical order (18:1–19:22). The third setback is the sin of Moses and Aaron (20:1–13, 22–29). These setbacks do not prevent ultimate progress (20:14–21; 21:1–35). Enemies both external (22:1–24:25) and internal (25:1–5), are defeated, and priestly leadership, as embodied in Phinehas, ultimately justifies itself (25:6–18).

C. *Final Preparations for Settlement* (26:1–36:13)

This section puts the setbacks of the past behind, beginning with the reconstitution of the community, measuring its dimensions again, and raising the question of the division of the land (26:1–65). The right of women to inherit land is discussed (27:1–11) (and again in an appendix [36:1–13]), and a renewed commitment to a Mosaic succession follows with the selection of Joshua (27:12–23). A calendar and pattern of daily observances for use in the land is set out (28:1–29:40), and the status of female vows discussed (30:1–16). In 31:1–54 the community, through the spoils of war, renews its commitment to the priestly theocracy, and the commitment of all to the settlement of the land is tested in 32:1–42. This crucial point in Israel's history warrants a review of the journey through the wilderness (33:1–49), and this is followed by indication of how the land is to be divided, and of its boundaries (33:50–34:29). The concluding sections take up the themes of Levitical possessions in the land (35:1–8), and of the handling of the question of refuge in cases of homicide in the land.

Redaction

There is no doubt that in some sense the book of Numbers is part of a larger literary whole. It continues a story already begun in the books of Genesis, Exodus, and Leviticus, and a story which requires for its completion some attention at the very least to the story of the death of Moses in Deut 34:1–12 and the settlement in the book of Joshua. It is widely held that all of these six books are in their present form the product of a priestly school of writers, working in the sixth and/or fifth centuries B.C. In some (e.g. Deuteronomy) the influence is slight. In others (e.g. Leviticus) it is massive. The criteria by which the influence is perceived are stylistic, linguistic, conceptual, and ideological, and are best set out in such works of classical criticism as S. R. Driver's *Introduction to the Literature of the Old Testament* (Edinburgh: Clark, 1913, 9th ed.) and *The Composition of the Hexateuch* (London: Longmans, Green, 1902) by J. E. Carpenter and G. Harford-Battersby. The confidence of these earlier analysts is not often shared by more recent investigators, particularly in matters of detail, but there remains a very wide measure of agreement as to the identity and extent of the priestly material (P). In the book of Numbers there is very general acceptance of a total priestly contribution in the following chapters—1–9, 15, 17–19, 26–31, 33–36—and of a substantial influence in

10, 13–14, 16, 20, 25, 32. The only chapters lacking such influence would appear to be 11–12, 21–24.

The reasons for tracing P to the exilic or early post-exilic periods are also accessible in the works of classical criticism cited above. The most sustained assault on this position has come from a succession of Jewish scholars— see particularly Y. Kaufmann, *The Religion of Israel* (London: Allen & Unwin, 1961), M. Weinfeld, *Deuteronomy and the Deuteronomic School* (Oxford: Clarendon, 1972), and M. Haran, *Temples and Temple Service in Ancient Israel* (Oxford: Clarendon, 1978). These scholars are inclined to argue for the priority of P over Deuteronomy (D), and for its pre-exilic origin. An attempt has been made to support an early view of P on linguistic grounds—see A. Hurvitz, "Evidence of Language in Dating the Priestly Code; a Linguistic Study in Technical Idioms and Terminology," *RB* 81 (1974) 24–56. Since those who give P a late date recognize within it some codification of pre-exilic practice, and since Haran, for example, recognizes that P was not a significant factor in Jewish life until the time of Ezra, the argument is not as polarized as may be supposed. The main problems attaching to the acceptance of a significant and recognizable pre-exilic version of P have to do with the relationship between Pentateuchal legislation and that contained in Ezek 40–48 (which at all points appears to be the earlier), the difficulty of demonstrating beyond reasonable doubt that D was familiar with P, and the difficulty of finding an exclusively Aaronite priesthood, as required by P, before post-exilic times. This third point is not a weak argument from silence since there are many texts, even as late as Malachi (the first half of the fifth century B.C.), where some allusion to the priesthood of the sons of Aaron is positively to be expected had that been the normative position.

The view adopted here is that as recognizable entities the priestly revisions of tradition belong essentially with that influential movement in Judaism which originated in Babylon in exilic times, and which effected a resettlement in Palestine from the late sixth century onward. The revisions provide both an apologia for this group of Jews, and also some programmatic proposals for the restoration. Ezek 40–48 (and perhaps other elements in that book), and Lev 17–26 (the so-called Holiness Code) are among the earliest responses of this group to the fact of exile and to the possibility of restoration, and it may be better to date the priestly traditions to the latter part of the fifth century. The book of Malachi does not appear to reflect them, and they may have some association with the mission of Ezra. They appear to provide for Israel's early traditions what the Chronicler was later to do for the deuteronomic history and the period of the monarchy to make a major revision reflecting the concerns and point of view of what may be termed "Babylonian Judaism."

Does the book of Numbers have any individuality and integrity as a unit within this process of revision? A typical view is that offered by O. Eissfeldt (*The Old Testament. An Introduction* [Oxford: Blackwell, 1965] 156–57) who suggests that though there are meaningful divisions between the various books of the Pentateuch these divisions are essentially secondary, deriving from a desire to divide the whole literary complex into five manageable and approximately equal parts. There are some signs, however, that the book of Numbers is not necessarily an artificial creation. At the very least the possibility that it was constructed as a unit, albeit as one in a closely connected series of books, deserves closer consideration that it usually receives. There is no *a priori* objection to the possibility, and there is every reason to suppose that problems of handling and manageability were there from the outset. The massive scope of the priestly revision made certain of that. It is clearly impossible to determine how the whole enterprise was planned and put into effect, and in the last resort the question cannot be resolved with any degree of certainty, but there are distinctive features and emphases in the book of Numbers, the significance of which deserves attention.

As the discussion of *Contents* has revealed, the book is by no means as disordered and incoherent as is sometimes claimed. Though there is room for disagreement about where the various components begin and end there is a basic threefold structure, covering the progress from Sinai to the borders of the land, and proceeding in a disciplined and ordered fashion. In points of detail there are few totally inexplicable connections between the various sections (see *Commentary*). The exploration of the shape and character of the community (1:1–9:14), and the description of the journey with its various sins (9:15–25:18), both proceed with some pattern and purpose. The problem of coherence is most acute in the third major section (26:1–35:34), but as the *Commentary* shows, many of the apparently disconnected items handled there embody themes in which Numbers wishes to develop or interpret the teaching of Deuteronomy. This in itself gives a degree of coherence to the material. That it should come at this point, on the plains of Moab and before the great farewell discourse in Deuteronomy, is entirely appropriate.

The two outstanding religious contributions in the book of Numbers concern the Levitical order and the Tent of Meeting. Both are handled in a distinctive fashion as compared with Exodus and Leviticus, the two preceding books which have been subject to priestly revision. The existence of a separate and subordinate order of Levites is hinted at in Exod 38:21–31, but this section is arguably supplemental. It presupposes the appointment of Ithamar as the head of the Levites, an appointment not made until Num 4:28, 33. Elsewhere in Exodus it seems perfectly proper to describe Aaron as a Levite, and to think of Levites generally as priests (Exod 4:14; 6:16–25; 32:25–29). The significant contribution made by Numbers is the description of Levites as a subordinate order, and the discussion of their relationship to the priests proper—the sons of Aaron. The distinction is formulated in the first major section of the book (1:47–54; 3:1–4:49), is pursued in the second (16:1–18:32), and is returned to at the end of the third (35:1–8). In a massive re-interpretation of tradition the author/editor adapts the distinction between Zadokites and degraded Levites, as made in Ezek 40–48, and constructs a hierarchy with the sons of Aaron at its head and with Levites occupying a subordinate but dignified position.

As for the Tent of Meeting the book of Numbers makes a major contribution in centralizing it. In Exodus the external position for the Tent appears to be accepted, as advocated in earlier tradition (Exod 33:7–11). To earlier contributors in the priestly school this may have had a particular attraction, symbolizing the authenticity of the way of faith sustained by the exiles at a distance from the land itself. To the author/editor of Numbers, working in the context of an assured restoration under Nehemiah and Ezra, the centralization of the Tent of Meeting, within the camp, carried its own appropriate meaning.

There are also a number of minor features which may suggest that Numbers is a distinct and in some degree independent production. The explanation for the altar covering (17:1–5) differs from that given in Exod 38:2, and the author/editor gives his own adaptation of the traditional story of water at Meribah (20:1–13; cf. Exod 17:1–17). The Levitical genealogy given in 26:57–60 does not deviate significantly from the more detailed picture in Exod 6:16–25, but the need for repetition may be a witness to a degree of independence. The use of money for purposes of redemption is another distinctive feature of Numbers within the priestly traditions as a whole (3:44–51; 18:14–18; cf. Exod 13:13; 34:20).

These observations, of course, are not conclusive. There are other theories about the growth of the priestly literature which might explain the phenomena in question. On the other hand they do fit in with the view that the book has a degree of independence and integrity as a unit. Even if its independence is judged to be secondary it is not entirely artificial as a unit, and it deserves consideration and interpretation as such.

Sources

To what extent is the book of Numbers an editing of existing material? To what extent is it a new production by an author? The view that the book had from the outset a degree of independence carries with it the assumption that "authorship" is in some measure an appropriate idea. The further question must be asked as to whether the author had substantial entities of tradition at hand which he incorporated and left virtually unaltered.

The Priestly Material

G. von Rad (*Die Priesterschrift im Hexateuch.* BWANT 4/13. Stuttgart: Kohlhammer Verlag, 1934) attempted to disentangle parallel threads of law and narrative in P. The basis of this approach was effectively criticized by P. Humbert ("Die literarische Zweiheit des Priester-Codex in der Genesis," *ZAW* 58 [1940/41] 30–57), and it has hitherto been customary to view the structure of P in terms of a coherent base text (PG), and supplementary elements of varied vintage (PS). It has proved very difficult, however, to reach widespread agreement on the identity and extent of PG. M. Noth (*A History of Pentateuchal Traditions* [Englewood Cliffs: Prentice Hall, 1972] 8–19) argued for a view of PG as essentially narrative, while others find the link between "law" and "narrative" to be inseparable or too close to justify such an assessment (cf. e.g. G. Fohrer, *Introduction to the Old Testament* [London: SPCK, 1970] 182–83). Noth also opposed the classical view that PG is well represented in the book of Joshua. For him it is angled, not toward the settlement, but toward Sinai. Among those who maintain the more traditional view are S. Mowinckel (*Tetrateuch-Pentateuch-Hexateuch: Die Berichte uber die Landnahme in den drei altisraelitischen Geschichtswerken* [BZAW 90; Berlin: Töpelmann, 1964]) and J. G. Vink ("The Date and Origin of the Priestly Code in the Old Testament" [*The*

Priestly Code and Seven Other Studies ed. P. A. H. de Boer. Leiden: Brill, 1969]). Whatever choice is adopted it remains notably difficult to identify with confidence and precision a coherent PG narrative. Form criticism can sometimes make tenable suggestions about the origin and growth of the literature (see e.g. R. Rendtorff, *Die Gesetze in der Priesterschrift.* Göttingen: Vandenhoeck & Ruprecht, 1954; K. Koch, *Die Priesterschrift von Exodus 25 bis Leviticus 16, eine über-lieferungsgeschichtliche und literarkritische Untersuchung.* FRLANT 71. Göttingen: Vandenhoeck & Ruprecht, 1959), but offers little in the way of confident conclusions about the identity and extent of PG.

Difficulties do not of course negate the validity and appropriateness of an enquiry, but they may very well invite alternative approaches—in this instance to the nature of P as a whole. The view that P is in some sense "midrashic commentary" deserves attention—see e.g. R. H. Pfeiffer, *Introduction to the Old Testament* (London: Black, 1952) 207; F. M. Cross, "The Priestly Tabernacle," *Old Testament Issues* (ed. S. Sandmel. London: SCM, 1969) 39–67. There are certainly points at which P interprets earlier tradition, but if it were merely "commentary" it would be unlikely to exhibit the degree of coherence and completeness which it often does. M. Noth (*Pentateuchal Traditions,* 11–17) concludes from this that the earlier material has been edited into and used to enrich an already complete and coherent narrative, namely PG. The difficulty with Noth's view is that the "fragmentariness" of the earlier material depends on the units of tradition chosen for study. In the Abraham traditions, for example, P is much more likely to be an interpretative accretion than a component of PG. It seems best to evaluate P as a fresh presentation of tradition, incorporating older material and in places interpretative comment, but providing a distinctive theological structure. There are signs of this even in Genesis where P is at its briefest. It may be that the Chronicler's work provides a proper analogy. He evidently uses earlier tradition from the books of Samuel and Kings, and draws material from other sources, but it scarcely seems necessary to posit a base narrative (CG?) comparable to the proposed PG. To reject PG, and to see Numbers as a unit in an overall program of revision, does not of course preclude the possibility of minor supplementation, as for example in Exod 38:21–31 and Num 36:1–13.

The Yahwistic Material

The nonpriestly material is found in Num 11–12, 21–24, and in parts of Num 10, 13–14, 16, 20, 25–32. It is widely recognized that this is part of a wider complex of narrative and legal traditions, traceable in all essentials to the pre-exilic period. It is sometimes designated JE, reflecting the "Yahwistic" (J) and "Elohistic" (E) blocks of tradition which are often held to be its major components. The works of classical criticism previously cited indicate certain stylistic criteria by which JE as a whole can be distinguished from the other major literary influences in the Pentateuch—D (Deuteronomy) and P. Similar criteria, on a smaller scale, are used for distinguishing J from E. It is true that the meticulous division of verses or half verses into various documents has been widely abandoned, but general acceptance of where the earlier tradition is to be found in Numbers still exists.

There is still discussion about the overall extent, nature, and date of the early tradition, and in some respects issues are more open than hitherto. There have been recent suggestions that the tradition lacks an overall theological coherence, and that investigation would more profitably proceed on the basis of the "larger units" (e.g. the patriarchal stories) than on the basis of the usual source strata—see especially R. Rendtorff, *Der überlieferungsgeschichtliche Problem des Pentateuch* (BZAW 147. Berlin: Töpelmann, 1977). This approach arguably undervalues the threads of inner coherence in the sources revealed by such as P. Ellis (*The Yahwist. The Bible's First Theologian.* London: Chapman, 1969) and H. W. Wolff ("The Kerygma of the Yahwist," *Int* 20 [1966] 131–58), and is also inclined to ignore the more important stylistic phenomena isolated by earlier critics. On the other hand it is unwise to suppose it possible, or methodologically necessary, to attribute all the early material to either J or E. Greater weight must be given to the possibility that the tradition is a compendium of materials from a variety of sources. There must obviously have been some point at which this material was forged into a pre-settlement "history" of Israel, a compendium of traditional material and the author's own contributions. It seems reasonable to describe this author/editor as "the Yahwist," and his work as JE, if only to indicate the dominant components in its varied background.

It has been supposed that this work culminated in the story of the triumphs of the Davidic empire. For a recent exposition of this theory see H. Schulte, *Die Entstehung der Geschichtsschreibung im alten Israel* (BZAW 128. Berlin: Töpelmann, 1972) 203–24. Most analysts, however, have found it hard to attribute much extant material beyond the Hexateuch to JE. The supposition that the story reaches its goal in some account of the settlement remains a reasonable one. The inner movement of the traditions seems to require some climax which brings Israel into Canaan, and for this it seems best to look to the book of Joshua. The covenant making of Josh 24:1–28, though influenced by Deuteronomy in its present form, is perhaps a more probable climax than the fragmentary settlement traditions of Judg 1:1–36. It shows Israel with a firm foothold in central Palestine, and renewing the Sinaitic commitments in the new context.

Attempts to identify the larger strata within the Yahwist's work are bound to be provisional. It is reasonable to suppose that from relatively early times there were stories celebrating in prose some of the main themes of the story. Though the debate is still an open one there are grounds for suspecting the presence of a distinct "Elohistic" tradition—see J. F. Craghan, "The Elohist in Recent Literature," *BTB* 7 (1977) 23–35 and A. W. Jenks, *The Elohist and North Israelite Traditions* (Missoula, MT: Scholars Press, 1977). Whether this was a genuinely independent source of information for the Yahwist, or whether it represents an interpretative growth from within the tradition, remains difficult to judge. In any event the attribution of texts in Numbers to E is an uncertain enterprise. Arguments for a "lay" source (L) (O. Eissfeldt, *The Old Testament. An Introduction* [Oxford: Blackwell, 1965] 189–204), a "nomadic" source (N) (G. Fohrer, *Introduction to the Old Testament* [London: SPCK, 1970] 146–65), or for J1/J2 distinctions (see e.g. C. A. Simpson, *The Early Traditions of Israel* [Oxford: Blackwell, 1948]) remain highly conjectural. Eissfeldt and Fohrer have not convincingly shown that the material isolated by them constitutes coherent and independent strands of narrative, while the fragmentation of the text which is a constant feature of Simpson's work becomes all the more hypothetical the more it is pursued.

The date and provenance of this earlier tradition is difficult to determine. The earliest dating widely proposed for any of its major components is the period of the united monarchy. Classical analysis was more inclined to assign both J and E components to the separate kingdoms, during the divided monarchy. Recent protagonists for a major exilic contribution to the tradition have not been lacking. It is usually recognized that much of the data cited in this debate is scarcely strong as evidence, and it seems very likely that there is material of varied age—within the pre-exilic period—preserved within the tradition. There must however have been a point at which the Yahwist gave the tradition something of its essential present shape and content. Many of the arguments for a Solomonic date are indecisive, while the historical allusion in Gen 27:40 better fits the events of 2 Kgs 8:20–22 (c. 850 B.C.) than those of 1 Kgs 11:14. On the other hand it is true that the tradition is permeated with a strong sense of national identity and unity, and it may be that the Yahwist's essential work of editing and authorship should be traced to those periods after the fall of the northern kingdom when Judaean kings, notably Josiah (2 Kgs 23:15–20, 29–30), exercised significant control in the north. Perhaps the components of Israel's history had been given their earliest verbal form in the celebrations of worship. Earlier written records (proto-J? and E) were used by the Yahwist, and forged into the present history. This is above all an etiology of an Israel in possession of the land, and readily fits the circumstances of Josiah's time. In the ordering of the patriarchal narratives it affirms that Israel's possession of the land is not an accident of history but the fruit of a divine promise. The Joseph story in particular is an impressive reminder of what the ancestor of the northern tribes, Ephraim and Manasseh, was able to achieve, even in adversity in a foreign land. The traditions of escape from Egypt bear witness to the spirit of confident independence which was a mark of the times, and are an implicit criticism of those who still sought security in alliances with Egypt. Above all, the tradition of covenant-making at Sinai and Shechem bears witness to the need for new commitment (cf. 2 Kgs 23:3). Only so can the settlement and possession of the land under Yahweh be secured. In Numbers the Yahwist's main contribution is the exploration of Mosaic authority (Num 11–12)—important to the Josianic concept of a Mosaic book of the law, the bringing together of traditions of settlement from the south and the east (Num 13–14), and the incorporation of the confident oracles of Balaam (Num 22–24). The shadow of the fall of Samaria remained in the background, and its causes had to be properly understood (Exod 32:1–35; Num 25:1–5).

Such a view of the Yahwist's work can only be a tenable perspective, but it deserves serious consideration. The Yahwist may have been one of the court faction which was able to shape the early years of Josiah's reign (2 Kgs 21:24; 22:1), and to influence its course throughout. His emphasis on the principles of Mosaic leadership and of a Mosaic mediation of Sinaitic law prepared the way for the idea of Mosaic authority—the foundation of the first edition of Deuteronomy, and the main stimulus to the reformation of 621 B.C.

Religious Contribution

The book of Numbers makes a major contribution in several areas.

1. It presents an understanding of Israel, the people of God, as a community on the march. It has yet to reach its goal, but the journey has begun (10:11–36). The author is offering here a major theological development of a theme already present in the earlier Yahwistic tradition. The life of the community is organized around the Tent of Meeting (2:1–34), the centrality of which bears witness to the presence of God *within* and *among* the community. God is thus the focal point of the community, and the center from which it draws its resources. The people of God are dependent at all points on the continuing guidance of God (10:11–12, 35–36), and must be ready to listen to his directives regarding their future patterns of life (3:1–6:27; 18:1–19:22; 27:1–11; 28:1–30:16; 35:1–36:13). The community must not only understand the style of life which under God is its goal, but must also be wholly dedicated in its self-giving (7:1–88; 31:1–54). Only so can the inheritance be possessed and secured (32:1–34:29).

2. The book also reveals the goal of Israel's journey as land. The obviousness of the point must not lead to its neglect. The earlier tradition traces in detail the course which leads to land, at times a tortuous one (13:1–14:45; 21:1–25:5), and it presents a community well able to reach its goal (32:1–42). This too is integral to the wider content and structure of the book, as formulated by the author. The details of the settlement are not integral to his purpose; the preconditions for a successful occupation are. Thus land, the access to the resources which it secures, is seen to be fundamental to the divine intention. The cardinal sin of the community is rejection of the land (14:1–38), and other acts which in various ways constitute a failure to accept the scope of the divine intention lead to exclusions from the land and its resources, even at the highest level (16:1–17:26; 20:1–13; 21:4–9; 25:1–18).

3. The book also offers a major exploration of the nature of authority in the journeying community. The earlier tradition embedded in Num 11:1–14:45; 16:1–35 examined the theme of Mosaic leadership, asserting recognition of it as a fundamental priority. This naturally carried with it the idea of Mosaic authority, and that in turn is presented in the book as a whole as requiring a major priestly component in the hierarchical patterns of leadership and authority. The successor of Moses himself retains a significant function (27:12–23), but there is also a major area of responsibility presided over by the sons of Aaron, and their assistants the Levites. The various dimensions of authority are thus analyzed, and a more sophisticated structure of priestly authority is established in order to secure the community's need for stability.

4. The book also examines the nature and consequences of the rejection of authority in the community. This theme was also present in the earlier tradition in the stories of Israel's disaffection during the journey (11:1–12:16; 16:12–15; 21:4–9). There the patterns of rebellion are essentially a rejection

of Mosaic leadership, and the policy Moses pursued to secure the land. The preference expressed is for the experience of captivity in Egypt. The theme is amplified by the author in the book as a whole with separate studies of the rebellion of the people (Num 14:1–38), the rebellion of the Levites (Num 16:1–35), and the rebellion of the leadership (Num 20:1–13). All three are presented as ways of death, leading ultimately to loss of land. There is a despising of land as "evil." There is self-assertiveness on the part of the Levites. There is failure to respect the holiness of Yahweh on the part of Moses and Aaron.

From a universalistic perspective the book offers an insight into the divine purpose for man at large—access to land and its resources. This remains as yet an ideal, but the author offers ideas which may be a fundamental precondition for its realization, and explores the patterns of human behavior which may in the short term frustrate it.

Numbers and History

Our investigations have proceeded on the assumption that the book of Numbers is a complex accumulation of tradition, and not a simple factual account of Israel's journey from Sinai to the border of the land. This assumption is rooted in the findings of literary and historical criticism, and has been shown to be justified at every stage of the enquiry. The book of Numbers lacks many of the essential data that the modern historian requires—a clear witness to the use of sources close to or contemporary with the period described, in the form of annals, chronicles, inscriptions, and a firm backbone of dates which can be worked in with the known history of the second half of the second millenium B.C. The question must necessarily be raised as to what value if any the book has to the historian of the second millenium. In general the prospects are not very promising. The book appears to lack the kind of information the historian of the second millenium requires.

These observations should not be taken to mean that the book is of no interest to the historian. The point is rather that the search for history has to be undertaken with care, that it cannot be assumed to be present at all points, and that results must necessarily be tentative and provisional. It is obvious enough that at the core of the tradition is a historical fact—the presence of Israel in the land of Canaan—and that the book of Numbers is part of a larger explanation of that fact. The difficult question for the modern historian to determine is how much of that "explanation" can help him understand the particular patterns of cause and effect in human affairs which interest him.

It seems proper that the historian should begin with the inescapable historical core—the presence of Israel in the land of Canaan—and the associated fact that that presence begins at some point in the latter part of the second millenium B.C. and the beginning of the first. It has become customary, in view of the paucity of secure historical evidence about Israel's origins, to discuss the processes of settlement in terms of models, and to identify the model which the historian believes best fits the available evidence, from within the OT and without. N. K. Gottwald (*The Tribes of Yahweh*, 191–233) identifies three such models—those of conquest, immigration, and revolt. J. Maxwell Miller (*Israelite and Judaean History*, 264–79) notes five—pan-Israelite exodus and invasion, independent migrations and settlement by separate tribal groups, gradual penetration in search of pasturage, forced entry, and internal revolt. However many are identified they are not always mutually exclusive. Each has strengths and weaknesses, and a sophisticated account of Israel's origins may have to allow for elements from all the models. Even so some may have had a greater potential for refinement, and one may be more fundamentally accurate than others.

It is impossible and inappropriate to attempt such an account here, but it would be fitting to ask what contribution the book of Numbers can make to the discussion. It is natural to look to the early traditions for an answer. This is not to preclude the possibility that the later priestly material is capable of carrying historical information pertaining to the period. The trouble is that for the modern historian this material is extraordinarily hard to penetrate. It is arguable that such history as it preserves is mediated to it through the earlier narrative tradition; at no point have we discovered an independent witness from priestly texts which is likely to be of great value to the historian. Turning to the pre-priestly material the results of our investigation can be analyzed as follows:

1. *Liturgical Material*

We include here the psalm incorporated in the story of Hobab and the ark (10:29–36), and the traditions about manna and quail as desert food (11:7–9, 31–33). The latter certainly appear to have been a theme of cultic celebration (Pss 78:23–28; 105:40). In the former the liturgical use of such texts may be based on the earlier use of the ark in war. The dating of the text (pre- or post-settlement) is impossible to determine, and nothing of substance emerges with respect to the wilderness experience.

The food traditions certainly reflect a familiarity with conditions of life in the desert areas to the south, and in the Sinai peninsula, but what should be deduced from this in historical terms is uncertain. There is certainly a liturgical tradition of Yahweh's desert march (Ps 68:8; Deut 33:2, Judg 5:4), and there is every reason for associating this with the holy mountain. It seems likely that this tradition has its roots in the custom of pilgrimage to and from Yahweh's earlier sanctuary, and that the desert food theme belongs here. For the historian, however, the tradition is hard to penetrate. The theme of desert march may well be telling us more about the transference of the worship of Yahweh from Sinai to Jerusalem than about Israel's wilderness wanderings.

2. *Temple Material*

We include here the story of the serpents (21:4–9). The text appears to have as its background a priestly etiology justifying the cult of Nehushtan. The ideological interests at the root of such stories and their adaptations make it very difficult for a historian to extract ancient history from them.

3. *Prophetic Material*

We include here a number of stories where the Yahwist has incorporated or embellished material which appears to have a prophetic background. This is true of the traditions about elders and prophets (11:16–17, 24–30) and about Miriam and Aaron (12:1–15). As with the temple tradition about serpents, there are strong apologetic interests in this material. The vindication of particular outlooks and stances by means of appeal to Moses and the wilderness period is central. It is difficult for the historian to know whether there were any real historical grounds for such an appeal (there may have been other grounds for it), and in the absence of supporting witness or appeal to earlier sources the historian is likely to conclude that he can make little direct use of such material.

The original Balaam oracles (23:7–10, 18–24; 24:3–9, 15–19) look more promising. They have archaic features, and in parts at least are arguably pre-Davidic compositions. They reflect a confident spirit which probably takes us back close to Israel's beginnings in the land. Unfortunately they provide no information by which those beginnings may be reconstructed or explained. The Balaam material has an integrity of its own, and is very loosely attached to the rest of the Transjordanian material. The suggestion that it is filler material for the Transjordanian journey means that it has no particular significance as first hand witness to such a journey.

The traditions about Baal Peor (25:1–5) may also have been preserved in prophetic circles, and though they doubtless bear witness to the existence of such a cult at an early period, it is very difficult to be certain that such a cult was encountered during a Transjordanian journey prior to the settlement and establishment of Israel in Canaan.

4. Disaffection Material

The tradition of Israel's rebelliousness prior to the settlement is firmly rooted in the Yahwist's stories (Num 11:1–3, 4–6; 13:31; 14:23b–24, 40–45; 16:12–15; 21:5; 25:1–3), in the book of Exodus as well as in Numbers. Here again there would appear to be apologetic interests at work, and it is very hard to determine how ancient the tradition is. There was certainly a liturgical tradition which viewed the desert quail positively as a gracious gift of God (Ps 105:40), and it is difficult to see how this could ever have been asserted had the tradition always been one of disaffection and punishment. A development in the other direction—from gracious gift to punishment for rebellion—is altogether more credible. The disaffection tradition may have been stimulated in part by a recollection that there were some unwilling to settle in the land (16:12–15), but this is the most that the historian could justifiably claim.

5. The Itineraries

Here we include some of the sites mentioned in 21:10–20, and the larger compilation in 33:1–49. The historian must ask from where the authors drew this information, and some form of royal archive is the most likely solution. It is difficult to envisage the circumstances under which a list compiled by Moses might have been preserved, and the possibility remains that the lists are from later routes for travelers, designed for commercial or other purposes. The point is not that this can be proved, but that the uncertainty is real.

6. Ancient Poetic Material

Here we include those ancient texts which have no obvious contact with Israel's later liturgical tradition or with prophetic circles—in particular the citation from the book of the Wars of Yahweh (21:14–15), the Song of the Well (21:17–18), and the taunt song against Heshbon (21:27–30). These are undoubtedly ancient texts, but the question of their specific origin and background remains.

The citation from the book of the Wars of Yahweh appears to describe land occupied and controlled, presumably, in view of the source, as a result of war. The difficulty of knowing whether it is Davidic or earlier remains. The Song of the Well reflects the experience of a community dependent on occasional sources of water, and probably in some sense a mobile community. The word "nomadic" may imply more than the evidence allows. It could be that this is also a citation from the book of the Wars of Yahweh, and that the background is of a community on a campaign. The taunt song against Heshbon, like the citation from the book of the Wars of Yahweh, is a witness to war in Transjordan, though its ultimate origin is uncertain. So also is to the date of the campaign to which the song bears witness.

7. Settlement Traditions

Here we have the material which is arguably of most value to the historian of the settlement period, though it is patchy and disconnected. We include what may be fragments of Kenite tradition in 10:29–32, and Calebite tradition in 13:30, 14:24. There is also Judah tradition in general in 21:1–3, and traditions of the Transjordanian tribes in 21:21–35; 32:34–38, 39, 41–42. The Kenite and Calebite material must all have become incorporated in the wider Judah tradition, and it is this wider Judah tradition which was available to the Yahwist. It is difficult to know precisely what this Judah tradition claimed about the occupation of the land. It may have attested an incursion from the south, as has sometimes been supposed from 21:1–3, but this is scarcely certain, and the difficulty remains of explaining why a Judah tradition above all should come to be suppressed. There were other ways in which the traditionists could have maintained invasions from south and east within the context of an essentially pan-Israelite operation. The most that the historian can deduce from the traditions is that Calebites occupied territory in and around Hebron, and that there was a successful anti-Canaanite campaign in the vicinity of Hormah. The possibility that the latter is a folk etiology, built on the name Hormah ("devoted to destruction"), must be reckoned with. Little can be learned about the Kenites, except what may also be deduced from Judg 1:16—that they were one of the various groups who took over what later became Judah, along with Calebites, Othnielites, Kenizzites, Jerahmeelites, and perhaps the Simeonites.

The Transjordanian traditions in 20:14–21 and 21:21–35 (the song excluded) are too dominated by Yahwistic and deuteronomistic interests to be of much use for our purpose. It is difficult to be certain that they relate directly to the period with which we are concerned. The fragmentary references to the Manassite clans Machir, Jair, and Nobah (Num 32:39, 41–42) are important. They speak of the successful dispossession of Amorites in

Gilead, and of the occupation of cities there. The evidence of Judg 10:3–4, on the other hand, makes it very difficult to be sure that we are here pushing back beyond the period of the judges. The oldest settlement traditions of Gad and Reuben (32:34–38) seem to imply a peaceful occupation of the land of Jazer. There is no reference to war—only to the building of towns and sheepfolds. It is difficult to establish that this in any way relates directly to the activity of Moses.

This survey demonstrates the difficulty of establishing a clear picture of the period with which we are concerned. Some of the traditions, as we have argued, are probably pre-Davidic, but it is difficult to be more precise about them. It is likely that the processes of settlement should be thought of as continuing up to the time of the monarchy, and that they are only effectively secured under David, but the problem of putting the fragmentary traditions into a coherent picture persists. We have suggested evidence of reluctance to settle on the part of some, of war in Transjordan as well as peaceful occupation in that area, and of dispossession and occupation in Judah.

The evidence from Numbers gives no clear answer as to which of the basic settlement models is to be preferred. That there was war is reasonably certain. Even folk etiologies deserve attention here, not so much for the history they record, as for the recollection of a warlike past that they preserve. What does seem difficult to maintain is the theory of a pan-Israelite invasion in association with a Transjordanian journey. Though this tradition tends to dominate in the present form of the biblical text there are good grounds for suspecting that this view is a product of systematization in the period of the monarchy, intended to demonstrate and secure the unity of the nation. Archaeology appears to offer some kind of tacit support for this view. Recent Transjordanian study seems to indicate that the territories of Edom and Moab were not significantly occupied in the thirteenth century. The ancient kingdoms cited in the biblical text do not appear to have existed then in anything like the form required by the biblical witness itself. The same seems to apply to Arad and the suggested sites for Hormah. We have suggested that this last part of the journey is essentially a literary construct. It provides for a crossing of the Jordan which can be genuinely pan-Israelite, and also vindicates Israelite settlement in Transjordan. How much it tells us about the history of Moses and his refugees from Egypt must remain uncertain.

Any reconstruction of the settlement must allow for a sense of cohesiveness and common outlook which David in the course of time was able to forge into a powerful nation-state. That there was a significant influx of refugees from Egypt (in terms of influence and not necessarily numbers) is very probable, under the initial leadership of Moses. It also seems likely that they joined in common cause with groups in Canaan, and that they were able to set up alternative communities independent of the Canaanite city-states. This independence, buttressed by Yahwistic faith, made for a natural antagonism against Canaanite politics, religion, and culture, but where Canaanite influence was slight, the occupation and independent life style could be carried through in a relatively peaceful way.

To suggest that the book of Numbers is somewhat hard to penetrate in the interests of modern historiography is not to devalue it or necessarily to raise problems for religious faith. It must be remembered that we have addressed ourselves to a narrow historiographical question—the processes of settlement in the last two centuries of the second millenium—and the historiographical interest of the book as a witness to the developing consciousness of Israel as a community of faith in the first millenium is permanent and inescapable. The search for origins is not the be-all and end-all of history. Judaeo-Christian religion in particular is concerned with a God who continues to guide and engage in the patterns of cause and effect which the modern historian seeks to identify.

Theological Postscript

The importance of the OT, as with other ancient literature, lies in its capacity to reflect at a deep level the persistent problems and aspirations of communities across the centuries and across cultures, and to speak effectively to them. Coming as one of a series after the book of Exodus, the book of Numbers deals with what is in a sense a liberated community. But how can such a community continue to live freely? How can it secure its political and economic stability, and maintain its religious freedom? Without in any way forcing the OT into a univocal mold, these are persistent and pervasive themes, not least in the book of Numbers itself.

As we have sought to show, the possession of the land is the goal of the journey and much attention is given, particularly in the latter part of the book, to certain principles which must control the life of the community in the land. Access to the land itself speaks above all of access to the resources which it provides. The whole enterprise calls for action, faith, and courage. Obedience is not an abstract value, but a commitment to the enterprise, with a view to securing the land in a way that gives religious freedom and economic and political security. In taking up the Yahwist's etiology of landed Israel the priestly author of Numbers renews, albeit in different circumstances, this basic perspective and commitment.

Self-determination is a crucial aspect of the discussion. If possession of the land has to do fundamentally with access to resources, self-determination has to do with access to power. People without influence are in bondage. The rejection of the Canaanites and their culture, the particularism of the laws, the stress on fulfillment of an ancient promise and on single-minded loyalty to Yahweh are all part of the determination to establish an identity and societal self-consciousness which are essential to the self-determination of the community. The census, the laws on purity, the Balaam and the Baal Peor traditions all contribute to this sense of community identity. The non-visibility of Yahweh is a further crucial factor in this sense of distinctiveness, and it also helps to make faith-action more important that mere religiousness. There are times when return to Egypt, to economic and political subservience, seems to offer the only way, but the Mosaic alternative of independence and self-determination, despite its difficulties, is shown to be the only way of true freedom. Ties of subservience can never be a way to ultimate security and well-being.

A third crucial aspect of the discussion is the meaning of community itself.

Access to resources and to influence are important—so too is the creation of a life style which enables the community to function justly and cohesively. In this, ritual and religious observance have their part to play—particularly in their capacity to place all on a fundamentally equal footing before the deity. Hierarchical forms and structures there may be, but these are constantly shown in the book of Numbers to be platforms, not for the exercise of individual power and privilege, but for forms of community service. Any failure in this respect emerges as devastating in its consequences for the individuals concerned. The presentation of the cult in the book of Numbers helps to support this view of the community. The centrality of the Tent of Meeting, and the need to give from resources on an equal footing, are two elements which help to make it real.

Access to resources, to power, and to true community are deeply scored into the OT witness as preconditions to the kind of securities which are fundamental to all human needs and aspirations. In its own distinctive way the book of Numbers affirms and elaborates all of them. Ideals may not always be attainable, and the post-exilic situation in the short term offered less in terms of practical possibilities, but the vision cannot be abandoned, and new ways for effecting it must be constantly sought.

The Dimensions of the Community (1:1–47)

Bibliography

Albright, W. F. "The Administrative Divisions of Israel and Judah." *JPOS* 5 (1925) 17–54. **Barnouin, M.** "Les Recensements du Livre des Nombres et l'Astronomie Babylonienne." *VT* 27 (1977) 280–303.———. "Tableaux numériques du Livre des Nombres." *RB* 76 (1969) 351–64. **Lucas, A.** "The Number of Israelites at the Time of the Exodus." *PEQ* 76 (1944) 164–68. **Mendenhall, G. E.** "The Census Lists of Numbers 1 and 26." *JBL* 77 (1958) 52–66. **Noth, M.** *Die Israelitischen Personennamen im Rahmen der Gemeinsemitischen Namengebung.* BWANT 3/10 Stuttgart: Kohlhammer, 1928.———. *Das System der zwölf Stämme Israels.* BWANT 4/1 Stuttgart: Kohlhammer, 1930. **Petrie, W. M. F.** *Researches in Sinai.* London: Murray, 1906. **Schedl, C.** "Biblische Zahlen unglaubwürdig?" *TPQ* 107 (1959) 58–62. **Weinberg, J. P.** "Das *Beit ʾAbot* im Jh. v.u.Z.." *VT* 23 (1973) 400–14. **Weippert, H.** "Das geographische System der Stämme Israels." *VT* 23 (1973 76–89. **Wenham, J. W.** "Large Numbers in the Old Testament." *TB* 18 (1967) 19–53.

Translation

[1] *And Yahweh spoke to Moses in the wilderness of Sinai, in the Tent of Meeting, on the first day of the second month, in the second year after their departure from the land of Egypt, saying,* [2] *"Take a census* [a] *of all the congregation of the people of Israel, by clans and fathers' houses, name by name, every male, head by head.* [3] *You and Aaron shall number* [a] *those aged twenty and upwards, all eligible for military service in Israel, company by company.* [4] *And you shall have with you a man from each tribe, each one being head of his fathers' house.* [5] *And these are the names of the men who shall accompany you: From Reuben* [a]*—Elizur, son of Shedeur.* [6] *From Simeon—Shelumiel, son of Zurishaddai.* [7] *From Judah—Nahshon, son of Amminadab.* [8] *From Issachar* [a]*—Nethanel, son of Zuar.* [9] *From Zebulun—Eliab, son of Helon.* [10] *From the sons of Joseph. From Ephraim—Elishama, son of Ammihud. From Manasseh—Gamaliel, son of Pedahzur.* [11] *From Benjamin—Abidan, son of Gideoni.* [12] *From Dan—Ahiezer, son of Ammishaddai.* [13] *From Asher—Pagiel, son of Ochran.* [14] *From Gad—Eliasaph, son of Deuel* [a]. [15] *From Naphtali—Ahira, son of Enan "* [16] *These were those called* [a] *from the congregation, leaders of the tribes of their fathers, heads of the families of Israel.*

[17] *And Moses and Aaron took these men* [a] *who have been named.* [a] [18] *And they assembled all the congregation on the first day of the second month. And they were registered by clans and fathers' houses, name by name, from the age of twenty and upwards, head by head.* [19a] *As Yahweh commanded Moses,* [a] *so he numbered them* [b] *in the wilderness of Sinai.*

[20] *The sons of Reuben, the first born of Israel, their tribal list, by clans and fathers' houses, name by name, head by head, every male from the age of twenty and upwards, all eligible for military service.* [21] *The number of the tribe of Reuben was 46,500.*

22 *To the sons of Simeon, their tribal list, by clans and fathers' houses,*[a] *name by name, head by head, every male from the age of twenty and upwards, all eligible for military service.* 23 *The number of the tribe of Simeon was 59,300.*

24 *To the sons of Gad, their tribal list, by clans and fathers' houses, name by name, from the age of twenty and upwards, all eligible for military service.* 25 *The number of the tribe of Gad was 45,650.*[a]

26 *To the sons of Judah, their tribal list, by clans and fathers' houses, name by name, from the age of twenty and upwards, all eligible for military service.* 27 *The number of the tribe of Judah was 74,600.*

28 *To the sons of Issachar, their tribal list, by clans and fathers' houses, name by name, from the age of twenty and upwards, all eligible for military service.* 29 *The number of the tribe of Issachar was 54,400.*

30 *To the sons of Zebulun, their tribal list, by clans and fathers' houses, name by name, from the age of twenty and upwards, all eligible for military service.* 31 *The number of thé tribe of Zebulun was 57,400.*

32 *To the sons of Joseph. To the sons of Ephraim, their tribal list, by clans and fathers' houses, name by name, from the age of twenty and upwards, all eligible for military service.* 33 *The number of the tribe of Ephraim was 40,500.*

34 *To the sons of Manasseh, their tribal list, by clans and fathers' houses, name by name, from the age of twenty and upwards, all eligible for military service.* 35 *The number of the tribe of Manasseh was 32,200.* 36 *To the sons of Benjamin, their tribal list, by clans and fathers' houses, name by name, from the age of twenty and upwards, all eligible for military service.* 37 *The number of the tribe of Benjamin was 35,400.* 38 *To the sons of Dan, their tribal list, by clans and fathers' houses, name by name, from the age of twenty and upwards, all eligible for military service.* 39 *The number of the tribe of Dan was 62,700.*

40 *To the sons of Asher, their tribal list, by clans and fathers' houses, name by name, from the age of twenty and upwards, all eligible for military service.* 41 *The number of the tribe of Asher was 41,500.*

42 *To* [a] *the sons of Naphtali, their tribal list, by clans and fathers' houses, name by name, from the age of twenty and upwards, all eligible for military service.* 43 *The number of the tribe of Naphtali was 53,400.*

44 *These were those numbered, whom Moses counted, with Aaron and the twelve leaders of Israel (*[a] *each one represented his fathers' house* [a]*).* 45 *And so all those numbered of the people of Israel, by fathers' houses,*[a] *from the age of twenty and upwards, all eligible for military service in Israel,*[b] 46 *all those numbered came to 603,550.* 47 *But the Levites were not numbered along with them by their ancestral tribe.*

Notes

2.a. The plural שׂאוּ is unexpected in view of the command to Moses alone in v 1. It must include Aaron (v 3). The singular in S is probably a recognition of the difficulty.

3.a. *Sam* and *S* use the second person sing. in order to adjust to the singular form of address of v 1.

5.a. On the use of *lamed* in vv 5–14 cf. F. Nötscher, "Zum Emphatischen Lamed," *VT* 3 (1953) 378.

8.a. The form of the word is an example of *Q^ere perpetuum* (cf. GKC § 66).

14.a. The form *Deuel* occurs again in Num 7·42, 47; 10:20, and also in many MT mss in

Num 2:14. The form *Reuel* has some MT support in Num 2:14, and is preferred throughout by *G* and *S*, *G* reading Ραγουηλ. *BHS* recommends *Deuel*.

16.a. The *Q*ᵉʳᵉ, giving the usual form of the passive participle, is preferable.

17.a.-a. J. A. Paterson (*The Book of Numbers* [Leipzig: Hinrichs'sche, 1900] 41) considers the clause to be a marginal gloss, but it is hard to see what purpose such an addition would serve.

19.a.-a. The clause may belong with v 18, as in *G*. Paterson (*Numbers*, 41) prefers to transpose v 19a and v 19b, thus concluding the paragraph with a customary formula. It would be possible to take v 19b as the beginning of the next paragraph, introducing the details of the census.

19.b. The verb can be repointed to give a plural subject (cf. *BHS*), thereby including Aaron and the leaders. This is not essential since the ultimate responsibility of Moses is made clear in v 1.

22.a. The word פְּקֻדָיו ought probably to be deleted, as in some MT mss, *G*, *S*, *Tg*ᴶ., thereby bringing v 22 into conformity with the rest of the census returns.

25.a. *G* places the census information about Gad after v 37, between the returns for Benjamin and Dan. This unusually early position for Gad in MT may be due to that tribe's association with Reuben and Simeon in the encampment of chap. 2. On tribal lists generally in the OT cf. M. Noth, *Das System der zwölf Stämme Israels*; H. Weippert, "Das geographische System der Stämme Israels."

42.a. In view of the stylized turn of phrase throughout the paragraph it is better to include the preposition, as in some MT mss, *G*, *S*, Vg, Sam.

44.a. The clause is curious, and could be reconstructed after the pattern of v 4 (*BHS*). SP and *G* both witness to the presence of מַטֵּה "tribe." If MT be retained the phrase is loose, since the leaders are essentially tribal representatives.

45.a. Sam and *G* have לְצִבְאֹתָם "company by company" (cf. v 52). MT is more consistent with the general pattern in vv 1–46.

45.b. The lack of a predicate for וַיִּהְיוּ in the verse as a whole is striking, but is not necessarily a witness to editorial activity. The awkwardness arises from the author's insistence on incorporating much of the census terminology in v 45, and his desire to give final and special emphasis to the grand total.

Form/Structure/Setting

While there is general agreement among literary analysts that this section belongs to P the question of its traditio-historical growth is unresolved. J. Wellhausen (*Die Composition des Hexateuchs und der historischen Bücher des Alten Testaments.* [Berlin: Reimer, 1889] 178–79) took vv 17–47 to be a later addition on the ground that the order of tribes is different from that in vv 1–16. This is weak, since vv 1–16 clearly require a numbering of the tribes, and the distinctive ordering there is probably an anticipation of the pattern of encampment in Num 2 (see further A. Dillmann, *Die Bücher Numeri, Deuteronomium und Josua* [Leipzig: Hirzel, 1886] 4).

G. B. Gray (*A Critical and Exegetical Commentary on Numbers* [Edinburgh: Clark, 1912] 2–3) finds the overall ordering of material in Num 1:1–2:34 to be diffuse. The command *not* to number the Levites (v 47) is particularly remarkable in his view, coming as it does after the other tribes have already been numbered and details of their dimensions given. Gray believes that supplementation (PS) has involved the recasting of PG, and he suspects that the present awkwardness arises from the concern of PS to keep sacred and secular tribes entirely separate. He suggests that the original order in PG entailed the separation and functions of Levi, the appointment of assistants for the census, the numbering of the secular tribes, and finally the numbering of the Levites.

This reconstruction assumes the validity of a PG/PS analysis (see *Introduc-*

tion), and is entirely conjectural. There is clearly no textual ground for the supposition that the desire to keep sacred and secular apart is secondary rather than original. In any case the awkwardness should not be exaggerated. There is a sense in which v 47 enters with all the more force after the patient and meticulous enumeration of the other tribes.

An entirely different PG/PS analysis is offered by D. Kellermann (*Die Priesterschrift von Numeri 1:1 bis 10:10; literarkritisch und traditionsgeschichtlich untersucht* [Berlin: Töpelmann, 1970] 4–17). To PG he attributes vv 1a 2 (sing.), 3 (sing.—minus "Aaron"), 19b, 21b, 23b, 25b, 27b, 29b, 31b, 33b, 35b, 37b, 41b, 43b, 46. This amounts to a location of the incident in the wilderness of Sinai, a command to Moses to carry out a military census, the bare figures for each tribe, and the final total. At the next stage, according to Kellermann, Aaron is drawn into the tradition (vv 2–3). Most of the rest of the section comes in at a third level of expansion. This includes the dating in v 1b, the list of assistants in all essentials in vv 4–15, the stylized and repetitive phrases associated with the figures in vv 20–43, and v 45. Kellermann finds some stress on meticulous obedience at this level of the tradition. At a still later stage come vv 16, 44, the phrase "their tribal list" in vv 20–42, the making of the assistants into נְשִׂיאִים "leaders," and some other minor additions. The substantial accumulations are thus the incorporation of Aaron and the twelve assistants, and the stylized language associated with the census figures.

These arguments need a much broader base in P as a whole if they are to carry conviction. Aaron is firmly fixed in earlier tradition as a significant leader figure, and it is hard to envisage a form of PG in which he does not occur as the right-hand man of Moses. The well attested plural at the beginning of v 2 suggests that he is not an afterthought when named at the end of v 3. His absence in v 1 is explained by the author's conviction that the revelation itself comes to Moses alone in the Tent of Meeting. Ultimately it is his responsibility—hence v 19 and the awkward singular in v 44. The leader list is arguably something incorporated rather than a supplement. The repetitive turns of phrase linked with the census returns are likely to be formal legal language, integrally connected with the figures themselves. For the most part they are simply a taking up of the language in vv 2–3. If they really are supplementary the scribe concerned has achieved very little. It is difficult to see why such an individual needs to be posited at this point.

If the arguments for substantial supplementation are not persuasive what elements in the section may have been incorporated by the author from other sources? There are two topics deserving particular attention—the background of the tribal leader list in vv 5–15, and that of the census returns in vv 20–46.

The Tribal Leader List

A typical older view is offered by G. B. Gray (pp. 6–7). He maintained that the list is a relatively late compilation from post-exilic times, the names being a studied selection of ancient and more recent formulations.

M. Noth (*Die Israelitischen Personennamen*) offered a significant challenge to this point of view with his theory that the list is ancient and dates back to amphictyonic times. He points to the rough connection of the list with v 4, suggesting that this is an indication that the author has introduced earlier material at this point. In the names themselves he finds strong indications of antiquity—notably the absence of formations involving "Yahweh," and the components "zur" and "ammi" which suggest links with second millenium names at Mari. The unique order in the tribal list is also taken by Noth to be an indicator of old tradition, along with the unusual phrase in v 16—"leaders of the tribes of their fathers."

Some stylistic awkwardness in v 4 does indeed suggest the possibility that the list comes from an earlier source, though that in itself says nothing about its age. Equally indecisive is the order of the list—the position of Gad merely anticipates the camping arrangements in Num 2—and the unusual phrase in v 16, the components of which are easily found elsewhere in P.

The evidence of the names, on Noth's own analysis, is ambivalent. Noun sentence names tend to be more frequent in older literature, but there are only ten of these at most in the total list of twenty-four. These are Elizur "God is a rock," Shedeur "Shaddai is light," Shelumiel "God is prosperity," Zurishaddai "Shaddai is a rock," Eliab "God is father," Ammihud "the kinsman is glorious," Ahiezer "the Brother is a help," Ammishaddai "Shaddai is kinsman." The other two may belong to this category, but not certainly: Pagiel "God has encountered"(?), and Ahira (Ahida [S]?) "the Brother knows"(?).

Verb sentence names can also be early, though they are by no means exclusively so. Four in the list have the order noun/verb: Amminadab "the kinsman is generous," Elishama "God has heard," Abidan "the Father has judged," and Eliasaph "God has added." As Noth recognizes the verb/noun order in such names is common in late literature, and there are two such in the list: Nethanel "God has given" and Pedahzur "the Rock has redeemed."

D. Kellermann (*Priesterschrift*, 155–59) is unconvinced by Noth's conclusion. With respect to names associated with the family—"father," "brother"—the most that can be said is that they could be early. Names formulated with "kinsman" occur as late as the Chronicler (cf. e.g. 1 Chr 2:10; 6:7; 15:10–11), while the nine which incorporate "El" are impossible to date. They are certainly present in relatively late texts (cf. e.g. Jer 36:12, 20–21; 1 Chr 2:41; 2 Chr 17:8). The name Gamaliel "God is a reward" and Deuel (or Reuel "God is companion") seem to have the verb/noun pattern which is only frequently attested from the seventh century B.C. There are five names using "Shaddai" or "Zur." The former can occur in early contexts, but is familiar enough in P, and must thus be judged uncertain (cf. e.g. Gen 17·1; 28:3; 35:11; 48:3; Exod 6:3). In Pedahzur where "rock" is a name for God "Zur" does seem to be old, but in Elizur, and Zurishaddai it is the predicate, and it is thus less clear that these are ancient names.

The remaining six names give no clue as to their age: Nahshon "serpent," Zuar "little one," Helon "?," Gideoni "?," Ochran "?," and Enan "?" In Kellermann's view the absence of Yahweh names may just as well indicate a period when the divine name was considered too holy for use in personal names—i.e. at a relatively late date. It should also be noted that two-thirds of the names occur only in this list. The other eight tend to occur in later rather than earlier texts—Eliab (1 Chr 15:18, 20; 16:5), Elishama (2 Kgs 25:25; Jer 36:12, 20–21; 41:1; 2 Chr 17:8), Nethanel (Ezra 10:22; Neh 12:21, 36; 1 Chr 24:6; 26:4; 2 Chr 35:9), Ammihud (Num 34:20, 28; 1 Chr 9:4), Amminadab (Ruth 4:20; 1 Chr 15:10–11), Ahiezer (1 Chr 12:3), Nahshon (1 Chr 2:10–11; Ruth 4:20), Eliasaph (Num 3:24). In these contexts too, of course, the question of age is bound to arise, but caution about Noth's conclusions is wise.

Kellermann points out that names occurring in the OT can only be a sample of those in common use, and that this introduces a further element of uncertainty into the discussion. He also asks, assuming P to be post-exilic, how we should suppose that the list was preserved through the difficult times of 587 B.C., and why such a list, which on Noth's view had lost its original purpose, should have been preserved at all.

It has to be recognized that argument on the basis of names is largely indecisive. In the nature of the case names alone are an unreliable guide to the age of the literary context in which they occur. Ancient or not they tell us little about the age of the list. It also has to be recognized that haggadic method was capable of creating names where for some reason this was deemed desirable. The Targums find a wife for Cain, while the Book of Jubilees and Philo find names for her. On balance it seems unlikely that this list is the author's creation. There is some unevenness of style suggesting incorporation. The identity crisis posed by the exile may well have led to a Babylonian compilation of names of old tribal figures. Much of this work would have had to be done on the basis of unverifiable recollection, but it would have served a purpose in the reconstitution of Israel.

The Census Returns

The central difficulty here is the impossibly large number of fighting men recorded. The historical difficulties in accepting the figure as it stands are insuperable (see e.g. the older commentaries—Dillmann, 5–8; Gray, 9–15; B. Baentsch, *Exodus-Leviticus-Numeri* [HKAT 1/2; Gottingen: Vandenhoeck & Ruprecht, 1903] 446). According to A. Lucas ("The Number of Israelites at the time of the Exodus," *PEQ* 76 [1944] 164–68) the statistics given in Gen 46:27; Exod 1:5; 12:40, if accepted, mean that the total number of Israelites at the time could only have been about ten thousand.

One possibility is that the figures are simply the author's creation, an embellishment of tradition, depicting Israel under God as a mighty host. In this the author could be compared with the Chronicler who marshals massive armies for his wars (cf. e.g. 2 Chr 13:3; 14:8; 17:14–19; 26:13). Appeals to the possibility of textual corruption are entirely conjectural, and do not cope with the fact that this is in large measure a problem peculiar to P and the Chronicler. That the author was impressed by the army is a reasonable deduction, but the theory of total creation does not entirely explain the relative precision of the final figure, which is certainly not as "round" as it could be.

Some scholars have suggested that gematriya—a procedure involving the manipulation of the numerical value of certain letters—offers the best explanation (see e.g. H. Holzinger, *Numeri* [KHAT 4; Tübingen: Mohr, 1903] 5–6; A. Bentzen, *Introduction to the Old Testament. vol. 2* [Copenhagen: Gad, 1948] 34; G. Fohrer, *Introduction to the Old Testament* [London: SPCK, 1970] 184). This theory builds on the numerical value of the letters in בְּנֵי יִשְׂרָאֵל "people of Israel." If added together (2 + 50 + 10 + 10 + 300 + 200 + 1 + 30) these make 603, which is the total in thousands of the whole army. The remaining 550 have to be dealt with in some other way.

Holzinger drew attention to two possibilities. By taking the value of the letters in the phrase כָּל־זָכָר לְכָל־יֹצֵא צָבָא "every male, all eligible for military service" the figure 551 is reached. The additional "one" could be Moses himself. Alternatively, the figure 563 can be obtained from the word לְצִבְאֹתָם "company by company," with Moses and the twelve leaders perhaps constituting the additional thirteen. P. Heinisch (*Das Buch Numeri* 17) worked with כָּל־רֹאשׁ "every head," pointing out that without the quiescent aleph the letters added together make 550 exactly. If the aleph is included the figure is 551; the final total in that event would be a simple "rounding down" to 603,550.

The ease with which different kinds of answers can be found for the 550 suggests that the correspondence between "sons of Israel" and the figure 603 may be coincidental. Kellermann (p. 161) points to Rev 13:8 as the first certain biblical example of gematriya, and it may well be that the use of letters for figures is no earlier than the Hellenistic period. It is most unlikely that these figures are as late as that. No comparable suggestions have been offered for the twelve figures given for individual tribes. If there is a randomness about them there is some likelihood that the same obtains for the final figure.

W. F. Albright (*JPOS* 5 [1925] 17–54) suggested that the problem could be solved by regarding the figures as a variant of the census taken under David (2 Sam 24:1–9). This begs the question of how the figures in 2 Sam 24:9 are to be understood. For many they are at the least improbably large (see R. de Vaux, *Ancient Israel. Its Life and Institutions* [London: DLT, 1961] 65–67). The tribute payable in 2 Kgs 15:19–20 suggests a figure of only sixty thousand landowners in the state of Israel in the year 738 B.C. In any case the explanation seems to create a new problem. Why do the figures for Davidic census vary so much?

Another line of explanation involves a reduction of the figures through a reinterpretation of אֶלֶף "thousand." This approach was pioneered by W. M. F. Petrie (*Researches in Sinai*). There are certainly a number of texts where אֶלֶף arguably refers to a subdivision within a tribe (Num 1:16; 10:4, 36; Josh 22:14, 21, 30; Judg 6:15; 1 Sam 10:19; 23:23; Mic 5:1, and perhaps Isa 60:22). Petrie suggested that these subdivisions were "tent groups." The figure given for Reuben should therefore be understood as 46 tent groups and 500 warriors. This gives an overall total for Israel of 598 tent groups, and a more manageable figure of 5,500 warriors.

G. E. Mendenhall (*JBL* 77 [1958] 52–66) offers a variation of this. Against Petrie, and with the present form of the biblical text, he regards this as a military census. The אֶלֶף was certainly a subsection of a tribe, but in due course it was applied, in Mendenhall's view, to a contingent of troops under its own leader. So we have here a tribal military list, dating from the time of the Judges, giving a total of 598 contingents, and 5,500 warriors. Since this is probably too small a figure for the time of the judges Mendenhall suggests that the tribal figures are quotas rather than a complete enumeration of those liable for service. This would account for the degree of "roundness" about the figures. Under David אֶלֶף came to mean, on this theory, a military unit roughly one thousand strong, and hence the scope for misunderstanding and inflated figures. M. Noth (*Numbers* [OTL. London: SCM, 1968] 21–23) has some sympathy for this kind of approach, and points out, on the basis of more general ancient near eastern practice, that contingents or units of only nine or ten men are by no means a difficulty.

If a solution of this kind is adopted it should be recognized that the original figures have been misunderstood. J. W. Wenham (*TB* 18 [1967] 19–53) wishes to avoid this, but his method is unconvincing. Whether אֶלֶף can fairly be repointed to make אַלּוּף or not, MT refuses to read the plural אֲלֻפִים, and evidently intends the meaning "one thousand." Verse 46, with its final total of 603,550, is unintelligible on any other basis. Nor, for that matter, are Petrie, Mendenhall, and Noth entirely convinving. That אֶלֶף could mean some kind of tribal subdivision is clear, but it is far from certain that it was essentially a military unit. Mendenhall's awareness that the returns are intended to be a military census is preferable to Petrie's idea of a nationwide count. The figures for warriors on Petrie's view are too "round." On the other hand, with Mendenhall's view, the numbers of men per unit in the figures for Simeon and Manasseh (about five or six) seem too low to be convincing. Why a Simeonite unit should consist of five men and a Gadite of fourteen has not been adequately explained.

A novel approach is offered by M. Barnouin (*VT* 27 [1977] 280–303). He finds some correlation between the figures and the Babylonian calendar. The purpose in linking Israel's population with calendrical mathematics would be to give the people a sense of their own place, fixed and unalterable, within the harmonious order of the cosmos. It has to be asked whether these alleged astronomical data in the figures are any more obvious than those perceived in gematriya. It seems an obscure way of making the point, and it is reasonable to wonder how many contemporary readers would have grasped it.

There may in fact be a simpler solution to hand. There were texts available to the author in Yahwistic tradition which offered a figure of some six hundred thousand Israelites—presumably the whole community, and not merely fighting men (Exod 12:37; Num 11:21). In developing the tradition the author suggests that this figure applies in fact to the men over twenty eligible for military service. The precise figure is to be traced perhaps to Exod 38:26. That text suggests a simple answer to the question of how 603,550 was calculated. The bases and hooks of the Tabernacle, as envisaged in vv 27–28, require 100 talents and 1775 shekels of silver. There were 3,000 shekels to the talent, making a total requirement of 301,775 shekels. Evidently half a shekel per head was the sanctuary offering (v 26 cf. Exod 30:13), payable by all men over the age of twenty. The thought naturally occurs therefore that there must have been 603,500 men liable for the tax. In short, the large number derives, not from misunderstanding, but from haggadic contemplation of the priestly Tabernacle, and from what was doubtless a post-exilic level of Temple tax. There is good reason for seeing Exod 38:21–31 as a supplement to the Book of Exodus (see *Introduction*), and it is widely held that the same applies to Exod 30. This supplementation may have been the work of the author of Numbers himself. He prepares the way for the census in Exod 30:11–16, indicates his thinking about the size of the community in Exod 38:26, and then in Num 1 tells of the count, indicating that tax liability is also a liability for military service, and providing a breakdown of the total figure among the different tribes. This breakdown was probably rough and ready, as the "roundness" of the figures tends to suggest. It may have been based on intuition, or on an intelligent assessment of the fortunes of the tribes, as set out in Gen 49 and Deut 33.

Comment

1. בְּמִדְבַּר סִינַי "in the wilderness of Sinai." The tradition identifying Mount Sinai with Jebal Musa, near the southern tip of the Sinai Peninsula is no earlier than the fourth century A.D. Other suggestions look to Midianite territory in northwest Arabia, or to the neighborhood of Kadesh-barnea. For recent thorough discussion of the question see G. I. Davies, *The Way of the Wilderness* (Cambridge: CUP, 1979).

1. אֹהֶל מוֹעֵד "Tent of Meeting." This is the most favored in P for the wilderness sanctuary (131 times). The root יָעַד means "to appoint," and since the tent in question is regularly a place of divine communication, the "Tent of Meeting" may mean the place appointed for revelations of God's will to Israel. In P it is evidently the place where the Ark resides (cf. e.g. Num 7:89). The word מִשְׁכָּן can also be used of the same tent (cf. e.g. Exod 25:9; Num 1:50). The expressions are combined in Exod 40:2, 6, 29, and overall there is no clear indication that the מִשְׁכָּן is a definite part of the אֹהֶל מוֹעֵד, or that the two terms are used consistently in significantly different contexts. They are best understood as offering different dimensions to P's understanding of the sanctuary. מִשְׁכָּן, derived from the verb "to dwell," draws attention to the divine presence, and אֹהֶל מוֹעֵד to divine communication. As Num 2:1 makes plain P's "Tent of Meeting" stands at the center of the camp.

In earlier Yahwistic tradition the אֹהֶל מוֹעֵד stands outside the camp (Exod 33:7–11; Num 11:16–30; Num 12:4–10). There too it is a place where God appears and communicates. The author of Numbers (P) has linked this revelatory tradition with the Temple traditions of the divine presence. The tent is thus centralized within the camp, and becomes a symbol of the Temple, the place of revelation *par excellence*. For further discussion of this process see B. S. Childs, *Exodus* (London: SCM, 1974) 530–37; R. E. Clements, *God and Temple* (Oxford: Blackwell, 1965); F. M. Cross, "The Priestly Tabernacle," *Old Testament Issues*. ed. S. Sandmel (London: SCM, 1969) 39–67; M. Gorg, *Das Zelt Begegnung Untersuchungen zur Gestalt der sakralen Zelttraditionen Altisraels* (BBB 27; 1967); M. Haran, "The Nature of the 'Ohel Mo'edh' in Pentateuchal Sources," *JSS* 5 (1960) 50–65; M. Haran, *Temples and Temple Service in Ancient Israel* (Oxford: Clarendon, 1978) 260–75; R. Hartmann, "Zelt und Lade," *ZAW* 37 (1917/18) 209–44; A. Kuschke, "Die Lagervorstellung der priesterschriftlichen Erzählung," *ZAW* 63 (1951) 74–105; J. Morgenstern, "The Ark, the Ephod and the 'Tent of Meeting'," *HUCA* 17 (1942/43) 153–266; 18 (1944) 1–52; G. von Rad, "The Tent and the Ark," *The Problem of the Hexateuch and Other Essays* (Edinburgh: Oliver & Boyd, 1966) 103–24. The process is an example of the haggadic reinterpretation of tradition going on at the priestly levels of the literature.

2. J. Wijngaards ("הוצא and העלה, a twofold approach to the Exodus," *VT* 15 [1965] 91–102) sees יצא as a technical term for the freeing of slaves. This idea is sometimes very obvious in P (cf. e.g. Exod 6:6, 7; Lev 26:13). The word is a favored formula of the Deuteronomists with respect to the Exodus. Wijngaards believes it has its origin in the earliest Sinaitic tradition.

2. שְׂאוּ אֶת־רֹאשׁ literally "lift" or "take" "the head." This is a common technical term in P for the calculation of totals, cf. e.g. Num 1:49; 4:2, 22; 26:2; 31:26, 49.

2. כָּל־עֲדַת בְּנֵי־יִשְׂרָאֵל "all the congregation of the people of Israel." The description of Israel as עֵדָה is common in P. It appears to be connected with the root יָעַד (BDB), and can occur in the context of divine assemblies (Ps 82:1). It was evidently an appropriate description of Israel gathered in worship (Ps 74:2; 111:1), and is used by P to depict בְּנֵי־יִשְׂרָאֵל as a worshiping community. In the opinion of B. Luther (" 'Kahal' und 'edah' als Hilfsmittel der Quellenscheidung im Priesterkodex und in der Chronik," *ZAW* 56 [1938] 44–63) the word עֵדָה offers a valid tool for further analysis within P. Whether or not this is true it is clear that P as a whole is offering a new understanding of the nature of Israel in the wilderness.

2. לְמִשְׁפְּחֹתָם לְבֵית אֲבֹתָם "by clans and fathers' houses." It appears that within each tribe there were clan groupings (מִשְׁפָּחֹת), and that within each clan there were fathers' houses (בֵּית אָבוֹת). J. P. Weinberg ("Das Beit Abot") shows how prominent the בֵּית אָבוֹת are in post-exilic literature, and argues that they constitute a new and significant post-exilic social grouping, linked to the pre-exilic מִשְׁפָּחָה or בֵּת אָב, and arising from the social disruption caused by exile and dispersion. The scope of the "fathers' house" may have varied, but essentially it seems to represent the extended family. On the subject of tribal organization generally, see R. de Vaux, *Ancient Israel. Its Life and Institutions* (London: DLT, 1973) 4–10.

2. לְגֻלְגְּלֹתָם "head by head." The word means "skull" and is used thus in Judg 9:53; 2 Kgs 9:35; 1 Chr 10:10. It is used for the enumeration of heads on a number of other occasions in P, and also in the Chronicler (e.g. Exod 16:16; 38:26; Num 3:47; 1 Chr 23:3, 24).

3. כָּל־יֹצֵא צָבָא "all eligible for military service." The root יָצָא occurs in connection with war in Judg 2:15; Isa 41:12—see also P. D. Miller, "The Divine Council and the Prophetic Call to War," *VT* 18 (1968) 100–07. The link between יָצָא and צָבָא is also attested in Num 31:14, 36; 1 Chr 5:18; 7:11, where the context is clearly military. The link is evidently conventional in post-exilic times, but is also to be found in Deut 24:5; 31:27. The plural of צָבָא occurs in the title "God of Hosts"—a form not to be found in the books from Genesis to Judges, but quite commonly in some of the prophetic books. The term may mean that Yahweh is God of Israel's warriors. For earlier use of the root in connection with fighting men see Gen 21:22; Judg

4:2; 2 Sam 3:23; 1 Kgs 1:25; 2:32; 2 Kgs 5:1; Ps 68:12. It can also be used of the heavenly bodies (Isa 34:4), and of astral cults in particular (Deut 17:3; 2 Kgs 17:16; 21:3; 23:4–5; Jer 8:2).

3. וְאַהֲרֹן "and Aaron." In P Aaron is often given a nominal role alongside Moses. For studies of the history and tradition associated with Aaron see A. Cody, *A History of Old Testament Priesthood* (Rome: PBI, 1969) 146–74; A. H. J. Gunneweg, *Leviten und Priester* (Göttingen: Vandenhoeck & Ruprecht, 1965) 81–98, 138–88.

4. מַטֶּה "tribe." This is the regular word in P. In JE and D שֵׁבֶט is preferred (but see Num 4:18). מַטֶּה is used in earlier Pentateuchal tradition of a "staff" or "rod" (Gen 38:18, 25; Exod 4:2, 4, 17; 7:15, 17, 20; 9:23; 10:13; 14:16; 17:5). It continued to carry this sense at priestly levels of the tradition (Exod 7:9–10, 12, 19; 8:1, 12–13; Num 20:8–9, 11). Play is made with both meanings in the story of Aaron's rod (P—Num 17:17–25).

4. רֹאשׁ "head." It appears that each "fathers' house" had a "head" or "heads." On the use of the word generally see J. R. Bartlett, "The Use of the word רֹאשׁ as a title in the Old Testament," *VT* 19 (1969) 1–10. Bartlett concludes that the title originally belonged to the tribal leader, who would be responsible for both military and judicial matters. By post-exilic times these, he suggests, had ceased to be essentially tribal responsibilities, and the position of רֹאשׁ is now focussed on the family, the fathers' house. In genealogical contexts, however, they still appear as military commanders (see M. D. Johnson, *The Purpose of the Biblical Genealogies* [Cambridge: CUP, 1969] 63–64).

16. נְשִׂיאֵי "leaders of." The use of this word for leading laymen with some kind of official position in Israel is typical of P (sixty-three times in Numbers alone, eighty-three in all). The נָשִׂיא is cited in the Book of the Covenant (Exod 22:27), and is some kind of judicial figure, perhaps even the king himself, in view of the penalties attaching to the cursing of a king (2 Sam 16:9; 1 Kgs 21:10). In Genesis the word is used of foreign potentates (17:20; 25:16; 34:2), and of Abraham himself (23:5–6). With the possible exception of 34:2 these are priestly texts. The word is used of Israel's king in 1 Kgs 11:34, and on several occasions in Ezekiel (12:10, 12; 21:30; 34:24; 37:25). Ezekiel also uses it of foreign rulers (26:16; 27:21; 30:13; 32:29; 37:2–3; 39:1, 18). There are some references in Ezekiel where leading laymen could be in mind (21:17; 22:6; 45:8–9), but even here a royal interpretation is not impossible. It is clear from Ezek 45:8–9 that the proper exercise of justice is central to the function of the נָשִׂיא. According to Noth (*zwölf Stämme*) the נָשִׂיא was originally a tribal representative in the Israelite amphictyony. Even if the amphictyonic theory is accepted it is arguable that the שַׂר is a more likely candidate for such a role (cf. e.g. Judg 5:15). De Vaux (*Ancient Israel*, 8) suggests a function corresponding to that of sheik, some kind of tribal leader. For P the נָשִׂיא is a tribal representative, possibly exercising some function in relation to Israel as "congregation" (cf. v 16; Exod 16:22; Num 4:34; 16:2; 31:13; 32:2; Josh 9:15, 18; 22:30). For further discussion see J. van der Ploeg, "Les Chefs du Peuple d'Israel et Leurs Titres," *RB* 57 (1950) 40–61; E. A. Speiser, "Background and Function of the Biblical Nāsî'" *CBQ* 25 (1963) 111–17.

17. נִקְבוּ בְּשֵׁמוֹת "who have been named," literally "picked by name." This expression occurs often in the Chronicler's work (Ezra 8:20; 1 Chr 12:32; 16:41; 2 Chr 28:15; 31:19).

18. וַיִּתְיַלְדוּ "and they were registered." M. Noth (*Numbers* 20) renders this "so that they could be entered in the register of births." This occurrence of the *Hithpael* of יָלַד "to bear" or "to beget" is an *hapax legomenon*. In all probability it means "to get one's descent acknowledged."

19. כַּאֲשֶׁר צִוָּה יהוה אֶת־מֹשֶׁה "as Yahweh commanded Moses." A common phrase in P (cf. Exod 39:1, 5, 7; Lev 8:9, 17, 21, 29).

20. תּוֹלְדֹתָם "their tribal list," literally "their generations." On the use of the word generally in P, and the question of the so-called Toledoth Book see G. von Rad, *Die Priesterschrift*, and for a brief survey M. D. Johnson, *Biblical Genealogies*, 14–28. The word is derived from the root יָלַד "to bear," "to beget," hence "their generations." In this context "their tribal list" is reasonable (cf. NEB).

Explanation

It has been maintained (see *Introduction*) that the books of Genesis, Exodus, Leviticus, Numbers, Deuteronomy, and Joshua, in their present form, constitute massive revisions of tradition, dating probably to the fifth century B.C. The scope of Numbers is to move Israel from the wilderness of Sinai to the borders of the land, and thus to provide the immediate platform from which Deuteronomic law is given. Its story of a community preparing to settle is of obvious relevance to the circumstances of the sixth and fifth centuries B.C. From an apologetic point of view it engages in the search for authenticity. The priestly theocracy, advocated by Babylonian Judaism, is found to have its roots in the pre-settlement period. From the programmatic point of view it offers the style of life, faith, and organization which the post-exilic community must pursue, embodying convictions which also have their roots in the Babylonian communities of Jews.

The concern of the first of the three major sections (1:1–9:14) is to analyze the constitution and character of the community in the wilderness. It is natural enough to find at the outset some specific interest in the community's dimensions. The wilderness of Sinai is the point to which the author of Exodus had brought Israel in Exod 19:1, the location which for him was marked supremely by the setting up of the Tabernacle (Exod 35:1–40:38). The author of Numbers must clearly begin the story here. He allows a month to pass from the setting up of the Tabernacle (Exod 40:1, 17), a sufficient period for the events and law-giving of the book of Leviticus. The precision of priestly authors with respect to time and place is characteristic. The shaping of the tradition in terms of historiography does not begin with them, but there is no doubt that they introduce a new interest and expertise into this aspect of what was believed about the past. It may be that the "priestliness" of their work relates more to the kind of community they advocated, and perhaps to some of the influence acting upon them, than to their own origins, which in some respects seem academic and possibly scribal.

The author thus begins his work with a military census, incorporating a list of the twelve tribal leaders who acted as assistants, and a precise figure for each of the twelve tribes. That earlier Yahwistic faith was suspicious of censuses seems clear from 2 Sam 24:1–3. David's action is described there as an incitement by Yahweh which was bound to bring evil consequences. This conviction probably stems from theocratic ideas which antedated the setting up of the monarchy. The holding of a census could be considered, in some circles at least, an infringement of God's prerogatives. This opinion probably weakened, and later, in exilic and post-exilic times, there were new and pressing reasons for conducting censuses. Given the facts of exile and dispersion the key question of the day was "Who are the people of God?" On the view widely held among Babylonian Jews that foreign entanglements— religious and marital—had been largely responsible for the exile, it was reasonably certain that lists of names and pedigrees, guaranteeing authenticity, would come into their own (cf. e.g. Ezra 2:1–70/Neh 7:6–69). That in turn made the validity of a census feasible. The pressure of the old faith may still have been felt, and was perhaps alleviated by means of the idea of a census tax as described in Exod 30:11–16. In practice this appears to have become a regular commitment for Temple maintenance (2 Chr 24:6, 9; Matt 17:24– 27). The Chronicler (1 Chr 21:1–6) is unable to alter the basic perspective of 2 Sam 24:1–3, nor is he able to ignore it, since it provides preliminary material for his Davidic Temple, but he is able to depict it as Satanic. The suggestion of Josephus that David failed to collect the census tax does not apparently occur to him.

The author puts some stress on the fact that this is a military census. It is true that the criteria for the count also offered a basis for taxation, and, as Noth points out (*Numbers*, 20) that the census is essentially "one element in the external organisation of the people." This is indeed a measurement of the dimensions of the community at large. On the other hand the author does envisage a significant Midianite war (Num 31:1–54), and Noth's reasons for refusing this war to P are not entirely convincing. It may be true that in a sense the priestly writers "theologize" both war and settlement, but it also seems that the author of Numbers does wish to depict Israel as a mighty army.

The different ordering of the tribes in the leader list as opposed to the order in the census returns suggests that the author has indeed drawn his list of names from some earlier source. This was probably a list of early tribal representatives, drawn up in Babylon in early exilic times, on the basis of memory and recollection, as a way of perpetuating the shell of the twelve-tribe system. That system was already well attested in earlier Yahwistic tradition and in Deuteronomy. One of the author's prime concerns in Numbers, however, is to set up the Levites as a separate functional group within a new priestly hierarchy. They are entirely separate from the secular tribes, and hence are not included in the count (v 47). The twelve tribe pattern is maintained by separating the Joseph tribe into Ephraim and Manasseh.

The immense size of the community at large is drawn from faith rather than demonstrable history. That faith is expressed in passages such as Gen 17:1–8 and Exod 1:7 where God's intention with respect to Israel's strength and well-being is indicated. The precise figure seems to have been reached on the basis of reflection on Exod 38:25 and the size of the Temple tax.

These overall conclusions do not mean that the priestly material is totally divorced from history. It is rather a creative engagement with tradition which itself rests with reasonable certainty on historical events—see the discussion of the first Yahwistic section of the book in Num 10:29-36.

A major contribution of the book of Numbers is its theology of Israel, the people of God. Three aspects emerge in this initial section.

1. Israel's location in the wilderness of Sinai sets the scene for an understanding of the people of God on the march. The idea of Israel as a people, under God and on the move, toward an inheritance as yet unattained, is here given strong expression. The idea is present in earlier tradition—Yahwistic and Deuteronomic, and in the final form of the book of Exodus—but what the author of Numbers is able to do is to show the people, devoid of both land and king, as the fully constituted and authentic worshiping "congregation." Thus one of the essential dualisms in biblical theology emerges in a distinctive way—the tension between the "now" and the "not yet," between the "possessed" and the "looked for."

2. The ordered organization of the community emerges in the hierarchy of Moses, Aaron, and the twelve tribal representatives. These patterns of control and authority offer a reinforcement to one side of another pervasive dualism in biblical theology—the tension between the "institutional" and the "charismatic." Post-exilic Judaism, in its struggle for a foothold in Palestine, and in its suspicion of the "freedom" which had led to false prophecy, was inclined to lay great stress on recognized patterns of authority. There is thus a sense in which theology is given shape by the requirements of the time, though there may always be a need for fruitful interaction between institution and charisma. While the overall stress here is on patterns of authority and control, the maintenance of the twelve tribe scheme indicates a readiness to recognize the idea of shared responsibility and of some diversity within the community. No concern was felt to press the claims of one secular tribe above those of others, or to exclude any who could genuinely show themselves to be of the people of God.

3. The counting of the people is intended to indicate the dimensions of the community at large. To that extent it is an expression of a community consciousness. At the same time it gives some significance to the individual. Each person falling within the terms of the census has recognition as a component of the total community. The size of the final figure is a witness to the conviction that God's faithful community experiences healthy and vigorous growth.

The Distinctiveness of the Levites within the Community (1:48–54)

Bibliography

Abba, R. "Priests and Levites in Ezekiel." *VT* 28 (1978) 1–9. **Berry, G.** "Priests and Levites." *JBL* 42 (1923) 227–38. **Cody, A.** *A History of Old Testament Priesthood.* Rome: PBI, 1969. **Emerton, J. A.** "Priests and Levites in Deuteronomy." *VT* 12 (1962) 129–38. **Gaster, T. H.** "The Name לֵוִי." *JTS* 38 (1937) 250–51. **Gunneweg, A. H. J.** *Leviten und Priester.* Göttingen: Vandenhoeck & Ruprecht, 1965. **Halpern, B.** "Levitic Participation in the Reform Cult of Jeroboam I." *JBL* 95 (1976) 31–42. **Meek, T. J.** "Moses and Levites." *AJSL* 56 (1939) 113–20. **Möhlenbrink, K.** "Die levitischen Überlieferungen des Alten Testament." *ZAW* 52 (1934) 184–231. **Nielsen, E.** "The Levites in Ancient Israel." *ASTI* 3 (1964) 16–27. **Snijders, L. A.** "The Meaning of 'zar' in the Old Testament." *OTS* 10 (1954) 1–154. **Waterman, L.** "Some Determining Factors in the Northward Progress of Levi." *JAOS* 57 (1937) 375–80. **Wright, G. E.** "The Levites in Deuteronomy." *VT* 4 (1954) 325–30.

Translation

[48] And Yahweh spoke to Moses, saying, [49] "Only [a] the tribe of Levi you shall not number; you shall not count their heads among the people of Israel. [50] And you [a] shall appoint the Levites over the Tabernacle of the Testimony, over all its implements, and over everything which belongs to it.[b] They shall carry the Tabernacle, and all its implements, and they shall minister to it, and shall encamp around the Tabernacle. [51] And when the Tabernacle is to leave the Levites shall take it down. And when the Tabernacle is to be pitched the Levites shall raise it. And any unauthorized man who comes near shall be put to death. [52] And the people of Israel shall encamp, each with his own group, and each by his standard,[a] according to their companies. [53] But the Levites shall encamp around the Tabernacle of the Testimony, so that there shall not be wrath [a] against the congregation of the people of Israel. And the Levites shall be responsible for the Tabernacle of the Testimony." [54] And the people of Israel did everything which Yahweh commanded Moses.[a] This they did.

Notes

49.a. *G* translates as ὁρα "see to it," "take heed."

50.a. The emphatic pronoun is not necessarily intended to exclude Aaron, as suggested by A. Dillmann (*Numeri*, 11). Its effect is to emphasize the antithesis—between "numbering" and "appointing."

50.b. *BHS* suggests reading בּוֹ "in it."

52.a. Sam has דֹרֹתָיו "in his place" (?) (cf. Num 2:17). The reading lacks substantial support, and is therefore improbable.

53.a. *G* reads ἁμάρτημα "failure," "error," "sin." This seems to be an attempt to interpret *MT*.

54.a. *G* has "and Aaron" here. There are no plural verbs in *MT* to suggest Aaron's presence in the original text. *G* is probably to be rejected.

Form/Structure/Setting

There is complete agreement among analysts that the section belongs to the priestly strata of tradition, but no general consent about its place within those strata. According to J. Wellhausen (*Hexateuch*, 178–79) vv 48–54 should precede vv 17–47. In his view the command not to number the Levites should precede the census itself. A. Kuenen (*An Historico-Critical Inquiry into the Origin and Composition of the Hexateuch* [London: Macmillan, 1886] 94) dissented from this view on the ground that strict logic is not to be expected in narratives of this kind. G. B. Gray (*Numbers*, 2–3) takes the view that in PG the separation of Levi and the description of his functions probably came before the census. M. Noth (*Numbers*, 17) considers vv 48–54 to be dependent upon v 47, and to be from a later writer—one who anticipates the theme about the organization of the camp in Num 2:1–34, and who is anxious to secure an early reference to the special position of the Levites. D. Kellermann (*Priesterschrift* 17–32) takes the whole of Num 1:48–2:34 as a unit, and like Noth considers vv 48–54 to be a late accretion to the material in Num 2:1–34. He is inclined to see the earlier elements of this accretion in vv 48, 50 (minus the clause וְעַל כָּל אֲשֶׁר־לֹו, and possibly הַמִּשְׁכָּן), 52, 54. The texts forbidding a counting of the Levites, and grounding it in a command of Yahweh (vv 47, 49) are judged to be later, while vv 51, 53, and the glossing in v 50 are later still. These latter elements are said to come from one author who was particularly interested in the question of Levitical service. J. de Vaulx (*Les Nombres* 57) is also inclined to view vv 47–54 as redactional.

The grounds for seeing v 48 as the beginning of a new section are clear enough. The *waw* consecutive cannot properly be rendered "for" as in RV and RSV. It is less obvious that the command not to number the Levites necessarily precedes the census. The author's ultimate concern in Num 1:1–54 is to affirm the separateness of Levites. Instead of revealing this intention at the outset he works toward it, a method which ultimately makes the point with just as much effect. The fact that the section "anticipates" material in Num 2:1–4:49 is not of itself an indication of secondary editing. The concern to assert the separateness of Levites fully justifies the inclusion of the material at this point, in close association with the lay census. The forthcoming material in Num 2:1–4:49 can just as well be viewed as further interpretative expansion of this section.

The most pressing critical problem is the census prohibition itself (v 49). As J. Bright observes ("The Apodictic Prohibition: Some Observations," *JBL* 92 [1973] 185–204) the prohibition seems on the face of it to have permanent validity, and to be a basis for not including Levites in any census. Yet in Num 4:1–43 a census of Levites *is* conducted. If Bright is correct then the possibility that the command of v 49 is temporary has to be excluded. On the other hand the author of Numbers must have found some way of understanding the problem. Perhaps he took the view that since the Levites are entirely separate from the lay tribes they cannot be numbered as part of a lay census. That does not mean that they cannot be numbered on their own account in a clerical census.

If Bright is correct the problem could be solved by suggesting that the author has incorporated and partly rewritten some earlier Levitical tradition in vv 48–50, a suggestion which makes use of some of Kellermann's analytical findings. This would be broadly traceable to Deuteronomic levels in the tradition where "the tribe of Levi" (v 49) exercised overall priestly responsibility. In fact vv 48–50 contain all the essentials of the section as a whole—the census prohibition, responsibility for the oversight and transport of the Tabernacle, and the obligation of encampment around it. In vv 51–54 the author may himself be offering further elaboration of these themes, repeating and developing those relating to Levitical responsibilities, and stressing specific Levitical obligations. This might explain why the "Tent of Meeting" (v 1) is now the "Tabernacle" (v 50). The latter term could be an element of earlier sanctuary tradition with which the tribe of Levi had become associated. It is conceivable that the ancient suspicion of the census (see *Explanation* on Num 1:1–47 was, at Deuteronomic levels of the tradition (from the seventh to the fifth centuries B.C.), channeled into a refusal to number the tribe of Levi.

Comment

49. On the vexing question of Levitical history see *Bibliography*. Though the matter is far from certain the Levites may well have had lay origins (Gen 49:5–7). From an early stage some at least seem to have acquired oracular expertise (Deut 33:8), and Levites in general became recognized for their commitment to Yahwism (Exod 32:25–29; Judg 17:13). Deuteronomy asserts their peculiar rights as priests (33:10; 18:5). The question of their relationship to the "sons of Zadok" raised problems which are reflected in Ezek 44:10–27. These problems are ultimately resolved by the author of Numbers.

50. The use of פָּקַד in its other sense—"to appoint"—is striking. On its place within Levitical tradition see M. Gertner, "The Masorah and the Levites," *VT* 10 (1960) 241–72 (especially p. 252).

50. מִשְׁכַּן הָעֵדֻת "the Tabernacle of the Testimony." "Tabernacle" indicates that the sanctuary is a place where God dwells (see *Comment* on Num 1:1). The full phrase is uncommon in P, occurring only in this section and in Exod 38:21; Num 10:11. It entails some reference to the ark and the tables of the law within it; cf. the phrases "Tables of the Testimony" (Exod 31:18; 32:15; 34:29), "Ark of the Testimony" (Exod 25:22; 26:33–34; 30:6, 26; 31:7; 39:35; 40:3, 5, 20–21; Num 4:5; 7:89; Josh 4:16), "Tent of the Testimony" (Num 9:15; 17:22–23; 18:2; 2 Chr 24:6), "Veil of the Testimony" (Lev 24:3). It is possible that "testimony" originally referred to some written seal of God's promise to dwell with Israel. Its use in association with the law tablets stresses the fact that law is a constant reminder to Israel of the nature and content of obedience.

50. יְשָׁרְתֻהוּ "they shall minister to it." This root is widely used of the "service" rendered by a subordinate to a superior—to an official (Gen 39:4; 40:4), a prince (2 Sam 13:17–18), a king (1 Kgs 10:5; 2 Chr 17:19; 22:8; Prov 29:12; Esth 1:10; 2:2; 6:3), or a prophet (1 Kgs 19:21; 2 Kgs 4:43). The service rendered by Joshua to Moses may have had some connection with the Tent of Meeting (Exod 24:13; 33:11; Num 11:28). P uses the root

exclusively of service rendered at the sanctuary by the priestly hierarchy (cf. also Deut 10:8; 17:12; 21:5; 1 Sam 2:11, 18; Jer 33:21–22; Joel 1:9; 2:17, and possibly Ps 103:21). The author of Exodus can use it of Aaron's ministry (Exod 28:35, 43; 29:30; 30:20; 35:19; 39:1, 26, 41). The author of Numbers limits its use to Levitical service, as here (Num 3:6, 31; 4:9, 12, 14; 16:9; 18:2).

51. וְהַזָּר "any unauthorized man." Here the word clearly means anyone not belonging to the tribe of Levi. Essentially it denotes something alien (cf. Deut 25:5; Hos 5:7). In P it means, in effect, "the layman." See further L. A. Snijders (OTS 10 [1954] 1–154).

52. דִּגְלוֹ "his standard." G. B. Gray (Numbers, 20) favors "company" (cf. J. de Vaulx, Nombres, 71; G; Syr; Tg.; Vg). KB suggests some kind of tribal division. The root occurs elsewhere in Ps 20:6; Cant 2:4; 5:10; 6:4—a conspicuous object seems to be intended. It seems to involve here something visible and striking which marked off one tribe from another, so that the traditional renderings in terms of "standard" or "banner" seem justified.

53. קֶצֶף "wrath." A breach of the clerical/lay distinction would lead at once to some disastrous demonstration of divine anger (cf. Num 8:19). This represents a continuation of an older faith concerning the ark (1 Sam 6:19; 2 Sam 6:6–8). The word itself occurs only in exilic or post-exilic texts.

53. וְשָׁמְרוּ . . . אֶת-מִשְׁמֶרֶת "and they shall be responsible for," literally "they shall keep the service of." This is a typical expression in P for particular clerical duties. The usage can be traced to Ezekiel (e.g. 40:45–46; 44:8, 14–15). As Gray points out (Numbers, 16) the phrase has a more general frame of reference in earlier writings (e.g. Gen 26:5; Deut 11:1).

Explanation

Having established the dimensions of the lay community the author introduces one of his major preoccupations—the distinctiveness of the Levites in relation to the rest of the community. Because of this they are not to be counted along with the other tribes, and they have special responsibilities with respect to the Tabernacle. They, and they alone, erect it, take it down, and carry it. When in camp they, and they alone, pitch their tents around it. It may well be that the author has drawn in older Levitical tradition to the effect that members of the tribe of Levi were not to be counted. For him this means that they are not to be numbered as a mere component of the larger mass of lay tribes. Moreover any lay person who dares to engage in their ministry must be put to death. Israelites at large must be aware of the cruciality of Levitical ministry for their own safety and well-being.

This concern is part of a wider programmed design to secure an ordered hierarchical pattern in the priestly leadership. Deuteronomy had already established that the tribe of Levi was the only tribe with rights of priestly ministry. Ezek 40:1–48:35 identifies "the sons of Zadok" as the true Levitical priesthood of Deuteronomy (34:19; 34:15). They were the established pre-exilic priesthood at Jerusalem whose ministry is authenticated in 1 Sam 2:27–36. Ezekiel contrasts these sons of Zadok with apostate Levites who are to be excluded from priesthood as such, and restricted to certain limited functions within the sanctuary (44:10–14). For them this is humiliating. It entails bearing their "shame." There is little doubt that this reflects dissension within the priesthood, traceable to the traumatic events associated with the exile. These dissensions became more critical once the prospect of return became a reality. Ezekiel, as representative of Babylonian Judaism, is perhaps taking the side of the first deportees (598 B.C.) over against those who functioned in Jerusalem under Zedekiah from 598–587 B.C. Alternatively he may be taking the side of exiled priests in general over against those who had remained in the land. In any event the search for authenticity in the exilic and post-exilic period was important. The author of Exodus was able to validate exiled priests by identifying them as "sons of Aaron." Their priesthood had roots in the pre-settlement period, and does not therefore depend upon possession of the land. The author of Numbers accepts this, but is exercised by further uncertainty and dissension about the priestly hierarchy. He accepts the basic division of function between an altar priesthood and subsidiary ministers as set out in Ezekiel. His great contribution to the developing tradition is the addition of a significant functional sense to the word "Levite," and his recognition that the subsidiary ministry was not originally a thing of "shame," but was providentially constituted in the wilderness by God himself. It was a ministry of dignity involving a care for the Tabernacle which only they could exercise, and one which was crucial to the security of the Israelites in general. In this recognition of the validity of Levitical tradition there may well be a conciliatory dimension. Thus the author formulates at the outset his Levitical theology, and proceeds in Num 2:1–4:49 to build on the insights of this section and of Num 1:1–54 as a whole.

It thus appears that one response of post-exilic faith to the crises of the times was to secure fixed and recognized patterns of leadership and control. There was a profound sense of the possibility of disaster (v 53), and illegitimate leadership and claims to authority were identified as the greatest source of danger. The priestly programs are in part a solution to the crisis of authority. They aim to secure authentic religion through structures of authority and control. The dangers in this as a permanent response are the exclusion of charisma, and slowness to adapt to new needs. Furthermore the priestly hierarchy and the Tabernacle structure it served were inclined to put the ordinary man at some distance from God, highlighting the awesomeness of a deity able to bring the worst of disasters on Israel. The analysis involved the conviction that too much freedom on the part of king, false prophets, and the people generally had led pre-exilic Israel to destruction. The new order was intended to provide the security of a structure giving an authentic but controlled contact between God and people. Compensation for the structured distance between God and people generally was found in the notion of God's dwelling at the center of the community's life—a theme explored in the following section.

The Community As a Priestly
Theocracy   (2:1–34)

Bibliography

Douglas, C. E. "The Twelve Houses of Israel." *JTS* 37 (1936) 49–56. **Kuschke, A.** "Die Lagervorstellung der priesterschriftlichen Erzählung." *ZAW* 22 (1951) 74–105. **Roach, C. C.** "The Camp in the Wilderness: A Sermon on Numbers 2:2." *Int* 13 (1959) 49–54. **St. Clair, G.** "Israel in Camp: A Study." *JTS* 8 (1907) 185–217.

Translation

[1] *And Yahweh spoke to Moses and to Aaron, saying,* [2] *"The people of Israel shall encamp, each by his standard, with the emblems of their fathers' houses. They shall encamp in sight of the Tent of Meeting, and round about it.* [3] *And those who pitch on the east side,[a] toward the sunrise, shall belong to the standard of the camp of Judah, company by company. And the leader of the people of Judah shall be Nahshon, son of Amminadab.[b]* [4] *And his company, as numbered,[a] came to 74,600.* [5] *And those who pitch next to him shall be the tribe of Issachar.[a] And the leader of the people of Issachar shall be Nethanel, son of Zuar.* [6] *And his company, as numbered,[a] came to 54,400.* [7] *And[a] the tribe of Zebulun. And the leader of the people of Zebulun shall be Eliab, son of Helon.* [8] *And his company, as numbered, came to 57,400.* [9] *All those numbered of the camp of Judah came to 186,400, company by company. And they shall leave first on the march.*

[10] *The standard of the camp of Reuben shall be to the south, company by company. And the leader of the people of Reuben shall be Elizur, son of Shedeur.* [11] *And his company, as numbered, came to 46,500.* [12] *And those who pitch next to him shall be the tribe of Simeon. And the leader of the people of Simeon shall be Shelumiel, son of Zurishaddai.* [13] *And his company, as numbered, came to 59,300.* [14] *And the tribe of Gad. And the leader of the people of Gad shall be Eliasaph, son of Reuel.[a]* [15] *And his company, as numbered, came to 45,650.* [16] *All those numbered of the camp of Reuben came to 151,450, company by company. And they shall leave second on the march.*

[17] *And the Tent of Meeting shall leave next, with the camp of the Levites in the middle of the camps. As they encamp so shall they leave on the march, each in his place according to their standards.[a]*

[18] *The standard of the camp of Ephraim company by company shall be to the west. And the leader of the people of Ephraim shall be Elishama, son of Ammihud.* [19] *And his company, as numbered, came to 40,500.* [20] [a] *And next to him the tribe of Manasseh. And the leader of the people of Manasseh shall be Gamaliel, son of Pedahzur.* [21] *And his company, as numbered, came to 32,200.* [22] *And the tribe of Benjamin. And the leader of the people of Benjamin was Abidan, son of Gideoni.* [23] *And his company, as numbered, came to 35,400.* [24] *All those numbered of the camp of Ephraim came to 108,100, company by company. And they shall leave third on the march.*

[25] *The standard of the camp of Dan shall be to the north, company by company.*

And the leader of the people of Dan shall be Ahiezer, son of Ammishaddai. [26] *And his company, as numbered, came to 62,700.* [27] *And those who pitch next to him shall be the tribe of Asher. And the leader of the people of Asher shall be Pagiel, son of Ochran.* [28] *And his company, as numbered, came to 41,500.* [29] *And the tribe of Naphtali. And the leader of the people of Naphtali shall be Ahira, son of Enan.* [30] *And his company, as numbered, came to 53,400.* [31] *All those numbered of the camp of Dan came to 157,600.*[a] *They shall leave fourth on the march, standard by standard.''*

[32] *These are those who were numbered of the people of Israel, by fathers' houses. All those numbered in the camps, company by company, came to 603,550.* [33] *But the Levites were not numbered* [a] *along with the people of Israel, as Yahweh commanded Moses.*

[34] *And the people of Israel did everything which Yahweh commanded Moses. So they pitched camp by their standards, and so they set out, each one by his clan and fathers' house.*

Notes

3.a. G^B reads κατα νοτον "on the south side" (cf. *L*)—apparently an error. Other *G* witnesses read πρωτοι "the first." The word מִזְרָחָה "toward the sunrise" is strictly superfluous, but MT poses no serious difficulty, and it need not be omitted.

3.b. On the nominal clause here and in the chapter as a whole see J. Hoftijzer, "The Nominal Clause Reconsidered," *VT* 23 (1973) 500, 504.

4.a. J. Paterson (*Numbers*, 42) exaggerates the tautology here. The singular suffix in צְבָאוֹ, followed by a plural in וּפְקֻדֵיהֶם, is admittedly awkward, but there are no good textual grounds for omitting one word or the other. The awkwardness arises from the author's interest in a wide variety of technical terms.

5.a. See note on Num 1:8.

6.a. The singular suffix occurs again in vv 8, 11, and throughout in *S*. The plural is the norm (nine times in this chapter), and may be original. The singular is not necessarily the result of the editing of separate traditions (J. Paterson, Ibid, 42; G. B. Gray, *Numbers*, 20). It could easily be scribal, reflecting the consistent use of the singular suffix in צְבָאוֹ.

7.a. The conjunction should probably be added, as in vv 14, 22, 29, and as attested in Sam, *G, S*.

14.a. See note on Num 1:14.

17.a. *BHS* recommends the removal of v 17b to the end of v 2. This produces a better ordered text, but lacks textual support (see further under *Form/Structure/Setting*).

20.a. It may be that וְהַחֹנִים has fallen out here (cf. vv 5, 12, 27).

31.a. In the corresponding phrases in vv 9, 16, 24 לְצִבְאֹתָם is used. Such deviations are striking in formal contexts such as this, and may be attributable to scribal error.

33.a. See note on Num 1:47.

Form/Structure/Setting

There is general recognition that the section belongs to priestly levels in the Pentateuch, and for those accepting PG/PS theories there is wide acknowledgment that PG is present. J. Wellhausen (*Hexateuch*, 179) sees the whole of the chapter as groundwork. G. B. Gray (*Numbers*, 3) suggests that the original order in PG consisted of an initial description of the central position of the Tent, followed by an account of the Levitical encampment (as in chap. 3), and finally of the encampment of the lay tribes (as in chap. 2). According to D. Kellermann (*Priesterschrift*, 17–32) the original elements from PG are to be found in vv 1 (not "Aaron"), 2 (most), 3a, 5a, 7a, 10a, 12a, 14a, 18a, 20a, 22a, 25a, 27a, 29a, 34 (most). The word וְהַחֹנִים "and those who pitch" (vv 3, 5, 12, 27) is excluded. Kellermann's suggestion thus eliminates the names of tribal leaders, and the statistics about tribal dimensions. A subsequent redactor would have drawn in all this material from chap. 1, computing the figure for each of the four groups (vv 9, 16, 24, 31), and adding vv 32–33. At a third level comes the idea of "pitching" the tents, which in Kellermann's view serves to show that the ordering of the camp held for every station on the march. This third author is reputedly thinking beforehand in terms of Num 10:14–28. The word וּצְבָאוֹ "and his company" (vv 4, 6, 8, 11, 13, 15, 19, 21, 23, 26, 28, 30) and elements in v 34 are taken to reflect the same perspective. Further minor elaboration, including the incorporation of Aaron in v 1, is assumed to follow at later levels.

Both Gray and Kellermann, in their search for PG, are looking for an ideal of good order and succinctness. The likely danger in this procedure is the imposition of subjective patterns of coherence. Occasional awkwardness in syntax is not in itself a necessary sign of editorial activity. Indications of some purposeful accretion to tradition are desirable. If an editor saw grounds for the incorporation of material from chap. 1, then the author himself may have had grounds for simply repeating his material. There is certainly no good reason for positing an original text in which the idea of a journey and of regular encampments is absent. The more restrained view of editorial activity exemplified by J. de Vaulx (*Les Nombres*, 57–58) is preferable.

B. D. Eerdmans (*OTS* 6 [1949] 101–216) suggests that an ancient source lies behind the existing text. He understands v 2 to indicate close proximity to the Tent on the part of the lay tribes—a pre-exilic view, he suggests, which betrays no fear of its holiness. Another ground for his suspicion that the tradition is historically uneven is his belief that v 34 sees the beginning of the march, though in fact no command to such purpose has been given. These are not very strong grounds for the conclusion drawn. In v 2 neither מִנֶּגֶד nor סָבִיב necessarily implies close proximity. The former can readily mean "in sight of" (*KB*), or even "at a distance" (Deut 32:52; 2 Kgs 2:15), and the latter means merely "on all sides." If a priestly author had understood v 2 to mean close proximity he would probably have modified it. The reference to a march in v 34 is not necessarily specific. It simply indicates the customary procedure.

The only serious difficulty in seeing the essentials of vv 1–34 as an integral unit is v 17. The thought appears to have moved rather abruptly from the arrangement of the camp to the order of the march. The reference in v 24 to the Ephraim group, and its third position in the column might seem to take no account of v 17. Moreover the order of movement suggested here does not entirely cohere with the more detailed provisions of Num 10:17–21.

Even here, however, the problems should not be overpressed. The thought of movement is present in vv 9, 16, 24, 31, and there are no very good reasons for eliminating these references as secondary. To indicate as v 17 does that the Tent takes a central position on the march, as in an encampment, seems entirely desirable. Since the author has not yet analyzed the encampment of the Levites, the third position of the Ephraimites (v 24) should not be pressed as a problem. The tension with Num 10:17–21 may be explicable in terms of detail, and the author's real center of attention. Here the author is preoccupied with the details of the lay encampment, but wishes the reader to remember that this is an army on the march. In Num 10 he is preoccupied with the details of the march, and tackles there a particular problem (which need not concern him here) by distinguishing between the Tent structure and the holy objects it contains. The latter move at the center of the army, while the former occupy the position between the Judah and Reuben groups. The literary technique may very well be deliberate (see further under *Explanation*). For the present the author is concerned only that the Levites should not be forgotten. It is sufficient to indicate their central position on the march, along with the Tent (v 17a), and to hint that they too are organized into groups (v 17b). He has more to say on the latter topic in chaps. 3–4.

Comment

2. בְּאֹתֹת "emblems." This word is widely used in the OT of different kinds of "signs." Within P it can be used of some aid to memory, calling duties to mind, God's activity in the past, or basic aspects of his will (Gen 9:12; 17:1; Exod 31:13, 17; Num 17:25). Such signs can be a deterrent (Num 17:3). The use of the word as here of some kind of emblem is rare (cf. Ps 74:4). For further discussion see B. O. Long, *The Problem of Etiological Narrative in the Old Testament* (BZAW 108; Berlin: Töpelmann, 1968) 65–78. According to L. E. Binns (*The Book of Numbers*): the אוֹת represented the whole group of three tribes, but it is just as possible that each tribe had one, and that the אוֹת was an emblem of some kind for each fathers' house.

3. קֵדְמָה מִזְרָחָה "toward the sunrise" is strictly tautological (see *Notes*), but this kind of style is not uncommon in P (Exod 27:13; 38:13; Num 3:38; 34:15; Josh 19:13).

5. עָלָיו "alongside." We should probably take the reference to Zebulun in v 7 as part of the predicate, in which case Judah takes the central position among the three tribes on the eastern side. The same would apply to Reuben, Ephraim, and Dan on the other three sides.

10. תֵּימָנָה "to the south," literally "on the right hand." The perspective is of one facing east, and "to the south" seems a satisfactory rendering (cf. Exod 26:18, 35; 27:9; 36:23; 38:9; Num 3:29; 10:6). The idiom occurs in Ezekiel (21:2; 47:19; 48:28) and in Deut 3:27—cf. also Ps 78:26; Jer 39:26; Cant 4:16 where the root denotes "south wind."

17. עַל-יָדוֹ "in his place," literally "upon his hand." The expression must mean "in his recognized position" (cf. Num 13:29; Deut 23:12; Jer 6:3).

Explanation

This section contains detailed information about the organization of Israel in camp. The Tent of Meeting is at the center, and the twelve lay tribes are arranged around it in a square, with three on each side. There is a Judah group to the east, including Issachar and Zebulun, a Reuben group to the

south, including Simeon and Gad, an Ephraim group to the west, including
Manasseh and Benjamin, and a Dan group to the north, including Asher
and Naphtali.

Having established the dimensions of the community, and indicated the
distinctiveness of the Levites as a clerical group (Num 1:1–54), the author
is ready to lay the foundations for his understanding of the community as a
priestly theocracy. It has to be remembered that the books of the Pentateuch
were widely used in Judaism for purposes of public recitation, and it is entirely
reasonable to suspect that such a concern was a factor in their final shaping
and formation. From this perspective techniques of literary construction can
be discerned which rule out the need to posit complex processes of redaction.
The technique involves:

1. The further explanation of material already given—in this instance of
the encampment referred to in Num 1:52.

2. The simple repetition of material already given, as an aid to memory
and for purposes of enforcement—in this instance the names of the tribal
leaders, the census figures, and the emphasis on the distinctiveness of the
Levites (v 33).

3. The presentation of new ideas, many of which receive further attention
and elaboration in sections yet to come—in this instance information about
the order of the march.

The fundamental theme of the section is that of the community gathered
round the Tent of Meeting. This is an important foundation for the further
examination of the priestly theocracy in Num 3–4. The community is gathered
around the sanctuary, which is therefore the real focal point of its continuing
life. The Tent of Meeting is not an external institution as in earlier tradition
(Exod 33:7–11; Num 11:24–30), but the hub of the community's life. The
priestly author was anxious to establish the second Temple as just such an
institution, and he argues that his program has deep roots in Mosaic times.

The inspiration for such a view was already present in Ezek 40:1–48:35.
The lay tribes are fulfilling something of the function of the walls of the
outer court in Ezek 40:1–27, or of the city in Ezek 48:30–35. The primacy
of the east side is attested in Ezek 47:1, while the idea of holiness at the
center is present in Ezek 48:8–22. As M. Noth suggests the pattern of tribal
assembly on four sides may have deeper roots (*Numbers*, 24). Though the
evidence is scarcely decisive such texts as 1 Sam 4:4–8, Judg 18:20, and 2
Sam 11:11 may bear witness to a central position for the ark. In any event
it seems likely that reflection on Ezekiel is the immediate influence as far as
Numbers is concerned.

The ordering of the tribes is rather different from that proposed in Ezek
48:30–35, but it is not hard to suggest a basis on which it was reached.
The author works from his list of tribal leaders in Num 1:5–15. This has an
inner logic with respect to its order. The five Leah tribes (minus Levi) come
first, in their traditional order of birth. Then come the three Rachel tribes,
with the supremacy which tradition gave to Ephraim (Gen 48:19) duly acknowledged. The four tribes of the concubines follow, though there is no obvious
reason for the ordering within this group. The author of Numbers evidently
wishes to place Judah in the prime position. This is entirely appropriate in

the post-exilic situation, and it may also be reflected in the high census figure for that tribe. Since in Gen 49:2–27 and Deut 33:2–29 there are evident traditions of decline associated with Reuben and Simeon, the promotion of Judah, given the exclusion of Levi, is entirely justified. So Judah heads the group in the prime position, the eastern side, while Reuben and Simeon are relegated to the southern side. The two Leah tribes which follow Judah in the original list of Num 1:5–15 are represented as accompanying Judah on the eastern side. There is obviously good reason for keeping the Rachel triad together, and they, maintaining roughly their overall position in the original list, are placed on the western side. This necessitates the promotion of one of the concubine tribes to accompany Reuben and Simeon on the southern side. In Ezek 48:32 Dan appears to get this kind of preferential treatment. Here Gad is selected, possibly because he is the firstborn of Leah's handmaid. The remaining concubine tribes are placed on the north side, and follow the order of the list. Dan is by tradition the eldest, and occupies the central position.

This picture of the organization of Israel in camp is an expression of the author's understanding of the theology of the divine presence. There are barriers which divide a holy God from a fallible Israel. The structure of the Tent itself and the construction of a sophisticated priestly hierarchy has the effect, at least potentially, of emphasizing the difference and distance between man and God. This is valuable to theology as a perspective, but requires the compensating search for nearness and presence. The priestly author sought to affirm this in and through his insistence that God is to be found, tabernacled among his people, at the center of their life as a community.

The Structure and Dimensions of the Priestly Hierarchy (3:1-51)

Bibliography

Abérbach, M. & Smolar, L. "Aaron, Jeroboam, and the Golden Calves." *JBL* 86 (1967) 129–40. Auerbach, E. "Die Herkunft der Sadokiten." *ZAW* 49 (1931) 327–28. Bartlett, J. R. "Zadok and His Successors at Jerusalem." *JTS* 19 (1968) 1–18. Bentzen, A. "Zur Geschichte der Sadokiten." *ZAW* 10 (1933) 173–76. Brin, G. *The First-Born in Israel in the Biblical Period* Diss.: Tel-Aviv, 1971. Gradwohl, R. "Das 'fremde Feuer' von Nadab und Abihu." *ZAW* 75 (1963) 288–96. Greenberg, M. "A New Approach to the History of the Isarelite Priesthood." *JAOS* 70 (1950) 41–46. Haran, M. "The Uses of Incense in the Ancient Israelite Ritual." *VT* 10 (1960) 113–29. Hooke, S. H. "Theory and Practice of Substitution." *VT* 2 (1952) 2–17. Judge, H. G. Aaron, Zadok and Abiathar." *JTS* 7 (1956) 70–74. Kennett, R. H. "The Origin of the Aaronite Priesthood." *JTS* 6 (1905) 161–86; *JTS* 7 (1906) 620–24. Laughlin, J. C. H. "The Strange Fire of Nadab and Abihu." *JBL* 95 (1976) 559–65. Meek, T. J. "Aaronites and Zadokites." *AJSL* 45 (1929) 149–66. Morgenstern, J. "A Chapter in the History of the High Priesthood." *AJSL* 55 (1938) 1–24, 360–77. North, F. "Aaron's Rise in Prestige." *ZAW* 66 (1954) 191–99. Robinson, G. "The Prohibition of Strange Fire in Ancient Israel." *VT* 28 (1978) 301–17. Westphal, G. "Aaron und die Aaroniden." *ZAW* 26 (1906) 201–30. Valentin, H. *Aaron. Eine Studie zur vor-priesterschriftlichen Aaron Überlieferung.* Göttingen: Vandenhoeck & Ruprecht, 1978. On the Levites see Num 1:48–54 (*Bibliography*).

Translation

[1] And this is the genealogical list of Aaron and Moses [a] on the day when Yahweh spoke [b] to Moses on Mount Sinai. [2] And these are the names of the sons of Aaron— Nadab, the first born, and Abihu, Eleazar and Ithamar. [3] These are the names of the sons of Aaron, the anointed priests, who were consecrated to the priesthood. [4] And Nadab and Abihu died before Yahweh [a] when offering strange fire before Yahweh in the wilderness of Sinai. And they had no sons. And Eleazar and Ithamar served as priests in the presence of Aaron their father.

[5] And Yahweh spoke to Moses, saying, [6] "Bring near the tribe of Levi, and make them stand before Aaron the priest, and they shall minister to him. [7] And they shall be in attendance on him and on all the congregation before the Tent of Meeting, performing the work of the Tabernacle. [8] And they shall keep all the implements of the Tent of Meeting, and be in attendance on the people of Israel, performing the work of the Tabernacle. [9] And you shall give the Levites to Aaron and to his sons. They shall be wholly given [a] to him [b] from among [c] the people of Israel. [10] And you shall appoint Aaron and his sons [a] and they shall keep their priestly office. [b] And any unauthorized man who comes near shall be put to death."

[11] And Yahweh spoke to Moses, saying, [12] "Behold, I have taken the Levites from among the people of Israel in place of all the firstborn from among the people of Israel. [a] And the Levites shall be mine. [13] For all the firstborn are mine. On the day that I struck all the firstborn in the land of Egypt I sanctified for myself all the firstborn in Israel, both man and beast. They shall be mine. I am Yahweh."

[14] *And Yahweh spoke to Moses in the wilderness of Sinai, saying,* [15] *"Count the sons of Levi, by fathers' houses and clans, every male. You shall count those aged one month and over."* [16] *And Moses* [a] *counted them, in accordance with Yahweh's word, as Yahweh had commanded him.* [b] [17] *And these were the names of the sons of Levi—Gershon, and Kohath, and Merari.* [18] *And these were the names of the sons of Gershon by their clans—Libni and Shimei.* [19] *And the sons of Kohath by their clans—Amram and Izhar, Hebron and Uzziel.* [20] *And the sons of Merari by their clans—Mahli and Mushi. These are the clans of the Levites by their fathers' houses.*

[21] *To Gershon belonged the clan of the Libnites and the clan of the Shimeites. These were the Gershonite clans.* [22] *Their number, counting all the males from the age of one month and upwards, was 7,500.* [a] [23] *The clans of the Gershonites shall encamp behind the Tabernacle, to the west.* [24] *And the leader of the fathers' house of the Gershonites shall be Eliasaph, son of Lael.* [25] *And the ministry of the sons of Gershon in the Tent of Meeting shall concern the Tabernacle and the Tent, its covering, and the screen for the door of the Tent of Meeting,* [26] *and the hangings of the court, and the* [a] *screen for the door of the court which is round about the Tabernacle and the altar, and its cords, and all pertaining to it.*

[27] *And to Kohath belonged the clan of the Amramites and the clan of the Izharites and the clan of the Hebronites and the clan of the Uzzielites. These were the Kohathite clans.* [28] *Counting* [a] *all the males from the age of one month and upwards there were 8,600* [b] *engaged in the ministry of the sanctuary.* [c] [29] *The clans of the sons of Kohath shall encamp beside the Tabernacle to the south.* [30] *And the leader of the fathers' house of the clans of the Kohathites shall be Elizaphan, son of Uzziel.* [31] *And their ministry shall concern the ark and the table and the candlestick and the altars,* [a] *and the implements of the sanctuary which they use, and the screen, and all pertaining to it.* [32] *And in charge of the leaders of the Levites* [a] *shall be Eleazar son of Aaron the priest. He is appointed over* [b] *those exercising the ministry of the sanctuary.*

[33] *And to Merari belonged the clan of the Mahlites and the clan of the Mushites. These were the clans of Merari.* [34] *And their number, counting all the males from the age of one month and upwards, was 6,200.* [35] *And the leader of the fathers' house of the clans of Merari was Zuriel, son of Abihail. They shall encamp beside the Tabernacle to the north.* [36] *And the duties of ministry of the sons of Merari shall concern the frames of the Tabernacle and its bars, its pillars, and its bases, and all its implements, and all pertaining to them,* [37] *and the pillars of the court round about, and their bases, and their pegs, and their cords.*

[38] *And those who encamp in front of the Tabernacle to the east,* [a] *before the Tent of Meeting, toward the sunrise, shall be Moses, Aaron and his sons, exercising the ministry of the sanctuary on behalf of the people of Israel. And any unauthorized man who comes near shall be put to death.* [39] *The total number of Levites which Moses and Aaron* [a] *counted, in accordance with the word of Yahweh, by clans, every male from the age of one month and upwards, was 22,000.*

[40] *And Yahweh said to Moses, "Count all the firstborn of the people of Israel, from the age of one month and upward, and calculate the number of persons.* [41] *And you shall take the Levites for me (I am Yahweh) in place of all the firstborn of the people of Israel, and the cattle of the Levites in place of all the firstborn of the cattle of the people of Israel."* [42] *And as Yahweh commanded him Moses counted all the firstborn of the people of Israel.* [43] *And all the firstborn, calculating the number of persons, from the age of one month and upwards, came to 22,273.*

⁴⁴ *And Yahweh spoke to Moses, saying,* ⁴⁵ *"Take the Levites in place of all the firstborn of the people of Israel, and the cattle of the Levites in place of their cattle. And the Levites shall be mine. I am Yahweh.* ⁴⁶ *And for the* ᵃ *redemption of the 273 from the firstborn of the people of Israel who exceed the Levites,* ⁴⁷ *you shall take five shekels per person, reckoning by the sanctuary shekel. This shekel is equal to twenty gerahs.* ⁴⁸ *And you shall give the money to Aaron and to his sons, for the redemption of the surplus."* ⁴⁹ *And Moses took the redemption* ᵃ *money paid for those in excess of the number redeemed by the Levites.* ⁵⁰ *He took the money from the firstborn of the people of Israel—1,365 (shekels),* ᵃ *reckoned by the sanctuary shekel.* ⁵¹ *And Moses gave the redemption money to Aaron and to his sons, in accordance with the word of Yahweh, as Yahweh commanded Moses.*

Notes

1.a. *BHS* suggests the deletion of "Moses." His genealogy is not given. Some commentators support this. "Moses" is present in all versions, and ought probably to be accepted. The author is concerned only with the genealogy of Aaron, but wished to remind readers of Aaron's close relationship to Moses.

1.b. Taken by GKC § 520 to be the *Piel* perfect.

4.a. "Died before Yahweh" is lacking in one MT ms, Sam, and Vg. J. Paterson (*Numbers*, 42) suggests that the same phrase after זָרָה אֵשׁ has caught the copyist's eye too soon; but cf. Lev 10:2.

9.a. The repetition is for emphasis; see GKC § 123e.

9.b. Some MT mss, Sam and *G* have "to me" (cf. Num 8:16). The idea that the Levites belong to Yahweh emerges in vv 11–13, and is best excluded here. See discussion under *Explanation*.

9.c. The correct reading may be מֵאִתּוֹ (Sam, *S*), as in v 12 and Num 8:16.

10.a. *G* appears to have added "over the Tent of Meeting."

10.b. *G* has further material concerning the altar and priestly ministry (cf. Num 18:7). It is probably a secondary explanation of "keeping their priesthood."

12.a. Sam and *G* read פְּדֻיֵיהֶם יִהְיוּ "and they shall be for their redemption." This is probably an insertion based on the themes of vv 44–51.

16.a. The reference to Aaron in *G* is probably secondary—n.b. the singular verb.

16.b. *BHS* suggests that וַיְהִי (beginning of v 17) should be read as יהוה, and incorporated in v 16, with צִוָּה emended to צִוָּהוּ "as Yahweh commanded him." Verse 17 would begin with וְאֵלֶּה. The usual Pual is צֻוֵּיתִי (Lev 8:35; 10:13; Ezek 12:7; 24:18; 37:7). *BHS* seems acceptable.

22.a. The word is absent in Syr and Vg. J. Paterson (*Numbers*, 42) argues that the sentence is too short for the word to be repeated in this way—in his view a transcriptional error (cf. also G. B. Gray, *Numbers*, 27). *BHS* suggests its deletion.

26.a. *BHS* suggests the deletion of אֵת here, and later in the verse, but for explanation of its presence see GKC § 117l; P. P. Saydon, "Meanings and Uses of the Particle אֵת," *VT* 14 (1964) 192–210. J. Macdonald, "The Particle את in Classical Hebrew," *VT* (1964) 263–75.

28.a. One MT ms, Syr and Vg read פְּקֻדֵיהֶם, as in vv 23, 24. This is probably to be preferred (see *BHS;* G. B. Gray, *Numbers*, 28).

28.b. *G*ᴸ has τριακοσιοι "three hundred," reading שְׁלֹשׁ. This is widely accepted. It entails the omission of a single consonant, and the figure is thereby brought into line with the total in v 39.

28.c. J. Paterson (*Numbers*, 42) takes the whole clause "engaged in the ministry of the sanctuary" to be a gloss deriving from v 32. The clause is certainly absent in the parallel sections (vv 22, 34), but Kohath was responsible for the holiest things (Num 4:19), and this may have justified the special reference here.

31.a. *S* has the singular "altar." This is insufficient reason for rejecting MT. The author is aware of the incense altar in Exod 30:1–10.

32.a. Sam, Syr, Tg., read הַלְוִיִּם (cf. Num 1:50). הַלְוִי occurs in v 20 with the support of Sam and should perhaps be accepted (cf. Deut 12:19; Judg 17:7).

32.b. פְּקֻדַּת can be taken as construct of פְּקֻדָּה "oversight" (BDB). *G* reads καθεσταμενος, which is smoother. The construction is awkward, but is best accepted; see G. B. Gray, *Numbers*, 30.

38.a. *G* lacks "in front of the Tabernacle to the east."

39.a. "Aaron" is lacking in some MT mss, Sam, and Syr. The singular verb suggests its deletion; but cf. J. Sturdy, *Numbers* 32.

46.a. On וְאֵת here see GKC §117m; J. Blau, "Zum Angeblichen Gebrauch von אֵת von dem Nominative," *VT* 4 (1954) 7–19; P. P. Saydon. "Meanings and Uses," 208.

49.a. *BHS* recommends הַפְּדֻיִם as in Sam and in the *Qere* and Sam of 51. This is supported by GKC §85t. פְּדוּיִם would be an *hapax legomenon*. The alteration involves the transposition of only two letters and seems desirable.

50.a. *G*[BFL], Syr, *Tg.*[OJ] add שֶׁקֶל "shekel."

Form/Structure/Setting

There is general recognition among analysts that the section belongs to the priestly stratum, but much uncertainty about its literary history. J. Wellhausen (*Hexateuch*, 179–80) took vv 1–4 to be supplementary on the grounds that they simply repeat material from Lev 10:1–7, and that they assume, in contrast to e.g. Exod 29:7 that Aaron's sons are anointed, as well as Aaron himself. Other pointers identified by Wellhausen were the awareness of two altars (v 31—the incense altar of Exod 30:1–10 being widely regarded as secondary), and an interest in a Levitical census—in contrast to Num 1:47. G. B. Gray (*Numbers*, 2–3) took up most of these points, and also drew attention to the "cords" of vv 26, 37—unknown apparently in Exod 25:1–29:46, but present in arguably supplementary texts such as Exod 35:18; 39:40. Gray was inclined to attribute one of the two Levitical censuses (cf. also Num 4:34–39) to PS, but was unable to say which. His search for PG involves discovering what he judges to be a more coherent original pattern, with the counting of the Levites following immediately the numbering of the lay tribes. Information about their position in camp would have come later, following a statement of the centrality of the Tabernacle, but preceding statements about the positioning of other tribes. An observation with more weight (p. 26) is that in vv 11–13 the Levites are "given" to Yahweh, contrasting somewhat with vv 5–10 where they are given to Aaron. For Gray vv 11–13 and related texts (vv 40, 41, 45) could come from a later hand.

More recent analysts find some of these features to be evidence of unevenness. M. Noth (*Numbers*, 30–31) draws attention to new introductions (vv 5, 11, 14), to different formulations of the same material (vv 18–20// vv 21, 27, 33), and to repetition of the substance of vv 25–26, 31, 36–37 in Num 4:4–15. The contact between vv 11–13 and vv 40–51 has been widely recognized, though differing conclusions are based upon it. For Noth vv 11–13 are a correction, favorably disposed to the Levites, of vv 5–10 (see also J. Sturdy. *Numbers*, 26–27). They, along with vv 40–51, are an addition to PG. By contrast D. Kellermann (*Priesterschrift*, 32–49) finds the "given to Yahweh" motif to be earlier (see also N. H. Snaith, *Numbers* 190).

A key question for recent analysis has been the isolation of the original element in vv 14–39. Noth suspects that the classification of Levites and the information about their various duties are the essential core to be attributed to PG (along with vv 5–10). The formulations in vv 21, 27, 33 are judged to be older than those in vv 18–20. Data about the census, the camping positions, and the Levitical leaders are all taken to be accretions. Kellermann is inclined to identify the census rather than the duties as the core of the section, and of the chapter as a whole. For him there is no PG material. The position in the camp and the names of the leaders constitute the first accretion, with duties of each group coming later still—extracted, according to Kellermann, from information in Num 4. A different genealogy of Levi's sons appears at the next stage (vv. 17–20), and later still some minor additions in vv 28, 32. The next stage, according to Kellermann, is the production of a framework for vv 14–39, namely vv 11–13 and most of vv 40–51. This author has grounded his work theologically in Exod 12, and depicts the Levites as substitutes for the first born. The material in v 41 and the reference to cattle in v 45 are minor additions here. The next significant expansion in Kellermann's view is the addition of vv 5–10, 38 which depict the Levites as given to Aaron and provide a position in the camp for Moses and Aaron. Kellermann finds the view that Levites serve Aaron to be in fundamental conflict with vv 25–26, 31, 36. The addition of vv 1–4 is the final step in a long and complex process.

There is no doubt of the complexity of the chapter, and to approach it from the point of view of the final author/editor does not give easy solutions to all problems. On the other hand it does offer a new perspective, and arguably a firmer base for discussion. J. de Vaulx (*Nombres*, 57–58) believes there to be an identifiable redactional framework in Num 1–4 as a whole, and finds evidence of it here in vv 14–16, 42–43, 49–51. Into this has been worked some legislative (vv 5–10, 44–51) and theological (vv 11–13, 40–41) material. The substance of vv 5–10 is developed in vv 14–39, and that of vv 11–13 in vv 40–51. The legislative/theological distinction is questionable, but the perspective adopted here can certainly ease some of the literary problems.

The following is an attempt to see the section as a unit. In vv 1–4 the author draws in material from Lev 10:1–7. This is desirable because his book has not yet indicated the composition and constitution of the priesthood proper, and because a new understanding of the Levitical office required some preliminary indication of where the summit of clerical authority lay. The point that Nadab and Abihu had no sons had not been previously made. It is arguable that the anointing of all priests (v 3) is a development of an earlier more limited custom reflected in H (Lev 21:10). This view is widely held, though K. Elliger (*Leviticus* [HAT 4: Tübingen: Mohr, 1966] 131–34) argues for change in the opposite direction. Whatever the truth of the matter our view of the authorship of Numbers is unaffected. The books of Exodus and Leviticus both reflect the limited (Exod 29:7, 29; Lev 8:12) and the wider (Exod 28:41; 29:21: 30:30; 40:15; Lev 8:30; 10:6–7) views of anointing. The reference to "altars" in v 31 is simply a sign that the composition of Exodus is effectively complete. Moreover the Levitical census is not a contradiction of Num 1:47. The author's view is that the distinctiveness of the Levites demands an *entirely separate* census. The reference to cords (vv 26, 37) may indeed be supplementary where it occurs in the book of Exodus. It could indeed be attributable to the author of Numbers himself. Once again it is arguable that the search for a coherent and tidy PG is missing the *kind* of methodical approach the author has chosen.

Some, though not all, of the issues raised by more recent analysts are more pressing. The question of new introductions in vv 5, 11, 14, however, is not necessarily evidence of literary unevenness. In a text designed essentially for recitation it is desirable that the divine origin of stipulations be affirmed repeatedly. The search for a single theme in vv 14–39, to be regarded as the core of those verses, is also unnecessary. This involves the real risk of imposing a pattern of order on an alleged original author while failing to observe a pattern that exists in the text as we have it. The author, having classified the three Levitical groups (vv 14–20), might well wish to take each family in turn (vv 21–26, 27–32, 33–37), and indicate in each case the census figure, the position of encampment, the leader, and the specific responsibilities of each. The repetition of some of this material in Num 4 is not an indication of literary disunity, but of a technique of recollection entirely appropriate in a text constructed for recitation. The idea of Levites serving the sanctuary (vv 25–26, 31, 36) is not a serious point of tension; it is surely of a piece with the idea that they are given to Aaron.

The threads of coherence in the section as a whole can be traced in diagrammatic form:

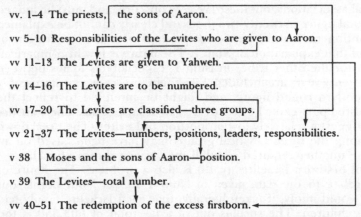

vv. 1–4 The priests, the sons of Aaron.

vv 5–10 Responsibilities of the Levites who are given to Aaron.

vv 11–13 The Levites are given to Yahweh.

vv 14–16 The Levites are to be numbered.

vv 17–20 The Levites are classified—three groups.

vv 21–37 The Levites—numbers, positions, leaders, responsibilities.

v 38 Moses and the sons of Aaron—position.

v 39 The Levites—total number.

vv 40–51 The redemption of the excess firstborn.

While it is true that vv 40–51 take up the precise ideas of vv 11–13, they are not totally disconnected to vv 14–39. The number of Levites has to be established before the principles of redemption can be put into effect.

An attempt to see the section as a purposeful unit is not to deny tensions traceable to the adaptation by the author of traditional material. The possibility of an older formulation of the Levitical genealogy in vv 21, 27, 33 is entirely acceptable, and there are three other topics which deserve particular attention.

1. *The Levites as "given to Yahweh"* (*vv 11–13*)

The "given to Yahweh"/"given to Aaron" tension in vv 5–13 may mean that older Levitical material has been incorporated in vv 11–13 (cf. J. Sandys-

Wunsch, *The Book of Numbers* [Diss., Oxford, 1961] 20). A Levitical foundation legend (v 12), asserting the special sanctity of the tribe as a substitute for the offering of the firstborn, is incorporated as valid. This would serve the author's purpose in that it recognizes Levitical status as a position, not of shame, but of the greatest dignity. Nevertheless the author gives this traditional Levitical claim a new context. The "giveness" to Yahweh is to be understood essentially as a "giveness" to Aaron, Yahweh's priest. The gift to Yahweh operates through the Aaronic channel. The validity of the tradition is recognized, but it is reinterpreted in halakhic fashion. The content of v 13 probably comes from the author. The reference to animals as well as men suggests that he has Exod 13:12–13 in mind. He is simply refreshing the reader's memory. This approach is altogether preferable to Noth's view that vv 11–13 are an adaptation of vv 5–10. In fact there would have to be a major revision of Numbers as a whole before vv 11–13 could fairly be considered a "correction." They are unlikely to be a secondary reminder of the dignity of Levitical service because there is nothing in the preceding material which would suggest a position of shame (cf. e.g. Num 1:53; 2:17; 3:7), and which would therefore require such a reminder.

2. *The Levitical Census* (vv14–39)

As in Num 1 the origin and significance of the census figures is an important and difficult question. M. Barnouin ("Nombres et l'Astronomie") again claims to find calendrical associations, but these are very obscure, and must be judged uncertain. The total figure of twenty-two thousand clearly cannot be explained in terms of "contingents" and "warriors," perhaps a further indication of the inadequacy of that explanation in Num 1. The figure is low in comparison with those given for the other tribes in Num 1, especially as males between one month and twenty years are included. Like them, however, it is impossibly large. It is evidently a round figure, and might be intended to reflect the balance of accredited post-exilic Levites over against lay people. The statistics given in Neh 7 suggest a relatively low proportion of Levites. The breakdown of the figure among the three Levitical groups may have been based on an assessment of the number required to fulfill the varying duties of each.

The surplus of firstborn Israelites (v 43) is also a problem. The figure of 273 is hard to relate to the data given in Num 1:46. As Noth points out (*Numbers*, 40) it would imply, if taken literally, that each Israelite family had some forty male children. The surplus out of a lay total of 603,550 is too small. It seems clear that the author's interest in supplying these figures lies elsewhere. It was suggested that in Num 1 the figure for lay Israelites was reached by means of a financial computation. The same could obtain here. The redemption money of v 50 may be the starting point. For some reason the figure of 1,365 shekels seemed appropriate to the author as the priestly income from this particular source. At the rate of five shekels per head (v 47) this necessitated a surplus of 273 persons.

3. *The Levitical Leaders* (vv 24, 30, 35)

The genealogical detail in vv 17–20 is probably drawn from Exod 6:16–19, but the author also has to hand the names of three Levitical leaders—

Eliasaph, Elizaphan, and Zuriel. These are sons respectively of Lael, Uzziel, and Abihail. The kind of name represented here is inclined to occur in late texts. The combination of preposition and noun, as in Lael, is unusual, but does occur in Prov. 31:1 (for Elizaphan cf. 1 Chr 15:8; 2 Chr 29:13; and for Abihail cf. Esth 2:15; 1 Chr 5:14; 2:29; 2 Chr 11:18). As in Num 1 little can safely be deduced from this about the antiquity or otherwise of the author's information. The most likely explanation is that suggested for the list of leaders given in Num 1. Its basis is perhaps an early exilic Babylonian compilation of names of old tribal figures.

Comment

3. אֲשֶׁר־מִלֵּא יָדָם "who were consecrated to the priesthood," literally "whose hand was filled." This is evidently a technical term associated with the installation of priests, and is generally considered to be ancient. Commentators have associated the phrase with the giving of money to the priest (cf. Judg 17:5, 12; 18:4), with some divinatory object, or with some part of the sacrificial offering (cf. 2 Chr 13:9). The act of consecration could have involved any or all of these things at different periods. H. F. Beck ("Consecrate," *IDB* a-d 677) draws attention to Deut 26:13 which speaks of the removal of the sacred portion from a house. This was God's, and was passed into the hands of the priest, the only person who had the right of approaching God. The phrase could simply denote the giving of the office itself. G. B. Gray (*Numbers*, 21) draws attention to an Assyrian custom in which the god fills the hand of the king with his kingdom. The evidence in Judg 17–18 is arguably the oldest available in the OT. There to fill a priest's hand is apparently to hire him.

4. אֵשׁ זָרָה "strange fire." The nature of the sin is not entirely clear. Some have suggested that the action was presumptuous. N. H. Snaith (*Numbers*, 75–76) compares the story with 2 Chr 26:16. R. Gradwohl ("Das 'fremde Feuer.' ") thinks that they may have lacked the right to enter the holiest place, or, if they had the right, that they neglected to take the precautions required in Lev 16:12–13. Other possibilities, offered with varying degrees of conviction, are that the act of censing in itself was wrong (M. Noth, *Leviticus*. [OTL London: SCM, 1965] 84–85), that the fire came from the wrong place (M. Haran, *VT* 10 [1960] 113–129), that the mixture for the incense was incorrect (considered by A. T. Chapman & A. W. Streane, *The Book of Leviticus* [Cambridge. CUP, 1911] 54), or that the timing was wrong (preferred by Chapman and Streane; cf. also L. A. Snijders, *OTS* 10 [1954] 1–154; K. Elliger, *Leviticus*, 136–39).

The fault surely lies in the "strangeness" of the fire. If the action was simply presumptuous the point would surely be clearer, as indeed it is in e.g. Num 16:8–11; 2 Chr 26:16–21. Equally doubtful is an opposition to censing itself. The tradition now functions in a stratum in which the offering of incense is legitimate, and in some circumstances vital (cf. e.g. Num 17:6–15). If timing were the point at issue it would be reasonable to expect some indication of what was wrong about that moment, and what time would have been right. The technical offense of Eleazar and Ithamar in Lev 10:16–20 is no less serious than an error of timing, but is treated very leniently. This also makes the idea that the incense was incorrectly mixed a doubtful one. In any case the objection seems to relate more to the "fire" than to the "incense." Haran's suggestion that the fire was not taken from the altar remains one of the stronger possibilities, though even here the point is not as clear as might be expected. The root *zr* (see *Comment* on Num 1:51) is widely used of foreigners (e.g. Exod 29:33; 30:33; Isa 61:5; Jer 5:19; 30:8; 51:51; Ezek 7:21; 11:9; 28:7, 8, 10; 30:12; 31:12; Hos 7:9; 8:7) and alien deities (Deut 32:16; Isa 17:10; 43:12; Jer 2:25; 3:13; Ps 44:21; 81:10). It is quite possible that "strange fire" involved procedures considered by the author to be foreign and apostate. This would well explain the peremptory punishment. (See further M. Aberbach and L. Smolar, (*JBL* 86 [1967] 129–140), J. C. H. Laughlin (*JBL* 95[1976] 559–65), G. Robinson (*VT* 28 [1978] 301–17). Laughlin suggests Zoroastrian practice. Robinson mentions some rabbinic theories on this matter).

4. עַל־פְּנֵי "in the presence of." This is the usual meaning though the phrase could denote "in the lifetime of" (RSV; cf. Gen 11:28).

7. וְשָׁמְרוּ אֶת־מִשְׁמַרְתּוֹ "and they shall be in attendance on him," literally "and they shall keep his service." Duties for the congregation must have entailed some function in connection with the offering of sacrifices by the laity (cf. 2 Chr 29:34).

9. נְתוּנִם נְתוּנִם "wholly given," literally "given given." The repetition is essentially for emphasis, but there could also be some allusion to the low order of Temple servants known as Nethinim (Ezra 2:36, 40–43; Neh 10:28). Ezra 2:58 suggests that they were closely connected with Solomonic slaves, though distinguishable (v 55). Their tasks were probably among the most menial. They may originally have been of foreign extraction—hence perhaps Ezek 44:6–7 (cf. Num 31:30, 47; Josh 9:27). Their status in the post-exilic period appears to have improved. They belonged to the congregation (Neh 10:28), and shared in the privilege of tax exemption (Ezra 7:24; cf. 1 Chr 6:48). The author here and in Num 18:6 may be thinking of the Levites as Nethinim to Aaron.

10. תִּפְקֹד "you shall appoint." The context requires this rather than the verb "to number."

12. There are no grounds for believing that the sacrifice of the firstborn child was anything other than exceptional in Israel (see R. de Vaux, *Ancient Israel*, 441–46), but it is clear that there was a special sanctity attaching to the firstborn of man and beast. There is no strong reason for supposing that this entailed a priesthood of the firstborn. The sanctity probably stems from a recognition of man's dependence upon God for life and fertility. The principle is asserted in some of the oldest available OT laws (Exod 22:28), along with the idea of redemption—for man and some animals (Exod 13:11–13; 34:19–20). A redemption involving finance is first explicit in P (cf. vv 46–51; Num 18:15–16). In this unit (vv 11–13) the Levites themselves are seen as the substitute for the human firstborn.

13. אֲנִי יהוה "I am Yahweh." A solemn formula which occurs occasionally in P (v 41; Exod 6:8; 12:12), but which is particularly characteristic of H (Lev 17–26), occurring forty-two times.

15. The numbering is to include those over one month old (contrast Num 1:3). The difference probably lies in the fact that the clerics are not men of war, but substitutes for the firstborn.

17. M. Noth (*Numbers*, 35–36) favors the view that Gershon is to be identified with the Gershom who was son of Moses (Exod 2:22), and who in Judg 18:30 is linked with the Danite priesthood. Noth conjectures that the Gershonites were Levitical groups who lived in close proximity to the Danite sanctuary. No comparable suggestion can be offered for Kohath and Merari, and the matter must remain open. The most that can be said with confidence is that these were the three basic groups to which post-exilic Levites aligned themselves. Clear evidence concerning them is found only in P, Ezra/Nehemiah, and the Chronicler. Among the Gershonite functions were music making (the Asaphites belonged to them—1 Chr 6:39, 43), and administration of the temple treasuries (1 Chr 23:7–9; 26:21). Some Kohathites were responsible for the shewbread (1 Chr 9:32). Merarites are depicted as accompanying Ezra on his journey in order to be Temple ministers (Ezra 8:18–19).

18. In 1 Chr 23:7 Libni is Ladan. Noth (*Numbers*, 36) considers linking the Libnites with the town of Libna in the west Judean hill country, but recognizes the difficulty this would pose for his theory of a northern provenance for the Gershonites. Shimei was probably originally, in Noth's view, a personal name.

19. Noth suggests that Amram, Ishar, and Uzziel were originally personal names. Hebron naturally suggests the southern city of that name, and Noth considers the possibility that a Kohathite Levitical group was resident in and around Hebron.

20. For a sophisticated theory of pre-exilic Mushite history see F. M. Cross, *Canaanite Myth*.

23. אַחֲרֵי "behind." Since the Tabernacle was understood to be facing east this means that the Gershonites pitched on the west side. The word "west" incorporates the idea "toward the sea"—i.e. the Mediterranean. This could easily have become a conventional term for "west," and does not necessarily mean that the narrator was in Palestine (against A. H. McNeile, *Numbers* 15).

25. הַמִּשְׁכָּן "tabernacle." The word is used precisely here— of that part of the Tent of Meeting which is described in Exod 26:1, 6.

25. הָאֹהֶל "tent." Here the word is used of the covering for the "tabernacle" as described in Exod 26:7, 11, 13.

25. מִכְסֵהוּ "covering." This is the overall covering described in Exod 26:14.

26. וְאֶת מֵיתָרָיו "and its cords." These are assigned to Merari in v 37. Since Gershon appears to be responsible for the fabric hangings of the Tent of Meeting and Merari for the wooden framework it may be that in the author's mind cords were attached to both hangings and framework. If not, there must be some oversight on his part.

31. These items are described in Exod 25:10–40; 27:1–8, 19; 30:1–10, 17–21. Since most of the door hangings are the responsibility of the Gershonites (v 25) the "screen" must be the curtain which separates the Holy of Holies from the Holy Place (Exod 26:31–33).

37. These items, excluding the "cords," are described in Exod 26:15–30; 27:10–18.

38. On the approach of unauthorized persons see *Comment* on Num 1:51.

41. בֶּהֱמַת הַלְוִיִּם "the cattle of the Levites." This is surprising since the author clearly intends that the sacrifice of the animal firstborn should continue (Num 18:17). A. Dillmann (*Numeri*, 19–21) limits "cattle" to unclean animals. M. Noth (*Numbers*, 41) describes v 41 as purely theoretical in this respect, and J. Sturdy (*Numbers*, 33) thinks that in the course of time the sacrifice of all firstborn cattle might have proved impracticable. The reference may simply be an artificial reflection on v 13 where the author has already mentioned the firstborn of all living things. His intention is not to bring the sacrifice of animal firstlings to an end, but to see in the Levites, in their persons and animal possessions, the symbolic firstfruits of Israel's offering to God. The point at issue is the dignity of the Levitical office, not the operation of the law of the firstborn.

46. וְאֵת פְּדוּיֵי "and for the redemption of." The word apparently indicates the ransom price (G. B. Gray, *Numbers* 31; J. Blau, "Zum Angeblichen Gebrauch von אֵת"). In general the root denotes a process by which something lost to the original owner can be recovered through the payment of money. The other "redemption" root (גאל) is used essentially of family law, but in a broadly similar way. S. H. Hooke (*VT* 2 [1952] 11) describes the redemption of the firstborn as a compromise between an old practice of substitution as a means of averting supernatural danger, and the recognition of Yahweh's right to the firstborn. He describes this part of Num 3 as a legal fiction intended to bring together Yahweh's right to the firstborn and the claim of the priesthood to maintenance. Substitution is thus transformed into a Temple tax.

46. הָעֹדְפִים "who exceed." This root is found only in P (cf. 48; Exod 16:18, 23; 26:12–13; Lev 25:27).

47. שֶׁקֶל הַקֹּדֶשׁ "the sanctuary shekel." This is a weight of about 11.5 grams of silver. On this and "gerahs" see R. B. Y. Scott, "Weights and Measures of the Bible," *BA* 22 (1959) 22–39; A. Segré, "A Documentary Analysis of Ancient Palestinian Units of Measure," *JBL* 64 (1945) 357–75.

Explanation

The section as a whole opens up the priestly hierarchy, reminding the reader that the priesthood as such belongs to the sons of Aaron, namely Eleazar and Ithamar (vv 1–4), and exploring the special relationship between priests and Levites (vv 5–10) and between Levites and Yahweh (vv 11–13). The three Levitical groups are identified (vv 14–20), and the number, position of encampment, and special responsibilities of each group is duly noted (vv 21–39). The final part (vv 40–51), developing ideas in vv 11–13, indicates that the Levites fulfill the role of firstborn, and illustrates the principle of redemption in action.

The author's method may seem complex, but the section does have its own patterns and coherence, and whatever its pre-history can be understood as a unit. The method is much as before:

1. There is further explanation of material already given. Moses, Aaron and the Levites had been introduced in Num 1:3, 47; now their relationship to one another, in terms of status and responsibility, is further explored in vv 1–10, 32, 38. The crucial and distinctive role of the Levites as set out in Num 1:48–54 is given theological grounding in vv 11–13, 40–51 (vv 40–51 are themselves a further exploration of vv 11–13). The possibility of a separate Levitical census (Num 1:49) is here carried through (vv 14–16, 22, 28, 34, 39). The meaning of encampment around the Tabernacle (Num 1:50, 53) is here explained (vv 23, 29, 35, 38), and the meaning of Levitical ministry, first raised in Num 1:50, 53, is given some precise content (vv 25–26, 31, 36–37).

2. There is no direct repetition of information previously given, but many of the motifs are familiar—Levites, clans, leaders, encampment, and the census.

3. The essentially new information given is to be found in the classification of the Levitical clans (vv 17–20, 27, 33), and in the names of the Levitical leaders (vv 24, 30, 35).

Since the chapter touches on many themes it would be as well to consider each distinguishable section in turn:

1–4. Here the author indicates the peak of the priestly hierarchy. The priests are those who were anointed. Here he is recalling material in Exod 29:21 and Lev 8:30. In the same way the names of Aaron's four sons were already available to him (Exod 6:23), while the fate of the two eldest had already been described in Lev 10:1–2. This is the familiar technique of repetition and recollection. The only point the author needs to add is that Nadab and Abihu had no children, thus opening the way for Eleazar and Ithamar to complete, along with Aaron himself, the priestly triad.

It is not certain whether specific historical circumstances are reflected here. It is clear that Nadab and Abihu were figures from earlier tradition, standing alongside Aaron and the elders of Israel (Exod 24:1). At this point they have no obvious relationship to Aaron or to the priesthood. Moses alone "draws near" (v 2). R. Gradwohl ("Das 'fremde Feuer' ") has suggested that the tradition of the peremptory deaths of Nadab and Abihu is based on the fate of the sons of Jeroboam—Nadab and Abijah—both of whom die prematurely (1 Kgs 14:1, 20). Some support for this is given by M. Aberbach & L. Smolar ("Aaron, Jeroboam"). The priestly authors may have been aware of certain resemblances here, but there is in fact no association of Nadab and Abijah with incense or strange fire, and they die for the sins of Jeroboam, not their own (1 Kgs 14:10). Some "good thing" is found in Abijah (1 Kgs 14:13), and he dies as a child (1 Kgs 14:17). Though Nadab the king dies violently, and has followed the sins of Jeroboam, his fate, after ruling Israel for two years, is not really comparable to the immediate demise of Nadab the priest in Lev 10:2.

It seems then that priestly authors have simply reinterpreted the tradition of Exod 24:1, understanding Nadab and Abihu as sons of Aaron, and therefore as priests. The idea of their premature death has obvious attractions. At its simplest the story shows how priests can be displaced for sin. Precedence and impeccable genealogy are not a safeguard against disqualification. The priests from Babylon, resettling and establishing their status in Jerusalem, are not usurpers, but the properly accredited priesthood. The Palestinian priests, who by virtue of their presence might have a claim to precedence, have forfeited that right by apostasy. They are the ones who authorized the apostate incense burning of Ezek 8:11. There is thus a sense in which Nadab and Abihu may symbolize the priesthood which functioned in Jerusalem during the exile, or perhaps those who operated from the time of the first deportation in 598 B.C. The Zadokites of Babylon clearly understood their relationship to Aaron in and through Eleazar and Ithamar.

The priestliness of Aaron was another important idea to them. It gave them identity in its implication that their priesthood was older than land and temple, and did not depend on either for its existence and authenticity. The idea also gave them access to the right hand of Moses himself. Tradition in any case judged Aaron to be a Levite (Exod 4:14–16), and the story of Aaron's failure in Exod 32 was not sufficient reason for looking elsewhere for their roots. After all in their view many priesthoods, northern and southern, had shown themselves weak and unworthy.

5–10. The author is now ready to introduce more clearly one of his major programmatic proposals. He has already indicated the distinctiveness and dignity of the Levites (Num 1:48–51; 2:17). He now has to define their relationship to the sons of Aaron. In vv 7–8 he recalls material from Num 1:50. In vv 6, 9 he introduces the new ideas. The Levites are "given to Aaron." M. Noth (*Numbers*, 33) is quite wrong to describe this as a debasing of the Levites. There is no hint of that, either in intention or effect. The author's principal objective is to tone down, and in a sense supercede, the sharpness of the division in Ezek 40–48 by recognizing that the admitted subordination of Levites is nevertheless a position of dignity. At the same time the idea of Levitical "ministry" in association with the Tent of Meeting does some necessary justice to the Deuteronomic view that all Levites are priests, or at least have full ministerial rights (Deut 18:1–5). This solution offers the best possible interpretation of the traditions to hand.

11–13. As further evidence of his desire to bring order and harmony to the hierarchy the author incorporates an older Levitical tradition (v 12), and adds his own observation (v 13) based on Exod 13:12. The older tradition was one which asserted the Levitical right to priesthood. The author is able to retain the idea of Levites as substitutes for the firstborn, but may have had to drop some clear indication that "the Levites shall be mine" means that they are Yahweh's priests.

It is arguable that this program takes us a step beyond the position as it exists in the books of Exodus and Leviticus. The author of Exodus accepts an older Levitical ordination tradition (Exod 32:25–29), but depicts the sons of Aaron as the Levites *par excellence*—those who are specially anointed to serve as priests (Exod 29:1). This was not difficult since Aaron was already recognized as a Levite (Exod 4:14). But what does the consecration of the sons of Levi mean in Exod 32:29? It is above all this question which the author of Numbers has answered.

14–20. Having dealt with the question of the relationship of the Levites to the sons of Aaron the author can now deal with the question of their numbers. He does not see this as a contradiction of Num 1:48–49. It is just that Levitical figures must be computed entirely separately from those of the lay tribes. Calculations of population were important in the circumstances of the return (Ezra 2:40 = Neh 7:43), and as far as priests and Levites were concerned would have been part of the business of establishing an authentic pedigree (Ezra 2:61–63 = Neh 7:63–65). The count includes those as young as one month, mainly because of the idea of the Levites as substitutes for the firstborn in v 12. The author is anxious to show that accepting the Levitical ideas of v 12 does not mean that the principle of redemption is invalidated (vv 40–51). This is indeed a major reason for holding this particular Levitical census. Before the figures can be given he needs to indicate how they are to be broken down, and for this purpose he recollects the genealogical material in Exod 6:16–19 in vv 17–20.

Gershon, Kohath, and Merari were probably the leading Levitical priest-hoods with whom the Zadokites of Babylon would have had to come to terms. Deuteronomy demanded it, while Ezekiel's proposal to downgrade Levites was either not practicable or else not applicable to these Levitical groups, who may well have resisted the charge of idolatry. The author outlines the way in which these problems were solved.

21–39. In a systematic fashion the author now supplies the details of the census. His figure of 22,000 appears to be an estimate—so too the breakdown of the figure among the various Levitical groups (see discussion under *Form/ Structure/Setting*). In each case he has chosen to supply three additional pieces of information—the camping position of the group, its leader, and its particular duties with respect to the Tent. There is no strong reason for regarding this information as out of place in the overall context, and therefore supplementary. It is an integral part of the process whereby the overall picture is slowly pieced together. The description of the camp in Num 2 naturally raises the question of where the Levitical groups camp. What do Num 1:50, 53 mean? The author's desire to emphasize the essential separateness of the Levites precluded his answering these questions at that point. It is appropriate to answer them here. The same goes for the information about the Levitical leaders. The list of laymen in Num 1:5–15 raises the question about Levitical leadership. Because of the author's premise that the Levites are a wholly distinct clerical group he prefers to answer that question here. Similarly Num 1:50 raises a host of unanswered questions about particular Levitical duties. The author finds it easier to answer these now that the basic group divisions among the Levites have been made. This may not be precisely the kind of order and coherence we would choose in handling the author's information, but there is coherence—based on recollection, repetition, and slow advance—and the kind of coherence which is appropriate for teaching based on oral recitation.

The positions of encampment are given in vv 23, 29, 35, 38. The favored eastern position is reserved for Moses himself, and for Aaron and his sons. The author has thus discovered another way of distinguishing between priests and Levites, and of asserting the primacy of the former. Levitical status is one of honor and dignity, but the status of the sons of Aaron is closely linked with that of Moses himself. Though listed in second place behind

Gershon the Kohathites are given the next favored position to the south. This may be because they are the largest Levitical clan and/or because their responsibilities for the items cited in v 31 are the most important. At heart it is probably attributable to the fact that the author of Exodus has made Aaron and his sons Kohathites (Exod 6:16–25). Gershon may originally have been the more significant group, but in any event Gershon-Kohath-Merari is the order of Exod 6:16, and the author retains it for the basic framework in vv 21–39. That Gershon should pitch to the west and Merari to the north is logical enough in terms of the criteria just discussed.

The author has also drawn in names of Levitical leaders (vv 24, 30, 35), possibly from early exilic records based on recollection. The duties of each group are based on a logical division of the Tabernacle as described in Exod 25–29. It is hard to see how these responsibilities might correspond very closely to functions in the second Temple, and the division may be in large measure a construction of the author. The responsibilities are not meant to be menial or debasing. They imply care and protection, and an office of great dignity. The Chronicler offers some elaboration of this view of Levitical functions—the most notable development being the ministry of music (cf. e.g. 1 Chr 23:28–32). Doorkeeping (cf. e.g. 1 Chr 26:1) may well be an interpretation of the view in Numbers that the clerical orders camp on all four sides of the Tabernacle. The Chronicler even notes the superior diligence of Levites as compared with priests, justifying some involvement for them in particular priestly duties (2 Chr 29:34).

For his part the author of Numbers is anxious to secure the primacy of the sons of Aaron, as well as the dignity of the Levites. To this end he insists that Eleazar is to be in charge of the Levitical leaders. There is no reason to regard v 32 as a late addition. It comes at this point because the Kohathites, in their involvement with the ark and other implements, are exposed to the most danger (cf. Num 4:17–20). In this, as elsewhere, the author is able to sow the seed of ideas yet to come. Since he also wishes to associate Aaron himself as closely as possible with Moses, in order to establish the idea of a priestly theocracy, the practicalities of day-to-day priestly ministry are inclined to devolve upon the sons. Ithamar is given general supervision of the Levites (Exod 38:21; Num 4:33), and Eleazar a specific responsibility for the Kohathites in view of their special needs (cf. Num 4:17–20).

The priesthoods of Eleazar and Ithamar are evidently those to which the exilic priests aligned themselves. There is no sign that these names, like Nadab and Abihu, come from earlier Pentateuchal tradition. If the grave tradition for Eleazar is early (Josh 24:33) then there are deep historical roots linking the Eleazar priests with Gibeah. There was also a tradition of a son of Abinadab called Eleazar who was consecrated to serve the ark (1 Sam 7:1). M. Noth (*Pentateuchal Traditions*, 185–86) suggests that the Zadokites usurped the Eleazar tradition, but if the link with 1 Sam 7:1 is substantial the Eleazar/Zadok link was probably established from the very beginnings of the Solomonic Temple. There are no such hints about the Ithamar group, but they too were evidently Zadokites.

40–51. The author is now in a position to make his point that acceptance of the Levitical tradition in v 12 does not entail the abandonment of the principle of redemption. There is nothing unusual about the position of this section in relation to vv 11–13, and thus no need to posit a very complex process of literary growth. The author cannot illustrate how the principle of redemption is to continue until he has conducted a Levitical census, since redemption is to be based on the surplus of lay firstborn. So a census of firstborn males is conducted from the relevant age (one month) (vv 40–43), and there are found to be 22,273, thus creating a surplus of 273.

The author is in fact the first to introduce the idea of financial redemption for the firstborn (contrast Exod 13:13; 34:20), and this is certainly a developing pattern in post-exilic Judah (cf. Lev 27:1–10 where financial payments are a substitute for vows, and also Ezek 45:12). The difficulties in relating the population figures of the Levites and of the firstborn to the census figure of 603,550 in Num 1:46 are not to be taken too seriously. The author's prime concern is to show ways in which the post-exilic priesthood is to be maintained, and his population figures here are simply a construction to illustrate a point. The figure of 1,365 shekels seemed appropriate for the needs from this source of the priests in the wilderness, and the surplus is constructed accordingly.

Theologically the section as a whole explores the theme of God's holiness. Viewed in one way the priestly hierarchy is a means of protecting Israel from divine holiness. The introduction of another sacred order between priests and people emphasizes the difference between the fallibility of man and the perfection of God. Even the priests are at peril if they wilfully disobey. Divine perfection is such that direct contact would be fatal for erring humanity. Goodness, the essence of perfection, must be respected. Viewed in another way the hierarchy constitutes the recognized channel through which God brings stability and well-being to his people. Priestly ministry functions "on behalf of the people of Israel" (v 9). It is thus essential that it be exercised conscientiously by priests and Levites together, and that they in turn be financially maintained by the people. In claiming the firstborn as his own God reveals his good will and commitment toward his people. The theology of leadership among the people of God is seen to include a recognition by leaders of the perfection of God's will, and a thoroughly conscientious commitment to the responsibilities of leadership. The duty of those who are led is held to include respect for what is learned of God through the leadership, and thus a proper recognition and support for the work of those who lead.

Levitical Service Within the Priestly Hierarchy (4:1–49)

Bibliography

See Num 3:1–51 (*Bibliography*)

Translation

¹ *And Yahweh spoke to Moses and to Aaron,*[a] *saying,* ² *"Take a census*[a] *of the sons of Kohath from among the sons of Levi, by clans and fathers' houses,* ³ *from the age of thirty years*[a] *up to fifty, all eligible for service, for the work of the Tent of Meeting.*[b] ⁴ *This is the service of the sons of Kohath in the Tent of Meeting— responsibility for the holiest things.* ⁵ *When the camp sets out Aaron and his sons shall go and take down the veil of the screen, and cover the ark of the testimony with it.* ⁶ *And they shall put upon it a covering of skin,*[a] *and shall spread over it a cloth entirely of violet, and shall put in its poles.* ⁷ *And on the table of the presence they shall spread a violet cloth, and they shall put on it*[a] *the bowls and the dishes and the cups and the flagons with which to pour. And the regular bread shall also be on it.* ⁸ *And they shall spread upon them a cloth of scarlet, and they shall cover it with a covering of skin, and they shall put in its poles.* ⁹ *And they shall take a cloth of violet, and they shall cover the lampstand, its lamps, its tongs, its firepans, and all its vessels for oil with which they minister to it.* ¹⁰ *And they shall put it and all its vessels in a covering of skin, and shall put it upon the carrying frame.* ¹¹ *And on the gold altar they shall spread a violet cloth, and cover it with a covering of skin, and shall put in its poles.* ¹² *And they shall take all the implements of ministry with which they minister in the sanctuary, and put them in a violet cloth, and cover them with a covering of skin, and shall put them on the carrying frame.* ¹³ *And they shall take away the ashes from the altar,*[a] *and they shall spread on it a purple cloth.* ¹⁴ *And they shall put on it all its implements with which they minister around it, the firepans, the forks, the shovels and the basins—all the implements of the altar. And they shall spread on it a covering of skin, and shall put in its poles.*[a] ¹⁵ *And when Aaron and his sons have finished covering the sanctuary, and all the implements of the sanctuary, whenever the camp is ready to set out, then the sons of Kohath shall come forward to carry it. But they shall not touch the holy things, lest they die. These things are the burden of the sons of Kohath in the Tent of Meeting.*

¹⁶ *"And the responsibility of Eleazar son of Aaron the priest shall be the oil for the light, and the sweet incense, the regular cereal offering, and the anointing oil, as well as the responsibility of all the Tabernacle and of everything in it, the sanctuary and its implements.*[a]*"*

¹⁷ *And Yahweh spoke to Moses and to Aaron, saying,* ¹⁸ *"Do not expel the tribe of the clans of the Kohathites from among the Levites,* ¹⁹ *but do this for them, and they will live and not die when they approach the holiest things. Aaron and his sons shall go and appoint each man*[a] *to his service and to his burden.* ²⁰ *But they must not come to see the holy things, not even for a moment, lest they die."*

²¹ *And Yahweh spoke to Moses, saying,* ²² *"Take a census of the sons of Gershon also, by fathers' houses and clans.* ²³ *From the age of thirty years up to fifty you shall number them, all eligible to go to serve* ᵃ *in the Tent of Meeting.* ²⁴ *This is the service of the clans of the Gershonites, to serve and to carry.* ²⁵ *And they shall carry the curtains of the Tabernacle, and the Tent of Meeting, its covering and the covering of skin which is on it, and the screen for the door of the Tent of Meeting,* ²⁶ *and the hangings of the court, and the screen for the door of the gate of the court,* ᵃ *which is by the Tabernacle and by the altar round about,* ᵇ *and its cords and all the implements for their service. And they shall do all that must be done with regard to these things.* ²⁷ *All the service of the sons of the Gershonites shall be at the command of Aaron and his sons, all their burdens and all their service. And you shall appoint to those in charge* ᵃ *all that they are to carry.* ²⁸ *This is the service of the clans* ᵃ *of the sons of the Gershonites in the Tent of Meeting, and their work is to be supervised by Ithamar son of Aaron the priest.*

²⁹ *"You shall count* ᵃ *the sons of Merari by their clans and fathers' houses,* ³⁰ *from the age of thirty years up to fifty you shall number them, all eligible to serve in the Tent of Meeting.* ³¹ *And this is what they are to carry, as their service in the Tent of Meeting—the frames of the Tabernacle, its bars, its pillars and its bases,* ᵃ ³² *and the pillars of the court round about, and their bases,* ᵃ *their pegs and their cords, with all their implements and accessories. And you shall assign by name the implements* ᵇ *they are to carry.* ³³ *This is the service of the clans of the sons of Merari, for all their service in the Tent of Meeting, under the hand of Ithamar son of Aaron the priest."*

³⁴ *And Moses and Aaron and the leaders of the congregation numbered the sons of the Kohathites by their clans and fathers' houses,* ³⁵ *from the age of thirty years up to fifty, all eligible to engage in the service of the Tent of Meeting.* ³⁶ *And those numbered by clans were 2,750.* ᵃ ³⁷ *These were those numbered of the clans of the Kohathites, all who served in the Tent of Meeting, whom Moses and Aaron numbered according to the commandment of Yahweh, by the hand of Moses.*

³⁸ *And those numbered of the sons of Gershon, by clans and fathers' houses,* ³⁹ *from the age of thirty years up to fifty, all eligible to engage in the service of the Tent of Meeting,* ⁴⁰ *and those numbered by clans and fathers' houses were 2,630.* ⁴¹ *These were those numbered of the clans of the sons of Gershon, all who served in the Tent of Meeting, whom Moses and Aaron counted, according to the commandment of Yahweh.* ᵃ

⁴² *And those numbered of the clans of the sons of Merari, by clans and fathers' houses,* ⁴³ *from the age of thirty years up to fifty, all eligible to engage in the service of the Tent of Meeting,* ⁴⁴ *and those numbered by clans were 3,200.* ⁴⁵ *These are those numbered of the clans of the sons of Merari, whom Moses and Aaron counted, according to the commandment of Yahweh, by the hand of Moses.*

⁴⁶ *And all those numbered of the Levites, whom Moses and Aaron and the leaders of the congregation counted, by clans and fathers' houses,* ⁴⁷ *from the age of thirty years up to fifty, all eligible to engage in service and burden bearing in the Tent of Meeting,* ⁴⁸ *and those numbered were 8,580.* ⁴⁹ *According to the commandment of Yahweh by the hand of Moses* ᵃ *they* ᵇ *counted them, each man according to his service and his burden. And they were appointed* ᶜ *just as Yahweh commanded Moses.*

Notes

1.a. A few MT mss lack "to Aaron." The singular verb in vv 34, 46 (of פָּקַד) suggests that "Aaron" may be secondary here.

2.a. An emphatic imperative (GKC 113bb). The verb is an infinitive absolute with imperative force.

3.a. G^B has "twenty-five" as in Num 8:24, and again in vv 23, 30, 35, 39, 43, 47. G^A has "twenty" as in 1 Chr 23:24, 27. G is probably seeking to harmonize disparate texts.

3.b. BHS suggests הַבָּא as in Sam and in vv 23, 30.

6.a. G (ὑακίνθινον) appears to have read תְּכֵלֶת "violet." The same obtains in vv 8, 10, 14.

7.a. G lacks "and they shall put on it."

13.a. Instead of "they shall take away the ashes from the altar" G reads "and he shall place the cover upon the altar" (see v 14.a.).

14.a. G and Sam have a substantial section here which is probably an addition. It tells of a purple cloth for the laver and its base, and of a further covering of skin. For discussion of the Midrashic tendencies in G, here and in v 13, see D. W. Gooding. "On the Use of LXX for Dating Midrashic Elements in the Targums," JTS 25 (1974) 1–11.

16.a. G has "and all its service" at this point.

19.a. Two MT mss omit the second אִישׁ "man."

23.a. Dagesh lene would be normal in לַצָּבָא (see GKC § 45g).

26.a. The clause "and the screen for the door of the gate of the court" is absent in G. This could easily be an error due to homoeoteleuton—n.b. the dual occurrence of הֶחָצֵר.

26.b. G lacks "and by the altar round about"—perhaps another accidental omission.

27.a. BHS suggests בְּשֵׁמוֹת "by name" as in v 32, a reading supported by G.

28.a. "Clans" is lacking in a few MT mss and in G.

29.a. G has a plural here—contrast MT cf. also v 30.

31.a. G adds material about the coverings here.

32.a. G adds material about the curtain here.

32.b. BHS suggests אֶת-כָּל "all" in place of אֶת-כְּלִי "the implements." This has good support from one MT ms, Sam, G, and Tg^J., and may be correct.

36.a. There is a varied G witness to this figure. It seems best to retain MT.

41.a. A few MT mss, G and Tg^J have "by the hand of Moses" here.

49.a. If the BHS suggestion is accepted (see v 49.b.) the clause "by the hand of Moses" fits best here after "Yahweh."

49.b. BHS suggests a plural. It is hard to see what the subject of the singular פָּקַד could be. If it is Moses then the clause "by the hand of Moses" would have to be dropped.

49.c. MT is impossible here. Some identify a misplaced fragment. It seems best to read וַיִּתְפָּקְדוּ "and they were appointed" (cf. Num 1:47; 2:33), supported by G, S, Tg., and Vg. If so אֲשֶׁר is best read as כַּאֲשֶׁר.

Form/Structure/Setting

The passage continues the previous section's investigation into the priestly hierarchy. There is thus little doubt that it belongs to the priestly stratum. Older commentators were inclined to see much supplementary work in the chapter. J. Wellhausen (Hexateuch, 179–80) points to the repetitions and elaborations, and draws the customary supplementary conclusion. Much of vv 1–33 is a repetition of the precautions in Num 3:14–39 against Levitical contact with the sacred vessels. In v 11 there is the gold altar of incense, and in v 16 there is reference to the incense and the oil of anointing. Both allusions are held to depend on supplementary strata in the book of Exodus (Exod 30:1–10, 22–33, 34–38). A. Kuenen (Hexateuch, 92) pointed out that the author himself could have expanded his own ideas on Levitical service. Additional grounds for a supplementary theory are offered by G. B. Gray (Numbers, 3).

The "cords" in vv 26, 32 are held to reflect PS elements in Exod 35:18; 39:40—items apparently unknown in Exod 25–29. Small divergencies from the phraseology of other parts of P are also observed.

M. Noth (*Numbers*, 41–44) looks at the chapter in a similar way. He points to the fact that much of the subject matter has already been discussed in Num 3:25–26, 31, 36–37, and adds that the peculiar forms of expression mean that the author cannot simply be identified with the PS author in Exodus. The phrase "put in its poles" (v 6) with regard to the ark is found to be a contradiction of the ruling in Exod 25:15 that the poles are not to be removed. The references to Ithamar in v 28b and v 33b are likely to be secondary in Noth's view because they follow concluding formulae in v 28a and v 33a.

D. Kellermann (*Priesterschrift*, 49–62) discovers two main independent elements in the chapter, one to do with the numbering of Levites, and the other with Levitical service. In his view the chapter consisted originally of the census (vv 1–3, 34–39), but without the references to Aaron, the leaders, and the hand of Moses. He thinks that this material probably belongs to PG since it has a good deal in common with the frame of mind in Num 1 and less with that in Num 3. The description of Levitical service is held to reveal a different use of language, and comes from a different author. This includes most of vv 21–33, and the corresponding material in vv 4–15. A third author introduces more Kohathite material in vv 5–15, while a fourth, working on those same verses, emphasizes the need for the covering of the various holy objects. The Eleazar material in v 16 is added, and then vv 17–19 with their special stress on Kohathite discipline. After minor additions elsewhere v 20 is added, prompted by the ideas of vv 17–19. The addition of "Aaron," the "leaders," and "the hand of Moses" comes at the very latest stages of compilation.

It is clear that our attempt to see Numbers as essentially a redactional unit and as a work of authorship in a significant sense is in no way threatened by evidence of dependence on any part of the book of Exodus. Numbers is produced as one in a series, and in close association with Exodus. Repetition is entirely consonant with the idea of a work designed for recitation in some such institution as the synagogue. It is arguable that repetition is *harder* to explain in terms of literary supplementation. Why has the supplementer not inserted his material at the obvious point in Num 3 where the subject matter has already been discussed? It would seem entirely open for him to do so. Repetition of course is not the sum of the matter. The subject in Num 4 is Levitical service for the journey. The stress in Num 3 is on care and protection, and in Num 4 on transport. The peculiarities of language are discussed under *Comment*. They are not very substantial, and they tend to show a divergence from usage in other priestly books, not within Numbers itself.

The sharp separation, suggested by some, between sections dealing with Levitical numbers and those dealing with Levitical service seems unjustified. There is scarcely enough evidence to posit confidently a difference of authorship on linguistic or literary grounds, and there is a kind of coherence about most of the material as it stands. Having raised the matter of Levitical service in Num 3 it seems entirely appropriate to pursue it here, particularly as there is to be a new emphasis on "transport" rather than "care." The matter of another census is integral, since it is designed to identify precisely the numbers of Levites eligible for service. There is a reasonably clear structure to the chapter. The divine command for a census (vv 1–3, 21–23, 29–30) for each Levitical clan is followed in each instance by a description of each clan's service for the journey (vv 4–20, 24–28, 31–33). Each clan is then numbered (vv 34–45), the total figure of Levites eligible for service is calculated (vv 46–48), and a concluding observation about Israel's obedience is made (v 49).

It is true enough that the three commands are not linguistically uniform, and less so than is usual in this kind of material. Nevertheless the structure of each command section is essentially the same, including the sequence of ideas used. It is also true that the description of Kohathite service is long in comparison with that for Gershonites and Merarites. This however is understandable in view of the fact that they are most exposed to danger through their handling of the holiest things. Much of this particular section is given over to an extended statement that the sons of Aaron, and not the Kohathites themselves, must make the preparations for the journey. The Kohathites must carry, but must not come into direct contact with or even see, the holiest things. The Eleazar material (v 16) is appropriate here in that it indicates some sanctuary items which lie outside Kohathite responsibility, and in that it reaffirms the ultimate supervision exercised by the sons of Aaron.

These observations do not of course preclude the possibility of minor glossing and supplementation. The singular verbs in vv 34, 46 suggest that this may be true of "Aaron" and the "leaders of the congregation." Furthermore the possibility that traditional elements have been incorporated into the section has still to be considered. J. de Vaulx (*Nombres*, 53) locates the narrative redactional frame in vv 1–3, 21–23, 29–30, 34–35, 49, and suggests a process of assembly by the author which combines new information with material already used. He also recognizes in the section a retouching and reorganization of existing written tradition (p. 85). It is hard to be certain where traditional elements may be, but two areas deserve special attention:

1. *Levitical Tradition*

One striking feature of the chapter is the statement that the period of active service for Levites is between thirty and fifty years of age. In contrast the period in Num 8:23–26 is between twenty-five and fifty. In 1 Chr 23:24, 27; 2 Chr 31:17; Ezra 3:8, service begins at the age of twenty, with no upper limit specified. The section in Num 8:23–26 is a clear divine pronouncement on the matter, and doubtless represents the author's final view. The information here emerges somewhat in passing. It is at least possible that the "thirty-fifty" tradition represents an older Levitical pattern which is here accorded some temporary validity. J. Sandys-Wunsch (*Numbers*, 29) suggests that the problem about the removal of poles (v 6) could come into the same category. He is not convinced by Gray's idea that "adjustment" rather than "insertion" might be meant, it being difficult to see what kind of adjustment could be made. Whether he is correct in seeing here a very ancient tradition of a mobile ark is less certain—the argument being that pole removal would be more likely in such a tradition. He is inclined to see the greater part of the

Kohathite section as embodying old Tent traditions traceable to Kohathite circles. The strongest hint in favor of such a supposition is the strong protestation in vv 15, 17–20 *against* their involvement, implying perhaps some contrary claim that they had the right to do the jobs assigned here to Aaron. This can scarcely be more than a theory, but the section as a whole does indicate an anxiety to set down clear lines of demarcation, and doubtless reflects post-exilic tensions in this kind of area. These are arguably the tensions between Babylonian and Palestinian Judaism, and the "coverings" are a way of preventing Kohathite encroachment on the proper preserves of the sons of Aaron.

One hint that written tradition may have been incorporated in vv 4–15 is the nature of vv 17–20. De Vaulx (*Nombres,* 85) correctly calls them a short halakic commentary. They could well come from the author himself, and seem to be addressed to a specific issue—the possibility that Kohathites actually be excluded from Levitical service. This issue may have been of such immediate concern and relevance that he saw fit to give his ruling, with its own divinely authenticated introduction (v 17), an additional insistence that what is proposed in vv 4–15 is the good and right way for all concerned (v 19), and a firm statement in v 20 of the implications of the assertion in v 5 that "Aaron shall go in." It is to be he and he alone. The Kohathites must not even see the holiest things.

There is no strong reason for supposing that v 16 contains very ancient tradition from a specific Eleazar priesthood. Some at least of these responsibilities were doubtless traditional to the exilic Zadokites generally. In granting sanctuary rights to non-Zadokite Levites they were anxious to preserve certain areas of responsibility for themselves.

2. *The Census*

The figures given here relate reasonably well to those in Num 3:22, 28, 34, though the proportions of men in this age bracket are higher than would be expected in relation to the total of 22,000. It seems unlikely that these relatively round figures constitute the results of an actual census—post-exilic or otherwise. The precise figures given in Ezra 2:40–58 = Neh 7:43–60 are modest in comparison. The figures are probably the author's own construction, based in general terms on the size of the community as it has been depicted in Num 1–3. His concern is to show that a proper computation of those eligible for Levitical service is essential. The proportions (Kohath–2,750, Gershon–2,030, and Merari–3,200) may have been based on a rough assessment of the balance each group would need to carry out its functions properly

Comment

2. נָשֹׂא אֶת-רֹאשׁ "take a census" (cf. v 22) See *Comment* on Num 1:2.
2. On "clans" and "fathers' houses" see *Comment* on Num 1:2.
3. לְצָבָא "for service." The root here is more often used for "warfare" or "military hosts." In vv 23, 30, 35, 39, 43 and Num 8:24–25 it occurs again of service in the Tabernacle. It is used of the sanctuary service of women in Exod 38:8; 1 Sam 2:22, the former a late text, and the latter often

considered a gloss by commentators. The military idea is thus probably original. The root could also be used of hard work and trouble (Isa 40:2; Job 7:1). The author of Numbers wishes to show that Levitical service is just as integral to Israel's military advance as the carrying of weapons.

4. On "the Tent of Meeting" see *Comment* on Num 1:1.

4. קֹדֶשׁ הַקֳּדָשִׁים "the holiest things." The point of this reference is not entirely clear. N. H. Snaith (*Numbers*, 194) thinks it a gloss (meaning "holy of holies") on "the Tent of Meeting." The phrase could be a reference to the special sanctity of Kohathite service. More probably it refers to those specially holy objects for which the Kohathites are responsible (cf. Exod 30:10, 29).

5. אֵת פָּרֹכֶת הַמָּסָךְ "the veil of the screen." P has three screens in all. There is one at the gate of the court (Exod 27:16), one at the entrance of the Tent (Exod 26:36; Num 3:25), and one inside the Tent (Exod 35:12). The one described here hides the ark, and is doubtless the innermost.

5. On "the ark of the testimony" see *Comment* on Num 1:50, 53.

6. תַּחַשׁ "skin" (cf. also vv 8, 10–12, 14, 25). There is no certainty as to what is meant here. Suggestions include "badger skin" (AV), "sealskin" (RV), "goatskin" (RSV), "porpoise-hide" (NEB), or "hide of the sea cow" (NEB note), "fine leather" (JB). In Arabic *taḫas* is a "dolphin," hence the preference among some for the skin of a sea creature. J. Sturdy (*Numbers*, 38) wonders whether such creatures would be clean for the purpose intended here. He is confident that "goatskin" must be ruled out. "Leather" is derived from an Egyptian loanword (cf. Ezek 16:10). *G* has understood a color ὑακίνθινον "hyacinth blue," but is probably perplexed by the word. Some kind of leather is probably intended—in Ezek 16:10 the material seems to be usable for footwear. Since the Merarite burdens do not seem to require it, the material is apparently needed to protect the more holy items carried by Kohathites and Gershonites.

6. תְּכֵלֶת "violet." According to Snaith (*Numbers*, 194–95) the color is probably a bluish purple. *G* uses ὑακίνθινον again.

7. שֻׁלְחַן הַפָּנִים "the table of the presence." This phrase is unique. The table intended is described in Exod 25:23–30.

7. הַקְּעָרֹת "the bowls." See Snaith, *Numbers*, 195.

7. הַכַּפֹּת "the dishes." The root means "hand." These objects are perhaps for incense (cf. *G*).

7. הַמְנַקִּית "cups"—for drawing wine from a bowl (cf. *G*).

7. קְשׂוֹת הַנָּסֶךְ "flagons"—for pouring libations. These various vessels are first mentioned in Exod 25:29.

7. לֶחֶם הַתָּמִיד "the regular bread." This expression is unique (cf. Exod 25:30). The bread is the twelve loaves which have to be set out in the sanctuary, and replaced each week (Lev 24:5–9). This bread may originally have been thought of as food for God, but in P it is probably a sign of Israel's dependence on God for daily provision.

9. מְנֹרַת הַמָּאוֹר "the lampstand." This expression occurs only here and in Exod 35:14. The reference is to the seven-branched lampstand described in Exod 25:28; Lev 24:4.

9. מַחְתֹּתֶיהָ "its firepans." The word apparently denotes some utensil for catching falling material from the fire. The word can be used of a utensil

for moving ashes (Exod 27:3), and of one for holding incense (Lev 10:1; Num 16:6).

10. הַמּוֹט "the carrying frame" (RSV). NEB has "slung from a pole." The word occurs again in v 12, in Num 13:23 (where some kind of pole may well be involved), and in Nah 1:13 where "yoke" gives a reasonable rendering.

11. מִזְבַּח הַזָּהָב "the gold altar." This is the altar of incense first described in Exod 30:1–10. It was probably no older than the second temple.

13. אַרְגָּמָן "purple." This was probably of a reddish tint in contrast to the תְּכֵלֶת of v 6. Both colors may have been obtained from shellfish on the Phoenician coasts.

14. הַמִּזְלָגֹת "the forks." The fork in 1 Sam 2:13 was three-pronged and used for extracting the priestly portion of the sacrifice.

14. הַמִּזְרָקֹת "the basins" or "the tossing bowls" (NEB). These were used for throwing blood against the altar, as required in many of the sacrificial laws.

16. Eleazar is given special responsibility for four items. This could mean that he, and not the Kohathites, was required to carry them. Certainly he must take special responsibility for them: שֶׁמֶן הַמָּאוֹר "the oil for the light" (cf. Exod 27:20). קְטֹרֶת הַסַּמִּים "the sweet incense" (cf. Exod 25:6; 30:34–38). מִנְחַת הַתָּמִיד "the regular cereal offering." This phrase occurs in Neh 10:33, but is unique in the Pentateuch. It is probably the offering cited in Lev 6:13–15. שֶׁמֶן הַמִּשְׁחָה "the anointing oil" (cf. Exod 30:22–33).

18. שֵׁבֶט "tribe." The use of this word for a *subdivision* of one of the twelve tribes seems to be unique—see the discussion in G. B. Gray, *Numbers*, 37.

21.–28. For the various items associated with Gershonite service see *Comment* on Num 3:24–26.

26. וְאֵת כָּל-אֲשֶׁר יֵעָשֶׂה לָהֶם "all that must be done with regard to these things." This might include the undoing of hooks and loops, and the rolling up of curtains to facilitate transport.

29.–33. For the various items associated with Merarite service see *Comment* on Num 3:36–37.

34. The involvement of the נְשִׂיאִם "leaders" reflects their involvement in the census in Num 1:16. This particular phrase "leaders of the congregation" occurs again in Num 16:2 and Exod 16:22.

Explanation

This section provides another Levitical census—in this instance of all those between thirty and fifty years of age, and who are thus eligible for the service of the Tent. The command is given for each of the Levitical clans to be counted (vv 1–3, 21–23, 29–30), and the results are collected (vv 34–39). More specific detail about the different functions of each clan is also given, particularly that detail which concerns the moving of the various objects of the sanctuary when Israel is on the march. There is information for the Kohathites (vv 4–20), the Gershonites (vv 24–28) and the Merarites (vv 31–33).

Once again there are complexities in the structure of the chapter, but there are also patterns of coherence which enable the essence of it to be understood as a unit. There are the familiar techniques whereby new material is incorporated in the repetition and further explanation of information already given. There is little need to posit different origins for the census material and the service material. The kind of census envisaged, one identifying those eligible for service, makes it appropriate to recall what that service involves, particularly as there is more to be said in this area when it comes to the matter of preparation for the journey.

1–3, 21–23, 29–30. Here the author sets out the divine commands for a second Levitical census. The repetition in similar though not identical words reminds hearers, in a text intended for recitation, that the census is conducted on the highest authority. The author is building, in characteristic fashion, on foundations already laid—the idea of counting Levites (Num 3:15), and the idea of Levitical service with respect to the fabric and contents of the Tent of Meeting (Num 1:50). In recognising the period of service as one of twenty years (from thirty to fifty) he may well be incorporating older Levitical tradition. A specific divine judgment on the period of service finally appears in Num 8:24.

4–16. Since there is to be a census of Kohathites eligible for service, what precisely is Kohathite service to be, particularly when Israel is ready to move on? Here the author recollects and repeats ideas already developed in Num 3—that Kohathite service entails responsibility for the objects at the very center of the Tabernacle, and that Eleazar must exercise overall supervision (Num 3:31–32). The author is now ready to offer some further explanation of this information. Kohathite responsibility does not include the right to *handle* these objects. This is the author's main point in this extended section on the Kohathites. When the time comes to dismantle the Tabernacle Aaron and his sons are the ones who must make the preparations, placing various cloths and coverings on the holy objects to ensure that the Kohathites do not handle them.

In all Aaron and his sons make six large packages. These are the ark (covered with the screen), the table with utensils and loaves on top, the lampstand and its utensils, the gold altar of incense, miscellaneous utensils not belonging specifically to any one item of furniture, and the altar of burnt offering. The author is particularly interested in the coverings since these protect the Kohathites from direct contact with the objects. The covering for the first five objects is of a violet color, though the table has also a scarlet covering over its loaves and utensils. The covering for the altar of burnt offering is purple. All six packages have a covering of skin for further protection. Only the ark has its colored covering over the skin, perhaps for ease of identification. It is possible that behind this information lies older Levitical tradition, but it is difficult to separate this with any confidence from the constructive originality of the author himself. The key issue is the protection of the Kohathites.

Once the packages have been assembled by Aaron and his sons the service of the Kohathites is to carry them (v 15). In granting Levites this privilege with respect to the ark the author is anxious to do justice to tradition. It may be that transport by cart is the oldest transport tradition (1 Sam 6:8; 2 Sam 6:3), both references occurring in older parts of the Deuteronomic history which validate Jerusalem as a Yahwistic sanctuary. Even there a Levitical right to handle the ark seems to be recognized (1 Sam 6:15), and this is maintained in 2 Sam 15:24 in the Succession Narrative, though v 29 is less clear about the point and the possibility of glossing in v 24 has to be recognized. Other tradition saw handling the ark as a priestly function (Josh 3:6, 8, 13–15, 17), and the Deuteronomic historian was anxious to identify these as Levitical priests (Josh 3:3). The author of Numbers finds it easiest to bring these traditions together by granting the principle of Levitical transport (within the terms of his definition of "Levite"), but to assert the principles of preparation for transport by the sons of Aaron, and of general supervision by them. The items reserved for Eleazar doubtless indicate a traditional claim of the Zadokites in Babylon. The author is not prepared to make any adjustment or compromise at this point.

17–20. The author offers here a halakic observation on the material he has just presented. Does all this mean that the Kohathites must not even see the holy objects? The answer is—yes. It seems very likely that the returning exiles had a particularly awkward "Kohathite problem." Perhaps this was the point at which the author's new ideas were exposed to the greatest strain. The problem emerges again in connection with Korah the Kohathite in Num 16–17, and it may be that the items reserved to Eleazar were one of the points at issue. The pressure from the Kohathites may well have been such that there were advocates for their expulsion (v 18). The author is anxious to avoid this, but intends to maintain the basic stance of the returning priests. The Kohathites must be persuaded that the stipulations are not intended to degrade them or to rob them of privilege, but to protect them from danger.

24–28, 31–33. With the Kohathite question clarified it now remained to complete the picture by setting out the service of the Gershonites and the Merarites. In practice this meant the familiar method of repeating material (from Num 3:25–26, 36–37) with the further explanation that "service" includes carrying the items in question. In Exod. 38:21 Ithamar is given supervisory responsibilities regarding the Levites. The author, having taken the view that Kohathites need the special supervision of Eleazar, leaves the Gershonites and Merarites under the care of Ithamar (vv 28, 33).

The clarification of the relationship between priests and Levites, as offered in Num 3–4, was important in the post-exilic period. The basic distinctions are traced back to the wilderness period, and given the ultimate authority of a divine command through Moses. It would be relatively easy to apply these principles of distinction to the second Temple, and the Chronicler does this in some measure, attributing singing, gate-keeping and assistance with the sacrifices to the Levitical duties of David's time. There is an honorable Levitical ministry of care and protection with respect to the fabric, furniture, and utensils of the Temple, and also of assistance to Aaron, but there are certain qualifications and clarifications which have to be made. This ministry does not extend to all such items (v 16), and the Kohathites, who are responsible for the items of the holiest place, must be closely supervised, and at all costs must not see or handle directly the objects involved.

34–49. The author is now ready to reveal the results of the census. The figures are probably his own construction (see *Form/Structure/Setting*), based perhaps on an assessment of what each group would need to carry out its functions. The census clearly played an important part in post-exilic Judaism, in its struggle for authenticity through the elimination of what was alien, and for the identification of true Jewishness. For the author the figures also function as a further enforcement to readers and hearers of the importance of Levitical ministry. They help to set it apart as something distinct.

Theologically the section continues to explore the theme of God's holiness. The clarification of the distinction between priests and Kohathites brings a further sharpening of the hierarchical pattern. This pattern, as was suggested in the discussion of Num 3, is designed to secure protection from divine holiness, and also an authentic structure through which the holy God can reveal himself and be met by Israel.

The section also highlights the mobility of the Tabernacle and the ark it contains. The picture of Israel on the march persists, even in this major introductory section which is intended to set out the structure of the community. The God of the book of Numbers is not to be tied down to time or place. There is dismantling, journeying, and burden-bearing to be done.

The meticulous concern to clarify hierarchical distinctions may seem archaic and legalistic in the light of the NT. It was nevertheless an integral part of the post-exilic "Jewish revolution"—that movement in which Ezra and Nehemiah played leading parts that was aimed at the elimination of alien religion and culture, and the rediscovery of Jewishness. It involved both influencing and adjusting to the realities of the situation. This search for true identity, and for the meaning of authenticity, remains a proper and necessary quest of the people of God throughout history.

Priests and the Purity of the Community (5:1-4)

Bibliography

Douglas, M. *Purity and Danger. An Analysis of Concepts of Pollution and Taboo.* Londøn: Routledge and Kegan Paul, 1966. **Milgrom, J.** "Two Kinds of *hatta't.*" *VT* 26 (1976) 333–37. **Neusner, J.** *The Idea of Purity in Ancient Judaism.* Leiden: Brill, 1973. **Tucker, G. M.** "Covenant Forms and Contract Forms." *VT* 15 (1965) 487–503.

Translation

¹ *And Yahweh spoke to Moses, saying,* ² *"Command the people of Israel that they expel from the camp every person who has a skin disease or a bodily discharge, or who is unclean through contact with a corpse.* ³ *You shall expel both male and female. You shall expel them from* ª *the camp, so that they do not defile the camp within which I dwell."* ⁴ *And the people of Israel did so, and expelled them from the camp. The people of Israel did as Yahweh ordered Moses.*

Notes

3.a. According to GKC § 119e the combination of prepositions here has each retaining its full force—"out in front of." In English "from" seems sufficient when associated with the word "expulsion."

Form/Structure/Setting

It has been widely held that the section is supplementary to more basic forms of the P narrative (cf. e.g. J. Wellhausen, *Hexateuch*, 176; A. Kuenen, *Hexateuch*, 92–93; M. Noth, *Numbers*, 44–45). Its stipulation that discharges and contact with death are also grounds for exclusion seems to take us beyond the position in Lev 13–15, where the penalty applies only to skin disease. G. B. Gray (*Numbers*, 39) is less sure, thinking that these verses, along with Num 6:22–27, could have formed an appropriate conclusion to the PG narrative in Num 1–4.

D. Kellermann (*Priesterschrift*, 63–65) judges the section to be relatively late. He sees it as law based on Lev 13–15, and with an idealized view of the wilderness. The inclusion of women in v 3a and a minor addition in v 4a are the only elements which Kellermann takes to be supplementary to the law itself.

It is clear that connections with Lev 13–15 present no difficulty to the view of redaction and authorship we have adopted. The whole is a halakhic comment on those chapters, incorporated and possibly composed by the author of Numbers, extending the principle of exclusion in Lev 13:46 to all forms of tangible uncleanness. It may be that v 3, framed as it is in the second person, reflects the ongoing process of teaching and interpretation. The purpose may be to prepare the way for the exclusion of Miriam in Num 12 (v 3a), and to provide solid theological ground for the ruling (v 3b).

Comment

2. צָרוּעַ "skin disease." The word apparently covers a wide variety of skin complaints, particularly those with open sores. The traditional translation "leprosy" is thus misleading.

2. זָב "bodily discharge"—particularly those associated with sexuality as in Lev 15. The ultimate origins of ideas of religious pollution are uncertain. For discussion and suggestions see M. Douglas, *Purity and Danger.*

2. J. Milgrom (*VT* 26[1976] 333–37) argues that "outside the camp" refers not to an unclean place, but to one that is ceremonially neutral. The danger to the sanctuary and camp is the real point at issue.

Explanation

This section demands the exclusion from the camp of all unclean persons. The kind of uncleanness in mind is ceremonial and tangible, including skin diseases of many kinds, some types of bodily discharge, and contact with corpses.

Some commentators are inclined to call this and the other laws in Num 5–6 "miscellaneous." M. Noth (*Numbers,* 44–45) speaks of "additions joined together without any particular plan." This does less than justice to the author's work. Having explored the inner structure of the priestly hierarchy (Num 3–4) he is now ready to enter a new area in his overall discussion of the community's constitution. One thing he wishes to stress is the purity of the camp, and J. de Vaulx (*Nombres,* 89–90) and J. Sturdy (*Numbers,* 41) correctly identify this as a thread of inner coherence in Num 5–6 as a whole. It seems entirely appropriate that the issue should be raised here after the detailed discussion of the camp's organization in Num 1–4. Clearly the point must be established before the march begins.

It also seems that the author is now venturing into the realm of the relationship between priests and people. That between priests and Levites has been examined extensively in Num 3–4. Now is the time to extend the consideration of relationships. Though there is no specific reference here to priests—it is "the people of Israel" who obey in v 4—there can be little doubt in the light of Lev 13–15, where there is great stress on priestly diagnosis, that priests are at the center of affairs here. It was obviously important for the priestly theocracy of returning exiles that principles be set out in this area. Civil power was ultimately in Persian hands, and it was imperative that priesthood should mark out its role within the community. The content of vv 1–4 is probably one aspect of this. Taking responsibility for the ceremonial purity of the community was a primary function which priesthood was free to exercise. It may have been practiced for many years in Babylon. Some of these principles of purity may well have fallen into neglect in Palestine, and their reaffirmation was integral to the rediscovery of Jewishness. It could also be that the continuing stress on the camp's purity reflects a degree of antagonism to the "people of the land" of post-exilic times.

The author's approach to purity was already well established in Deuteronomy. Still older texts indicated that certain activities required special care in the matter of ceremonial purity. War was certainly one of these (2 Sam 11:11–13 and probably 1 Sam 21:6), possibly because it was often understood as a holy activity. Deuteronomy, in its search for a new spirit of aggressive independence, revives many of these old principles, and seeks a fresh adherence to them (cf. e.g. Deut 23:9–14). The author of Numbers follows in this general tradition, extending the principles of purity to the whole community, and specifying those phenomena which traditionally pollute. Skin diseases in particular had involved exclusion in relatively early tradition (Num 12:15; 2 Kgs 7:3; 15:5). The recognition of what pollutes evidently reflects deep-seated abhorrences, whose cause and origin are difficult to discover. M. Douglas (*Purity and Danger*) shows how many of these abhorrences offend a sense of "order" and "harmony."

The principles affirmed here are a logical consequence of the author's theological understanding of the God who dwells at the center of the community (v 3b). All in contact with such a God must be ceremonially clean. All that is polluted offends his holiness, and must be rigorously excluded. The NT undermines a purely ceremonial understanding of "pollution" (cf. e.g. Mark 7:19), thereby accentuating the commitment to moral holiness (cf. e.g. 1 Pet 1:15).

Priests and Restitution   (5:5-10)

Bibliography

Kellermann, D. "'*Asham* in Ugarit?" *ZAW* 76 (1964) 319–22. Latley, C. "Vicarious Solidarity in the Old Testament." *VT* 1 (1951) 267–74. Saydon, P. P. "Sin-Offering and Trespass-Offering." *CBQ* 8 (1946) 393–98. Thomson, H. C. "The Significance of the Term '*Asham* in the Old Testament." *TGUOS* 14 (1953) 20–26.

Translation

⁵ *And Yahweh spoke to Moses, saying,* ⁶ *"Speak to the people of Israel, when a man or woman does any of the sins which men commit, thereby breaking faith with Yahweh, and that person be found guilty,* ⁷ *then they shall confess the sin they have done, and make restitution for the guilt in full, with the addition of one fifth, and shall give it to the one to whom restitution is due.* ⁸ *But if the man has no next of kin to whom restitution can be paid, the restitution shall be* ᵃ *to the priest—in addition to the ram of atonement with which he, the priest, makes atonement for him.* ⁹ *And every contribution of all the holy things of the people of Israel which they offer to the priest* ᵃ *shall be his.* ¹⁰ *He shall have* ᵃ *each man's holy gifts;* ᵇ *whatever a man gives the priest shall be his."*

Notes

8.a. G reads יְהְיֶה "shall be" instead of לַיהֹוָה "to Yahweh," and is probably to be preferred (so *BHS*).

9.a. G also has "to Yahweh" at this point, along with 1 MT ms. It is probably an addition, reminding hearers of the one to whom offerings are ultimately given.

10.a. Some MT mss, SP, S, Tg. read a singular verb here.

10.b. Two MT mss read the negative לֹא here, but it seems easier to make sense of the majority reading.

Form/Structure/Setting

This section is often taken to be supplementary (cf. e.g. J. Wellhausen, *Hexateuch*, 176; A. Kuenen, *Hexateuch*, 93, 309; M. Noth, *Numbers*, 44–45). In this instance, G. B. Gray (*Numbers*, xxxvi, 39) also was unable to find little connection with the preceding and following material. The principle of restitution, with the addition of one fifth and the offering of a sacrifice, squares with the requirements of Lev 5, which itself is widely considered to be secondary. The law here in vv 5–10 is seen to take the discussion one stage further by giving rights to the priest if no legal owner is to be found. Thus vv 5–10 are seen to be dependent on Lev 5, and must themselves be a late accretion. A significant development is the fact that the sacrifice is called a "ram of atonement" (v 8) and not a "guilt offering." The latter term is reserved for the compensation paid (v 7). This is often taken to be a further indication of lateness, and of complex processes of growth within P. Noth points out (*Numbers*, 46) that the unusual formulations of v 6 are best explained on the hypothesis that this is comment on the specific text of Lev 5:20–26. The expression "any of the sins that men commit" looks to Noth like a deliberate contraction of the formula of Lev 5:22. The fact that it is "the priest" in vv 8–10 and not "Aaron" or "the sons of Aaron" is to him a further reflection of Lev 5:25–26.

D. Kellermann (*Priesterschrift*, 66–69) is inclined to the same kind of view. He points out that the observation in v 9 is very general, relating to offerings at large, and as such is only loosely linked with vv 5–8. For Kellermann it is an addition, with v 10 a possible tradition variant to v 9.

That Num 5:5–10 is some kind of halakhic comment on Lev 5 seems clear enough. The author is evidently anxious to resolve a matter concerning restitution when payment is no longer possible. The links with Lev 5 reveal his use of that text, while the differences reveal his independence, the shift of meaning in relation to the "guilt offering" being the most important of these. The idea of priestly maintenance in v 8 prompts him to make a general observation on the subject in v 9, while v 10, not necessarily a variant, serves to reinforce the point. There may be minor traces of glossing and editing (J. de Vaulx, *Nombres*, 91), but essentially vv 5–10 are an intelligible unit.

Comment

6. מִכָּל-חַטֹּאת הָאָדָם "any of the sins which men commit," literally "any sins of men." The genitive can be taken subjectively, as proposed (cf. *G*, RV), or objectively—"any of the sins committed against men" (NEB). On the analogy of Lev 5:22 the subjective interpretation is probably preferable. Social sins of this kind are also against Yahweh—Lev 5:21.

6. לִמְעֹל מַעַל "breaking faith," literally "treacherously to do an act of treachery." The kinds of offense in mind are those described in Lev 5:21–22.

7. וְהִתְוַדּוּ "they shall confess." Other priestly laws calling for some kind of verbal acknowledgment of guilt are Lev 5:5 (the sin offering) and Lev 16:21 (the Day of Atonement).

7. וְהֵשִׁיב אֶת-אֲשָׁמוֹ "make restitution for the guilt," literally "restore his guilt."

7. בְּרֹאשׁוֹ "in full," literally "with its head."

7. וַחֲמִישִׁתוֹ יֹסֵף עָלָיו "with the addition of one fifth." This is the normal figure for such purposes in Leviticus (cf. e.g. 22:14; 27:11–13, 31; cf. also Lev 5:24).

8. גֹּאֵל "next of kin." This root is widely used in connection with redemption. Here it is evidently a technical legal term. In the first instance the next of kin would be a brother, and then uncles and cousins on the father's side, and after them some other near kinsman. It was the duty of the "next of kin" to buy back property temporarily lost to the family (Lev 25:25), and perhaps a relative who has become a slave through poverty (Lev 25:47–52). The next of kin is also the "avenger of blood" in Num 35:9–34.

8. אֵיל הַכִּפֻּרִים "the ram of atonement." The expression occurs only here.

It appears to be the guilt offering required in Lev 5:25. On the idea of "atonement" see *Comment* on Num 17:6-15.

9. וְכָל־תְּרוּמָה "and every contribution." The root means "to lift off," and denotes that which is lifted off or set apart for sacred purposes. It can be used of the produce of the earth (Num 15:19-21) or of spoils taken in war (Num 31:29, 41, 52). It can be used of tithes (Num 18:24, 26-29) or of material for the Tabernacle (Exod 35:5, 21, 24), and even of the half shekel (Exod 30:13-16). In sacrifices it is applied to the shoulder of the peace offering (Exod 29:27; Lev 7:34; Num 6:20). These varied items are all in some sense dedicated to Yahweh. There is no real justification for taking the *terumah* to be a specific offering, as in the traditional translation "heave offering" (RV). J. Milgrom (*IDB* Sup 391) notes that the *terumah* is never offered "before" Yahweh, but always "to Yahweh." He concludes convincingly that it was a dedication without ritual outside the sanctuary, effected by oral declaration (Judg 17:3) or physical act (Lev 27:32). As such it contrasted with the *tenuphah*.

In general vv 9-10 wish to stress that each gift becomes the personal property of the priest to whom it is given, and does not therefore belong to the priestly community as a whole.

Explanation

Though many commentators are at a loss to perceive the connection of vv 5-10 with vv 1-4 there are threads of coherence. Both J. de Vaulx (*Nombres,* 90, 92-93) and J. Sturdy (*Numbers,* 41-42) discern a movement from a concern for ceremonial purity to one of concern for ethical purity. The overall context of vv 5-10 continues to be essentially ceremonial, and it may be unwise to press this distinction too firmly, but it is broadly true that the pollutions of vv 1-4 preclude contact with God, and that those of vv 5-10 divide man from man (cf. Lev 5:21-22) thereby giving them a distinctly moral dimension.

The section calls for the righting of wrongs within the community, the kind of wrong in which damage has been done and loss sustained. Confession, full restitution, and additional payment of twenty percent is required of the guilty party, in addition to the ram of atonement. If the man is dead and there is no next of kin to whom payment can be made then the money, along with the ram and other offerings, goes to the priest.

As in vv 1-4 there is in this section a marking out of priestly rights with respect to the community at large. The principle of restitution was well established in ancient collections of law (cf. e.g. Exod 21:32, 34-36; 22:2-6, 11, 13, 15-16). There the compensation might in some cases be decided by the victim (Exod 21:22), or in other cases be as high as double (Exod 22:3, 6, 8). There is no clear indication that restitution plus twenty percent was a widespread pre-exilic rule. It was evidently part of the tradition among Babylonian Jews, and was part of the program they brought to Palestine.

In these verses the author is also able to make a claim on behalf of the priests. The destination of restitution where there was no kinsman may have been a matter of dispute, or more probably a Palestinian slackness in the matter had led to the total non-payment of restitution in such cases. Here too the priests are able to stake a claim. It need not be assumed that this was entirely selfish. The books of Ezra and Nehemiah make it plain that much slackness in the maintenance of the priesthood had had a damaging effect on priestly practice and morale. D. Kellermann makes a plausible suggestion about the relevance of such law in the post-exilic context. The departure into exile of the upper strata of Jewish society left a vacuum in Palestine, and many possessions and properties must have been taken over by those who remained. This stipulation guaranteed to returning Jews the right of repossession and compensation. The extent to which the twenty percent norm could be enforced was immaterial; the principle mattered.

The author's method is to offer a halakhic interpretation of texts already available in Lev 5—hence the description of the official as simply "the priest." J. Sandys-Wunsch (*Numbers* 58) conjectures that in vv 9–10 there is a concern to protect the rights of individual priests, and to prevent favoritism among the returning Zadokites. Whether or not this is true the author uses the compensation question to affirm the principle of proper priestly maintenance by the community, through the system of sacrifices and offerings. He has more to say about this later on. For the moment the principle is sufficient.

The section removes any suspicion that priestly theology lacked moral seriousness. The procedures of cultic observance are not a substitute for the proper rebuilding of relationships between man and man within the community. To the guilty party this is bound to be costly. Moreover an effective leadership must be properly supported, and in the eyes of the priestly theologians this responsibility devolved upon the community at large.

Priests and the Ordeal   (5:11–31)

Bibliography

Blank, S. H. "The Curse, the Blasphemy, the Spell, and the Oath." *HUCA* 23/1 (1950/1) 73–95. **Brichto, H. C.** The Case of the *Sota* and a Reconsideration of Biblical Law." *HUCA* 46 (1975) 55–70. **Driver, G. R.** and **Miles, J. C.** "Ordeal by Oath at Nuzi." *Iraq* 7 (1940) 132. **Driver, G. R.** "Two Problems in the Old Testament Examined in the Light of Assyriology." *Syria* 33 (1956) 70–78. **Fensham, F. C.** "Malediction and Benediction in ANE Vassal Treaties and the Old Testament." *ZAW* 74 (1962) 1–9. **Fishbane, M.** "Accusations of Adultery: A Study of Law and Scribal Practice in Numbers 5:11–31." *HUCA* 45 (1974) 25–46. **Hempel, J.** *Die Israelitischen Anschauungen von Segen und Fluch im Lichte altorientalischer Parallelen.* BZAW 81 Berlin: Töpelmann, 1961, 30–113. **Lehmann, M. R.** "Biblical Oaths." *ZAW* 81 (1969) 74–92. **Morgenstern, J.** "Trial by Ordeal among the Semites in Ancient Israel." *HUCA Jub. Vol.* (1925) 113–43. **Press, R.** "Das Ordal im alten Israel." *ZAW* 51 (1933) 121–40, 227–55. **Rinaldi G.** "La dònna che 'ha deviatio'. Considerazioni su Nu. 5, 11–31." *Euntes Docete* (Roma) 26 (1973) 535–50. **Sasson, J. M.** "Nu. 5 and the Waters of Judgment." *BZ* 16 (1972) 249–51. **Scharbert, J.** "Fluchen und Segnen im Alten Testament." *Bibl* 39 (1958) 1–26. **Stade, B.** "Die Eiferopferthora." *ZAW* 15 (1895) 166–78. **Schotroff, S.** *Der altisraelitische Fluchspruch.* WMANT 30 Neukirchen: Kreis Moers, 1969.

Translation

[11] *And Yahweh spoke to Moses, saying,* [12] *"Speak to the people of Israel, and say to them, If any man's wife goes astray, and acts unfaithfully to him,* [13] *and a man lies with her* [a] *carnally, and it is hidden from the eyes of her husband, and she is both undetected and defiled, and there is no witness against her, and she was not taken in the act,* [14] *and a spirit of suspicion comes upon him, and he is suspicious of his wife, and she is defiled, or if a spirit of suspicion comes upon him, and he is suspicious of his wife, and she is not defiled,* [15] *then the man shall bring his wife to the priest, and shall bring the offering required to her—a tenth of an ephah of barley meal. He shall pour no oil upon it, and put no frankincense on it, for it is a cereal offering of suspicion, a cereal offering of memorial, bringing iniquity to light.*

[16] *"And the priest shall bring her near, and shall set her before Yahweh.* [17] *And the priest shall take holy water* [a] *in an earthen vessel, and of the dust which is on the floor of the Tabernacle* [b] *the priest shall take, and shall put it into the water.* [18] *And the priest shall set the woman before Yahweh, and shall loosen the hair of the woman's head, and put the cereal offering of memorial in her hands, the cereal offering of suspicion. And the priest shall have in his hand the water of testing* [a] *which brings the curse.* [19] *And the priest shall make her swear, and shall say to the woman, 'If no man has lain with you, and if you have not gone astray to uncleanness, while under your husband's authority, be free* [a] *from this water of testing which brings the curse.* [20] *But if you have gone astray, while under your husband's authority, and if you are defiled, and some man other than your husband has lain with you,'* [a] [21] *(then the priest shall make the woman swear with the oath of the curse, and the*

priest shall say to the woman) '*Yahweh make you a curse and an oath among your people, if Yahweh makes your thigh fall away and your body swell.*[a] [22] *And this water that brings the curse shall pass into your belly, and make your body swell* [a] *and your thigh fall away.*' [b] *And the woman shall say 'Amen, Amen.*'

[23] "*And the priest shall write these curses in a book, and shall wash them into the water of testing,* [24] *and he shall make the woman drink the water of testing which brings the curse. And the water which brings the curse shall enter her for the testing.* [25] *And the priest shall take from the hand of the woman the cereal offering of suspicion, and shall present the cereal offering as a special contribution before Yahweh, and shall bring it to the altar.* [26] *And the priest shall take* [a] *a handful of the cereal offering as a token, and shall burn it on the altar, and afterwards shall make the woman drink the water.* [27] *And he shall make her drink the water,* [a] *and it shall be,* [b] *if she is defiled, and has acted unfaithfully toward her husband, that the water which brings the curse shall enter into her for the testing, and· her body shall swell, and her thigh shall fall away. And the woman shall be a curse among her people.* [28] *But if the woman is not defiled, and she is clean, then she shall be free, and shall conceive children.*

[29] "*This is the law of suspicion, when a wife, being under the authority of her husband, goes astray and is defiled,* [30] *or when a spirit of suspicion comes upon a man, and he is suspicious of his wife. Then he shall set the woman before Yahweh, and the priest shall deal with her according to all this law.* [31] *And the man shall be free from iniquity, and the woman shall bear her iniquity.*"

Notes

13.a. אָתָהּ should probably be pointed אִתָּהּ "with her" (cf. also 19).

17.a. Sam has קדישים "sanctified." *G* has καθαρον ζων "pure running water." *Tg.* understands this to be water from the laver (Exod 38:8). J. Paterson (*Numbers*, 44) rejects this on the grounds that there is no mention of the laver, that its water is nowhere described as "holy," and that there is no ceremony for the consecration of such water. The water of purification in Num 19:9 is judged to be entirely different. Paterson prefers *G*. Perhaps a holy spring is to be understood. A. Dillmann (*Numeri*, 28) argues similarly on the basis of the unique adjectival use of קדוש. If the author is indeed drawing on ancient custom (see *Form/Structure/Setting*) something comparable to *G* may well sum up the original intention behind the text.

17.b. *G* has "Tent of Meeting" and *S* has "the altar." There is no strong reason for rejecting MT.

18.a. RV and RSV take the root to be מרר (cf. *Tg.* and Vg). This is usually understood to mean "to be bitter"—hence "bitterness." *G* reads τουἐλεγμου "proof"—hence "contention" (NEB) and "testing." Either seems possible, though the latter gives a more precise indication of the water's function, and is easier to translate in vv 24, 27 (cf. also vv 19, 23). N. H. Snaith (*Numbers*, 202) draws on Arabic words, and suggests that the idea "to cause an abortion" may be intended.

19.a. An imperative expressing a consequence which is to be expected with certainty (GKC § 110f [b]).

20.a. An example of aposiopesis—in which a clause has to be supplied from the context to complete the sense (GKC § 167/1). The content of v 21b or v 22 is required.

21.a. The root occurs in Isa 29:7. It seems best to see צבא in Sam as an emendation.

22.a. On the vocalization see GKC § 53q.

22.b. On the vocalization see GKC § 53q, 66f.

26.a. This is a rare verb, but it is found elsewhere in P (Lev 2:2; 5:12) and is preferable to Sam and Syr.

27.a. The whole of the first clause is omitted in *G* and *S*, perhaps through homoeoteleuton—note the repetition of המים. This view also removes the difficulty posed by the third drinking (see *Form/Structure/Setting*).

27.b. וְהָיְתָה may be an error. וְהָיָה is normal (Sam, *Tg.*ʲ; cf. GKC § 112 y, gg; J. Paterson, *Numbers*, 44).

Form/Structure/Setting

The section has been universally recognized as priestly by analysts, and many assume it to belong to a supplementary stratum (cf. e.g. J. Wellhausen, *Hexateuch*, 177; A. Kuenen, *Hexateuch*, 92, 93; G. B. Gray, *Numbers*, 39; M. Noth, *Numbers*, 44–45). The grounds for such a view are that the cereal offering of Lev 2 (itself secondary) is presupposed, and that the section has little or no connection with the preceding and succeeding material. The dependence on Lev 2 is entirely consonant with the approach to the view of the tradition we have proposed, and threads of coherence, linking this with surrounding sections, are not entirely absent (see. *Explanation*).

Problems within the law itself have long been recognized. B. Stade ("Die Eiferopferthora") drew attention, among other things, to the fact that the woman is twice brought to Yahweh (vv 16, 18), twice takes an oath (vv 19, 21), and twice drinks the water (vv 24, 26, 27). Moreover v 20 is incomplete, and v 22 duplicates v 21. Stade concluded that there was a fusion here of two ordeal laws:

1. A cereal offering of remembrance consisting of most of vv 11–13, 15–20, 22a, 23–26a, 31.
2. A cereal offering of jealousy consisting in the main of vv 14, 21, 22b, 25, 27–29, 30a.

An alternative analysis favored by H. Holzinger (*Numeri*), R. Press ("Das Ordal") and R. Rendtorff (*Die Gesetze in der Priesterschrift*. Göttingen: Vandehoeck & Ruprecht 1954) distinguishes between a rite in which holy water is drunk, and another involving a cereal offering and a curse. J. de Vaulx (*Nombres*, 93) is looking for solutions in a broadly similar direction. He concludes that the ordeal is for two purposes—to give a judicial decision in a reasonably definite case of adultery (vv 12–13, 29, 31), and to assuage the jealous suspicions of a husband. He posits a bitter water ordeal to fulfill the first purpose (vv 15a,ᵃ 16–17, 19–20, 22a, 23–24). The second, a case in which there is much less certainty includes the offering (vv 14a,ᵇ 18a, 21, 22b, 25–26). He is led in this direction by two distinct procedures in the Hammurabi code (131–132), one for a case of reasonable certainty, and the other for a case where the issue is much less clear. Whether this is a correct interpretation of the Hammurabi stipulations is another matter. The point that the woman has not been caught is common to both rites. The difference is whether a husband makes the accusation (in which case an oath is taken) or whether somebody else points the finger (in which event an ordeal is performed). Nor is it obvious that any part of vv 11–31 necessarily envisages a case of a reasonable certainty. The selection of texts designed to show this is somewhat arbitrary. It is true that guilt is the center of attention in vv 13–14a, but this is balanced in some measure by v 14b. In the overall context the case is evidently an open one. In the same way v 28 is balanced by v 29.

D. Kellermann (*Priesterschrift*, 70–83) argues that the problems are created by expansion rather than amalgamation. The groundwork is found in the bulk of vv 14a, 15a,[a] 17, 18a,[b] 21a, 22–24. The man brings his wife to the priest, who takes water, adds dust, and loosens the woman's hair. She is made to pronounce an oath-curse, and the priest in turn makes the pronouncement of v 22a. The woman concurs (v 22b), and the priest writes down the curse, washing it into the water, and making the woman drink. According to Kellermann, most of the rest of the section belongs to secondary expansion. It stresses the occasion on which such an ordeal is to be used, brings what is essentially a magical rite under the aegis of Yahweh and his power, and emphasizes the question of guilt or innocence. The third and final expansion, according to Kellermann, introduces the offering, thus linking the ordeal with rituals in Leviticus, and bringing the rite to the Temple.

M. Noth (*Numbers*, 49) seeks to penetrate the earliest literary tradition, and suggests the possibility of three different kinds of divine judgment. These he suspects are so closely amalgamated that they cannot confidently be separated in literary terms. He sees in the simple designation "the priest" an indication of earlier tradition, and suspects that the earliest elements in the text take us back to fairly ancient practice. The forms of divine judgment are:

1. The powerful effect of "holy" water mixed with sanctuary dust (v 17). This causes bodily deformities and prevents childbearing (vv 27–28).

2. An oath in the form of a curse. This also would be spontaneous in its effects (vv 19, 21).

3. The writing of words in a book (v 23). Noth suggests that the consumption of these words would have the effect of a curse. It is the amalgamation of these diverse practices that produces the complexities in the present form of the text.

It is hard to reach any great degree of certainty in this kind of discussion, but there can be little doubt that the ordeal was an ancient custom (cf. e.g. de Vaulx, *Nombres*, 89). Though the ordeal of bitter waters has no direct parallel in the ancient near east, there are many other such judicial procedures, particularly in Mesopotamia (cf. e.g. S. N. Kramer, "Ur-Namu Code," *Or* 23 [1954] 48; G. R. Driver & J. C. Miles, *The Assyrian Laws* [Oxford: Blackwell, 1935] 86; *The Babylonian Laws* [Oxford: Blackwell, 1956, vol. 2] 53). A widely attested Mesopotamian practice is the casting of the accused into a river. R. de Vaux (*Ancient Israel*, 158) conjectures that lack of a suitable river might have precluded such a custom in Israel. In any event, the ordeal principle was doubtless ancient, and the combination of different rites as an explanation for some of the text's difficulties is reasonable. The drinking of water, and the writing of curses may possibly have been linked at a relatively early stage. Such a law survives perhaps in vv 17, 18 (most), 21a[b]b, 23–24. Apart from the matter of the oath this agrees in most respects with Kellermann's groundwork. It does seem likely however that the involvement of Yahweh would have been there at the outset. This is what makes the procedure acceptable. It is perfectly possible that the rest of the section comes from the author of Numbers, all the unevenness in the text being now explained. It may be that the rite had been used for a somewhat wider range of tests, and that the author in vv 11–14, 16, 29–31 is anxious to limit the precise circumstances in which it can be used. He also builds into the ritual a cereal offering (vv

15, 18 (part), 25–26), an oath (vv 19–21a,ᵃ 22) and some further comment
emphasizing the consequences (vv 27–28). The introduction of the oath would
help to bring the ordeal into line with the legal tradition of Exod 22:7–8,
10.

Comment

12. Contrary to the impression given by N. H. Snaith (*Numbers*, 200–01)
שָׂטָה "to go astray" is rare, occurring elsewhere only in Prov 4:15; 7:25.
The latter text speaks of seduction.

13. Two witnesses were required (Deut 17:6; 19:15; Num 35:30), particularly if an adulteress is to be put to death (Deut 22:22–27; Lev 20:10).

14 רוּחַ "spirit." This word has many uses. It can denote human breath
(e.g. 1 Kgs 10:5), nothingness (Prov 11:29), wind (e.g. Gen 3:8), and in some
sense the spirit of man (e.g. Gen 6:3). It is very often used of God's spirit
(e.g. Judg 3:10). It can also denote a human mind, disposition, or mood.
Sometimes this can be desirable: e.g. courage (Josh 2:11)—but the word can
also be used of apostasy (Hos 4:12). This idea of "disposition" or "mood"
must be closest to the sense required here.

15. עֲשִׂירִת הָאֵיפָה "a tenth of an ephah." This is a dry measure, and is
a relatively small amount (7½ pints or 3–4 litres).

15. קֶמַח שְׂעֹרִים "barley meal." This is a coarse flour, unlike the סֹלֶת
required elsewhere (e.g. Num 6:15; Ezek 46:14). For earlier references to
קֶמַח cf. Judg 6:19; 1 Sam 1:24; 1 Kgs 5:2, and to שְׂעֹרִים; cf. Judg 7:13; 1
Kgs 5:8; Ruth 2:17.

15. Oil and frankincense are used in the normal cereal offering (Lev 2:1).
Another dry cereal offering is the poor man's sin-offering (Lev 5:11). It is
perhaps the possible association with sin that makes this ordeal offering a
dry one.

15. Unlike most "memorials" (cf. e.g. Lev 23:24) this is a somber occasion,
bringing iniquity to light.

16. לִפְנֵי יהוה "before Yahweh." Probably before the altar (cf. 1 Kgs 8:31).

17. Originally the holy water was probably derived from a holy spring.
The author of Numbers probably intended that it should come from the
laver mentioned in Exod 38:8 (see *Notes*).

17. כְּלִי-חָרֶשׂ "an earthen vessel." As in Lev 14:5, 50.

17. The dust was doubtless considered sacred by virtue of its presence
in the Tabernacle.

18. The loose hair of the leper (Lev 13:45) is a sign of uncleanness (cf.
Lev 21:10). It may also be a sign of mourning (Lev 10:6). Some see subjection
to shame in the loosening of hair here.

18. מֵי הַמָּרִים "water of testing." Though this is perhaps the best rendering (see *Notes*) the root מָרַר "to be bitter" underlies the word. The use of
bitter tasting water was probably a regular feature of early ordeals.

21. To become "a curse and an oath" means to be quoted by people in
such forms of expression (cf. Jer 29:22).

21. אֶת-יְרֵכֵךְ נֹפֶלֶת וְאֶת-בִּטְנֵךְ צָבָה "your thigh fall away and your body
swell." These ideas are expressed in the reverse order in vv 22, 27. The
root צָבָה is often understood as "to swell," but NEB n. suggests "to melt

away." It is unlikely that a disease as such is intended. Most commentators take the expressions to be euphemisms for a miscarriage and/or stillbirth. There is to be no fruit from an illicit union (cf. v 28). Jewish tradition, and probably the author himself, considered this a most fitting punishment for the sin in question.

22. בִּטְנֵךְ "your body." The word appears to include most of the internal organs associated with the belly.

23. בַּסֵּפֶר "in the book." A piece of parchment is probably intended.

25. וְהֵנִיף The root probably means "to present a special contribution"— see G. R. Driver, "Three Technical Terms in the Pentateuch," *JSS* 1 (1956) 97–105.

26. אֶת-אַזְכָּרָתָה "as a token." This is a technical term occurring elsewhere only in Lev 2:3, 9, 16; 5:12, 6:8; 24:7. It seems to be a portion of the offering which is burnt on the altar. The rest is the priest's (Lev 2:2). The meaning is not entirely clear—see further G. R. Driver *JSS* 1 [1956] 97–105; L. Kopf, "Arabische Etymologien und Parallelen zum Bibelwörterbuch," *VT* 59 (1959) 247–87. Driver suggests "token."

28. The "freedom" relates to the "water of testing" (cf. v 19). It is clear that moral as well as ceremonial matters affect the question of ritual pollution.

29. זֹאת תּוֹרַת "this is the law of." This expression is characteristic of priestly law (cf. Lev 6:2, 7, 28; 7:1, 11; 11:46; 12:7; 13:59; 14:32, 57; 15:32; Num 6:13, 21).

31. This verse appears to mean that the man is free of guilt, even if his suspicions proved false. If they were correct than of course the woman must bear the consequences of her guilt.

Explanation

This section consists of a trial by ordeal whereby a woman suspected of adulterous relationships can be brought to the sanctuary and made to undergo certain rites, the outcome of which determines the accuracy or otherwise of the suspicion. The central rite is the consumption of a mixture of water and dust. The taking of an oath by the woman also occurs. The result of the procedure either condemns or clears the woman.

As with Num 5:1–10 there has been an inability among a number of commentators to perceive the patterns of organization and coherence which link this section with those which precede and follow it. J. de Vaulx (*Nombres*, 90) and J. Sturdy (*Numbers*, 41) have properly observed that Num 5 as a whole is about the sanctification of the community. A crucial part of this process, beginning in vv 1–10, is the unmasking of hidden sin, and the vindication of those unjustly accused. This is why the old ordeal procedures of vv 11–31 are incorporated here.

It would be fair to add that this section is another step toward the marking out of a priestly role within the restored community. The "hard case" had been legislated for in the Book of Covenant with some form of oath (Exod 22:9–10; cf. also Exod 22:7–8). Though not provided for in those laws the ordeal was probably widely practiced in earlier times, particularly in the provincial country areas. The administration of both oath and ordeal would have been a significant priestly responsibility. The lot-casting of Josh 7:16–18; 1 Sam 14:38–42 may also have been conducted by priests, albeit under the supervision of leader figures. The establishment of the monarchy apparently brought the king some responsibility for hard cases (cf. e.g. 2 Sam 15:1–6; 1 Kgs 3:16–22). Such evidence as exists suggests that judgments were reached on a more rational basis, through enquiry and the hearing of evidence. This receives some support from Deuteronomy which sets up a central bureaucracy of priests and judge, and lays stress on "enquiry" without mentioning mechanical techniques, though the possibility that these are presupposed cannot be entirely precluded (Deut 17:8–9; 19:17–18). The author of Numbers naturally accepts such an arrangement, and the Chronicler confirms it, tracing a significant movement in that direction in the reign of Jehosphaphat (2 Chr 19:8–11). Nevertheless the author of Numbers is ready to recognize the validity of a traditional method, seeing in it particularly a means of securing a priestly role in another aspect of the community's life.

Another distinct possibility is that the exile, with the collapse of the central bureaucracy, led to a revival in Palestine of the traditional method of ordeal. The author of Numbers is anxious to come to terms with it, but at the same time introduces important adaptations. We have suggested that there was an older rite in vv 17–18, 21^{ab}b, 23–24, and this may have been in current use among the Palestinians. One of the author's aims may have been to limit the ordeal to this particular kind of case—hence the precise and meticulous description of the circumstances in the casuistic formulations of vv 12–14. Such a case was both notoriously hard and notoriously serious—particularly in its implications for the holiness of individuals and the community at large. So there was justification in the author's view for submitting this case in particular to the processes of the ordeal. The introduction of a cereal offering by the author (vv 15, 18, 25–26) brought the ritual into the mainstream of the post-exilic sacrificial system, and helped to ensure that it would only be conducted by the priests at Jerusalem. The author's additions in vv 19–21a,^{a} 22 put special stress on the oath rather than the water as the significant factor in the rite. They repeat the circumstances of the case as set out in vv 12–14, and involve the woman positively in the procedures of the ritual through her verbal response. His summary of the consequences of the ritual (vv 27–28) is in line with these fundamental concerns. These adaptations may not be quite the battle against superstition suggested by de Vaulx (Nombres, 97). The author's main purpose may be to bring the oath-taking traditions of Exodus 22 into contact with the ordeal. It is arguable though that oath-taking and the positive involvement of the woman point the ordeal in a less superstitious direction.

Theologically the section bears further witness to the moral seriousness of the priestly literature. Marital deceit is a matter of such seriousness that the truth must be discovered. It is harmful to the sanctity of the community at large, and destructive of one of the bases of community life. That the ordeal as a judicial method is inadequate, and possibly unjust, is obvious enough to modern perceptions. Nevertheless it does bear witness to a proper concern for objectivity in justice, and in this particular instance, the only one cited in the OT, the procedures demanded proof of guilt and favored the defendant. The water drinking of Exod 32:20 is not an ordeal but a punishment; there guilt is already known. In Num 5 miscarriage is most unlikely from the purely physical effects of drinking water and dust. Only a guilty conscience, prompted perhaps by the oath and the solemnity of the occasion, might produce one. In any event there seems little danger to the innocent in such a procedure. The advantage of it was that, to the ancient mind, it was sufficient to remove the destructive effects of suspicion and fear within relationships. Modern practice of the ordeal would obviously be indefensible, but a modern moral seriousness, aiming for healthy relationships, has to recognize the destructive effect of suspicion, and find means to allay and eliminate it.

Priests and the Nazirites (6:1–21)

Bibliography

Eichrodt, W. *Theology of the Old Testament.* Vol. 1. London: SCM, 1959, 303–06. **Gray, G. B.** "The Nazirite." *JTS* 1 (1899–1900) 201–11. **Milgrom, J.** "Sin Offering or Purification Offering?" *VT* 21 (1971) 237–39. **Peritz, I. J.** "Woman in the Ancient Hebrew Cult." *JBL* 17 (1898) 111–48. **Smith, W. Robertson.** *The Religion of the Semites.* London: Black, 1907, 323–35, 479–85. **Weisman, Z.** "The Biblical Nazirite, Its Types and Roots." *Tarbiz* 36 (1967) 207–20.

Translation

¹ *And Yahweh spoke to Moses, saying,* ² *"Speak to the people of Israel, and say to them, If a man or a woman makes a special* ª *vow, the vow of a Nazirite, to dedicate himself to Yahweh,* ³ *he shall abstain from wine and strong drink. He shall drink no vinegar of wine, or vinegar of strong drink, nor shall he drink any juice of grapes, or eat fresh grapes or dried.* ⁴ *All the days of his dedication he shall eat nothing that is made from the grape vine, from the seeds to the skins.*
⁵ *"All the days of his vow* ª *of dedication a razor shall not touch his head. Until the days are complete during which he is dedicated to Yahweh, he shall be holy. He shall let the locks of the hair of his head grow long.*
⁶ *"All the days of his dedication to Yahweh he shall not come near to a dead body.* ⁷ *Even for his father, his mother, his brother, or his sister* ª *he shall not make himself unclean when they die, because his dedication to his God is upon his head.* ⁸ *All the days of his dedication he is holy to Yahweh.*
⁹ *"And if a man beside him dies suddenly, and he defiles his dedicated head, then he shall shave his head on the day of his cleansing. On the seventh day shall he shave it.* ¹⁰ *And on the eighth day he shall bring two turtledoves or two young pigeons to the priest, to the door of the Tent of Meeting.* ¹¹ *And the priest shall offer one for a purification offering, and the other for a whole offering, and shall make atonement for him, because he sinned on account of the dead, and he shall sanctify his head on that day.* ¹² *And he shall dedicate to Yahweh the days of his dedication,* ª *and he shall bring a male lamb of the first year for a reparation offering.* ª *And the preceding days shall not be reckoned, because his dedication was defiled.*
¹³ *"And this is the law for the Nazirite when the days of his dedication are completed. He shall be brought* ª *to the door of the Tent of Meeting.* ¹⁴ *And he shall make his offering to Yahweh, one* ª *male lamb of the first year without blemish for a whole offering, and one female lamb of the first year without blemish for a purification offering, and one ram without blemish for a shared offering,* ¹⁵ *and a basket of unleavened bread, cakes of fine flour mixed with oil, and unleavened wafers covered with oil, along with the proper cereal and drink offerings.* ¹⁶ *And the priest shall present them before Yahweh, and shall offer his purification offering and his whole offering.* ¹⁷ *And he shall offer the ram for a shared offering sacrifice to Yahweh, with the basket of unleavened bread. The priest shall also offer the proper cereal offering and drink*

offering. [18] *And the Nazirite shall shave his dedicated head at the door of the Tent of Meeting, and shall take the hair of his dedicated head, and put it on the fire which is under the shared offering sacrifice.* [19] *And the priest shall take the boiled shoulder of the ram, and one unleavened cake out of the basket, and one unleavened wafer, and shall put them into the hands of the Nazirite, after he has shaved his dedicated head.* [20] *And the priest shall present them as a special gift before Yahweh. This is a holy portion for the priest, together with the breast of the special gift, and the thigh of the special contribution. And afterwards the Nazirite may drink wine.*

[21] *"This is the law of the Nazirite who makes a vow, his offering to Yahweh for his dedication, apart from anything else that he can give. According to his vow* [a] *which he makes so must he do, in accordance with the law of his dedication."*

Notes

2.a. cf. Lev 27:2 for another Hiphil of this root. Contrast the Piel in Lev 22:21; Num 15:3, 8. *BHS* suggests that the vocalization of Lev 27:2 be adopted.

5.a. נִדְרוֹ may be dittographic, and could thus be deleted—as in a few MT mss, *G* (cf. v 8).

7.a. On the vocalization see GKC § 96.

12.a. *BHS* raises the possibility that the whole clause is an addition; see further under *Comment*.

13.a. *BHS* suggests יָבוֹא or יָבִיא. It is hard to see why and by whom a Nazirite should be "brought" to the Tent of Meeting. J. Paterson (*Numbers*, 45) suggests that אֹתוֹ could be transposed with אֶת-קָרְבָּנוֹ in v 14 to make good sense. For further suggestions see G. B. Gray, *Numbers*, 70.

14.a. The numeral "one" is in a rare position (but cf. 1 Sam 6:7). *BHS* suggests its possible removal to a position after כֶּבֶשׂ (cf. also J. Paterson, *Numbers*, 45; G. B. Gray, *Numbers*, 70).

21.a. Some MT mss read נְדָרוֹ here (cf. v 4), but נִדְרוֹ has no serious difficulty, and is probably to be accepted.

Form/Structure/Setting

Analysts have recognized the work of priestly writers in this section, and there has been a general tendency to see a secondary stratum here (cf. e.g. J. Wellhausen, *Hexateuch*, 177; A. Kuenen, *Hexateuch*, 91–93; G. B. Gray, *Numbers*, 39; M. Noth, *Numbers*, 53–55). Points raised in this discussion are the dependence of vv 9–11 on Lev 14:9; 15:14–15, 30, and of v 15 on Exod 29:2–3, and a general dependence in the rituals on Lev 1–7. Gray is unable to find any organic connection to the priestly narrative, and therefore rules out PG. He attributes the section to PX—his legal source coming from varied hands. Some analysts have found phraseology approximating closely to that of the Holiness Code (Lev 17–26), but Gray was unconvinced, and drew attention to small details in the present form of the law suggesting a comparatively late date, including the use of a male lamb (v 14), the sin offerings, and precision about quantities. Noth finds evidence of a basic form of the law characterized by "the priest" rather than "Aaron." It has been adapted to the P narrative as a whole, but is probably not very old because it is quite reminiscent of the rituals of Lev 1–7. The law is far removed, in Noth's view, from the older Nazirite principles evident in Judg 13:4–5; Amos 2:12.

The Nazirite vow is now a meritorious work by the individual with little general significance for the community as a whole. Noth sees vv 13–20 as an addition, since v 13a, now an introduction, must originally have been in his view a concluding formula (cf. v 21a).

D. Kellermann (*Priesterschrift*, 83–95) finds two basic components in the section—a law and an expansion. The law is found in vv 2b (most), 3–8, 9 (most), 12 (most). The expansion includes the reference to the seventh day in vv 9–11, the male lamb in v 12, and the termination rite in vv 13–21, as well as the introduction in vv 1–2a. Other additions identified by Kellermann are relatively minor. On the basis of Judg 13:5; 1 Sam 1:11 he posits an earlier form of the basic law in vv 2–8. This includes abstinence from the fruit of the vine (Iv 3aᵇb), the non-use of the razor (v 5aᵇ), and avoidance of the dead (v 6b). The oldest element he judges to be v 5aᵇ. Rechabite influence may have led to the inclusion of abstinence (v 3aᵃ), while the corpse commandment, though possibly old in itself, must be the latest element to be included in the Nazirite rule of life.

J. de Vaulx (*Nombres*, 89–90, 99–102) also finds signs of an adaptation of earlier customs and texts. He argues that vv 2–3, in contrast to v 8, do not envisage a temporary vow. In vv 9–12 the purification of the Levite ignores the possibility of expulsion from the camp (Num 5:1–3), or of washings (Num 19:11–13). The essential dependence is on the rituals of Lev 12–15. He also sees in v 11 and v 12 two analagous rites which use different vocabulary, the parallels being provided by words such as חַטָּאת and אָשָׁם, קָרְשׁ and הַזִּיר. He finds the whole to be a synthesis of diverse texts, but sees an overall purpose from an editorial perspective to be the replacement of the ancient charismatic Nazirite by a formal invitation to all laymen to engage in special vows.

It is obvious that the evident dependence on Exodus and Leviticus is completely consonant with the view of Numbers we have proposed. Kellermann's theory of a law which has undergone expansion is essentially acceptable, and the expansions may very well be the work of the author of Numbers himself. There is a feasibility about Kellermann's theory of the history of the three component parts of the vow, but the evidence is sparse. Certainly Judg 13:4–5 and Amos 2:12 suggest that abstinence from wine and the refusal to cut the hair are fundamental at a relatively early stage to the commitments of a Nazirite (n.b. also a reference to unclean food in Judg 13:4). According to R. de Vaux (*Israel*, 467), the hair commitment is likely to be earliest. The abstinence from wine may indeed be traceable to Rechabite influence (Jer 35:6). It is quite likely that the text in Judg 13 is not the earliest element in the Samson stories, and the fact that it is possible for the stories to think of a man who engages in slaughter as a Nazirite makes it certain that separation from death is a relatively late accretion to the tradition.

It may be that the laws employed by the author are contained essentially in vv 3–5, though even v 4 has something of the character of an interpretation. Though the point is not entirely clear it may be that these laws at this stage envisage a life-long commitment. The inclusion of proximity to death could have been the author's own contribution, based on ideas associated with the priest in H (Lev 21:10–15). The incorporation of a rite to deal with accidental cases of defilement would naturally follow (vv 9–12). As de Vaulx shows the author is drawing here on Lev 12–14. It seems unnecessary to press the differences in vv 11–12 in terms of varying traditions. The author is following fairly closely the procedures envisaged in Lev 12–14, and the three offerings mentioned in vv 11–12 are in fact required of the man purified in Lev 14. The use of a male lamb does indeed contrast with Lev 5:6, but not with Lev 14:12. The third part of the ritual (vv 13–20) follows naturally, and does not have to be supplementation to what precedes. It follows the procedures of Lev 1–7 closely, while adding the rite involving the burning of the hair in accordance with the special circumstances of Num 6. Noth's point is of little substance. Since v 8 clearly envisages a vow of limited duration the inclusion of rites to mark its end seems entirely appropriate. The use of the title "the priest" in vv 10–11, 16–17, 19–20 is not surprising in view of the fact that the author is writing in the idiom of the rituals of Leviticus.

Comment

2. יַפְלִא "special." The root seems to mean "to be marvelous." A similar idea occurs in Lev 22:21; 27:2; Num 15:3, 8. It is apparently used to make the point that the vow is exceptional.

2. נָזִיר "Nazirite." *G* conveys the idea of "purity" or "chastity," but these ideas are not obviously present. In essence the root speaks of the dedication of a man or woman who has made a vow to Yahweh. Samson's mother is bound by rules of this kind (Judg 13:4, 7), though neither she nor her husband are called "Nazirites."

3. שֵׁכָר "strong drink." This is a general term covering all intoxicating liquids.

3. חֹמֶץ "vinegar." This is probably a preparation which has been allowed to go sour.

3. מִשְׁרָה "juice." This word is a *hapax legomenon*. It may be derived from the root שָׁרָה "to water," "to be moist," hence perhaps the "juice" of the grape.

4. חַרְצָן "seed." Another *hapax legomenon*. RSV proposes "seeds." NEB has "shoot." A. Dillman (*Numeri*, 33) suggested "unripe grapes."

4. זָג "skin." Another *hapax legomenon*. RSV suggests "skins." NEB has "berry." Dillman (*Numeri*, 33) suggested the "tendrils" of the vine. A connection with זָגַג "to be clear" has been suggested, and so possibly some reference to the "clear" skin of the grape may be intended. The matter must remain open.

5. גַּדֵּל "grow long" (cf. Judg 5:2). The same root is used of the woman's hair in Num 5:18. Many religions attach special significance to the hair; n.b. the idea that Samson's strength resides in his hair (Judg 16:17).

7. This rule is stricter than that applied to ordinary priests (Lev 21:1–2). It is the rule that the high priest must observe (Lev 21:11).

7. נֵזֶר אֱלֹהָיו "his dedication to his God." This root is used for the untrimmed vine in Lev 25:5, 11.

9. The hair has become unclean, and has to be removed. According to the Mishnah, it was to be buried.

10. The birds prescribed are an inexpensive offering (Lev 5:7; 12:8; 14:30–31; 15:14–15, 29–30; Luke 2:24). It may be that the author was anxious to ensure that the poor were not precluded from such vows. In v 21 it is made clear that extra offerings are encouraged if a person is able to make them when his vow comes to an end.

11–12. The offerings are discussed again in Num 28–29. A "purification offering" (better than "sin offering"—see J. Milgrom, *VT* 21 [1971] 237–39) restores a person to a state of ritual purity when, as in this case, some taboo has inadvertently been broken. The "whole offering" (sometimes translated "burnt offering") involves the burning of the whole of the sacrificial animal, and may be a sign of the worshiper's total dedication to God. The "reparation offering" (sometimes translated "guilt offering") is essentially compensation for damage done. On the distinctions see further N. H. Snaith, "The Sin Offering and the Guilt Offering," *VT* 15 (1965) 73–80; R. de Vaux, *Israel,* 418–21. It is often held that the later editors and redactors of the priestly stratum did not entirely understand the original significance of the various sacrifices, and that this explains some of the confusion and lack of precision evident overall. On the idea of "atonement" see under Num 17:6–15.

14. The use of a male lamb seems to be contrary to earlier custom (1 Sam 6:14). The male lamb is also employed in Lev 1:3, 10; 14:12; 22:18–19. The use of a female lamb for the purification offering squares with Lev 4:32; 5:6, and the ram for the reparation offering with Lev 3:1–6.

14. For the "whole offering" and the "purification offering" see *Comment* on vv 11–12. The "shared offerings" (often translated "peace offerings") contrast with the "whole offering" in that only part of the sacrificial animal is burned, the rest being consumed by priest and offerer. The sacrifice probably denotes a state of harmony between God and worshiper, expressed through the shared meal—hence the ideas of "peace" and "communion" sometimes associated with this sacrifice. Connections with the word שָׁלוֹם "peace" and with שָׁלֵם "to make restitution" or "pay what is due" have been suggested, but it seems best to focus on that which distinguishes the sacrifice in practice—hence "shared offering."

15. The law here squares with the principles of Lev 7:12. The intention is to indicate that the usual accompaniments to animal sacrifices are to be made in this case too. These consist of cakes, wafers, and oil, along with a proper cereal offering and drink offering. The latter would be wine poured out on the ground as an offering to God.

18. Some commentators see the burning of the hair as an offering (e.g. A. H. McNeile, *Numbers,* 35; G. B. Gray, *Numbers,* 68). M. Noth (*Numbers,* 57) rejects this, perceiving rather the annihilation of a sacred thing once it has fulfilled its function. Its destruction removed the danger of its being profaned or used superstitiously (cf. R. de Vaux, *Israel,* 436).

19–20. These verses deal with those parts of the cereal offerings and the shared offerings which belong to the priest. It has often been thought that these items were held out toward the altar (hence "waved") but retained by the priest, the action symbolizing the idea that they are given by the offerer to God, and then by God to the priest (cf. Exod 29:27; Num 5:10). It is now thought by some that the words signify "special gifts" and "special contributions" (cf. NEB)—see *Comment* on Num 5:10. As Lev 7:34 makes clear the שׁוֹק "thigh" and the חָזֶה "breast" are always the priest's in shared offerings, and so the special reference to them in v 20.

21. The stipulations made are only a minimum requirement. The Nazirite is encouraged to offer more if he can.

Explanation

This section begins by defining the Nazirite vow. The three fundamental commitments are abstention from everything connected with the vine, a refusal to cut the hair, and the avoidance of all proximity to death (vv 1–8). An accidental infringement of this third commitment requires ritual action (vv 9–12). These commitments are however of a temporary nature, and provision is made for the ending of the vow with ritual procedures, and the return of the Nazirite to normal life (vv 13–21).

The links between this section and those in Num 5 are not as hard to perceive as some commentators suggest. As J. Sturdy observes (*Numbers*, 49) the section deals with an institution whereby people could consecrate themselves to God in a special way, thus linking it with the theme of holiness evident throughout Num 5. J. de Vaulx (*Nombres*, 89) sees here, as in Num 5:11–31, an updating of ancient custom in such a way as to reject magical and superstitious beliefs.

It would be proper to add that the section reveals, as do those in Num 5, the priests relating to the community. How do the hierarchical patterns of the priesthood, established in Num 1–4, affect other holy men, and in particular the vows of the Nazirite? It may well be that the author is anxious to regulate Nazirite vows, and to ensure that they do not rival the priesthood itself. He makes it clear in vv 10, 16–17, 19–20 that the vow is exercised under the jurisdiction of the priesthood, and most important of all transforms it into a commitment which is normally of limited duration. It is true of course that the vow could still be for a substantial period, but the setting up of a rite to mark its completion (vv 13–21) creates a new framework within which the vow will normally be taken, and so predisposes the future toward vows of a limited kind. In this terminating rite the author is also able to find additional means by which his priests are to be supported.

It would be wrong to imply by this that the author undervalues the commitment of the Nazirites. He has in fact opened up the role of Nazirite to lay people at large, and has no wish to discourage such vows. His concern is to adapt and to regulate. In tradition Nazirites were men specially devoted to God at birth (Judg 13:5; cf. 1 Sam 1:11), and that dedication was a lifelong commitment. In Samson there is a strong charismatic dimension to the Nazirite's activity, while in Amos 2:11–12 the Nazirites are set alongside the prophets as a group of God-given and God-inspired individuals. The adaptation achieved by the author of Numbers not only ensures that Nazirites are not a significant rival to the priests, but at the same time removes the charismatic element and extends the possibility of a serious Nazirite commitment to the laity at large, making sure that even the poor are not excluded. In the process he includes contact with death as a third element in the vow, alongside the traditional commitments of uncut hair and abstinence from alcohol. He makes the rules in connection with the vow very strict, applying the same principles that affect the high priests (Lev 21:11). His aim then is not to devalue the commitment of the Nazirite, but to control and regulate it. It may well be that he was confronted with a situation of some laxity in the matter. He certainly considered the breaking of Nazirite vows to be a serious danger to the purity and well-being of the community in general. The best way forward was to ensure that those Nazirites involved in accidental defilement took proper steps to safeguard themselves and the community (vv 9–12), and to encourage a responsible and realistic attitude to the taking of such vows by implying that they are of limited duration and by providing a procedure which would terminate them (vv 13–20). His method in making these adaptations is to apply as far as possible the ritual principles of Leviticus to this specific issue.

Theologically the section provides another witness to the religious serious- ness and discipline which priestly writers encouraged. At an earlier stage this may, as W. Eichrodt suggests (*Theology of the Old Testament I* 306), have been a witness to the distinctiveness of Israelite faith and its separation from all things Canaanite. For the priestly writer this seriousness and discipline was the obvious outcome of his understanding of divine holiness. Vows to a God of such holiness must be treated with the utmost seriousness. Without the disciplines of such commitment the life of the community at large was in danger. The vows in question may seem merely external, though compara- ble commitments are still attested in NT texts (cf. e.g. Luke 1:15; Acts 21:23– 24), and the content of the commitment is clearly partial and limited in the light of the biblical witness as a whole. Christian disciplines focus mainly on a different kind of commitment, with different methods and different objec- tives. The pattern of discipleship presented by Jesus is nevertheless a commit- ment and a discipline, and there is a sense in which this is prefigured in the seriousness of OT vows.

Priests and the Blessing of the Community (6:22–27)

Bibliography

Begrich, J. "Das priesterliche Heilsorakel." *ZAW* 52 (1934) 81–92. **Kuchler, F.** *Das priesterliche Orakel in Israel und Juda.* BZAW 33. Giessen: Töpelmann, 1918, 285–301. **Liebreich, L. J.** "The Songs of Ascents and the Priestly Blessing." *JBL* 74 (1955) 33–36. **Miller, P. D.** "The Blessing of God. An Interpretation of Numbers 6:22–27." *Int* 29 (1975) 240–51. **Murtonen, A.** "The Use and Meaning of the Words L^E Barek and B^E raka^H in the Old Testament." *VT* 9 (1959) 158–77.

Translation

²² *And Yahweh spoke to Moses, saying,* ²³ *"Speak to Aaron and to his sons, saying, This is the way you shall bless the people of Israel, saying* ᵃ *to them,*
²⁴ *May Yahweh bless you and keep you.*
²⁵ *May Yahweh make his face shine on you, and be gracious to you.*
²⁶ *May Yahweh look favorably upon you, and give you well being.* ᵃ
²⁷ᵃ *"So shall they put my name upon the people of Israel, and I* ᵇ *will bless them."*

Notes

23.a. The only example of the infinitive absolute of אָמֹר standing on its own. J. Paterson (*Numbers*, 45) suggests that haplography has led to the omission of ל—n.b. its occurrence at the end of the preceding word. G. B. Gray (*Numbers*, 74) points out that this would produce a very unusual construction involving אָמֹר plus ל and a pronominal suffix. Another possibility is to emend to אָמְרוּ. MT may be unique, but is not untenable.

26.a. On the use of the jussive here see *GKC* § 109b.

27.a. In *G* this verse follows v 23.

27.b. *G* has "Yahweh" here—probably an addition.

Form/Structure/Setting

The involvement of Aaron and his sons makes it clear that the section belongs to the priestly stratum. Attention has been drawn to the fact that it builds on Lev 9:23 where a priestly blessing is referred to (J. Wellhausen, *Hexateuch*, 177). This passage provides the words for such a blessing. That the passage is an addition has also been widely accepted (cf. e.g. A. Kuenen, *Hexateuch*, 90–93; M. Noth, *Numbers*, 44–45). G. B. Gray (*Numbers*, 39) was not so sure, and entertained the possibility that this, along with Num 5:1–4, was the conclusion of PG's description of the camp order. D. Kellermann (*Priesterschrift*, 95–98) sees the section vv 22–26 as a unit and v 27 as an addition developing the priestly role.

Clearly any dependence on Lev 9:23 is acceptable on the view of authorship we have adopted. The introductory material in vv 22–23 comes from the author himself, and there is little reason to deny v 27 to him. The latter is an halakhic comment on the significance of the priestly blessing. The blessing itself in vv 24–26 has been widely recognized as earlier and traditional. Its linguistic characteristics link it with the psalms, and it may have influenced Ps 67, and possibly Ps 4:7 (see further under *Comment*). It is metrical, with three lines (consisting of three words, five words, and seven words respectively), and it uses the second person singular mode of address which is not typical of P. A priestly responsibility in this matter is attested in Deut 10:8; 21:5, and there seems good reason for believing that this form of blessing was actually used in the pre-exilic Temple, and that this was the text preserved among the exiled Zadokites.

Comment

23. For a good description of the high priest's ministry, and its climax in the blessing, see Sir 50:21–22.

25. M. Noth (*Numbers*, 59) calls the shining face a "figure of speech for benevolence and favour." It is an idea widely used in cultic texts (Pss 4:7; 31:17; 44:4; 67:2; 80:4, 8, 20; 89:16; 119:135; cf. Dan 9:17), and probably has its roots in the theophanies of the pre-exilic Temple.

26. אֵלֶיךָ פָּנָיו . . . יִשָּׂא "look favorably upon you," literally "lift up his face to you" (cf. Deut 31:18; Pss 30:8; 44:25; 104:29 for the hiding of the face as a picture of divine disfavor or withdrawal of support). This precise phrase is not used of God elsewhere. The nearest parallels appear to be in Pss 4:7; 33:18; 34:16.

26. שָׁלוֹם "well being." This is the root often rendered "peace." It denotes what Noth (*Numbers*, 59) calls "the state of 'wholeness,'" and refers to every aspect of life; cf. Lev 26:6; Job 21:9 for similar uses of the root.

27. עַל שְׁמִי-אֶת וְשָׂמוּ "they shall put my name upon." The pronunciation of the divine name over Israel was thought of as an effective means of blessing. It indicates that the people belong to Yahweh, and that he will bring them prosperity.

Explanation

This short section indicates that the cultic blessing of Israel is to be carried out by Aaron and his sons, and gives the form of words to be used. It follows naturally enough from the sections which precede it. J. Sturdy (*Numbers*, 54) suggests that it shows God's gracious response to the kind of voluntary devotion evident in a Nazirite vow. J. de Vaulx (*Nombres*, 90, 103) sees the priestly benediction as the obvious conclusion to the material dealing with the sanctification of the community in Num 5:1–6:21. He also draws attention to Gen 49:26 and Deut 33:16 with their references to blessings on him who is separated, suggesting that this may partly explain the editor's inclusion of the blessing here after the material on the Nazirites. All these observations seem to make valid points against those who see in these chapters a not very coherent miscellany of materials.

The author's particular concern is to standardize the text of the priestly blessing, the one preserved from the pre-exilic Temple by the Zadokites, and to ensure that this responsibility is confined to the sons of Aaron. There is witness in tradition to blessing as a royal function (2 Sam 6:18; 1 Kgs 8:14, 55), but Deuteronomy itself links blessing firmly with the priests (10:8; 21:5), who, in the terms of Deuteronomic law, are members of the tribe of Levi in general. Given the new hierarchical patterns advocated by the author of Numbers it was necessary to specify that priestly blessings were the responsibility of the sons of Aaron alone. That there was also some uncertainty at the time about the proper text is also feasible. The author provides the answers in both areas.

Looking at Num 5–6 as a whole the author has evidently succeeded in marking out a role for the priests in the community, depicting them as the ones who, through their various privileges and responsibilities, safeguard the purity of the people and bring divine blessing and well-being upon them. The author's method is based essentially on the exegetical application of principles in Leviticus in particular to current issues in the developing Palestinian scene.

Theologically the blessing provides the context in which the commitments and disciplines of purity are to be understood. Each of the three clauses, in a different way, gives expression to God's commitment to Israel—a commitment which promises earthly security, prosperity, and general well-being. That commitment is attested by the imposition of the divine name, in and through the pronunciation of the blessing. Prophetic eschatology makes clear that the divine will and commitment operates on a universal level (cf. e.g. Isa 2:2–4; Mic 4:1–5). It is to the exercise of this latter commitment, under the lordship of Christ, that the Christian gospel bears witness.

The Community's Commitment to the Priestly Theocracy   (7:1–88)

Bibliography

Levine, B. A. "The Descriptive Tabernacle Texts of the Pentateuch." *JAOS* 85 (1965) 312–13. Rainey, A. F. "The Order of Sacrifices in Old Testament Ritual Texts." *Bib* 51 (1970) 485–98.

Translation

¹ *On the day when Moses had finished setting up the Tabernacle, and had anointed it, and dedicated it, and all its implements, and the altar and all its implements, and had anointed them, and consecrated them,* ² *the leaders of Israel, the heads of their fathers' houses, made an offering.* [a] *They were the leaders of the tribes. They were the ones who supervised the numbering.* ³ *And they brought their oblation before Yahweh, six covered wagons and twelve oxen—a wagon for every two of the leaders and a bullock for every one. And they offered them before the Tabernacle.* ⁴ *And Yahweh spoke to Moses, saying,* ⁵ *"Take it from them, and the offering shall be for the service of the Tent of Meeting. And you shall give it to the Levites, to each man according to his service."* ⁶ *And Moses took the wagons and the oxen and gave them to the Levites.* ⁷ *He gave two wagons and four oxen to the sons of Gershon, according to their service.* ⁸ *And he gave four wagons and eight oxen to the sons of Merari, according to their service—under the hand of Ithamar the son of Aaron the priest.* ⁹ *But he did not give to the sons of Kohath, because theirs was the service of the sanctuary. They carried it on their shoulders.* ¹⁰ *And the leaders offered for the dedication of the altar, on the day when it was anointed. And the leaders offered their oblation before the altar.* ¹¹ *And Yahweh said to Moses, "They shall offer their oblation, each leader on his day, for the dedication of the altar."* [a]

¹² *And he who offered his oblation on the first day was Nahshon, son of Amminadab,* [a] *of the tribe of Judah.* ¹³ *And* [a] *his oblation was one silver bowl, weighing 130 shekels, one silver tossing bowl, weighing 70 shekels, according to the sanctuary shekel. Both of them were full of fine flour mixed with oil for a cereal offering.* ¹⁴ *One gold dish, weighing 10 shekels, full of incense.* ¹⁵ *One young bullock, one ram, one male lamb a year old, for a whole offering.* ¹⁶ *One male goat for a purification offering.* ¹⁷ *And for the sacrifice of shared offerings, two oxen,* [a] *five rams, five male goats, five male lambs a year old. This was the oblation of Nahshon son of Amminadab.*

¹⁸ *On the second day Nethanel son of Zuar, leader* [a] *of Issachar, offered.* ¹⁹ *He offered for his oblation one silver bowl, weighing 130 shekels, one silver tossing bowl, weighing 70 shekels, according to the sanctuary shekel. Both of them were full of fine flour mixed with oil for a cereal offering.* ²⁰ *One gold dish, weighing 10 shekels, full of incense.* ²¹ *One young bullock, one ram, one male lamb a year old, for a whole offering.* ²² *One male goat for a purification offering.* ²³ *And for the sacrifice of shared offerings, two oxen, five rams, five male goats, five male lambs a year old. This was the oblation of Nethanel son of Zuar.*

²⁴ *On the third day Eliab son of Helon, leader of the sons of Zebulun:* ²⁵ *his*

oblation was one silver bowl, weighing 130 shekels, one silver tossing bowl, weighing 70 shekels, according to the sanctuary shekel. Both of them were full of fine flour mixed with oil for a cereal offering. [26] *One gold dish, weighing 10 shekels, full of incense.* [27] *One young bullock, one ram, one male lamb a year old, for a whole offering.* [28] *One male goat for a purification offering.* [29] *And for the sacrifice of shared offerings, two oxen, five rams, five male goats, five male lambs a year old. This was the oblation of Eliab son of Helon.*

[30] *On the fourth day Elizur son of Shedeur, leader of the sons of Reuben:* [31] *his oblation was one silver bowl, weighing 130 shekels, one silver tossing bowl, weighing 70 shekels, according to the sanctuary shekel. Both of them were full of fine flour mixed with oil for a cereal offering.* [32] *One gold dish, weighing 10 shekels, full of incense.* [33] *One young bullock, one ram, one male lamb a year old, for a whole offering.* [34] *One male goat for a purification offering.* [35] *And for the sacrifice of shared offerings, two oxen, five rams, five male goats, five male lambs a year old. This was the oblation of Elizur son of Shedeur.*

[36] *On the fifth day Shelumiel son of Zurishaddai, leader of the sons of Simeon:* [37] *his oblation was one silver bowl, weighing 130 shekels, one silver tossing bowl, weighing 70 shekels, according to the sanctuary shekel. Both of them were full of fine flour mixed with oil for a cereal offering.* [38] *One gold dish, weighing 10 shekels, full of incense.* [39] *One young bullock, one ram, one male lamb a year old, for a whole offering.* [40] *One male goat for a purification offering.* [41] *And for the sacrifice of shared offerings, two oxen, five rams, five male goats, five male lambs a year old. This was the oblation of Shelumiel son of Zurishaddai.*

[42] *On the sixth day Eliasaph son of Deuel,*[a] *leader of the sons of Gad:* [43] *his oblation was one silver bowl, weighing 130 shekels, one silver tossing bowl, weighing 70 shekels, according to the sanctuary shekel. Both of them were full of fine flour mixed with oil for a cereal offering.* [44] *One gold dish, weighing 10 shekels, full of incense.* [45] *One young bullock, one ram, one male lamb a year old, for a whole offering.* [46] *One male goat for a purification offering.* [47] *And for the sacrifice of shared offerings, two oxen, five rams, five male goats, five male lambs a year old. This was the oblation of Eliasaph son of Deuel.*

[48] *On the seventh day Elishama son of Ammihud, leader of the sons of Ephraim:* [49] *his oblation was one silver bowl, weighing 130 shekels, one silver tossing bowl, weighing 70 shekels, according to the sanctuary shekel. Both of them were full of fine flour mixed with oil for a cereal offering.* [50] *One gold dish, weighing 10 shekels, full of incense.* [51] *One young bullock, one ram, one male lamb a year old, for a whole offering.* [52] *One male goat for a purification offering.* [53] *And for the sacrifice of shared offerings, two oxen, five rams, five male goats, five male lambs a year old. This was the oblation of Elishama son of Ammihud.*

[54] *On the eighth day Gamaliel son of Pedahzur, leader of the sons of Manasseh:* [55] *his oblation was one silver bowl, weighing 130 shekels, one silver tossing bowl, weighing 70 shekels, according to the sanctuary shekel. Both of them were full of fine flour mixed with oil for a cereal offering.* [56] *One gold dish, weighing 10 shekels, full of incense.* [57] *One young bullock, one ram, one male lamb a year old, for a whole offering.* [58] *One male goat for a purification offering.* [59] *And for the sacrifice of shared offerings, two oxen, five rams, five male goats, five male lambs a year old. This was the oblation of Gamaliel son of Pedahzur.*

[60] *On the ninth day Abidan son of Gideoni, leader of the sons of Benjamin:* [61] *his*

oblation was one silver bowl, weighing 130 shekels, one silver tossing bowl, weighing 70 shekels, according to the sanctuary shekel. Both of them were full of fine flour mixed with oil for a cereal offering. ⁶² *One gold dish, weighing 10 shekels, full of incense.* ⁶³ *One young bullock, one ram, one male lamb a year old, for a whole offering.* ⁶⁴ *One male goat for a purification offering.* ⁶⁵ *And for the sacrifice of shared offerings, two oxen, five rams, five male goats, five male lambs a year old. This was the oblation of Abidan son of Gideoni.*

⁶⁶ *On the tenth day Ahiezer son of Ammishaddai, leader of the sons of Dan:* ⁶⁷ *his oblation was one silver bowl, weighing 130 shekels, one silver tossing bowl, weighing 70 shekels, according to the sanctuary shekel. Both of them were full of fine flour mixed with oil for a cereal offering.* ⁶⁸ *One gold dish, weighing 10 shekels, full of incense.* ⁶⁹ *One young bullock, one ram, one male lamb a year old, for a whole offering.* ⁷⁰ *One male goat for a purification offering.* ⁷¹ *And for the sacrifice of shared offerings, two oxen, five rams, five male goats, five male lambs a year old. This was the oblation of Ahiezer son of Ammishaddai.* ᵃ

⁷² *On the eleventh day Pagiel son of Ochran, leader of the sons of Asher:* ⁷³ *his oblation was one silver bowl, weighing 130 shekels, one silver tossing bowl, weighing 70 shekels, according to the sanctuary shekel. Both of them were full of fine flour mixed with oil for a cereal offering.* ⁷⁴ *One gold dish, weighing 10 shekels, full of incense.* ⁷⁵ *One young bullock, one ram, one male lamb a year old, for a whole offering.* ⁷⁶ *One male goat for a purification offering.* ⁷⁷ *And for the sacrifice of shared offerings, two oxen, five rams, five male goats, five male lambs a year old. This was the oblation of Pagiel son of Ochran.*

⁷⁸ *On the twelfth day Ahira son of Enan, leader of the sons of Naphthali:* ⁷⁹ *his oblation was one silver bowl, weighing 130 shekels, one silver tossing bowl, weighing 70 shekels, according to the sanctuary shekel. Both of them were full of fine flour mixed with oil for a cereal offering.* ⁸⁰ *One gold dish, weighing 10 shekels, full of incense.* ⁸¹ *One young bullock, one ram, one male lamb a year old, for a whole offering.* ⁸² *One male goat for a purification offering.* ⁸³ *And for the sacrifice of shared offerings, two oxen, five rams, five male goats, five male lambs a year old. This was the oblation of Ahira son of Enan.*

⁸⁴ *This was the dedication offering for the altar by the leaders of Israel, on the day when it was anointed: twelve silver bowls, twelve silver tossing bowls, twelve gold dishes,* ⁸⁵ *each silver bowl weighing 130 shekels, and each tossing bowl 70— all the silver of the implements amounting to 2,400 shekels, according to the sanctuary shekel,* ⁸⁶ *the twelve gold dishes, full of incense, weighing ten shekels each, according to the sanctuary shekel—all the gold of the dishes was 120 shekels.* ⁸⁷ *The cattle for the whole offering were twelve bullocks, the rams twelve, the male lambs a year old twelve, and their cereal offering,* ᵃ *and the male goats for a purification offering twelve.* ⁸⁸ *And the cattle for the sacrifice of shared offerings were twenty-four bullocks, the rams sixty, the male goats sixty, the male lambs a year old sixty. This was the offering for the dedication of the altar,* ᵃ *after it had been anointed.*

Notes

2.a. It may be that the Qal is to be read here and in v 10 (cf. Sam and *BHS*).

11.a. For discussion of the repetition of words in a distributive sense see GKC § 123d.

12.a. *G* and *S* read נָשִׂיא "leader" here. Since it occurs in the corresponding clauses throughout the section the omission in MT is probably accidental.

13.a. *G* has the words "and he offered for" (cf. v 19). MT has the norm for the section as a whole, and is probably to be accepted.

17.a. *G* reads "two calves" here and throughout the section.

18.a. *G* and *S* have מַטֶּה "tribe" here, as in v 12.

42.a. On the form of the name here and in v 47 see *Notes* on Num 1:14.

87.a. *G* reads וְנִסְכֵּיהֶם "and their drink offerings" (cf. Num 6:15). This is probably a mistaken addition—see G. B. Gray, *Numbers*, 77).

88.a. *G* appears to have read אַחֲרֵי מִלָּא יָדֵיו literally "after the filling of its hands" at this point (cf. Ezek 43:26). Gray (*Numbers*, 77) thinks that the translators must have had the phrase before them, but there is no good reason for thinking MT to be in error.

Form/Structure/Setting

Analysts have been in complete agreement that this section belongs to the priestly material, and it has been widely held to be supplementary and relatively late. A. Dillmann (*Numeri*, 39) was among the first to suggest that since the events of the section are dated to the day on which Moses erected and consecrated the Tabernacle (v 1) the section ought to come immediately after Exod 40. He also observed that the names of the leaders as given in Num 1–2 are presupposed, and that the order of offering is based on the order of encampment as given in Num 2. The section can be seen as an expansion of Num 3–4 in that it provides Gershon and Merari with wagons of which there is no hint in the earlier chapters. J. Wellhausen (*Hexateuch*, 181) and A. Kuenen (*Hexateuch*, 94) endorsed this, the latter suggesting that the new author of Num 7 has reached a new level of monotony in the priestly strata as a whole! G. B. Gray (*Numbers*, 74) accepts most of these points. According to him even if PG did have some account of offerings by leaders that account has evidently been moved and recast in the light of Num 1–4.

M. Noth (*Numbers*, 63–64) takes the section to be one of the very late additions to the P narrative. The references to the setting up, anointing, and consecrating of the Tabernacle, and to the anointing of the altar (vv 10, 84) are taken to be dependent on material in Exod 40, while the names and ordering of the leaders are dependent on Num 1–4. Noth also refers to Lev 9 which purports to tell of the first sacrifices offered after the setting up of the sanctuary. These to all appearances were sufficient to consecrate the altar. So Num 7:1–88 is awkwardly placed in relation to Lev 9 as well as to Exod 40. N. H. Snaith (*Numbers*, 208) takes a similar view of the lateness of the section. J. de Vaulx (*Nombres*, 109–11) also sees it as late, tracing its composition to a short time before the definitive redaction of the book. He argues that the vocabulary confirms this, with the use of the word קָרְבָּן for "gift" or "offering" being unusual in P. A very high degree of idealism is discerned in the section as a whole.

D. Kellermann (*Priesterschrift*, 98–111) sees the whole section as formulated by one author, but considers that that author had material about the offerings of wagons available to him. This would be found in vv 2a, 3a (most), 4–9. In Kellermann's view this material is influenced by Num 10:11–28 in that it is aware of the difficulties of travel. Since the material in Num 3–4 clearly implies to Kellermann that the Levites are to carry all the sacred objects themselves, he concludes that the section as a whole is very late. Not only is there dependence on Exod 40 and Num 1–4, but also on the offering rituals in Leviticus.

It is clear that evidence of dependence on Exodus and Leviticus or on any part of those books, is entirely in keeping with the idea of an author/ editor of Numbers as previously propounded. This author wished to say more about the day of consecration as described in Exod 40, and the days which followed it as set out in Lev 8–9. He would of course have been free to include his material as an appendix to Exodus, or to insert it after Lev 9, but there was good reason for the decision to include it here. He wishes to name the leaders of Num 1, and to develop the theme of offering in the light of Num 3–4. To insert the material at an earlier point in the story would have necessitated the inclusion of much of the content of those chapters in one of the earlier books. In particular this would have involved his view of the priestly hierarchy, and such a procedure would thus have forestalled one of his major distinctive contributions—the separation of priests and Levites. Another sound reason for including the material here is the fact that wagons imply the movement of the fully constituted camp, and this is another central and crucial theme to the book of Numbers. The journey is shortly to begin again in Num 10:11, and it is not inappropriate to prepare for it here.

The notion of literary dependence on Num 1–4 cannot simply be assumed. Clearly the names and ordering of the tribal leaders could just as well come from the compiler of Num 1–2 as from later sources. The fact that Num 3–4 seem to imply that Levites carry all the sacred objects is not a serious difficulty. Clearly Gershon and Merari must still be considered handlers of the sacred objects since the Tent must be erected and dismantled, the wagons loaded and the oxen driven. The author's method is arguably of a piece with that suggested for Num 1–4—the didactic technique of building a picture slowly, piece by piece. This section is simply the fitting in of another piece. The author is scarcely more "monotonous" than in Num 1, and the method of meticulous repetition is appropriate in texts intended for oral recitation. The author is evidently aiming at massive effect and emphasis. Whether or not the modern mind finds this successful is not a satisfactory criterion of analysis. There are certainly some points of contact between this section and Num 1–4, including the phrase "leaders of Israel" itself (vv 2, 84; cf. Num 1:44; 4:46). The awkwardness of expression in vv 10–11 is real, but this is not necessarily a good reason for wondering with Gray (*Numbers*, 76) whether the offering on separate days is an intrusion. The technique of making a broad statement (v 10) and then sharpening or clarifying it (v 11) is intelligible, and does not of itself imply diversity of authorship.

Whether Kellermann is correct in identifying a text about wagons which the author has taken up must remain uncertain. There is certainly no obvious need for positing such a text. One reason the author himself could have had for constructing a section on wagons as a mode of transport was to do some justice to a wider tradition, a motive evident elsewhere in his work. Faced by the fact that the ark could be transported by cart (1 Sam 6:8, 11; 2 Sam 6:3), apparently legitimately, and also by the fact that it was to be carried by priests (Josh 3:8), and given the author's own differentiation between priestly and Levitical functions, it was open to the author to suggest that originally wagons were used for some of the Levitical duties, but that the ark itself, in the first instance, was carried by hand.

Comment

1. וַיִּמְשַׁח אֹתוֹ "he anointed it," cf. Exod 40:9–10; Lev 8:10–11.
2. וַיַּקְרִיבוּ "they offered." The object must be "their oblation" in v 3.
3. עֶגְלֹת צָב "covered wagons." This is a traditional translation, and is attested in many of the ancient versions. It is a reasonable hypothesis, but not a certain rendering. The word צָב seems to be that used in Isa 66:20, though the meaning there is also unclear. Some *Tg* witnesses suggest "made ready," and *Syr* implies wagons for military service. The singular after עֶגְלֹת is certainly, strange, and Gray (*Numbers*, 76) suggests that צָב may be a gloss. It may have some connection with the Accadian *ṣumbu* "cart."
9. The use of a cart for carrying the ark is attested in 1 Sam 6:8, 11; 2 Sam 6:3. J. Sturdy (*Numbers*, 57) suggests that its transport on the shoulders of men (2 Sam 6:13; 15:24) arose from the difficulty of using carts in Jerusalem itself.
10. חֲנֻכָּה "the dedication," meaning probably a dedication gift. The verbal root is ancient and means "to train," but the noun as here is used only by P, the Chronicler, and a late editor of the Psalms (Ps 30:1).
13. קַעֲרַת-כֶּסֶף "silver bowl" (cf. Num 4:7; Exod 25:29; 37:16). The weight was about 1,500 grams (cf. R. de Vaux, *Israel*, 203–06).
13. מִזְרָק "tossing bowl" (NEB)—i.e. a bowl used to throw the blood of animals against the altar. Its weight was about 800 grams.
13. For a note on the "cereal offering" see *Comment* on Num 4:16, and for more general discussion see Num 28–29.
14. כַּף "dish" (cf. Num 4:7). Its weight was about 115 grams.
15. For a note on the "whole offering" see *Comment* on Num 6:11, and for more general discussion see Num 28–29.
16. For a note on the "purification offering" see *Comment* on Num 6:11, and for more general discussion see under Num 28–29.
17. For a note on the "shared offering" see *Comment* on Num 6:14, and for more general discussion see Num 28–29.

Explanation

In this section the twelve tribal leaders bring gifts for the Tabernacle. The first group of gifts consists of transport for the use of the Levites (vv 1–9)—twelve oxen and six wagons in all. The Kohathites, however, are not allowed to use them, their responsibility being the holiest things. The second group of gifts (vv 10–83) is for use in worship—each leader making an identical offering to cover the needs of cereal and incense offerings, and of whole, purification, and shared offerings. These gifts were presented on successive days. The section ends with a calculation of the grand total of offerings (vv 84–88).

Having discussed in Num 5–6 various ways in which the new priesthood is to be involved in the life of the community the author is now ready to discuss the commitment of the community to the new priestly theocracy. An effective restored community in Palestine requires generous support from the Jews of the diaspora. The scene is set for discussion of this commitment by the introduction of the wagons. This in turn prepares the way for the beginning of the march to the land in Num 10:11–12, perhaps the book's major overall theme. It could be, as J. Sturdy (*Numbers,* 56) suggests that an association of ideas led the author to include this material here. The sacrifices and offerings of the Nazirite vow lead on to the thought of the offerings made before the departure. It could also be that the return of the Temple vessels, as described in Ezra 8:33, had involved the wagons as a major mode of transport, particularly in view of the distance involved. There were also old traditions about wagons and their use in cultic transport (1 Sam 6:8, 11; 2 Sam 6:3), and this offering proved to be a way of appropriating and developing the tradition. The fact that the wagons are a lay contribution is intended to encourage popular support for and involvement in the processes of return and restoration.

The provision of vessels and materials for the offerings (vv 10–83) is depicted as a lay responsibility for similar reasons. No attention is given to the historical problem about where in the wilderness such a wealth of gifts, including those of precious metals, was to be found. The sole objective was the encouragement of generosity and commitment among the post-exilic laity. The delineation of the separate offerings of each tribe on separate days, in the camp order of Num 2, serves to emphasize the point about the involvement of the whole community. If the new community, organized around the second Temple, is to flourish then there must be disciplined and generous giving, as there had been in the wilderness. It is on a commitment of this order that the health of the community is based. The massive and meticulous repetitions are also designed for effect and as an aid to memory. This is appropriate in a text intended essentially for oral recitation.

There is no strong reason for doubting that in principle the section is the author's own construction, and that its content embodies one of his major concerns—one which is to emerge again in Num 31.

The theological dimensions of the section develop themes already touched on in earlier sections. The holiness of the sanctuary, the visible witness to God's presence at the center of the community, is in some measure presupposed. In addition there is some stress on the fact of its being "anointed" (vv 1, 10, 84, 88). This has the effect of linking traditional faith about royalty and the divine spirit with the sanctuary itself, which thus becomes the new focal point for these themes of faith. The extension of the rites of dedication to twelve days further enhances the significance of that event. Above all the section throws light on the character of man's involvement with God. It expects from man a wholehearted commitment of resources in a spirit of generosity. This is not intended to facilitate the perpetuation of a mere institution, though the danger of such tendencies is ever present, but is rather a symbol of man's commitment to the place where God reveals himself and is met by his people. It is in principle a commitment to the revelation itself.

Divine Revelation in the
Community   (7:89–8:4)

Bibliography

Cross, F. M. "The Tabernacle." *BA* 10 (1947) 1–68. Fretheim, T. E. "The Priestly Document: Anti-Temple?" *VT* 18 (1968) 313–29. Gorg, M. *Das Zelt der Begegnung. Untersuchung der Gestalt der Zelt traditionen alt Israels.* BBB 27. Bonn: Hanstein, 1967. Haran, M. "The Nature of the 'ohel mo'edh' in Pentateuchal Sources." *JSS* 5 (1960) 50–65. ———. "The Priestly Image of the Tabernacle." *HUCA* 36 (1965) 191–226. Meyers, C. L. *The Tabernacle Menorah. A Synthetic Study of a Symbol from the Biblical Cult.* AASOR 2 Missoula: Scholars Press, 1976.

Translation

[89] *And when Moses entered the Tent of Meeting to speak with him (Yahweh), he heard the Voice* [a] *speaking* [b] *to him from above the cover which was on the ark of the covenant, from between the two cherubim. And he spoke to him.*
    [8:1] *And Yahweh spoke to Moses, saying,* [2] *"Speak to Aaron, and say to him, When you set up the lamps, see that the seven lamps shed their light in front of the lampstand."* [3] *And Aaron did so. He set up the lamps so as to shed light in front of the lampstand, as Yahweh had commanded Moses.* [4] *And this was the workmanship of the lampstand—beaten work in gold—its* [a] *stem and its petals were of beaten work. In accordance with the pattern which Yahweh had showed to Moses, so he made the lampstand.*

Notes

89.a. *G* has "the voice of Yahweh." The divine name is almost certainly an addition.
89.b. The pointing should probably be מְדַבֵּר. The Hithpael participle does occur in Ezek 2:2; 43:6 (cf. 2 Sam 14:13), but the Piel of the verb occurs elsewhere in this verse, and is preferable here. G. B. Gray (*Numbers*, 77) suggests that the pointing in MT stems from traditional exegesis.
4.a. Sam has plural suffixes here (cf. also *G* and *Tg*), as the text seems to require.

Form/Structure/Setting

Analysts are agreed that the section belongs to P, and most see it as relatively late. It is widely held that 7:89 is an isolated fragment which belongs neither to 7:1–88 nor to 8:1–4. G. B. Gray (*Numbers*, 77) points out that it is in effect the fulfillment of the promise made in Exod 25:22. Arguments for its fragmentary character are offered by A. H. McNeile (*Numbers*, 43) who suggests that the words "with him" imply that Yahweh has already been mentioned, and that the verbs are not frequentative, indicating what customarily happened, but relate to a single incident, the content of which is now lost. By contrast M. Noth (*Numbers*, 65) argued that the supposition that something is missing after v 89 is a "pure expedient of embarrassment." The unusual language of the verse, particularly the description of God as "the Voice," suggests to Noth the essential independence of the verse. It can however be understood as an addition to 7:1–88, expressing Yahweh's pleasurable acceptance of the gifts offered, and this is the solution Noth prefers. D. Kellermann (*Priesterschrift*, 109–11) is also inclined to link v 89 with 7:1–88, seeing it as a late addition and as an expansion of Exod 25:22.

Analysts are inclined to see 8:1–4 as an amplification of the laws in Exod 27:20–21 and Lev 24:1–4. A. Dillmann (*Numberi*, 41–42) took the view that vv 1–3 had been displaced, and that v 4 was an addition, but J. Wellhausen (*Hexateuch*, 180–81) and A. Kuenen (*Hexateuch*, 92) took vv 1–4 as a relatively late unit. G. B. Gray (*Numbers*, 77) gives detailed evidence of dependence on earlier material. Thus vv 1–2a are a typical formula, v 2b repeats Exod 25:37, v 3 tells of the execution of the command in v 2b (omitted in Exod 37:17–24), v 4a adds nothing to Exod 25:37, and v 4b is very close to Exod 25:9, 40. That Aaron has the care of the lamps is already clear in Exod 27:21; Lev 24:1–4. Gray attributes the whole of vv 1–4 to PS. Noth also sees these verses as a general appendix to Exod 25:31–40, and in particular as an amplification of v 37b, though lacking significant new information. D. Kellermann (*Priesterschrift*, 111–15) takes the view that vv 1–3 are late, being in general dependent on Exod 25:31–40. He also believes however that Exod 25:37b is dependent on Num 8:1–3, a contention hard to prove. As for v 4 this in Kellermann's view is a later addition.

It is clear that the dependence on texts in Exodus and Leviticus is entirely consonant with the view of authorship previously proposed. In essence the passage is dependent on Exod 25:22, 31–40; 27:20–21; 37:17–24; Lev 24:1–4.The author is well acquainted with these texts, but does not develop them in any substantial way. He is anxious to show that the promise of Exod 25:22 did indeed take effect. He may also be preparing the way for the special consultations with God which are to follow in Num 9:8; 15:34; 27:5. His other interest is to recall important data about the lamp—the simple technique of repetition—and also to indicate a point not clearly made in Exod 37:17–24 that Aaron did indeed obey the command. He evidently intends that Aaron must ensure that the light of the lamps is cast in the right direction, and in v 2b uses rather different phraseology from that in Exod 25:37, but it is hard to see that he is offering any significant reinterpretation of the Exodus text. He can only mean here, as there, that the lamp must light up the table on the north side of the Tabernacle (cf. also Exod 40:22–25). Given that the information of vv 1–4 is derived in toto from earlier texts there is little reason for not treating the section as a unit.

The difficulty of relating 7:89 to the context is real, and the possibility of a late addition to 7:1–88 or of a fragmentary narrative cannot be excluded. On the other hand Noth's theory that "the Voice" accepts the offering of 7:1–88 is without obvious foundation in the text, and it is hard to see how the important substance of a narrative could be lost in the way some have proposed. The first verb could be frequentative, and may possibly be providing a customary kind of context for the other verbs. Even if the frequentative sense is excluded it would be entirely feasible to envisage the author describing a specific incident in which Exod 25:22 is fulfilled. The words "with him" are linked fairly closely with "the Voice," and do not necessarily imply lost material. The reference to "the Voice" seems to be an influence from Deut 4:12, and the whole is intended to bear witness to the mysteries of such consultation. The possibility that the subject of the last clause is Moses must be reckoned with. In that event the verse does have a completeness of its own. Moses went in to speak to God, but before he could do so found God speaking to him, in accordance with the promise of Exod 25:22. Only then was it proper and possible for Moses to speak his mind.

Though the link between 7:89 and 8:1–3 is relatively loose there is some justification for regarding all five verses as one section. On balance this seems preferable to attempts to link v 89 with 7:1–88. The scene in 7:89–8:4 is the same throughout—inside the Tent of Meeting, and the author throughout is drawing on material from Exodus. The positioning of the lights (8:1–4) is evidently intended to cast light toward the place from which God communicates with Moses (7:89).

Comment

89. מִבֵּין שְׁנֵי הַכְּרֻבִים "from between the two cherubim." These figures were of one piece with the הַכַּפֹּרֶת "cover," which constituted the top of the ark (cf. Exod 25:18–22; 37:7–9)—contrast the figures in Solomon's Temple (1 Kgs 6:23–28; 8:6–7). The whole was considered to be the throne and/or footstool of the invisible God. R. de Vaux (*Israel,* 299–301) notes how the "cover" can be distinguished from the "ark" (Exod 35:12), the lengthy independent description of it (Exod 25:17–22; 37:6–9), and its importance in certain rituals (Lev 16:14–15), and concludes that it was a post-exilic substitute for the ark. In view of 1 Chr 28:11 where "room of the cover" means "the Holy of Holies" this supposition may be correct.

2. אֶל-מוּל "in front of." The intention of the verse is to give guidance on how the lampstand is to cast its light. It must be positioned, so it seems, to cast light on the table opposite (cf. Exod 25:37; 40:22–25).

4. מִקְשָׁה זָהָב "beaten work in gold." This would be hammered from a single plate of gold.

4. עַד-יְרֵכָהּ עַד-פִּרְחָהּ "its stem and its petals." The author wishes to emphasize that the "beaten" work included even these parts of the lampstand. The root ירך usually means "side"—hence "stem" (cf. *G*) may be better than "base" (RV, RSV).

Explanation

This section tells how God communicated with Moses in the Tent of Meeting from above the ark, and goes on to give instructions to Aaron about the lighting of the lamps. The light must be cast in the right direction. The section concludes with information about the manufacture of the lampstand.

The author has stressed the community's commitment to the priestly theocracy (Num 7:1–88), and is now ready to describe the rites by which the Levites were set apart for their new subordinate functions (Num 8:5–26). Before doing so, however, he finds it necessary to lay stress on the source of the community's authority (Num 7:89). Divine revelation is no longer sought outside the camp (Exod 33:7–11), but at the center, from within the Tent of Meeting. The voice of Yahweh speaks in effect from the temple precincts. T. E. Fretheim's arguments ("The Priestly Document") that P is anti-temple are ineffectual when it is appreciated that the priestly perspective was shaped in Babylon, that it sought among other things authentication outside the land, and that it is therefore specially interested in the wilderness period. The shrine was bound to be the Tent. In tracing the divine voice to the Temple precincts the author subjects the "freedom" of prophetic inspiration to priestly control. It is scarcely surprising that from the middle of the fifth century onward prophecy assumes a different and less decisive role in the life of the community. The author is also concerned to tell of the fulfillment of the promise of Exod 25:22; in so doing he brings the story one step nearer to the point of departure from Sinai. Since there are also more laws to come v 89 provides necessary authentication for them.

The inclusion of material about the lamp at this point (Num 8:1–4) is not inexplicable. The thought of consultation in the Tent of Meeting prompted thought about the illumination of the sanctuary, and in particular of the direction from which God spoke. C. L. Meyers (*The Tabernacle Menorah*) shows that the lampstand is a stylized tree or plant with associations of "life" and "fertility." It speaks of that which sustains the community, and is thus appropriately associated with the divine voice. J. de Vaulx (*Nombres*, 117) shows something of the symbolic significance of the sanctuary light, and there is no reason for supposing that this is entirely later interpretation. The section also serves to show that Aaron did indeed position the lamp as commanded in Exod 25:37, information that is absent from Exod 37:17–24. In his obedience Aaron is shown to be worthy of the high honor accorded to him and his sons. It is possible that priestly responsibility with respect to the lights was a point at issue between the returning priests and the Levite priests of Palestine (cf. Num 4:16). It seems that the traditions of Shiloh allowed for the sanctuary lights to go out at night (1 Sam 3:3), but at Jerusalem, in the course of time if not from the outset, the lamps burned only at night (Exod 30:8; Lev 24:1–4). Josephus bears witness to a later custom which kept the lights burning all the time (*Antiq.* 3:8:3). Solomon's temple appears to have had separate candlesticks (1 Kgs 7:10). The priestly pattern for the lampstand is based apparently on the custom of the second temple.

Theologically the section reinforces the author's concern for religious controls. That these can ultimately stifle the word of God is easy to see. That there may also be proper controls must also be appreciated. In the eyes of the returning exiles it was religious "freedom" which had ruined the two kingdoms, a "freedom" tantamount to anarchy. In their view, this anarchy persisted in exilic and early post-exilic Palestine. It is hard to make value judgments about their achievement. The perennial problem, to which they bear witness, is the need to test "words of God," and to establish criteria whereby their authenticity can be assessed. Man's persistent fallibility demands safeguards if the God who speaks, sustains life, and brings light is to be truly heard and experienced.

The Purification of the Levites (8:5-26)

Bibliography

See Num 3:1–51 (*Bibliography*). **Péter, R.** "L'Imposition des Mains dans l'Ancien Testament." *VT* 27 (1977) 48–55.

Translation

[5] *And Yahweh spoke to Moses, saying,* [6] *"Take the Levites from among the people of Israel, and cleanse them.* [7] *This is what you shall do to cleanse them. Sprinkle the water of purification upon them, and let them shave all their flesh, and let them wash their clothes and cleanse themselves.* [8] *And let them take a young bull,[a] and its cereal offering, fine flour mixed with oil, and let them take a second young bull for a purification offering.* [9] *And you shall present the Levites before the Tent of Meeting. And you shall gather the whole congregation of the people of Israel.* [10] *And you shall present the Levites before Yahweh, and the people of Israel shall lay their hands upon the Levites.* [11] *And Aaron shall offer the Levites as a special contribution before Yahweh from the people of Israel. And they shall do the work of Yahweh.* [12] *And the Levites shall lay their hands on the heads of the young bulls, and you[a] shall offer one for a purification offering to Yahweh, to give protection for the Levites.* [13] *And you shall make the Levites stand[a] before Aaron, and before his sons, and offer them as a special contribution to Yahweh.*

[14] *"And you shall separate the Levites from among the people of Israel, and the Levites shall be mine.* [15] *And after this the Levites shall go in to do the work of the Tent of Meeting, and you shall cleanse them, and offer them as a special contribution.[a]* [16] *For they are wholly given to me from among the people of Israel in the place of[a] all the first born from the womb of all[a] the people of Israel. I have taken them for myself.* [17] *For all the firstborn among the people of Israel are mine, both man and beast. On the day that I struck all the firstborn in the land of Egypt I consecrated them for myself.* [18] *And I have taken the Levites in the place of all the firstborn among the people of Israel.* [19] *And I have given the Levites as a gift to Aaron and to his sons from among the people of Israel, to do work for the people of Israel in the Tent of Meeting, and to give protection for the people of Israel. And there will not be any plague among the people of Israel when the people of Israel come near to the sanctuary."*

[20] *And Moses, Aaron and all the congregation of the people of Israel did so to the Levites. According to all that Yahweh commanded Moses concerning the Levites so the people of Israel did to them.* [21] *And the Levites purified themselves and washed their clothes, and Aaron offered them as a special contribution before Yahweh. And Aaron made atonement for them to cleanse them.* [22] *And after this the Levites went to do the work in the Tent of Meeting before Aaron and before his sons. As Yahweh commanded Moses concerning the Levites so they did to them.*

[23] *And Yahweh spoke to Moses, saying,* [24] *"This[a] concerns the Levites. From the age of twenty-five years old and upward they shall go in to engage in service in*

the work of the Tent of Meeting. [25] *But from the age of fifty they shall cease from the service of the work. And they shall work no more.* [26] *They may minister with their brothers in the Tent of Meeting who engage in the service, but they shall do no work. So you shall arrange for the Levites in their service."*

Notes

8.a. *G* specifies that it must be a year old.

12.a. *G* reads וְעָשָׂה "and he shall offer" (i.e. Aaron). *BHS* suggests that the infinitive absolute וְעָשֹׂה might be read.

13.a. *G* has "before Yahweh and before Aaron" at this point.

15.a. *G* has "before Yahweh" at this point. J. Paterson (*Numbers*, 46) considers the whole of v 15b to be a gloss (n.b. elements of repetition from v 13b).

16.a. Sam reads the whole clause as כָּל בְּכוֹר פֶּטֶר רֶחֶם. This makes better grammatical sense. *BHS* suggests that כָּל be read before בְּכוֹר. This makes a reasonable clause, and involves little disturbance in MT.

24.a. The reading "the law" at this point in Syr is not widely supported and is probably an insertion.

Form/Structure/Setting

That the section is a continuation of P is accepted on all sides among analysts. There is evidently some close connection with Num 3:5–13. A. Dillmann (*Numeri*, 42–45) took the cleansing and formal presentation of the Levites (vv 6b–13) to belong to PG, but most of the earlier analysts took the basic text to belong to PS (cf. e.g. J. Wellhausen, *Hexateuch*, 180–81; A. Kuenen, *Hexateuch*, 92, 93; G. B. Gray, *Numbers*, 78). Fairly complex patterns of expansion were often envisaged. Kuenen took the view that the author of Num 3–4 believed the Levites to be already fitted for their task, and that no rites were required. The text must thus be an addition. In vv 5–22 the only substantially new material is contained in vv 6b–13. The rest consists of stereotyped formulae, restatements of material in Num 3:5–13, and some variants on parts of vv 6b–13. There seem to be two commands to purify the Levites (vv 6, 15), and three "offerings" of the Levites (vv 11, 13, 15), the first by Aaron and the other two by Moses. Gray judges the basic PS text to have been constructed as a parallel to the consecration of priests in Lev 8, and then to have been expanded, partly to emphasize Aaron and partly to assimilate the text to Num 3:5–13. He believed that some unevenness in the text can be explained by taking v 11 as an interpolation. Dillmann took vv 13b–14 to have been originally in the place of v 11. The further "cleansing" and "offering" of v 15 must be an expansion in his view.

The short passage in vv 23–26, with its new information about the age for Levitical service, was generally understood to be a further expansion. The age of entry differs from that given in Num 4:3 (twenty-five instead of thirty), and Gray claims to find certain stylistic peculiarities. These verses speak of entering service (יָבוֹא) and retirement (יָשׁוּב) in rather different terms from Num 4, and there are several peculiar combinations of words (p 82). These suggest to Gray the possibility of a late hand.

M. Noth (*Numbers* 67–70) took the position of vv 5–26 to indicate that in general it is an appendix to Num 3–4, though the precise patterns of relationship are in his view more complex than that. He believes that the basic form of the passage is connected closely to Num 3:11–13 in particular, and is both simpler and older than that text, though he recognizes that this gives no clue to the literary date of Num 8:5–22. Noth's view of the literary structure of the text is broadly similar to Gray's. The same holds for vv 23–26, which according to Noth must be a later correction explained by a need for extra Levitical strength (cf. also N. H. Snaith, *Numbers*, 215).

G. von Rad (*Priesterschrift*, 95–97) claimed to find two parallel rites in the passage, an older tradition in which Levites are offered for the firstborn, and an exilic compromise which gave the Levites a subordinate place to Aaron. These two have been welded together to create the present text. Though von Rad correctly identifies some of the more significant points of unevenness, the theory of parallel rites has not been widely accepted.

D. Kellermann (*Priesterschrift*, 115–24) finds the basic text essentially in vv 5–9a, 12–16a, 21. This in his view was a purification rite involving the shaving of the body, the washing of clothes, and the sprinkling of the water of purification. These procedures were rounded off with an act of offering. Kellermann thinks that this may reflect a post-exilic ordination ceremony for Levites. A second author has introduced vv 9b–11, 20, 22 (most), and in v 21 has changed the subject from Moses to Aaron. The introduction of Aaron and the attendance of the whole congregation are this author's main contribution. A further addition in vv 16b–19 depicts the Levites as a substitute for all the firstborn. Kellermann concludes that it is better to assume that the author was familiar with both Num 3:5–10 and 3:11–13, and that he therefore stands in time at some distance from both passages. Kellermann also concludes, on linguistic grounds, that vv 23–26 are a very late addition.

J. de Vaulx (*Nombres*, 117, 119–20) also notes the extreme complexities of the passage. There are second person singulars with Moses as subject in vv 6, 9–10, 13–14, and third person plurals with the Levites as subject in vv 7b–8. There seem to be two formulae of introduction (vv 6–7) and of conclusion (vv 12, 14). In de Vaulx's view the fusions and retouching of the passage are too numerous to make it possible to reconstruct the basic text and the process of compilation. He thinks it likely that some of the ancient usage associated with the consecration of the priests has been preserved here.

It is obvious that the text poses considerable difficulty, but it is not impossible to make reasonable suggestions about its background in the light of the author's purpose as discussed in connection with Num 3–4. As there, it seems very likely that the author is bringing older Levitical tradition into line with his new view of the relationship between priests and Levites. It is too much to speak of the downgrading of Levites here. Despite the "water of purification" (v 7) the position to which the Levites are ultimately brought is one of dignity (v 16). This continues to be so even in those texts which speak of the Levites as given to Aaron. These Levites are vital to the protection of Israel (v 19). The author has Levitical tradition to hand. He recognizes its validity (he need not have done so), and is anxious to do justice to it, but he must also square it with his understanding of the relationship between priests and Levites.

Given this understanding of the author's objectives, it is reasonable to locate the Levitical material in vv 7–8. This may well represent the tradition of the Palestinian priests. Their consecration involved the procedures described here. There are a number of distinctive features as compared with the rites for the consecration of priests in Exod 29 and Lev 8, which probably represent the Babylonian tradition. There is the water of purification, a term whose uniqueness may confirm the view taken, and also a sprinkling rather than a washing as in Lev. 8. Instead of the new clothes of Lev 8:13 the Levites here wash their clothes, as do laymen in Exod 19:14; Lev 14:8. In this rite two bullocks are used rather than one plus other animals. The contrast between the third person plural and the second person singular may be further confirmation of this view of vv 7–8. The author thus accepts this tradition as a legitimate rite for his Levites, but calls it a "cleansing" rather than a "consecration."

The author locates this command about the Levites in the wilderness, and incorporates an assembly of the whole congregation at the Tent of Meeting, a presentation of the Levites, and a laying on of hands by the whole community (vv 5–6, 9–10). It is quite possible that the author is also responsible for the continuation of the rite in vv 11–13. He may well have envisaged two "offerings." The first in v 11 is conducted by Aaron. It does justice to the Levitical tradition of Num 3:11–13 that the Levites are given by Israel to Yahweh in place of the firstborn. Then, when the sacrifices have been made (v 12) Moses conducts another "offering" (v 13), one which does justice to the author's reinterpretation of tradition in terms of the Levites as given to Aaron.

It is easy to see vv 14–19 as the author's further comment on this rite of purification. In his typical didactic fashion he repeats what the rite is about (v 15b), and calls to mind his previous teaching about the separation of the Levites (v 14a), their functions (v 15a) and their protective work (v 19b). In particular he is anxious to reaffirm his commitments in Num 3:5–13. There is a validity about that aspect of Levitical tradition which sees the Levites as given to Yahweh (vv 14b, 16–18; cf. Num 3:11–13, 40–51). But that givenness has to be understood in the new context of subordination to Aaron. Levites can thus be viewed as a gift to Aaron (v 19a). In vv 20–22 the author simply asserts that all was done as God had commanded.

In the final section (vv 23–26) a definitive view of the proper age for Levitical service is given. Though the possibility that this is a later addition to the book, updating Num 4:3, cannot be excluded, it is also arguably the author's. He has let the traditional age, deriving probably from Levitical sources, stand for a time, having linked it more particularly with the census than with service. Here he makes a final statement on the matter which doubtless takes into account the needs of his own time. The linguistic peculiarities may point to influence later than the author, but there is little evidence with which to work. The link between "service" and "warfare" is held in common with Num 4:3, and a contribution at this point by the author himself is perfectly possible.

This general view of the text and its history does not of course preclude minor glossing and retouching of the text.

Comment

7. מֵי חַטָּאת "water of purification." This is a unique term. The root is
the same as that used for "purification offering" (cf. *Comment* on Num 6:11),
and it should probably be understood in the same way (cf. the "water of
impurity" in Num 19:9). *G* has "purification." Whether this water was specially
prepared in any way cannot be determined.

10. וְסָמְכוּ . . . אֶת־יְדֵיהֶם "and they shall lay their hands." The author
may have envisaged the leaders engaging in this action, as representatives
of the people, though he may not seriously have considered the practicalities
of the action. This rite gives expression to the idea in v 16 that the Levites
are given to Yahweh by the people in place of the firstborn. R. Péter ("L'Imposition") is uncertain about the significance of the laying on of hands in this
text. He is inclined to think that it is an act of substitution or identification
rather than of consecration.

11. תְּנוּפָה "special contribution." See *Comment* on Num 5:25. N. H. Snaith
(*Numbers*, 216) may be overly precise in suggesting that it is an offering allocated to the whole priesthood.

12. For the "purification offering" and the "whole offering" see *Comment*
on Num 6:11.

12. לְכַפֵּר "to make atonement" (cf. v 19). The sense in this context seems
to be "to give protection." It is usually believed that the basic meaning of
the word is "to cover." Here it speaks of protection from divine wrath. See
further *Comment* on Num 17:6–15.

19. נְתָנִים "a gift." See *Comment* on Num 3:9.

26. The general meaning seems to be that the Levite can continue to
offer assistance beyond the age of fifty, but that he has no regular commitment,
probably on a rota.

Explanation

Having stressed in Num 7:89–8:4 the focal point of the theocracy's authority—the divine word speaking from the sanctuary—the author returns to his
familiar Levitical theme, providing a rite by which Levites can be purified
and begin their new mode of service. His inclusion of the material at this
point has reason and purpose in it. It could of course have come at the
end of Num 4, but there is a logic in its presence here. The principles by
which the life of the community are to be governed have been set out in
Num 2:1–8:4. It is now time to act upon these principles, and in particular
to initiate the Levites into their new form of ministry. If it was proper for
the priests to be ordained by ritual procedure (Lev 8–9) then it is appropriate
that Levitical ministry should be marked in a similar fashion.

The author's method in formulating this rite is to incorporate some elements of older Levitical tradition in vv 7–8 (see *Form/Structure/Setting*). The
position to which the Levites are called is one of dignity and distinction,
and is vital to the well-being of the community (v 19). There is no strong
reason for supposing that the author is stressing the inferiority of Levites
in the distinctive features of the rite—i.e. the water of purification, the sprin-

kling, the washing of old clothes rather than the use of new ones, and the use of two bullocks rather than one. These procedures may well reflect established custom among the Palestinian priest Levites. What the author does do is to call the rite a "cleansing" of the Levites rather than a "consecration" or "ordination." This description does indeed enforce the distinction between priests and Levites, and may have been necessary, in the author's view, because of the involvement of Levites in cultic irregularities. As in Num 3 the older Levitical idea of Levites as those "given to Yahweh" is reinterpreted in terms of a gift to Aaron.

Finally the age of service for Levites is fixed as twenty-five to fifty (vv 23–26). The older Levitical tradition about the age at which service is to begin (Num 4:3) is thus extended, probably in the light of contemporary need. With the question of pedigree paramount in post-exilic times, properly authenticated Levites may have been at a premium. The earlier tradition had been so closely tied to the Levitical census in Num 4 that it was possible to approach the issue of service directly at this point, and to give a different and definitive age at which it was proper for service to begin. It was appropriate enough to add this note after the rite for the cleansing of Levites had been described.

Theologically the section continues the theme of the importance of ministry, particularly in the light of divine holiness. Those engaged in holy work have to be properly prepared and set apart for their responsibilities in a significant and specific way. Through these rites the Levites are distinguished from the rest of the community, and the importance of such ministry for the community's well-being is duly stressed. This is a continuation of the main theological themes in Num 3–4. The distinctive emphasis of this section is that the Levites are nevertheless not remote from the community. Through the laying on of hands they in some sense represent the people at large, and constitute an offering from the people. Unlike the priests they do not receive anointing or special vestments. Like laymen they wash their clothes for the special rites. They are perhaps something of a bridge between priests and people. Distinctiveness in ministry combined with a significant solidarity with those ministered to constitute a fuller picture of service and ministry among the people of God.

Observing Passover—the Community's Foundational Rite   (9:1–14)

Bibliography

Auerbach, E. "Die Feste im alten Israel." *VT* 8 (1958) 1–18. **Haran, M.** "The Passover Sacrifice," *Studies in the Religion of Ancient Israel.* VTS 23 Leiden: Brill, 1972. ———. *Temples and Temple Service in Ancient Israel.* Oxford: Clarendon, 1978, 317–48. **Kraus, H. J.** "Zur Geschichte des Passah-Massot-Festes im AT." *EvT* 18 (1958) 47–67. **Kutsch, E.** "Erwägungen zur Geschichte der Passafeier und des Massotfestes." *ZTK* 55 (1958) 1–35. **May, H. G.** "The Relation of the Passover to the Feast of Unleavened Cakes." *JBL* 55 (1936) 65–82. **Morgenstern, J.** "Two Ancient Israelite Agricultural Festivals." *JQR* 8 (1917–18) 39–50. **Segal, J. B.** *The Hebrew Passover.* London: SPCK, 1963. **Talmon, S.** "Divergencies in Calendar Reckoning in Ephraim and Judah." *VT* 8 (1958) 48–74. **Vaux, R. de.** *Ancient Israel. Its Life and Institutions.* London: DLT, 1961, 484–93. **Wellhausen, J.** *Prolegomena to the History of Israel.* Cleveland & New York: World Publishing Co., 1957 (1885), 83–120.

Translation

¹ *And Yahweh spoke to Moses in the wilderness of Sinai in the first month of the second year after they came out from the land of Egypt, saying,* ² *ᵃ The people of Israel shall keep the Passover at its appointed time.ᵇ* ³ *On the fourteenth day of this month ᵃ you shall keep it at its appointed time in the evening. In accordance with all its statutes and judgments you shall keep it.ᵇ"* ⁴ *And Moses spoke to all the people of Israel that they should keep the Passover.* ⁵ᵃ *And they kept the Passover ᵃ in the first (month), on the fourteenth day of the month ᵇ in the evening, ᵇ in the wilderness of Sinai. In accordance with all that Yahweh commanded Moses so the people of Israel did.* ⁶ *And there were men who were unclean through contact with a corpse, and they could not keep the Passover on that day. And they approached Moses and Aaron ᵃ on that day.* ⁷ *And those men said to him, "We are unclean through contact with a corpse. Why are we debarred from offering Yahweh's oblation at its appointed time along with the people of Israel?"* ⁸ *And Moses said to them, "Wait, and I will see what Yahweh will command for you."*

⁹ *And Yahweh spoke to Moses, saying,* ¹⁰ *"Speak to the people of Israel, saying, If any man among you is unclean through contact with a corpse, or is away on a long journey, one of you or your descendents, he shall keep a Passover to Yahweh.* ¹¹ *In the second month on the fourteenth day at evening he shall keep it. They shall eat it with unleavened bread and bitter herbs.* ¹² *They shall not leave any of it until morning, and they shall not break a bone of it. In accordance with all the statues of the Passover they shall keep it.* ¹³ *But the man who is clean and who is not on a journey,ᵃ and who fails to keep the Passover, that person shall be cut off from his people, because he did not offer the oblation of Yahweh at its appointed time. That man shall bear his sin.* ¹⁴ *And if an alien settles with you and will keep the Passover to Yahweh, then in accordance with the statute of the Passover and its judgment,ᵃ so shall he do. There shall be one statute for you, both for the alien and for the person born in the land."*

Notes

2.a. The text seems to require אָמַר before וְיַעֲשׂוּ (G, BHS). A. Dillmann (*Numeri*, 46) suggested that originally the tense was historical—וַיַּעֲשׂוּ.

2.b. Sam reads "times" here and in vv 3, 7, 13 (cf. G of v 3).

3.a. G reads "of the first month." MT seems acceptable.

3.b. Sam, Syr read יַעֲשׂוּ, taking the verse historically. The strongest G witness favors a second person sing.

5.a.-a. This note is absent in G. MT is acceptable.

5.b.-b. This clause is absent in G. MT is acceptable.

6.a. The third person singular "to him" in v 7 suggests that "Aaron" is an addition here.

13.a. G makes it a "long" journey.

14.a. Sam, Syr, V, favor a plural here, as in v 3. G. B. Gray (*Numbers*, 85) supports this.

Form/Structure/Setting

Analysts are agreed that the section is priestly, and the majority recognize it as a late accretion (e.g. J. Wellhausen, *Hexateuch*, 177; A. Kuenen, *Hexateuch*, 92–93; G. B. Gray, *Numbers*, 82–83). A. Dillmann (*Numeri*, 45–47) took a similar view but considered that the original P narrative underlies the present text in the form of a simple historical account of the keeping of the Passover. The main arguments for a late accretion are the dating in v 1 which places us in the first month of the second year (Num 1:1 had already reached the second month of that year), and the general lack of an organic connection with the context. Gray recognizes that the chief interest of the passage— the supplementary Passover—*is* concerned with the second month, and he sees this as the reason for its insertion at this point. He believes that if the section had been original to P the main concern would have been stated first and dated in the second month, with the historical clause set out in a pluperfect paragraph.

More recent analysts are inclined to the same kind of view of the section (e.g. M. Noth, *Numbers*, 71; N. H. Snaith, *Numbers*, 218). D. Kellermann (*Priester-schrift*, 124–33) finds in vv 10b–12 the beginning of the processes of growth, a passage which clearly presupposes Exod 12. According to Kellermann this legal text (vv 10b–12) probably belongs to the exilic period, permitting those traveling to observe the Passover in the second month. Most of the rest of the section is taken to be a single relatively late addition (vv 1–8, excluding "Aaron" in v 6 9–10a). This addition links the legal text of vv 10b–12 with the wilderness period, and incorporates contact with death as a further ground for late observance. Kellermann takes the remaining elements (vv 13–14, "Aaron" in v 6) to be further additions.

It seems reasonably clear that vv 2–5, 11–12 are drawing on Exod 12. That the author should work in this way is completely in accordance with his method and interest elsewhere. Nor is there any serious difficulty in taking the section as essentially a unit from the author's hand. That he should wish to tell of Passover observance is entirely credible. The only possible difficulty is his failure to include the section in what might seem to be its proper chronological place at the beginning of the book, or alternatively why he dates the census to the second month. The reason may lie in Gray's observations noted above, though the conclusions he draws run the risk of circularity. If reason can be found for the insertion of a text at a particular point it seems perfectly possible that that same reason may have operated in an original author's mind. It may be worth pointing out again that the text is intended in the first instance not for historiographical study but for recitation with a didactic purpose. As Gray observes, the main interest is the supplemental Passover to be observed in the second month. This therefore is not unreasonable as a position for the appropriate information, particularly as the author intends to move Israel on six days later (Num 10:11). In any event it is certainly possible to read the perfects of vv 1–8 as pluperfects, and the divine response (vv 9–14) as set in the second month. It is true enough that the stipulations are not closely or organically linked with 8:23–26 or 9:15–23, but it is not true that the incorporation of the material here is random. That the author should wish to refer to a Passover observance just before the departure from Sinai is quite likely. This observance provides an excellent parallel to the first Passover immediately prior to the departure from Egypt (cf. Ezra 6:16–22 for another significant Passover following the dedication of the second Temple).

Kellermann's arguments about the evolution of the text are not particularly convincing. It seems just as likely that the reference to traveling reflects a relatively stable post-exilic situation than the circumstances of the exile itself. The author is perhaps formulating what had already become a custom regarding contact with death. This custom is given divine authentication, and a further exceptional case is included by the author—that of merchant travelers. S. Talmon ("Divergencies") suggests that the date in the second month reflects northern tradition (cf. 2 Chr 30:1–3). If so it would seem that the author has found a means of incorporating this tradition in the circumstances of the exceptional case. It is easy enough to see v 13 as an integral part of the whole. The author is anxious to ensure that the exceptions do not become a rule, or an encouragement to laxity. All Israelites in normal circumstances are obliged to observe the Passover at its proper time. It is arguable that v 14 is less closely linked with the rest of the section, but if the information is to be included at all this is as appropriate a place as any. There is no reason for doubting that the author would be interested in the Passover rights and responsibilities of aliens. As J. de Vaulx shows (*Nombres*, 125) comparison with the Elephantine texts on this matter of the supplemental Passover gives some ground for dating the author's work towards the end of the fifth century.

Comment

2. It is widely believed that in origin Passover was a spring feast involving rites to keep away evil spirits and/or to secure fertility in the flocks of a nomadic community. This conclusion is reached by separating the most distinctive features of the rite (as set out in Exod 12:1–13, 21–27, 43–50) from their current setting in the account of the Exodus, and considering them in isolation. According to Wellhausen (*Prolegomena*) the rites were first linked with the originally Canaanite rite of Unleavened Bread under Josiah (Deut 16:1–8), and in his view this development provided a significant thrust towards the historicising of Passover. Much would depend here on the dating of the Yahwistic material in Exod 12:21–27. Kraus ("Passah-Massot-Festes") finds a much earlier assimilation of the two rites at Gilgal, along with the tendency

to historicise them. This depends on their being ancient tradition in texts such as Josh 4:19–23; 5:10–12, and to some extent on the acceptability of the amphictyonic hypothesis. Haran (*Temples*, 317–48) argues that in the oldest injunctions of Exod. 23:18; 34:25 Passover and Unleavened Bread are already linked, and conceived of as pilgrimage festivals.

3. This was the fourteenth of Nisan which, following the acceptance of a spring new year in post-exilic times, had become the first month.

3. בֵּין הָעַרְבָּיִם "in the evening" (vv 5, 11), literally "between the two evenings" (cf. Exod 16:12; 29:39, 41; Lev 13:5; Num 28:4, 8). Jewish tradition is imprecise about the meaning of this (cf. N. H. Snaith, *Numbers*, 152). A narrow period of time seems to be required in Exod 16:12, where it is the complement to "daybreak" or "first light," and so perhaps "between dusk and darkness" is the time intended.

3. On "statutes" and "judgments" see R. Hentschke, *Satzung und Setzender* (Stuttgart: Kohlhammer, 1963); G. Liedke, *Gestalt und Bezeichnung alttestamentlicher Rechtsätze* (WMANT 39; Neukirchen: Neukirchener, 1971); P. Victor, "A Note on 'hoq' in the Old Testament," *VT* 16 (1966) 358–61.

6. Uncleanness prevented any involvement in feasts (cf. Lev 7:20).

7. לָמָה נִגָּרַע "why are we debarred . . . ?" For use of the root elsewhere see Exod 5:8; Lev 27:18; Num 27:4; 36:3; Deut 4:2. It has to do in general with the idea of "withdrawal."

8. Other special consultations of this kind occur in Lev 24:12; Num 15:34; 27:5.

11. מַצּוֹת וּמְרֹרִים "unleavened bread and bitter herbs." This reflects the link between the Feasts of Passover and Unleavened Bread (see above on v 2). The regulations here and in v 12 specify three important features of Passover (cf. Exod 12:8, 10, 46). These are doubtless representative; the rest of the requirements in Exodus 12 are taken for granted (cf. v 12b).

13. נִכְרְתָה "shall be cut off." Some commentators take this to be a reference to execution (e.g. G. B. Gray, *Numbers*, 84–85). Others think of it as a threat of death by divine not human hand (e.g. A. H. McNeile, *Numbers*, 48). Others take the phrase to mean excommunication (e.g. J. de Vaulx, *Nombres*, 125; B. Lindars, "Ezekiel and Individual Responsibility," *VT* 15 [1965] 452–67). The third suggestion seems most likely.

14. גֵּר "alien." Such a person was not Israelite by birth, but had been settled in the community for a considerable period, and in many respects was a member of it. He was distinguished from the temporary visitor (Num 35:15) who was not entitled to engage in the Passover (Exod 12:45). The alien would probably have been circumcised, and was entitled to the care and protection of the community. In D Israel's status in Egypt was likened to that of the alien, and this was used as a motive for respect towards that class of person (cf. e.g. Deut 10:19).

Explanation

This section tells of the keeping of Passover (vv 1–5). This description serves as a starting point for discussion of a special case concerning Passover observance—the situation of people who are unclean through contact with death at the time of the Passover (vv 5–8). The answer, secured by Moses at a special consultation with God, is that such persons must observe the Passover a month later, in the second month (vv 9–12). The answer also indicates another special case—that of those on a journey in a foreign country. Concluding observations make it clear that this supplemental celebration is entirely exceptional (v 13), and that aliens are fully entitled to take part in the Passover (v 14).

The author is now approaching the end of his discussion of the constitution of the community. He has discussed its dimensions (1:1–46), and indicated something of its character as a priestly theocracy (2:1–34). He has discussed the rights and responsibilities of the priests (5:1–6:27), and the community's commitment to the new order (7:1–88). In particular he has elaborated a new structure for the priestly hierarchy, involving an honored and responsible status for Levites, but one of subordination to the sons of Aaron (1:47–54; 3:1–4:49; 7:89–8:26). In this, the concluding section, he describes the observance of Passover, the community's foundational rite. This comes most appropriately as the immediate prelude to the journey from Sinai to the land. The observance of Passover in Exod 12 had been the immediate prelude to the journey from Egypt.

This description of the observance of the community's foundational rite gives the author an opportunity to legislate concerning a particular issue that had arisen in post-exilic times. How important is the Passover? Under what circumstances, if any, may it not be observed at the proper time? Uncleanness necessarily involved exclusion from the celebration, and the author confirms this with an authenticating word of God. But in his view Passover was so fundamental to the community's existence and identity that a second observance on the fourteenth day of the second month was permitted. This rule also covered those traveling in foreign countries on the fourteenth of the first month. This rule reflects either an awareness of the special circumstances raised by the diaspora, or the commercial problems of merchants, or both. These exceptions are not however an open door to general laxity. Failure to observe the Passover at its proper times brings a severe penalty—probably excommunication—an appropriate fate for one who values his identity within the community so slightly. The rights of aliens to take part are also protected. These people were not Jewish by birth, but were committed to Jewish faith and practice. So crucial aspects of the observance of this key festival are set out—the observance which above all other defines the community and sustains its self-consciousness.

It has been suggested that the date in the second month has a northern background (see *Form/Structure/Setting*), and if so the author has found a means of incorporating this in the exceptional cases. In 2 Chr 30:1–3 Hezekiah celebrates a late Passover when he includes the people of the northern kingdom in the nation's observance. The dating may have been available to the author of Numbers as a Palestinian tradition, in which case he resolves the issue in one of his characteristic compromises.

The dominant concern of the section is the overriding obligation to celebrate this foundational feast. The exceptions enforce the point rather than detract from it. No one has a case for failure to observe it. This obligation

entails also the recognition of a great privilege. The people of God find
their identity in those rites which constantly re-enact and call to mind the
historical roots of faith. This "identity" has to do with their own distinctiveness
as a group, and with the meaning and purpose of their existence in the world
at large. In the incorporation of the alien there is a prefiguring of the calling
of the Gentiles (see J. de Vaulx, *Nombres*, 126–27).

Means of Guidance on the Journey—The Cloud (9:15–23)

Bibliography

See under Num 7:89–8:4 (*Bibliography*). **Dus, J.** "Herabfahrung Jahwes auf die Lade und Entziehung der Feuerwolke." *VT* 19 (1969) 290–311. **Harrelson, W.** "Guidance in the Wilderness." *Int* 13 (1959) 24–36. **Sabourin, L.** "The Biblical Cloud. Terminology and Traditions." *BTB* 4 (1974) 290–311. **Schmidt, W.** "מִשְׁכָּן als Ausdruck Jerusalemer Kultsprache." *ZAW* 75 (1963) 91–92.

Translation

[15] And on the day when the Tabernacle was set up [a] the cloud covered the Tabernacle, [b] the Tent of the Testimony.[b] And in the evening it was [c] over the Tabernacle like the appearance of fire until morning. [16] So it was continually. The cloud covered it (by day),[a] and there was the appearance of fire at night. [17] And whenever the cloud was taken up from over the Tent, then the people of Israel set out, and in the place where the cloud settled, there the people of Israel encamped. [18] At the commandment of Yahweh the people of Israel set out, and at the commandment of Yahweh they encamped. All the days that the cloud settled upon the Tabernacle they remained encamped. [19] And when the cloud stayed long over the Tabernacle, for many days, then the people of Israel engaged in the service of Yahweh, and did not set out. [20] It was the same when the cloud was on the Tabernacle for a few days.[a] At the commandment of Yahweh they encamped, and at the commandment of Yahweh they set out. [21] And there were some times when the cloud remained only from evening to morning, and when the cloud was taken up in the morning they set out. Whether it was by day [a] or by night, [b] when the cloud was taken up they set out.[b] [22] Whether it was for two days, a month, or for longer, that the cloud waited [a] over the Tabernacle,[a] settling thereon, the people of Israel encamped and did not set out. [b] And when it was taken up they set out.[b] [23] At the commandment of Yahweh they encamped, and at the commandment of Yahweh they set out. They engaged in the service of Yahweh [a] according to Yahweh's commandment by the hand of Moses.

Notes

15.a. Sam reads the word as הוּקַם, a third sing perfect *Hophal*.
15.b.-b. Possibly a gloss (cf. J. Paterson, *Numbers,* 47).
15.c. The perfect is required here (*BHS;* Paterson, *Numbers,* 47).
16.a. *G* reads יוֹמָם at this point. The sense seems to require it (cf. *Syr, Tg., Vg*) (cf. also Paterson. *Numbers,* 47; N. H. Snaith, *Numbers,* 220).
20.a. *BHS* favors יָמִים here (cf. also G. B. Gray, *Numbers,* 87; L. E. Binns, *Numbers,* 56). See also GKC § 131e.
21.a. The singular seems preferable (see *BHS*).
21.b.-b. This clause is lacking in *G.* Gray (*Numbers,* 87) suggests that its presence in MT is dittographic.
22.a.-a. This clause is absent in *G.* Gray (*Numbers,* 87) suggests that it may have been a gloss on עָלָיו. It replaces עָלָיו in *S.*
22.b.-b. This clause is lacking in *G.* It is probably a gloss.
23.a. There are some minor variations in *G,* but MT is acceptable.

Form/Structure/Setting

The connection of this passage with Exod 40:36–38 makes it certain that this too is priestly material. There is a tendency among analysts to suspect that it belongs to the original, or at least to an early stage in the history of P (cf. e.g. J. Wellhausen, *Hexateuch,* 181; A. Kuenen, *Hexateuch,* 92). G. B. Gray (*Numbers,* 85) points out that the date in v 15 links the section directly with Exod 40:2, 17, and claims that it would have stood most naturally at the conclusion of the story of the erection of the Tabernacle. In its present form however he judges that it is best linked to PS. He seeks support for this in the numerous clauses which are lacking in *G,* and in a few expressions not found elsewhere in texts attributable to PG.

M. Noth (*Numbers,* 75) took key elements in Exod 40 to be additions to P, and had no doubt that these anticipations of the wilderness wandering came from a later author. Others also speak of this section as an "expansion" or "extension" of material in Exod 40 (e.g. A. H. McNeile, *Numbers,* 49; N. H. Snaith, *Numbers,* 220). D. Kellermann (*Priesterschrift,* 133–40) concludes, on stylistic and linguistic grounds, that the section is late. He finds the original material in vv 15–19. The comments about the varied duration of encampments (vv 20–23a) come in his view from another author, and v 23b is a still later gloss. The reference to the Tent of the Testimony (v 15) is another gloss which it is impossible to place according to Kellermann.

It is clear enough that the connections with Exod 40 are readily intelligible in the light of the theory of authorship we have proposed. The author is anxious to take up ideas about the divine presence from that chapter, and to use them to develop a theory of divine guidance in the wilderness. Each variation in *G* has to be considered on its own merits (see *Notes*), and no very obvious support for theories of supplementation in P emerges. The few peculiar expressions identified by Gray can very well be a witness to the distinctiveness of the author of Numbers. There is indeed a good deal of meticulous repetition in the section. The purpose may be didactic—to emphasize and enforce the points made. When this is appreciated there is much less reason for positing substantial accretions (not excluding the possibility of minor glosses) to a basic text. There seems to be a natural enough movement from v 19 to v 20. The first part (vv 15–19) is concerned to explain the processes of guidance, movement and encampment, with the concluding verse (v 19) indicating that encampment could be for many days. The second part (vv 20–23) goes on to explore this theme of duration, and to explain that though the periods of encampment varied greatly Israel always obeyed. There is thus no strong reason for calling in question the substantial unity of the section, or for denying it to the overall author.

Comment

21. אוֹ יוֹמָם וָלַיְלָה "whether it was by day or by night" (thus NEB). The meaning is not entirely clear. RSV takes it to be a reference to a day and a night—i.e. a twenty-four hour period.

22. יָמִים "for longer," literally "days." RV understands this to be "a year"

(cf. Lev 25:29; 1 Sam 27:7). N. H. Snaith (*Numbers,* 221) and L. E. Binns (*Numbers,* 56) accept this, but Gray (*Numbers,* 87) rejects it. It may simply be an indefinite period longer than a month—hence "for longer." F. S. North ("Four Month Seasons of the Hebrew Bible," *VT* 11 [1961] 446–48) makes the suggestion that the word is used as a technical term here for a season of four months.

Explanation

This section is the first of two which are clearly preparatory to the beginning of the march. Having discussed the constitution of the community in Num 1:1–9:14 the author is now ready to begin this second major division of the book which tells of the journey from Sinai to Canaan. This preparatory section explains how Isrealites were led on the journey. The cloud of Exod 40:36–38 which indicated God's presence in the Tent of Meeting was also the guide. When it rose from the Tent the people followed. Where it rested the people encamped. This was the unchanging rule.

The author's main achievement here is his adaptation of the theology of divine presence in Exod 40 in the interests of the guidance and leadership themes. He has brought together various elements in the early narrative tradition of the Pentateuch. In Exod 13:21–22 (J?) the cloud takes the form of a column which at night becomes a column of fire. Its function is to move in front of the people as a guide. In Exod 33:7–11 (E) (cf. also Num 11:25; 12:5, 10; Deut 31:15) it is again a column, associated closely in these texts with the external "Tent of Meeting" where it appears from time to time when God communicates with men. Here in Num 9:15–23 the cloud is not a column, but at night it does have a fiery appearence (cf. Exod 13:21). In priestly tradition it makes its first appearance at Sinai (Exod 24:15–18), and as in Exod 33:7–11 is associated with the Tent of Meeting, an institution at the center of the camp. The leadership of the cloud is apparently conducted from the center of the marching column. The author's picture thus draws together, as far as possible, the varied elements in the earlier narrative tradition—the idea of leadership by a cloud from Exod 13:21–22, and of association with the Tent from Exod 33:7–11—putting both in a new context, that of a centralized Tent.

This description of the patterns of guidance and leadership helps to enforce some of the principal points made in the book's first major division (Num 1:1–9:14). The covering of the Tabernacle by the cloud (vv 15, 18–22) emphasizes the theocratic theory of Num 2:1–34. Even when the cloud moves to indicate the time for departure, the author defines that movement only in terms of being "taken up" (vv 17, 21–22). He is unwilling to lose the theory of the centrality of the divine presence, even when the issue of leadership through the wilderness is at stake. It is pointless to ask how the author precisely believed the guidance by the cloud operated. It is sufficient for him that it did so. He would not have wished of course to contest the theory in Exod 13:21–22 of leadership at the head of the host by columns of cloud and fire. His concern is to put the emphasis in a different place, preserving the centrality of the divine presence, even when Israel is on the march.

Another theme stressed in this opening section to the second main division of the book is Israel's faithful and obedient response to the guidance of God. The alternating patterns of obedience and disobedience are an important feature of this central part of the book. For the moment at least, Israel is depicted as faithful in her response, whether the periods of encampment required by the cloud were long or short.

For the priestly theologians the cloud was always the means whereby the invisible and exalted God made his nearness evident to his people. Previously it has borne witness to the priestly theology of the divine presence. Here it points to God's guidance and protection in danger and uncertainty. Experience of such benefits is dependent however on a proper recognition of the realities of the divine dimension. The movement of God, symbolized by the cloud, and God's times may not always be subject to rational explanation. Man's commitment is to follow in faith.

The Signal for the Journey—The Silver Trumpets   10:1–10

Bibliography

Finesinger, S. B. "Musical Instruments in the Old Testament." *HUCA* 3 (1926) 21–76. ———. "The Shofar." *HUCA* 8–9 (1931–32) 193–228. **Werner, E.** "Musical Instruments." *IDB* r-z 469–76.

Translation

¹ *And Yahweh spoke to Moses, saying,* ² *"Make for yourself two silver trumpets. You shall make them of beaten work. And they shall be for you to call the congregation, and for the setting out of the camps.* ³ *And they* ᵃ *shall blow with them, and all the congregation shall gather themselves to you at the door of the Tent of Meeting.* ⁴ *And if they blow with one (trumpet), the leaders, the heads of the thousands of Israel, shall gather themselves to you.* ⁵ *And when you blow an alarm the camps on the east side shall set out.* ⁶ *And when you blow a second alarm the camps on the south side shall set out.* ᵃ *They shall blow an alarm for their setting out.* ᵇ ⁷ *And when the assembly is to be gathered you shall blow, but not an alarm.* ⁸ *And the sons of Aaron, the priests, shall blow with the trumpets. And they shall be to you for a statute throughout your generations.* ⁹ *And if you go to war* ᵃ *in your land against the oppressor who oppresses you, then you shall sound an alarm with the trumpets. And you will be remembered before Yahweh your God, and you will be saved from your enemies.* ¹⁰ *And on the day of your gladness, and on your feast days, and at the beginning of your months you shall blow with the trumpets over your whole offerings and over the sacrifices of your shared offerings. And they shall be to you for a remembrance before your God. I am Yahweh your God."*

Notes

3.a. *G* reads a second person singular here.

6.a. SP has צפונה here, probably mistakenly (cf. G. B. Gray, *Numbers*, 89).

6.b. MT lacks all reference to the third and fourth divisions of the army (cf. Num 2:1–34). *G* has a full description, which, in view of author's liking for full detail, should probably be accepted (cf. J. Paterson, *Numbers*, 47).

9.a. The expression וְכִי-תָבֹאוּ מִלְחָמָה is unusual (cf. the discussion in J. Paterson, *Numbers*, 47). *BHS* suggests לְמִלְחָמָה.

Form/Structure/Setting

Analysts are agreed that the section is priestly. J. Wellhausen (*Hexateuch*, 181) took the view that it belonged to the kernel of P. Unevenness however has long been recognized, and conclusions about a complex literary history have been drawn. In vv 5–6a, 7, 9–10 there are second person plural verbs, but third person plural verbs in vv 3–4, 6b, 8. A Dillmann (*Numeri*, 48–50) took the second person material to be redactional. In vv 9–10 a different use of the trumpets is discussed, and this too was considered additional, along with the incomplete material about the camps in vv 5–6a.

D. Kellermann (*Priesterschrift*, 140–47) offers a modern analysis along broadly similar lines. He finds the kernel of the section in vv 3–4—the stipulations for the assembling of the community and the leaders. Since vv 5–6a presuppose Num 2 these verses are taken to be an addition to vv 3–4. The main author of vv 1–8 incorporates this material, according to Kellermann, within vv 1–2, 7–8. He notes that elsewhere these trumpets occur only in secondary priestly strata, and concludes that this section cannot belong to PG. In vv 9–10 he sees two separate additions to vv 1–8.

The value of this kind of analysis is uncertain, and the possibility of viewing the section in more holistic terms deserves attention. It is true enough that vv 3–4 stand out. They are framed in the third person plural, and are imprecise about who is to blow the trumpets. This tradition of a two-trumpet peal for the whole community and a one-trumpet peal for the leaders may therefore be older festal material incorporated by the author. It could be Palestinian rather than Babylonian, and be further evidence of his willingness to exercise a controlled assimilation of such material. If this is correct the author has certainly written up the tradition in his own style, speaking of the "congregation," the "Tent of Meeting," and the "leaders."

The rest of the section can very well be the author's work. He specifies the making and two-fold function of the trumpets in his schema (v 2), and includes material illustrating the second function in vv 5–6. In introducing this second function the author wishes to do justice to the battle traditions of earlier texts (cf. e.g. Josh 6:1–20). The third person plural is not a serious difficulty, its form aligning it with the form in which the first function is expressed in vv 3–4. In v 7 the author makes clear that there are two kinds of trumpet peals to distinguish the two functions. In v 8 he stressed in typical fashion that this is a priestly responsibility of the sons of Aaron, indicating quite clearly that any acceptance of Palestinian tradition operates under overall Babylonian control. In vv 9–10 the author shows what the two functions of the trumpet would mean after the settlement, and there is no problem in seeing them as integral to the whole. Since the author is obviously concerned with post-settlement problems it is natural that these verses should form the climax of the section.

Comment

2. חֲצוֹצְרֹת "trumpets." The word is rarely used in pre-exilic texts (cf. Hos 5:8; 2 Kgs 11:14). It occurs most often in cultic and military contexts in the Chronicler's work (cf. also Ps 98:6). Earlier narrative tradition tends to lay stress on the "ram's horn" (cf. e.g. Exod 19:13; Josh 6:5).

3. N. H. Snaith (*Numbers*, 221) suggests long blasts for the gathering of the community, and in v 5 a rapid succession of three notes for the תְּרוּעָה "alarm." This can only be conjecture.

6. לְמַסְעֵיהֶם "for their setting out." This seems to mean that a separate alarm is blown for each of the four groups of tribes.

7. הַקָּהָל "the assembly." This word for the community is an alternative within P for "congregation." It denotes the idea of being "called together," and is often used in contexts where the community is gathered at the Tent of Meeting. This is a better explanation of its use than the theory of literary supplementation based on the assembly/congregation distinction as offered by B. Luther (" 'Kahal' und "edah' als Hilfsmittel der Quellenscheidung im Priesterkodex und in der Chronik," *ZAW* 56 [1938] 44–63).

9. For a good illustration of the use of trumpets in battle see 2 Chr 13:12–16.

10. וּבְיוֹם שִׂמְחַתְכֶם "and on your feast days." These are set out in Num 28.

Explanation

This section contains information about the second means of guidance for the journey to the land, the first being the cloud in Num 9:15–23. The two silver trumpets are a means of assembling the Israelites, and also of signalling the beginning of the march. The use of both trumpets assembles the whole community (v 3); the use of one summons the leaders. The signal to march is a different sound—an "alarm" (vv 5–7). Priests are responsible for blowing the trumpets (v 8). This two-fold use persists after the settlement—the alarm is for war (v 9), and the other peal for festal assemblies (v 10).

Whereas the cloud in Num 9:15–23 represents the divine initiative in leadership the trumpets constitute the response of the human leadership as it summons the congregation to gather at the Tent, and signals the moment of advance for each tribal group. The author may be adapting Palestinian tradition in vv 3–4—tradition associated with the various ways of summoning leaders and people at feasts. Having incorporated this he describes the kind of trumpet to be used (v 2), and introduces another function—the trumpet peal which puts Israel on the move (vv 5–7). By insisting on this as a role for the sons of Aaron the author further enforces priestly status and authority (v 8). The two functions of the trumpet described here are strongly reminiscent of the activities of the major judges (cf. e.g. Judg 3:27; 4:10; 6:34; 7:20; 8:1). Thus the author imprints on the priests some traditional functions of the judge. When Israel reaches the land the priestly trumpets are to sound for war (v 9), and also for the great festal occasions (v 10). A role for priests prior to battle had already been established in Deut 20:2–4. This was probably based on the fact that the priest handled the ark in time of war (1 Sam 4:1–11).

Theologically the section bears witness to the need for a human response to divine initiative. The divine guidance, symbolized by the cloud, calls forth the response of Israel and her leaders. The trumpet peal is the audible sign which prompts the exercise of the obedience of faith. One aspect of man's commitment is his willingness to follow in faith, whatever the dangers and obstacles.

The trumpet sounds are also depicted as a reminder, on Israel's behalf, before God (vv 9–10). This idea may seem strange in the context of a faith where God is thought both to take the initiative and to be wholly dependable. In what sense can he need reminding? It may be that this is a way of expressing man's complete dependence on God. From the perspective of faith God can never be taken for granted or exploited.

The Beginning of the Journey 10:11-28

Bibliography

See under Num 2:1-34 (*Bibliography*).

Translation

¹¹ᵃ *And it was in the second year, in the second month, on the twentieth day of the month, that the cloud was taken up from over the tabernacle of the testimony.* ¹² *And the people of Israel set out on their journey from the wilderness of Sinai. And the cloud rested in the wilderness of Paran.* ¹³ *And they set out according to the commandment of Yahweh by the hand of Moses.* ¹⁴ *And the standard of the camp of the sons of Judah set out* ᵃ *first, company by company. And Nahshon son of Amminadab was over this company.* ¹⁵ *And Nethanel son of Zuar was over the company of the tribe of the sons of Issachar.* ¹⁶ *And Eliab son of Helon was over the company of the tribe of the sons of Zebulun.*
¹⁷ *And the tabernacle was taken down.* ᵃ *And the sons of Gershon and the sons of Merari who carried the tabernacle set out.* ¹⁸ *And the standard of the camp of Reuben set out, company by company. And Elizur son of Shedeur was over this company.* ¹⁹ *And Shelumiel son of Zurishaddai was over the company of the tribe of the sons of Simeon.* ²⁰ *And Eliasaph son of Deuel* ᵃ *was over the company of the sons of Gad.*
²¹ *And the Kohathites set out, carrying the holiest things. And they set up the tabernacle before they came.* ²² *And the standard of the camp of the sons of Ephraim set out, company by company. And Elishama son of Ammihud was over this host.* ²³ *And Gamaliel son of Pedahzur was over the company of the tribe of the sons of Manasseh.* ²⁴ *And Abidan son of Gideoni was over the company of the tribe of the sons of Benjamin.*
²⁵ *And the standard of the camp of the sons of Dan, which was the last of all the camps, set out, company by company. And Ahiezer son of Ammishaddai was over this host.* ²⁶ *And Pagiel son of Ochran was over the company of the tribe of the sons of Asher.* ²⁷ *And Ahira son of Enan was over the company of the sons of Naphtali.* ²⁸ *Thus the people of Israel set out, company by company. And they went forward.*

Notes

11.a. Sam has an evident expansion of the text at this point, including the substance of Deut 1:6b–8.
14.a. יִסַּע or יָסַע seems to be required here (see *BHS;* cf. v 17).
17.a. *G* and *Syr* read וְהוֹרִידוּ here (cf. Num 1:51; 4:5).
20.a. See *Notes* on Num 1:14.

Form/Structure/Setting

The section is evidently priestly, and in J. Wellhausen's view (*Hexateuch,* 181) belonged to the kernel of the priestly tradition. The date in v 11, the

conception of the cloud, and the tribal arrangements for the journey all serve
to link the section with priestly tradition already considered. G. B. Gray (*Numbers*, 90) was inclined to assign vv 11–12 and perhaps v 28 to PG, with the
rest taken as a later insertion. The disagreement between vv 17–21 and Num
2:17 is the point which justifies, in Gray's view, an ascription of the tribal
material to PS (cf. also A. Dillmann. *Numeri*, 50–51). More recent analysts
tend to be less confident about making such distinctions within P, but M.
Noth (*Numbers*, 76–77) observes the phenomena of vv 17, 21, and concludes
that vv 13–28 probably do not belong to the basic form of P.

There is no very serious difficulty however in seeing the section whole,
and judging it to be from the overall author of the book. He is faithful here
to the dating and cloud traditions from earlier parts of the book, and to
the essential tribal arrangements of Num 2. The information in vv 17, 21 is
not so much a disagreement with Num 2:17 as an elaboration of it, in the
light of the picture as it has developed in Num 3–4. This is in accordance
with what we have suggested in the author's general method—the slow but
progressive construction of an overall picture. The further developments
which emerge in Num 3–4 demand some consideration of the mechanics
by which the sanctuary and its contents are carried and housed. It comes
appropriately at this point because Israel is now on the march. We are less
concerned now with the constitution of the community, more with the journey.
If the sons of Gershon and Merari move on ahead of the Kohathites then
the structure could be ready erected for the housing of the ark when it arrived.

Comment

11. The date is nineteen days after the census in Num 1:1, and ten months
nineteen days after the arrival at Sinai (Exod 19:1; 40:17).

12. The wilderness of Paran cannot be identified with precision. It probably
lies to the north of the Sinai peninsula, south of Kadesh-barnea and the
Negeb, and with its eastern border running roughly from the Dead Sea to
the Gulf of Akaba (cf. its link with Edom in Deut 33:2; Hab 3:3 and other
references in Gen 21:21; 1 Kgs 11:18). M. Noth (*Numbers*, 76) suggested
that it might be identified with the *wādi fērān* in the mountainous southern
part of the peninsula, but this has not been widely accepted.

17. The verbs are perfects with *waw*, and are probably meant to be frequentative (cf. A. H. McNeile, *Numbers*, 53; G. B. Gray, *Numbers*, 91). They indicate
what was customary.

21. Since the sacred structure is already being carried by the Gershonites
and Merarites שׁדְקִּמַּה must mean the "holiest things"—i.e. those carried
by the Kohathites (cf. Num 4:1–15).

Explanation

This section tells of the beginning of the journey. The cloud is taken
up, and the various tribal groups move, in the order suggested by Num 2.
The only significant addition to the information contained there is an indication in v 17 of the fact that Gershon and Merari carry the Tabernacle in a

position between the Judah and Reuben groups rather than at the center. In this latter position are the holiest things, carried by the Kohathites (v 21). These distinctions are not made in Num 2:17. The first stage of the journey takes the Israelites to the wilderness of Paran. For the author this journey may be a distant echo of his own experience, and a significant encouragement to others to engage in the return.

In effect the section mobilizes the arrangements for encampment as set out in Num 2:1–34. The clockwise order of movement—from east to north—may be an order of precedence. Since the mechanics of movement are now at the forefront of attention, the author offers further elaboration of Num 2:17. There must be a place for the ark to inhabit as soon as it arrives at the place of encampment, and so the Gershonites and Merarites are sent on ahead, between the Judah and Reuben groups (v 17). The ark itself, and the other objects for which the Kohathites are responsible, remain at the central position in the order of the march. The author in fact does not mention the ark by name, perhaps because of the Yahwistic tradition he intends to include in v 33. In characteristic fashion he builds on material previously provided, and for the same didactic purposes repeats in detail information already known—in this instance the names of the tribal leaders (cf. Num 1:5–15; 2:1–34).

In the whole section Num 9:15–10:28 the priestly author of the book is giving a massive haggadic interpretation of the Yahwistic material he is shortly to incorporate (Num 10:29–36). The bare information given there about the ark leading the way, and the liturgical verses which accompanied its movement, are substantially elaborated with cloud and trumpets and with the ordered advance of each tribal group, along with the sanctuary.

The section's overall importance lies in the fact that it marks the beginning of the second major phase of the book—the journey to the borders of the land. Its emphasis on ordered obedience is the dominant motif. The changing pattern of obedience/disobedience is the most striking feature of this part of the book.

Hobab and the Ark 10:29–36

Bibliography

Albright, W. F. "Jethro, Hobab and Reuel in Early Hebrew Tradition." *CBQ* 25 (1963) 1–11. Binns, L. Elliott. "Midianite Elements in Hebrew Religion." *JTS* 31 (1930) 337–54. Coats, G. W. "Moses in Midian." *JBL* 92 (1973) 3–10. Dus, J. "Herabfahrung Jahwes auf die Lade und Entziehung der Feuerwolke." *VT* 19 (1969) 290–311. ———. "Noch zum Brauch der Ladewanderung." *VT* 13 (1963) 126–32. (cf. Erratum— *VT* 13 (1963) 475). Fritz, V. *Israel in der Wüste*. Marburg: Elwert, 1970. Leiman, S. Z. "The Inverted *Nuns* at Numbers 10:35–36 and the Book of Eldad and Medad." *JBL* 93 (1974) 348–55. Levine, B. A. "More on the Inverted *Nuns* of Num 10:35–36." *JBL* 95 (1976) 122–24. Mitchell, T. C. "The Meaning of the Noun *HTN* in the Old Testament." *VT* 19 (1969) 93–112. Mazar, B. "The Sanctuary of Arad and the Family of Hobab the Kenite." *JNES* 24 (1965) 297–303. Seebass, H. "Zu Num X 35f." *VT* 14 (1964) 111–13.

Translation

[29] And Moses said to Hobab, son of Reuel the Midianite, the father-in-law [a] of Moses, "We are travelling to the place of which Yahweh said, 'I will give it to you.' Come with us, and we will do good to you. For Yahweh has promised good to Israel." [30] And he said to him, "I will not go. I will depart to my own land, and to my relatives." [31] And he said, "Do not leave us, I pray, because you know how we are to encamp in the wilderness, and you will be our eyes. [a] [32] And if you go with us it shall be that whatever good Yahweh does for us we will do the same for you."

[33] And they set out from the mount of Yahweh and went three days' journey. And the ark of the covenant of Yahweh went before them [a] (three days' journey) [a] to seek out a place for them to rest. [34a] And the cloud of Yahweh was over them by day, when they set out from the camp. [a]

[35] And whenever the ark set out Moses said, "Rise up, O Yahweh, and let your enemies be scattered; and let those who hate you flee from before you." [36] And when it rested he said, "Return, [a] O Yahweh, to the countless [b] thousands of Israel."

Notes

29.a. The pointing חֹתֵן is preferable (see *BHS*, N. H. Snaith, *Numbers*, 224).

31.a. *G* has πρεσβύτης "elder statesman"?

33.a.-a. There is some ground for omitting this clause (cf. *BHS*). It could be an accidental repetition (N. H. Snaith, *Numbers*, 225; J. Paterson, *Numbers*, 47). *S* has "one day's journey."

34.a.-a. In *G* the whole verse comes after v 36. MT is probably preferable.

36.a. Perhaps שָׁבָה should be read, corresponding with קוּמָה in v 35.

36.b. *BHS* makes various suggestions, including the root ברך "to bless." MT is unusual but not unintelligible, and is best accepted.

Form/Structure/Setting

There is general agreement that the author has incorporated for the first time some substantial material from the Yahwistic early narrative tradition (cf. e.g. J. Wellhausen, *Hexateuch*, 100–101; A. Kuenen, *Hexateuch*, 242; A. Dillmann, *Numeri*, 51–54; G. B. Gray, *Numbers*, 92–93). The usual grounds for this view are that the section parallels vv 11–28, and is not strictly consecutive with it. It describes in somewhat different terms from Num 9:15–23 and 10:11–28 how the journey was conducted. It is quite clear in 10:21 that the ark is in the middle of the column—in Num 4:15 it is evidently one of the holy things to be carried by Kohathites—though the author, perhaps because of the difficulty, refrains from mentioning it precisely. In v 33, by contrast, the ark leads the way. In v 12 the Israelites have moved from Sinai to the wilderness of Paran. In v 33 they are still at "the mount of Yahweh." The three-day journey (v 33) is typical of the Yahwist (cf. e.g. Gen 30:36; Exod 3:18; 5:3; 8:27; 15:22).

Some analysts have also sought grounds for distinguishing J and E within the section. There has been a general suspicion that it is substantially J. The father-in-law of Moses in E is Jethro (Exod 3:1; 4:18; 18:1), whereas here it is Hobab (cf. Exod 2:18). Gray (*Numbers*, 93) points out some finer and correspondingly weaker linguistic points of distinction. E elements have been detected by Dillmann and Kuenen, mainly in v 33. A priestly view of the cloud has been widely recognized in v 34 (cf. G. B. Gray, *Numbers*, 93; A. H. McNeile, *Numbers*, 56), thus making v 34 an insertion. The old poetical fragments in vv 35–36 are generally judged to have been part of the overall early narrative tradition (JE).

More recent analysts are less convinced of the effectiveness and value of fine documentary distinctions, though the presence of older material here is widely accepted. Interest tends to focus less on documentary distinctions and more on the history of the tradition. A common starting point is the question of the father-in-law of Moses. Assuming this to be an accurate translation of חֹתֵן, there are three named fathers-in-law. According to Judg 4:11 he is Hobab, in Exod 2:16 he is Reuel, while in Exod 3:1; 18:2 he is Jethro. Here in Num 10:29 he is either Hobab or Reuel, the text being not entirely clear. To complicate matters he is described as a Midianite here and in Exod 2:16, 18, but as a Kenite in Judg 4:11 and arguably Judg 1:16 (see *G*). M. Noth (*Numbers*, 77) detects harmonizing influences at work in this section with the Kenite/Hobab tradition brought into connection with the Midianite/Reuel tradition. Noth suspects that this harmonizing process would be later than J itself. Noth also follows a widely held view that originally the story must have told explicitly of Hobab's acceptance of the second invitation. Since in the present form of the story the ark leads the way (v 33) it was easy and natural to drop this element from the story. Noth finds a different view of the ark in vv 35–36, and hence another distinct unit of tradition. The issue here, in his view, is not leadership, but enemies and war.

H. Seebass ("Zu Num X 35f.") also argues for the replacement of Hobab by the ark, but H. Schmid (*Mose. Überlieferung und Geschichte* [Berlin: Töpelmann, 1968] 75–76) is unconvinced. He points out that the reference in Judg

4:11 is to the *sons* of Hobab, while Judg 1:16 makes it plain that they entered the land from the south not the east as did the Moses group. Schmid thinks that Hobab was the brother-in-law of Moses (cf. RV text) and following the analyses of the early tradition favoured by O. Eissfeldt (*Hexateuch-Synopse*) and G. Fohrer (*Introduction to the Old Testament*) he assigns Jethro to J and Reuel to L/N, reflecting Kenite and Midianite tradition. V. Fritz (*Israel*, 63–68) conducts a traditio-historical investigation, and concludes that originally vv 29–32 were an etiological narrative about the dwelling place of a small Midianite group of Hobabites, dating to pre-monarchic times. In his view Moses is drawn into the tradition at a pre-literary stage.

There are obviously many uncertainties in this kind of discussion, but a reasonably certain starting point is that the author of Numbers has here incorporated material from Yahwistic tradition. There can be no great certainty about the question of the father-in-law. Various hypotheses have been offered which if correct may ease the problem—e.g. that Reuel was a tribal name, that Hobab may be a brother-in-law (as in RV text of Judg 4:11), or that the word חֹתֵן should be rendered more loosely as "relative by marriage." Nevertheless it may be best to assume that the difficulties arise from the redaction of variant traditions. Presumably the Yahwistic author had clarified the matter to his own satisfaction. So "the priest of Midian" (Exod 2:16) he identifies as Jethro (Exod 3:1; 18:1). Reuel may already have been present in Exod 2:18, in which case he must have assumed that Reuel and Jethro were one and the same, but preferred the Jethro tradition to dominate. If Reuel in Exod 2:18 is a later accretion—and there is no strong reason for supposing this—there is no evidence for believing it to be a very late gloss. For the Yahwist Hobab in Num 10:29–32 may simply have been "the Kenite." He is this in Judg 4:11, and the Yahwist may well have wished to draw in ancient witness to Kenite links with Israel at the settlement. The real problem confronts the priestly author of Numbers. He was familiar with the wide range of literary tradition in Exodus and Judges, and in particular with the tradition of Hobab's relationship by marriage to Moses in the latter. He therefore makes the link in Num 10:29. Hobab is thus חֹתֵן to Moses, meaning perhaps a "relative by marriage." Though there is an ambiguity in Num 10:29 it seems most likely that Hobab not Reuel is חֹתֵן in this verse. The author clarifies the relationship by making Hobab son of the Reuel of Exod 2:18 rather than the Jethro of Exod 3:1. This may have been because Jethro did not in fact accompany the Israelites (Exod 18:27).

The Yahwistic author does not give Hobab's response to the second invitation, but from v 33a it must be assumed that he accompanied the people. There is no very serious conflict between v 31 and v 33. The former contains the tradition (J or E) available to the Yahwistic author, while the latter indicates his own concern to stress that this was divine and not merely human guidance. In vv 35–36 he goes on to include traditional liturgical material associated with the ark in the processions of the cult. This in turn may well have deeper roots in the traditions of the Yahweh war. In incorporating the material here the Yahwist gives liturgical material even deeper roots in the wilderness period.

Comment

29. On "Hobab" and "Reuel" see discussion under *Form/Structure/Setting*.
29. "The place of which Yahweh said, I will give it to you." This clause links the section with the Yahwist's work in Exod 33:1. According to J. De Vaulx (*Nombres,* 145) the discussion between Moses and Hobab probably had to do with a non-aggression pact.
30. For discussion of the location of Sinai see *Comment* on Num 1:1. It is wrong to assume from Hobab's words that the traditional location is wrong, as does A. H. McNeile (*Numbers,* 55). Hobab is not saying that his destination (Midian) lies in a different direction, but that he does not intend to settle where Israel does.
31. לְעֵינָיִם "our eyes" (cf. Job 29:15). This is apparently a reference to Hobab's greater familiarity with the conditions of desert existence.
33. הַר יהוה "the mount of Yahweh," an unusual expression in the Pentateuch for the holy mountain, but commonly used in cultic texts for Zion. In the Pentateuch "Sinai" (J/P) and "Horeb" (E/D) are the more usual terms.
33. וַאֲרוֹן בְּרִית־יהוה "and the ark of the covenant of Yahweh." This description of the ark is generally recognized as Deuteronomic (cf. Deut 10:8; 31:9, 25; Josh 4:7, 18; 6:8; cf. Num 14:44). Links of this kind are not surprising if the Yahwistic author does indeed belong to the seventh century (see *Introduction*).
35. The liturgical words are those of Ps 68:1 (cf. Ps 132:8 and Judg 5:31 for ancient links with war; see *Form/Structure/Setting*). For "arise" as a battle cry cf. Deut 19:11; Ps 27:3. For the use of the ark in battle cf. 1 Sam 4:1–10; 2 Sam 11:11.
36. The poetry is probably liturgical, with roots in earlier battle songs. In this case there are no extant cultic texts with a comparable form of words. Whether the ark "rests" or "returns" is unclear. Variable pointing would give either sense.

Explanation

This section tells how Hobab, a relative of Moses by marriage, accepts the invitation of Moses to join Israel in the settlement. The section goes on to tell how the ark leads the way, and determines the place where Israel is to rest. The section concludes with some liturgical material associated with the movement of the ark.

For the first time the author of Numbers has incorporated an element from the earlier Yahwistic tradition. This particular section is the nucleus of tradition which he has so extensively elaborated in Num 9:15–10:28. One of the Yahwistic author's great interests is the theme of land possession (Gen 12:1; Exod 33:1), and it emerges here in v 29. His is arguably a late preexilic work of the seventh century (see *Introduction*), probably from Josianic times, and providing in general a great etiology of landed Israel. The preceding extant section is Exod 34:1–28 with its description of the renewal of the covenant. There must have been intervening material of some kind, describing perhaps the first contact with Hobab, and the origin of the ark. The Yahwistic author's interest in Hobab the Kenite stems in part from his interest in the land and the facts of settlement. The story he provides (vv 29–33) explains the close relationship between Israel and the Kenites (cf. Judg 1:16; 4:11; 1 Sam 15:6). As the Yahwistic author understands it, Hobab, after an initial refusal, accompanies Moses and the Israelites on the journey. There is probably some kind of treaty or alliance. Hobab's special experience of the desert is recognized and appreciated, but the Yahwistic author is anxious to indicate that it was God, represented by the ark, who led Israel (v 33), and not man alone. He includes liturgical material from the Temple—texts which probably had their origin in battle songs, but which in the course of time had become associated with the festal processions involving the ark (vv 35–36).

The priestly author of Numbers readily accepts this material as worthy of preservation. It is after all the text he has chosen to elaborate in Num 9:15–10:28. The liturgical material fitted in particularly well with his concept of the journey to Canaan as a liturgical procession, with the ark and each of the tribes in its proper place. The text also gives him an opportunity to indicate, as Judg 4:11 had done, that Hobab was indeed related by marriage to Moses. Since these relationships had been established prior to the settlement they could not be judged an apostate association with the people of the land. The priestly author also wishes to align the tradition of leadership by the ark in v 33, which he has no wish to dispute, with the priestly conception he had set out in Num 9:15–23, and so he includes v 34.

Overall the priestly author points to the ordered obedience of the people of God as they begin the march. The journey has something of a liturgical celebration about it as the procession sets forward, an impression heightened by the inclusion of the Yahwistic material in vv 35–36. Lines of division between the obedience of faith and the life of worship are scarcely recognized by the priestly author. Worship and practical obedience merge into a single activity of faith.

Disaffection at Taberah (11:1-3)

Bibliography

Blank, S. H. "Men against God—The Promethean Element in Biblical Prayer." *JBL* 72 (1953) 1–14. ———. "Some Observations concerning Biblical Prayer." *HUCA* 32 (1961) 75–90. **Brueggemann, W.** "From Hurt to Joy, from Death to Life." *Int* 28 (1974) 3–19. **Buis, P.** "Les Conflits entre Moise et Israël dans Exode et Nombres." *VT* 28 (1978) 257–70. **Childs, B. S.** "The Etiological Tale Re-examined." *VT* 24 (1974) 387–97. **Coats, G. W.** *Rebellion in the Wilderness.* Nashville: Abingdon, 1968. **Culley, R. C.** *Studies in the Structure of Hebrew Narrative.* Philadelphia: Fortress, 1976. **DeVries, S. J.** "The Origin of the Murmuring Tradition." *JBL* 87 (1968) 51–58. **Engnell, I.** "The Wilderness Wandering." *Critical Essays on the Old Testament.* London: SPCK, 1970, 207–14. **Fichtner, J.** "Die etymologische Ätiologie in den Namengebungen der geschichtlichen Bücher des Alten Testament." *VT* 6 (1956) 372–96. **Fritz, V.** *Israel in der Wüste.* Marburg: Elwert, 1970. **Golka, F. W.** "The Aetiologies in the Old Testament." *VT* 26 (1976) 410–28; *VT* 27 (1977) 36–47. **Long, B. O.** *The Problem of Etiological Narrative in the Old Testament.* BZAW 108. Berlin: Töpelmann, 1968. **Seebass, H.** "Num. XI, XII und die Hypothese des Jahwisten." *VT* 28 (1978) 214–23. **Thomas, D. R.** "Some Notes on the Old Testament Attitude to Prayer." *SJT* 9 (1956) 422–29. **Tunyogi, A. C.** "The Rebellions of Israel." *JBL* 81 (1962) 385–90.

Translation

¹ *And the people complained in the hearing of* [a] *Yahweh. And Yahweh heard it, and his anger was kindled. And the fire of Yahweh burned among them, and consumed some at the extremities of the camp.* ² *And the people cried to Moses and Moses prayed to Yahweh. And the fire abated.* ³ *And the name of that place was Taberah, for there the fire of Yahweh burned among them.*

Notes

1.a. Many mss read בְּעֵינֵי "in the eyes of" (cf. v 10), but MT is probably to be preferred (cf. v 18).

Form/Structure/Setting

Analysts are in general agreement that the section belongs to JE. Israel is depicted as עַם rather than עֵדַת "congregation" or קָהָל "assembly" as in P. Those analysts who assign it to J tend to be the ones who query the independent existence of E, or who require very firm indications of E's presence (e.g. H. Holzinger, *Numeri* [HKAT 4; Tübingen: Mohr, 1900] 42–43; B. Baentsch, *Exodus-Leviticus-Numeri* [HKAT 1 /2; Göttingen: Vandenhoeck & Ruprecht, 1904] 504; H. Gressmann, *Mose und seine Zeit* [Göttingen; Vandenhoeck & Ruprecht, 1913] 124; W. Rudolph, *Der 'Elohist' von Exodus bis Josua* [BZAW 68; Berlin: Töpelmann, 1938] 63; M. Noth, *Numbers,* 83–84; G. W.

Coats, *Rebellion*, 124–25; V. Fritz, *Israel*, 16–17). Most other analysts prefer E, pointing particularly to the root פלל "to pray," "to intercede." This is rare in the Pentateuch at large, but occurs twice in a Genesis text readily identifiable as E (Gen 20:7, 17; cf. Num 21:7; Deut 9:20, 26). This suggests that the role of Moses, like that of Abraham, is prophetic, and the point tells against the views of O. Eissfeldt (*Hexateuch*, 161) and G. Fohrer (*Introduction*, 159–65) that the material is lay or nomadic. A. W. Jenks (*The Elohist and North Israelite Traditions* [Missoula: Scholars, 1977]) provides a modern discussion of the Elohistic stratum, and believes this section is part of it. He makes a reasonable case for the distinctiveness and common origin of some of the material he designates as "Elohistic," but it is still far from clear that the narratives in question are part of an independent parallel tradition rather than accretions, and there can be no great certainty about the milieu from which they come.

The most striking differences between this story and those in Exodus where Israel complains (cf. Exod 14:11–12; 15:24; 16:2–3; 17:2–3) have to do with structure and content. The divine intervention comes much earlier in the development of this story, and brings punishment rather than aid. The role of Moses changes accordingly. Instead of being the leader who appeals for aid in situations of deprivation and danger he has become the great intercessor, averting divine wrath, and saving Israel, not from some external crisis, but from herself. It seems reasonable to suggest that this adaptation of the murmuring tradition is traceable to the Yahwistic author himself. The etiological element is a possible indication of this. The concern to fix the wilderness traditions into an itinerary is likely from a traditio-historical perspective to be later rather than earlier. The Massah/Meribah etiologies in Exod 17:1–7 are fairly loosely connected with the tradition of water from the rock in vv 3–6, and could likewise be traced to the Yahwist. The literary form of the etiology in Num 11:3 is close to that in Exod 17:7.

The etiological character of the story as a whole is widely recognized by modern commentators (e.g. M. Noth, *Numbers*, 83–84; G. W. Coats, *Rebellion*, 124–27; V. Fritz, *Israel*, 68–70; B. O. Long, *Etiological Narrative*, 42–43). It is difficult however to find a significant pre-history for the tradition. The story could in fact be a literary construction on the part of the Yahwist. H. Cazelles ("Review of V. Fritz, *Israel in der Wüste*," *VT* 21 [1971] 506–14) suggests that the theme of divine fire has some cultic connection with the "ʾwn" ritual (1 Sam 15:23; Hos 10:8). The story in 2 Kgs 1:10, 12, 14 suggests that it may have been current in northern prophetic circles. M. Noth (*Pentateuchal Traditions*, 123) draws attention to an Arabic root baʿr(a) "animal dung," but the relevance of this is to the present story is far from obvious. At most these various observations tell only of possible influences. There is little to suggest that the story is other than literary in its essential origin. J. de Vaulx (*Nombres*, 148–55) seeks to link the story much more closely with the tradition in Num 11:4–35 (and in particular vv 4a, 5, 18, 20, 33b), arguing that vv 1–3 are the primitive part of the story. This is unlikely. The schematic character of vv 1–3 is likely to be a sign not of antiquity, but rather the reverse. The "ear of Yahweh" is not an obviously primitive anthropomorphism (cf. Num

14:28; 2 Chr 6:40; Neh 1:6, 11; Dan 9:18 for late texts in which it occurs). The force-like character of divine wrath is as evident in later priestly texts (e.g. Num 17:11) as in earlier tradition. In general it seems best to treat vv 1–3 and vv 4–35 as separate traditions, though the priestly author in omitting Taberah in Num 33:16 may have treated them as one.

The background against which the theme of Israel's disaffection must be understood has been widely discussed, but without any general measure of agreement. M. L. Newman (*The People of the Covenant* [London: Carey Kingsgate, 1965] 72–101) argues for a clash at Kadesh between the Rachel tribes and Kenite Yahwists (including Judah). H. Schmid (*Mose*, 39–48) also argues for tensions between different Israelite groups prior to the settlement. These arguments are difficult to sustain in detail, but it is feasible that access to resources (e.g. land and water) and the viability of settlement were divisive factors in early tribal experience. Whether these "facts" had much influence on the disaffection theme in the Pentateuch is more doubtful. G. W. Coats (*Rebellion*, 221–24, 251) concludes that the murmuring motif arises from within the Jerusalem cult as anti-northern polemic, while V. Fritz (*Israel*, 122) sees it as a warning to the newly formed state under David and Solomon that rebellion against Yahweh would threaten its unity and independence. A. C. Tunyogi ("Rebellions") argues that disaffection is the explanation offered by northern Yahwists, from Elijah onwards, of Israel's disloyalty in the land. She had been disloyal from earliest times. For a thorough discussion of these and other suggestions see P. J. Budd, *Tales of Disaffection—a Pentateuchal Motif Examined and Assessed* (Diss. Bristol University, 1977) 342–77. Since the disaffection theme is inclined to focus on the means and origins of economic and political security it is possible that disaffection represents the attitudes of those who sought security in foreign alliances. These issues had been crucial policy matters in Hezekiah's time (cf. e.g. Isa 28:15; 30:1–5; 31:1–3), and returned to the surface in the early years of Josiah's reign when the Yahwistic author was probably at work.

Comment

1. כְּמִתְאֹנְנִים רַע "complained." The root אנן is rare, and occurs only here and in Lam 3:39 where its meaning is equally uncertain. There are similar words in a number of a cognate languages, and the Accadian *unninu* "to sigh" could be the most relevant. The root is rendered "to complain" or "to murmur" by BDB, and "to indulge in complaints" by KB. G evidently understood the word in these general terms using γογγίζων, the word it consistently used to translate לון "to murmur." N. H. Snaith (*Numbers*, 226) wonders whether the verb is really אנה "to seek a pretext" (cf. 2 Kgs 5:7), but this idea is based on the assumptions that vv 1–3 and vv 4–35 were closely connected from the outset, that the people already have the flesh (the flocks and herds which accompany them), and that therefore the request arises, not from need, but from a concern to oppose Moses and Yahweh. These assumptions are doubtful, and it is best to think of some form of "complaint." The word may have some technical significance now lost associ-

ated with communal lamentation. The root רַע "evil" has been emended by Snaith (*Numbers*, 226) to רָעָב "hunger," thus making it a deprivation story, but textual warrant is lacking. רַע could be rendered "misfortune" (RSV) (its opposite טוֹב can mean "good fortune"; cf. e.g. 1 Kgs 22:8, Job 2:10).

1. אֵשׁ יהוה "the fire of Yahweh." In general terms this denotes the divine presence (cf. Exod 3:2; 19:18; Lev 10:2; Num 16:35; 1 Kgs 18:38; 2 Kgs 1:10, 12; Isa 33:14; Mal 3:2; Job 1:16). The notion of a fire that "devours" (אָכַל) is taken up by P in Exod 24:17.

2. וַיִּתְפַּלֵּל "and he prayed." The word is used particularly when divine wrath has to be averted (cf. Gen 20:7, 17; Deut 9:20, 26).

3. The site of Taberah is unknown.

Explanation

This story tells of an incident located at Taberah in which the people provoke Yahweh's anger by their complaints. Divine fire burns at the extremities of the camp, and only the intercession of Moses averts a major disaster.

The story is the continuation of the Yahwist's account of Israel's journey from Sinai to the land. The site of Taberah is unknown, but its name—"burning"—evidently suggested to the author a site for a story of disaffection. The simple schematic structure of the story, and its absence from cultic texts dealing with the wilderness period, suggests that it is a literary construct by the author himself. The celebration in song of Yahweh's mighty acts in the wilderness had already led to the growth of a prose tradition as exemplified in such stories as "water from the rock" (Exod 17:3–6). The expression of Israel's fear and doubt may reflect the attitude of those who sought security in foreign alliances. In any event it helps to accentuate the magnitude of Yahweh's mercy.

The Yahwist takes up the theme of fear and doubt, and makes a significant development in the disaffection theme. He provides an etiology for water from the rock, possibly both Meribah and Massah, thereby providing new dimensions to the nature of disaffection. He also makes disaffection itself the problem. In the various stories of complaint in Exod 14–17 the problems are real and external, involving genuine dangers of death. Here, however, the problem is internal faithlessness. It may also be that since God has revealed himself in a new way at Sinai such fears and doubts are no longer warranted. The Yahwist has already provided a serious example of apostasy (Exod 32:1–6) in the incident concerning the golden calf. Despite the renewal of the covenant in Exod 34 the danger persists. The role of Moses in this new situation becomes ever more crucial. As Exod 32 itself makes clear Moses is the one who stands between Israel and destruction. Here too his intercession is critical in the turning aside of divine wrath.

Pre-exilic Judaeans would be inclined to see the continuation of the Mosaic role and authority in the Judaean king (cf. J. R. Porter, *Moses and Monarchy. A Study in the Biblical Tradition of Moses.* Oxford: OUP, 1963). The cruciality of Moses and his unwavering faithfulness to the policy of independence express a faith in the duty of the Davidic king, Josiah for the Yahwist, to lead the nation in an independent direction, and to ensure its well being. The story mentions no specific grievance, and we must assume that the people's complaint concerns the general hardships of desert life. The policy of independence may seem to have led to hardship, but complaint is an expression of faithlessness, and incurs divine judgment.

The Gift of Quail at Kibroth-hattaavah (11:4–35)

Bibliography

Bodenheimer, F. W. "The Manna of Sinai." *BA* 10 (1947) 1–6. **Haran, M.** "From Early to Classical Prophecy: Continuity and Change." *VT* 27 (1977) 385–97. **Leiman, S. Z.** "The Inverted *Nuns* at Numbers 10:35–36 and the Book of Eldad and Medad." *JBL* 93 (1974) 348–55. **Malina, B. J.** *The Palestinian Manna Tradition.* Leiden: Brill, 1968. **Parker, S. B.** "Possession, Trance and Prophecy in Pre-Exilic Israel." *VT* 28 (1978) 271–85. **Rabe, V. W.** "The Origins of Prophecy." *BASOR* 221 (1976) 125–28. **Ruppert, L.** "Das Motiv der Versuchung durch Gott in vordeuteronomischer Tradition." *VT* 22 (1972) 55–63. **Seebass, H.** "Num. XI, XII und die Hypothese des Jahwisten." *VT* 28 (1978) 214–23. **Walters, S. D.** "Prophecy in Mari and Israel." *JBL* 89 (1970) 78–81. **Wilson, R. R.** "Early Israelite Prophecy." *Int* 32 (1978) 3–16. On disaffection in the wilderness see Num 11:1–3 (*Bibliography*). On the Tent of Meeting see Num 7:89–8:4 (*Bibliography*).

Translation

⁴ And the rabble among them had an inordinate craving. And the people of Israel sat down,ᵃ and said, "Who shall give us flesh to eat?." ⁵ We remember the fish we ate in Egypt for nothing, cucumbers, and watermelons, leeks and onions and garlic. ⁶ But now our appetite is taken away, and there is nothing at all but this manna to look at.

⁷ The manna looked like coriander seed, and had the appearance of bdellium. ⁸ The people went about collecting it, and ground it in mills or beat it in mortars, and boiled it in pots, and made cakes from it. Its taste was like that of cakes baked with oil. ⁹ When the dew fell upon the camp in the night, the manna fell with it.

¹⁰ Moses heard the people weeping, all of them in their families, each man at the door of his tent. And the anger of Yahweh blazed hotly, and Moses was troubled. ¹¹ And Moses said to Yahweh, "Why have you done ill to your servant? And why have I not found ᵃ favor in your sight, that you lay on me the burden of all this people? ¹² Did I conceive all this people? Have I brought them into the world, so that you should say to me 'Carry them in your bosom like a nurse with her baby to ᵃ the land you promised on oath to their fathers?' ¹³ Where am I to get meat to give to all this people? For they weep before me and say, 'Give us meat that we may eat.' ¹⁴ I am not able to carry all this people alone. The burden is too heavy for me. ¹⁵ If this is what you want me to do ᵃ then kill me at once if I find favor in your sight, that I may not see my wretchedness."

¹⁶ And Yahweh said to Moses, "Assemble seventy men for me from the elders of Israel, men known to you as elders and officers over them, and bring them to the Tent of Meeting, and there let them take their stand with you. ¹⁷ And I will come down and talk with you there. And I will share ᵃ some of the spirit which is upon you with them. And they shall bear the burden of the people with you, that you may not bear it yourself alone. ¹⁸ And say to the people, "Sanctify yourselves for tomorrow, and you shall eat meat, for you have wept in the hearing of Yahweh, saying, 'Who

will give us meat to eat? For it was well with us in Egypt.' Therefore Yahweh will give you meat, and you shall eat. **19** *You shall not eat one day, or two days, or five days, or ten days, or twenty days,* **20** *but for a whole month, until it comes out at your nostrils* ᵃ *and becomes loathsome to you,* ᵃ *because you have rejected Yahweh who is among you, and have wept before him, saying, 'Why did we come forth out of Egypt?' "* **21** *But Moses said, "The people among whom I am number six hundred thousand on foot, and you have said, 'I will give them meat that they may eat a whole month.'* **22** *Are there sufficient flocks and herds to be slaughtered for them? Are there enough fish in the sea to be caught for them?"* **23** *And Yahweh said to Moses, "Is Yahweh's hand shortened? Now* ᵃ *you shall see whether my word will come true for you or not."*

24 *And Moses went out* ᵃ *and told the people the words of Yahweh. And he gathered seventy men from the elders of the people, and placed them round about the Tent.* **25** *And Yahweh came down in the cloud and spoke to him, and shared* ᵃ *the spirit that was upon him with the seventy elders. And when the spirit rested upon them they prophesied. But they did so no more.* ᵇ

26 *And two men remained in the camp, one named Eldad, and the other Medad,* ᵃ *and the spirit rested upon them. They were among those registered, but they had not gone out to the Tent, and so they prophesied in the camp.* **27** *And a young man ran and told Moses, "Eldad and Medad are prophesying in the camp."* **28** *And Joshua the son of Nun, the minister of Moses, one of his chosen men,* ᵃ *said, "My lord Moses, forbid them."* **29** *But Moses said to him, "Are you jealous for my sake? Would that all Yahweh's people were prophets, and that Yahweh would put his spirit upon them."* **30** *And Moses and the elders of Israel returned to the camp.*

31 *And a wind from Yahweh sprang up, and it brought* ᵃ *quail from the sea, and let them fall beside the camp, about a day's journey on both sides, round about the camp, and about two cubits above the face of the earth.* **32** *And the people rose all that day, and all night, and all the next day, and gathered the quail. He who gathered least gathered ten homers. And they spread them out* ᵃ *for themselves all around the camp.* **33** *While the meat was yet between their teeth, before it was bitten,* ᵃ *the anger of Yahweh was kindled against the people. And Yahweh smote the people with a great plague.* **34** *Therefore the name of that place was called Kibroth-hattaavah, because there they buried the people who had the inordinate craving.* **35** *From Kibroth-hattaavah the people travelled to Hazeroth, and they remained at Hazeroth.*

Notes

4.a. This is to read וַיֵּשְׁבוּ as in *G* and Vg rather than וַיָּשֻׁבוּ as in MT. If MT is preferred (cf. e.g. J. Paterson, *Numbers*, 48) the idea of "weeping again" must be involved. *G* is preferred by P. Beirne ("A Note on Numbers 11:4," *Bib* 44 [1963] 201–03). There is also communal weeping in Judg 20:23, 26, and it is interesting to note that in Judg 20:26; 21:2 MT reads "sat down." A. H. McNeile (*Numbers*, 59) is thus not necessarily correct in claiming that *G* and Vg "escape the difficulty."

11.a. Sam includes the quiescent *aleph*.

12.a. אֶל "to" is preferable (Sam, *G, Syr, Tg.*ᴶ).

15.a. This pointing is unusual (cf. GKC § 32g. It may be better to emend the text to הָעֹשֶׂה or אַתְּ הָעֹשָׂה (*BHS*).

17.a. The root אָצַל means "to share" (v 25; Gen 27:36; Ezek 42:6; Eccl 2:10). *G* understands the text to mean "take from" (RSV), possibly reading Sam's וְהִצַּלְתִּי (cf. Gen 31:9, 16; Hos 2.11). G. B. Gray (*Numbers*, 112) thinks הַצִּיל to be too violent for the context.

20.a.-a. J. Paterson (*Numbers*, 48) takes the clause to be a gloss, noting particularly the Aramaic form לְזָאנ (cf. GKC § 113r). Gray (Numbers, 113) raises the possibility of a copyist's error for הרז.

23.a. Sam has the personal pronoun אתה here.

24.a. *BHS* proposes וַיֵּב־א here, but the support is not strong.

25.a. Probably an imperfect *qal* rather than *hiphil* (cf. GKC § 68f).

25.b. on the use of יסף with a negative to express non-recurrence of an action see GKC § 120d.²

26.a. The form "Modad" may be original (Sam, *G*).

28.a. A *hapax legomenon*. Syr and *Tg.* understand as "from his youth" (cf. RV mg.). Sam and *G* take it to come from בחר, and render it "one of his chosen."

31.a. The *Hiphil* וַיָּגָז seems to be required here.

32.a. Some *G* mss read שָׁחַט "to slaughter" instead of שָׁטַח, probably mistakenly.

33.a. *G*, Vg, *Tg⁰* understand this to mean "ran short," a translation preferred by Gray (*Numbers*, 118).

Form/Structure/Setting

There are three distinguishable "events" within this section—the sending of quail in response to Israel's complaints, the appointment of seventy elders to assist Moses in the responsibilities of leadership, and the "unofficial" prophetic ministry of Eldad and Medad.

Analysts are agreed that there is no priestly material here, and the whole can be attributed to the Yahwist. Israel is regularly depicted as "the people," and the "Tent of Meeting" (vv 16, 24–25, 30) is evidently outside the camp (as in Exod 33:7–11). Older analysts were inclined to draw into the discussion what are arguably less decisive linguistic data. More difficult to determine is the relationship between the various elements within the story. Since the Eldad/Medad incident is fairly closely connected with the story of the seventy elders, and since the quail tradition is essentially self-contained it seems reasonable to make an initial distinction between vv 4–10, 13, 18–23, 31–35 (quail) and vv 11–12, 14–17, 24–30 (elders and prophets).

Quail

This story has some very obvious similarities with two Yahwistic stories in Exodus—the tradition of bitter water at Marah (Exod 15:22–26), and the smiting of the rock at Massah/Meribah (Exod 17:1–7). In all three there are complaints about physical need, a Mosaic appeal to Yahweh, and a divine response. The essential content of the story is found in vv 4b–6, 10, 13, 31, 33. There is very general agreement among analysts that this material must be attributed to J. The attempt of H. Cazelles ("Review of V. Fritz. *Israel in der Wüste." VT* 21 [1971] 506–14) to find E in vv 4–9 is based on his denial of vv 4a, 7–9 to J. In fact he has nothing positive to offer in favor of E, and the crucial verses as far as the story is concerned are in any event vv 4b–6.

As in Exod 17:1, 7 the etiology (in vv 4a, 34) is very loosely linked to the essential story. The offenders are "the rabble" rather than "the people of Israel" (v 4b). Their offense is that they had an "inordinate craving," not that they "wept." The etiology evidently depends on the story since it builds on the notion of a plague in v 33 by explaining how those who craved came to be buried. This localization of the story is attributable to the Yahwist, and likewise the itinerary of v 35.

The dialogue in vv 18–23 is unusual in these stories of deprivation, and may well be a further additional element. The punishment threatened in vv 19–20 does not correspond precisely with that administered in v 33. The allusion to "consecration" on the morrow (v 18) is not taken up in the narrative of v 31, where some indication of a response to the command would naturally be expected. The reference to "consecration" is reminiscent of a few other texts attributable to the Yahwist (Exod 19:10; Josh 3:5; 7:13). The use of מאס (v 20) to express "rejection" is rare in the Pentateuch, occurring elsewhere only in P (Lev 26:15, 43–44; Num 14:31), and there is some distinctive interest in the divine word (v 23 cf. Isa 50:2; 59:1). There are no overwhelming indications of deuteronomistic or priestly influence in the section, and it is probably best to attribute it to the Yahwist.

The parenthetical description of manna (vv 7–9) is difficult to assign. H. Cazelles ("Review") and O. Eissfeldt (*Hexateuch*, 161–64) favor E, and W. O. E. Oesterley and T. H. Robinson (*An Introduction to the Books of the Old Testament* [London: SPCK, 1961] 38) prefer P, but these are very much minority views. The description might conceivably come from the author of Numbers, but it may well come from the Yahwist's account.

If this analysis is broadly correct then the Yahwist was evidently taken up a story about the provision of quail and elaborated it. It remains very difficult to decide whether the negative view of quail as punishment was already integral to the story, or whether the Yahwist himself has developed the story in this particular way, perhaps with a view to making the link with the graves of craving in the etiology. In any event it seems reasonably certain that originally the quail theme was celebrated positively in worship (Pss 78:26–28; 105:40). This is in opposition to the view held by C. Barth ("Zur Bedeutung der Wüstentradition," [VTS 15: 1966] 14–23) and B. S. Childs (*Exodus* [London: SCM, 1974] 254–64). It is scarcely credible that these positive assertions in the psalms could ever have been made if the negative view of quail was traditio-historically original. A positive view of the wilderness in general is preserved in Hos 2:13; Jer 2:2–3, and of quail in particular in the essentially priestly account of quail and manna in Exod 16. Quail like manna reflect a familiarity with desert life (see *Comment*) and belong arguably with an old cultic "march from Sinai" theme (cf. Judg 5:4–5; Ps 68:8–10; Deut 33:2). The process by which the hexateuchal history of Israel was forged is not entirely clear, but its ultimate roots probably lie in the celebrations of the worshipping community.

M. Noth (*Pentateuchal Traditions*, 122–45) took the view that the motif of disaffection in the wilderness had its roots in this story, and in the Kibroth-hattaavah etiology in particular, and that it spread from here to the tradition as a whole. His method was to search for the story or stories in which the motif was arguably the creative nucleus, and therefore indispensable. In his view only this story fulfills the requirements. The difficulties of this view have been thoroughly exposed by G. W. Coats (*Rebellion*, 100–15). Our argument suggests that the etiology is in any case a loose accretion to the story.

Coats (*Rebellion*, 163–68) suggests that the story of Dathan and Abiram in Num 16 has a number of distinctive features which could make it the point of departure for the spread of murmuring, while S. J. DeVries (*JBL* 87 [1968] 51–58) looks to the traditions of Num 13–14. For him murmuring is a "theological reflex" arising from the need to square a tradition of conquest from the south with one of conquest from the east. As Childs points out (*Exodus*, 257), this does not adequately explain the content of murmuring with its repeated emphasis on the Exodus. The question that needs to be raised in this discussion is whether the whole theory of "spread" from one tradition to the whole is justified. The radical development of the tradition in terms of disaffection is more likely to be a literary phenomenon inspired by other motives (see further *Explanation*, and *Explanation* on Num 11:1–3).

Elders and Prophets

This material is evidently an accretion to the basic story about the giving of quail. Its content has been widely recognized as Elohistic (A. Kuenen, *Hexateuch*, 158; B. Baentsch, *Numeri*, 276–77, 504; H. Holzinger, *Numeri*, 42; O. Eissfeldt, *Hexateuch*, 39, 57; G. Beer, *Numeri*, 156–57; G. Fohrer, *Introduction*, 167; A. W. Jenks, *The Elohist*, 54–55). The main arguments focus on the interest in prophecy (cf. Gen 20:7) and the conviction that there is a distinct E view of revelation, contrasting with J's, and which can be found here and in Exod 33:7–11. It seems fair to suggest that these arguments depend on preconceived views of the nature and purpose of E. The concentration on prophecy can scarcely be decisive when v 23 (part of the quail story) also reveals some such interest in its stress on the divine word.

A number of analysts have suspected that the material is independent of J and E, or is the work of the JE redactor (e.g. J. Wellhausen, *Hexateuch*, 101–03; G. B. Gray, *Numbers*, 98–99; H. Gressman, *Mose*, 240 n.3; M. Noth, *Numbers*, 83; V. Fritz, *Israel*, 17; J. Sturdy, *Numbers*, 83–84; W. Rudolph, *Der "Elohist,"* 55). The Elohistic character of the story in Exod 18 makes it unlikely that this somewhat similar story comes from the same background. It seems best to associate this and the material in Exod 33:7–11 with the Yahwist as we have conceived him. It may be that the material came to him with some distinctive features, but it would be hard to identify it as a significant parallel source to J and E. In any event the story evidently builds on the idea of disaffection in the quail tradition, and to that extent must be later rather than earlier. The Yahwist finds in this idea of faithless weeping an opportunity to explore the theme of authority in the community. In vv 11–12, 14–15 we have the welding which locks the material about elders and prophets into v 13, which is in any event a piece from the Yahwist about quail.

M. Noth (*Numbers*, 90) suggests that behind the stories are "prophets" or "prophetic groups" battling for recognition, and using the story of elders to give their spirit-authority some literary validity. Eldad and Medad are probably fictitious and forward the claims of spirit prophecy in general. J. de Vaulx (*Nombres*, 155) argues that the pair safeguard the independence of "prophecy" over against more institutional forms of authority. Their authority is challenged by Joshua, but approved by Moses. In both components—the empowering of the elders and the activity of Eldad and Medad—there is evidently a concern that possession of the spirit should play its part in the professional institutions, represented by the elders, and in the charisma of men freely raised up by God to declare his word (see further *Explanation*).

Comment

4. הָאסַפְסֻף "the rabble." The word occurs only here, and might mean literally "a gathering of people," from אסף "to collect." Some commentators associate this group with the "mixed multitude" of Exod 12:38 (e.g. A. Dillmann, *Numeri*, 56; G. B. Gray, *Numbers*, 102). The root, however, is different, and there is no clear warrant for the assumption. There may be a degree of contempt in the word—hence possibly "riff-raff" or "rabble"—those governed not by powers of discrimination and insight, but by sensual appetite.

4. הִתְאַוּוּ תַּאֲוָה "had an inordinate craving." The root אוה means "to desire." The Piel stem generally denotes ordinary wishes which may be perfectly legitimate (cf. e.g. Josh 23:13; Ps 132:13–14). The Hithpael seems stronger, but is not necessarily sinful (cf. e.g. Deut 18:6). Where it is so, as it must be here, the idea seems to be of an undiscriminating passion controlled only by the senses (cf. Deut 5:21; Jer 2:24).

4. The fact that they had flocks and herds (Exod 12:32, 38; 17:3; 19:13; 34:3) is an indication that these stories grew up independently, and that their incorporation into the history of Israel belongs to a later stage in the history of the literature. On the use of the interrogative clause "who will give us flesh to eat?" see GKC § 476; B. Jongeling, "L'expression *my ytn* dans l'ancien Testament," *VT* 24 (1974) 32–40.

5. The fruit, fish and vegetables mentioned here reflect a genuine familiarity with Egyptian diet. חָצִיר "leeks" can mean green vegetables generally, but "leeks" appears to be supported by *G* and Vg.

6. וְעַתָּה "and now." On this expression see H. Brongers, "Bemerkungen zum Gebrauch des adverbialen *we ʿattah* im Alten Testament," *VT* 15 (1965) 289–99.

6. נַפְשֵׁנוּ "our appetite," literally "our life." יְבֵשָׁה means literally "is dried up," and M. Noth (*Numbers*, 86) reads נֶפֶשׁ as "throat." The whole expression is best taken to mean "to take away the appetite" (cf. A. Dillmann, *Numeri*, 57; N. H. Snaith, *Numbers*, 227). In theory this could be a complaint that the manna is inadequate to meet their needs, though the author obviously dissents from this view. For him this is culpable discontent arising from what is judged to be a monotonous diet.

7–9. On "manna" see F. W. Bodenheimer, "The Manna of Sinai." It is the Arabic *mann*, a juice from the tarfa tree, found particularly in the western part of the Sinai peninsula. Coriander is a plant, the small seeds of which can be used for flavoring. Bdellium is a gum resin. Broadly speaking the description of the manna and its use is close to that given in Exod 16:13–14, 31, with some slight variation as to its taste. In Exod 16:31 it is like "wafers made with honey." Here it is like "cakes mixed with oil."

8. בָּרֵחַיִם "in mills." These were household implements, handmills consisting of two millstones for grinding (cf. Jer 25:10).

10. The last clause provides the Yahwist with the springboard for his exploration of the problems faced by Moses in leadership.

11. The modes of expression in this verse are typical of the early narrative tradition in the Pentateuch; see G. B. Gray, *Numbers*, 107–08 and cf. e.g. Gen 6:8; 18:3, 5; 19:9; 43:6; Exod 33:1–3, 12, 13, 16.

12. For the idea of Israel as Yahweh's son see Exod 4:22; Hos 11:1. For the idea of a foster parent see 2 Kgs 10:1, 5; Isa 49:23. The word הָאֹמֵן "the nurse" is in fact masculine, although הַיֹּנֵק "the sucking child" suggests a female foster parent. M. Noth (*Numbers*, 86–87) presses the metaphor too far in seeing here an implicit reference to Yahweh as mother.

16. מִזִּקְנֵי "from the elders." These people occur frequently in the Yahwist's work, but rarely in P (cf. Lev 4:15; 9:1). They are apparently leading members of the various tribes, and roughly equivalent to P's "leaders." See further J. de Vaulx, *Nombres*, 153–54.

16. וְשֹׁטְרָיו "and officers." This may indicate some distinct administrative function. *G* translates the word as "scribes." On men of rank and influence generally see R. de Vaux, *Israel*, 69–70.

17. Yahweh's appearance is as promised in Exod 33:9, 11.

17. הָרוּחַ "the spirit." This is evidently a divine endowment giving all necessary resources for the leadership of God's people (cf. Num 24:2; Judg 3:10; 11:29; 1 Sam 10:6; 19:20; Isa 11:2; 61:1; Ezek 11:5). The endowment received by Moses is thought of quantitatively (cf. 2 Kgs 2:9–10), and is to be shared out among the seventy. G. B. Gray (*Numbers*, 111) is unnecessarily literalistic in claiming that v 17b with its offer of human assistance is not a genuine reply to Moses' plea for divine assistance in v 14. The nub of his complaint is not that Yahweh should bear some of the burden, but that he is chosen to carry the responsibility on his own (vv 11, 14–15). It is in this context that v 12 must be understood.

18. הִתְקַדְּשׁוּ "sanctify yourselves." This is to be a sacred meal and ritual cleanness is essential (cf. Gen 35:2; Exod 19:10). The Hithpael is used again in Josh 3:5; 7:13 to signify a solemn preparation for a holy appearance. The idea may however be double-edged. It is also to be a day of slaughter along the lines envisaged in Jer 12:3 (cf. also Isa 34:6; Jer 46:10; Ezek 39:17, 19; Zeph 1:7–8).

18. לְמָחָר "for tomorrow" (cf. Exod 8:6, 19, 25; 9:5, 18; 10:4; Num 14:25).

20. לְזָרָא "loathsome," a word occurring only here and in Sir 39:27. *G* interprets it as actual sickness, and G. B. Gray (*Numbers*, 112) suggests violent vomiting. It may however be merely nausea—the deleterious effect of overeating.

21. שֵׁשׁ־מֵאוֹת אֶלֶף "six hundred thousand." This is the figure given in Exod 12:37. It is impossible to determine how it is calculated.

25. The text implies that this is ecstatic prophecy, the kind in which men are seized and overpowered by divine spirit (cf. 1 Sam 10:10–13; 19:20–24). The author seems anxious to stress that this is a once-for-all experience associated with their installation in office.

26. בַּכְּתֻבִים "among those registered." It is not clear whether this means that Eldad and Medad were two of the seventy. The balance of probability is against that supposition. There is no indication earlier in the story that

the seventy are "registered," and vv 24–25 seem to assert that all seventy went out and received the spirit. It may be that "registration" is to eldership or the role of officer, and that Eldad and Medad were among those elders not chosen—see further G. B. Gray, *Numbers*, 114.

28. The reference to Joshua is another piece of evidence linking this story with the tradition of Exod 33:7–11. The future leader of Israel is here depicted as the close assistant of Moses himself at the Tent of Meeting. On Joshua in tradition see M. Noth, *Pentateuchal Traditions*, 175–78.

29. הַמְקַנֵּא "jealous." The root can denote a right and proper zeal (cf. e.g. Num 25:11). In this instance Joshua's zeal is misplaced.

31. נָסַע "sprang up." The root is translated "burst forth" by KB. For other meanings see Gen 33:12; Judg 16:3, 14; Isa 33:20.

31. שַׂלְוִים "quail." These birds cross certain parts of the Sinai peninsula in spring and autumn; see J. Gray, "The Desert Sojourn of the Hebrews and the Sinai Horeb Tradition," *VT* 4 (1954) 148–54. The vicinity of Kadesh rather than the southern part of the peninsula is a more likely location for the experience of this phenomenon. The birds fly short distances and can be captured fairly easily.

31. וּכְאַמָּתַיִם "two cubits," approximately three feet. The meaning may be that the birds were flying at this height.

32. עֲשָׂרָה חֳמָרִים "ten homers," a large quantity, believed to be approximately two thousand litres.

33. טֶרֶם יִכָּרֵת "before it was bitten," literally "before it was cut off." For discussion of the textual witness see *Notes*.

34. The site of Kibroth-hattaavah cannot now be identified.

35. The site of Hazeroth cannot now be identified. On both places see further G. I. Davies, *The Way of the Wilderness* (Cambridge: CUP, 1979).

Explanation

Having provided a story in Num 11:1–3 which deals with disaffection in a general way the Yahwist here produces a disaffection story of a specific kind. He takes the tradition of the miraculous provision of quail and gives it a new twist. Originally the theme of quail was almost certainly celebrated, along with manna and the provision of water, as a gracious gift (see *Form/Structure/Setting*). For the Yahwist the quail were indeed a response to a request, but faithlessness was the keynote of the request, and the gift itself becomes the means of punishment.

The precise form and content of the complaint (vv 4–6) may reflect circumstances in Hezekiah's time when the question of the source of political and economic security came to a head (see *Introduction*). The Yahwist, writing in Josiah's time, faced similar questions, and saw, in the hankering after Egypt, the faithlessness of those who advocated pro-Egyptian policies as the answer to Judah's ills. Just as he had done in Exod 17:2, 7 he provides an etiology (vv 4a, 34) which serves to locate the incident at a particular place on the journey. The tradition of a Mosaic appeal to Yahweh (as in v 13) was a feature of the stories available to the author (cf. Exod 15:25; 17:4), and it called to mind the burdens of leadership that Moses must have borne. As is clear

from Exod 33 as a whole these burdens were very much at the forefront of
the Yahwist's mind. It is for this reason that he interrupts the story of the
quails and introduces the complaint of Moses in vv 11–12, 14–15, along with
the divine response in vv 16–17. The seventy elders who share the "spirit"
of Moses may help to legitimize the system operative in the Judaean court.
The Elohistic material in Exod 18 shares a similar concern, but the issues
are not the same. There the king, in the person of Moses, is encouraged to
share his responsibility for the judging of cases. Here the burden of leadership
itself is to be shared. This legitimates perhaps the principle of having royal
advisers on all matters of policy. The fact that they share the king's spirit is
a guarantee of the propriety of this development.

Having begun this excursus it seemed appropriate to the Yahwist to carry
it through to the end, and thus include the content of vv 24–30 at this point.
This gives to the chapter as a whole a seemingly fragmentary character which
has led some to posit complex theories of supplementation. The fragmentariness is perhaps more apparent than real. The impression of complexity is
created by the Yahwist's decision to expand upon the Mosaic appeal to Yahweh. Once this decision had been taken and is recognized there is a reasonable
logic about the way the rest of the chapter develops. The overall story divides
neatly into two between v 23 and v 24, a division indicating the movement
from "words" to "action." It is because the Yahwist has more "words" on
the subject of quail that he returns to that theme in v 18. The effect of vv
18–23, as compared with the similar stories in Exod 14–17, is to make the
gift of the quail an altogether more solemn and momentous occasion. It is
a sacred event requiring ritual purification (v 18), and even Moses is puzzled
as to how Yahweh can achieve his promise. The further dialogue between
Moses and Yahweh gives the Yahwist an opportunity to introduce one of
his prophetic interests—the fulfillment of the divine word (v 23). It is failure
to listen to the divine word through Yahweh's prophets that has led kings
astray.

Having set the scene, the author is now ready to turn from "words" to
"action." He turns first in vv 24–30 to the seventy elders. The spirit they
are given leads them to prophesy. They are not prophets as such, and so it
is a once-for-all experience, but the spirit of leadership and the spirit of
prophecy are closely related. For the Yahwist a leadership which has no place
for prophetic insights is doomed to be misled. The Yahwist's work may thus
be described as an etiology of Davidic Israel. He is concerned not only with
how the land is possessed, but also with how the community is led. In vv
25–29 the point is made very clearly that there must be a sensitivity to the
voice of Yahweh through "unregistered" agencies. Joshua in this story represents a kind of sanctuary clericalism. The leadership must be prepared to
hear the authentic voice of prophecy in such as Eldad and Medad who here
represent the nonprofessional prophets. In v 29 the meekness of Moses is
a sign of strength, and his example should be followed by kings. The verse
is essentially an assertion of the distinctive importance of prophecy.

In locating the Tent of Meeting outside the camp, the Yahwist is probably
handling one of two distinct traditions available to him concerning the focal
point of Yahweh's presence, traditions about the ark on the one hand and

about the tent on the other. It is probably his view that the ark was placed within the tent. In all probability the tent was southern, and specifically Judaean. In 2 Sam 6:17 the ark is brought from the north, and placed in the tent which is already pitched for it.

It is a debatable point as to why the Yahwist introduces the story of the elders at this point rather than after Exod 18 where it might be considered more appropriate. It may be that he thought the passage of more time was necessary for the burdens of leadership to take their full effect, and that a story such as that about quail was necessary to bring matters to a head.

In vv 31–34 the Yahwist brings the wheel full circle and tells of the "action" concerning the quail. The gift turned out to be a terrible means of judgment, involving a plague and death for the rabble whose inordinate desire is apparently judged all the more severely through their deaths. It is the blindness and unbelief of these false roads to security that most concern the author. Mere sensual desire, or the more sophisticated hankering after Egypt, are both evidence of lack of faith.

Theologically Num 11 raises the questions of means to ends and of leadership in the community. From the seventh to the fourth centuries the story of how Israel came initially to possess the land, and the factors that hindered or prevented possession, were of constant relevance. It is from this period that much of the Pentateuchal story in its present form comes. The questions of political identity and independence, and of economic viability, necessarily loomed large. It is with the search for political stability and economic security, those elusive goals of freedom from war and from hunger, that many of these Yahwistic stories are concerned. For the Yahwist the chief threats to the fulfillment of what God intends are doubt, unbelief, and a preference for foreign domination. "Egypt" functions in some measure as the "anti-Christ" of the Old Testament. M. Buber (*Moses* [Oxford: OUP, 1946] 88) interprets murmuring generally as symptomatic of the "permanent passion for success," and of the attempt to identify God with success. This is true if "success" is understood as a means. The author evidently does believe in possession of the land, and in the political and economic security that should properly go with it. What he recognizes is that these goals call for a commitment to the land, and to Yahweh whose gift it is. Faith however is not blind optimism, and the Yahwist is anxious to secure proper patterns of leadership. There are great safeguards in his view in patterns of shared leadership and responsibility. There must also be a sensitivity to the voice of the living God, wherever it may be heard and whoever speaks it.

Miriam and Aaron Oppose Moses   (12:1-16)

Bibliography

Kselman, J. S. "A note on Numbers 12:6-8." *VT* 26 (1976) 500-04. On the Tent of Meeting and Prophecy see Num 11:4-35 (*Bibliography*).

Translation

¹ *Miriam and Aaron spoke against Moses because of the Cushite* ᵃ *woman whom he had married, for he had married a Cushite woman.* ² *And they said, "Has Yahweh spoken only through Moses? Has he not also spoken through us?" And Yahweh heard it.* ³ *Now Moses was in fact very humble, more so than all men who were on the face of the earth.* ⁴ *And suddenly Yahweh said to Moses, to Aaron, and to Miriam, "Come out, you three, to the Tent of Meeting." And the three of them came out.* ⁵ *And Yahweh came down in a pillar of cloud, and stood at the door of the Tent, and called Aaron and Miriam. And they both came forward.* ᵃ ⁶ *And he said, "Hear my words: If there is a prophet among you* ᵃ *I Yahweh make myself known to him in a vision. I speak with him in a dream.* ⁷ *It is not so with my servant Moses. He is entrusted with all my house.* ⁸ *I speak with him face to face, openly* ᵃ *and not in riddles. And he sees the very form* ᵇ *of Yahweh. Why then were you not afraid to speak against my servant Moses?"*

⁹ *And the anger of Yahweh was roused against them, and he departed.* ¹⁰ *And when the cloud moved from over the Tent, behold, Miriam was leprous, as white as snow. And Aaron turned towards Miriam, and behold, she was leprous.* ¹¹ *And Aaron said to Moses, "O my lord, do not punish us because we have been foolish and have sinned.* ¹² *Do not let her be as the dead,* ᵃ *as one whose flesh is half consumed when he comes out of his mother's womb."* ¹³ *And Moses cried to Yahweh, "O God,* ᵃ *please heal her, I pray."* ¹⁴ *But Yahweh said to Moses, "Suppose her father had spat in her face, would she not have to remain in disgrace for seven days? Let her be shut up outside the camp for seven days, and after that she may be brought in again."* ¹⁵ *So Miriam was shut up outside the camp for seven days. And the people did not set out on the march till Miriam was brought in again.* ᵃ ¹⁶ *And afterwards the people set out from Hazeroth, and encamped in the wilderness of Paran.*

Notes

1.a. G reads "Ethiopian" here. Tg⁰ reads "beautiful." For discussion of the meaning of "Cushite" see *Comment*.

5.a. The suggestion that וַיָּבֹא "and they came" or "came forward" (*BHS*) has some support in Num 11:24. In any event this seems to be the sense required.

6.a. It is customary to emend וּנְבִיאֲכֶם to נְבִיא בָכֶם "a prophet among you." MT is not intelligible, and the emendation involves the introduction of one consonant only. For further discussion, and other possibilities see J. Paterson, *Numbers*, 48; G. B. Gray, *Numbers*, 126; GKC § 128d.

8.a. MT is acceptable, and attempts at textual emendation are not strictly necessary; see e.g. J. Paterson, *Numbers*, 48; G. B. Gray, *Numbers*, 126-27.

8.b. *G* reads בָּבוֹד "glory" here, but is almost certainly interpreting the text in line with a major theme in the priestly parts of the wilderness tradition.

12.a. *G* has ὡσεὶ ἔκτρωμα "as an abortion," probably an emphatic gloss.

13.a. Most commentators prefer the pointing אַל־נָא "no, I pray" (cf. Gen 19:18), a better solution than the emendation to אֱלֹהֵנוּ "our God" occasionally proposed.

15.a. *G* adds ἐκαθαρίσθη "she was cleansed," probably to make it clear that the rules about skin diseases (Lev 14:9) were observed.

Form/Structure/Setting

Analysts are agreed that this section belongs to the early narrative (J/E) level of the Pentateuch. The itinerary in v 16 uses הָעָם "the people," and is thus most unlikely to belong to P. The Tent is apparently outside the camp (v 4), as in Exod 33:7–11 and Num 11:26, and in contrast to P. Aaron is prominent, but not as in P. As in Exod 32 he stands over against Moses. The pillar of cloud (v 5) gives a further point of contact with Exod 33:7–11, and with Num 11:25.

It has often been suspected that the section is not a simple literary unit. Two distinct grounds for opposition to Moses have been noted—his marriage (v 1) and his claim to be unique (v 2). The occurrence of the feminine singular וַתְּדַבֵּר "and she spoke" (v 1) has been taken as an indication that Aaron may be an addition here and elsewhere in the story. The restriction of punishment to Miriam, when Aaron seems equally culpable, has been seen as support for this view. There may also be a double summons in v 4 and v 5, and a double departure in v 9b and v 10a. Most analysts who are impressed by these phenomena are inclined to the view that there is a base narrative which has been supplemented with "Aaron" material, though opinions differ as to the precise extent of the supplementation. B. Baentsch (*Numeri*, 510–14) and M. Noth (*Numbers*, 92–96) limit it to vv 2–8. G. W. Coats (*Rebellion*, 261–64) finds it in vv 2–9, 11b, and V. Fritz (*Israel*, 18–19) in vv 2–9b, 10b–12. W. Rudolph (*Elohist*, 69–74) finds additions in vv 2–8, 10a, 11, essentially the position of J. de Vaulx (*Nombres*, 158–59). Attempts to identify parallel sources are unusual. O. Eissfeldt (*Hexateuch*, 164–66) distinguishes E (what most regard as supplementary) from L, his lay source (what most regard as the base narrative). This approach is not very convincing, and is not widely supported.

It is reasonable to ask whether the evidence for literary disunity is in fact very strong. Most of the phenomena are explicable on the view that the Yahwist created the story on the basis of two "hard" facts from tradition—that Moses had married a Cushite, and that Miriam had suffered from leprosy. Given these basic data it would not have been hard to construct the existing story, using the data to depict an incident of opposition to Moses, which in turn provided means for asserting the uniqueness of Moses. The grounds for opposition to Moses are thus not incompatible, while the use of a singular in v 1 where a plural is in fact involved is far from unique, see GKC § 146g. The restriction of the punishment to Miriam would thus reflect the tradition received. The Yahwist chose to implicate Aaron, as he had done in Exod 32, in order to highlight the supremacy and uniqueness of Moses. In vv 4–5 the first summons brings out all three main characters, the second isolates and addresses the offenders. In vv 9–10 there is not necessarily a double departure; in v 10 the interest is in what is revealed as the departure takes effect.

Many analysts would assign the basic narrative to E or to ES, the latter in the light of the section's "advanced" reflection on prophecy. For a recent defense of the Elohistic character of the story see A. W. Jenks, *The Elohist*, 54–55. The Tent of v 5 is certainly situated outside the camp (the three "come out" from the camp), and the passage can readily be linked with traditions such as Exod 33:7–11 and Num 11:16–17, 24–30. The grounds for identifying this kind of material as E are far from overwhelming. Arguments hinge largely on the prophetic interest (allegedly characteristic of E), and the fact that Joshua is a minister of Moses in Exod 33:7–11 as in Exod 24:13, the latter text being judged to be E on other grounds (e.g. the use of the phrase "the mountain of God"). Small linguistic indicators of E have been perceived in דִּבֶּר בְּ (v 1 cf. Num 21:5, 7, a story in which "Elohim" is used) and עַל־אֹדוֹת (v 1 cf. Gen 21:11, 25; Exod 18:8; Num 13:24). Others, often more recent analysts, prefer the designation J (W. Rudolph, *Elohist*, 70–74; M. Noth, *Numbers*, 92–96; G. W. Coats, *Rebellion*, 261–64; V. Fritz, *Israel*, 18–19; J. de Vaulx, *Nombres*, 158–59). M. Noth (*Pentateuchal Tradition*, 32 n.120) argued that since Miriam was a Kadesh figure (Num 20:1), and thus from the south, the story was more probably J's. It is hard to resolve this kind of discussion, but there is evidently no difficulty in assigning the story to the Yahwistic author of the overall early tradition. Since we have already attributed passages such as Exod 33:7–11 and Num 11:16–17, 24–30 to the Yahwist it is natural enough to do so here. Various words and phrases have affinities with the Yahwistic style elsewhere, e.g. "the face of the earth" (v 3 cf. Gen 2:6; 4:14; 6:1, 7; 7:4, 23; 8:8, 13b; 33:16), the address בִּי אֲדֹנִי "O my lord" (v 11 cf. Gen 43:20; 44:18; Exod 4:10, 13), and תֶּשֶׁת "punish" (v 11 cf. Gen 3:15; 4:25; 30:40; 41:33; 46:4; 48:14, 17; Exod 7:23; 10:1; 33:4; Num 24:1). The reflection on the character of Moses in v 3 may be a gloss, but it is certainly not inappropriate in the context. The phrase "the man Moses" can be found elsewhere in the Yahwist's work (Exod 11:3).

The claim that the Yahwist has built a story from brief isolated data in tradition can be sustained on other grounds. The marriage of Moses with a Cushite is such a datum, and it looks at first sight as though intermarriage is to be the topic of discussion. In the event, no answers or even general principles in that area are forthcoming. The question the story answers is not whether you should marry a Cushite, but whether you should challenge the uniqueness of Mosaic authority.

F. M. Cross (*Canaanite Myth and Hebrew Epic* [Harvard: HUP, 1973] 203–4) has proposed that behind the story lies a priestly controversy, and that its function is to affirm the legitimacy of the Mushite priesthood, represented by Moses, despite its mixed blood. The second stratum, in Cross's view, presses the superiority of the Mushites over the house of Aaron as mediator of the divine command. The theory seems doubtful. No trace of "priestliness" survives in the narrative—prophetic issues seem to be more to the fore—and the tradition conspicuously fails to return to the question of mixed blood. The point at issue seems to be wider than any struggle between rival priesthoods. It is possible that some priests did seek "Mosaic authority" for their status, but it is not certain that this particular story was used by them, or indeed that such interests were confined to them. The question of Mosaic revelation and its relationship to other modes of revelation became a widespread and fundamental concern in the seventh century (see *Explanation*).

H. Gressmann (*Mose und seine Zeit* 264–75) attempted to find an etiology for Hazeroth (v 16) in the story, based on מְצֹרַעַת "leprous" (v 10), but the theory is forced and improbable. The itinerary in v 16 has the loosest of connections with the main story, and is unlikely to have had any role in its creation. Gressmann also suggested a distinct pattern of conflict in stories of this kind to do with the battle between El-religion, represented by such figures as Aaron, Miriam, Nadab, Abihu, and Korah, and Yahweh religion, represented by such as Moses and the Levites. This may have some validity for the story in Exod 32, but as an overall explanation of conflict it runs the risk of forcing other stories, especially this one, into a false mold. Essentially Miriam represents those who speak against the representatives of Mosaic authority. This and nothing more is the point of the story.

If this view is correct the choice of Miriam as opponent calls for some explanation. J. de Vaulx (*Nombres*, 161) finds natural "family jealousy" at the root of the tradition, but it is far from certain that the idea of Miriam as sister of Moses is original or even early (cf. e.g. M. Noth, *Numbers*, 96; G. W. Coats, *Rebellion*, 262–64). In Mic 6:4 she, along with Aaron and Moses, are depicted as leader figures, and the description of her as "prophetess" (Exod 15:21) may mean that she was a "southern Deborah"—southern because of the tradition of her death at Kadesh (Num 20:1). As previously argued there may well have been an old tradition that she had contracted leprosy (cf. V. Fritz, *Israel*, 75–79), but it seems that the essential composition of the story as one of opposition to Moses is to be traced to the Yahwist. The suitability of Miriam as opponent lies simply in the fact that she is a leader figure from the past. Her "prophetic" connections were valuable because they showed that even those who claimed such inspiration had no right to speak against Moses. There is a uniqueness and supremacy about Mosaic revelation which must be recognized and acknowledged by all. This stress on the part of the Yahwist paved the way for Mosaic authority as propounded by the Deuteronomists and for the ultimate and absolute character of Mosaic law in the post-exilic period. Even prophetic revelation is subordinate to Mosaic religion.

There are some signs that in the divine response of vv 6–8 the Yahwist has taken up older poetic material. The regular 3–3 epic meter is discernible, and some resemblances to Ugaritic poems about Baal have been found (see W. F. Albright, *Yahweh and the Gods of Canaan*, 37). One can only conjecture about the origin and provenance of such material. It would presumably belong to those who had cherished and maintained Mosaic connections prior to the seventh century. The Levites are perhaps the most likely contenders for this role. There are ancient texts which associate them with Massah and Meribah in the vicinity of Kadesh (Deut 33:8), and a tradition which indicates their devotion to Mosaic Yahwism (Exod 32:25–29). In Judg 18:30 there is a Danite genealogy, linked with the story of Micah the Levite, which claims Mosaic

origin, and which deserves attention, if only because of the embarrassment
it caused to later scribes—n.b. the reading "Manasseh" for "Moses."

Comment

1. בְּ דִּבֶּר "spoke against." This is also used of hostile speech in Num
21:5, 7 (cf. Job 19:18; Pss 50:20; 78:19). It seems to fulfill much the same
function as לוּן "to murmur" in the water stories available to the Yahwist
(Exod 15:22–26; 17:3–6). The Yahwist may have judged it a more culpable
sin, in that there are no external threats to give it some justification. For a
detailed note see G. B. Gray, *Numbers*, 122–23. In v 2 the same expression
is used of divine communication to a prophet (cf. also vv 6, 8; 2 Sam 23:2;
1 Kgs 22:18; Hos 1:2; Hab 2:1).

1. הָאִשָּׁה הַכֻּשִׁית "the Cushite woman." The nature of Miriam's objection
is not wholly clear. There is no attempt to identify this woman with Zipporah
(Exod 2:21), and such a connection cannot simply be assumed. Cush is usually
Ethiopia in Biblical tradition (cf. e.g. 2 Kgs 19:9; Isa 20:3, 5; 37:9; 43:3;
45:14; Ezek 30:4–5; 38:5; Nah 3:5). *G* makes this identification. Another possibility is the region of the Cassites—east of Babylonia (cf. Gen 10:18). M.
Noth (*Numbers*, 94) draws attention to the Cushan of Hab 3:7, apparently
close to Midian, and prefers this on the grounds that it is closest to the
sphere in which Moses worked (see also W. F. Albright, *Archaeology and the
Religion of Israel* 205 n. 49). A link with Ethiopia/Egypt remains feasible. The
name "Moses" appears to be of Egyptian origin (see A. Cody, *A History of
Old Testament Priesthood* [Rome: PBI, 1969] 39–41), and it is reasonable to
believe that he was there, and that he married. The tradition was naturally
awkward for later faith, and is not likely to have been created for apologetic
purposes of any kind.

2. The two questions here are not explanation-seeking, as is often the
case in speeches of disaffection, but rhetorical assertions. The first queries
the uniqueness of Moses as communicator of the divine word. The two words
for "only" (רַק and אַךְ) emphasise the fact that the issue is uniqueness. In
the second rhetorical question Aaron and Miriam claim for themselves the
status Moses has.

3. עָנָו "humble." The word is often used of a trustful attitude (e.g. Pss
25:9; 37:11). The point here seems to be that Moses is not self-assertive.
His uniqueness is something conferred by God.

5. For a similar descent in the pillar of cloud see Num 11:25, and for
"standing" at the door of the Tent of Meeting see Exod 33:9–10; Num 11:16–
17, 25.

6. בַּמַּרְאָה . . . בַּחֲלוֹם "in a vision . . . in a dream." This form of revelation
is often mentioned in the early narrative tradition, usually in texts regularly
identified by analysts as E (cf. e.g. Gen 15:1; 20:3; 28:11–12; 31:11, 24; 37:5–
7; 40:5–7; 41:1–3; 46:2; Num 22:8, 20). In some other texts revelation by
dreams and revelation through prophets are clearly distinguished (1 Sam
28:6, 15; Deut 13:1; 27:9). Sometimes revelation by dreams is denigrated
(cf. e.g. Jer 23:25–27).

7. עַבְדִּי מֹשֶׁה "my servant Moses." This description "servant" is reserved

for distinguished personages in Israel's history (cf. e.g. Gen 26:24; Exod 14:31; Num 14:24; Deut 34:5; Job 1:8) but is used most often of David.

7. בְּכָל-בֵּיתִי נֶאֱמָן הוּא "he is entrusted with all my house." An alternative reading is "he is trustworthy in all my house."

8. פֶּה אֶל-פֶּה "mouth to mouth." According to M. Noth (*Numbers*, 95–96), this denotes equality of rank, but that idea seems improbable in this context. A unique immediacy and directness about revelation to Moses seems to be the point. Even "friendship" is an acceptable image for the relationship (cf. Exod 33:11; Deut 34:10).

8. בְּחִידֹת "in riddles" (cf. Ezek 17:2; Hab 2:6; Prov 1:6).

8. תְּמֻנַת יהוה "the very form of Yahweh." This is another way of expressing the uniqueness of Moses. The elders are said to have seen God on one special occasion (Exod 24:10), and the people not at all (cf. Deut 4:12, 15). The direct contact Moses has with God is regular and familiar. It may be misleading to call this the ultimate prophetic experience (H. W. Robinson, *Inspiration and Revelation in the Old Testament* [Oxford: Clarendon, 1946] 186). This appears to be something different in kind—something peculiar to the experience of Moses. According to M. Noth (*Numbers*, 95–96) the clause is an addendum, disturbing the rhythm of the passage. If so its sentiment is very much in keeping with the whole.

10. מְצֹרַעַת כַּשָּׁלֶג "leprous as snow." The word "leprous" probably covers a wide range of skin disease as in Num 5:2, though the Yahwist does not make this plain in the way that the priestly elements in Leviticus do. "Leprous" seems as convenient a rendering as any in this context. The comparison with snow could be an allusion to a mild form of the disease (cf. Exod 4:6). Cross (*Canaanite Myth*, 204) makes the speculative comment that if there are connotations of blackness in "Cushite" (v 1), then this would be a peculiarly appropriate punishment. N. H. Snaith (*Numbers*, 236) suggests more probably that the comparison is not with the "whiteness" of snow, but with its "moistness," and that the reference is therefore to open wounds and ulcers. The phrase may be a technical reference to a particular kind of skin disease.

11. בִּי אֲדֹנִי "O my lord." An expression of profound respect. It can be addressed to God (cf. e.g. Exod 4:10, 13; Josh 7:8; Judg 6:13, 15; 13:8).

12. The disease is compared with the birth of a stillborn child.

14. יָרֹק יָרַק בְּפָנֶיהָ "had spat in her face." The repetition of יָרַק is emphatic. The reference is to a degrading custom which would have caused Miriam to hide or to be excluded for seven days, had she experienced it (cf. Deut 25:9; Isa 50:6; Job 30:10). Her crime is comparable to those which would provoke such action, and hence she is to be excluded from the camp for that period of time. This may mean that she has been healed at once, in response to the prayer of Moses, in which case only the ritual pollution remains. The failure to mention healing and subsequent inspection suggests that this is the case. Mosaic prayer is normally effective at once. There is no attempt to establish a principle or precedent in the matter since the author fails to give all the guidance that would be necessary. The Yahwist's real interest lies in the opposition to Moses and the divine response it receives.

16. The site of Hazeroth cannot be identified with certainty.

Explanation

In this story the Yahwist tells of the opposition of Miriam and Aaron to Moses, and in particular of their challenge to the uniqueness of his relationship to Yahweh and therefore of the supremacy of his word. Miriam is stricken with leprosy, and after Mosaic intercession on her behalf, has to be excluded from the camp for seven days before the journey can proceed.

The Yahwist appears to have built the story round two "facts" of tradition—the marriage of Moses to a Cushite, and Miriam's leprosy. His real purpose is to highlight the error of opposing Moses. It is possible that there were those who opposed the principle of foreign marriage, but there is no clear indication that the author wishes to address himself directly to this subject. He is content to use it as a starting point for discussion of the question of Mosaic authority. We have seen in Num 11 that Moses may be functioning for the Yahwist as a "Davidic" figure. Elders and prophets are both given significant and authentic roles there, but in the last resort the king is Yahweh's man in a special sense, and must not be spoken against. The choice of Miriam lies in the fact that she is a well established leader figure in tradition with prophetic associations (Exod 15:20). The Yahwist tells of the consequences of such temerity, and this is evidently at the center of his interest. The concluding details (vv 14–15) serve only to link the tradition to the story of the journey, which continues in v 16. The structure, with punishment coming early in the story, with disaffection itself the problem, and with an act of Mosaic intercession as the means by which the situation is retrieved, is precisely that which the Yahwist has established in the Taberah story of Num 11:1–3.

Throughout Num 11–12 it is possible to perceive the Yahwist's interest in "Mosaic validation." For him this probably bears on the role of the Davidic king. The interest in Moses as intercessor, the one through whom disaster is averted, begins to emerge very strongly in these stories. This probably reflects the greatly increased interest in the figure and function of Moses during the seventh century. He is less of a leader in difficulties with his awkward followers (as in the Yahwistic traditions of Exodus), and more the heroic savior of the nation. This is an important movement in the direction of Deuteronomy (cf. especially Deut 3:26; 9:18, 26). This idea of crucial intercession gives a useful context for the idea of a unique Mosaic revelation and its ultimate development—a faith which could be described as "Mosaic religion." It is generally recognized that the first significant indications of this process are to be traced to Josiah's reign. This tradition, with its affirmation that it was wrong to oppose those who represented Moses, would have been very much in place at that time. Mosaic revelation has a unique and supreme authority, and thus the way is paved for the "Mosaic law" of the post-exilic period. Miriam and Aaron together appear to represent the claims of prophetic inspiration. Their challenge in v 2 suggests this, and the answer in vv 6–8 tends to confirm it. Even prophetic revelation is subordinate to Mosaic religion. There are no clear signs that for the Yahwist Aaron represents priestly interests. Even in Exod 32 the activity of Aaron is not peculiarly or necessarily priestly (see A. Cody, *Priesthood*, 147–50). If anything the points of contact are closest between Aaron and Jeroboam I. It may be best not to press this as an identification in the author's mind. For the Yahwist Aaron is essentially the respected, if somewhat shadowy, leader figure from tradition, with an identity of his own as the close associate of Moses. In any event all forms of leadership and revelation are shown to be subject to the ultimate authority of Mosaic religion.

Theologically the section draws attention to the question of authority in religion. The need for a clear understanding of its nature and of the patterns of authority is fundamental. Neglect of these themes is intrinsically dangerous.

There remains the question of why the author of Numbers draws in this particular material from the Yahwist. He evidently sees himself as an interpreter of tradition through supplementation, and it is obviously appropriate that he should preserve elements of that which he interprets. In this particular case what interests him is probably the theme of Israel's disaffection which is prominent throughout Num 11–12. The traditional material thus provides a springboard for his own treatment of wilderness disaffection. He has three special interests in this theme (see *Introduction*), and the first of these is to be discussed at length in Num 13–14. Moreover since the principle of supreme Mosaic authority is the *sine qua non* of his own work it is natural that he should use traditional material to reveal how integral it is.

Reconnaissance of the Land   (13:1–33)

Bibliography

Beltz, W. *Die Kaleb-Traditionen im Alten Testament.* BWANT 98, Stuttgart: Kohlhammer, 1964. **Lohfink, N.** "Die Ursünden in der priesterlichen Geschichtserzählung." *Die Zeit Jesu* (H. Schlier Festscrift: ed. G. Bornkamm & K. Rahner). Freiburg: Herder, 1970. 38–57. **McEvenue, S. E.** *The Narrative Style of the Priestly Writer.* Rome: PBI, 1971. **van Seters, J.** "The terms 'Amorite' and 'Hittite.' " *VT* 22 (1972) 64–81. **Wagner, S.** "Die Kundschaftergeschichten im Alten Testament." *ZAW* 76 (1964) 255–61. On the tribal leader list see Num 1:1–47 (*Bibliography*). On disaffection see Num 11:1–3 (*Bibliography*).

Translation

1a *And Yahweh spoke to Moses saying,* **2** *"Send men to spy out the land of Canaan, which I give to the people of Israel. You* [a] *shall send a man from each tribe of their fathers, every one a leader among them."* **3** *And Moses sent them from the wilderness of Paran, in accordance with the commandment of Yahweh. All of them were heads over the people of Israel.* **4** *And these were their names. From the tribe of Reuben— Shammua, the son of Zaccur.* **5** *From the tribe of Simeon—Shaphat, the son of Hori.* **6** *From the tribe of Judah—Caleb, the son of Jephunneh.* **7** *From the tribe of Issachar— Igal, the son of Joseph.* [a] **8** *From the tribe of Ephraim—Hoshea, the son of Nun.* **9** *From the tribe of Benjamin–Palti, the son of Raphu.* **10** *From the tribe of Zebulun— Gaddiel, the son of Sodi.* **11** *From the tribe of Joseph (that is from the tribe of Manasseh)—Gaddi, the son of Susi.* **12** *From the tribe of Dan—Ammiel, the son of Gemalli.* **13** *From the tribe of Asher—Sethur, the son of Michael.* **14** *From the tribe of Naphtali— Nahbi, the son of Vophsi.* **15** *From the tribe of Gad—Geuel, the son of Machi.* **16** *These were the names of the men whom Moses sent to spy out the land. And Moses called Hoshea the son of Nun Joshua.*

17 *Moses sent them to spy out the land of Canaan, and said to them, "Go up into the Negeb, and go up into the hill country,* **18** *and see what the land is like, whether the people who live in it are strong or weak, whether they are few or many,* **19** *and whether the land that they live in is good or bad, and what the cities they live in are like,* [a] *whether they are camps or strongholds,* [a] **20** *and whether the land is rich or poor, and whether there is wood there or not. Be courageous, and bring some of the fruit of the land."* *Now the time was the season of the first ripe grapes.*

21 *And they went up* [a] *and spied out the land from the wilderness of Zin to Rehob by Lebo-hamath.* **22** *And they went up into the Negeb, and they* [a] *came to Hebron. And Ahiman, Sheshai, and Talmai, the descendants of Anak, were there. Hebron was built seven years before Zoan in Egypt.* **23** *And they came to the valley of Eshcol, and cut down from there a branch with a single cluster of grapes, and they carried it on a pole between two of them. They brought also some pomegranates and figs.* **24** *That place was called* [a] *the valley of Eshcol, because of the cluster which the people of Israel cut down from there.*

²⁵ At the end of forty days they returned from spying out the land. ²⁶ And they came to Moses and Aaron and to all the congregation of the people of Israel in the wilderness of Paran, at Kadesh. They reported to them and to all the congregation, and showed them the fruit of the land. ²⁷ And they told him, "We came to the land to which you sent us. It flows with milk and honey, and this is its fruit. ²⁸ But the people who dwell in the land are strong, and the cities are fortified and very large. And we also saw the descendants of Anak there. ²⁹ The Amalekites live in the land of the Negeb. The Hivites,ᵃ the Jebusites, and the Amorites live in the hill country. And the Canaanites live by the sea, and along the Jordan."

³⁰ But Caleb silenced the people before Moses, and said, "Let us go up at once, and occupy it, for we are well able to conquer it." ³¹ But the men who had gone up with him said, "We are not able to go up against the people, for they are stronger than we." ³² So they brought an evil report of the land which they had spied out, saying, "The land through which we have travelled, to spy it out, is a land that devours its inhabitants, and all the people that we saw in it are giants. ³³ And we saw there the Nephilim, ᵃ the sons of Anak who come from the Nephilim.ᵃ We felt like grasshoppers beside them, and so we seemed to them.ᵇ

Notes

1.a. In Sam and some *G* witnesses there is additional material at this point. It is almost certainly an accretion to the text, and appears to have been drawn from Deut 1:20–23a.

2.a. Sam, *G*, and Syr all have a singular, as v 1 and v 2a require.

7.a. J. Paterson (*Numbers*, 49) thinks that "Joseph" belongs in v 8, and that the name of Igal's father has fallen out of the text. In the light of this it is surprising that he takes "Joseph" in v 11 to be a gloss.

19.a.-a. Paterson (*Numbers*, 49) takes this clause to be a gloss, but the preceding clause deserves some further clarification, and there being no textual evidence to the contrary, MT is preferable.

21.a. Sam has וַיֵּלְכוּ וַיָּבֹא literally "and they went and they came" (cf. v 26). Sam is probably mistaken.

22.a. There is very wide textual support for the plural here.

24.a. The plural occurs in Sam, *G*, Syr, *Tgʲ*, but MT is acceptable.

29.a. The reading "Hivite" rather than "Hittite" (MT) is supported by Sam and *G*, and is probably preferable (See *Comment*).

33.a.-a. This clause is lacking in *G*, and may be a redactional addition made in the light of v 28.

33.b. As in v 1 Sam appears to have additional material at this point from Deuteronomy, in this case Deut 1:27–33.

Form/Structure/Setting

There are a number of problems of analytical detail in this section, but analysts are generally agreed that there is a Yahwistic and a priestly presence. The priestly material is in general the easiest to identify. It can certainly be found in vv 1–17a, 21, 25. It envisages a reconnaissance of the whole land. There is an evident geographical link in v 3 with the priestly text in Num 10:12. The list of tribal names is typical (cf. Num 1:5–15), while the interest in name changes in v 16 is readily attested elsewhere in P (cf. e.g. Gen 17:5, 15; 35:10). The words מַטֶּה "tribe" and נָשִׂיא "leader" are among the most widely acknowledged signs of P. It is clear that v 21 and v 25 fulfill the commands of vv 2, 17a, so that they too must be priestly. It seems reasonable to attribute this material as a whole to the author of Numbers.

There is every indication, however, that the priestly work is an interpretation of older tradition, and that that tradition, coming from the Yahwist, survives in parts of the section. In vv 17b–20, 22–24 there is a survey of the land which penetrates the southern hill country alone. It apparently extends only as far as Hebron. The joining of טוֹב "good" and רָע "bad" (v 19) is a familiar feature of Yahwistic tradition (cf. e.g. Gen 2:9, 12; 3:5, 22; 24:50; 31:24, 29; 44:4; 50:20; Num 24:13). Some analysts have argued that J and E can be disentangled here with a measure of confidence (A. Dillmann, *Numeri*, 71–79; H. Holzinger, *Numeri*, 43–44; B. Baentsch, *Numeri*, 514–32; B. W. Bacon, *The Triple Tradition of the Exodus* [Hartford: Student Publishing Co., 1894] 177–89; J. E. Carpenter & G. Harford, *Hexateuch*, 519; H. Gressmann, *Mose*, 291 n.1; O. Eissfeldt, *Hexateuch*, 166–72; G. B. Gray, *Numbers*, 130–65; C. A. Simpson, *The Early Traditions of Israel* [Oxford: Clarendon, 1948] 230–36). Other analysts, particularly among the more recent, are doubtful about the appropriateness or feasibility of this (W. Rudolph, *Elohist*, 74–80; M. Noth, *Numbers*, 101–12; G. W. Coats, *Rebellion*, 137–56; V. Fritz, *Israel*, 19–24; J. de Vaulx, *Nombres*, 164–69, 171–75). Arguments for the presence of E are relatively weak. The expression עַל אֹדֹוֹת "because of" (v 24 cf. Gen 21:11, 25; Exod 18:8; Num 12:1) needs supporting evidence, and occurs in any case in Gen 26:32, which most would identify as J. Moreover if E is really northern it is unlikely to have been interested in an Eshcol etiology. It is just possible that the Yahwist engaged in some supplementation of an earlier text. If he did, then the second half of v 17b, where the range of the survey is identified precisely as the hill country, literally "the mountain," may have been part of it. It could be that v 18 is a complete commission in an original story, and that vv 19–20 offer some elaboration of it. Certainly there is no obvious duplication in vv 19–20, justifying a theory of parallel sources. The "scholarly" supplement in v 22b may be the Yahwist's addition to an earlier story. The account of an arrival at Eshcol (vv 23–24) would probably be the Yahwist's. It seems to correspond to the command to go up into the hill country (v 17b), and the etiological interest (v 24a) is characteristically his. It is obvious that suggestions of this kind can only be tentative. That the material overall is Yahwistic is altogether clearer.

In the rest of the material so far undiscussed there are signs of both the Yahwist and the author of Numbers. In v 26 there are indications of both J and P. The reference to Kadesh and to the fruit (v 23) must be Yahwistic, while the involvement of Moses and Aaron, the "congregation" and the reference to Paran (v 3) are indications of the author of Numbers. Essentially the verse must be his in its present form. He has simply incorporated some of the data from the Yahwist's account.

In vv 27–31 there is again a substantial Yahwistic presence. The gathered fruit of vv 23, 26b is shown in v 27, and the root סָפַר "to tell" is quite common in the Yahwist (e.g. Gen 24:66; 29:13; 37:9–10; 40:8–9; 41:8, 12; Exod 9:16; 10:2; 18:8; 24:3). The report in vv 27–28 seems to correspond with the commission in vv 19–20, and would therefore be Yahwistic. The scholarly note in v 29 may also be his. In v 30 it is not easy to see to what

Caleb's silencing of the people relates. A tentative suggestion is that it relates to the "weeping" of Num 14:1 in the original story, and that it has been displaced in editing by the Yahwist. The counter argument of the other spies would also be the Yahwist's.

Many analysts have supposed that P's report was of a barren land (v 32ab),[a] while the Yahwist's focussed on the strength and hostility of human adversaries (vv 32b,[b] 33). There are no persuasive linguistic grounds for this assumption. It is thus arguable that the author of Numbers reported fearsome adversaries in his own way, as well as a barren land. In short there is no difficulty in agreeing with those who attribute vv 32–33 to P (M. Noth, *Numbers*, 106–7; G. W. Coats, *Rebellion*, 138; V. Fritz, *Israel*, 20).

If this analysis is broadly accurate then the author of Numbers has provided a haggadic expansion of the Yahwist's story of the reconnaissance of the land, incorporating key elements of that story, and elaborating and expanding them. There is also the possibility that the list of tribal names in vv 4–15 constitute traditional material of some kind. M. Noth (*Numbers*, 103–4) is doubtful of this. He argues that the choice of one spy from each tribe clashes with the remark that each of them is to be a leader (v 2b). In Num 1:5 the position of "leader" is an office which could not be taken on from time to time in an *ad hoc* fashion. For Noth the phraseology of v 2b[b] suggests a supply of leaders in each tribe from which a choice could be made. In his view the list gives an impression of being freely composed. For the most part the enumeration of tribes follows the pattern in Num 1:5–15. There is a reversal of order with respect to Manasseh/Ephraim and Naphtali/Gad. The fact that Caleb appears for Judah, and Joshua for Ephraim shows that the list has been constructed on the premise of the author of Numbers that Joshua and Caleb were faithful spies (Num 14:6). The absence of names compounded with "Yahweh" is explained by Noth in terms of the conscious reflection that those born before the revelation of the divine name in Exod 6:2–3 could not have had such names. Hence it is Moses who at this point gives Hoshea the name Joshua. Among the names themselves only Ammiel (v 12) has what Noth calls an old formation. Some of the names can be found in earlier texts—Palti (1 Sam 25:44), Ammiel (2 Sam 9:4), Shaphat (1 Kgs 19:16), Shammua (2 Sam 5:14), and Igal (2 Sam 23:36)—but the precise textual form of some of them is far from certain (especially in vv 14–15), and arguments based on this kind of evidence are inconclusive. For further discussion of the names see G. B. Gray, *Numbers*, 135–36. On balance it seems best to accept Noth's arguments, and to assume that the author of Numbers compiled the list on his own account. He was anxious to have Joshua as a faithful spy, along with Caleb, and names for the other ten seemed desirable. As was suggested for Num 1:5–15 it may be that the other names were gathered from exilic sources, based on recollections of the names of distant ancestors.

It was suggested that the Yahwist may also have adapted traditional material (proto-J), and that some elements of this survive. Other elements of this may well survive in Num 21:1–3. Perhaps it suggested a settlement from the south on the part of the Judah group. If this is the case then the tradition of a detour around Edom and of settlement from the east is a major Yahwistic adaptation of tradition. The old Judah tradition may well have been specifically Calebite—a local tradition dealing with Caleb's settlement in and around Hebron. For further discussion of Calebite history and tradition see H. Gressmann, *Mose*, 291–300; M. Noth, *Pentateuchal Traditions*, 130–36; H. Seebass, *Der Erzvater Israel und die Einführung der Jahweverehrung in Kanaan* (BZAW 98; Berlin: Töpelmann, 1966) 63; V. Fritz, *Israel*, 79–84; W. Beltz, *Die Kaleb-Traditionen*, 30–37. Caleb's occupation of favorable land, including the fertile valley of Eshcol, was possibly explained in terms of his special bravery, as compared with other groups who were reluctant to move in. This would explain the courage of Caleb as expressed in Num 13:30. In Josh 15:13–14 and Judg 1:20 there are further hints of what this earlier stage of the tradition would have contained. Caleb was apparently a Kenizzite (Num 32:12; Josh 14:6, 14; 15:17; Judg 1:3; 3:9, 11), a group of Edomite extraction (Gen 36:11, 42). At an early stage this group must have entered into friendly relations with Judah (Nabal was a Calebite, 1 Sam 25:3), and though reckoned with Judah for genealogical purposes, their distinctness was long recognized (1 Chr 2:4–5, 9, 18–19, 24–26, 42–43). On the relationship between Caleb and Abraham see R. E. Clements, *Abraham and David* (London: SCM, 1967) 37–39. A settlement tradition was thus transformed in proto-J into a story set on the edges of the land immediately prior to the settlement and involving a reconnaissance which only Caleb responds to positively. S. Wagner ("Die Kundschaftergeschichten") has attempted to show that the spy story is a fixed form of a traditional kind. As S. E. McEvenue argues (*Priestly Writer*, 96 n.13) there seems to be too much variability in the stories to justify so firm an assertion, though the story we have proposed for proto-J does in fact fit the pattern suggested by Wagner quite well.

Comment

17. בַּנֶּגֶב "into the Negeb." This is the semi-desert area to the south of Palestine.

20. וְהִתְחַזַּקְתֶּם "be courageous," or "determined" (cf. 2 Sam 10:12; 1 Kgs 20:22; 1 Chr 19:13).

20. בִּכּוּרֵי עֲנָבִים "first ripe grapes." This suggests a setting for the story towards the end of July.

21. For the author of Numbers, the wilderness of Zin represents the southern edge of Canaan. It is identified by N. H. Snaith (*Numbers*, 238) as an area to the southwest of the southern end of the Dead Sea, and northwest of Edomite territory.

21. Rehob is probably the Beth-rehob of 2 Sam 10:6, a city to the west of Hermon.

21. Lebo-hamath was a city close to the source of the Orontes. It was in the far north, and reference to it here emphasizes the fact that for the author of Numbers the reconnaissance covers the whole land.

22. Hebron is the modern el-Khalil, lying twenty miles to the south of Jerusalem. The name means "confederacy." Tradition held that it was the burial place of Abraham, Isaac, and Jacob, as well as Sarah, Rebekah, and Leah. It was David's capital when he was king of Judah alone. It had been known as Kiriath-arba (Gen 23:2; Josh 14:15) "city of four."

22. The three names—Ahiman, Sheshai, and Talmai—probably represent three clans known to have been in the Hebron area (cf. Josh 15:14; Judg 1:20).

22. יְלִידֵי הָעֲנָק "the descendants of Anak." M. Noth (*Numbers*, 105–06) proposes "necklace descendants" (cf. Judg 8:26; Prov 1:9). "Anak" probably signifies that they were believed to have been exceptionally tall. See also 2 Sam 21:18–22.

22. Zoan was the city of Tanis. It had been called Avaris, the capital of the Hyksos Pharaohs in the first half of the second millenium B.C. The modern site is Şân el-Ḥagar.

23. Eshcol means "cluster." The valley of Eshcol may be the modern Beit Ishkahil, a few miles north west of Hebron; see further G. W. Coats, *Rebellion*, 144–45.

26. Kadesh, meaning "sanctuary," is the modern ᶜAin Qadeis. It lies about fifty miles south of Beer-sheba. It is called Meribah Kadesh in Num 27:14 and Kadesh-barnea in Num 32:8.

27. זָבַת חָלָב וּדְבָשׁ "flows with milk and honey." This is a common description of the fruitfulness of Canaan. There is no strong evidence in favor of the conjecture that milk and honey were originally food of the gods. For special studies see B. Stade, "Ein Land wo Milch und Honig fliesst," *ZAW* 22 (1902) 321–24; I. Guidi, "Une terre coulant du lait avec du miel," *RB* 12 (1903) 241–44; F. C. Fensham, "An Ancient Tradition of the Fertility of Palestine," *PEQ* 98 (1966) 166–67.

29. Amalek was a nomadic group belonging to the deserts to the south of the Negeb. It always appears to have been at enmity with Israel—see Saul's campaign (1 Sam 15:1–9). The Hivites were a pre-Israelite group in Palestine. If the reading "Hittites" (MT) can be accepted then the reference must be to the great empire based in southern Asia Minor. Its power was at a peak between 1400–1200 B.C. There are hints of its greatness in Josh 1:4; Ezek 16:3. The Jebusites were the inhabitants of the city Jebus, to be identified with Jerusalem (Judg 1:21). The Amorites are here distinguished from the Canaanites. They appear to be the hill country dwellers of Palestine, while Canaanites belonged to the lowlands. The Babylonians appear to have called the whole of the land Amurru. For further comment on these various peoples see D. J. Wiseman (ed.), *Peoples of Old Testament Times.* (Oxford: Clarendon, 1973).

32. דִּבַּת "an evil report." N. Lohfink ("Die Ursünden") argues persuasively that this constitutes a defamation of the delivering grace of God—the *Heilsgabe.*

32. אֶרֶץ אֹכֶלֶת יוֹשְׁבֶיהָ "a land that devours its inhabitants." This may be a reference to infertility (A. H. McNeile, *Numbers*, 71; B. Baentsch, *Numeri*, 522–23; G. B. Gray, *Numbers*, 151; S. E. McEvenue, *Priestly Writer*, 135–36 tend to favor this view). It has been suggested that the metaphor represents the Canaanites as cannibals (L. E. Binns, *Numbers*, 30), that it denotes a land filled with "warlike dissensions" (M. Noth, *Numbers*, 107—cf. Lev 26:38; Ezek 36:13–14), or that it indicates a land "geared for battle" (G. W. Coats, *Rebellion*, 140–41). It may be that the phrase is meant to denote "destruction" generally. The land is both infertile and insecure. McEvenue suggests that the metaphor is a way of saying that Yahweh's land is like Sheol, a devouring monster.

33. The Nephilim were a legendary race of semi-divine beings whose origin

is explained in Gen 6:1–4. The etymology is uncertain. The word may have some connection with נָפַל "to fall." *Něphîlāʾ* is the Aramaic of Orion, giant of the sky.

33. It would be possible to read כֵּן "so" as "gnats" (cf. Exod 8:13; Isa 51:6).

Explanation

This section tells of how the Israelites conducted a survey of the land prior to the settlement. Moses sends out a spy from each tribe to investigate the land's strength and weaknesses. The report about the land's fertility is positive, but there is a general pessimism about Israel's ability to occupy it. Only Caleb is confident that the land can be possessed.

For the author of Numbers this story marks the beginning of a major section (Num 13–14) in which the journey to the land is interrupted and delayed by the sin of the people. It is possible that he saw in this some foreshadowing of the exile, and that it reflects some interpretation of the exilic experience. He may also see in this failure possible hindrances to the return and resettlement of the land in post-exilic times. The Yahwistic tradition he handles is also critical of Israel, but the priestly revision gives extensive supplementation, much of which reveals his special interest, namely loss of land. There is obviously a warning in this, but at the same time a note of encouragement. God's plan to give the land is not ultimately thwarted, though those who reject that plan must expect to suffer the consequences.

The first major elaborative component he offers is the assertion that the survey of the land is at God's command. The preparations, as depicted in vv 1–17a, are ordered and methodical. In Deut 1:22–25 the reconnaissance is instigated by the people, and in all probability this was the pattern in the Yahwist's work. The fact of God's initiative emphasizes divine control and purpose in the whole operation. The author's list of spies is probably his own compilation (see *Form/Structure/Setting*), but he may well have derived the names from the relevant tribal sources in Babylon. It is important to him that Joshua be one of the spies, because as Num 14 makes clear only the faithful spies of Joshua's generation survive to reach the land.

The second major contribution of the priestly author of Numbers is the idea of a reconnaissance covering the whole land. This development is an important symbolic feature, making clear the scope of God's purpose. Since the gift is the whole land it is artistically appropriate that the whole be surveyed and appreciated. The third major division of the book (see *Introduction*) reveals a major interest in life in the land, and for this reason too a total survey of the land is appropriate.

A third contribution is the priestly author's magnification of the unbelief of the spies. They bring up a negative assessment of the land (v 32). This contrasts somewhat with the Yahwistic picture (vv 27–28) in which the land itself is good, though its occupants are powerful. In this way the sin is heightened, and the grave consequences of Num 14 justified.

The Yahwist, like the priestly author, was interested in the land and the conditions attaching to its occupation. He adapts earlier Calebite and Judahite traditions of settlement, partly in the interests of aligning such traditions with those who spoke of settlement from the east across the Jordan. It was the sin of Israel which led to the detour, and further material in Num 14 emphasizes the point. In the meantime the Judahite tradition of a reconnaissance as far as Hebron can be left as it stands. The importance of the land, and the conditions attaching to its occupation, were key issues in late pre-exilic Judah. Further discussion of the meaning of this particular story for the Yahwist occurs in connection with Num 14 (*Explanation*). In Num 13 his main emphasis is on the excellence of the land (vv 27–28), and on the role of Caleb as the one who seeks to silence the disquiet of the people.

Theologically, the section emphasizes the goodness and graciousness of divine provision. God's control of circumstances is massive, his provision abundant, and the essential response of man must be simple faith. The failure of the majority of the spies is not their recognition of the difficulties and obstacles in Israel's way. Faith is not depicted here as an ignorant or unseeing optimism. The failure consists primarily in an inability to see these difficulties in their true perspective. Caleb's observation (v 30) is not that their difficulties are imaginary, but that Israel is well able to overcome them. Faith seeks to view the circumstances of existence from a divine perspective.

Rejection of the Land and Defeat at Hormah (14:1–45)

Bibliography

Bartlett, J. R. "The Use of the Word ראש as a Title in the Old Testament." *VT* 19 (1969) 1–10. **Sakenfeld, K. D.** "The Problem of Divine Forgiveness in Num 14." *CBQ* 37 (1975) 317–30. See also Num 13: 1–33 (*Bibliography*). On disaffection, see Num 11:1–3 (*Bibliography*).

Translation

¹ *And all the congregation raised a loud cry, and the people wept* [a] *that night.* ² *And all the people of Israel murmured against Moses and Aaron. And the whole congregation said to them, "O that we had died* [a] *in the land of Egypt! Or that we had died in the wilderness!* ³ *Why does Yahweh bring us into this land, to fall by the sword? Our wives and our little ones will become a prey. Would it not be better for us to go back to Egypt?"* ⁴ *And they said to one another, "Let us choose a captain, and go back to Egypt."* ⁵ *And Moses and Aaron fell on their faces before all the assembly* [a] *of the congregation of the people of Israel.* ⁶ *And Joshua, the son of Nun, and Caleb, the son of Jephunneh, who were among those who spied out the land, tore their clothes,* ⁷ *and they said to all the congregation of the people of Israel, "The land through which we passed to spy it out is an exceptionally good land.* ⁸ *If Yahweh delights in us, he will bring us into this land and give it to us, a land which flows with milk and honey.* ⁹ *But do not rebel against Yahweh, and do not fear the people of the land, for they are our bread. Their protection* [a] *is removed from them, and Yahweh is with us. Do not fear them."* ¹⁰ *But all the congregation said* [a] *to stone them with stones.*

And the glory of Yahweh appeared at the Tent [b] *of Meeting to all the people of Israel.* ¹¹ *And Yahweh said to Moses, "How long will this people despise me? And how long will they not believe in me in spite of all the signs I have shown among them?* ¹² *I will strike them with the pestilence and disinherit them. And I will make of you* [a] *a nation greater and mightier than they."* ¹³ *But Moses said to Yahweh, "If the Egyptians hear of it,* [a] *for you did bring up this people in your might from among them,* ¹⁴ *then they will tell the inhabitants of this land.* [a] *They have heard that you, Yahweh, are in the midst of this people. For you, Yahweh, are seen* [b] *face to face, and your cloud stands over them, and you go before them in a pillar of cloud by day and in a pillar of fire by night.* ¹⁵ *Now if you kill this people as one man, then the nations who have heard of your fame* [a] *will say,* ¹⁶ *'Because Yahweh was unable to bring this people into the land which he swore to give to them, therefore he has killed* [a] *them in the wilderness.'* ¹⁷ *And now, I pray, let the power of Yahweh be great, as you have promised, saying,* ¹⁸ *'Yahweh is slow to anger, and totally faithful,* [a] *forgiving iniquity and transgression,* [b] *but by no means clearing the guilty,* [c] *visiting the iniquity of fathers upon children, upon the third and fourth generation.'* ¹⁹ *Pardon the iniquity of this people, I pray, in accordance with the greatness of your faithfulness, and because you have forgiven this people, from Egypt even until now."*

20 *Then Yahweh said, "I have pardoned according to your word.* 21 *But truly, as I live, and as all the earth shall be filled with the glory of Yahweh,* 22 *none of the men who have seen my glory and my signs which I performed in Egypt and the wilderness, and who yet have put me to the test these ten times and have not listened to my voice,* 23 *none shall see the land which I swore to give to their fathers.*ª *And none of those who despised me shall see it.* 24 *But my servant Caleb, because he has a different spirit and has followed me wholeheartedly, I will bring into the land which he entered, and his descendants shall possess it.* 25 *[And the Amalekites and the Canaanites live in the valley.]*ª *Turn tomorrow, and set out for the wilderness, by the way to the Sea of Reeds."* 26 *And Yahweh spoke to Moses and to Aaron,* 27 *"How long must I bear*ª *this evil congregation which murmurs against me? I have heard the murmurings of the people of Israel which they murmur against me.* 28 *Say to them, 'As I live,' says Yahweh, 'what you have said in my hearing I will do to you.* 29 *Your carcasses shall fall in this wilderness. And of all your number, of those counted from twenty years old and over, who have murmured against me,* 30 *not one shall come into the land where I swore that I would make you live, except Caleb, the son of Jephunneh, and Joshua, the son of Nun.* 31 *But your little ones, whom you said would become a prey,*ª *I will bring in, and they shall know*ᵇ *the land which you have despised.* 32 *But as for you, your carcasses shall fall in this wilderness.* 33 *And your children shall be shepherds*ª *in the wilderness for forty years, and you shall suffer for your faithlessness, until the last of your carcasses lies in the wilderness.* 34 *In accordance with the number of days in which you spied out the land, forty days, for every day a year,*ª *you shall bear your iniquity, forty years, and you shall know me as an enemy'.*ᵇ 35 *I Yahweh have spoken. Surely I will do this to all this evil congregation which is gathered together against me. In this wilderness they shall come to a full end, and there they shall die."* 36 *And the men whom Moses sent to spy out the land, and who returned and made all the congregation murmur against him, by bringing up an evil report against the land,* 37 *the men who brought up an evil report of the land, died by plague before Yahweh.* 38 *But Joshua, the son of Nun, and Caleb, the son of Jephunneh, remained alive, of those men who went to spy out the land.* 39 *And Moses told these words to all the people of Israel, and the people mourned greatly.* 40 *And they rose in the morning, and went up to the heights of the hill country, saying, "Behold, we are on our way up to the place which Yahweh has promised, for we have sinned."*ª 41 *But Moses said, "Why now are you transgressing the command of Yahweh, for that will not succeed?* 42 *Do not go up lest you be struck down before your enemies, for Yahweh is not among you.* 43 *For there the Amalekites*ª *and the Canaanites are before you, and you shall fall by the sword. Because you have turned back from following Yahweh, Yahweh will not be with you."* 44 *But they presumed to go up to the heights of the hill country, although neither the ark of the covenant of Yahweh, nor Moses, departed out of the camp.* 45 *And the Amalekites and the Canaanites who lived in that hill country came down,*ª *and defeated them and pursued them, as far as Hormah.*ᵇ

Notes

1.a. Sam, *G, Syr,* Vg have the singular here.

2.a. On this use of the perfect see GKC § 106 p.

5.a. קָהָל "assembly" is lacking in *G, Tg*ᴶ. The complete expression in MT is unusual (cf. only Exod 12:6), but not to be rejected.

9.a. *G* has ὁ καιρὸς "the time." MT is acceptable (for further discussion see *Comment*).

10.a. *BHS* suggests the root מאן "to reject," "to refuse," but MT is not unintelligible, and is best accepted (see *Comment*).

10.b. *G* has ἐν νεφέλῃ ἐπὶ τῆς σκηνῆς "in a cloud over the Tent," but MT is acceptable (see *Comment*). *G* is probably interpretative.

12.a. Sam and *G* read וְאֶת-בֵּית אֲבִיךָ "and the house of your father" at this point. It is probably expansionary, as *G* and Sam often seem to be in this chapter.

13.a. This verse is best taken as the protasis; see S. R. Driver, *Hebrew Tenses* (Oxford: Clarendon, 1881) 185–87; J. Paterson, *Numbers*, 49.

14.a. *G* is easier to construe at this point (see J. Paterson, *Numbers*, 49). MT is probably corrupt.

14.b. This should probably be read as וְרָאָה, a Niphal participle.

15.a. *G* reads this as שִׁמְךָ "your name."

16.a. *G* reads the root שָׁחַט "to scatter." The same variation is found in Num 11:32. J. Paterson (*Numbers*, 49–50) provides further discussion of the words.

18.a. Sam and *G* have וֶאֱמֶת "and truth," probably an addition.

18.b. Sam and *G* have וְחַטָּאָה "and sin," probably an addition.

18.c. *G* has "the guilty" here (followed by RSV), probably a further addition.

23.a. *G* has material here, apparently based on Deut 1:39, and seeming to anticipate v 31. It must be additional.

25.a. This bracketed clause is probably a gloss; see J. Paterson, *Numbers*, 50, and further discussion under *Comment*.

27.a. It seems likely that לִי has fallen out here (*BHS*); cf. Jer 2:18).

31.a. *S* has some material based on Deut 1:39 here. See v 23 above.

31.b. *G* has κληρονομήσουσιν "and they shall possess," reading וְיָרְשׁוּ (cf. Deut 1:39). *BHS* suggests the root רָעָה (cf. v 33), but prefers MT.

33.a. רֹעִים "shepherds." Other suggestions are "shall wander" (J. Paterson, *Numbers*, 50; cf. Num 32:13), and "shall stray" (Tgᴶ, Vg), reading נָעִים and תֹּעִים respectively. "Be shepherds" seems to some to be insufficiently condemnatory. On the other hand MT is intelligible, and in the context of a promise of a land flowing with milk and honey is sufficiently judgmental. MT is thus preferable.

34.a. On this expression see *GKC* § 123d.

34.b. *G* has τὸν θυμὸν τῆς ὀργῆς μου "the anger of my wrath," and Vg has "my vengeance." These are almost certainly paraphrases. For discussion of the difficulties in the verse see *Comment*.

40.a. The content of Deut 1:42 has been added here in Sam.

43.a. J. Paterson (*Numbers*, 50) prefers "Amorite" to "Amalekite" here. This is posited on the ground that Amorite and Canaanite are respectively the hill and lowland dwellers in Palestine, and on the basis of Deut 1:19–20, 44. There is no textual support, however, and "Amalekites" is perfectly possible (see *Comment* on Num 13:29; 14:25).

45.a. Sam has additional material here based on Deut 1:44.

45.b. Sam and *G* have additional material based on Deut 1:45.

Form/Structure/Setting

The combination of priestly and Yahwistic material noted in Num 13 persists in this section. In v 1 there are features of both, particularly the Yahwist. The picture of "the people" (הָעָם) "raising their voices" (קוֹלָם . . . וַתִּשָּׂא) and "weeping" (וַיִּבְכּוּ) is Yahwistic (cf. Gen 21:16; 27:38; 29:11; 33:4; 37:5; 42:24; 43:30; 45:14–15; 46:29; 50:1, 3, 17; Exod 2:6; Num 11:4, 10). The use of נָתַן in association with the voice can also be found in the Yahwist (Gen 45:2). All the same his text in v 1 is not entirely smooth—n.b. the use of both נָשָׂא and נָתַן, and some of the awkwardness may arise from the suggested dislocation and editing by the Yahwist of an original text (see *Form/Structure/Setting* in relation to Num 13:1–33). The sure sign of the priestly author's influence is כָּל־הָעֵדָה "all the congregation."

In vv 2–10 there are very evident signs of priestly influence. Israel is הָעֵדָה "the congregation." Aaron is linked closely with Moses, the pair fall on their faces (v 5; cf. Gen 17:3, 17; Lev 9:24; Num 16:4, 22; 17:10; 20:6), and the priestly כָּבוֹד "glory" appears (v 10). Joshua appears alongside Caleb in the role of faithful spy (cf. Num 13:6). Some analysts find a Yahwistic presence in v 3 (B. W. Bacon, *Triple Tradition*, 185–86; H. Holzinger, *Numeri*, 50–59; H. Gressmann, *Mose*, 291 n.1; O. Eissfeldt, *Hexateuch*, 166–72; W. Rudolph, *Der Elohist*, 74–80; C. A. Simpson, *Early Traditions*, 230–36. S. E. McEvenue [*Priestly Writer*, 90–92] is uncertain, but denies it to P). On the other hand v 3 is not really a duplicate of v 2. In v 2 Israel laments her lot, whereas in v 3 she questions the course of events. This transition from lament to questioning is logical enough, and is attested elsewhere in material generally assigned to P (cf. e.g. Num 20:3b–4). The linguistic features are sufficiently attested in P—וְלָמָה "and why?" (Gen 27:46; Num 9:7; 20:4; 27:4; 32:7), נָשֵׁינוּ וְטַפֵּנוּ "our wives and our little ones" (Gen 34:29; Num 31:9, 17–18). S. E. McEvenue (*Priestly Writer*, n.200) denies v 3 to P on the grounds that it would come as an "awful anticlimax" after v 2. This is a baffling remark. The Israelites, as they see things, have come a long way, all to no purpose. They thus bemoan the fact that they have not died hitherto. They are certain that the best course of action for the present is to return to Egypt. This line of argument is entirely coherent. A stronger case for Yahwistic origins can be made for v 4. From the point of view of coherence this also could be P. There is no strict duplication. The suggestion of v 3b turns into a positive resolve in v 4. On the other hand the use of the word ראֹשׁ "captain" does suggest that the priestly author has taken up here an element from the Yahwist's speech of disaffection. The word does occur in P (cf. e.g. Exod 6:14; Num 1:4; 13:3), but of heads of families or of distinct offices, rather than, as here, of overall leadership—a position evidently comparable to that held by Moses. The expression נִתְּנָה ראֹשׁ "let us make a captain" agrees with a Yahwistic text in Exod 18:25 (cf. Num 25:4), though there too the word seems to relate to judicial officials. Perhaps the closest parallels to the usage here occur in Judg 10:18; 11:8–9, 11. Ultimately the arguments in either direction are indecisive. A majority of analysts do indeed assign the verse to JE (including M. Noth [*Numbers*, 101–02] who finds little of the Yahwist elsewhere in the chapter), and it is probably best to accept this provisionally.

The material in vv 8–9 also poses problems. There are some features which point to the Yahwist, and some analysts assign them accordingly (V. Fritz, *Israel*, 19–24; J. de Vaulx, *Nombres*, 171; and most older analysts). In favor of this is the injunction not to fear (cf. Gen 15:1; 21:17; 26:24; 35:17; 43:23; 46:3; 50:19, 21; Exod 14:13; 20:20), and the idea of Yahweh as "with us" (cf. Gen 21:22; 26:3, 28; 28:15, 20; 31:3, 5; 35:3; 48:21; Exod 3:12; 10:10; 18:19; Num 14:43; 23:21). If this view is correct we must assume that the author of Numbers, who is certainly responsible for v 7, has taken up an element from Caleb's speech as it appeared in the Yahwist's work. There are in fact a number of unusual words and expressions which give the passage a character of its own. This is the only place in the Pentateuch where מְרֹד is used of rebellion against God. It occurs elsewhere in relatively late texts (cf. Josh 22:16, 18, 29; Ezek 2:3; 20:38; Dan 9:5, 9). In Gen 14:9 it is used of rebellion against the human king. The expressions "for they are our bread" and "their protection (literally "shadow") is removed from them" are both unusual for the main Pentateuchal sources (cf. Deut 7:16; Judg 9:15; Pss 14:4; 17:8; Isa 32:2; Jer 10:25). Though the verses lack all the best distinguishing marks of P it may be best to regard them as a free creation by the author of Numbers.

There is general agreement that there is supplementary material in vv 11–25, but uncertainty as to its precise extent, and to the level of the tradition to which it belongs. A majority of analysts assign it in some way to the Yahwist, either to the redactor, or to a supplementer of JE (cf. e.g. J. Wellhausen, *Hexateuch*, 103–04; B. Baentsch, *Numeri*, 515–16; H. Gressmann, *Mose*, 291 n.1; L. E. Binns, *Numbers*, xxx–xxxi; H. Holzinger, *Numeri*, 50–59; V. Fritz, *Israel*, 19–24). The presence of deuteronomistic material has long been recognized (e.g. B. W. Bacon, *Triple Tradition*, 186–88), and some see this as extensive (e.g. M. Noth, *Numbers*, 108–10; G. W. Coats, *Rebellion*, 138–39). There are evident Yahwistic elements in vv 24–25. The singling out of Caleb (v 24), and the command to turn back (v 25) follow well the pattern of the Yahwist's story thus far. The "despising" (נאץ) of Yahweh (vv 11a, 23b) is also a Yahwistic feature (Num 16:30). In vv 11b–23a there are various deuteronomistic words and phrases. The אתות "signs" (vv 11b, 22) are perhaps most typical of D (cf. e.g. Deut 4:34; 6:22; 7:19; 11:3; 13:1–2; 26:8; 28:46; 29:2; 34:11). In v 12b there are obvious linguistic and conceptual links with Deut 9:13; Exod 32:10 (RD?). The essential ideas of vv 13–16 can be found in Exod 32:7–14 (RD?) and Deut 9. D is certainly aware of the pillar of cloud and fire (Deut 1:38), and the ideas of vv 15–16 are particularly close to Deut 9:28. The phraseology of v 18b occurs in Deut 5:9, and the notion of forgiveness (v 19) in Deut 29:19; 1 Kgs 8:30, 34, 36, 39, 50. The "testing of Yahweh" (v 22) is familiar in D (cf. Deut 6:16; Exod 17:2, 7), and so also is the "hearkening" to Yahweh's voice (v 22) (cf. Deut 4:30; 8:20; 9:23; 13:4, 18; 15:5; 26:14, 17; 28:1–2, 15, 45, 62; 30:2, 8, 10, 20). In v 23a there appears to be a shortened version of Deut 1:35, while v 22 has some affinity with Deut 5:24. There are other words and phrases which seem quite distinctive—in v 14 the expression "eye to eye," and the notion of a cloud standing *over* Israel. The former occurs elsewhere only in Isa 52:8, while the latter is P-like (cf. Exod 40:34–38). The plea for forgiveness (vv 16–19) has a marked affinity with Exod 34:6–7, which may belong to the Yahwist. The notions of "forgiveness" and "transgression" are both well represented in his work. Ultimately these words may have a cultic background (Pss 86:15; 103:8; 145:8). The idea of the ten tests (v 22) is distinctive, and v 21b has some affinity with prophetic eschatology (cf. e.g. Hab 2:14), while v 20b seems to have closest contacts with the Yahwist. Thus the section reveals Yahwistic, deuteronomistic, and other influences. It may therefore be best to take it that vv 11b–23a, along with Exod 32:7–14, are an expansion of the Yahwist's text, probably of exilic date. In view of the prominent deuteronomistic elements it would not be inappropriate to call it a deuteronomistic gloss, but this should not be taken to preclude influences from elsewhere. In Deuteronomy there is special interest shown in this story and that of the golden calf, and this confirms the general appropriateness of the description as deuteronomistic. At the same time the section evidently builds closely on the Yahwist's work, and in particular on the theme of the cruciality of Mosiac intercession, as set out in the stories of Taberah (Num 11:1–3) and Miriam (Num 12:1–16).

In vv 26–38 there is a major elaboration of the tradition by the priestly author. It offers a broad parallel to vv 11–23. Israel is "the congregation," and the idea of "murmuring" (לון) is picked up from the P complaint of v 2, in vv 27, 29, 36. Joshua is clearly one of the faithful spies (v 38), and in v 29 there is a clear reference to the census earlier in the book. Some analysts, however, deny vv 30–34, in whole or in part, to P (e.g. B. W. Bacon, *Triple Tradition*, 188; H. Holzinger, *Numeri*, 50–59; H. Gressmann, *Mose*, 291 n.1; G. B. Gray, *Numbers*, 161–64; L. E. Binns, *Numbers*, xxx–xxxi; O. Eissfeldt, *Hexateuch*, 166–72; J. de Vaulx, *Nombres*, 171–75. S. E. McEvenue [*Priestly Writer*, 90–92] regards vv 30–34 as a gloss). The arguments are not very persuasive. In v 30 there is a satisfactory continuation of the P material in v 29, while v 30b, with its reference to Joshua, must in any case belong to P. Clearly v 31 belongs to the same stratum as v 3. The ascription of v 3, as we have shown is unnecessary, and in fact v 31 provides a good continuation of v 30b. The idea of "despising" or "rejection" (מאם) does occur of disaffection in the Yahwist (Num 11:20), but is common enough in later texts (Lev 26:15; Ezek 5:6; 20:13, 16, 24; 21:5). In vv 32–33 there seems to be a reversion to the themes of vv 29–31, but if this really is a difficulty it is best explained in terms of an emphatic gloss rather than as a parallel source. In verbal content v 32 is essentially a repetition of v 29a. The idea of Israel being "shepherds" during their sojourn (v 33) is unusual, but not out of place in priestly material (cf. Num 27:17 for its use in a different sense). The idea of "suffering for your faithlessness," "bearing whoredoms" (RV v 33) has a strong affinity with Ezek 23:35, and is probably late. The content of v 34 links it firmly enough with P. There is a reconnaissance in v 34 of the whole land, and the idea of "bearing iniquity" is present (cf. Exod 28:38, 43; Lev 5:1, 17; 7:18; 10:17; 17:16; 19:8; 20:17, 19; 22:16; Num 5:31; 18:1, 23; 30:15—all P). In sum there may be some minor accretions to P in these verses, but there is little reason for supposing that any part of the text belongs to the Yahwist Arguments by J. de Vaulx (*Nombres*, 174–75) for two priestly points of view in Num 13–14 are tenuously based.

It was tentatively suggested in Num 13:1–33 (*Form/Structure/Setting*) that the Yahwist adapted earlier tradition in this story. The encouragement of Caleb (Num 13:30) may originally have been a response to the "weeping" of Num 14:1. It would therefore be to the Yahwist that we owe the serious disaffection of Num 14:4, which calls in turn for the drastic judgment of Num 14:25. In Deut 1:19–46, D is probably following the Yahwist's pattern of events quite closely. The shape of the earlier pre-Yahwistic tradition can only be guessed, but it is possible that that tradition told of a faithful response, of victory over the Canaanites at Hormah (underlying Num 21:2–3), and of a successful invasion of the land from the south. In Num 21:1 there is an allusion to "the way of the spies," and the tradition in Josh 15:13–19 may also reflect the memory of incursion from the south (cf. Judg 1:11–20).

There is very general agreement that vv 39–45 belong to the Yahwist. Israel is הָעָם "the people," and there are no certain signs of P. Some analysts believe that J and E are closely interwoven (e.g. A. Dillmann, *Numeri*, 80–81; B. Baentsch, *Numeri*, 532), and others that the two sources have been joined adjacently (e.g. J. E. Carpenter & G. Harford, *Hexateuch*, 519). For some the story is an essential unit, apart from minor glosses, to be attributed to J (e.g. W. Rudolph, *Der Elohist*, 78–79; O. Eissfeldt, *Hexateuch*, 172–73; C. A. Simpson, *Early Traditions*, 230–36; M. Noth, *Numbers*, 101–03; G. W. Coats, *Rebellion*, 139; V. Fritz, *Israel*, 19–24) or E (A. Kuenen, *Hexateuch*, 153 n.14; B. W. Bacon, *Triple Tradition*, 189; H. Gressmann, *Mose*, 291 n.1 [minor traces of J]). Arguments for E would have to be based largely on the assumption that Num 21:1–3 is a parallel tradition, and is to be assigned to J. Convincing linguistic arguments are lacking, while the reference to "Canaanite" rather than "Amorite" tends to tell against E. Many analysts are uncommitted on the matter, and simply link the passage with the JE redactor. If the theory of interweaving is correct then there should be clear signs of duplication. The story in fact moves steadily and coherently from theme to theme. The report (v 39a) is followed by mourning (v 39b), ascent (v 40a), resolve to go forward and confession (v 40b), questioning rebuke (v 41), command (v 42a), reasons (v 42a, 42b, 43), disobedience (v 44), defeat (v 45). The only serious point of tension is the assertion in v 40a that Israel reached the top, and that in v 44 which claims she presumed to go there. Even this need not be the sort of duplication indicative of interwoven sources. It is possible that v 44 *interprets* the act of v 40a as presumption. It would therefore be possible that v 40 (minus the last clause) contains the pre-Yahwistic link between the encouragement of Caleb in Num 13:30 (to which Israel faithfully responded) and the victory at Hormah in Num 21:3. The rest of the story (Num 14:41–45) would be the Yahwist's adaptation of the tradition. Israel's faithlessness justifies the long detour, and enables the Yahwist to tell of settlement from the east. For him whatever later success may have been gained at Hormah (Num 21:1–3) it did not materially affect the course of events. There was in any case for the Yahwist an initial catastrophic defeat there, the outcome of Israel's presumptuous spirit, and a further vindication of the judgment of Num 14:25. The Yahwist's supplementation would include the mourning of v 39, and the confession of sin in v 40 (cf. Num 12:11).

M. Noth (*Pentateuchal Traditions*, 133–36) thought that Hormah may originally have featured in Calebite settlement tradition associated with Hebron. If so it was probably taken up into the Judah conquest traditions. In Judg 1:16–17 there is a description of Judah's success in the company of Kenites against Hormah. The text is uncertain, but an attack on Arad is probably implied (cf. Num 21:1–3). According to this story Judah renames the city Hormah. In the story in its present form there may be an etiological motive, explaining the ban in war—i.e. the total destruction of all booty. The suggestion of J. de Vaulx (*Nombres*, 177–78) that Num 14:39–40, 44a allude to some ceremony on a Canaanite high place is not very probable. If some such theme had been at the core of the tradition it is reasonable to suppose that precise allusions would have survived, and been developed further. It is best to suppose that, as in the story of the spies, some ancient tradition of settlement has been taken up into Judah's story of invasion from the south. For further discussion of the theory of invasion from the south see H. H. Rowley, *From Joseph to Joshua* (London: OUP, 1950) 101–04.

The history of the tradition in Num 13–14 may be summarized thus:

1. Calebite settlement traditions associated with Hebron, and possibly Hormah.

2. These traditions are incorporated into a history of Judah which told of a reconnaissance penetrating as far as Hebron, and after initial hesitation of a successful invasion from the south, inspired by Caleb's foresight and courage. There is victory at Hormah.

3. A Yahwistic adaptation builds on Israel's hesitation, making it an instance of unbelief which incurs divine judgment—i.e. a major detour which results ultimately in an approach to the land from the east. The initial contact with Hormah is a disaster.

4. An exilic expansion focuses on the crucial Mosaic intercession which makes a second chance possible.

5. The priestly expansion by the author of Numbers which extends the reconnaissance to the whole land, makes Joshua one of the faithful spies, and which builds on the theme of Israel's murmuring as rejection of the land, and on the necessary divine judgement.

Comment

1. וַיִּבְכּוּ "and they wept." The verb covers all kinds of weeping—joy (Gen 43:30), grief (1 Sam 1:10), lamentation (Lam 1:2), repentance (2 Kgs 22:19), supplication (2 Kgs 20:3). Here the context suggests vexation regarding their plight as in Num 11:4. Fear of the Canaanites, and a general sense of hopelessness regarding the settlement are the decisive factors. The closest parallels are in Judg 20:23, 26. Both contexts are concerned with intractable military situations.

2–3. The speech of murmuring contains the usual formal elements of such complaints—a lament (v 2), an interrogative challenge (v 3), and an attempt at justification (v 3). The theme "return to Egypt" is an important symbol in the OT of apostasy and alienation from Yahweh (Deut 17:16; Hos 7:11; Isa 30:1–7; 31:1–3; Jer 2:18, 36; Ezek 17:15). It can also denote Yahweh's rejection of Israel (Hos 8:13; 9:3; 11:5). Note also Jeremiah's attitude toward the migration to Egypt (Jer 42:7–22).

3. וְטַפֵּנוּ "and our little ones." The root suggests taking quick or little steps; see N. H. Snaith, *Numbers*, 242 (cf. Num 31:17–18; Deut 2:34).

4. רֹאשׁ "captain." J. R. Bartlett ("The Use of the Word "רֹאשׁ "") suggests that the title belonged originally to tribal leaders who were competent to

judge in both military and judicial matters. It remained in use for men with such responsibilities, and for senior men in families or clans, and could easily develop new uses of a special kind.

5. The act of prostration by Moses (and Aaron) is typical of P (Num 16:4, 22; 17:10; 20:6) in the book of Numbers. In Amos 3:5 the root is used of the fall of a bird in a trap and in 2 Kgs 19:14 of Hezekiah's response to the letter (cf. also Gen 17:17; 24:64; Lev 9:24; Josh 7:10; 1 Sam 25:23; 2 Sam 9:6; 1 Kgs 18:7; Ezek 1:28; 3:23; 11:13; 43:3; 44:4; Dan 8:17). It seems reasonable to see an intercessory element here. The action denotes at the very least an attitude of self-abasement or deference before one of higher rank (cf. Lev 9:24; Josh 7:6; 1 Sam 25:3; 2 Sam 9:6; Ruth 2:10). This makes it unlikely that the prostration is before the people. In that case לִפְנֵי must mean "in front of" (see BDB, 816–18). J. de Vaulx (*Nombres*, 175) is unconvincing when he seeks to associate the idea with threats to the life of Moses. Where such danger is present (as in v 10) there is no prostration. There is thus no reason for supposing that Moses and Aaron are pleading to the people for their lives. The prostration before Yahweh, however, is not merely an act of deference. M. Weinfeld (*Deuteronomy and the Deuteronomic School* [Oxford: Clarendon, 1972] 205) is not strictly accurate in claiming that prostration is a normal response to the theophany in P. On the whole the appearance of the divine glory tends to come later in these stories (as here in v 10). Nor is it quite correct to say with G. W. Coats (*Rebellion*, 173) that prostration signifies a willingness to stand aside and let Yahweh react as he chooses. If that were true it would make little difference to the course of the story. In Num 17:6–15 prostration is clearly intercessory, aimed at averting divine wrath, and this is probably its usual significance. Here it averts immediate wrath, holding up the flow of events, thereby giving Joshua and Caleb opportunity to argue their case in vv 6–7.

8. On "a land which flows with milk and honey" see *Comment* on Num 13:27.

9. לַחְמֵנוּ הֵם "they are our bread." Israel is assured that the conquest will be as easy as eating bread (cf. Num 13:32; 24:8; Deut 7:16; Jer 10:25; Ps 14:4).

9. צִלָּם "their protection" or "their shadow." This may be an allusion to the protection afforded by their deities (M. Noth, *Numbers*, 108; L. E. Binns, *Numbers*, 92; J. Sturdy, *Numbers*, 100—n.b. that סוּר מֵעַל is used of the divine presence in Judg 16:20; 1 Sam 28:15). Some think of it simply as an appropriate figure of speech for a hot country (G. B. Gray, *Numbers*, 153; N. H. Snaith, *Numbers*, 243)—cf. Judg 9:15; Isa 25:4; 32:2; Ps 17:8.

10. Stoning is a typical response in such rebellious contexts (cf. 1 Sam 30:6; 1 Kgs 12:18).

10. וּכְבוֹד יהוה "and the glory of Yahweh." The root suggests "weight" or "heaviness," and the noun is widely used of an external appearance of splendor or wealth. It can be used of riches (Gen 31:1; Isa 10:3; Hag 2:7; Ps 49:17), of success (Gen 45:13; 1 Kgs 3:13), and of beauty (Isa 35:2). In P the "glory" is depicted as a visible shining splendor which accompanies Yahweh when he draws near to reveal himself to Israel (Exod 14:4, 17–18;

16:10; Num 17:7). In some of these texts "glory" in the eyes of Israel's enemies is what Yahweh seeks. In P "glory" is the only form in which Yahweh's presence can be visibly apprehended, and essentially it speaks of his majesty. The idea does not originate with P. It is used extensively and daringly by Ezekiel (see von Rad, *Studies in Deuteronomy* [London: SCM, 1953] 39–42), and should probably be traced to the pre-exilic temple (see M. Weinfeld, *Deuteronomy*, 201–06; R. E. Clements, *God and Temple*, [Oxford: Blackwell, 1965] 104). The "glory" in P is described by E. Jacob (*Theology of the Old Testament* [London: Hodder, 1974] 79–82) as a "veritable *theologoumenon* of the divine presence," and by Weinfeld (*Deuteronomy*, 201–06) as a "systematised glorified version befitting learned priests of a speculative bent of mind." Prophetic and deuteronomistic literature give to the idea an eschatological dimension. The difference between the "priestly" and "prophetic" developments is drawn sharply by W. Eichrodt (*Theology of the Old Testament. 2* [London: SCM, 1967] 29–35). By contrast to the cloud the glory in P appears intermittently, generally at critical points in the wilderness story which require some divine speech or action. It is common in P's stories of disaffection, and appears also in Exod 24:16–17; 40:35; Lev 9:23. Here in Num 14:10 the glory appears "in" the Tent; in Num 16:19; 20:6 the "door" of the Tent is specified. Since the appearance in v 10 is witnessed by all Israel we must assume that this appearance also takes place at the door.

11. עַד־אָנָה "how long." The expression has strong prophetic connections (e.g. Hos 8:5; Jer 23:26; 47:6).

11. יְנַאֲצֻנִי "will they despise me" (cf. Num 16:30). The root means "to condemn," "to spurn" (BDB), or "to despise," "to treat without respect" (KB). For other occurrences in the *piel* see Deut 31:20; 2 Sam 12:14; Isa 1:4; 5:24; 60:14; Jer 23:17; Pss 10:3, 13; 74:10, 18. In some texts, as G. W. Coats points out (*Rebellion*, 146–47), it seems to indicate actual "rejection" or "renunciation" (e.g. Isa 1:4; 5:24), and this would make good sense here, since Israel (Caleb excepted) is to be rejected by God. This does not preclude a sense of distaste ("spurning") or ridicule ("despising"); n.b. that in Num 11:20 the Yahwist uses מָאַס to express the idea of "rejection."

11. הָאֹתוֹת "the signs." These are tokens of God's power and evidence of his presence. Israel has witnessed them, but failed to act trustfully (cf. Deut 4:34; 6:22; 7:19; 28:8; 29:3). The word is widely used, and can relate to any physical object to which some special meaning is attached (cf. e.g. Gen 9:12; 17:11; Exod 31:13, 17). Events and people (particularly their names) can also function as "signs" (cf. e.g. 1 Sam 2:34; 10:7, 9; 14:10; Isa 7:11, 14; 8:13; 20:3). See further B. O. Long, *Etiological Narrative*, 65–78.

11. לֹא־יַאֲמִינוּ "they will not believe." Israel's failure is often expressed in these terms in Deuteronomic texts (e.g. Deut 1:32; 9:23; cf. Ps 78:22). The word has to do essentially with "trust" and "credibility," and this accords with D's tendency to see disaffection in terms of faulty inner dispositions. Can all be staked on the word of Yahweh? (cf. Gen 15:6; 45:26; Exod 4:1, 5, 8–9, 31; 14:31; 19:9; Num 20:12; 1 Kgs 10:7; 2 Kgs 17:14). According to G. von Rad (*Old Testament Theology. 1* [London; SCM, 1975] 171) to "believe" means "to make oneself secure in Yahweh."

12. בַּדֶּבֶר "with pestilence" (cf. 2 Sam 24:13, 15; Jer 14:12; 21:9). *G* describes it simply as "death."

14. עַיִן בְּעַיִן "face to face," literally "eye to eye." The phrase occurs elsewhere only in Isa 52:8, and is clearly intended to express the closest of contact.

14. וַעֲנָנְךָ עֹמֵד עֲלֵהֶם "and your cloud stands over them." This conception differs from that in the following clauses (the Yahwist's picture). The words may possibly be harmonizing influence from the author of Numbers (cf. Num 10:34).

18. אֶרֶךְ אַפַּיִם "slow to anger." For further descriptions of the divine forbearance in this kind of context see Ps 78:38–39; Neh 9:19.

18. וְרַב-חֶסֶד "and totally faithful." The idea is often rendered "steadfast love." Notions of "loyalty" and "reliable commitment" are integral to the word in many OT contexts. For further discussion and references see N. H. Snaith, *Numbers*, 244–45.

18. נֹשֵׂא עָוֹן "forgiving iniquity." This probably means the taking away of the punishment sin deserves. The root נָשָׂא means "to lift up," and the idea of the carrying away of sin seems integral.

18. וָפֶשַׁע "and transgression." Snaith (*Numbers*, 245) argues that "rebellion" is preferable since the word denotes opposition to a person rather than infringement of rules. "Transgression" is the more usual rendering, and can be taken to imply rebelliousness.

18. RSV, following *G*, adds "the guilty" here. For the use of the root נָקָה elsewhere see Isa 3:26; Zech 5:3. NEB thinks of the phrase, not in judicial terms, but of Yahweh's unwillingness to "sweep them clean away." This is a possibility, but the ancient understanding in *G* deserves respect.

18. פֹּקֵד "visiting." In P this root is used quite differently with the senses "to appoint" or "to number" (cf. e.g. Num 1:3, 50).

19. נָשָׂאתָה "you have forgiven." In view of the fact that נָשָׂא can also mean "to carry" N. H. Snaith (*Numbers*, 245–46) suggests a double meaning here (cf. Exod 19:4; Deut 32:11).

21. חַי-אָנִי "as I live." A common oath form. In the Pentateuch, however, it occurs only here and in v 28.

22. וַיְנַסּוּ אֹתִי "they have put me to the test" (cf. Deut 6:16; Exod. 17:2, 7). According to N. Lohfink (*Das Hauptgebot. Eine Untersuchung literarischer Einleitungsfragen zu Dtn. 5–11* [Rome: PBI, 1963] 80) the "testing" motif belongs to the cult. This "testing" of Yahweh seems to be a reversal of the original idea in D of Yahweh's "testing" Israel (Deut 8:2; 29:2). The "testing" of Yahweh may well have an earlier background (cf. e.g. Isa 7:12). In D it indicates an attitude of mind dissatisfied with simple trust. The sin at Meribah (Exod 17:7) involved lack of trust. Yahweh's presence was queried, and so the place was also called Massah (see V. Fritz, *Israel*, 53 n.23).

22. זֶה עֶשֶׂר פְּעָמִים "these ten times." "Ten" is understood by most commentators as a round figure. F. V. Winnett (*The Mosaic Tradition* [Toronto: TUP, 1949] 121–54) takes it literally, and builds a wide-ranging theory on that assumption. On the subject generally see H. A. Brongers, "Die Zehnzahl in der Bibel und ihrer Umwelt," *Studia Biblica et Semitica* (Ed. W. C. van Unnik & A. S. van der Woude; Wageningen: Veeman & Zonen, 1966) 30–45. A hyperbolic use of "ten" is well attested (cf. e.g. Gen 31:7, 41; Job 19:3).

24. רוּחַ אַחֶרֶת "a different spirit," cf. Num 11:17 for a further example of a psychological use of רוּחַ.

24. וַיְמַלֵּא אַחֲרָי "he has followed me wholeheartedly," cf. Deut 1:36; Josh 14:8.

25. For comment on the Amalekites and Canaanites see *Comment* on Num 13:29.

25. דֶּרֶךְ יַם-סוּף "the way to the Sea of Reeds." This probably indicates a specific route that they are to take, but it also threatens to nullify the great victory secured at the Sea (Exod 14:1–15:21). The precise location of the sea remains uncertain.

29. פִּגְרֵיכֶם "your carcasses." The root can be used of the corpses of men (Amos 8:3) or animals (Gen 15:11). The contemptuous use found here occurs also in Lev 26:30; Ezek 6:5.

30. נָשָׂאתִי אֶת-יָדִי "I swore," literally "I lifted up my hand." The lifting of the hands to heaven would probably have accompanied the taking of oaths (cf. Exod 6:8; Deut 32:40; Dan 12:7).

33. רֹעִים "shepherds." The next generation will be deprived of the benefits of the land for forty years, and will have to exist as shepherds on its perimeters.

33. וְנָשְׂאוּ אֶת-זְנוּתֵיכֶם "you shall suffer for your faithlessness," literally "you shall carry your whoredoms" (cf. RV).

33. עַד-תֹּם "until the last of." The root תָּמַם has the general sense "to complete" (cf. e.g. Deut 31:24, 30). The idea here and in v 35 (cf. also Num 32:13) seems to be "until all your deaths have been completed." For this eliptical use of the verb cf. e.g. Gen 47:15; Deut 2:15).

34. וִידַעְתֶּם אֶת-תְּנוּאָתִי "and you shall know me as an enemy." The phrase conveys a sense of active opposition and hostility. The noun occurs elsewhere only in Job 33:10, and there the text is uncertain. The verb from תְּנוּאָתִי occurs in Num 30:6; 32:7 with the sense of "to disallow" or "to discourage." R. Loewe ("Divine Frustration Exegetically Frustrated," *Words and Meanings* [Ed. P. R. Ackroyd & B. Lindars. Cambridge: CUP, 1968] 137–58) subjects the word to meticulous analysis, and concludes that "what it means to thwart me" is the best translation. Some element of "abandonment" in the word may have been understood (cf. Num 32:15).

36. On "an evil report" see *Comment* on 13:32.

37. בַּמַּגֵּפָה "by plague," literally "by a smiting," though a plague seems usually to be understood (cf. Exod 9:14; Ezek 24:16; Zech 14:12, and the use of the root נָגַף for "plague" in Exod 7:27; 12:13; 30:12; Josh 22:17).

39. וַיִּתְאַבְּלוּ "and they mourned." The word is rare in the Hexateuch (cf. Gen 37:34; Exod 33:4). It is often used of mourning for the dead (Gen 37:34; 1 Sam 6:19; 2 Sam 13:37; 14:2; 19:2; 1 Chr 7:22; 2 Chr 35:24), but it can readily be used, as here, of bad news (Exod 33:4; 1 Sam 15:35; 16:1; Isa 66:10; Ezek 7:12, 27; Dan 10:2; Neh 1:4, 8–9).

40. חָטָאנוּ "we have sinned," cf. Num 21:7; 32:3; Deut 1:41; 9:16, 21; Ps 78:17, 32 for other occurrences of the root in connection with disaffection in the wilderness. The root is generally understood to mean "to miss the mark" (see e.g. KB; E. Jacob. *Theology,* 281), implying the transgression of specific commandments, received and known.

44. וַיַּעְפִּלוּ "but they presumed." N. H. Snaith (*Numbers*, 248) notes the Arabic ʿafala "swell"(?), and gafala "reckless," "headstrong." The word עֹפֶל can mean "tumour" or "rounded hill." The idea "to swell" may thus be the starting point, and hence self-important "presumption." The implication is probably that Israel was reckless and/or lighthearted.

44. A major function of the ark, in the view of older tradition, was to lead Israel into battle (cf. 1 Sam 4:1–22). Here it remains in the camp, as a witness to Yahweh's absence from the expedition.

45. וַיַּכְּתוּם "and they pursued them." The root denotes "crushing by beating," thus "pounded blow by blow" (N. H. Snaith, *Numbers*, 249). G understands it to mean "cut them in pieces."

45. Hormah "complete destruction." The place is possibly the modern Tell el-Mishash, not far to the east of Beersheba. See also the stories in Num 21:1–3; Judg 1:17.

Explanation

This section continues the story of the survey of the land in Num 13. Israel as a whole responds in a faithless fashion to the report of the spies, and the divine judgement is that the settlement of the land is to be delayed, and a long detour conducted, until the next generation is ready to enter the land. An attempt to defy this judgment results in total disaster at Hormah.

Once again the priestly author of Numbers makes a significant contribution to the tradition. In vv 1–4 he elaborates the Yahwist's speech of disaffection, building it up into the customary stylized speech pattern (cf. Exod 16:3). The people lament, ask challenging and faithless questions, and seek to justify their attitude. Some elements of the Yahwist's story survive in vv 1, 4. In vv 5–10 the priestly author depicts the climactic confrontation between Moses, Aaron, and the faithful spies on the one hand, and the rest of the people on the other. The story develops Joshua's role as a faithful spy alongside Caleb, and offers some further elaboration of the Yahwist's encouragement speech in Num 13:30. The confrontation comes to a head with the intervention of the divine glory. The idea of a theophany as the symbol of divine intervention at such critical points was important to authors of the priestly school. The author of Exodus employs it in Exod 16:10 in a similar context, when the people murmur for food and Yahweh intervenes to provide manna and quail. For the author of Numbers the intervention is invariably the prelude to punishment. The theophany appears to fulfill a two-fold function for the author. It provides the protection Moses and Aaron need from the wrath of the people, and it constitutes the introduction the author wants for the divine speech in vv 11–25.

The priestly author is happy to preserve this extended deuteronomistic gloss on the Yahwist's work in vv 11b–23. It helps to emphasize the seriousness of the situation, and it is precisely this theme which the author of Numbers wishes to develop further in vv 26–38. The Yahwistic idea of the rejection of the wilderness generation is extensively elaborated in vv 26–35. Israel's rejection of the land as "evil" perhaps prefigures an unwillingness to engage in the return in post-exilic times. The forty years of exclusion from the land (v 33) echo the experience of exile. The future lies with the children, with a new generation, and that too prefigures God's purpose in post-exilic times. In order to accentuate the seriousness of Israel's defection, and the gravity of the error of those who bore major responsibility for it, the author chooses to specify the manner of death suffered by the faithless spies, stressing the point that only Joshua and Caleb survive (vv 36–38).

Looking at the patterns in P as a whole this tradition clearly marks the point at which a special interest in the theme of disaffection in the wilderness begins to emerge. The priestly author of Exodus does indeed develop a story of murmuring in Exod 16, but there the outcome is a gracious divine response. Here, for the first time in the priestly view of the wilderness period, national disaffection brings divine judgment. The fact that the event occurs after the revelation at Sinai is probably a factor, but the nature of the sin, rejection of the land, gives this rebellion its particularly serious aspect. As in Exod 16:2–3 the people "murmur," but this time the situation becomes very ugly with the threat to stone Joshua and Caleb. The speech in vv 2–4 is above all a rejection of the policy that has taken Israel to the borders of the land. It is rejected and defamed. The congregation is "evil" and its apostasy is "faithlessness" ("whoredoms"), a word which as much as any probably interprets the exile. It is often applied to the worship of other gods (Hos 2:7; 9:1) or foreign alliances (Ezek 16:26; 23:1–5). Israel has gathered against Yahweh (v 35), a word which here must have sinister connotations (cf. Num 16:11; 27:3). She has rebelled (v 9), willfully rejecting Yahweh's lordship, and a word is used which often occurs as a general description of rebellion in the wilderness (Num 17:25; 20:10, 24; Deut 1:26, 43; 9:7, 23–24; 32:51; Ezek 20:8, 13, 24; Pss 78:8, 17; 106:7, 33, 43; Neh 9:17, 26). The whole section vv 26–38 is a long priestly commentary on the disaffection associated with the survey of the land. As has often been noted there is a marked tendency in P to replace "action" with "theology," and this commentary is an excellent example. What most interests the author is the kind of sin which can lead to exclusion from the land. This tradition provides an ideal base for the exploration of the theme, and for the author it is probably the most important thing which the motif of disaffection in the wilderness has to offer.

Much of this does speak directly to the circumstances of the fifth century. There are explanations here of what led to the exile, and encouragements to those who are part of the dispersion, and to those who are in the land, to consider their attitudes toward it. The involvement of all Israel in the survey of the land draws attention to the fact that the faithful spies are those from Judah and Ephraim. Their descendants are encouraged to hope for a new future, and to engage in a second settlement. There was always the risk that Jews, like the spies, would defame the land. There may well be implicit criticism of those who refuse to engage in the return. There is some "recognition of the uncertainty of the exilic age's position" (P. R. Ackroyd, *Exile and Restoration* [London: SCM, 1968] 101; cf. also K. Elliger, "Sinn und Ursprung der priesterlichen Geschichtserzählung," *ZThK* 49 [1952] 121–43). Will the Israel of the new age meet the challenge of faith more convincingly than the Israel of old? There may also be an apologetic function. The tradition shows that though one generation may be excluded the next may indeed possess the land (v 31), untainted by the "whoredoms" of their fathers (vv 32–33). Though the second generation may suffer some of the consequences it cannot ultimately be held responsible for the sins of the first. Any charge that the Babylonian exiles have forfeited their right to the land for all time is false.

An exilic editor, much influenced by deuteronomistic thinking, has offered his own elaboration of Yahwistic tradition in vv 11b–23. Deuteronomy, an exilic work in its present form, was particularly interested in this tradition because of its treatment of the theme of disinheritance. In Deut 1:39 only the very young children will enter the land. These are the ones who can be judged to have been without moral responsibility for the sin. Here in v 23 the act of disinheritance takes the form of a solemn oath by Yahweh that the sinful generation will not receive the promise made to the patriarchs (cf. Num 32:15; Ps 106:26–27). In v 12 disinheritance means to be driven away. That above all was Israel's exilic experience.

So it is that in D this story, along with that of the golden calf, is archetypal. It explains dispossession. In the aftermath of the fall of Jerusalem (587 B.C.) it was important to point out that possession was contingent upon obedience, to explain what had happened, and also to set the tone for the future. The earlier Josianic movement was in part a movement for political independence, and was imbued with the idea that there was a new war of occupation to be fought. The spirit of the holy war was to be revived, and the timidity evident in this story was to be eschewed.

The Yahwist is the one who provides the most radical reorganization of the tradition available to him. His adaptation of the survey of the land and of the events at Hormah has historiographical purpose in providing a base for the Transjordanian journey and for settlement from the east. The theological implications were also important, and the Yahwist's work prepares the way for the crucial role that the tradition has in both D and P. The command to Israel *not* to enter from the south, but to turn back (v 25), is a significant act of rejection. The Yahwist's final perspective, however, is far from sombre. In the providence of God the tragic failures of one generation can be retrieved in the experiences of the next. The purpose of God cannot ultimately be defeated. Nevertheless the reversal of the Judah tradition by the Yahwist adds a new and serious dimension to disaffection at this stage of the story. He has something of a chiastic pattern in his arrangement of the stories of disaffection from Sinai to the Jordan.

Apostasy—the golden calf (Exod 32:1–35)
    Discontent—Taberah/Quail (Num 11:1–35)
        Insubordination—individuals (Num 12:1–16)
            Insubordination—Israel (Num 13:1–14:45)
        Insubordination—individuals (Num 16:1–35)
    Discontent—serpents (Num 21:4–9)
Apostasy—Baal-Peor (Num 25:1–5)

The tradition in Num 13–14 thus occupies a central place in this phase of the Yahwist's story, and it also marks a major turning point in the wilderness itinerary. For the first time the Yahwist uses a variety of words of disaffection, relating to inner disposition and attitude, and this enforces the suspicion that for him as well the tradition is significant and serious. Having understood the events of 721 B.C. in terms of religious apostasy (Exod 32:1–35) the Yahwist could not escape the conclusion that Judah herself must have come close to destruction under Manasseh. This engendered in the Yahwist a new "pessimism" about Israel's loyalty to Yahweh. On the other hand the failures which led to the collapse of the northern kingdom do not negate the continuation of God's purposes in the southern kingdom. The inherent "optimism" in the story indicates that despite faithlessness and judgment the threads can be regathered. This mirrors perhaps the new mood and new policies in the early years of Josiah's reign.

The figure of Moses as ultimate authority is also important to the Yahwist. A central feature of his adaptation is the rejection of Moses. The people seek another "captain" (v 4) to lead them back to Egypt. In v 44 they ignore his warnings, and go off without his guidance and leadership. It is in the Davidic king, who is prefigured in the person of Moses, that Israel must find authoritative leadership. If the land is to be secured, and if there is to be a realistic political future in the land, then Josianic policy must be followed. To some, prefigured in the rebellious Israelites, this may have been national suicide, with the craving for Egypt representing a hankering after foreign alliances. The Yahwist's chief concern is thus to deepen Judah's awareness of the insidiousness and perils of disaffection, to advance the cause of what he believed to be true Mosaic faith, and to vindicate the principle of political independence as pursued under Josiah. The extension of Judaean control at this period to large parts of the north made the Yahwist's concern with settlement and possession a very appropriate theme. Josiah's cultic activities in the north (2 Kgs 23:15–20), his death at Megiddo (2 Kgs 23:29), and the fact that pilgrimages to Jerusalem from the north were established and sustained (Jer 41:5) are all indications of his control and influence.

The Judah tradition with which the Yahwist worked, in so far as it can be discerned, is essentially optimistic (see *Form/Structure/Setting*). After the weeping of the people Caleb encourages them to engage in a successful invasion from the south, epitomized by the victory at Hormah (Num 21:1–3). This too asserts that possession of the land can only be secured through policies of independence, and advocates a strong and distinctive Yahwism. In its final form this may have been shaped in Hezekiah's time, but its roots are probably much deeper in Judah's history, and can be traced ultimately to Calebite settlement traditions associated with Hebron. The allusion to "weeping" (v 1) may reflect at a distance some unwillingness on the part of those who were associated with Caleb to engage in the settlement, but it is also important to the fully developed Judah tradition. Judah must trust Yahweh, and not faithlessly bewail her plight. Her future lies in non-alignment with respect to the nations, and total commitment to Yahweh. The message is comparable to that of Isaiah himself (cf. e.g. Isa 28:14–16; 30:1–5; 31:1–3).

In the broadest theological terms the section addresses itself to the theology of land. Access to the land, and to its resources, is contingent upon a whole-hearted commitment to the land, and to Yahweh who has given it. The dimensions of this theme within the OT at large are discussed by W. Brueggemann (*The Land*, Philadelphia: Fortress, 1977). It is with the search for security, for political and economic stability, the elusive goals of freedom from war and hunger, that the OT theology of land is concerned. The wilderness traditions make an important contribution to the whole.

Additional Cereal and Drink Offerings   (15:1–16)

Bibliography

Abba, R. "The Origin and Significance of Hebrew Sacrifice." *BTB* 7 (1977) 123–38. **Gray, G. B.** *Sacrifice in the Old Testament.* Oxford: Clarendon, 1925. **Levine, B. A.** *In the Presence of the Lord—A Study of Cult and Some Cultic Terms.* Leiden: Brill, 1974. **McCarthy, D. J.** The Symbolism of Blood and Sacrifice." *JBL* 88 (1969) 166–76. ———. "Further Notes on the Symbolism of Blood and Sacrifice." *JBL* 92 (1973) 205–10. **Milgrom, J.** "Sin Offering or Purification Offering." *VT* 21 (1971) 237–39. **Snaith, N. H.** "Sacrifices in the Old Testament." *VT* 7 (1957) 308–17. ———. "The Sin Offering and the Guilt Offering." *VT* 15 (1965) 73–80. **Stevenson, W. R.** "Hebrew *Olah* and *Zebach* Sacrifices." (Ed. W. Baumgartner, O. Eissfeldt, K. Elliger, L. Rost) *Festschrift für A. Bertholet.* Tübingen: Mohr, 1950. **Thompson, R. J.** *Penitence and Sacrifice in Early Israel.* Leiden: Brill, 1960. **de Vaux, R.** *Studies in Old Testament Sacrifice.* Cardiff: Univ. of Wales, 1964.

Translation

[1] And Yahweh spoke to Moses, saying, [2] "Speak to the people of Israel, and say to them, When you come into the land where you are to live, which I am giving to you, [3] and when you offer to Yahweh from the herd or from the flock an offering by fire or a whole offering, or any sacrifice, to fulfill a vow, or as a freewill offering or at your appointed feasts, to make a soothing odor to Yahweh, [4] then he who brings his offering shall offer to Yahweh a cereal offering of a tenth of an ephah [a] of fine flour, mixed with a quarter of a hin of oil. [5] And wine for the drink offering, a quarter of a hin, you shall prepare with the whole offering, or for the sacrifice, for each lamb. [a] [6] Or for a ram, [a] you shall prepare for a cereal offering two tenths of an ephah of fine flour mixed with a third of a hin of oil. [7] And for the drink offering you shall offer a third of a hin of wine, a soothing odor to Yahweh. [8] And when you prepare a bull for a whole offering, or any sacrifice, to fulfil a vow, or for shared offerings to Yahweh, [9] then you [a] shall offer with the bull a cereal offering of three tenths of an ephah of fine flour, mixed with half a hin of oil. [10] And you shall offer for the drink offering half a hin of wine, as an offering by fire, a soothing odor to Yahweh.

[11] "So it shall be done for each bull or ram, or for each of the male lambs or the kids. [12] According to the number that you prepare, so shall you do with every one according to their number. [13] Every native Israelite shall do these things in this way, in offering an offering by fire, a soothing odor to Yahweh. [14] And if a resident alien, or someone permanently settled among you, wishes to offer an offering by fire, a soothing odor to Yahweh, he shall do as you do. [15] For the assembly [a] there shall be one statute for you, and for the resident alien, [b] a permanent statute throughout your generations. As you are, so shall the resident alien be before Yahweh. [16] There shall be one law and one ordinance for you, and for the resident alien with you."

Notes

4.a. *G* reads τοῦ οἰφι "of an ephah" here (RV, RSV, NEB). This meaning is evidently intended.
5.a. *G* has "as a soothing odor to Yahweh" here (cf. vv 7, 10). It is probably an addition.
6.a. *G* has "when you prepare it for a whole offering or for a sacrifice" (cf. v 8). This is probably another addition.
9.a. *BHS* proposes a second person singular here. An interchange of persons in this section is quite common, and may be a form critical rather than a text critical problem (see *Form/Structure/Setting*).
15.a. הַקָּהָל "the assembly" is lacking in *S* and Vg. J. Paterson (*Numbers*, 50) takes its occurrence in MT to be a gloss. In Sam and *G* the verse is linked closely with v 14.
15.b. On the linguistic features of this expression see GKC § 161c. *BHS* suggests the insertion of אִתְּכֶם "with you."

Form/Structure/Setting

There is total agreement among analysts that the section is the work of priestly editors, and also wide agreement that it is a relatively late accretion within P. J. Wellhausen (*Hexateuch*, 177–78) took the view that the whole of Num 15 came from the editor (not the author) of H (Lev 17–26). He drew attention to similarities between Num 15:2, 18 and Lev 19:23; 23:10; 25:2, and between Num 15:3 and Lev 22:21. A. Kuenen (*Hexateuch*, 96) described vv 1–16 as a "novella to Lev 2, intended to regulate what was there left to the free will of the sacrificer or to usage." The extension of precepts to aliens (vv 14–16) is shown to be paralleled in H (Lev 17:8, 10, 13; 24:22). G. B. Gray (*Numbers*, 168–69) argues that the laws in this chapter have little connection with one another, and none with the story of the spies in Num 13–14, or for that matter with the revolt of Korah in Num 16–17. Gray is at a loss to say what reasons induced the editor to refer this particular group of laws to this point in the period of wandering. M. Noth (*Pentateuchal Traditions*, 9) finds the insertion to be "without apparent motivation." Because of his particular belief that the P narrative is oriented to Sinai, and not the occupation of the land, the introductory formula in v 2 indicates for him a very late connection with the Pentateuch at large (see also Noth, *Numbers*, 114). J. Sturdy (*Numbers*, 108) conjectures that the final editor simply felt that narratives should alternate with laws. For Sturdy the laws are probably later than P, and intended as a supplement to it.

Some comparison with the laws of Ezek 46:5–7, 11, 14 is relevant. A similar scale of quantities is found there for the same purposes, but the amounts in Ezekiel are larger, they are not graduated so directly to the size of the animal, and there is no offering of wine. It may be that Ezekiel's scheme represents the tradition of the priests in Babylon in late exilic times, immediately prior to the first return of exiles. As G. B. Gray points out (*Numbers*, 170) there are some reasons for thinking that Num 15:1–16 is a later adaptation of this. The weakness of Kuenen's attempt to link vv 1–16 with Lev 2 is that vv 1–16 are not concerned with independent cereal offerings, as is Lev 2, but with cereal offerings that are demanded as an accompaniment to animal offerings. If vv 1–16 are linked rather with Ezek 46 we see in them a major extension of the scales of offering from the public offerings of the prince to the private offerings of the people. The continuation of the optional element present in Ezekiel, and the systematic grading of the scale according to the size of the animal give a general impression that vv 1–16 are the later development.

It may be that these adaptations represent an adjustment on the part of returning exiles. An important motive may be to involve the laity more fully in sacrificial procedures. The cereal and drink offerings which accompany the daily offerings of the priests (Exod 29:38–42) are also to be part of the lay offerings. This principle is also clear in Lev 7, but in vv 11–14 the quantities to accompany such private offerings are not specified, and so the author of Numbers has clarified the matter.

It may also be that the various changes of person throughout this section (see e.g. G. B. Gray, *Numbers*, 176) indicate that the author has assimilated older written material. The second person plural in vv 1–3, 12–16 is doubtless the author's own material. It may be that the third person singular material in vv 4, 9, containing the cereal and oil offering for flock and herd, contains the oldest stipulations. In Ezek 46 there is no wine offering. To this a second person singular accretion has been made (vv 5–8, 10–11), distinguishing between lambs and rams, and introducing regulations for wine offerings as well. It is this amplified text (vv 4–11) which the priestly author has taken, providing an appropriate introduction (vv 1–3), and extending the laws to the alien (vv 12–16). The findings of P. Grelot ("La Dernière Étape de la Rédaction Sacerdotale," *VT* 6 [1956] 174–89) suggest that the extension of the law to the alien indicates that the priestly author was at work in the second half of the fifth century. The tendency in *G* and *Sam* to use the second person plural throughout is probably a smoothing out of the unevenness in the text which the author's editorial work has produced.

Though the text in its earliest form may be no earlier than late exilic times it seems clear that the offering of cereal, oil, and wine was well established in pre-exilic custom. There are stories of the offering of oil and wine (Judg 9:9, 13), cereal and wine (1 Sam 1:24; 10:3), and prophetic allusions to wine (Hos 9:4) and oil (Mic 6:7). The stipulation of fixed quantities may have some background in the custom of the pre-exilic Temple, but there can be no certainty in the matter.

The question of why this material is included here by the priestly author may not be as difficult as commentators suggest. The assertion in v 2 provides the link with the disastrous events of Num 13–14—"when you come into the land where you are to live." If the nature of Israel's sin in Num 14 is perceived as rejection of the land this statement in Num 15:2 becomes a massive reassertion of faith in God's purpose. Israel will indeed inherit, and this sudden turn to the minutiae of observance in the land is a startling assertion of a practical and pragmatic faith.

Comment

3. אִשֶּׁה "an offering by fire," a general term covering all sacrifices burned on the altar.

3. נֶדֶר There seems no reason for accepting McNeile's view (*Numbers*, 80)

that "sacrifice" refers to the "shared offering" (see *Comment* on Num 6:14). It is best to understand it as a general reference.

3. רֵיחַ נִיחֹחַ "a soothing odor" (NEB), "sweet savor" (RV), "pleasing odor" (RSV). It is generally believed that this is an ancient term, reflecting the idea that God smells and delights in the sacrifice in an anthropomorphic way (cf. Gen 8:21 for its use in earlier tradition). According to J. Sturdy (*Numbers*, 109) the phrase in P has become a "vivid metaphor for acceptable worship."

4. It is impossible to be certain what the modern equivalents of these quantities would be. It may be 7½ pints (4.5 litres) of flour and 3 pints (1.8 litres) each of oil and wine. These quantities are also used in the laws of Exod 29:40 and Num 28–29.

7. לַנֶּסֶךְ "for the drink offering." According to Sir 50:15 this would be poured out at the foot of the altar (cf. Josephus, *Anti. Iud.* 3:9:4). The custom is ancient, as evidence from the Canaanite texts from Ras Shamra shows; see J. de Vaulx, *Nombres*, 179–80.

14. On the "alien" see *Comment* on Num 9:14. This verse seems to cite also another class of person who is resident in the land, but who lacks the status of native and alien (see A. H. McNeile, *Numbers*, 81). The NEB takes both clauses to refer to the alien, the difference being whether the alien is temporarily resident or permanently settled.

Explanation

This section tells of the quantities of flour, oil, and wine required for the various offerings. These quantities are described as the cereal and drink offerings. It appears that these are to accompany any offering, though the whole offerings and those connected with vows or the voluntary offering are specified. The quantities are fixed in terms of the animal offered. For every lamb it is one tenth of an ephah of flour, one quarter of a hin of oil, and one quarter of a hin of wine. For every ram it is two tenths of an ephah of flour, one third of a hin of oil, and one third of a hin of wine. For every bullock it is three tenths of an ephah of flour, half a hin of oil, and half a hin of wine.

Having described Israel's rejection of the land, and then her presumptuous attempt to take it (Num 14), the author of Numbers reaffirms God's commitment to the land and to his intention to give it to Israel. It is essentially the people as a whole who failed in Num 13–14, but nevertheless there is a future, and these are laws for their descendants to observe when they do in fact reach the land. The author's particular interest in the section reveals his continuing confidence in God's willingness to give the land. The cereals, the wine, and the oil are above all else the products of the land, and this is probably a good reason for the author's decision to discuss the quantities of these items to be used at sacrifices.

In all essentials the author is providing some elaboration of material in Ezekiel, in this instance Ezek 46:5–7, 11, 14. The scale of the offerings is more carefully graded in relation to the size of the animal, and the procedures are extended to the private offerings of people in general. There had been some mention of this in Lev 7:11–14. Here the author is able to specify precisely what their quantities should be. It appears that the author has taken up an already complex text in vv 4–11, and added vv 1–3 and vv 12–16 (see *Form/Structure/Setting*). The author's main contribution is thus the assertion that these principles apply to aliens as well as to native Israelites. Israel will indeed inherit the land, and Israelites along with resident aliens will be free to offer of its fruit, cereal, wine and oil, to Yahweh.

Offering the First Fruits (15:17–21)

Translation

¹⁷ *Yahweh said to Moses,* ¹⁸ *"Say to the people of Israel, When you come into the land to which I bring you,* ¹⁹ *and when you eat of the food of the land, you shall present a contribution to Yahweh.* ²⁰ *Of the first of your dough* ᵃ *you shall present a cake as a contribution. As a contribution from the threshing floor, so you shall present it.* ²¹ *Of the first of your dough you shall give to Yahweh, a contribution throughout your generations."*

Notes

20.a. עֲרִסֹתֵכֶם "your dough." The normal form of the word is found in v 21, and should probably be read here.

Form/Structure/Setting

Analysts are agreed that the material is priestly, and most take it, along with the whole of Num 15, to be a relatively late accretion. It has been observed by A. Kuenen (*Hexateuch,* 96) that v 18 is very similar to v 2, suggesting a common origin. G. B. Gray (*Numbers,* 177) points out a minor phraseological link between v 18b and the Holiness Code (Lev 17–26). In view of the link between v 18 and v 2 it is reasonable for us to attribute the section to the priestly author of Numbers. Affinities with H in vv 1–22 as a whole demonstrate only a familiarity with Leviticus, and in no way threaten the view of P we have adopted. In content the stipulation is the same as that given in Ezek 44:30. The only other reference to this particular offering is in Neh 10:38, and it is impossible to judge how old the practice is. The priestly author commits himself, as in v 2, to the graciousness of God's purpose. Despite the rejection of the land by the faithless in Num 14, God looks forward to the time when Israel will enter the land to which he is bringing them. Despite the chaos, and destruction brought about by human sin, the possibility of an ordered and detailed religious life in the land can still be perceived by the eye of faith.

Comment

19. תְּרוּמָה "a contribution." See *Comment* on Num 5:9. For further discussion in this context see M. Noth, *Numbers,* 115–16.

20. רֵאשִׁית עֲרִסֹתֵכֶם "the first of your dough." The meaning is uncertain. The expression occurs elsewhere in Ezek 44:30; Neh 10:37. The Talmudic use of ערס suggests "dough." N. H. Snaith (*Numbers,* 251) prefers "kneading trough"—"a batch of loaves from one kneading trough"—i.e. the first batch of your baking.

Explanation

This section prescribes a small offering, to be made regularly from the first fruits of the land in the form of a cake made from dough. This is a *terumah* offering.

As in vv 1–16 there is witness here to God's commitment to the land and to his promise, in spite of the sin of Num 14. In v 18 there is the same confidence as in v 2 concerning Israel's ultimate occupation of the land. In regulating such an offering there is implied a faith that Israel will indeed be free to till the land, and benefit from its produce. From the first of its bounty the Israelites are to make an offering to Yahweh. Here, as previously, the priestly author reveals an interest in bringing stipulations from Ezekiel (in this instance 44:30) within the ambit of Mosaic law. Despite Israel's faithlessness there will be an ordered religious life in the land, which is God's ultimate purpose.

Inadvertent Offenses   (15:22–31)

Bibliography

Kellermann, D. "Bemerkungen zum Sündopfergesetz in Num. 14:22ff." ed. H. Gese. *Festschrift für K. Elliger.* Neukirchen: Keuelaer, 1973, 107–14. **Toeg, A.** "טו במדבר: כב-לא-מדרש הלכה. An Halakhic Midrash in Num 15: 22–31." *Tarbiz* 43 (1973) 1–20.

Translation

[22] *"But if you err, and do not observe all these commandments which Yahweh has spoken to Moses,* [23] *all that Yahweh has commanded you by the hand of Moses, from the day that Yahweh commanded, and onward throughout your generations,* [24] *then if it was done inadvertently [a] without the knowledge of the congregation, all the congregation shall offer one young bull for a whole offering, a soothing odor to Yahweh, with its cereal offering and its drink offering, according to the ordinance, and one male goat for a purification offering.* [25] *And the priest shall make atonement for all the congregation of the people of Israel. And they shall be forgiven because it was an error, and they have brought their offering, an offering by fire to Yahweh, and their purification offering before Yahweh, for their error.* [26] *And all the congregation of the people of Israel shall be forgiven, and the resident alien with them, because the whole population was involved in the error.*

[27] *"If one person sins inadvertently, he shall offer a female goat a year old for a purification offering.* [28] *And the priest shall make atonement before Yahweh for the person who commits an error, when he sins inadvertently, to make atonement for him. And he shall be forgiven.* [29] *You shall have one law for him who does anything inadvertently, for him who is native among the people of Israel, and for the resident alien with them.* [30] *But the person who does anything with deliberate defiance, whether he is native or an alien, reviles Yahweh, [a] and that person shall be cut off from among his people. [b]* [31] *Because he has despised the word of Yahweh, and has broken his commandment, [a] that person shall be utterly cut off. His guilt shall be on him."*

Notes

24.a. לִשְׁגָגָה "inadvertently." The form is usually בִּשְׁגָגָה, as in vv 27, 29; Lev 4:22.
30.a. G reads "God" here.
30.b. Sam reads the plural noun (cf. Gen 17:14; Exod 31:14; Lev 7:20–21; Num 9:13).
31.a. The plural is more usual in such contexts, as in Sam, G, Syr and Tg.

Form/Structure/Setting

The priestliness of the material is universally recognized among analysts. Though its present position in Num 15 is widely believed to be relatively late the substance of the law itself is often considered to belong to the earlier levels in P (see e.g. A. Dillmann, *Numeri,* 83–84). The argument is based essentially on a comparison with other laws, apparently on the same subject, in Lev 4. Those in Lev 4 seem to be more elaborate, and are therefore likely to be later. They envisage two further categories of sinner—the high priest and the leader. Moreover in Lev 4 there is no whole offering for the congregation and one young bull (not a male goat as here) is required for the purification offering. In the case of an individual the purification offering may be a female goat (as here), though its age is not specified. It may in fact be a female lamb (Lev 4:32).

It has sometimes been suggested that Lev 4 refers to acts of commission and Num 15 to acts of omission. G. B. Gray (*Numbers*, 179) rejects this on the grounds that the phraseology of vv 24, 29 and the antithesis in v 30 show that the writer has in mind positive acts that violate the law. Gray himself is not committed to a simple view of Num 15 as the older legislation and Lev 4 as the later. The present form of Num 15:22–31 presupposes, in his view, Num 15:1–16, since he takes v 24b to refer to vv 8–10. This, however, he takes to be the influence of the compiler, and in substance he is inclined to accept Num 15:22–31 (and Lev 5:1–6) as older than Lev 4.

If this view is accepted it seems to threaten our view that the priestly author of Numbers was familiar with Leviticus in something like its present form. Gray's conclusion is in fact far from necessary. M. Noth (*Numbers*, 116) argues that the purpose of this section (vv 22–31) is to *expand* on Lev 4, especially with regard to the sacrifices to be offered. Thus v 24 goes beyond Lev 4 in laying down that the congregation must offer more than a purification offering. The young bull is to be a whole offering, with the male goat functioning as the purification offering. The author of Numbers also adds the cereal and drink offerings to the requirements of Lev 4. In the case of individuals the choice given in Lev 4 between goat and lamb is not necessarily unknown to Num 15. The author is concerned simply to specify the age of the goat. Viewed in this way the compiler of vv 22–31 is giving additional stipulations for two of the categories of person specified in Lev 4. He is also anxious to affirm that these principles apply to aliens as well as to native Israelites, and to insist that there are no sacrifices for deliberate offenses. J. Sturdy (*Numbers*, 111–12) also sees this section as expanding the details of the sacrifices to be made. N. H. Snaith (*Numbers*, 252) suggests that whereas Leviticus 4 deals with purification offerings in general Num 15 is concerned with inadvertence relating to the specific offering mentioned in vv 17–21. There is no indication in vv 22–31 that it should be understood so narrowly, and the approaches of Noth and Sturdy seem preferable.

It is difficult to make confident suggestions about the handling of inadvertence prior to the age of the present text. There were probably some provisions in the procedures of the pre-exilic Temple, but it is hard to say what they involved. It is easier to see why the author of Numbers placed this expansion of Lev 4 at this particular point. In vv 1–21 he has reasserted faith in the gracious purpose of God after the disasters of Num 14. Having introduced the expansionary stipulations he is able to make the point that for deliberate and defiant sin (such as that in Num 14) there is no sacrifice. The judgment of God in that chapter is right, and cannot be averted by sacrifice.

Comment

24. לִשְׁגָגָה "inadvertently." There is no indication of how such an offense might happen within the community, nor are any details given of the kind of offence in mind.

25. וְכִפֶּר "he shall make atonement." See *Comment* on Num 17:6–15.

30. בְּיָד רָמָה "with deliberate defiance," literally "with a high hand" (cf. Exod 14:8; Num 33:3).

30. As A. H. McNeile (*Numbers,* 83) points out the emphatic position of the word "Yahweh" (or "God," see *Notes*) emphasizes the seriousness of the offence.

31. הִכָּרֵת תִּכָּרֵת "he shall be utterly cut off." See *Comment* on Num 9:13.

Explanation

This section deals with the offerings to be made when inadvertent transgressions occur. There are separate requirements for those committed by the congregation as a whole (vv 22–26) and for those committed by individuals (vv 27–29). The congregation is required to make a whole offering (one young bull), with its accompanying cereal and drink offerings, and also a purification offering (one male goat). The individual is required to make a purification offering (one female goat). The point is made that these offerings are only appropriate for sins of inadvertence; there is no sacrifice for deliberate sin.

The author's purpose here is to offer some expansion of material in Lev 4. The congregation must offer more than a purification offering. The young bull is to be a whole offering, while a male goat is to be used for the purification offering. The priestly author also draws in the cereal and drink offerings of vv 1–16. His particular concern is to give additional stipulations regarding two of the categories of person mentioned in Lev 4—the congregation as a whole, and the individual. There is again, as in vv 12–16, a concern to apply these principles to the alien as well as to the native. This is doubtless a contemporary question in the fifth century. The author has applied this to a number of laws already, thereby resolving a point of discussion, and perhaps dissension.

The author's purpose in discussing inadvertent sin at this point is not hard to discover. Faith in the ultimate purpose of God for Israel and the land is one thing (vv 1–21), but Israel must be ready to reckon with certain hard realities. There are indeed sacrifices for sins of inadvertence, but there is no sacrifice for sin "with a high hand"—defiant and deliberate sin. The rejection of the land, and the presumptuousness which led to the debacle at Hormah (Num 14) both fall within this category. Faith in the good purpose of God cannot be allowed to become a form of complacency or presumptuousness. There are further illustrations of defiant and deliberate sin to follow, in Num 16–17. If these hard realities are unrecognized by Israel then the judgment of God is both appropriate and unavoidable.

Gathering Sticks on the Sabbath
(15:32–36)

Bibliography

Bamberger, B. J. "Revelations of Torah after Sinai." *HUCA* 16 (1941) 97–113. **Phillips, A.** "The Case of the Woodgatherer Reconsidered." *VT* 19 (1969) 125–28. **Weingreen, J.** "The Case of the Woodgatherer (Numbers XV 32–36): *VT* 16 (1966) 361–64.

Translation

³² *While the people of Israel were in the wilderness, they found a man gathering sticks on the sabbath day.* ³³ *And those who found him gathering sticks brought him to Moses and Aaron, and to all the congregation.* ³⁴ *They put him in custody, because it had not been made clear what should be done to him.* ³⁵ *And Yahweh said to Moses, "The man shall be put to death. All the congregation shall stone him with stones outside the camp."* ³⁶ *And all the congregation brought him outside the camp, and stoned him to death with stones, as Yahweh commanded Moses.*

Form/Structure/Setting

It is widely accepted among analysts that this story is a relatively late element within P. The resemblance to a story in H (Lev 24:10–14, 23) is unavoidable, and the midrashic character of the stories is widely recognized (e.g. G. B. Gray, *Numbers*, 182). O Eissfeldt (*Introduction*, 31–32) likens them to Islamic Hadiths, and thinks of them as late fictions. N. H. Snaith (*Numbers*, 249) thinks that the story may come from H, but overlooks the likelihood that the corresponding story in Lev 24 is an accretion to the collection of H laws in Lev 24:15–22. It seems reasonable to attribute vv 32–36 to the priestly author of Numbers.

The author was clearly concerned to secure proper observance of the sabbath, and this particular issue concerning the gathering of sticks was doubtless a matter of contemporary concern. He introduces it here because it illustrates sin "with a high hand" (v 31) (cf. J. De Vaulx, *Nombres*, 187).

Comment

32. The case requires special revelation (v 34). Sabbath breaking was already recognized as a capital offense (Exod 31:14–15; 35:2). What needs to be established is whether the gathering of the wood constitutes Sabbath breaking (cf. M. Noth, *Numbers*, 117). J. Weingreen ("The Case of the Woodgatherer") argues that something of the Rabbinic principle of setting a fence around the Torah is evident here. In other words there is a prescription of acts which, though harmless in themselves, may lead to the violation of very fundamental principles. The gathering of wood is a prelude to the kin-

dling of fire, and thus reveals a culpable intent. The dilemma of Moses consists in working through to this conclusion. A. Phillips ("The Case of the Wood-gatherer Reconsidered") sees the story as an illustration of the extension of Sabbath principles to all forms of domestic activity. Earlier Sabbath laws, he suggests, referred to occupation rather than domestic work. It is hard to draw confident conclusions in this area. What is clear is that the application of a great principle, such as abstention from work, is bound to raise questions as to what falls within its orbit, and as to what precisely constitutes "work." This story is certainly part of the process whereby answers were found, and it provides a ruling on one particular form of activity.

36. The stoning avoids the shedding of blood, and subsequent blood guilt (see N. H. Snaith, *Numbers*, 135). It must take place outside the camp, thus ensuring that a holy place (the camp) is not contaminated by death (cf. 1 Kgs 21:13).

Explanation

This story provides an individual case of sin "with a high hand" (v 31). The story is essentially legal, and it rules that the gathering of sticks on the Sabbath is indeed an infringement of the Sabbath law, incurring the death penalty.

This particular question was probably one of high contemporary relevance in the latter part of the fifth century. Is the gathering of sticks an infringement of Sabbath, and if so, how is it to be handled? The issue is settled here by means of a midrashic story with a definitive ruling. The story is a further reminder (see also vv 22–31) that confidence in God's good purpose is no ground for indifference to his commandments. Essentially however the story belongs to the legal realm, and particularly to the application of principles to specific situations. Is this action work? Is it evidence of a defiant and willful cast of mind?

Tassels of Remembrance (15:37–41)

Bibliography

Bertman, S. "Tasseled Garments in the Ancient East Mediterranean." *BA* 24 (1961) 119–28. **Stephens, F. J.** "The Ancient Significance of Sisith." *JBL* 50 (1931) 59–71.

Translation

[37] *Yahweh spoke to Moses, saying,* [38] *"Speak to the people of Israel, and tell them to make tassels for themselves for the corners of their garments throughout their generations, and to put upon the tassel of each corner a violet thread.* [39] *And it shall be [a] to you a tassel to look upon and remember all the commandments of Yahweh, to do them, and not to follow after your own heart and your own eyes, which you are inclined to go after wantonly.* [40] *So you shall remember and do all my commandments, and be holy to your God.* [41] *I am Yahweh your God, who brought you out of the land of Egypt, to be your God. I am Yahweh your God."*

Notes

39.a. Sam has a plural verb and noun in this clause.

Form/Structure/Setting

There is no doubt that this also belongs to P, as the introduction to the law (vv 37–38) makes clear. Some find in the section a fragment of H (e.g. N. H. Snaith, *Numbers*, 253; W. E. Addis, *Hexateuch*, 405). The divine "I" in association with "holiness" (vv 40–41) is the strongest argument in favor of this. A. Kuenen (*Hexateuch*, 54) notes affinities with Deuteronomy (6:8–9; 11:18–20; 22:12), but observes also the distinctively priestly character of v 38, as well as the affinities with H in vv 40–41. G. B. Gray (*Numbers*, 183) concludes that either the law is derived from H, or deliberately cast in the manner of H (cf. Lev 17:7; 19:29, 36; 20:5–6; 22:33; 26:13). As Gray points out the use of מִצְוֹת "commandments," rather than חֻקּוֹת "statutes" or מִשְׁפָּטִים "judgments," is not characteristic of H.

These various literary phenomena square well enough with the view that essentially the section comes from the priestly author of Numbers. Linguistic connections with D or H need mean only that the author was familiar with the D and H traditions. The use of the third person plural in v 38 may possibly indicate the presence of an older written law which the author has taken up and incorporated into his second person plural address. The custom of wearing tassels is already attested in Deut 22:12, though the word employed there is different. It is hard to know what the original significance of such tassels may have been. M. Noth (*Numbers*, 117) proposes some apotropaic function. It is easier to see why the author should have wished to incorporate some visible reminder of this kind at this point. The tassels are a reminder that God's Sabbath laws, as discussed in vv 32–36, must be kept. In the wider context they function as a fitting conclusion to the section dealing with Israel's sin, specifically the rejection of the land in Num 14, but more generally the whole section of disaffection in Num 11–14. The tassels ought to be a safeguard against these besetting sins.

Comment

38. צִיצָת "tassels." Some prefer the reading "fringes." *G* has κρασπηδα "edges."

38. פְּתִיל תְּכֵלֶת "a violet thread" (cf. Exod 28:37).

39. וְלֹא־תָתֻרוּ "and not to follow." The root used is the same as that employed in Num 13:21 for the reconnaissance conducted by the spies. This may support the idea that the author has the sin of Num 14 in view as he constructs this section (see *Form/Structure/Setting*).

39. אֲשֶׁר־אַתֶּם זֹנִים אַחֲרֵיהֶם "which you are inclined to go after wantonly" (RSV). A. H. McNeile (*Numbers*, 84) thinks of this as a reference to earlier superstitions connected with the tassels. More probably the author has Num 14:33 in mind.

Explanation

This section prescribes the wearing of tassels on garments. These tassels are to function as a reminder to the Israelites to obey God's commandments.

The author provides a neat conclusion to the chapter as a whole. The tassels will help to keep Israel faithful to God's laws. The author has probably taken up an older law (v 38). His purpose is to stress that the Sabbath law of vv 32–36 must be kept, that rejection of the land and presumption (Num 14) must be eschewed, and that general disaffection (Num 11–12) is dangerous and unworthy. Thus the tassels conclude a major section dealing with the sin of Israel as a whole and its consequences. That sin does not negate God's ultimate good purpose, but Israel must be very careful to obey. It seems likely that something of the author's situation in the fifth century is reflected here. His attitude to the problems of resettlement and dispersion is subtle. He affirms the principle of rightful authority (Num 11–12), the Mosaic authority as preserved and exercised by the Jews of Babylon. He likewise rejects those attitudes of fear or faithlessness which lead Jews of the dispersion to reject the land, preferring the perceived safety and comfort of "Egypt" to the perils of faith (Num 14:1–38). Nevertheless there can be a presumptuous attitude among those seeking to enter the land. God's time and God's way are crucial (Num 14:39–45). The ultimate test of faith is obedience to God and his commandments (Num 15:37–41).

The broad theological thrust of Num 15 in its context is to indicate that God's good purpose cannot ultimately be defeated. But God has ways of being true to himself which may be beyond human perceptions at any given time. Rejection of that purpose, and its consequences, is always feasible. Man's duty and responsibility is thus the obedience of faith.

The Rebellion of Korah, Dathan, and Abiram (16:1–35)

Bibliography

Gillischewski, E. "Die Geschichte von der 'Rotte Korah' Num 16." *Archiv für Orientforschung* 3 (1926) 114–18. **Hanson, H. E.** "Num. XVI 30 and the meaning of *bārā'*." *VT* 22 (1972) 353–59. **Hort, G.** "The Death of Qorah." *ABR* 7 (1959) 2–26. **Lehming, S.** "Versuch zu Num. 16." *ZAW* 74 (1962) 291–321. **Liver, J.** "Korah, Dathan and Abiram." *Studies in the Bible* (ed. C. Rabin) *Scripta Hierosolymitana 8.* Jerusalem: Magnes, 1961, 189–217. **Meek, T. J.** "Some Emendations in the Old Testament." *JBL* 48 (1929) 167–68. **Nyberg, H. S.** "Korah's Uppror (Num. 16f.)." *SEA* 11 (1946) 214–36. **Richter, G.** "Die Einheitlichkeit der Geschichte von der Rotte Korah." *ZAW* 39 (1921) 123–37. **Wanke, G.** *Die Zionstheologie der Korachiten.* BZAW 97 Berlin: Töpelmann, 1966.

Translation

¹ Now Korah the son of Izhar, son of Kohath, son of Levi, and Dathan and Abiram the sons of Eliab, (and On the son of Peleth),ᵃ sons of Reuben ᵇ were insolent. ᶜ ² And they rose up against Moses with men from the people of Israel, two hundred and fifty leaders of the congregation, chosen from the assembly, well-known men. ³ And they assembled themselves together against Moses and against Aaron, and said to them, "You have gone too far! ᵃ For all the congregation are holy, every one of them, and Yahweh is among them. Why then do you exalt yourselves above the assembly of Yahweh?" ⁴ When Moses heard it his face fell,ᵃ ⁵ and he spoke to Korah and to all his congregation, saying, " ᵃ In the morning Yahweh will show ᵃ who is his, and who is holy, and will make him come near to him. The one whom he will choose he will make to come near to him. ⁶ Do this, Korah and all his congregation, take censers for yourselves. ⁷ Put fire in them, and put incense upon them before Yahweh tomorrow. And the man whom Yahweh chooses shall be the holy one. You have gone too far, you sons of Levi!" ⁸ And Moses said to Korah, "Hear now,ᵃ you sons of Levi. ⁹ Is it too small a thing for you that the God of Israel has separated you from the congregation of Israel, to bring you near to himself, to do service in the tabernacle of Yahweh, and to stand before the congregation to minister to them, ¹⁰ and that he has brought you near him, and all your brothers the sons of Levi with you? And would you also seek the priesthood? ¹¹ Therefore it is against Yahweh that you and all your congregation have gathered together. What is Aaron that you murmur ᵃ against him?"

¹² And Moses sent to call Dathan and Abiram the sons of Eliab. And they said, "We will not go up. ¹³ Is it a small thing that you have brought us up out of a land flowing with milk and honey, to kill us in the wilderness, that you must also make yourself a prince over us? ¹⁴ Moreover you have not brought us into a land flowing with milk and honey, nor given us an inheritance of fields and vineyards. Will you continue to mislead these men? We will not go up."

¹⁵ And Moses was very angry, and said to Yahweh, "Do not respect their offering.ᵃ I have not taken one ass ᵇ from them, and I have not harmed one of them." ¹⁶ And

Moses said to Korah, "Be present, ᵃ you and all ᵃ your congregation, before Yahweh
tomorrow, you and they and Aaron. ¹⁷ And let every one of you take his censer, and
put incense upon it, and every one of you bring before Yahweh his censer, two hundred
and fifty censers, you as well as Aaron, each man with his censer." ¹⁸ So every man
took his censer, and they put fire in them and laid incense upon them, and they
stood at the entrance of the Tent of Meeting with Moses and Aaron. ¹⁹ Then Korah
assembled all the congregation against them at the entrance of the Tent of Meeting.
And the glory of Yahweh appeared to all the congregation.
        ²⁰ And Yahweh said to Moses and to Aaron, ²¹ "Separate yourselves from among
this congregation, that I may consume them in a moment." ²² And they fell on their
faces, and said, "O God, the God of the spirits of all flesh, shall one man sin, and
will you be angry with all the congregation?" ²³ And Yahweh said to Moses, ²⁴ "Say
to the congregation, Get away from around the tabernacle ᵃ of Korah, Dathan, and
Abiram."
        ²⁵ Then Móses rose and went to Dathan and Abiram. And the elders of Israel
followed him. ²⁶ And he said to the congregation, "Depart, I urge you, from the
tents of these wicked men, and touch nothing of theirs, lest you be swept away ᵃ
with all their sins." ²⁷ So they got away from around the tabernacle of Korah, Dathan,
and Abiram. And Dathan and Abiram came out, and stood at the door of their
tents, together with their wives, their sons, and their little ones. ²⁸ And Moses said,
"By this you shall know that Yahweh has sent me to do all these works, and that it
has not been of my own accord. ²⁹ If these men die the common death of all men, or
if they are visited by the fate of all men, then Yahweh has not sent me. ³⁰ But if
Yahweh creates something new, ᵃ and the ground opens its mouth and swallows them
up, ᵇ with all that belongs to them, and they go down alive into Sheol, then you
shall know that these men have despised Yahweh."
        ³¹ And when he had finished speaking all these words, the ground under them
split, ³² and the earth opened its mouth ᵃ and swallowed them up, with their households
and all the men that belonged to Korah and all their possessions. ³³ So they and all
that belonged to them went down alive into Sheol. And the earth closed over them,
and they perished from the midst of the assembly. ³⁴ And all Israel round about fled
at their cry, for they said, "Lest the earth swallow us up!" ³⁵ And fire came out
from Yahweh, and devoured the two hundred and fifty men offering the incense.

Notes

1.a. It seems likely that "On" should be dropped as a piece of dittography. His absence
from the rest of the story supports this view. Some have sought to find an original role for
On in vv 13–14a, 15, now absorbed into the tradition about Dathan and Abiram, but there is
no evidence for this. It may be that "Peleth" should be read as "Pallu" (cf. Num 26:8–9; cf.
also Gen 46:9; Exod 6:14; 1 Chr 5:3).
    1.b. Sam and G read the singular "son" (cf. Deut 11:6). This helps to make the genealogy
of v 1b correspond with that of v 1a. All three are great-grandsons of patriarchs.
    1.c. Since נִקַּח "he took" lacks an accusative many commentators prefer to read נָקָם "he
arose" (e.g. A. Dillmann, Numeri, 89–90; J. Paterson, Numbers, 51). A better solution may be
to read the root קרח (same consonants), meaning perhaps "to be bold" or "insolent" (cf. Job
15:12) (see M. Noth, Numbers, 122–23; N. H. Snaith, Numbers, 255–56). G has ἐλάλησεν "and
he spoke," apparently an attempt to deal with the difficulties. The suggestion that the original
object was "offerings" (B. W. Bacon, Triple Tradition, 194; L. E. Binns, Numbers, 109) is unlikely.

On the subject generally see T. J. Meek, "Some Emendations in the Old Testament," *JBL* 48 (1929) 167–68.

3.a. J. Paterson (*Numbers*, 51) wishes to insert "you sons of Levi" here, drawing it in from v 7. Since Korah's band included more than Levites it is inappropriate here. There are no textual witnesses offering support for this view—for further discussion see *Form/Structure/Setting*.

4.a. *BHS* proposes reading עַל פְּנֵי וַ as וַיִּפְּלוּ, and the whole expression might then be taken as "and his face fell" (cf. Gen 4:5). This is without specific textual support, but since there is a prostration later in the story (v 22), at a point where an act of intercession is obviously appropriate, this emendation is acceptable.

5.a.-a. G appears to have read בָּקַר וַיֵּדַע "has examined and known," and uses "God" rather than "Yahweh."

8.a. G has read שְׁמָעוּנִי "listen to me."

11.a. We should probably read תֵּלִינוּ, with the *Qere*.

15.a. Neither of the emendations suggested by *BHS* are necessary—תִּ כָחֲתָם "groaning," אַנְחָתָם "sighing." Moses prays that the status of Dathan and Abiram before God be as that of Cain.

15.b. G has read חֲמֹד-ἐπιθύνημα "desirable things." This makes little difference to the Hebrew text, but a reference to asses, as a means of asserting innocence, is attested elsewhere (1 Sam 12:3; cf. 1 Sam 8:16), and MT is acceptable.

16.a.-a. G reads ἁγίασον "consecrate."

24.a. Since "tabernacle" is invariably used of Yahweh's dwelling place elsewhere *BHS* suggests that originally the text read "Yahweh" rather than "Korah." But it may be that Korah has in fact set up a rival מִשְׁכָּן. The term "tabernacle of Korah" might thus be disparaging. Most see redactional influences in the clause as a whole (see further *Form/Structure/Setting*). The same problem arises in v 27. In both places G reads "congregation of" in place of "tabernacle of," but this is probably an attempt to deal with the difficulty.

26.a. This reads the root סָפָה. G seems to have read סוּף "come to an end."

30.a. G appears to have found this difficult, and reads possibly יַרְאֶה בְּרָאִי "if Yahweh shows in a portent," but cf. Exod 34:10; Isa 48:6; Jer 31:22.

30.b. G has some words from v 32 at this point, probably mistakenly.

32.a. G lacks "its mouth."

Form/Structure/Setting

In this section there appears to be a very complex combination of traditions. It is generally accepted that there is a major priestly element in the chapter, but also a well preserved Yahwistic tradition. It is customary to associate the Korah material with P, and the Dathan/Abiram texts with JE. G. Richter ("Die Einheitlichkeit der Geschichte von der Rotte Korah") argues for a single narrative, but his observations show only how the final editor understood and worked together the various traditions. Richter does little to explain the literary tensions which remain in the chapter. Proceeding on the basis that Korah belongs to P and Dathan/Abiram to the Yahwist it is reasonable to go ahead and seek to differentiate the literary strata in the section.

1.–2. Since these verses introduce all the rebels they are in some degree editorial, reflecting the work of the priestly author of Numbers. The phrase "well-known men" is priestly (Gen 6:4), and designations such as "leaders of the congregation" and "assembly" are characteristic of his work earlier in the book. He has drawn in the names of the Yahwist's rebels (v 1b) (eliminate "On" see *Notes*) in order to give a degree of cohesion to the chapter as a whole. It may be that v 2a also comes from Yahwistic tradition. The word קוּם "rise up" is not found elsewhere as a word of disaffection in P, and v 2a as a whole is a good parallel to v 3a, which is certainly priestly. S. Lehming

("Versuch zu Num 16") sees 250 Israelites as opponents of Moses at the earliest level of the tradition (cf. also J. de Vaulx, *Nombres,* 189–96). This may well be another tradition handled by the priestly author, independent of the Yahwist's, but there are no means of determining its age.

3–11. There is general agreement that this section belongs to P. The "assembly" and the "congregation" are cited, and the idea of "assembly against" (vv 3, 11) occurs in Num 20:2 (P). The preoccupations of the section are typical—"incense," "censer," and the issue of priestly service, expressed by the root קרב "to draw near." The use of בָּתוֹךְ of the divine presence (v 3) is also typical (cf. Exod 25:8; 29:45–46; Lev 15:31; 16:16; Num 5:3; 18:20; 35:34; Josh 22:31). The Yahwist is inclined to prefer בקרב for this idea.

There are doubts nevertheless about the unity of the section. In vv 4–7 an incense offering test is proposed, and it is reasonable to suppose that this is designed to test the right to engage in that activity. In that event the right may have been claimed by the 250 lay leaders mentioned in v 2. In vv 8–11 the issue appears to be different. Here, and in the last clause of v 7, the rebels are evidently Levites who oppose Aaron's exclusive right to the priesthood. The sharp distinction between priests and Levites is of course a preoccupation of the priestly author of Numbers, and vv 8–11 must be his distinctive contribution. The claim in v 3 that the whole community is holy could belong to either level in the tradition. It is clear that stylistically vv 3–11 are of a piece. The incense tradition may therefore be an early priestly adaptation of the Dathan/Abiram story. The author of Numbers has built Korah upon it.

12–15. This is evidently a major element from the Yahwist. It is true that v 12 does not link easily with v 2a, but a fragmentary Yahwistic tradition is not unusual. The expression of wrath by means of חָרָה לְ (v 15) is typical of the Yahwist (cf. e.g. Gen 4:5–6; 18:30, 32; 31:36; 34:7). So too is עָלָה (v 13) of the exodus (cf. Gen 46:4; 50:24; Exod 3:8, 17; 17:3; 20:5; 32:1, 4, 23; 33:1, 12, 15. In P it occurs only in Lev 11:45). J. G. Vink ("The Date and Origin of the Priestly Code in the Old Testament," *The Priestly Code and Seven Other Studies* [Leiden: Brill, 1969] 119–20) makes an unconvincing attempt to attribute the Dathan/Abiram tradition to P. To cite words not found elsewhere in the Yahwist as evidence against an attribution to the Yahwist is, on its own, a weak line of argument. The use of מִנְחָה (v 15) is not a difficulty (cf. e.g. Gen 4:4). The presence of Dathan and Abiram (but not Korah) in Deut 11:6; Ps 106:17 is a strong indication that these individuals were in the Yahwist's work, but not in P, and Vink does not explain these passages. The content of the missing material between v 2a and v 12 can only be guessed from the substance of vv 12–15.

Some analysts have sought to disentangle J and E in vv 12–15 (cf. e.g. A. Dillmann, *Numeri,* 92–95; B. W. Bacon, *Triple Tradition,* 194–95; J. E. Carpenter & G. Harford, *Hexateuch,* 519; H. Gressmann, *Mose,* 251 n.3; B. Baentsch, *Numeri,* 539–53). Others prefer to identify a single source with some minor elaboration (e.g. A. Kuenen, *Hexateuch:* 154 n.14; O. Eissfeldt, *Hexateuch,* 173–75; W. Rudolph, *Elohist,* 81–84; C. A. Simpson, *Early Traditions,* 238; M. Noth, *Numbers,* 121; G. W. Coats, *Rebellion,* 156; V. Fritz, *Israel,* 24–26; J. de Vaulx, *Nombres,* 189–96). Others are content to assign the material to JE. The search for parallel threads of tradition is thinly based. It has been argued that On and others wished to exercise sacrificial functions (vv 13–14a, 15) while Dathan and Abiram are rejecting the leadership of Moses. Quite apart from the status of On in the story (see *Notes*) vv 13–14a go very well with a dispute about the leadership of Moses, which leaves only v 15a as a possible dispute about sacrifice. In fact such an interpretation is scarcely necessary (see *Comment*). All in all it seems best to regard vv 12–15 as a single unit of tradition from the Yahwist. Dathan and Abiram refuse to obey (v 12). They set out their reasons (vv 13–14) (v 14b fits well if read figuratively). Moses is angry and asks that Yahweh's favor be withdrawn from them (v 15) (cf. Gen 4:4–5). Linguistic features support the view that the story is the Yahwist's. The expression "fields and vineyards" (v 14) occurs in other Yahwistic texts (Num 20:17; 21:22), in connection with the journey through Transjordan. It is possible that the refusal "to go up" (v 12) is drawn from earlier tradition (proto-J), in which some refused to join the triumphant settlement from the south (see on Num 13–14 *Form/Structure/ Setting*). Reluctance to settle is still an issue in the Yahwist's form of the story, but the emphasis is on the status of Moses, and a willingness or otherwise to accept his leadership.

16–17. This clearly belongs to P, and should probably be assigned to the author of Numbers. It appears to duplicate the instructions of vv 5–7, possibly another indication that there is an earlier tradition in those verses. It is easy to see why the author would wish to repeat the instructions of preparation for the test after the inclusion of the Yahwistic material in vv 12–15. The verses also make it clear that the battle is between Korah on the one side and Aaron on the other, the view of the situation the author wishes to emphasize.

18–19. This is also priestly. Elements of the earlier tradition about incense offering survive in v 18. Here the instructions of vv 5–7 are carried out. In v 19 the whole congregation is implicated, and Korah is cited by name. This is probably the work of the author of Numbers.

20–24. The continued presence of P is clear. Israel is "the congregation," the words are given to Aaron as well as Moses (v 20), and there is a prostration (v 22). There is also the formulation "and he spoke . . . saying" (vv 20, 23). In all probability this is the author of Numbers providing his continuation of the story. The text continues well from v 19 with its theophany, and contains a scathing reference to the rival tabernacle, presumably a Levitical one (v 24). The reference to Dathan and Abiram at this point is made in the interests of overall cohesion.

25–26. There are grounds for seeing important elements of the Yahwist's story here. In v 25 Dathan and Abiram are cited on their own, and the elders appear here as companions of Moses rather than Aaron (cf. Gen 50:7; Exod 3:16, 18; 4:29; 12:21; 17:5–6; 18:12; 19:7; 24:1, 9, 14; Num 11:16, 24–25, 30). There are no strong linguistic grounds for deciding the origin of v 26. It may be from the priestly author, since the word "congregation" evidently indicates his influence.

27–29. Clearly v 27a belongs to the priestly author (cf. v 24), and v 27b to the Yahwist. The issue is less clear in vv 28–29. Linguistic evidence does not point strongly in either direction. The point at stake is whether Moses has a commission to do "works" or not. It is possible to relate this to the Yahwist's tradition of vv 12–15 with the "works" referring to the exodus and the general leadership Moses has given. Was Moses "sent" by Yahweh (v 29), or not? The alternative is to suppose that the "works" have something to do with the construction of the Tabernacle, and the assertion by Moses of his authority over the assembly at large. On the whole it seems best to attribute these verses to the Yahwist.

30–35. Analysts have often been content to assign vv 30–34 to JE and v 35 to P with the two kinds of death marking the difference. Evidently v 35 is priestly, but there are some grounds for dividing vv 30–34. Tensions have long been noted, but have generally been supposed to lie within the Yahwistic stratum (see e.g. A. Dillmann, *Numeri*, 93–95; J. Wellhausen, *Hexateuch*, 105–106, 339–41; B. W. Bacon, *Triple Tradition*, 199–200). The marks of the Yahwist in v 30 are clear enough—the allusion to Sheol (cf. Gen 37:35; 42:38; 44:29, 31), and the despising of Yahweh (cf. Num 14:11, 23). These marks continue in vv 31, 33a. In this tradition the "ground" "splits open" (v 31), and the rebels descend alive into Sheol (v 33a). In vv 32a, 33b^a, 34 there seems to be a parallel tradition which speaks of the "earth" which "opens up," and swallows the rebels (v 32), with the earth closing over them (v 33b). This causes Israel to flee (v 34). Only in the use of בלע "to swallow" does this tradition have linguistic contact with the other. On the words "its mouth" (v 32) see *Notes*. Since there are no clear indications of P here this material is probably a gloss on the Yahwist's work. The priestly author has made his own contribution indicating that Korah is killed along with Dathan and Abiram (v 32b), adding the reference to the assembly (v 33b), and indicating the fate of the 250, a distinctive fate derived probably from the earlier incense tradition.

The suggested literary history of the section may be summarized thus:

1. A pre-Yahwistic tradition tells of the refusal of Dathan and Abiram, two Reubenites, to engage in the successful settlement from the south (v 12).

2. The Yahwist takes up this story into his tradition of a Transjordanian journey, interpreting the refusal as an unwillingness to wait on Moses, and seeing the whole as an overt challenge to the leadership of Moses. They, and all belonging to them, are swallowed by the ground and go down to Sheol (vv 1b, 21, 12–15, 25, 27b–31, 33a).

3. Some elaboration of the disaster is made (vv 32a, 33b^a, 34).

4. An early priestly accretion introduces 250 laymen whose claim to the right to offer incense is refuted by a test. The substance of this survives in vv 2b, 4–7, 18, 35.

5. The author of Numbers introduces Korah as a rebel, identifying him as a Levite, and elaborating the existing tradition in the interests of establishing his distinction between priests, the sons of Aaron, and Levites, and confirming the supremacy of the former. His contribution is evident in vv 1a, 3, 8–11, 16–17, 19–24, 26–27a, 32b, 33b^b.

Various attempts have been made to establish a convincing prehistory for these varied and essentially literary traditions. J. de Vaulx (*Nombres*, 190–

93) and S. Lehming ("Versuch zu Num 16") cite various pre-exilic situations out of which certain of the priestly parts of the tradition might have grown. The weakness of this is its tendency to neglect the linguistic evidence of the chapter, and particularly the fact that all the Korah material is unmistakably priestly. In the absence of a radically new and thoroughly tested theory about the date and origins of P these approaches appear very tenuous.

The introduction of Korah as one of the rebels is evidently important to the priestly author. Unlike the names Nadab and Abihu (see *Comment* on Num 3:1–4) Korah does not appear to have been drawn from earlier written tradition. The name was probably an eponym for an important Levitical family in the author's time (see particularly the discussions of A. Cody *A History of Old Testament Priesthood* [Rome: PBI, 1969] 172–73) and A. H. J. Gunneweg (*Leviten und Priester* [FRLANT 89; Göttingen; Vandenhoeck & Ruprecht, 1965] 171–84). Korah's Levitical connections are widely attested in the Chronicler, and assumed in a number of superscriptions in the Psalter. Various attempts to show that the Levitical connection is secondary are not very persuasive. G. B. Gray (*Numbers*, 193–94) noted a Korah in 1 Chr 2:43 who is descended from Judah, and who is a son of Hebron. He notes too that the Levitical Korah is a nephew of Hebron (Exod 6:18, 21). He suggests that the Korah of Judah was converted by later genealogists into Korah the Levite. On the other hand the Hebron in 1 Chr 2:43 has a different lineage from that in Exod 6:18. The argument hinges partly on Gray's unfounded belief that Moses and Aaron in PG are Levites who are opposed by laymen. H. Gressmann (*Mose*, 259–63) shares this misapprehension. J. de Vaulx's suggestion (*Nombres*, 189–96) that Num 16:3 reflects the epoch of 1 Kgs 12:31, and the anti-Levitical stance of Jeroboam, is unconvincing. His analysis tends to confuse the literary strata of the chapter, and to that extent renders his conclusions doubtful. The claim that P reflects a conflict as early as this needs to be argued more thoroughly. J. Liver ("Korah, Dathan, and Abiram") does accept that Korah is Levite from the outset, and sees the story as coming from Jerusalem priests seeking to defend their position against Levites. His tracing of the tension to the early period of the monarchy stems largely from his acceptance of a pre-exilic date for P. There are arguments against this (see *Introduction*), and on the whole it seems best to search for the author's purpose in introducing the Korah tradition in the circumstances of the fifth century (see *Explanation*).

There have been various attempts to uncover the roots of the tradition used by the Yahwist, but many have difficulties attaching to them. Some scholars have sought etiological explanations in terms of certain geophysical phenomena (cf. e.g. H. Gressmann, *Mose*, 255; A. H. McNeile, *Numbers*, 90). Others posit a historical recollection of some natural disaster (cf. e.g. G. Hort, "The Death of Qorah"; G. W. Coats, *Rebellion*, 163–68). Both suggestions seem unlikely. The story implies very strongly that the event is without precedent (v 30). It is not an earthquake, but a totally unique incident. It is also clear that Dathan and Abiram disappear without a trace. The earth closes over them and leaves no new phenomenon which the story might be held to explain. Other scholars have found cultic conflicts behind the story. H. S. Nyberg ("Korah's Uppror [Num. 16f.]") suggested that the story reflects ancient opposition between the central Mosaic cult, and the decentralization inherent in the gradual decay of the amphictyony. The refusal to "go up" is a refusal to engage in the amphictyonic cult. A. H. J. Gunneweg (*Leviten und Priester*, 171–72) offered support for this on the basis of a specifically cultic interpretation of מִנְחָה in v 15 (but see *Comment* for a rejection of this). A considerable doubt now attaches to the value of the concept of amphictyony (cf. e.g. G. Fohrer, *History of Israelite Religion* [London: SPCK, 1973] 89–94; A. D. H. Mayes, *Israel in the Period of the Judges* [London: SCM, 1974]), and the value of this approach is affected accordingly. Others focus on the fact that Dathan and Abiram are Reubenites. The story is held to explain Reuben's loss of dignity and influence, as attested in Gen 49:3 and Deut 33:6. On the other hand the story gives no hint that it seeks to explain the fate of Reuben as a whole. It seems best to assume that the root of the story is the refusal of some Reubenites to join Judah in their successful settlement from the south.

Comment

2. וַיָּקֻמוּ לִפְנֵי מֹשֶׁה "and they rose up against Moses." This idea fulfills much the same function as the root קָהַל עַל "assemble against" in v 3. It could have a legal background, denoting the attitude of an adversary in court (Deut 19:15–16; Ps 27:12). A literal appearance before Moses is not necessarily implied; the essence is a rebellious affront to Moses. Their objection is contained in the speech of vv 12–14.

2. קְרִאֵי מוֹעֵד "chosen from the assembly." This may mean that they were counselors of some kind (L. E. Binns, *Numbers*, 110; G. B. Gray, *Numbers*, 9, 196).

2. אַנְשֵׁי־שֵׁם "well-known men," literally "men of a name" (cf. Gen 6:4; Prov 22:1; Job 30:8; 1 Chr 5:24; 12:30).

3. רַב־לָכֶם "you have gone too far!" It could mean "enough of your pretensions!" (G. B. Gray, *Numbers*, 197), but "you are overreaching yourself" is probably better (M. Noth, *Numbers*, 123 n.). The supremacy claimed by Moses and Aaron is unjustified in view of the fact that the whole congregation is "holy." G. W. Coats (*Rebellion*, 168–71) claims that the issue is not about priesthood at all. This is true in so far as Korah is not claiming for himself a unique priestly status, but it is unlikely that Korah is simply anti-clerical, recognizing no special responsibilities in the area of priestly ministry. It is the exclusiveness of the system Moses has introduced to which he objects. He affirms the holiness of the whole congregation as a means of challenging the *unique* system represented by Moses and Aaron.

4. וַיִּפֹּל עַל־פָּנָיו "and he fell upon his face," though the correct meaning may be "his countenance fell" (see *Notes*). For the prostration see Num 14:5 (*Comment*). The fact that Moses alone "prostrates" himself—it is usually Moses and Aaron together—may favor the emendation. G. B. Gray (*Numbers*, 198) explains Aaron's absence in terms of fusion of sources, with v 3b as JE, but this is unnecessary and unlikely.

5. עֲדָתוֹ "his congregation" (cf. also vv 6, 11, 16; 17:5). This is an unusual word for P to use of a group other than Israel as a whole, but it is credible in this context. Korah has created a rival "Israel," and, from the author's

point of view, a caricature. The offering of incense will determine the validity or otherwise of Korah's claim. The syntax is awkward here. Gray (*Numbers*, 198) suggests that the best syntactical organization of the passage would produce—"Yahweh will make known him that is His; and him that is holy will He suffer to come near Him."

5. וְהִקְרִיב אֵלָיו "he will make him come near to him" (cf. Lev 16:1; 21:17; Num 17:5; Ezek 40:46; Pss 65:5; 145:18; 148:14). The word has previously been used by the author of the way in which Levites belong to, or are "brought near to" priests (Num 3:16; cf. Num 18:2).

5. יִבְחַר "he will choose." This word is used only of the priesthood in P. Where the choice of others is involved P texts are inclined to use הבדל (cf. e.g. Lev 20:26 [H]; Num 8:4; 16:9).

5. The idea of resolving a dispute by means of an offering test is earlier than P (cf. e.g. 1 Kgs 18:20–40).

6. מַחְתּוֹת "censers." See *Comment* on Num 4:9, 14.

8–11. The real interest of the priestly author now emerges. Korah is not merely siding with the 250 who wish to offer incense. He is one of the "sons of Levi" with rights of his own, and pressing for the special rights reserved for the sons of Aaron. He is challenging Moses and Aaron from *within* the priestly hierarchy, and not from outside.

12. לֹא נַעֲלֶה "We will not go up." The word can be used of going up to a superior (cf. Gen 46:31; Deut 25:7; Judg 4:5), and this is the way the Yahwist seems to understand it. There is something in favor of the view that in earlier tradition it referred to a refusal to settle (see *Form/Structure/Setting* and G. W. Coats, *Rebellion*, 164). The root is used of the exodus in v 13.

13. חָלָב וּדְבַשׁ "milk and honey." See *Comment* on Num 13:27. To talk in these terms is surprising, but it fits well the mentality of Dathan and Abiram, and justifies the severe consequences to follow.

14. שָׂדֶה וָכָרֶם "fields and vineyards." Like "milk and honey" the phrase is something of a convention. It denotes property (Exod 22:4; Num 20:17; 21:22; 1 Sam 22:7).

14. הַעֵינֵי הָאֲנָשִׁים הָהֵם תְּנַקֵּר "Will you continue to mislead these men?" The root speaks literally of "boring out the eyes" (cf. 1 Sam 11:2; Prov 30:17). The meaning appears to be metaphorical (for a literal use cf. Judg 16:21). In Deut 16:19 taking a bribe blinds the eyes, and something similar is probably intended here (A. Dillmann, *Numeri*, 92; B. Baentsch, *Numeri*, 546; G. B. Gray, *Numbers*, 201; A. H. McNeile, *Numbers*, 87; L. E. Binns, *Numbers*, 112; M. Noth, *Numbers*, 125–26; N. H. Snaith, *Numbers*, 257; J. Sturdy, *Numbers*, 117). Moses is a deceiver, beguiling the people with false promises. Gray (*Numbers*, 201) draws attention to the modern expression—"to throw dust in the eyes."

15. אַל-תֵּפֶן אֶל-מִנְחָתָם "Do not respect their offering." A prayer against Dathan and Abiram. The expression is probably a way of saying that Yahweh should not listen to Dathan and Abiram, or show them any favor when they come before him. The occurrence of מִנְחָה need not denote priestly activity on their part. The expression is probably a conventional way of talking about acceptance or nonacceptance in the presence of God (cf. Gen 4:4–5).

15. לֹא חֲמוֹר אֶחָד מֵהֶם נָשָׂאתִי "I have not taken one ass from them."
A protestation of integrity. This also appears to be a conventional turn of
phrase (cf. 1 Sam 8:16; 12:3).

19. כְּבוֹד-יהוה "the glory of Yahweh." See *Comment* on Num 14:10.

21. This is probably Korah's "congregation"; see G. W. Coats, *Rebellion*,
171–72.

22. This verse supports the view that acts of prostration in these stories
are essentially intercessory. The forms of expression in the prayer are widely
regarded as late. The phrase "god of the spirits of all flesh" is certainly
well represented in post-Biblical literature (cf. e.g. Jub 10:3; 2 Macc 3:24;
14:46). It occurs again in Num 27:16.

28. כִּי-לֹא מִלִּבִּי "and that it has not been of my own accord," literally
"from my heart." In Hebrew thought the "heart" is the spring of all thought,
emotion, and action.

29. The common death experienced by men in general is the withdrawal
of breath and divine spirit (cf. e.g. Job 12:10; Ps 104:28). This is clearly
distinguished from the abnormal intervention on God's part anticipated here.

30. וְאִם בְּרִיאָה יִבְרָא "if he creates something new," literally the idea
is "to create a creation" (cf. Exod 34:10; Isa 48:6; Jer 31:22).

30. שְׁאֹלָה "Sheol" (cf. Gen 37:35; 1 Sam 28:11–13; Isa 14:9–11; Job 3:17–
19; 21:23–26; Ps 6:6). Since they "go down alive" it may mean that they
feel deprivation there, and suffer in a way that the dead do not (see H. W.
Robinson, *Inspiration and Revelation in the Old Testament* [Oxford: Clarendon,
1946] 97).

35. For the use of fire to destroy offenders in P cf. Lev 10:2. The idea is
certainly older than P (cf. Num 11:1; 2 Kgs 1:10). There are occasions when
the appearance of divine fire is a sign of approval (cf. e.g. Lev 9:24; Judg
6:21; 1 Kgs 8:38).

Explanation

This section tells of a rebellion against Moses and Aaron by Korah, Dathan,
Abiram, and 250 leaders. A test is conducted, and Moses is vindicated through
the dramatic deaths of all the conspirators. Korah, Dathan, and Abiram are
swallowed by the earth, along with all their possessions, while the 250 are
destroyed by divine fire at the Tent of Meeting.

Having given insights into the sin of Israel on the journey (Num 13–14),
the author is ready to turn to the second great sin. Whereas the first entailed
rejection of the land, the second entails rejection of the new priestly hierarchy,
as previously set out in Num 3–4. Whereas the first involves Israel as a whole,
the second involves the leadership, lay and clerical. It is arguable that Num
13–14 provide a structural balance to Num 1–2. In Num 1–2 the constitution
of the community is discussed. In Num 13–14 Israel's failure to be the community of God is revealed. In a similar way, while Num 3–4 discusses the constitution of the priestly hierarchy, Num 16–17 reveal a failure to accept it, in
short an attempt to destroy it. The author has at hand a ready-made Yahwistic
tradition, about Dathan and Abiram and their rebellion against Moses, and
elaborates it accordingly.

The author's method is to build into the story of Dathan and Abiram a rebellion by Korah the Kohathite. He provides Korah with his Levitical genealogy (v 1), and shapes the rebellion in terms of a challenge to the unique authority claimed by Moses and Aaron (v 3). For the moment the challenge is expressed in fairly general terms (v 3), and in substance is not far removed from that offered by the Yahwist's Dathan and Abiram in vv 12–15. The author has resolved to settle the Korah dispute by means of the incense test which had already been built into the story. This earlier expansion told of 250 laymen who challenged the priests for the right to offer incense. The preparations for this survive in vv 4–7, and the rest is found in vv 2b, 18, 35. Apart from involving Korah with the 250 in vv 5–6, and an attempt to provide a transition to vv 8–11 at the end of v 7, there is little indication that the author of Numbers has modified or altered the incense tradition. It is in vv 8–11 that he develops his particular concern. The real issue for him is the right of a Levitical group led by Korah to share the privileges and responsibilities of the sons of Aaron, a claim he firmly rejects. After the Yahwistic material in vv 12–15 the author repeats the preparations for the test (vv 16–17). The earlier priestly adaptation had already moved the center of attention from the dwelling places of the rebels to the Tent of Meeting, thereby creating a significant tension within the story. In the later part of the story the author eases this slightly by linking Korah more closely with Dathan and Abiram than with the laymen (vv 24, 27, 32).

In broad terms the P tradition probably reflects something of the post-exilic power struggle within Judaism. The authority brought from Babylon by men such as Ezra and Nehemiah may well have been resented, and the accusation that Moses and Aaron are making themselves leaders, and thereby exalting themselves over the assembly (v 3) is readily intelligible in this context. Nehemiah's activities posed a considerable threat to various vested interests, and must have been deeply resented. Apart from Samaritan opposition (Neh 4:2) there was hostility among prophets (Neh 6:14), and also surely in influential priestly circles (Neh 13:4–9, 28). His policy on mixed marriages must have been disliked. Ezra's powers were wide-ranging (Ezra 7:12–26), extending to taxation, administration of law, and effective overall control. Whether or not he was actually granted these powers by the Persian authorities, he doubtless sought to exercise them, and newcomers with such power are readily resented.

It seems likely that the author of Numbers is addressing a specific issue in this broad overall context, and that Korah represents Levitical opposition to the priestly hierarchy proposed by the settlers from Babylon. The history of the Levites generally is obscure, but it is arguable that originally they were experts in a consultative technique with Urim and Thummim (Deut 33:8–11). The assertion in D that Mosaic priesthood was Levitical enhanced their status, but the position of the Zadokites was strong, and Zadokite pressure for a hierarchy may well have begun in Babylon. For the Korahite Levites, gradations of holiness within the clerical group were alien. Korah has status, as consultant, custodian, and perhaps teacher (Deut 33:8–11), but the hierarchy of holiness or privilege he does not recognize. The absence of Korahites from the list of returning exiles (Ezra 2:40–58) makes it possible that they were a prominent Levitical group who functioned in Palestine during the exile. The author is thus careful to exclude the sons of Korah from the fate suffered by the rebels (Num 26:11). The Korahites must ultimately have acceded to the pressures from Babylon, as Numbers itself makes clear. By the Chronicler's time they can be found performing subsidiary Levitical functions (1 Chr 9:19; 26:19; 2 Chr 20:19). They may even have developed a respected theological outlook of their own (G. Wanke, *Die Zionstheologie der Korachiten*).

It seems likely that these same pressures underlie the material in Num 4:17–20, where it is indicated that Kohathites (to whom Korah belonged) are not to be prevented from functioning as Levites. This may mean that at some point there had been grounds for so doing. The Kohathites may henceforth function as Levites, provided they do so under the strict supervision of Aaron himself. On this view Num 4:17–20 would be something of a conciliatory tradition, bridging the gap between Korah's rejection in Num 16, and his acceptance as a respected Levitical group in the Chronicler. The ascription of a Kohathite origin to Aaron (Exod 6:14–27) may stem from a concern to link the priesthood of Babylonian Judaism with this ancient Levitical group. The Chronicler's failure to refer to this particular pressure point in the books of Ezra and Nehemiah is not surprising; for him the sons of Korah are valued and respected ministers in the Temple.

Thus the author's main concern in this section is to substantiate his vision of the priestly hierarchy. That there is no sign of such a hierarachy in the pre-exilic period has long been recognized, and even Malachi (first half of the fifth century) gives no hint of it in contexts where it might well be expected (cf. e.g. Mal 2:1–9). The final shape of the hierarchy, as previously argued in relation to Num 3–4, is possibly a compromise between Zadokite interests in Babylon, and Levitical interests in Palestine. The supremacy of the Babylonian priesthood is secured, and a new Levitical office is defined, to be marked out by distinct functions. The role of Temple servant ceases to be degrading (as e.g. in Josh 9:23; Ezek 44:10–14), and becomes the dignified and respected ministry of Numbers generally, and whose range of function and responsibility increases with time, as in the Chronicler.

The suggested tradition of the 250 laymen with their incense also deserves attention from the point of view of its function and context. The Chronicler's story about Uzziah (2 Chr 26:16–21) shows that even in his day the issue was of some interest. It has often been observed that there is little evidence concerning the use of incense in the pre-exilic period. The gold altar (1 Kgs 6:20, 22; 7:48) is not specified as an altar for incense, and the "censer" in 1 Kgs 7:48–50 may really have been an implement for carrying fire. The Piel of קטר means "to cause to smoke" (1 Sam 2:15–16; Jer 19:13; 44:21, 23; Hos 4:13; 11:2; Hab 1:16) and probably has to do with sacrifice in general rather than incense in particular. Incense was familiar to Ezekiel (8:11), and since discovered incense altars appear to date from the seventh to fourth centuries it seems likely that incense was first introduced in the late pre-exilic period. In post-exilic times Mal 1:11 attests its acceptability, while P and the Chronicler insist that only the sons of Aaron are allowed to offer it. If older custom allowing laymen to offer incense still obtained in Palestine it is possible that the claim to exclusive rights in this area for priests is another move on the part of the priestly leaders of the restored community to secure their position. The justification for such a claim lay in the sort of peril to which Ezek 8:11 bears witness. It is also asserted very effectively in Num 17:6–15, where Aaron and his incense emerge as Israel's saviors.

Thus we see how the author of Numbers uses the theme of disaffection in the wilderness in the interests of establishing the post-exilic hierarchy. The issues raised are potentially divisive. Finding solutions in the pre-settlement purposes of God is the means of resolving them. The concern is both apologetic and programmatic. The claims of the restored community are affirmed, and the future structure of Judaism is shaped.

The interests of the Yahwist must also be considered. In all probability he has used a Judah settlement tradition in which certain Reubenites, Dathan and Abiram, refuse to engage in the successful incursion from the south. There have been various attempts to uncover other roots—in etiologies of geophysical phenomena, in recollections of some natural disaster, or in cultic conflicts, but various improbabilities attach to each of these (see *Form/Structure/Setting*). That there were those who preferred life in the desert or on the desert margins is intrinsically likely, and this view of the background to the Yahwistic tradition in Num 16 squares closely with that suggested for the Yahwistic material in Num 13–14. The Yahwist has created a story which makes these preferences and subsequent divisions an issue of insubordination to Moses himself.

To the seventh century, and to the Yahwist's contemporaries, the story sounds a note of warning to any disposed to reject "Mosaic" leadership, to reject those associated with the policies of the Davidic king Josiah who stood for Mosaic faith in his day. The tradition's interest in the land and the theme of possession was also important to the Yahwist. Interest in the land, and the conditions necessary to secure it, were paramount in a situation in which the northern kingdom had recently lost the land, and in which the southern, under Josiah, had repossessed it.

Korah, Dathan, and Abiram—the Aftermath (17:1–28)

Bibliography

See Num 16:1–35 (*Bibliography*).

Translation

¹⁽³⁶⁾ *And Yahweh spoke to Moses, saying,* ²⁽³⁷⁾ *"Tell Eleazar, son of Aaron the priest, to take up the censers out of the blaze, and to scatter* ᵃ *the fire from them far and wide, for they are holy.* ᵇ ³⁽³⁸⁾ *And the censers of these men who have sinned at the cost of their lives you shall make into beaten plates as a covering for the altar. Because they offered them before Yahweh they are therefore holy. So they shall be a sign to the people of Israel."* ⁴⁽³⁹⁾ *And Eleazar* ᵃ *the priest took the bronze censers, which those who were burned had offered. And they were beaten out as covering for the altar,* ⁵⁽⁴⁰⁾ *to be a reminder to the people of Israel, to the end that no unauthorized man, who is not a descendant of Aaron, should come near to burn incense before Yahweh, lest he be like Korah and his congregation—as Yahweh had said to Eleazar by the hand of Moses.*

⁶⁽⁴¹⁾ *But on the morrow all the congregation* ᵃ *of the people of Israel murmured against Moses and against Aaron, saying, "You have killed the people of Yahweh."* ⁷⁽⁴²⁾ *And as the congregation assembled against Moses and against Aaron, they turned towards the Tent of Meeting. And behold, the cloud covered it, and the glory of Yahweh appeared.* ⁸⁽⁴³⁾ *And Moses and Aaron came to the front of the Tent of Meeting.* ⁹⁽⁴⁴⁾ *And Yahweh spoke to Moses,* ᵃ *saying,* ¹⁰⁽⁴⁵⁾ *"Get away from the midst of this congregation, that I may consume them in an instant." And they fell on their faces.* ¹¹⁽⁴⁶⁾ *And Moses said to Aaron, "Take your censer, and put fire in it from the altar. Put incense on it, and carry it quickly to the congregation, and make atonement for them. For wrath has gone out from Yahweh. The plague has begun."* ¹²⁽⁴⁷⁾ *So Aaron took it as Moses had said, and ran into the middle of the assembly. And behold, the plague had already begun among the people. And he put on the incense, and made atonement for the people.* ¹³⁽⁴⁸⁾ *So he stood between the dead and the living, and the plague was stopped.* ¹⁴⁽⁴⁹⁾ *Now those who died by the plague were 14,700, in addition to those who had died in the affair of Korah.* ¹⁵⁽⁵⁰⁾ *And Aaron returned to Moses at the entrance of the Tent of Meeting. And the plague was stopped.*

¹⁶⁽¹⁾ *And Yahweh spoke to Moses, saying,* ¹⁷⁽²⁾ *"Speak to the people of Israel, and take from them rods, one for each fathers' house, from all their leaders according to their fathers' houses, twelve rods.* ᵃ *Write each man's* ᵇ *name upon his rod.* ¹⁸⁽³⁾ *And write Aaron's name upon the rod of Levi. For there shall be one rod for the head of each fathers' house.* ¹⁹⁽⁴⁾ *And you shall deposit them in the Tent of Meeting, before the Testimony, where I meet with you.* ᵃ ²⁰⁽⁵⁾ *And the rod of the man whom I choose shall sprout. So I will rid myself of the murmurings of the people of Israel, who keep on murmuring against you."* ²¹⁽⁶⁾ *And Moses spoke to the people of Israel, and all their leaders gave him rods, one for each leader, according to their fathers' houses,*

twelve rods. And the rod of Aaron was among their rods. ᵃ ²²⁽⁷⁾ *And Moses deposited the rods before Yahweh in the Tent of the Testimony.*

²³⁽⁸⁾ *And on the morrow Moses* ᵃ *went into the Tent of the Testimony, and behold, the rod of Aaron for the house of Levi had sprouted and put forth buds, and produced blossoms. And it bore ripe almonds.* ²⁴⁽⁹⁾ *And Moses brought out all the rods from before Yahweh to all the people of Israel. And they saw for themselves, and each man took his rod.* ²⁵⁽¹⁰⁾ *And Yahweh said to Moses, "Put back the rod of Aaron before the Testimony, to be kept as a sign for the rebels, that you may rid* ᵃ *me of their murmurings against me, so that they do not die."* ²⁶⁽¹¹⁾ *Moses did so. As Yahweh had commanded him, so did he.*

²⁷⁽¹²⁾ *And the people of Israel spoke to Moses, saying, "Behold, we shall perish,* ᵃ *we are undone,* ᵃ *we are all undone.* ᵃ ²⁸⁽¹³⁾ *Anyone who comes near,* ᵃ *who comes near to the Tabernacle of Yahweh shall die.* ᵇ *Are we all to perish?"* ᶜ

Notes

2.a. It may be better to read יזרה to parallel וירם. See W. Rudolph, *ZAW* 52 (1934) 114.

2.b. It would be possible to link this clause with the first in v 3 (cf. G. Syr, Vg)—"because these sinful men made their censers holy at the cost of their lives." See further J. Paterson, 51–52.

4.a. Sam and G have "son of Aaron" (cf. v 2).

6.a. G lacks reference to the "congregation."

9.a. G adds "and Aaron" here—also in vv 23, 26.

17.a. *BHS* proposes transferring the last clause of v 18 to this position.

17.b. On איש as "each man" see *GKC*, § 139b, c.

19.a. Sam, G, Vg and four MT mss read the singular (cf. Exod 25:22; 30:6, 36). The plural occurs in Exod 29:42.

21.a. Vg makes it clear that the rod of Aaron is not one of the twelve.

23.a. G adds "and Aaron."

25.a. The Qal וְתֵכֶל is preferable. See *BHS*, and W. Rudolph, *ZAW* 52 (1934) 114.

27.a. A good illustration of the prophetic perfect. The event is thought to be so certain as to be accomplished. See *GKC*, § 106n.

28.a. הקרב is lacking in G, Syr, and Vg. J. Paterson, 52 concludes that it is a mistaken addition in MT (cf. also *BHS*).

28.b. Sam reads the Hophal—"shall be put to death."

28.c. On the use of האם see *GKC*, § 150g.

Form/Structure/Setting

In vv 1–26 there are three related but distinguishable traditions. Taken together they all undergird the special priestly status enjoyed by Aaron. The covering for the altar (vv 1–5) is a permanent witness to Aaron's priesthood; so too is the rod (vv 16–26). The central section (vv 6–15) illustrates the cruciality of Aaron's ministry with the atoning incense. Some take vv 27–28 to be an introduction to Num 18 (G. B. Gray, 218; N. H. Snaith, 264); many others see them as a reaction to the deaths of the 250. There is no real need to choose between these possibilities; the verses can be seen as a bridge between Num 16:1–17:26 and Num 18. Since part of their function is to make the point that at last the people have understood the lessons of Num 16–17 it is appropriate to consider them in this context.

There is total agreement among analysts that the material belongs in its

entirety to the priestly stratum. There are many obvious words and phrases
pointing in this direction, and the themes are familiar priestly preoccupations.
The whole is evidently a continuation of the priestly elements in Num 16.
It has to be recognized that the use of העם "the people" in v 12 is most
unusual in priestly texts. It may have been prompted by the words of the
murmurers in v 6 which describe the rebels as "the people of Yahweh";
that term is familiar in P (cf. e.g. Exod 6:7).

Most commentators take vv 1–5 to be a supplementary element in P (e.g.
H. Holzinger, 66–67; B. Baentsch, 549–50; W. Rudolph, *Der "Elohist"* 81–
84), and many would now see the section as a supplement to the complete
P tradition of Num 16. It obviously continues the story of the 250 censers,
and is probably to be attributed to the priestly author of Numbers. All but
the "seed of Aaron" (v 5) are aliens as far as the altar is concerned, and
must not be allowed to come near. Only the sons of Aaron may engage in
incense ministry. There is no indication of a deep pre-history for the tradition.
It is the author's own explanation of the origin of the familiar bronze covering.
Insofar as the explanation conflicts with Exod 27:2 we have an indication
of the separate redaction of the book of Numbers.

The section vv 6–15 enforces the point that Aaron alone can engage in
incense ministry; it too is probably to be attributed to the priestly author
of the book. There have been some attempts to associate the section in part
or in whole with the original P narrative (PG) (e.g. H. Holzinger, 66–67; B.
Baentsch, 550–51; W. Rudolph, *Der "Elohist"* 81–84). H. Gressmann (275–
83) identified in vv 6, 12b, 13 the traces of an old etiological cult saga, the
kernel of which is the rod tradition in vv 16–28. He took this to be an explanation of how Moses the Levite, or the Levites in general, received the priesthood. The kernel of this saga was thought to go back to the time of Solomon
when the question of the Levites as priests was live. The Aaronic elements
are an accretion to this tradition.

The validity of this with regard to vv 6–15 is doubtful. The formal elements
in the section follow the customary pattern for stories of disaffection in the
wilderness, and it may not be correct to break them up in the search for
older components. A dilemma is posed by Israel's murmuring (v 6); is held
in suspense (vv 7–10) as a theophany, a command to separate, and a prostration occur; and is finally resolved by Aaron's atoning action (vv 11–13). The
calculation of the numbers involved (v 14), and the repetition of v 13b in v
15b may be glosses, but overall the story is well formed, and any search
for a significant pre-history is bound to be speculative. In vv 1–15 as a whole
the priestly author is addressing himself less to the issue of priests versus
Levites (though that is certainly present), and more to the question of incense
ministry. That this continued to be a live question to a relatively late period
is clear from 2 Chr 26.

In vv 16–26 the supremacy of Aaron is affirmed yet again. In this instance
he is brought into direct connection with the house of Levi and depicted as
its supreme representative (v 18). Here too various commentators have found
a base narrative from PG with variable glossing from supplementers (e.g.
H. Holzinger, 66–67; B. Baentsch, 551–53). In all essentials the section is
likely to be the work of the priestly author of Numbers. He is able to make

his fundamental point that the sons of Aaron, the priests of Babylonian Judaism, are indeed the central representatives of the house of Levi.

The previously cited suggestion of H. Gressmann that there is an adaptation of Levitical tradition in vv 6–26 deserves attention here, though little can be said with certainty about the age of such tradition. The priestly author evidently prefers to think of Levi as a tribe apart, quite distinct from the twelve (Num 1:1–2:34), but here there are only twelve rods, and Levi's is clearly one of them. It seems likely that a Levitical story telling how the rod of the tribe of Levi burst into flower has been taken up by the priestly author. Our investigations in Num 1–4 have suggested other examples of the incorporation and adaptation of earlier Levitical tradition. Originally the story was designed to validate Levitical priesthood. The author adapts it by indicating that Aaron's name was written on this Levitical rod (v 18). The story as a whole makes a good stylistic and formal unit, and the indications are that the author has rewritten rather than supplemented the Levitical tradition. Allusion in vv 20, 25 to the murmurings of v 6 ties in the section with the chapter as a whole. The author regards this event as a way of closing the hierarchical debate, at least insofar as it bears on Aaron's status, and he makes no further reference to it.

Comment

2. השרפה "the blaze." It is not clear whether this is the fire of Yahweh (Num 16:35) or the fire the rebels kindled (Num 16:18). In view of its proximity the former may be preferred.

3. רקעי פחים "beaten plates." This is a rare term which occurs only here and in Exod 39:3. The layers must have been very thin. In Exod 38:22 G provides a harmonization of the different traditions concerning the altar covering.

3. לאות "a sign" (cf. Num 14:11). This word is widely used (cf also v 25), and can relate to any physical object to which some special meaning is attached (cf. e.g. Gen 9:12; 17:11; Exod 31:13, 17). Events and people (particularly their names) can also function as "signs" (cf. e.g. 1 Sam 2:34; 10:7, 9; 14:10; Isa 7:11, 14; 8:13; 20:3). For further discussion see B. O. Long, *The Problem of Etiological Narrative in the Old Testament* (Berlin: Töpelmann, 1968) 65–78.

4. The choice of Eleazar for the role described here, rather than Aaron, is probably to be explained from the fact that the high priest must have no contact of any kind with the dead (Lev 21.10–15).

5. זכרון "a reminder." This word generally occurs in sacerdotal contexts, and gives a timeless dimension to the significance of the object (cf. e.g. Exod 13:9; Josh 4:7). For further discussion see B. O. Long, *Etiological Narrative*, 74. The "reminder" is a warning to those not among the sons of Aaron against assuming rights not theirs.

6. וילנו "murmured"—see *Comment* on Num 14:2. The murmuring consists of an assertion that Moses and Aaron have invoked the destructive power of Yahweh to vindicate their own positions.

7. כבוד "the glory"—see *Comment* on Num 14:10 (cf. Num 16:19; 20:6).

196   Numbers 17:1–28

The manifestations must have occurred at the door of the Tent of Meeting, since the observers are said to look toward the Tent.

7. בהקהל "assembled against"; see *Comment* on Num 16:3 (cf. Num 16:19; 20:2).

10. ואכלה "that I may consume"; cf. Num 16:21.

10. ויפלו על-פניהם "and they fell on their faces"; see *Comment* on Num 14:5 (cf. Num 16:4, 22; 20:6).

11. המחתה "your censer." The root means "to snatch away" (cf. Ps 52:7). In Isa 30:14 it means "to pick up coals from the hearth." The noun can apparently be used for any utensil designed for carrying hot items (cf. Exod 25:38; 27:3). A more precise word for censer is מקטרת (Ezek 8:11; 2 Chr 26:19).

11. קטרת "incense" from the root "to smoke." The noun also occurs in Deut 33:10; 1 Sam 2:28. For a thorough study of the topic see M. Haran, "The Uses of Incense in the Ancient Israelite Ritual." *VT* 10 (1960) 113–29.

11. וכפר עליהם "and make atonement for them" (cf. Num 8:12). The action of Aaron evidently appeases the wrath of God, and this idea must be central to the sense of the root, at least in this context. In Num 8:12 it was suggested that "protection" indicated the essential idea. The incense is perhaps conceived of as in some way obscuring and thus covering the transgression. B. Baentsch (550) describes the wrath as a *mechanische Kraft*—a mechanistic force. Perhaps the sight or smell of the incense turns the wrath aside. There is some uncertainty about the primary meaning of the root. A case can be made for a Godward interpretation—in other words in "atonement" God is appeased or propitiated. This is the idea here and also in Gen 8:21; Exod 29:25; 1 Sam 26:19. There are occasions, however, when God himself is the subject of the verb (e.g. Deut 21:8; Ezek 16:63; Ps 78:38). It can be argued that the primary meaning has to do with the effect on the sins. They are "covered," "blotted out," and generally rendered harmless (cf. e.g. Isa 6:7; Ps 65:3; Neh 4:5; Job 31:33). The search for "primary" meaning may not be very important. There are grounds for believing that the root could be used in various ways, so that each occurrence must be judged as far as possible on its merits. The averting of danger and reconciliation are generally the end result.

In many of the priestly laws blood-letting is regularly required to secure "atonement" (but cf. Exod 30:15). The use of incense here seems appropriate because of its use by the sinners. The cloud of incense in Lev 16:13 serves to separate sinful men from a holy God; for this reason too it serves a purpose here. Another story of atoning action, this time by death, follows in Num 25:7–10, 13.

11. הקצף "wrath"; cf. Lev 10:6 for the use of this root as a verb. The verb is impersonal here, but the intended subject must be Yahweh.

11. הנגף "the plague," literally "the smiting"; cf. Num 14:37; 25:8–9.

14. The figure 14,700 represents about one fortieth of the whole congregation, as counted in Num 1.

17. מטה "rods." The same word can mean "tribe," and hence its appropriateness here. G. B. Gray (215) thought "rod" was original. It seems likely

that the story develops from this double meaning. The dead "rod" or "stick" springs to life, and represents the "tribe" which God chose (cf. N. H. Snaith, 263). These rods are special symbols of authority, and are placed before the ark. The view that they were freshly cut sticks from trees (A. H. McNeile, 93) is less likely (cf. Gen 38:18, 25; 1 Sam 14:43).

17. לבית אב "fathers' house"; see *Comment* on Num 1:2. The phrase must mean a whole tribe here. N. H. Snaith (263) suggests that the unusual usage occurs here to avoid any confusion which would have arisen from the play on the word מטה "tribe," "rod."

19. לפני העדות "before the Testimony" (cf. also vv 22–23, 25; Exod 16:34). The idea occurs in Num 1:50, 53 where it was suggested that, as here, Levitical tradition is present. For the priestly author the word clearly means "before the ark" (cf. also Exod 27:21; 30:6, 36; Lev 16:13; 24:3). Some texts apply the word to the tablets only (Exod 25:16, 21; 40:20), and this may be an earlier understanding.

20. יפרח "shall sprout." This may mean that a complete process of growth is envisaged (G. B. Gray, 216–17). It may also be implied that when placed in position (v 25) the growth does not wither (M. Noth, 131).

20. והשכתי מעלי "I will rid myself of" or "make to cease" (cf. Gen 8:1). God is to give the definitive word on the matter.

23. שקדים "ripe almonds" (cf. Jer 1:11), perhaps an explanatory gloss.

25. לבני-מרי "rebels," literally "sons of rebellion." This kind of idiom is common in Hebrew (cf. e.g. 2 Sam 3:34; 7:10; 12:6; Prov 31:5). The phrase "sons of rebellion" is unique, but cf. Isa 30:9, and the frequent "house of rebellion" in Ezekiel (e.g. Ezek 2:5; 3:9; 12:2; 17:12; 24:3).

Explanation

The author provides here a triple reinforcement of the essential message of Num 16—that the sons of Aaron alone are the true priests of God. There is no explicit reference to the Levites, but the point is made emphatically that with regard to the priesthood all except the sons of Aaron are aliens.

In the first story (vv 1–5) the author deals with the immediate outcome of Num 16:35. The fire which consumed the 250 rebels is to be scattered far and wide. This means that the fire will go out, and that it therefore cannot be used for any purpose, holy or otherwise. The censers have been used irregularly, but since they have been employed in sanctuary service they can be put to some other holy purpose. The author therefore sees in the bronze covering of the altar the censers of the rebels. In so doing he has given an alternative explanation of its origin to that given in the book of Exodus. The purpose of this activity is to provide a permanent physical reminder to Israel of this tragic event—a "sign" of warning that only the sons of Aaron are entitled to engage in incense ministry at the altar. It may be that the author was addressing himself directly to a live issue of who was entitled to offer incense (cf. 2 Chr 26:16–23).

In the second story (vv 6–15) the people are depicted as murmurers regarding the deaths which are the outcome of the story in Num 16. Moses and Aaron are held responsible for substantial loss of life. Israel is slow to learn the lesson. The consequence of their rebelliousness is more death—this time by plague, with as many as one fortieth of the whole congregation as victims. The action taken by Moses, and above all by Aaron, is a further witness to the fact that only the sons of Aaron are entitled to engage in incense ministry. The story shows in dramatic fashion the atoning power of incense ministry, as exercised by Aaron, and many more deaths by plague are avoided. In this also the question of who is entitled to take part in incense ministry is very much to the fore. The author has therefore made very clear one of the fundamental privileges and responsibilities in his new hierarchical pattern. Incense ministry is confined to the priests, and no exception with respect to the principle can be tolerated.

In the third story (vv 16–26) the priestliness of the sons of Aaron is affirmed once and for all. The author takes over a Levitical ordination tradition about the sprouting of the rod of Levi, a tradition establishing the Levitical right to priesthood. This right must obviously be identified with the sole priestly prerogative of the sons of Aaron. The rod of Levi must therefore be the rod of Aaron. The distinctiveness and supremacy of the sons of Aaron as God's priests is thus affirmed, and the people are finally brought to a better frame of mind (vv 27–28). Answers to their fears are forthcoming in Num 18. Here, as in vv 1–5, a permanent tangible reminder to the people about God's order of things is given. The sprouting rod is committed to the ark, and continues forever as a witness to God's will.

The theological dimensions of Num 16–17 are much as in Num 3–4. In particular a warning is given about neglect of the principles contained in the earlier chapters, and the consequences of such neglect. The danger of presumption and disorder is the predominant concern. A theology of order is paramount. The priests of Babylonian Judaism perceived a need for this in the new Palestinian situation. Order was thought to be a prerequisite if the restored community was to find its identity and meaning, and to take deep and lasting root.

The Dues of the Priests and Levites
(18:1–32)

Bibliography

Cazelles, H. "La Dîme Israélite et les Textes de Ras Shamra." *VT* 1 (1951) 131–34. **Snaith, N. H.** "A Note on Numbers 18:9." *VT* 23 (1973) 373–75. **Speiser, E.** "Unrecognised Dedication." *IEJ* 13 (1963) 69–73. **Urie, D.** "Officials of the Cult at Ugarit." *PEQ* 80 (1948) 42–47. See also Num 1:48–54 (*Bibliography*) for literature on the Levites.

Translation

¹ *And Yahweh said to Aaron, "You and your sons and your fathers' house with you shall bear iniquity in connection with the sanctuary. And you and your sons with you shall bear iniquity in connection with your priesthood.* ² *And bring near your brothers also, the tribe of Levi, the tribe of your father, that they may be joined to you, and minister to you, while you and your sons with you are before the Tent of the Testimony.* ³ *They shall be in attendance on you, and be responsible for all the duties of the Tent, but they shall not come near to the vessels of the sanctuary or to the altar, lest they and you die.* ⁴ *And they shall be joined to you, and be responsible for the Tent of Meeting, for all the service of the Tent. But no unauthorized person shall come near you.* ⁵ *And you shall be responsible for the sanctuary and the altar so that wrath may fall on the Israelites no more.* ⁶ *And behold I myself have taken your brothers the Levites from among the people of Israel. They are a gift to you,* [a] *given to Yahweh, to do the service of the Tent of Meeting.* ⁷ *And you and your sons with you shall engage in your priesthood, in the duties that concern the altar or what lies within the Veil. And you shall serve.* [a] *I give your priesthood as a gift,* [b] *and any unauthorized person who comes near shall be put to death."*

⁸ *And Yahweh spoke to Aaron, "Behold I myself have given you responsibility for the contributions made to me, namely all the holy things of the people of Israel. I have given them to you as a portion, and to your sons as a perpetual due.* ⁹ *Out of the most holy things kept back from the altar fire* [a] *this part shall belong to you: every offering of theirs, every cereal offering and every purification offering and every reparation offering, which they render* [b] *to me shall be most holy to you and to your sons.* ¹⁰ *You* [a] *shall eat it in a most holy place. Every male may eat of it. It is holy to you.* ¹¹ *This also is yours:* [a] *the contribution from all their gifts which are presented as special contributions by the people of Israel. I have given them to you, and to your sons and daughters with you, as a perpetual due. Every one of your house who is clean may eat of it.* ¹² *All the best of the oil, and all the best of the wine and of the grain, of the firstfruits of what they give to Yahweh, I give to you.* ¹³ *The first ripe fruits of all that is in their land, which they bring to Yahweh shall be yours. Every one in your house who is clean may eat of it.* ¹⁴ *Every devoted thing in Israel shall be yours.* ¹⁵ *All the firstborn of man or beast which are brought to Yahweh shall be yours. Nevertheless the firstborn of man you shall redeem, and the firstling of unclean beasts you shall redeem.* ¹⁶ *And their redemption price (at a month old*

you shall redeem them) you shall fix at five shekels in silver, according to the sanctuary shekel which is five gerahs. **17** *But the firstling of a cow or the firstling of a sheep, or the firstling of a goat, you shall not redeem. They are holy. You shall throw their blood against the altar and burn their fat as an offering by fire, a soothing odor to Yahweh.* **18** *But their flesh shall be yours, as are the breast of the special contribution and the right thigh.* **19** *All the contributions from holy things which the people of Israel present to Yahweh I give to you, and to your sons and daughters with you, as a perpetual due. This is a perpetual covenant of salt before Yahweh with you and with your descendants with you."* **20** *And Yahweh said to Aaron, "You shall have no inheritance in their land, neither shall you have any portion among them. I am your portion and your inheritance among the people of Israel.*

21 *"To the Levites I have given every tithe in Israel for an inheritance, in return for the service they render, their service in the Tent of Meeting.* **22** *And henceforth the people of Israel shall not come near the Tent of Meeting, lest they incur sin, and die.* **23** *But Levi* ᵃ *shall do the service of the Tent of Meeting, and they shall bear their iniquity. It shall be a perpetual statute throughout your generations, and among the people of Israel they shall have no inheritance.* **24** *For the tithe of the people of Israel, which they present as a contribution to Yahweh, I have given to the Levites for an inheritance. Therefore I have said of them that they shall have no inheritance among the people of Israel."*

25 *And Yahweh spoke to Moses, and said,* **26** *"Moreover you shall say to the Levites, 'When you take from the people of Israel the tithe which I have given you from them for your inheritance, then you shall present a contribution from it to Yahweh, a tithe of the tithe.* **27** *And your contribution shall count for you as if it were grain from the threshing floor, and as the fullness of the winepress.* **28** *So you too shall present a contribution to Yahweh, one from all your tithes which you receive from the people of Israel. And from it you shall give Yahweh's contribution to Aaron the priest.* **29** *Out of all the gifts to you, you shall present a* ᵃ *contribution to Yahweh. And the gift which you hallow* ᵇ *must be taken from the best of them.'* **30** *Therefore you shall say to them, 'When you have set aside the best part of your contribution, the remainder shall count for the Levites as the produce of the threshing floor, and as the produce of the winepress.* **31** *And you may eat it anywhere, you and your households. It is your payment in return for your service in the Tent of Meeting.* **32** *And you shall bear no sin in respect of it, when you have set aside the best of it. And you shall not profane the holy things of the people of Israel, lest you die.'"*

Notes

6.a. "to you" is lacking in G, S, and Vg, but this is probably dropped to clarify the text—the gift is to Yahweh. MT is therefore preferable.

7.a. The text is awkward and *BHS* proposes the deletion of this as dittographic; see also W. Rudolph, *ZAW* 52 (1934) 116.

7,b. Literally in MT "a service of a gift." G understands the service rendered as "a gift of your priesthood."

9.a. G reads τῶν καρπωμάτων "the fruit," "the produce," and *BHS* prefers האשה "the fire offering." MT is intelligible, and seems acceptable.

9.b. Sam reads the root אשם—"to offend," tying the word in with the reference to the reparation offering.

10.a. The pronoun is singular in MT, but plural in G.

11.a. The pronoun is singular in MT, but plural in G.

23.a. MT reads the singular "Levi." This is unusual in this and other priestly contexts, and "the Levites" is found in Syr, Tg and Vg. It seems best to retain the singular (see *Form/Structure/ Setting*).

29.a. "Every" should probably be deleted (see J. Paterson, 52).

29.b. MT has "sanctuary" which is difficult to make intelligible. For the translation "you hallow," see J. Paterson, 52.

Form/Structure/Setting

This section deals principally with the means by which the clerical orders established in the book of Numbers are to be maintained, and analysts are agreed in attributing it to P. Earlier commentators were inclined to see earlier and even original elements of P here in the chapter. H. Holzinger (71–72) located such elements in vv 1, 3a, 5, 20–21, 23b, 24a and in parts of vv 2a, 8–19. B. Baentsch (555–60) attributed all but vv 16, 20, 22 to the basic form of P. The points at issue had already been raised by A. Dillmann (99–103) and J. Wellhausen (182–83). In vv 21–24 it is asserted, as in Deuteronomy, that the Levites are to have no inheritance of land in Israel. This is in contrast to the cities granted them in Num 35 (P). Some points of contact have been found between this section and Ezek 44:6–14, as for example the idea of "bearing iniquity" (Ezek 44:10; Num 18:23), and suggesting perhaps that the texts are of comparable age and from similar sources.

G. B. Gray (218–19) maintained this overall position. In addition to the seemingly irreconcilable inconsistency between v 20 and Num 35:1–8 he drew attention to the singular "altar" in vv 5, 17, which suggested to him an un-awareness of the second priestly altar of Exod 30. A further peculiarity, pointed out by Gray and many other of the earlier analysts, is the fact that laws are addressed here to Aaron alone (vv 1, 8, 20—cf. Lev 10:8, 12 for the only other occurrences). Moreover the usual priestly formula "spoke . . . saying" is not employed here.

More recent analysts are less inclined to attribute substantial parts to PG. M. Noth (133–34) finds the connections with Num 16–17 rather loose, and believes that originally the chapter was not intended for its present context. He judged the peculiarities and general content to be evidence of lateness, and suggested that the organization of the chapter is clumsy and inconsequential. The few connections with the P narrative are taken to be secondary additions. N. H. Snaith (267) thinks that the unusual use of technical terminology suggests a different stratum in P, and J. Sturdy (126) accepts the general lateness of the section.

J. de Vaulx (204–07) conducts a thorough study of the literary history of the tradition. In vv 1–7 he sees a restatement of the nature of the priestly hierarchy as previously established (Num 1:47–54; Num 3–4). In the remaining material he makes a major division between texts dealing with the special contribution (vv 8–19), and those dealing with tithes (vv 20–32). In vv 8–19 he finds the earliest material giving to the priests all the holy things (vv 8b, 10b, 11b, 12, 13b, 19), the best of oil, wine, and grain. Those of the priestly families who are male and clean may partake. Points of contact with Deut 18:4 and Lev 22:1–9 (H) help to establish this as earlier tradition. The second stage in the process of growth is the enumeration of the offerings, and other points of emphasis (vv 9c, 10c, 15a, 18a, 13a, 14, 18b). These are of varied origin, and according to de Vaulx belong in general to the post-exilic period. He sees the priestly redactor in vv 9, 11, while the redemption material in vv 15b–17 is understood as a further gloss. The material dealing with tithes is found in general to be more unified. The Levitical right to tithes is set out in vv 21–24 and a priestly right to tithes from Levites in vv 25–32.

In general terms it is not hard to see this chapter functioning within the overall approach we have proposed. The various subsections are easily distinguished by new words of introduction, and in the first instance they are best treated as units.

1–7. This in all its essentials is a composition by the priestly author. The links with Num 16–17 are not so loose as Noth suggests. The question of the right of access to the holiest places has been raised in detail in the preceding sections, and at the end of Num 17:28 a specific question is raised—"are all who draw near to the Tabernacle to perish?" This question gives the author an excellent opportunity to repeat the clerical principles he has established earlier in the book, and since this necessarily raises the question of duty and service it provides a fitting introduction to his stipulations about how such service is to be rewarded, and how the priestly ministry is to be maintained. There are indeed those who on Israel's behalf draw near. The Levites will exercise a general ministry in the Tent, while the privileged altar ministry belongs to the sons of Aaron. In v 6 as in Num 3:19; 8:19 the author adapts the older tradition of the tribe of Levi as given to Yahweh for the new situation. The Levites are "given" to Aaron, and only through him are they a gift to Yahweh.

8–20. The author's overall concerns are to establish means for the support of the clergy, and to adjust to existing tradition:

(1) He is aware of Ezek 44:29 and Lev 6:11, 22 (Heb.); 7:6 where cereal, purification, and reparation offerings are said to belong to the priest. This he reaffirms, and he links it with his own assertion made in Num 5:9 that *terumah* contributions (see *Comment* on Num 5:9) are also the priest's. This linkage occurs in vv 8–9.

(2) He is also anxious to establish a distinction between those offerings which are for the priests alone (vv 8–10), and those which are for the support of priestly families as a whole (vv 11–13). It appears that those which are purely *terumah* contributions, along with the perquisites attaching to the cereal, purification, and reparation offerings, are "most holy," and go to the priests alone, or to all mature males. Those *terumah* contributions which are also *tenuphah* special contributions (see *Comment* on Num 5:9) are not "most holy." They are for the use of all members of priestly families, along with the first-fruits of fields and vineyards. The legislation in Lev 6:11, 22 (Heb.); 7:6 had already established that the cereal, purification, and reparation offerings were for males alone. Exod 29:28 and Lev 7:34 had decreed that in ordination offerings and shared offerings the *tenuphah* breast and the *terumah* thigh were also for the priest. No indication had been given as to whether these were for males alone or for families as a whole. The general effect of the legislation

in Numbers as a whole is to extend priestly rights (more is defined as *terumah* and all such is the priest's) and to clarify issues, as in the present case.

(3) In vv 14–18 the author takes the opportunity of affirming again the redemption principles of Num 3:11–13. Here however he does not employ the Levitical tradition that the Levites themselves are a substitute for the offering of the human firstborn. Instead he finds in this basic idea, that all firstborn belong to Yahweh and must be offered to him, a ground for establishing the principle of redemption (cf. Num 3:40–51). In this way he secures a further means of support for the clergy. A fixed sum of money is here prescribed, in contrast to Exod 13:13; 34:20 where redemption is only possible by the sacrifice of a clean animal. The firstborn of clean animals are therefore not to be redeemed (v 17). They are offered to Yahweh in accordance with the laws established in Leviticus. The priest does have the right to the flesh, along with the *tenuphah* breast and the right thigh. In this way principles applicable to the shared offerings in Lev 7:28–34 are extended to the offering of the firstborn of clean animals.

The main theme of the section is then summarized (v 19), and given a theological grounding (v 20) in the conviction that the sons of Aaron, because of their special relationship to Yahweh, do not have access to the land, and therefore to their own means of support. Yahweh himself is that support. This is a traditional view, already established in relation to the Levites in Deut 10:9; 18:1–5 and the sons of Zadok in Ezek 44:28.

Noth is certainly correct to point out the linguistic awkwardness of many parts of the section, and de Vaulx's attempt to trace a literary history within the extant text may well be justified. In all probability the oldest traditions are contained in vv 12–15a. These give to priests a fairly imprecise measure of the firstfruits of the land—the "best" of them—and go on to specify that all clean members of priestly families may partake of them. They also include the priestly modification of the *herem* principle (see *Comment* on v 14), asserting that all items subject to the ban are "devoted," not to destruction, but to priestly use. This also applies to the firstborn of man and beast. Here arguably is the traditional material which the priestly author of Numbers has taken up. Since the Levitical interpretation of the firstborn principle is not apparent (see Num 3:11–13) it may have come from Zadokite circles. It is in general agreement with Ezek 44:30.

Earlier tradition regarding priestly upkeep can be found in 1 Sam 2:12–17 (Shiloh), and Deut 18:4, which granted shoulders, cheeks, stomachs, and firstfruits to the priests. The idea of a peculiar relationship to Yahweh which guaranteed a right to support was doubtless traditional in priestly circles of all kinds. The author here brings it into contact with his overall view of the priesthood, its nature and responsibilities.

21–24. Here the author reaffirms some of his basic beliefs (vv 21–22). The tribe of Levi exercises a crucial protective ministry at the Tent of Meeting. He goes on to assert that Levites, like priests, are not endowed with land, and must be supported by the giving of the people generally. The tithe of the contribution (v 24) would have been one tenth.

It seems likely that the author has again accommodated himself to Levitical tradition. The unusual occurrence of "Levi" in v 21 may be a literary indicator of this. Tithing was undoubtedly an ancient feature of cultic observance (cf. Amos 4:4; Deut 12:6, 11, 17; 14:23). H. Cazelles (*VT* 1 [1951] 131–34) suggests a royal background for the Levitical tithe (cf. Amos 7:1; 1 Sam 8:15). To the extent that Levites were cult specialists it seems likely that they had always laid claim to payment in return for their skills. Deuteronomy affirms this Levitical right throughout, and commends the landless unbeneficed Levites to the care of the community. The author of Numbers was bound to recognize this right, and to square it with his new view of the Levites. For him the tithe applies to animals as well as to produce (Lev 27:30–33), and it is clear that it could be converted into money (Deut 14:24–27). That financial giving came to be the norm seems to be implied by Neh 12:44; 13:5, 12.

25–32. The author also stipulates that the Levites must themselves pay a tithe of what they receive to the priests. This enforces the primacy of the sons of Aaron, and their sole right to priesthood, as affirmed in Num 16–17, without removing the Levitical right to tithes. It also ensured a further means of support for the priests, providing financial resources as well as the perquisites from sacrifices.

In summary, while it is true that the language and syntax of the chapter is often clumsy, and that there may well be textual glossing here and there, there are nevertheless no good grounds for thinking of its organization as inconsequential, or for regarding it as anything other than a fundamental unit. It follows Num 16–17 most appropriately, it enforces one of the author's fundamental convictions about the clerical hierarchy, and it examines the key question of how the clerical orders are to be maintained. There are only two difficulties which remain.

The first is the tension between this section and Num 35:1–8 where the Levites are granted cities to live in and pastureland for their cattle. The problem is considered in detail in relation to those verses. It may well be that ownership is not asserted in Num 35:1–8, that the situation reflected there is that of post-exilic provincial Levites (2 Chr 17:9), and that the ultimate origin of the provision made there is an adaptation of Levitical tradition necessitated by the Josianic program of centralization. The author of Numbers here incorporates the older Levitical tradition (Deut 10:9; 18:1–5). He cannot and does not wish to deny it, and it can be used to provide a means of support for his new Levitical order.

The second is the fact that Aaron is addressed directly in vv 1–24, without reference to Moses. This is certainly unusual, but is not necessarily an indicator of either unusually late or unusually early priestly material. There is another direct word to Aaron in Lev 10:8, 12, and it is significant that this also occurs in the aftermath of a disaster concerning priestly rights. Perhaps such situations warranted the direct approach, the effect of which is to increase the stature of Aaron, and to underline his unique priestly authority. The reversion to Moses alone in v 25 is entirely intelligible. The Levites must see this imposition on their resources (vv 26–32) as part of the divine order of things through Moses, and not acquisitiveness or exploitation on the part of the sons of Aaron. Other unusual technical terms and usages in the chapter are less impressive if Numbers is seen to have some identity of its own over against the priestly parts of other books.

Comment

1. תשאו את-עון "you shall bear iniquity" (RSV), "you shall be fully answerable for" (NEB). This may mean that they are to pay the penalty for all ritual errors. G. B. Gray (219) and N. H. Snaith (265) link it with the sin of coming too near in Num 17:27–28 (Heb.). The priests and Levites, as those chosen to approach God, will take all the risks and pay whatever penalties are incurred by drawing near. This is their protective role with regard to Israel at large. The phrase may have been drawn from Ezek 44:10–13 where it is used of the degraded ministry of the idolatrous Levites (cf Num 14:34 for its use in relation to the faithless congregation). There is no obviously adverse sense in its use here; its main point is to stress that the priests are fully responsible for the sanctuary, and for every aspect of priestly ministry.

2. וילוו עליך "that they may be joined to you." RSV ignores the passive, or understands the verb reflexively. The name "Levi" itself suggests the root לוה "to join" (cf. Gen 29:34), and so the author finds etymological grounds for his clerical hierarchy. The Levites are joined to the sons of Aaron as their assistants.

5. It is unclear whether this is addressed to the sons of Aaron alone or to priests and Levites together. The meaning of responsibility for the sanctuary cannot therefore be determined precisely.

6. On the Levites as "given" see *Comment* on Num 3:9.

7. ולמבית לפרכת "what lies within the Veil." This is that part of the sanctuary which only the high priests may enter once a year (Lev 16:2, 17).

8. משמרת "responsibility for." Some commentators translate "that which is kept" (of my contributions) (see e.g. G. B. Gray, 221–22; A. H. McNeile, 97; N. H. Snaith, 266). But the word is often used of a general responsibility and the *NEB* interpretation "control" seems preferable.

8. תרומתי "the contributions made to me." See *Comment* on Num 5:9.

8. לכל-קדשי "all the holy things." A general expression for those gifts which went to the Temple personnel, in contrast to the קרבנים which serviced the sanctuary.

8. למשחה "as a portion." An uncommon root. RV links it with the root משח "to anoint" (cf. Lev 7:35). A synonymous parallel with "perpetual due" is probably intended. This latter expression is regularly used of prescribed quantities (cf. e.g. Gen 47:22; Exod 29:28; Lev 6:11 (Heb.); 7:34; 10:15).

9. מן-האש "kept back from the altar fire," literally "from the fire." If this is the correct understanding (see *Notes*), then the reference is to those parts of the offerings which were not burned.

11. תרומת מתנם לכל-תנופת "the contribution from all their gifts which are presented as special contributions." This is a reference to the breast and thigh of Lev 7:34. See also *Comment* on Num 5:25. All *terumah* contributions are for the priests, and of these the breast and thigh are treated in some special way as *tenuphah* ("waved" before Yahweh?).

12. ראשית "the firstfruits." The author of Numbers appears to use this as a synonym for בכורים—"the first ripe fruits" (v 13).

13. בכורים "the first ripe fruits." In Lev 2:14 this word is used of grain only. A. Dillmann (101–2) took v 13 to be a generalizing repetition of v 12,

though בבורים in Lev 2:14 does appear to be fairly precise. G. B. Gray (225) conjectures that the ראשית of v 12 would go straight to the priests without ceremony, while the בכורים of v 13 called for some ceremonial in the Temple before passing to priestly use. Some evidence for this is offered in Neh 10:35–37. On the other hand the author of Numbers is not evidently interested in such distinctions, and may well be using the words synonymously. The firstfruits like the firstborn belong to God, and must therefore be presented to him.

14. כל-חרם "every devoted thing." This word is used of the ancient ban whereby persons or objects were considered "devoted" to Yahweh in an absolute way which required their total destruction (cf. e.g. Num 21:1–3; Deut 7:1–2; Josh 6:17, 21; 1 Sam 15:3). The priestly author employs the word as an alternative reference to the *terumah* contribution. This is appropriate, since even in the light of the older ideas, the wealth of a devoted place could be kept in a sacred treasury (Josh 6:19).

15. תפדה "you shall redeem." N. H. Snaith (268) suggests that פדה means to get by payment what was not originally yours, whereas גאל is to get back your own possessions. For alternative analyses of the usage see *Comment* on Num 3:46 and Num 5:8.

16. ופדויו "their redemption price." The figure given is the price for the firstborn of men (cf. Lev 27:6; Num 3:47). That for the firstborn of unclean animals appears to have varied (cf. Lev 27:11–12, 27).

17. תזרק "you shall throw." The translation "sprinkle" (RSV) seems too weak, and may lead to confusion with הזה, a word for which "sprinkle" is appropriate.

19. ברית מלח "covenant of salt." Salt was used regularly in offerings (cf. e.g. Ezek 43:24), and specifically the cereal offering (Lev 2:13). The importance of salt as a preservative in the ancient world is reflected here. Agreements between men were often attested by sacrifice (cf. e.g. Gen 31:51–54), and the phrase "covenant of salt" (cf. 2 Chr 13:5) witnesses to a binding and irrevocable agreement. On the use of salt generally in the Bible see J. F. Ross, "Salt," *IDB* Y-Z 167.

20. On the relationship of this to the notion that the Levites are to have forty-eight cities see *Form/Structure/Setting* on Num 35:1–8.

27. וכמלאה "the fullness" cf. Exod 22:28 where the word means "full harvest" (cf. also Amos 2:13).

29. את-מקדשו "which you hallow" a way of describing the tithe of the tithe. This revocalization of MT ("his hallowed thing") gives better sense.

30. The phraseological construction of this verse is awkward. NEB reorganizes it, and places the reference to the Levites earlier. J. Sturdy (132–33) suggests that בהרימכם "set aside" be rendered "demanded." The verse would then be addressed to the priests, telling them how to deal with the offerings of the Levites.

31. The tithe may be eaten anywhere because, unlike those offerings for the use of the priests, it is not a holy thing.

32. Since the tithe is apparently not a holy thing the profanation which Levites must avoid is the consumption of those items which properly belong to the priests.

Explanation

This section summarizes again in general terms the duties of the Levites, and the nature of their relationship to the priests, the sons of Aaron (vv 1–7). The author then turns to the dues payable to the priests (vv 8–20). Since the priests lack access to private means of support they are to receive the *terumah* contributions (the holy things) from the community at large. These include the appropriate parts of the cereal, purification and reparation offerings, along with the firstfruits of the produce of the land and all the firstborn of animals and men. Resources come from the firstborn by means of a system of financial redemption. The Levites also receive tithes (vv 21–24), the traditional exaction of one tenth, but from these receipts they must make their own contribution to the priests (vv 25–32).

It is natural enough that the author should wish at this point to reaffirm his view of the Levitical role and its relationship to that of the priests. The rebellion of Num 16–17 is essentially a dramatic rejection of the author's position. Its outcome vindicates the true divine order, and he therefore repeats the main outline of this order. It is equally natural to turn from this to the question of priestly dues. This material, along with that which describes the maintenance of the Levites, fulfills a function similar to that of the various sections in Num 15. The second great sin of the journey phase (Num 16–17) takes place within the priestly hierarchy, and disastrous though the outcome is it does not mark the end of God's purpose. In setting up this system for clerical maintenance God is seen to commit himself anew to the continuance of the priestly order. This graciousness is most evident in the provision for the Levites, who are granted their traditional claim to the tithes of the people. Despite the sin of Korah and his associates there is a future for the Levites within the purposes of God. On the other hand they must recognize their subordination by making a contribution themselves for the support of the priests. There must be no further profanations of the kind perpetrated by Korah. The author's method is to work with existing tradition, specifically in Ezekiel and earlier priestly texts (see *Form/Structure/Setting*), and to work it into his own perceptions of the true priestly order.

It is possible to suggest something of the value this might have in the latter part of the fifth century B.C. The author's chief objective within that context is the reordering of the clerical office in terms of a hierarchy giving preeminence to the sons of Aaron. These represent the Zadokite priests from Babylon. The Levites, among them some exiles and others who had remained in the land, are given a subordinate but dignified status as their assistants. This is the objective underlying much of the material in Num 1:47–54 and Num 3–4. It is quite possible that the stipulations regarding priestly dues are the outcome of Nehemiah's reforms in this area (Neh 10:36–40; 13:10–14). The account has probably been written in the light of the view of the Levites given in Numbers, but there is good reason for believing that Nehemiah did indeed engage in a serious reform of the tithing system.

Purification of the Unclean   (19:1–22)

Bibliography

Bowman, J. "Did the Qumran Sect Burn the Red Heifer?" *RevQ* 1 (1958) 73–84.
Gowan, D. E. "The Use of *ya'an* in Biblical Hebrew." *VT* 21 (1971) 168–85. **Milgrom,**
J. "The Paradox of the Red Cow (Num 19)." *VT* 31 (1981) 62–72. **Reif, S. C.** "A
Note on a Neglected Connotation of *NTN*." *VT* 20 (1970) 114–16.

Translation

[1] *And Yahweh spoke to Moses,*[a] *saying,* [2] *"This is the statute of the law*[a] *which
Yahweh has commanded, saying, Tell the people of Israel to bring you a red heifer
without defect, in which there is no blemish, and which has never borne the yoke.*
[3] *And you*[a] *shall give her to Eleazar the priest, and he shall take her outside the
camp, and she shall be slaughtered before him.*[b] [4] *And Eleazar the priest shall take
some of the blood with his finger, and shall sprinkle some of her blood toward the
front of the Tent of Meeting seven times.* [5] *And the heifer shall be burned*[a] *in his
sight. Her skin, her flesh, and her blood, with the intestines, he shall burn.* [6] *And
the priest shall take cedar wood, marjoram, and scarlet thread, and throw them into
the middle of the burning heifer.* [7] *Then the priest shall wash his clothes, and bathe
his body in water. After that he shall come into the camp. And the priest shall be
unclean until evening.* [8] *He who burns the heifer shall wash his clothes in water,*[a]
and shall be unclean until evening. [9] *And a man who is clean shall gather up the
ashes of the heifer, and deposit them outside the camp in a clean place. And they
shall be kept for the congregation of the people of Israel as the water for purification.
It is a purification offering.* [10] *And he who gathers the ashes of the heifer shall wash
his clothes, and shall be unclean until evening. And this shall be a perpetual statute
for the people of Israel and for the resident alien.*
[11] *"He who touches the corpse of any person shall be unclean for seven days.*
[12] *He shall cleanse himself with the water on the third day and on the seventh day,
and so be clean.*[a] *But if he does not cleanse himself on the third day and on the
seventh day, he will not become clean.* [13] *Whoever touches a corpse, the body of any
man who has died, and does not cleanse himself, defiles the Tabernacle of Yahweh.
And that person shall be cut off from Israel. Because the water for purification was
not thrown upon him he shall be unclean. His uncleanness is still on him.*
[14] *"This is the law when a man dies in a tent.*[a] *Everyone who comes into the
tent, and everyone who is in the tent, shall be unclean for seven days.* [15] *And every
open vessel, which has no cover fastened upon it, is unclean.* [16] *Whoever in the open
field touches one who has been killed with a sword, or any corpse, or a bone of a
man, or a grave, shall be unclean for seven days.* [17] *For the unclean they shall take
some ashes of the burnt purification offering, and they shall pour*[a] *running water
into a vessel.* [18] *Then a clean person shall take marjoram, and dip it in the water,
and sprinkle it upon the tent,*[a] *and upon all the furnishings,*[b] *and upon the people
who were there, and upon the one who touched the bone, or the slain, or the*

dead, or the grave. ¹⁹ *And the clean person shall sprinkle the unclean on the third and seventh days. So on the seventh day he shall cleanse him, and he shall wash his clothes and bathe himself in water. And at evening he shall be clean.* ᵃ

²⁰ *"But the man who is unclean and who does not cleanse himself, that person shall be cut off from the midst of the assembly, since he has defiled the sanctuary of Yahweh. Because the water for purification has not been thrown upon him he is unclean.* ²¹ *And it shall be a perpetual statute for you.* ᵃ *He who sprinkles the water for purification shall wash his clothes. And he who touches the water for purification shall be unclean until evening.* ²² *And whatever the unclean person touches shall be unclean. And anyone who touches it shall be unclean until evening."*

Notes

1.a. "And Aaron" is lacking in some mss, and should perhaps be rejected. The singular אליך "you" (v 2) suggests that Moses alone is addressed.

2.a. *BHS* considers an emendation to הפרה "the heifer." The phrase "the statute of the law" is uncommon but see Num 27:11; 31:21; 35:29. In view of these occurrences it is best accepted.

3.a. G and Vg have the singular, giving some support to the view that "Aaron" is not original in v 1. Aaron is not usually included in the reception of law (cf. Num 5:1, 11; 6:1; 15:1, 17).

3.b. NEB takes this clause to mean that the heifer is to be slaughtered "to the east" of the camp. This is uncertain, and the text is admittedly difficult. How can Eleazar take the heifer outside the camp, and slaughter it before him? It seems best to adopt an impersonal or passive rendering of the verb. G and Vg read "they shall burn it before him (Eleazar)," but this looks like an attempt to resolve the textual difficulty. J. de Vaulx (214) envisages a traditio-historical explanation in which "before Yahweh" (cf. Lev 4:4) once occurred.

5.a. As in v 3 a passive seems best. G and Vg have "they shall burn."

8.a. Omitted by some versions; cf. v 7.

12.a. Reading וְטָהֵר with Sam, G, Syr, and Vg.

14.a. G has "in the house."

17.a. Reading the plural with Sam, G, Syr, and Vg.

18.a. G has "in the house"; cf. v 14.

18.b. This reference to "furnishings" is lacking in some MT mss.

19.a. G and Vg read וטהר בערב "and he shall be unclean until evening" (as in vv 7–8, 10, 21–22). This is probably a standardization, and MT is acceptable.

21.a. Reading the second person plural with Sam, G, Syr, Tgᴶ and some MT mss.

Form/Structure/Setting

Analysts are agreed in attributing this section to P, though many recognize it as isolated, and as an accretion, if not to P, to some completed form of the Pentateuch. Many have seen vv 14–22 as an appendix to vv 1–13 (J. Wellhausen, 178; A. Kuenen, 96; H. Holzinger, 78–79; B. Baentsch, 560–64). Their purpose is to modify the original demand of Lev 5:2–3 that the restoration of the unclean requires a reparation offering. A. Dillmann (106–10) was less clear about the secondary status of vv 14–22, but pointed to a number of peculiar words and phrases, not easily paralleled elsewhere in P, and among them "the statute of the law" (v 2), the verb התחטא "to cleanse oneself from sin" (vv 12, 20; cf. Num 8:21; 31:19, 23), and "cut off from the midst of the assembly" (v 20). G. B. Gray (241–43) also notes such features, observes the isolation of the section from its surrounding material, and argues that it could in no way have formed part of PG. His inclination is to see vv

14–22 and vv 1–13 as originally distinct pieces of legislation which have been compiled by an editor in the interests of completeness (p 254). A. H. McNeile (101) sees in vv 14–22 an expanded and stricter form of vv 11–13 (cf. also L. E. Binns, 125). Whatever the literary age of the section, older analysts were in general agreed that the laws embody ancient practice and belief, particularly in their notion that contact with the dead causes pollution (cf. e.g. G. B. Gray, 243–44).

More recent analysts are inclined to agree about the literary lateness of the chapter, and also about the antiquity of the practice and belief exhibited here, but are more sophisticated in their attempts to analyze the chapter's literary history. M. Noth (139–40) observes how the subject of the text moves from Moses (and Aaron?) (v 1) to Eleazar the priest (v 3–4), to "the priest" (vv 6–7). There is no doubt in Noth's mind that there are independent laws here which originally cited "the priest" alone, and which have been adapted to suit the present context by the introduction of Moses and Eleazar. He sees the core of the chapter in vv 1–10a, the preparation of the ingredients for a water for purification; and in vv 14–22 instructions for its use, the removal of uncleanness caused by contact with a corpse. He sees vv 10b–13 as a likely addition. Their exposition of the necessity for cleansing is seen to have only a tenuous connection with the context through the subordinate clause in v 13b (p 141).

J. de Vaulx (213–15) also distinguishes three main components (vv 1–10, 11–13, 14–22). The complex history of vv 1–10 is evident, not only in the priestly subjects cited by Noth, but also in the use of second and third persons plural for the Israelites (vv 2b/3a) and in the indeterminate individuals cited in vv 8a, 9–10. He thinks that the most ancient elements of the rite survive in vv 3b, 5a, 6, 9. Responsibility for the performance of these rites has little by little been reserved to the priests, and finally to the sons of Aaron, represented by Eleazar. Some elements which recall the rites of Deut 21:3 are also found by de Vaulx. There the inhabitants of the town closest to the site of an unexplained murder must cleanse themselves. Here there is rather more ritual detail. Other developments of the original rite would be the purification of the participants (vv 7–8, 10), and some adaptation of the laws of Lev 4:3–12 in v 4 and possibly v 5.

In vv 11–13 de Vaulx finds a different literary genre. It is juridical in style, emphasizing the necessity of cleansing from contact with death, and it makes no reference to the red heifer. He goes on to make further form critical distinctions in vv 14–22. In vv 14–16 he sees a kind of *torah*, listing the persons and things to be purified, while vv 17–19 are rituals which may have belonged originally to the rites of vv 1–10. In style and content v 20 recalls vv 11–13, while vv 21–22 reaffirm the essential context of vv 7–8, 10. These are all additions of one sort or another, and make reference only to washing, not to the red heifer.

Whether or not this approach is accurate in all points of detail it is suggestive of ways in which the author of Numbers may have taken up and adapted traditional material. A somewhat simpler literary history for the chapter may be proposed along the following lines:

1. An ancient rite involving a red heifer. Its purpose is not clear, but it

may have had magical associations. The priest had a limited role in what was essentially a lay function taking place away from the sanctuaries. This may explain some of the linguistic awkwardness in vv 1–10 (vv 3b, 5–6, 9a).

2. The author of Numbers takes up this tradition, and makes it clear that the ashes of the heifer are ingredients for a water for purification, and demands washings for those who take part (vv 7a, 8, 9b, 10a). He also works it into the history of Israel's journey in the wilderness (vv 1–3a, 7b, 9—the reference to "the camp"), adds a reference to Eleazar's manipulation of the blood (v 4), thereby aligning the rite more closely with other sacrificial rituals in the Pentateuch and making it a sacrifice, and finally emphasizes its binding nature on all (v 10b). The involvement of Eleazar in these proceedings is probably to be explained in the light of Lev 21:12 which insists that Aaron himself, as high priest, is not to go out of the sanctuary.

3. The author of Numbers goes on to outline the circumstances in which this water for purification is primarily to be used, namely contact with death (vv 11–13). The timescale and the consequences of failure are specified.

4. It seems quite possible that vv 11–13 constitute a connecting link between the red heifer ritual (vv 1–10), and a quite different ritual for removing the uncleanness caused by contact with death. This second procedure is preserved in vv 14–19, and like the red heifer ritual, was taken up by the author of Numbers from tradition. J. Milgrom (*VT* 32 [1981] 62–72) prefers to see an ancient link between vv 1–10 and vv 14–19; for him the sprinkling of the ashes of the heifer on a corpse-contaminated person is the very ancient vestige in the tradition. In any event vv 14–16 deal with the problem of contact with death, specifying the conditions which cause uncleanness. If vv 14–19 can indeed be treated as an originally independent tradition then these verses indicate also that the ashes of the conventional purification offering may be used, if mixed with running water in a vessel (v 17). Any clean person may perform the cleansing ceremony (vv 18–19).

5. The author of Numbers then repeats in v 20 his warning of v 13, and adds further ritual requirements (v 21) and conditions (v 22).

If this overall view is broadly correct then the author of Numbers has taken up the red heifer ritual, which originally served some other purpose, and made it into the sole purification offering from which ashes may be taken to make the water for purification. The extent to which the section is internally loose and disconnected can thus be greatly exaggerated. This is also true of the chapter in its wider context. There is a sense in which it stands loosely in its present position, but even if this is judged a reason for considering it a late accretion, the question of "Why here, and not there?" is still valid. The supposition that its presence here is accidental or without recognizable purpose is a possibility, but it deserves to be questioned and tested. Just as the Levitical material in Num 18 has an appropriateness after the Levitical failures of Num 16–17 so too Num 19 can be understood as part of the aftermath of those decisive events. Its basic theme is contact with death, the red heifer rites being adapted to provide the ingredients for the water which removes the consequences of such contact. There are at least 250 who have died in Korah's rebellion, and a further 14,700 in the subsequent plague (Num 16:35; 17:14 [Heb.]). As part of the process of reconstruction

after such disasters it seems entirely appropriate that the author should incorporate here his stipulations about the consequences of contact with death,
and how these may be averted. In his view contact on a large scale must
have taken place, and it is essential that the community should know how
to reconstitute itself as the purified people of Yahweh. It is true that he has
no narrative account of this. Eleazar is commanded to prepare the water
and to lay it up for future use. On the other hand distinctions between law
and narrative are by no means sharp in priestly material; the important point
is to establish principles, and in the light of the events in Num 16–17 this
is a most appropriate place to do it.

Comment

2. אדמה פרה "a red heifer." Many modern translators prefer "cow." The
word is normally used of a full-grown animal (cf. Gen. 41:2–4; 1 Sam 6:7),
and "heifer" is thought to be a false influence from G. On the other hand
young animals are very widely prescribed in sacrificial laws, and it seems
unlikely that a cow of any age would be acceptable.

J. Milgrom (*VT* 31 [1981] 62–72) suggests that a bull cannot be chosen
because that is the purification offering of the high priests (Lev 4:1–12; 16:11)
or the community (Lev 4:13–21). A female is used for the individual (Lev
4:22–35; Num 15:27–29).

The adjective clearly means "red" in Isa 1:18, but in Cant 5:10 refers to
the tan derived from exposure to the sun. J. Sturdy (134) suggests "red-
brown" like the earth in which the dead are buried. It seems more likely
that "red," like the scarlet thread (v 6), suggested the color of blood, which
always had an important part to play in rites of purification (see J. Milgrom,
VT 31 [1981] 62–72, and references).

The cow would only be suitable for sacrifice if it was without blemish of
any kind, and had never been put to other forms of service. This latter point
supports the view that a young cow is intended.

3. Eleazar's part in this rite is probably explained by Lev 21:10–12 which
confine Aaron to the sanctuary.

4. שבע פעמים "seven times." "Seven" is a sacred figure, and is often
required if rites of purification are to be effective. For the significance of
"seven" in other contexts see Gen 17:12; 29:27; 50:10. J. Sturdy (135) sees
here an adaptation of this rite to that of Lev 4:3–12.

5. This is the only sacrificial rite which can take place outside the sacred
precincts, let along outside the camp.

6. עץ ארז ואזוב ושני תולעת "cedar wood, marjoram, and scarlet thread"
(cf. Lev 14:4). N. H. Snaith (272) points out that in Babylonian ritual the
efficacy of rites was enhanced by cedar and other aromatic woods. In Lev
14 it appears that the cedar wood and marjoram were bound together by
the thread to make an implement for sprinkling blood on the leper and his
house. The reason for burning them in this ritual is unknown, and may also
have been unknown to the priestly author. The identification of אזוב as "marjoram" (*NEB*) is not certain; cf. "hyssop" in RSV and older translations.

7. The author probably draws the ritual details here and in vv 8, 10 from

Lev 11:25; 15:8; 16:28. J. Sturdy (135) suggests that these people become unclean because the cow itself has become unclean prior to its actual use to remove uncleanness.

7. יכבס "he shall wash" (cf. vv 8, 10, 19, 21). The word can be used of cleansing from sin (Jer 2:2; 4:14; Ps 51:4, 9).

9. אפר "ashes." According to N. H. Snaith (272) this would be light ash-dust. A different word is normally used for the ashes of a sacrifice.

9. למי נדה "the water for purification," literally "the water for impurity." The word נדה can be rendered "abhorrent," and is used for various types of ritual impurity. As Snaith (273) points out it is used here in the sense of "de-impurifying," hence "for purification" is appropriate. Though the rite differs in some respects from that described in Lev 4 the author feels able to describe it as a "purification offering." This is fitting because as J. Milgrom (*VT* 31 [1981] 62–72) points out this offering transmits impurity from the purified to the purifier.

13. לא-זרק "was not thrown," a verb used of fluids which are flung against the altar. הזה (vv 4, 18) denotes "sprinkling."

16. Cf. Matt 23:27; Acts 23:3 for reflections of this law.

17. For the use of נתן "give, pour" here see S. C. Reif, *VT* 20 (1970) 114–16.

21. עד-הערב "until evening," the shortest period that ritual uncleanness can last.

Explanation

This section provides a ritual whereby the impurity caused by contact with death can be removed. Eleazar is required to witness the burning of a red heifer outside the camp, and to take some part in the rites with cedar wood, marjoram, and scarlet thread. The ashes are to be taken up and kept as an ingredient for the water for purification. Some indication is given of the circumstances which constitute contact with death. The production of the water for purification is described (v 17), and the procedures outlined.

Despite those who emphasize the lateness of the passage and its looseness in its present context it is not too difficult to suggest reasons why the author of Numbers chose to discuss the question of contact with death at this point. In the wake of Num 16–17 he needs to re-establish, not only the position of the Levites (Num 18), but also that of the community as ritually acceptable to Yahweh. The thousands of deaths recorded in Num 17 meant that the ritual effects of all contact with death must be thoroughly understood, and the procedures to deal with them duly recognized. It is true enough that the section is cast primarily in terms of the needs of the settled community (vv 14–16) rather than those of the wilderness generation—in other words as law rather than narrative. In view of the overall objective, however, this is scarcely surprising, and certainly not a serious difficulty. The author chooses to deal with the matter in terms of something first instituted in the wilderness. This accords with one of the priestly school's chief interests—to show that the rules shaping the community's life and faith are Mosaic, and therefore pre-settlement. Though not all such laws can be fully observed in exile or dispersion, it can nevertheless exercise a regulative and authoritative function for religious communities deprived of land but seeking restoration.

It may also be that the author is incorporating, and thereby controlling, rituals of an ancient date regarding the red heifer (see *Form/Structure/Setting*). Such rituals may originally have had magical associations. In the course of time they appear to have been transformed, but may still have retained or recovered some of these associations in Judaea during the exilic period. The author wishes to establish some rapprochement with Palestinian Judaism, and therefore retains rites which may well have been popular. They are strictly controlled, however, and become the means by which water for purification is prepared. This is the water to be used in cases of contact with death. The circumstances described in vv 14–16 and the procedures in vv 17–19 may have come in contrast from the traditions of the Jews in Babylon.

That the author's motive was in part to incorporate and transform the ritual of the red heifer is suggested by the fact that the book of Leviticus had already provided procedures to deal with unwitting contact with a dead animal (Lev 5:2, 5–13), with an unclean animal (Lev 11:24–28), and the pollution a priest would incur through contact with death (Lev 22:4–6). The author has already dealt with pollution suffered by a Nazirite (Num 6:6–10), and is able to use the red heifer rites by adapting them to further eventualities of contact with death experienced by people in general (vv 14–16).

Theologically the section has much in common with Num 5:1–4; 6:6–12. The community is encouraged to safeguard and preserve its condition of ritual purity. This concern is prompted by a sense of the holiness of God, and the realization that inward dispositions have to be confirmed and consolidated by outward actions. An awareness that such observance can be an empty shell is evident in Heb 9:13–14. The place of image, symbol, and ritual in religion is not however to be ignored, and the theology of Numbers acts as a stimulus to a consideration of the place of these phenomena in Judaeo-Christian religion.

The Exclusion of Moses and Aaron
(20:1–13)

Bibliography

Arden, E. "How Moses Failed God." *JBL* 76 (1957) 50–52. **Buis, P.** "Qadesh, un Lieu Maudit?" *VT* 24 (1974) 268–85. **Gray, J.** "The Desert Sojourn of the Hebrews and the Sinai Horeb Tradition." *VT* 4 (1954) 148–54. **Kapelrud, A. S.** "How Tradition Failed Moses." *JBL* 76 (1957) 242. **Kohata, F.** "A Tradition History of Num 20:1–13." *Seishogaku-Ronshu* 12 (1977) 31–62 (Japanese). **Lehming, S.** "Massa und Meriba." *ZAW* 73 (1961) 71–77. **Mann, T. W.** "Theological Reflections on the Denial of Moses." *JBL* 98 (1979) 481–94. **Margaliot, M.** "The Transgression of (Moses and) Aaron at Mey Merivah." *Beth Mikra* 19, 3 58 (1974) 375–400, 456. **Meshel, Z.** and **Meyers, C.** "The Name of God in the Wilderness of Zin." *BA* 39 (1976) 6–10, 148–51. **Porter, J. R.** "The role of Kadesh-Barnea in the Narrative of the Exodus." *JTS* 44 (1943) 139–43. On disaffection in the wilderness see Num 11:1–3 (*Bibliography*).

Translation

¹ And the people of Israel, the whole congregation, came into the wilderness of Zin in the first month, and the people stayed at Kadesh. And Miriam died there and was buried there.
² And there was no water for the congregation. And they assembled themselves together against Moses and against Aaron. ³ And the people contended with Moses, [a] and they spoke, saying, "Oh that we had died when our brothers died before Yahweh! ⁴ Why have you brought the assembly of Yahweh into this wilderness, that we should die [a] here, we and our cattle? ⁵ And why have you made us come up out of Egypt, to bring us to this evil place? It is not a place of seed, or figs, or vines, or pomegranates, and there is no water to drink." ⁶ And Moses and Aaron went from before the assembly to the door of the Tent of Meeting, and fell on their faces. And the glory of Yahweh appeared to them. ⁷ And Yahweh spoke to Moses, saying, ⁸ "Take the rod, and assemble the congregation, you and Aaron your brother, and you shall speak to the rock before their eyes, and it shall give of its water. So you[a] shall bring water for them from the rock, and give drink [b] to the congregation and their cattle." ⁹ And Moses took the rod before Yahweh, as he had commanded him.
¹⁰ And Moses and Aaron gathered the assembly together before the rock, and he said to them, "Hear now, you rebels. Shall we bring forth water for you out of this rock?" ¹¹ And Moses lifted up his hand, and struck the rock with his rod twice, and water came out abundantly. And the congregation drank, and their cattle. ¹² And Yahweh said to Moses and Aaron, "Because you did not believe in me, [a] to sanctify me in the eyes of the people of Israel, therefore you shall not bring this assembly into the land which I have given them." ¹³ These are the waters of Meribah, ·where the people of Israel contended with Yahweh, and he showed himself holy among them. [a]

Notes

3 a. "And with Aaron" is attested in one ms and Syr. There is no other support, and it is probably an addition.

4.a. G has "to kill us" (cf. Exod 17:3; Num 21:5), thereby accentuating the tension between Moses and the people.

8.a. A singular in MT, and a plural in G.

8.b. G again has a plural, involving Aaron more directly.

12.a. G and Vg lack "in me."

13.a. The tendency of Sam to add material from Deuteronomy is evident here — from Deut 3:24–25, 26b–28.

Form/Structure/Setting

That there is a significant priestly element in this section has been clear enough to analysts. In v 3 there is a reference back to the Korah traditions of Num 16–17, and the idea of being "sanctified" (v 13) is also characteristic of P (cf. e.g. Exod 29:43; Lev 10:3; 22:32). The rod "before Yahweh" (v 7) seems to refer to Num 17:25. In v 6 there are typical P theophanies and prostrations. Israel is regularly "the assembly" or "the congregation," and Aaron's involvement is also characteristic. There are decisive indicators of P in all but v 5.

Many analysts have also found traces of JE. These tend to be the older scholars, and there has been little overall agreement about its precise identity and extent (cf. e.g. A. Dillmann, 110–14; A. Kuenen, 100–01; J. Wellhausen, 109–10; B. W. Bacon, 202–04; H. Holzinger, 82–84; B. Baentsch, 565–70). Many chose to identify these fragments as E, and typical is Baentsch who discerns them in parts of vv 1b, 5, 8–9, 11. The main reasons for preferring E are the presence of Miriam in v 1, who is elsewhere associated with that source, and the suspicion that in parts of the story the rod is that of Moses (cf. the E plague stories). Others such as Holzinger (84), Gray (258), and McNeile (105) confine E to the note about Miriam, and are less precise about the rest of the analysis.

More recent investigators are much less certain that we have a substantial piece of early tradition here, and the dominant influence of P is given the weight it deserves (cf. M. Noth, 144–47; W. Rudolph, Der "Elohist" 84–87; G. W. Coats, Rebellion, 71–73; N. H. Snaith, 274; V. Fritz, Israel, 27–28). J. de Vaulx (221–24) argues for a succession of priestly accretions to an old narrative. In fact the only likely indicators of the early narrative tradition are the reference to Israel as "the people" in v 1b and v 3a, and the account of the death of Miriam in v 1b (cf. Exod 15:20–21; Num 12:1). The sojourn at Kadesh and the death of Miriam probably did have a place in the Yahwist's story, though they are not necessarily to be designated E. The reference to the fact that the people strove or contended with Moses (v 3) could well have been drawn directly from Exod 17:2. This would have been the work of the priestly author of Numbers who evidently wishes to retell the story of water from the rock with a new end in view—explaining the judgment on Moses and Aaron. It is true enough that use of the root עלה "go up" in connection with the exodus (v 5a) is typical of the early narrative tradition (cf. Gen 46:4; 50:24; Exod 3:8, 17; 17:3; 20:5; 32:1, 4, 23; 33:1, 12, 15; Num 16:13), and this is one of the subsidiary factors that encourages scholars to find a larger non-priestly presence in the text (cf. e.g. O. Eissfeldt's [Hexateuch, 177] ascription of major parts to L). On the other hand עלה is not unknown in P (cf. Lev 11:45), and as with the reference to "the people" in v 3 may simply be an echo of the Yahwist's story in Exod 17:1–7. There is therefore no need to posit the presence of a second water story in the early narrative tradition. At this point in his story the Yahwist told only of the sojourn at Kadesh and of the death of Miriam there.

Whether there is significant unevenness in the priestly tradition is difficult to determine. The use of such terms as "people of Israel," "the assembly," and "the congregation" does not fall into obvious patterns. The only possible point of tension is whether the sin lies in the speech of v 10, or in the action of striking the rock twice in v 11. If there is such tension then the rod material in vv 8a, 9, 11a may be an accretion culminating in the striking of the rock in v 11. On the other hand it is far from clear that the rod material really is intended to explain the sin of Moses and Aaron. Explanatory glossing usually makes its point in an obvious way, yet the sin of Moses and Aaron remains a difficult matter of debate (see *Comment*).

It seems reasonable to suppose therefore that the priestly author has rewritten the story of Exod 17:1–7, and used it as a basis for explaining the exclusion of Moses and Aaron from the land. There may be minor priestly editing, but essentially the story is his. He is encouraged to do this because the Yahwist has located the story of water from the rock at Meribah (Exod 17:1–7). For the priestly author Meribah and Kadesh are one and the same (cf. Ezek 47:19; 48:28), so that to tell his story of water from the rock in association with the sojourn at Kadesh, as reported by the Yahwist (v 1b), seemed entirely appropriate. The author's intentions are best appreciated on the basis of an exegesis of v 12 and the sin of Moses and Aaron (see *Comment* and *Explanation*).

Comment

1. The year is not mentioned. For P it is the fortieth. Only then does Israel arrive at Kadesh. The timescale in the Yahwist's account is difficult to judge, but the impression is given of an altogether speedier arrival.

2. ויקהלו על "and they assembled themselves together against," an idea of disaffection used by the priestly author in the Korah traditions (Num 16:3, 19; 17:7 [Heb]). The verb does not necessarily denote hostility (see G. B. Gray, 198), but the context here demands a measure of aggressive intent, born perhaps of despair rather than malice.

3. וירב "contended," a word with a broad frame of reference in terms of "strife" or "contention" (BDB). KB is inclined to render it more narrowly, in connection with legal processes. For discussion of the *rib* in a broader context see J. Limburg, "The Root '*rib*' and the Prophetic Lawsuit Speeches." *JBL* 88 (1969) 291–304. In the present context a struggle with words is obviously intended (cf. e.g. Gen 26:20; 31:36; Judg 6:32). For the use of the word in association with bodily struggles see Exod 21:18; Judg 11:25, and with the conduct of law see Isa 3:13; 57:16. The people's disputation or quarrel is apparently as serious as legal action. The idea has evidently been taken over by the priestly author from the Yahwist's etiological adaptation of the story of water from the rock (Exod 17:2).

3. The deaths cited here are probably an allusion to the Korah traditions (Num 16:35; 17:14 [Heb.]).

6. The prostration and theophany are typical of the priestly author's stories of disaffection see *Comment* on Num 14:5, 10 and cf. Num 16: 4, 19, 22.

8. המטה "the rod" is that which was placed "before the Testimony" in Num 17:25–26 (Heb.). The priestly contribution to the plague traditions in Exod 6:28–11:10 puts the rod in the hand of Aaron (cf. e.g. Exod 7:9, 12, 19–20; 8:1, 12), though Moses also has a rod in other apparently priestly material (Exod 14:16). It may be that the rod of Aaron in Exodus is a relatively late adaptation familiar with the events of Num 17. In any event for the author Moses has placed the rod of Aaron in the holy place (Num 17:25–26 [Heb.]), and it is appropriate that he should take it again.

10. שמעו-נא המרים "hear now you rebels," evidently an address by Moses to the people. Their "contention" is tantamount to rebellion.

11. Moses had been told to speak to the rock (v 8); here he strikes it twice.

12. The nature of the sin committed by Moses and Aaron has caused much debate. It has been defined as unbelief (M. Noth, 145–47), unwillingness (cited as a possibility by N. H. Snaith, 275), haste or ill-temper (G. W. Coats, *Rebellion*, 80–81; E. Arden, *JBL* 76 [1957] 50–52), and disobedience. The disobedience is often understood in terms of the action of v 11 (striking) as compared with the command of v 8 (speaking) (H. Gressmann, 151; V. Fritz, *Israel*, 27 n.3; P. Buis, *VT* 24 [1974] 268–85; S. Lehming, *ZAW* 73 [1961] 71–77). It has been proposed that Moses should have prayed (J. de Vaulx, 225–26), but it is far from clear that prayer or the lack of it is the real point at issue. One theory is that the original form of the story has been suppressed (cf. e.g. G. B. Gray, 263; A. H. McNeile, 107; L. E. Binns, 132). This approach generally involves the suggestion that Moses initially refused to obey Yahweh's command, and that the words of v 10b were originally Yahweh's words to Moses and Aaron. This is ingenious, but disturbs the text excessively and unnecessarily. A. S. Kapelrud (*JBL* 76 [1957] 242) suggests that the story is deliberately vague about the sin, so the story is able to explain why Moses and Aaron did not lead the invasion without incriminating them in an intolerable way.

Of these suggestions the tension between the command of v 8 and the action of v 11 is the most likely, though if the rod material is an accretion then disobedience of this kind cannot be the original sin. Moreover if the rod material is original, and if the striking is the sin, it is not very clear as to why Moses is commanded to take the rod in the first place in v 8. It seems best to concentrate on v 12, where it is claimed that Moses did not "believe in" (האמנתם) Yahweh, and that they did not "sanctify" him (להקדישני) in the eyes of Israel. The general effect is to suggest that they have prevented the full power and might of Yahweh from becoming evident to the people, and have thus robbed him of the fear and reverence due to him. This would correspond very well with the view that the speech to the people in v 10 was uncalled for, and that it was in some measure a claim that *they* had the power to provide the water. In Num 20:24; 27:14 the author accuses Aaron and Moses of "rebellion" (מרה), a root always used in the

Pentateuch of defiance against God. This in particular tends to tell against Kaplerud's view. In Ps 106:32–33 it is claimed that Moses spoke rash words, and this supports the view that the speech of v 10b is the root of the problem. The form of the Phinehas tradition in this psalm suggests that it is not a very late text (contrast Num 25:6–18), and it seems likely that the author knew it and is here giving flesh to those "rash words." The speech is uncalled for, and implies a claim that they, not God, will produce the water. In its arrogance it fails to foster true belief in and reverence for Yahweh.

13. וַיִּקָּדֵשׁ "he showed himself holy," essentially an etiological play on the place name Kadesh. It seemed appropriate both because of the sin of the leaders and also because of the holy power revealed in the provision of water.

Explanation

In this section the priestly author retells the story of the miraculous provision of water from the rock (cf. Exod 17:1–7). His particular purpose is to use the tradition to explain how it is that Moses and Aaron are excluded from the land. Israel's sin is in some respects understandable, but that of Moses and Aaron cannot be overlooked. Various factors suggested the feasibility of this. He had at hand Yahwistic tradition about the stay at Kadesh, in particular the account of the death of Miriam which he duly records (v 1b), but it was the name Kadesh which attracted his attention. Etiological reflection on the name, a feature of the Yahwist's own work in relation to other names, led him to think of "sanctification," and of the need to affirm the holiness of Yahweh. It is in this that he sees the failure of Moses and Aaron. The author was also familiar with the Yahwistic story of water from the rock, and it seemed appropriate that it should be murmuring which provokes the sin of Moses and Aaron (cf. the provocations in Num 11). The choice of this particular story was in no way arbitrary; after all, other tradition identified Meribah (the site of the Yahwist's story) and Kadesh (Ezek 47:19; 48:28). The Yahwist's etiological tradition associating Meribah with "contention" is also preserved (v 3a).

The story the author tells however is in all essentials his own, and it constitutes a major adaptation of the earlier tradition. It also plays a major part in the overall structure of the book as the third great sin in the book's central section (see *Introduction*). The failure of the people (Num 13–14), and the failure of the Levites (Num 16–17) is followed now by an account of the failure of the leadership itself. The deaths of Moses and Aaron outside the land were undeniable facts of tradition, and they required explanation by those for whom possession of the land constituted fulfillment of divine promise. The explanation offered in Deuteronomy, in exilic times, was that Moses suffered vicariously (Deut 3:26; 4:21), but the priestly author offers a quite different explanation. Exclusion from the land may be suffered by the greatest and most respected, but sin is such that any failure to inherit the divine promise must be traceable to specific failure. The author accepts of course the fundamental priestly view that Moses and Aaron, and the laws communicated to them, are the fountainhead of divine revelation and faith. On the

other hand both fail to possess the land. In both respects they resemble
the first leaders of Babylonian Judaism. Priestly interpretation did not seek
to soften or deny the sin which caused the exile, but it was anxious to affirm
the authenticity of the exilic community.

There is a sense therefore in which the author has an interest in interpreting
the failure of Moses to inherit in terms of sin. This is both daring and effective.
The place of Moses as law-giver was secure, certainly in Palestine and Babylon.
His fate is thus proof positive that exclusion from the land is not a sign of
inauthenticity. Establishing that principle was vital to the future and continuing
influence of Babylonian Judaism. This may also help to explain some of the
vagueness in the story. The rather generalized description of the sin in v
12 is more an explanation of the exile than a close elucidation of the tradition.
The vagueness is not an attempt to avoid incriminating Moses too much.
His punishment is affirmed with great clarity, and later in the book his sin
can be described as "rebellion." The vagueness arises rather from the author's
eye for the exilic situation.

What the author is able to do for Moses and Aaron is, in using the murmuring tradition, to show that the sin is provoked. The continued faithlessness
of the people, evident in their opposition and contention, tests the patience
of Moses to the limit. This does not exonerate him, but it sets his sin in a
particular context. The leaders are constantly subject to alien pressures from
the people at large. The tradition of Moses' death prior to the settlement
is thus in no way an embarassment to the author. On the contrary, it provides
him with an opportunity of showing that authenticity is not necessarily the
preserve of those who actually possess the land. The earlier Deuteronomic
tradition, with its more immediate need to establish Moses as fountainhead
of Jewish religion, is less able to think in terms of his sin. Its answer, in
terms of the vicarious sufferer, is also an authentication of the exilic community. For further discussion of the theme in Deuteronomy see T. W. Mann
(*JBL* 98 [1979] 481–94) and his references.

The story also gives the priestly author of Numbers an opportunity to
stress one of his principal theological interests. Moses and Aaron have failed
to "believe in" Yahweh, by claiming that they themselves can bring water
from the rock. In so doing they fail to "sanctify" him in the eyes of Israel,
and thereby deprive him of his due honor.

The Journey Around Edom (20:14-21)

Bibliography

Albright, W. F. "From the Patriarchs to Moses: 2. Moses out of Egypt." *BA* 36 (1973) 57–58, 63–64. **Bartlett, J. R.** "The Land of Seir and the Brotherhood of Edom." *JTS* 20 (1969) 1–20. ———. "The Rise and Fall of the Kingdom of Edom." *PEQ* 104 (1972) 26–37. ———. "The Brotherhood of Edom." *JSOT* 4 (1977) 2–27. **Glueck, N.** "The Boundaries of Edom." *HUCA* 11 (1936) 141–57. ———. "The Civilisation of the Edomites." *BA* 10 (1947) 77–84. **Mittmann, S.** "Num 20:14–21—eine redaktionelle Kompilation." *Wort und Geschichte,* ed. H. Gese and H. P. Rüger. Neukirchen-Vluyn: Neukirchener Verlag, 1973. **Sumner, W. A.** "Israel's Encounters with Edom, Moab, Ammon, Sihon and Og according to the Deuteronomist." *VT* 18 (1968) 216–28.

Translation

[14a] *And Moses sent messengers from Kadesh to the king of Edom,[b] "Thus says your brother Israel: you know all the adversity that has happened to us,* [15] *how our fathers went down to Egypt, and we lived in Egypt for many days. And the Egyptians dealt harshly with us and our fathers.[a]* [16] *And when we cried to Yahweh, he heard our voice, and sent an angel and brought us out of Egypt. And behold, we are here in Kadesh, a city on the border of your territory.* [17] *Now let us pass through your land.[a] We will not pass through field or vineyard, nor will we drink water from a well. We will go along the King's Highway. We will not turn aside [b] to the right hand or to the left, until we have passed through your territory."* [18] *But Edom said to him, "You shall not pass through, lest [a] I come out with the sword against you."* [19] *And the people of Israel said to him, "We will go up by the Highway, and if we drink of your water, I and my cattle, then I will pay for it. Let me only pass through on foot,[a] nothing more."* [20] *But he said, "You shall not pass through." And Edom came out against him with many men, and with a strong hand.* [21] *So Edom refused to give Israel passage [a] through his territory, and so Israel turned away from him.*

Notes

14.a. Sam has additional material from Deut 2:2–6 at this point.

14.b. "Saying" may have fallen out; cf. S, Vg, Num 21:21. "King" is lacking in vv 18, 20–21 and is thought by some to be an addition, but see *Form/Structure/Setting.*

15.a. *BHS* suggests that "fathers" is an addition.

17.a. In Sam the cohortative is absent, making the communication less of a request, and more a statement of intent.

17.b. Sam has a different verb (נסור "we will turn"), influenced perhaps by Deut 2:27.

18.a. On the use of פן "lest" see GKC, § 152w.

19.a. G has "by the mountain" at this point.

21.a. Perhaps לעבר should be read cf. Num 21:23, *BHS,* J. Paterson, 54. In Tg[J] it is explained that the time for vengeance on Edom had not yet come.

Form/Structure/Setting

There has been general agreement among analysts that this account of Edom's refusal to let Israel pass through is a preliminary to the JE account of the Transjordanian journey. There are no clear indicators of P, and that in itself would be remarkable in a passage of this length, were it in fact priestly. In vv 14, 16 the passage links well with the early narrative tradition of Num 20:1 that Israel is now at Kadesh. The description of the people as "Israel" (vv 14, 21) is a common feature of the Transjordanian journey (Num 21:1–3, 17, 21, 23–25, 31; 22:2; 23:10, 21, 23; 24:5, 17–18; 25:1, 3, 5; 32:13–14), and never occurs in obviously priestly texts. J. Wellhausen (110) saw here an indicator of J, citing Exod 14:30–31, but many older analysts preferred E (cf. e.g. A. Dillmann, 114–15; A. Kuenen, 151; B. W. Bacon, 195–97; B. Baentsch, 571). There was some doubt about the final words in v 20, but the reference to the angel (v 16; cf. Exod 14:19; 23:20) and the phrase "all the adversity that has happened to us" (v 14; cf. Exod 18:8) were held to be good indicators of E. G. B. Gray (264–65) offered support, pointing out also that the use of נתן "give" in v 21 occurs also in Gen 20:6; 22:13; 31:7; Num 21:23, all judged on other grounds to be E. Others noted that vv 19–20 appear to repeat v 17. This led L. E. Binns (xxxiii) to attribute vv 19–20 to J, a view also taken by H. Gressmann (300–04). O. Eissfeldt (*Hexateuch* 178–79), having assigned vv 14–18 to J, linked vv 19–20 with E, and v 21 with L. The uncertainties made it easy for W. Rudolph (*Der 'Elohist'* 87–88), in his opposition to E, to assign the whole of the section to J, with some unevenness in vv 17, 21.

More recent analysts have in some cases been inclined to accept the E indicators (cf. e.g. M. Noth, 149–50; N. H. Snaith, 276; J. de Vaulx, 227–30). Noth argues for a closely interwoven text with J and E components, but recognizes that minor inconsistencies may be the product of careless expression, and does not attempt a detailed analysis. He is impressed by the "obvious doublets," in particular the difference between vv 17–18 and vv 19–20. The latter give no indication that negotiations have been resumed, and promise to make payment for drinking water used (contrast v 17). De Vaulx is more interested in the ancient document which he thinks underlies the passage. This may have been an attempt to secure passage for Hebrew nomads through the territory of the Edomite kings, for traders from settled Israel to Elath, or a simple attempt to secure good relations with a near neighbor. Attractive as these suggestions may be we have to recognize that there are no clear linguistic signs of antiquity in the letter. The turn of expression constitutes a fairly conventional statement of Israel's faith about the Exodus, and there is no certainty that such creed-like recitals are early (see J. Sturdy, 142). W. A. Sumner (*VT* 18 [1968] 216–28) also accepts that the section is E (along with Num 21:21–31), and argues that these are a parallel account to Deut 2:1–3:11. He suspects that E and D are handling an earlier narrative tradition in a somewhat different way; they are essentially parallel accounts.

The most recent analytical tendency is to see the section as deuteronomistic and redactional in origin (see V. Fritz, *Israel*, 28–29; S. Mittmann, "Num

20: 14–21" in *Wort und Geschichte;* cf. also J. van Seters, "The Conquest of Sihon's Kingdom; a Literary Examination." *JBL* 91 [1972] 182–97). Mittmann finds the base narrative in vv 14abα, 17, 21, but he thinks this is only a copy of Num 21:21–23 (an E story). In vv 14bβ he sees a shortened version of the credo of Deut 26:5–9, while in vv 18–20 he sees an editorial piece, based on Num 21:23, which is anxious to picture the Edomites as on the march. This section (vv 14–21) is therefore wholly editorial with strong deuteronomistic influence; it is the base from which further expansion of the tradition takes place in Deut 2:4–6, 8a and Judg 11:17. J. R. Bartlett (*JSOT* 4 [1977] 2–27) is sympathetic to Mittmann's analysis. The main difference in the approach of van Seters (for fuller consideration see *Form/Structure/Setting* on Num 21:21–35) is to preclude E influences altogether, and to see the whole as the product of very late editors working on the texts in Deuteronomy and Judges. This overall approach receives the support of J. Maxwell Miller ("The Israelite Occupation of Canaan," *Israelite and Judaean History,* ed. J. H. Hayes and J. Maxwell Miller [London: SCM, 1977] 225).

It seems best to assume that the section is in all essentials a unit. The differences posited by Noth between vv 17–18 and vv 19–20 are not so sharp as he supposes. There is no reason why negotiations should not be reopened after v 18, and there is no serious tension in the matter of the drinking water. As J. Sturdy (142) suggests the repetition is to make the point more sharply. The Israelites have in any case made a concession. Through the payment of money Edom is being offered an incentive to grant passage. Making full allowance for the contributions of most recent analysis there is reason enough for associating the section with the Yahwist. We may side with Bartlett in suspecting that van Seters has not made a case for the dependence on this particular text in Numbers on Deuteronomy. Indeed, the shape of the Edom tradition in Deut 2 is arguably later, with all elements humiliating to Israel removed. The close connections with the story of Sihon in Num 21:21–23 do not of themselves make Num 20:14–21 editorial; they point just as well to common authorship. To point to deuteronomistic features may mean only that the Yahwist's work is seventh century, and that in certain respects, like Hosea, it is "proto-deuteronomic."

Any attempt to uncover the pre-history of the tradition will have to be guided by preconceptions about the Yahwist and his sources. We have suggested that the main settlement tradition available to the Yahwist was Judaean, suggesting settlement from the south. To provide a unified tradition, affirming a settlement from the east across the Jordan, a Transjordanian journey was necessary. As Noth (*Pentateuchal Traditions,* 206) has observed the story lacks any likely signs of an early tradition; it may therefore be the Yahwist's own composition. The belief that there was a journey through Transjordan in E depends largely on the assumption that E is an independent parallel tradition. This, as we have previously argued, is far from certain. The angel of v 16 is dependent on Exod 23:20 rather than Exod 14:19 (cf. N. H. Snaith, 277), and this is part of a passage which is best viewed as the Yahwist's concluding parenesis to the Book of the Covenant. The Yahwist has certainly affirmed E's "angel of God" tradition (Exod 14:19), but this does not mean that the text of Num 20:14–21 is properly described as Elohistic. The linguistic affinities with Exod 18:8 are admittedly strong, and the base narrative in Exod 18 is arguably E. There are nevertheless strong reasons for suspecting that vv 8–11 are an accretion, not least because of the consistent use of "Yahweh" in these verses. In that event Exod 18:8 and Num 20:14 are likely to be Yahwistic. The reference to field and vineyard (v 17) suggests connections with the Yahwistic material in Num 16:14.

Whether the Yahwist was familiar with some Edomite correspondence, along the lines suggested by de Vaulx, is a matter for conjecture. On the face of it there is nothing to demand such a supposition. The author wants a long journey from Kadesh in order to provide the base for yet another story of disaffection (Num 21:4–9). Edom's refusal provides such a base. It seems unlikely that any particular antagonisms underlie the story. The Yahwist is responsible for the incorporation of the Jacob-Esau stories, and though these reveal the former's cunning in securing the best, they end amicably enough (Gen 33:16–17). In the oracles the fact of Edomite independence is recognized (Gen 27:40), giving good ground for the spirit Edom adopts here. The exilic and post-exilic antagonisms have yet to emerge. In Deut 2:1–8 the deuteronomist does his best to eliminate the humiliating aspects of the Yahwist's account. The whole enterprise there is directed by Yahweh, and Edom is in fear of Israel. She for her part is to avoid any provocative act, and may in fact have commercial dealings with the Edomites on the journey. This is more likely to be an adaptation of the Yahwist's tradition, rather than the reverse.

The description of the people as "Israel," here and in the subsequent Transjordanian stories, is a feature already noted. It may stem from the Balaam oracles where it is firmly embedded, and these, along with the Balaam stories, form by far the greater part of the Yahwist's Transjordanian journey. It was also, as Exod 14:31 and Exod 17:8 suggest, the description the Yahwist preferred when describing direct contact with other nations.

Comment

14. J. R. Bartlett (*PEQ* 104 [1972] 26–37) shows that whatever the strength of the early Edomite settlers it is most unlikely that there was any national unity in Edom before the middle of the ninth century. He also believes that the kingdom flourished for a shorter period than is sometimes supposed, its decay beginning in the seventh century. These observations support our conclusions about the age of the story (see *Form/Structure/Setting*).

14. אחיך ישראל "your brother Israel." In the patriarchal traditions Esau and Jacob are the twin ancestors of Edom and Israel respectively (Gen 25:19–36:43). These traditions bear witness to a deeply rooted rivalry, stemming from the trickery whereby Jacob secures the best for himself, and also to an ultimate reconciliation (cf. Deut 2:4; 23:8 for further references to kinship with Edom). The prophet Amos spoke against Edom's ruthlessness in the eighth century (Amos 1:11). Edom appears to have gained some of Judaea during the exile, and hatred for her emerges most strongly in Obadiah.

14. כל-התלאה "all the adversity," the root לאה meaning "to be weary."

16. מלאך "an angel," an agent of God, in ostensibly human form, who brings divine reassurance and guidance.

17. דרך המלך "the King's Highway" (cf. Num 21:22; Deut 2:27), a through road running from Damascus to the Gulf of Akaba. It was fortified in some measure, and was a major trade route. B. Oded suggests that the name derives from the terminology of the Assyrian imperial administration ("Observations on Methods of Assyrian Rule in Transjordania after the Palestinian Campaign of Tiglath-Pileser III." *JNES* 29 [1970] 177–86). J. R. Bartlett (*PEQ* 104 [1972] 26–37) also supports the view that the name belongs to the Assyrian period, a further indicator of the story's relative lateness.

20. A battle is not necessarily to be supposed. Edom menaces Israel, and so she withdraws.

Explanation

The Yahwist tells here how the Edomites refused Israel a right of passage through their territory. In spite of a renewed request, offering payment for resources used, the Israelites are forced to make a long detour around the country. The author's main concern is to provide some basis for yet another story of disaffection, to follow later in Num 21:4–9. The Israelites are to complain yet again of the hardships of the long journey, and the Edomite refusal to cooperate provides the setting for this. In Deut 2:1–8 the humiliating aspects of the tradition are eliminated, with Yahweh directing the operation and Edom living in fear of Israel. For the Yahwist, however, the humiliating dimension fits well into his overall scheme. Israel has yet to recover from the debacle at Hormah (Num 14:39–45), and the dispiriting and futile rebellion of Dathan and Abiram (Num 16:12–15). The arrogance of Edom is a further deserved blow to their aspirations.

The story also helps the Yahwist's purpose of bringing Israel into the land, not from the south, but from the east. Nothing much is known of Israel's links with Edom during the resurgence of Josiah's time. Edom, like Judah, appears to have been an Assyrian vassal during the first half of the seventh century; whether the story reveals something of a weakened Judah's inability to challenge Edom in the circumstances following the collapse of Assyria is uncertain. The patriarchal traditions suggest that, for the Yahwist, relations between Israel and Edom are a mutual respect for each other's sphere of influence, and something of this may underlie the story here. For the Yahwist however it is essentially an illustration of Israel's weakness following her previous failure of nerve and presumptuousness. The priestly author retains the story for much the same reason. It is part of the journey tradition received by him, and he sees no reason for adapting or replacing it.

The Death of Aaron and the Investiture of Eleazar (20:22-29)

Bibliography

Cody, A. *A History of Old Testament Priesthood.* Rome: Pontifical Biblical Institute, 1969. **Elhorst, H. J.** "Das Ephod." *JBL* 30 (1910) 154–76. **Foote, T. C.** "The Ephod." *JBL* 21 (1902) 1–47. **Gunneweg, A. H. J.** *Leviten und Priester.* Göttingen: Vandenhoeck and Ruprecht, 1965. **Morgenstern, J.** *The Ark, the Ephod, and the "Tent of Meeting."* Cincinnati: Hebrew Union College, 1945. **Sellin, E.** "Zu Efod und Terafim." *ZAW* 55 (1937) 296–98. **Thiersch, H.** "Ependytes und Ephod." *ZAW* 53 (1935) 180–85. See also Num 3:1–51 (*Bibliography*).

Translation

[22] And they set out from Kadesh, and the people of Israel, the whole congregation, came to Mount Hor. [23] And Yahweh spoke to Moses and Aaron at Mount Hor, on the border of the land of Edom, saying, [24] "Aaron shall be gathered to his people,[a] for he shall not [b] enter the land which I have given to the people of Israel, because you rebelled against my word at the waters of Meribah. [25] Take Aaron, and Eleazar his son, and bring them up to Mount Hor.[a] [26] And you shall strip Aaron of his garments, and put them on Eleazar his son. And Aaron shall be gathered (to his people), and shall die there." [27] And Moses did as Yahweh had commanded. And they went up [a] Mount Hor in the sight of all the congregation. [28] And Moses stripped Aaron of his garments, and put them on Eleazar his son. And Aaron died there on the top of the mountain. And Moses and Eleazar came down from the mountain. [29] And all the congregation saw that Aaron was dead, and all the house of Israel wept for Aaron for thirty days.

Notes

24.a. Reading עמיו with Sam, G, Syr, Tg.
24.b. G has the second person plural.
25.a. G adds "in the sight of all the congregation"; cf. v 27.
27.a. Sam and G read the Hiphil, giving a causative sense.

Form/Structure/Setting

This account of the investiture of Eleazar and the death of Aaron is evidently priestly. Israel is "the congregation" (vv 22, 27, 29), Aaron and his son are priests, and v 24 makes a direct connection with the P version of water from the rock in v 13. Many earlier analysts saw it as part of the original P narrative (see the discussions of A. Dillmann, 115–17; A. Kuenen, 97; J. Wellhausen, 110; H. Holzinger, 88; B. Baentsch, 572–73; G. B. Gray, 269). Only v 22a with its reference to Kadesh was associated with JE; P would have referred to the wilderness of Zin. It was also observed that P's location for the death of Aaron (Mount Hor) differs from that cited in Deut 10:6 (Moserah). Some analysts suspected that in P Israel traveled across northern Edom without a detour at all. For those who worked with a basic PG/PS distinction, the former with a large narrative content and the latter primarily law, it was natural to associate this section with PG (see also W. Rudolph, *Der "Elohist,"* 89).

Some modern analysts do not dissent very much from this general view of the section. M. Noth (152–53) however finds additional material in vv 23–24. He suspects that Moses and Aaron could not have been addressed together before v 25, and believes that Mount Hor in v 23b, if original, should have stood in v 22b. In v 24 he thinks the death of Aaron is inappropriately anticipated. The main purpose of the addition in vv 23–24 would be to link the death of Aaron with the rebellion of vv 1–13. Noth also suspects that the story is modeled on that which recounts the death of Moses in Deut 34, but he is uncertain as to how Mount Hor became and remained the bearer of an Aaron tradition. There is no mention of burial here, and the site must in any case have been far beyond Israel's borders. He further observes that the tradition of Deut 10:6, which does have a burial reference, is unreconciled and unexplained here.

There are certainly problems in the passage, but it is easy to overpress them; there is no serious difficulty in seeing here the essential work of the author of Numbers. One of his key themes is the failure of the leaders to inherit the land (see Num 20:1–13, *Explanation*). The account of the death of Moses had probably already been formulated (Deut 34:1–12), and it remained to the author to tell of the death of Aaron the priest. This is recounted in a broadly similar fashion; there is again a mourning period of thirty days, and a successor to Aaron is immediately secured in Eleazar his son. The anticipation of events in vv 23–24 is not a serious difficulty. The fact that Yahweh knows and controls what is to happen is typical of P throughout, and is in no sense a necessary sign of literary unevenness. The reference to Kadesh in v 22a is probably drawn by the author from the earlier Yahwistic tradition. The assumption that there was a P tradition which did not envisage a detour around Edom is not soundly based. The site in fact is unknown (see *Comment*), and J. de Vaulx (231) offers some evidence for supposing that it was not far from Kadesh. The priestly author evidently thought that the peak of a mountain was an appropriate place for the death of a leader such as Aaron, as it was for Moses, and does not necessarily see this as irreconcilable with Deut 10:6. Since the death and burial of Aaron had already been traced to Moserah, the priestly author simply locates the death on the nearest available peak known to him. Alternatively הר may simply mean "mountain," and in that event the author, having no personal knowledge of peaks in that general vicinity, may simply have offered a vague indication of a high place for the site of Aaron's death.

Comment

22. הר ההר "Mount Hor." The traditional location is near Petra, a view as old as Josephus (*Ant:* 4:4;7). This is well into Edomite territory, and seems too far to the east. An alternative is Jebel Madurah on the northwest Edomite border, and not far from Kadesh; see also J. de Vaulx, 231. According to

Deut 10:6 Aaron died and was buried at Moserah. H. Gressmann (338–44) suggested that Moserah may have lain at the foot of Mount Hor just as Beth Peor apparently lay at the foot of Mount Pisgah.

26. These are the garments described in Lev 8:7–9. For discussion of the priestly garments in general see *Bibliography*.

29. The usual period of mourning was seven days. The thirty-day period links Aaron with Moses as a figure of comparable importance; cf. Deut 34:8.

Explanation

This section tells of the death of Aaron at Mount Hor. Moses is commanded to take Aaron and his son Eleazar up the mountain, and there Aaron dies. Eleazar is invested with the high priestly robes immediately before Aaron's death. The thirty-day period of mourning (cf. Deut 34:8) reveals something of Aaron's stature and status. According to Deut 10:6, Aaron dies at Moserah, but the same general location is probably intended. The priestly author is anxious to locate the death of Aaron on a mountain top, thereby establishing a close correspondence with the death of Moses (Deut 34:1–12; see *Form/ Structure/Setting*).

The section is in part the aftermath of the priestly author's third great sin (Num 20:1–13). In the material following the two earlier sins (Num 15; Num 18) the author was concerned to reassert God's commitment to the land and to the Levitical hierarchy. In this case the judgment on Moses is necessarily delayed. The account of his death was already in place at the end of Deuteronomy, and there is much Mosaic law still to be promulgated. The death of Aaron however can take place almost at once, and the judgment of Num 20:12 is thus recalled and in part fulfilled. As on the previous occasions however the priestly author is anxious to reassert God's commitment to the principle threatened by the sin, in this instance the priestly leadership of the sons of Aaron. So before Aaron dies his son Eleazar is clothed with Aaron's garments, and takes over Aaron's duties and roles. The purpose of God in constituting the priestly theocracy is not to be defeated by the sin of man.

Canaanites Defeated at Hormah   (21:1-3)

Bibliography

Aharoni, Y. and **Amiran, R.** "Arad: Its Inscriptions and Temple." *BA* 31 (1968) 1–32. **Aharoni, Y.** "The Solomonic Temple, the Tabernacle and the Arad Sanctuary." *AOAT* 22 (1973) 1–8. ———. "Arad." *Encyclopedia of Archaeological Excavations in the Holy Land,* ed. M. Avi-Yonah. London: Oxford University Press, 1975 (with bibliography). **Coats, G. W.** "Conquest Traditions in the Wilderness Theme." *JBL* 95 (1976) 177–90. **Fritz, V.** "Arad in der biblischen Überlieferung und in der Liste Schoschenk I." *ZDPV* 82 (1966) 331–42. ———. "Erwägungen zur Siedlungsgeschichte des Negeb in der Eisen 1—Zeit (1200–1000 v.Chr.) im Lichte der Ausgrabungen auf der Ḥirbet el-Mšāš." *ZDPV* 91 (1975) 30–45. **Gunn, D. M.** "The 'Battle Report'; Oral or Scribal Convention." *JBL* 93 (1974) 513–18. **Mazar, B.** "The Sanctuary of Arad and the Family of Hobab the Kenite." *JNES* 24 (1965) 297–303. **Noth, M.** "Num 21 als Glied der 'Hexateuch' Erzählung." *ZAW* 58 (1940/1) 161–89.

Translation

¹ *And the Canaanite* ᵃ *king of Arad,*ᵃ *who lived in the Negeb, heard that Israel was coming by way of Atharim.*ᵇ *And he fought against Israel, and took some of them captive.* ² *And Israel vowed a vow to Yahweh, and said, "If you will indeed give this people into my hand, then I will totally destroy their cities."* ³ *And Yahweh listened to the voice of Israel, and he gave over* ᵃ *the Canaanites. And they totally destroyed them and their cities. And the name of the place was called Hormah.*

Notes

1.a.-a. This is probably a gloss (J. Paterson, 54; G. B. Gray, 273; J. de Vaulx, 234). It is hard to identify Arad and Hormah as the same, as appears to be presupposed in vv 1–3. The collective noun הכנעני "the Canaanites" stands uneasily in apposition to "king of Arad." Syr reads "king of Godar."

1.b. The reading presupposed in Tg, Vg, Syr, Aq, Sym, appears to be התרים "by the way of the explorers." A proper name is probably intended.

3.a. It may be that בידו "into his hand" has fallen out from MT—cf. Sam, G.

Form/Structure/Setting

There was general agreement among older analysts that this short section belongs to JE (cf. A. Dillmann, 117–18; J. Wellhausen, 111; A. Kuenen, 334; H. Holzinger, 88–89; G. B. Gray, 272). Many were prepared to assign the passage with some confidence to J (cf. e.g. B. Baentsch, 573; W. Rudolph, *Der "Elohist,"* 89). It offers an alternative explanation for the name Hormah to that given in Num 14:39–45, a passage ascribed on other grounds to E. The use of the term "Canaanite" (vv 1, 3) was taken to be a clear indicator of J ("Amorite" in E) (cf. Gen 12:6; 24:3, 37; 34:30; 38:2). A contrary view is offered by A. H. McNeile (110), who was concerned about the passage's apparent lack of connection with the JE narrative, in particular the implied northward thrust of the Israelites as compared with the movement to the southeast described in Num 14:25. McNeile had already assigned Num 14:39–45 to J, and therefore tentatively favored E for this passage. O. Eissfeldt (*Hexateuch*, 180) resolved the difficulties by associating Num 21:1–3 with L, one of his three early sources.

This particular problem has been generally recognized, and M. Noth (154) sees the present position of the passage as a relatively late insertion. He thought that it could at one time have had some place in the J narrative. Other recent commentators are content simply to assign it to JE (e.g. N. H. Snaith, 279).

The best solution is to suppose that a further fragment of the Judaean tradition taken up by the Yahwist survives here (for a broadly similar approach see J. Sturdy, 144–46; J. de Vaulx, 233–34). These traditions told of conflict in the south, and possibly of an incursion from a southerly direction. Some support for this view comes from the fact of a similar tradition of victory at Hormah in Judg 1:17, where the victors are Judah and Simeon. The story may be in all essentials a folk etiology, explaining the name Hormah, but the fact that it takes the form of war and victory is probably a reflection and recollection of historical events.

The Yahwist is anxious to incorporate this tradition in order to show that Num 14:45 is not the last word about Hormah. He has not chosen to smooth out all the unevenness which his adaptation of tradition has produced, and so the sense of movement by way of Atharim survives. Within his story this event marks the turning point in Israel's fortunes. From this point onward the journey is to be a victory march.

Comment

1. "Arad" is the modern Tell Arad, about eight miles south of Hebron, and is notable for its Israelite temple dating from the time of the monarchy (for details see Y. Aharoni, *BA* 31 [1968] 1–32). The site has been thoroughly excavated, but appears to lack middle/late bronze age, and therefore Canaanite, settlements. It may be that Arad should be thought of as an area, and that Hormah (v 3) was its capital city. Alternatively another site may be sought for Canaanite Arad. Y. Aharoni (*BA* 31 [1968] 1–32) suggests Tell el-Milh, about seven miles to the southwest of Tell Arad, which had a good middle bronze fortification. The best solution is to treat the reference as a later gloss (see *Notes*), influenced by an awareness of the later settlements at Tell Arad.

1. "Atharim" is probably "Tamar," situated a few miles south of the Dead Sea (cf. "Tarim" in the ancient versions). The road is difficult to trace, but must have led from the southern deserts to the Judaean hills. Y. Aharoni ("Forerunners of the Limes: Iron Age Fortresses in the Negev," *IEJ* 17 [1967] 1–17) traces a route from Kadesh-barnea through the Negeb to Hormah.

2. והחרמתי "I will totally destroy," place under the ban (cf. Josh 6:24). There is a play here on the word "Hormah" in the following verse. For a discussion of the ban see N. K. Gottwald, *The Tribes of Yahweh*.

Explanation

This short section tells of a Canaanite attack on the Israelites. Some Israelites are captured, and the people address the matter to Yahweh, promising total destruction of the enemy as an offering to Yahweh, if success is assured. A battle ensues, the destruction takes place, and the site is named Hormah.

It seems likely that this section contains the Judaean Hormah tradition which the Yahwist has taken up. His own account of Hormah can be found in Num 14:39–45. The Judaean source told of successful conflict in the south against Canaanite settlements in the vicinity of Hormah (cf. Judg 1:17), and possibly of incursion and settlement from the south. The Yahwist uses the story to show that his own account of events in the area (Num 14:39–45) is not the last word on the matter. A true dedication to Yahweh, exhibited in a willingness to engage fully and single-mindedly in the Yahweh war, will indeed meet with success. This story marks a turning point therefore in Israel's military fortunes. There are still dangers to be faced, and temptations to avoid, but from this point onward Israel cannot be matched as a military force.

The Desert Snakes (21:4–9)

Bibliography

Jaroš, K. *Die Stellung des Elohisten zur kanaanaischen Religion.* Dissertation, Freiberg, 1973. **Joines, K. R.** "Winged Serpents in Isaiah's Inaugural Vision." *JBL* 86 (1967) 410–15. ———. "The Bronze Serpent in the Israelite Cult." *JBL* 87 (1968) 245–56. ———. *Serpent Symbolism in the Old Testament. A Linguistic, Archaeological and Literary Study.* New Jersey: Haddonfield House, 1974. **Noth, M.** "Num 21 als Glied der 'Hexateuch' Erzählung." *ZAW* 58 (1940/1) 161–89. **Rowley, H. H.** "Zadok and Nehushtan." *JBL* 58 (1939) 113–41. **Wiseman, D. J.** "Flying Serpents." *TB* 23 (1972) 108–10. **Zimmerli, W.** "Das Bilderverbot in der Geschichte des alten Israel. Goldenes Kalb, eherne Schlange, Mazzeba und Lade." *Alttestament liche Traditionsgeschichte und Theologie.* München: Kaiser, 1974.

Translation

⁴ *And they set out from Mount Hor by the way to the Sea of Reeds, to go around the land of Edom. But the people became impatient on the way.* ⁵ *And the people spoke against God* ᵃ *and against Moses, "Why have you brought us up* ᵇ *out of Egypt to die* ᶜ *in the wilderness? For there is no bread and no water, and we detest this worthless food."* ⁶ *And Yahweh sent fiery* ᵃ *snakes among the people. And they bit the people, and many of the people of Israel died.* ⁷ *And the people came to Moses and said, "We have sinned, because we have spoken against Yahweh and against you. Pray to Yahweh, that he take the snakes away from us." So Moses prayed for the people.* ⁸ *And Yahweh said to Moses, "Make a fiery snake,* ᵃ *and set it on a pole. And everyone who is bitten, when he sees it, shall live."* ⁹ *And Moses made a bronze snake, and set it on a pole. And when a snake had bitten a man* ᵃ *he would look at the bronze snake and live.*

Notes

5.a. G has "to God," and if that is correct the second person plural which follows in MT may be derived from Num 20:5, where Moses and Aaron are addressed together. On the unusual pronominal suffix see GKC § 59a.
5.b. Sam uses the root יצא here.
5.c. G uses the Hiphil again as in Num 20:4.
6.a. G understands as "deadly," Syr as "cruel."
8.a. "Snake" has to be understood here (cf. Sam, G). MT has simply שׂרף, the root used for "fiery" in v 6.
9.a. On the use of את here see GKC § 117d.

Form/Structure/Setting

There is general acceptance of the view that this passage belongs to JE (cf. e.g. A. Dillmann, 118–20; J. Wellhausen, 110–11; A. Kuenen, 334). The familiar features of P are absent, and Israel is consistently depicted as "the people." The use of the Hiphil of עלה "bring up" in relation to the exodus (v 5), and of the Hithpael of פלל "pray" for intercession (v 7; cf. Gen 20:7, 17; Num 11:2) are all indicators of JE.

Many of the older analysts assigned the section as a whole to E, or else detected a very strong E presence (see e.g. H. Holzinger, 89; B. Baentsch, 575–76; G. B. Gray, 274; O. Eissfeldt, *Hexateuch*, 180–81). The indicators are taken to be "God" (v 5), "speak against" (v 5; cf. Num 12:1), and the Hithpael of פלל (v 7) (cf. Gen 20:7, 17; Num 11:2). M. Noth (155–58) suspected an E original in what is now a relatively late tradition. Other more recent analysts are much less confident that this is E. A. W. Jenks (*The Elohist*, 68), a firm believer in the Elohist, does not include the story as part of E, and G. W. Coats (*Rebellion*, 115–17) identifies it as a late insertion. J. de Vaulx (235–37) sees the final product as a complex compilation of varied traditions. Among those prepared to identify the section as J are W. Rudolph, *Der "Elohist,"* 89–90 and V. Fritz, *Israel*, 29–30. That the introductory elements in v 4a link with the P account has been recognized by most.

The form and structure of the story are similar to that of the Taberah tradition in Num 11:1–3; it may be attributed therefore to the Yahwist. His main purpose seems to be to fill out the story of Israel's long detour. The reference to Mount Hor in v 4a is evidently a reflection of the P account of the death of Aaron in Num 20:22–29. In Num 20:1 the Yahwist told of the death of Miriam, and he may also have noted Aaron's death; if so, his account no longer survives.

There are no very serious points of tension within the narrative, and structurally it makes a coherent whole. Much of the unevenness discovered by H. Gressmann (284 n.1) (e.g. between v 5a and v 5b or within v 6b) is not very convincing. Grumblers may very well complain of the threat of death if they dislike the food they have, or think it inadequate. The description of the snakes as שרפים "fiery" (vv 6, 8), and the object made as נחשת "bronze" (v 9) arise from the Yahwist's concern to associate the tradition of a desert hazard (Deut 8:15) with familiar temple objects.

This story gives some support to the view that the Yahwist's work is relatively late. The background of the snake symbol is almost certainly Canaanite (see K. R. Joines, *JBL* 87 [1968] 245–56), and H. H. Rowley (*JBL* 58 [1939] 113–41) has proposed that the Jerusalemite snake Nehushtan, whose destruction by Hezekiah is described in 2 Kgs 18:4, was a Jebusite fetish with which Zadok was originally associated. The Jebusite origin of Nehushtan has been widely accepted, though the origins of Zadok remain obscure. The tradition received by the Yahwist was probably, as H. Gressmann argues (284–90), an etiological cult saga, explaining the name Nehushtan through the word "bronze," and establishing a connection with Moses. This the Yahwist is unwilling to contest, but he faces therefore a problem. How could the reforming Yahwists of Josiah's time, who claim above all to represent Mosaic faith and tradition, support Hezekiah's radical action against such a long standing Mosaic institution? The Yahwist's answer is to tell what in his view really happened in the wilderness. He uses a similar technique in his handling of the story of the calf in Exod 32:1–35. His method is not to deny the antiquity of such institutions, but to tell what really happened. Moses did not institute a snake cult, involving the offering of incense (2 Kgs 18:4), but provided a cult object to meet the needs of a specific crisis. Nehushtan was not to be worshiped, but to be looked upon by those who were sick.

On this view the Yahwist has received and altered a priestly etiology from the Temple at Jerusalem. The precise original form of this etiology cannot be determined with certainty. It is possible that Yahweh's protective power with regard to desert snakes was celebrated in worship (cf. Deut 8:15). In ancient Semitic mythology the desert was widely regarded as still in a state of primeval chaos (cf. the menace of snakes and the desert in Isa 30:6). At certain periods the idea may also have been encouraged that Moses was the representative of a serpent cult on Canaanite lines. It is precisely this notion which the Yahwist wishes to refute. The snakes are thus a punishment for sin rather than a natural desert hazard.

This approach precludes any likelihood that the story is to be associated with E. The literary indicators occur in contexts which we have been inclined to link with the Yahwist. The idea of speaking against God is rooted in a cultic text (Ps 78:19), and this confirms the suspicion that the roots of the story lie in a cult etiology. Gressmann's attempts to find also a place etiology associated with the name Phunon (Num 33:44) involve too much interference with the text to be convincing.

Comment

4. דרך ים סוף "by the way to the Sea of Reeds"; see *Comment* on Num 14:25.

4. ותקצר "impatient," literally "short," the opposite idea being "long suffering" (cf. Prov 14:29).

5. ונפשנו קצה בלחם הקלקל "we detest this worthless food." The root of the adjective seems to mean "to be light," and "worthless" or "unsatisfying" are good renderings (cf. 2 Sam 19:44; Isa 8:23; 23:9; Ezek 22:7 where the hiphil of קלל means "to treat with contempt"). N. H. Snaith (280) suggests that almost any derogatory word will do.

6. הנחשים השרפים "fiery snakes." It is often supposed that there is a reference here to the venomous bite of the snakes, and the burning inflammation produced (cf. e.g. G. B. Gray, 277–78; A. H. McNeile, 112; L. E. Binns, 138; N. H. Snaith, 280–81; J. Sturdy, 148). It is arguable that שרפים "fiery" is strictly a description of the creatures themselves, rather than of their bite (G. W. Coats, *Rebellion*, 117 n.51). For the Yahwist the שרף "seraph" is evidently a temple creature (cf. Isa 6:2; 14:29; 30:6).

7. For this type of response cf. Num 11:2; 12:10.

9. נחשת "bronze" (cf. Job 28:2 where the word apparently means "copper," a metal smelted directly from the ore). Bronze is an alloy of copper and tin, and is well attested in ancient times.

Explanation

This story tells of the discouragement which ensues from the long journey around Edom. This is expressed in typical words of disaffection, and there is an immediate response on the part of Yahweh who sends fiery snakes. Many die from the snake bites, and after the people implore Moses to intercede on their behalf he is instructed to make a bronze snake. Those who look at the snake are cured.

The story in its present form belongs essentially to the Yahwist. In form and structure it corresponds with Num 11:1–3, and in particular with the Yahwist's way of telling disaffection stories at this stage of the journey. There is no strong reason for suspecting an Elohistic base narrative in the text. The claim that the disaffection is against "God" (v 5) may have its background in cultic modes of speech (cf. Ps 78:19). The story has in fact a cultic orientation, and may be based on a cultic etiology of Nehushtan. In the Yahwist's hands the story is directed specifically against the cult, which was apparently attacked by Hezekiah (2 Kgs 18:4). This cult may have celebrated Yahweh's protective power, but it was probably also a healing cult with strong Canaanite associations, and deriving ultimately from Canaanite sources. At an early stage it had been associated with Moses, and the priestly etiology along these lines had developed. Something very similar probably obtained with regard to the bull cults of Dan and Bethel (cf. Exod 32:1–35).

The Yahwist's method in these cases is not to deny the Mosaic associations, but to give them their true content. In this instance Moses did not institute a snake cult involving the offering of incense (2 Kgs 18:4), but an object to meet the needs of a specific crisis. The possibility of the revival of the Nehushtan cult may have been a live issue in the Yahwist's time, and the truth about its background, as he understood it, should be made clear. It was easy to link the tradition with his account of the wilderness journey, and it provided very suitable filler material for the long journey around Edom.

The Transjordanian Journey (21:10–20)

Bibliography

Bennett, C. "Umm el-Biyara-Pétra." *RB* 71 (1964) 250–53; *RB* 73 (1966) 372–403. ———. "Tawilân (Jordanie)." *RB* 76 (1969) 386–90; *RB* 77 (1970) 371–74. ———. "Excavations at Buseirah, Southern Jordan." *Levant* 5 (1973) 1–11; *Levant* 6 (1974) 1–24. **Christensen, D. L.** "Num 21:14–15 and the Book of the Wars of Yahweh." *CBQ* 36 (1974) 359–60. **Coats, G. W.** "The Wilderness Itinerary." *CBQ* 34 (1972) 135–52. **Davies, G. I.** "The Wilderness Itineraries." *TB* 25 (1974) 46–81. ———. *The Way of the Wilderness.* Cambridge: University Press, 1979. **Dever, W. G.** "The EB IV—MB I Horizon in Transjordan and Southern Palestine." *BASOR* 210 (1973) 37–63. **Mendenhall, G. E.** "The Hebrew Conquest of Palestine." *BA* 25 (1962) 66–87. ———. "Change and Decay in All Around I See: Conquest, Covenant and the Tenth Generation." *BA* 39 (1976) 152–57. **Noth, M.** "Num 21 als Glied der 'Hexateuch' Erzählung." *ZAW* 58 (1940/1) 161–89. **Simons, J.** "Two Connected Problems Relating to the Israelite Settlement in Transjordan." *PEQ* 79 (1947) 27–39, 87–101. **Tur-Sinai, N. H.** "Was There an Ancient Book of the Wars of the Lord?" (Heb.) *BIES* 24 (1959/60) 146–48. **Vaux, R. de** "Notes d'histoire et de topographie transjordaniennes." *RB* 50 (1941) 16–47. **Walsh, J. T.** "From Egypt to Moab: a Source Critical Analysis of the Wilderness Itinerary." *CBQ* 39 (1977) 20–33. **Wüst, M.** *Untersuchungen zu den siedlungsgeographischen Texten des Alten Testaments. 1. Ostjordanland.* Wiesbaden: Reichert Verlag, 1975.

Translation

[10] *And the people of Israel set out, and encamped in Oboth.* [11] *And they set out from Oboth, and encamped at Iye-abarim,* [a] *in the wilderness which is opposite Moab, toward the sunrise.* [12] *From there they set out and encamped in the valley of Zered.* [a] [13] *From there they set out and encamped on the other side of the Arnon, which is in the wilderness which extends from the boundary of the Amorites.* [14] *That is why it is said in the Book of the Wars of Yahweh,*

" [a] *Waheb in Suphah,* [a]
and the valleys of the Arnon,
[15] [a] *and the slope of the valleys* [a]
that extends to the dwelling at Ar,
and leans to the border of Moab."

[16] *And from there they went to Beer. That is the well of which Yahweh said to Moses, "Gather the people together, and I will give them water."* [17] *Then Israel sang this song,*

" [a] *Spring up,* [a] *O well! Sing to it!*

[18] *The well which the princes dug,*
which the leaders of the people [a] *laid open,*
with the scepter and with their staves." [b]

ᶜ *And from the wilderness they went on to Mattanah,* ᶜ ¹⁹ *And from Mattanah to Nahaliel, and from Nahaliel to Bamoth,* ²⁰ *and from Bamoth to the valley lying in the region of Moab, by the top of Pisgah, which overlooks*ᵃ *the desert.*

Notes

11.a. G and the other versions show many divergencies here.

12.a. Sam appears to have inserted material from Deut 2:17–19 here.

14.a.-a. Sam has "Waheb on the Sea of Reeds." G reads "he has set Zoob on fire and the torrents of Arnon," reading זהב for והב, and taking סופה from the root ספף. Vg reads והב as the root יהב, and as equivalent to בים סוף (cf. Sam); hence AV—"what he did in the Red Sea." The assumption that there are two Moabite place names here seems best; cf. RSV, NEB.

15.a.-a. MT has literally "the descent of the torrents," referring probably to valley slopes (cf. Deut 3:17), or possibly a watershed.

The ancient witnesses show many textual variations in this poetic fragment—hence the extraordinary difficulties it poses. On the whole MT seems preferable; it gives a simplified geographical description of the area in question. Sam appears to have introduced the idea that God gave this region to the Hebrews, an attempt to understand the text theologically. G and Syr appear to make the text an account of epic victories, while Tg and Vg have the Sea of Reeds in mind.

17.a. D. N. Freedman ("Archaic Forms in Early Hebrew Poetry." *ZAW* 72 [1960] 101–07) suggested reading the Piel עלי "praise" or "celebrate," thereby giving a parallel to "sing." MT is intelligible, and perhaps to be preferred.

18.a. G has the plural.

18.b. Freedman (op. cit.). revocalizes to produce "with scepter—with staff."

18.c.-c. This is part of the song in MT, and might be rendered "a gift from the wilderness" (NEB cf. Ps 126:4). This has attractions, but creates difficulties in v 19 where "Mattaneh" has to be emended to "Beer."

20.a. Reading הנשקף as in Num 23:28 (cf. Sam, G, Syr, Tg, Vg).

Form/Structure/Setting

There is general recognition among older analysts that most of this material comes from JE (cf. e.g. A. Dillmann, 120–35; J. Wellhausen, 111; A. Kuenen, 334; H. Holzinger, 89–90; B. Baentsch, 576–81; G. B. Gray, 280–81; O. Eissfeldt *Hexateuch*, 181). Beyond that basic observation there were differences of opinion. Kuenen, Holzinger, and Baentsch discerned a major element from E, as also did Eissfeldt. There was general recognition that vv 21–30 were Elohistic because of their evident resemblance in style and structure to Num 20:14–21, and since vv 12–20 prepare the way for the incursion into Sihon's territory there seemed reason to associate them with E. The custom of citing old poetry in a similar kind of way was another common feature between vv 12–20 and vv 21–30. Dillman was disposed to assign only vv 12–18a to the Elohist, leaving the more formal itinerary in vv 18b–20 to J. There is particular reason for this since the stations cited lie to the north of the Arnon, actually within Sihon's territory, while according to vv 21–22 this territory has yet to be entered. Gray, having isolated the old poetry in vv 14–15, 17–18a, attributes vv 11b–13 to E and vv 16, 18b–20 provisionally to J. He held that the E story connects with Num 21:21–24a, 31 in telling a coherent story which resembles the E of Num 20:14–18. This story agrees with Judg 11:12–28 and Deut 2:24–37 in locating the Amorites between Arnon and Jabbok. The march formula in vv 12–13 was shown to agree with Deut 10:6–7. Gray was uncertain about the point at which the poetical fragments were introduced into the narrative. W. Rudolph (*Der "Elohist,"* 90–93), who denied the existence of E, saw only a collection of varied traditions within the section. The only material normally attributed to P by the earlier analysts was vv 10–11a, where the itinerary corresponds in form with that found elsewhere in P (cf. e.g. Num 1:4).

M. Noth (159) was particularly impressed by the unevenness and obscurity of the text, and concluded that we can scarcely attribute it to any of the Pentateuchal sources, or explain it as a compilation from several sources. He also believed that it is dependent on Num 33:43b–44; Judg 11:18; Deut 2:13, Num 22:41; 23:14, 28; Deut 3:29; 34:6. The passage must therefore be a late editorial attempt to compensate for the lack of connection between the stories set on the edge of the desert and the following accounts of the conquest. N. H. Snaith (281) sees no difficulty with the traditional approach, and accepts a substantial E presence in vv 13–20. J. Sturdy (150), while recognizing that J had a travel narrative with stations, follows Noth in raising the possibility that the present text is secondary borrowing from other passages. J. de Vaulx (239–44) is fairly traditional, recognizing two itineraries, the one priestly (vv 10–11a) and the other from an unspecified source. He is also inclined to see the poetic pieces as additions.

The difficulty with the view that the section is almost entirely dependent on other passages is that it is inclined to make the tradition of a Transjordanian journey very late indeed. If this is a late editorial attempt to fill gaps, then the gaps must have been there for a long time. The only alternative explanation is that there was some good reason for rejecting the Yahwist's account of the journey, and it is hard to suggest such a reason. The Yahwist certainly had an itinerary (Num 11:35; 12:16), and we have seen good reason for supposing that he also had a Transjordanian journey. In the absence of P indicators (vv 10–11a apart) it seems reasonable to suppose that here is part of the Yahwist's account—in vv 11b–20. So vv 10–11a would be attributable to the author of Numbers, filling in a small gap, as he perceived it, from his own itinerary, which he later sets out in full in Num 33. The material available to the Yahwist is an itinerary (vv 11b–13, 16, 18b–20), and two ancient songs (vv 14–15, 17–18a). There is no real difficulty in relation to vv 18b–20 and vv 21–22. Having begun the itinerary available to him the Yahwist chooses to continue copying from it as far as Pisgah, before telling of the difficulties with Sihon.

He also provides some color and variety with the two poems. The Book of the Wars of Yahweh (v 14) was probably a collection of victory songs. Its inclusion here is prompted by the reference to Arnon, which occurs in itinerary (v 13) and song (v 14). The provenance of the book, and the songs it contained, is hard to determine. This is the only reference to it. The victory songs need not be earlier than the time of the monarchy. The inclusion of the second song is prompted by the reference to Beer ("a well") in the itinerary (v 16), and the fact that the song itself is an ancient well song (vv 17–18).

O. Eissfeldt (*Introduction*, 88) categorizes it as a work song, sung during the digging of wells, but it may be better to see rather the celebration of a successful dig (cf. J. Sturdy, 151–52). It may be that the song belongs to an outlook in which word and song were not only aids to labor, but also endowed with a power of their own, which it was believed would bring success.

The section gives the general impression that the Yahwist does not have much traditional material from which to construct a Transjordanian journey. He appears to have an itinerary, derived perhaps from traveling and trading sources, indicating stages on the route along the King's Highway. To fill this out he has only the ancient songs. This is inclined to confirm the impression that the Transjordanian journey is his own construction.

Comment

10. The site of Oboth is unknown. ʿAin el-Weiba, some fifteen miles from the south end of the Dead Sea, has been proposed (for discussion of this and other topographical problems see J. Simons, *The Geographical and Topographical Texts of the Old Testament*, Leiden: Brill, 1959).

11. Iye-abarim may be the modern Mahay, at the southeastern corner of Moab, but the matter is very uncertain.

12. Zered (or Zarad) is a southern tributary of the Dead Sea.

13. Arnon is the modern Wady el-Mûjib. The land between the Arnon and the Jabbok (fifty miles to the north) was disputed in biblical times (cf. Judg 11:13). It was occupied by Ammon at a later stage (Jer 49:1–2). The Yahwist appears to have thought of the land to the south of the Arnon as natural Amorite territory. The land to the north was Moabite, though captured by Sihon.

14. The Book of the Wars of Yahweh was probably an ancient collection of songs celebrating military successes (cf. the Book of Jashar; Josh 10:13; 2 Sam 1:18). D. L. Christensen (*CBQ* 36 [1974] 359–60) provides a good reconstruction of the text which makes Yahweh the subject of the various clauses. Yahweh the divine warrior is depicted as coming in the whirlwind with his hosts to the very sources of the Arnon.

14. Waheb and Suphah cannot be identified—see *Notes*.

15. אֶשֶׁד "slope" (cf. Deut 3:17—"the slopes of Pisgah"). Some think the word means "watershed"—cf. NEB.

15. The site of Ar is unknown, but it was evidently an important Moabite city (cf. v 28; Num 22:36), and possibly a capital.

Many parts of this fragmentary song are obscure, but its inclusion is intended to prove that the Arnon is indeed a Moabite boundary (vv 13–14).

16. Beer has not been identified. There is a Moabite Beerelim in Isa 15:8. J. Simons (*Texts*, 262) considers Wady eṭṭemed, where water is close to the surface.

18. The involvement of "princes" (שָׂרִים) and "leaders" (נְדִיבִים) is curious in a supposed work song. It may be that credit is given to them because they direct where digging should commence, perhaps with the aid of scepter and stave in some divinatory procedure. A. H. McNeile (116) cites a suggestion that wells might have been lightly covered and then symbolically reopened

with a ceremony involving the leaders and their instruments of office. For discussion of the נדיבים see N. K. Gottwald, *The Tribes of Yahweh*, 539–40.

18. Mattaneh is unknown; but see J. Simons, *Texts*, 262. For an alternative way of understanding this clause see *Notes*.

19. Nahaliel is unknown, and so also is Bamoth (cf. Num 22:41). Both places were presumably located on the central plateau of Moab. On Bamoth see P. H. Vaughan, *The Meaning of 'bāmâ' in the Old Testament* (Cambridge: University Press, 1974) 62 n.50, 71 n.42.

20. J. Simons (*Texts*, 262–63) suspects that "the valley" is Wady ʿajūn Mūsā. Pisgah (cf. Num 23:14; Deut 3:27; 34:1) is evidently a high point, probably in the Abarim mountains. It gave a good view of the promised land, and also of the desert region to the northwest of the Dead Sea. The "desert" might be a place—"Jeshimon."

Explanation

This section tells of Israel's travels to the east of the Dead Sea, once Edom had been traversed. Many of the sites names cannot be identified with any certainty. The section can reasonably be attributed to the Yahwist. He apparently had at hand a list of places which he is able to present as the sites visited by Israel on her Transjordanian journey. It may be that the list derived from travelers and/or traders. It apparently begins at a point well to the south (vv 10–11a appear to come from P—see *Form/Structure/Setting*), and ends at Pisgah, overlooking the Jordan somewhere near Jericho. The Yahwist chooses to complete the list before telling of events that took place on the way (vv 21–31).

The Yahwist has supplemented the list of places with ancient poetic material. His choice of material is determined entirely by the correspondence of place names in the list with place names in the poetry. The reference to Arnon in the list (v 13) prompts the inclusion of part of a victory song from the Book of the Wars of Yahweh (vv 14b–15). The reference to Beer in the list (v 16) prompts the inclusion of an ancient well song (vv 17–18).

The section as a whole creates the impression of a determined and purposeful march toward the promised land.

The Defeat of Sihon and Og   (21:21–35)

Bibliography

Bartlett, J. R. "The Historical Reference of Numbers 21:27–30." *PEQ* 101 (1969) 94–100. ———. "Sihon and Og, Kings of the Amorites." *VT* 20 (1970) 257–77. ———. "The Moabites and Edomites." *Peoples of Old Testament Times*, ed. D. J. Wiseman. Oxford; Clarendon Press, 1973. ———. "The Conquest of Sihon's Kingdom: a Literary Re-examination." *JBL* 97 (1978) 347–51. **Dever, W. G.** "The EB IV—MB I Horizon in Transjordan and Southern Palestine." *BASOR* 210 (1973) 37–63. **Freedman, D. N.** "Archaic Forms in Early Hebrew Poetry." *ZAW* 72 (1960) 101–7. **Horn, S. H.** "The Excavations at Tell Hesban, 1973." *ADAJ* 18 (1973) 87–88. ———. "Heshbon." *Encyclopedia of Archaeological Excavations in the Holy Land*, ed. M. Avi-Yonah. London: Oxford University Press, 1976. **Mendenhall, G. E.** "The Hebrew Conquest of Palestine." *BA* 25 (1962) 66–87. ———. "Change and Decay in All Around I See: Conquest, Covenant and the Tenth Generation." *BA* 39 (1976) 152–57. **Mittmann, S.** *Deuteronomium 1:1–6:3. Literarkritisch und Traditions-geschichtliche Untersucht.* BZAW 139 Berlin: Topelmann, 1975. **Netzer, N.** "We ploughed the Amalekites . . . (Num 21:30)." *Beth Mikra* 56 (1973) 101, 114. **Noth, M.** "Num 21 also Glied der 'Hexateuch' Erzählung." *ZAW* 58 (1940/1) 161–89. ———. "Israelitische Stämme zwischen Ammon und Moab." *ZAW* 60 (1944) 11–57. **Rendtorff, R.** "Zur Lage von Jaser." *ZDPV* 76 (1960) 124–35. **Sumner, W. A.** "Israel's Encounters with Edom, Moab, Ammon, Sihon and Og according to the Deuteronomist." *VT* 18 (1968) 216–28. **Thompson, H. O.** "The Ammonite Remains at Khirbet al-Hajjar." *BASOR* 227 (1977) 27–34. **Tushingham, A. D.** "The Excavations at Dibon (Dhiban) in Moab, the Third Campaign 1952–53." *AASOR* 40 (1972) 93. **van Seters, J.** "The Conquest of Sihon's Kingdom. A Literary Examination." *JBL* 91 (1972) 182–97. ———. "Once Again—the Conquest of Sihon's Kingdom." *JBL* 99 (1980) 117–19. **Vaux, R. de** "Notes d'histoire et de topographie transjordaniennes." *RB* 50 (1941) 16–47. **Wright, G. R. H.** "The Bronze Age Temple at Amman." *ZAW* 78 (1966) 350–56. **Wüst, M.** *Untersuchung zu den siedlungs-geographischen Texten des Alten Testaments. 1. Ostjordanland.* Wiesbaden: Reichert Verlag, 1975.

Translation

[21] And Israel [a] sent messengers to Sihon king of the Amorites,[b] saying, [22] "Let me pass through your land.[a] We [b] will not turn aside into field or vineyard.[c] We will not drink water from a well. We will go by the King's Highway, until we have passed through your territory." [23] But Sihon would not let Israel pass through his territory.[a] He gathered all his men together, and went out against Israel to the wilderness and came to Jahaz, and fought against Israel. [24] And Israel put him to the sword, and took possession of his land from the Arnon to the Jabbok, as far as the Ammonite border. For Jazer was at the Ammonite border.[a] [25] And Israel took all these cities, and Israel settled in all the cities of the Amorites, in Heshbon and in all its villages. [26] For Heshbon was the city of Sihon the king of the Amorites, who had fought against the former [a] king of Moab and taken all his land out of his hand, as far as the Arnon.[b] [27] Therefore the ballad singers say,

"Come ^a *to Heshbon. Let it be built.*
Let the city of Sihon be established. ^b
²⁸ *For fire went out from Heshbon,*
and flames from Sihon's city.
It devoured Ar ^a *of Moab.*
It consumed ^b *the high place* ^c *of Arnon.*
²⁹ *Woe to you, Moab.*
You are undone, you people of Chemosh!
He has made his sons fugitives,
and his daughters the prisoners ^a *of Sihon the Amorite king.* ^a
³⁰ *And so their posterity* ^a *perished* ^b *from Heshbon to Dibon,*
And we laid waste ^c *until fire* ^d *spread* ^e *to Medeba."* ^f
³¹ *And Israel lived in the land* ^a *of the Amorites.* ³² *And Moses sent to spy out*
Jazer. And they took ^a *its villages, and dispossessed* ^b *the Amorites who were there.*
³³ *And they turned and went up by the way to Bashan. And Og the king of Bashan*
came out against them to battle at Edrei, he and all his people. ³⁴ *But Yahweh said*
to Moses, "Do not fear him, for I have given him into your hand, and all his
people, and his land. And you shall do to him as you did to Sihon king of the
Amorites, who lived at Heshbon." ³⁵ *So they killed him,* ^a *and his sons,* ^a *and all*
his people, until there was no survivor left. And they possessed his land.

Notes

21.a. G has "Moses" (cf. Num 20:14).
21.b. Sam and G read שלום דברי "words of peace," derived probably from Deut 2:26.
22.a. Sam appears to have added "we will go by the King's Highway" from Num 20:17 (cf.
Deut 2:27). G appears to be influenced by Deut 2:27.
22.b. Sam reads the singular אטה "I turn aside."
22.c. Sam is again influenced by D; cf. Deut 2:28–29a.
23.a. Sam adds Deut 2:31 at this point.
24.a. Following G, which seems reasonable in view of v 32. MT reads "for the border of
the people of Ammon was strong."
26.a. It would be possible to read this as "the first" (see J. de Vaulx, 246).
26.b. G reads "Aroer."
27.a. Sam reads the singular—therefore possibly "Come, O Heshbon."
27.b. D. N. Freedman (*ZAW* 72 [1960] 101–7) suggests minor changes.
28.a. Sam and G read עד "as far as." *BHS* suggests ערי "cities of."
28.b. Reading בלעה (cf. G), and providing good parallelism.
28.c. Perhaps a proper name "Bamoth Arnon"; see J. de Vaulx, 246, but see also *Comment*.
29.a.-a. This clause may be a gloss; see J. Paterson, 55; J. de Vaulx, 246 (cf. Jer 48:46). It
breaks up the poetry.
30.a. Following G. MT has "we have shot at them" which is hard to make intelligible. S
reads ונירם "their country," which is probably an interpretative attempt. (GKC § 76f) prefers
G.
30.b. MT has a masculine singular, and Sam a feminine singular.
30.c. G reads "and the women," reading ונשים, and providing some parallel with "their
posterity." MT is intelligible, and may be preferable.
30.d. This reading assumes that אשר "which" should be אש "fire" (cf. Sam, G). J. de Vaulx
(248) cites a conjecture by H. Cazelles reading אשים "men," thus completing a list of victims
in the verse as a whole—children, women, men.
30.e. Possibly a place name—Nophah (see J. de Vaulx, 248). The association with fire is
derived from the verb נפח "to breathe," "to blow," i.e. the spreading of fire.
30.f. G reads "Moab," and S "the desert." The text of v 30 is extraordinarily difficult, and

the original seems irrecoverable. The only secure elements are "Heshbon" and "Dibon." The overall context suggests that there is here a celebration of destruction.

31.a. Sam reads "towns" (cf. v 25).
32.a. G notes that Jazer itself was taken as well.
32.b. Reading ויירש (Sam, G, Tg).
35.a. Omitted by Sam (cf. Deut 3:3).

Form/Structure/Setting

There has been widespread acceptance of the view that this section belongs to JE (cf. e.g. A. Dillmann, 120–35; J. Wellhausen, 110–11; A. Kuenen, 334; H. Holzinger, 90–91; B. Baentsch, 581–89; G. B. Gray, 294). Wellhausen believed the base narrative to be J (as in Num 20:14–21), and was of course supported by W. Rudolph (*Der "Elohist,"* 93–97). Many of the earlier analysts found the base narrative in the Transjordanian journey to be Elohistic, and the conclusions of Gray and Baentsch are typical. They found E in vv 21–24a, essentially because of the connection with Num 20:14–21 already so assigned, and in v 31 with its reference to the "Amorites," allegedly an equivalent to J's "Canaanites." There was some uncertainty about vv 24b–26, 32 except that they appear to offer alternative settlement traditions and were not obviously uniform. O. Eissfeldt (*Hexateuch,* 181–83) proposed a very complex mix of J/E/L which was entirely his own.

The peculiar problem posed by vv 33–35 has long been recognized, with Dillmann suggesting that the text is an interpolation from Deut 3:1–3. Gray concurred, along with many other analysts, having already traced in vv 21–24a some influences from Deut 2:24–31. In vv 33–35 there are differences of grammatical structure from the preceding verses, while the defeat of Og recounted here does not seem to be taken account of in Num 22:2. The tendency in Sam to incorporate material from Deuteronomy (see *Notes*) appears to have affected MT in a major way. The original independence of the old song was widely recognized.

M. Noth (161–62) is fairly conventional in seeing the story of Sihon's defeat (vv 21–31) as essentially a unit, and he dissented from the view that vv 25–26 are in any way a duplication of vv 21–24. They are transitional and provide an explanatory introduction to the song. For Noth the "Amorites" of v 31 are sufficient indication of E. He also accepted the view that vv 33–35 come directly from Deut 3:1–3, and also saw v 32 as an ill-fitting deuteronomistic addition, made by an editor with reference to Num 32:1. J. de Vaulx (244–51) offers a broadly similar view, finding a base narrative in vv 21–25 (E or JE), and some additions in vv 26–30 comparable to those found in vv 14–15 and vv 17–18. The antiquity of the song is recognized, and also the independence of the Jazer tradition (v 32), its absence in Deut 2:24–27 and Judg 11:19–22 being particularly marked. J. Sturdy (153–55) is inclined to associate the Sihon material with J, but agrees that the Og tradition is derived from Deut 3:1–3.

As with Num 20:14–21 there have been a number of recent suggestions to the effect that the section is almost entirely deuteronomistic (V. Fritz, *Israel,* 28–29; J. van Seters, *JBL* 91 [1972] 182–97; *JBL* 99 [1980] 117–19; S. Mittmann, *Deuteronomium 1:1–6:3;* M. Wüst, *Untersuchungen,* 9–59). The argu-

ment as set out by van Seters is that the writers of the section are drawing
directly on Deut 2:26–37; 3:1–7; Judg 11:19–26, that v 32 is an artificial anticipation of the settlement in Num 32, and that the song with its close associations
with Jer 48:45–46 is also a late editorial accretion. Wüst also puts the emphasis
on redactional activity, arguing that many of the Transjordanian traditions
are editorial additions to P. For Wüst there is reliable basic tradition about
Jazer in v 24, and in vv 27–30 the earliest Sihon tradition. The earliest Og
material however is to be found in Josh 12:2–4 where it is already linked
with Sihon. It should be noted that not all recent analysts accept this approach.
J. R. Bartlett (*JBL* 97 [1978] 347–51) suggests that van Seters' line of argument
is in no way proven or necessary, and that Deuteronomy is inclined to remove
inconsistencies and clarify obscure points in Numbers. His own examination
of the Sihon and Og traditions (*VT* 20 [1970] 257–77) suggested that the
former was Gadite, while the Gileadite Og tradition was possibly appropriated
by Judah in David's time. Liturgical interests may have drawn the two traditions
together, and Gilgal seemed to Bartlett a likely place where this would occur.

It is not unreasonable to follow Bartlett in suspecting that the tradition
in Deuteronomy is a development of that contained in vv 21–31. W. A. Sumner's view (*VT* 18 [1968] 216–28) that the two texts provide parallel forms
of a common tradition also deserves attention. On either of these approaches
there is no difficulty in associating vv 21–31 with the Yahwist. There are
close connections with Num 20:14–21, and the incorporation of ancient poetic
material (vv 27–30) makes the section of a piece with vv 10–20. The people
are consistently described as "Israel" (vv 21, 23, 24, 25). It also seems reasonable to accept Noth's view that there is no duplication between vv 21–24 and
vv 25–26, and that the latter are essentially transitional. The concentration
on Heshbon is important because it provides the link word with the song
to be incorporated. It seems reasonable to take v 31 as the Yahwist's summariz-
ing conclusion to the preceding material. The reference to Jazer in v 32 is
problematic. It plays no part in Deut 2:24–27 or Judg 11:19–22, and may
not have been an original part of the Yahwist's story at this point. For him
Jazer is a feature of the specific settlement traditions of Reuben and Gad
(Num 32:1). This editorial reference to the dispossession of the Amorites
in this area is probably prompted by the Yahwist's allusion to the place in
v 24b. With regard to vv 33–35 it seems best to accept the commonly held
view that these are a deuteronomistic interpolation. The linking of Sihon
and Og in cultic texts (Pss 135:1; 136:19–20) is probably post-deuteronomic;
there is little in the psalms themselves to suggest an early date. It seems
clear that Deuteronomy is the first to have gathered legendary material about
Og (Deut 3:11), and it was readily assumed that the victorious Israelites must
have had a part in his downfall. The cultic tradition, already influenced by
the Yahwist's account of a Transjordanian victory journey, readily incorporated his defeat as part of the salvation story.

There remains the question of the origin of the Sihon tradition in vv 21–
26 and the song in vv 27–30. The tradition that Sihon was indeed king of
Heshbon (v 26; Deut 2:26) is probably original, but it is difficult to say how
old this is. Excavations at Tell Hesban have revealed no Late Bronze occupation, and only a minor presence in Iron 1 (1200–700 B.C.). It is only in Iron

2 (from the late eighth century) that Tell Hesban figures as a city of major proportions. Some look to Tell Jalul as a possible site for biblical Heshbon, but this is entirely speculative. It may well be that we should see the tradition of victory over Sihon as very late, the perhaps a construct by the Yahwist himself. Its creation is prompted by the song in vv 27–30 which is to be another piece of filler material for the Transjordanian journey. Sihon is a leading figure in the song. There is no need to discern an Elohistic base narrative here. The use of "Amorites" makes sense as the Yahwist's description of a Transjordanian kingdom and its people.

The provenance of the song is a matter of considerable dispute. Some have suggested that it is ultimately of Amorite origin. The direction of attack in v 30 can be interpreted as from north to south, and therefore perhaps non-Israelite, while the rest of the poem can be understood as the celebration of a defeat of Moab by Sihon the Amorite. A recent presentation of this theory is given by N. K. Gottwald, along with details of earlier expositions (*The Tribes of Yahweh*, 215, 738). The most that can be said is that the theory is feasible. It is true enough that the Yahwist's story supposes that Israel took the territory not from the Moabites but from the Amorites, and it is possible that they took the song along with the land. The obscurities of v 30 make any theory based on them necessarily tentative. Others prefer to see the song as Israelite in origin. J. R. Bartlett (*PEQ* 101 [1969] 94–100) summarizes a number of these, and states his own preference for the view that the song belongs to the Davidic period (cf. 2 Sam 8:2, 12). If it is a mocking song then the speakers would be Israelites taunting Moab to rebuild Heshbon.

Other suggestions have been that it celebrates a ninth century Israelite victory over Moab, perhaps Omri's (c. 880 B.C.), or a Gadite success against Amorite Heshbon. J. Sturdy (153–54) also thinks that the song is Israel's, and that it comes from a time when they themselves have occupied or reoccupied Heshbon. The relationship of the text with Jer 48:45–46 is obviously important, and Sturdy, among others, thinks that the song is borrowed from that source. J van Seters (*JBL* 91 [1972] 182–97) argues that the song could in fact be late post-exilic in origin. It seems unlikely that this is correct; the impression being given in the chapter as a whole is that the Yahwist has used rather more ancient texts for his purpose. Nevertheless it is certainly possible to argue that the original form of the song has nothing to do with a victory of Sihon over Moab. He is not mentioned in Jer 48:45–46, and the reference in Num 21:29b is probably a gloss (see *Notes*). This leaves only the references to "the city of Sihon" in vv 27–28, and these are merely descriptive rather than allusions to Sihon's agency and activity. There are no criteria for determining directions of influence between the song and Jer 48:45–46; it may be safest to suppose a common tradition behind both texts.

Our conclusion is that the Yahwist has taken up an old taunt song against Moab which was probably, though not certainly, of Israelite origin. The version available to him mentioned Heshbon as the city of Sihon. He took this Sihon to be an Amorite king, and assumed that he had previously dispossessed the earlier Moabites. Since in his view this was Israelite territory he

constructs the story of the defeat of Sihon by the Israelites. The view that
the Yahwist's all-Israel Transjordanian journey is a literary construct is supported by the evidence from the book of Judges which suggests at most
small enclaves of settlers in the area (Judg 3:12–30; 8:4–17; 10:17–12:6).

Comment

22. On "the King's Highway" see *Comment* on Num 20:17.

23. Jahaz is possibly the modern Khirbet Umm el-Idhâm, about five miles
north of Dibon (cf. Deut 2:32; Isa 15:4; Jer 48:34) cf. the form Jahzah/in
Josh 13:18; 21:36; Judg 11:20; Jer 48:21; 1 Chr 6:78.

24. Jazer is probably Kirbet Jazzir, about twelve miles south of the Jabbok
(Josh 21:39; Isa 16:8, 9; Jer 48:32). MT appears to be saying that the Israelites
did not move north of the Jabbok because the Ammonites there were too
strong (see *Notes.*) For an alternative view of v 24b, involving the emendation
of עד "as far as" to ארץ "land," see J. Simons, "Two Connected Problems
Relating to the Israelite Settlement in Transjordan,"*PEQ* 79 (1947) 87–
101.

25. Heshbon is the modern Hesbân, some twenty miles east of the northern
end of the Dead Sea. It has proved difficult to find any significant settlements
there prior to Iron 2 (see *Form/Structure/Setting;* cf. Josh 21:39; Isa 15:4; Jer
48:2; Cant 7:4).

27. המשלים—"ballad singers." The root משל, when a noun, is often rendered "proverb." It means "to be like," and probably refers to the parallelism
characteristic of Hebrew poetry. The present song is some form of ballad,
perhaps a taunt song. It begins with a call to assist in the rebuilding of Heshbon.

28. Some kind of successful campaign against the Moabites is envisaged.

28. במות ארנן "the high place of Arnon" may be a reference to a man-
made altar or cultic platform rather than to a geographical feature. It may
also be a proper name Bamoth Arnon (see *Notes*).

29. The song goes on to mock the Moabites. Chemosh has given them
into the hands of their enemies. There are references to the dealings of
Chemosh with Moab on the famous Moabite Stone.

30. This verse is exceedingly difficult (see *Notes*). The only certain elements
in the text appear to be the place names Heshbon and Dibon. It is not unreasonable to suppose that the text told something of the extent of destruction
associated with this uprising and/or campaign. For detailed discussion see
J. R. Bartlett, *PEQ* 101 (1969) 94–100.

Dibon is probably the modern Dhibân, in which case it lay well to the
south and not far north of the Arnon. For details of investigations there
see A. D. Tushingham, "Dibon," *Encyclopedia of Archaeological Excavations in
the Holy Land.* ed. M. Avi-Yonah (London: Oxford University Press, 1975).
The earliest occupational phase is dated to the middle of the ninth century.

Medeba is probably to be situated between Heshbon and Dibon—n.b. the
modern Mâdebâ to the south of Heshbon. An LB tomb has been discovered
there, but there is no evidence of a sizable population at that period. For
further details see M. Avi-Yonah, "Medeba," *Encyclopedia of Archaeological Exca-*

vations in the Holy Land. ed. M. Avi-Yonah (London: Oxford University Press, 1975).

33. הבשן דרך "by the way to Bashan," which implies a thrust to the north-east.

Edrei is about thirty miles east of the Sea of Galilee (Deut 3:1, 10). Bashan was noted for its rich pastures and well-fed cattle (cf. e.g. Amos 4:1). For legendary material about Og see Deut 3:11.

35. The ban—i.e. total destruction—is again the order of the day.

Explanation

The section tells in essence of the decisive defeat of two Transjordanian kingdoms—that of Sihon king of the Amorites, and that of Og king of Bashan. The story of the defeat of Sihon (vv 21–24) is constructed in a similar fashion to that found in Num 20:14–21. As with Edom messengers are sent requesting permission to pass through the land. Permission is once again refused, and Sihon threatens Israel. In this case battle is joined, and Israel is devastatingly successful. Sihon was thought to have occupied former Moabite territory, and this now falls into Israelite hands. The fall of Heshbon is celebrated in the older taunt song of vv 27–30. Linguistic evidence suggests that vv 33–35 are an intrusion from Deut 3:1–3, a feature of Sam in Numbers affecting here MT. The account of the occupation of Jazer (v 32) may well be influenced by v 24b. It too is probably an intrusion, because it is hard to reconcile with the Yahwist's account in Num 32:1.

The main part of the section (vv 21–31) appears to be the Yahwist's continuation of the Transjordanian journey. The list of stations in v 20 took us well inside Sihon's territory, and the Yahwist now takes us back to a decisive incident that took place at Jahaz. The account of the defeat of Sihon is in all essentials the Yahwist's own. It is structured in a stylized fashion comparable to the form adopted in Num 20:14–21. He is prompted to create the tradition by the contents of the old anti-Moabite taunt song (vv 27–30) which he proposes to include. This mentioned Heshbon as the city of Sihon, and led him to suppose that Israel must have crushed Sihon on her triumphant journey northwards.

The determined and purposeful progress of the people, which began in the previous section, gains further impetus with these crushing victories over the Transjordanian kingdoms.

The Story of Balaam (22:1–24:25)

Bibliography

Albright, W. F. "The Home of Balaam." *JAOS* 35 (1915) 386–90. ———. "The Oracle$ of Balaam." *JBL* 63 (1944) 207–53. ———. "From Patriarchs to Moses: 2. Moses out of Egypt." *BA* 36 (1973) 48–76. ———. "The Meaning of the Phrase še*t*ūm hā'ayin in Num 24:3, 15." *VT* 3 (1953) 78–79. **Bewer, J. A.** "The Literary Problems of the Balaam Story in Numbers, Chapters 22–24." *AJT* 9 (1905) 238–62. **Brichto, H. C.** *The Problem of "Curse" in the Hebrew Bible.* Philadelphia: Society of Biblical Literature and Exegesis, 1963. **Burrows, E.** *The Oracles of Jacob and Balaam.* London: Burns, Oates and Washbourne, 1938. **Canney, M. A.** "Numbers 22:21–31." *ExpTim* 27 (1917) 568. **Cheyne, T. K.** "Some Critical Difficulties in the Chapters on Balaam." *ExpTim* 10 (1898/9) 399–402. **Christensen, D. L.** *Transformations of the War Oracle in Old Testament Prophecy.* Missoula, MT: Scholars Press, 1975. **Cipriani, S.** "Il senso messianico degli oracoli di Balaam (Num 23–24)." *Attidella 18 settimana biblica: Il Messianismo.* Brescia, 1966. **Coats, G. W.** "Balaam: Sinner or Saint?" *BR* 18 (1973) 21–29. **Coppens, J.** "Les Oracles de Bileam: Leur Origine Littéraire et leur Portée Prophétique." *Melanges Eugene Tisserant Vol. 1.* Città del Vaticano: Bibliotheca Apostolica Vaticana, 1964. **Craigie, P. C.** "The Conquest and Early Hebrew Poetry." *TB* 20 (1969) 76–94. **Eising, H.** "Balaams Eselin." *BK* 13 (1958) 45–47. **Eissfeldt, O.** "Die Komposition der Bileam-Erzählung." *ZAW* 57 (1939) 212–41. ———. "Sinai Erzählung und Bileamsprüche." *HUCA* 32 (1961) 179–90. **Freedman, D. N.** "Archaic Forms in Early Hebrew Poetry." *ZAW* 72 (1960) 101–7. ———. "Pottery, Poetry, and Prophecy: An Essay on Biblical Poetry." *JBL* 96 (1977) 5–26. **Franken, H. J.** "Texts from the Persian Period from Tell Deir 'Alla." *VT* 17 (1967) 480–81. **Gemser, B.** "Der Stern aus Jacob (Num 24:17)." *ZAW* 2 (1925) 301–2. **Gross, W.** " 'Ein Zepter wird sich erheben aus Isreal' (Num 24:17). Die messianische Hoffnung im Alten Testament." *BK* 17 (1962) 34–37. ——— . Bileam. Literar- und formkritishce Untersuchung der Prosa in Num 22–24. Munich: Kösel Verlag, 1974. **Guillaume, A.** "A Note on Num 23:10." *VT* 12 (1962) 335–37. **Guyot, G. H.** "The Prophecy of Balaam." *CBQ* 2 (1940) 330–40. ———. "Balaam." *CBQ* 3 (1941) 235–42. **Hertz, J. H.** "Numbers 23:9b, 10." *ExpTim* 45 (1933/4) 524. **Hoftijzer, J.** "The Prophet Balaam in a 6th Century Aramaic Inscription." *BA* 39 (1976) 11–17. **Johnson, A. R.** *The Cultic Prophet in Ancient Israel.* Cardiff: University of Wales, 1962. **Kosmala, H.** "Form and Structure in Ancient Hebrew Poetry." *VT* 14 (1964) 423–45. **LaVerdiere, E. A.** "Balaam Son of Peor." *TBT* 89 (1977) 1157–65. **Lipiński, E.** "הימים באחרית dans les textes preexiliques." *VT* 20 (1970) 445–50. **Liver, J.** "The Figure of Balaam in Biblical Tradition." *Eretz-Israel* 3 (1954) 97–100. **Lock, W.** "Balaam." *JTS* 2 (1901) 161–73. **Loewe, H.** "Numbers 22:6." *ExpTim* 26 (1914/15) 378. **Löhr, M.** "Bileam, Num 22:2–24, 25." *AfO* 4 (1927) 85–89. **Loretz, O.** "Die Herausführungsformel in Num 23:22 und 24:8." *UF* 7 (1975) 571–72. **Mackensen, R. S.** "The Present Literary Form of the Balaam Stories." *The Macdonald Presentation Volume.* Princeton: Books for Libraries Press, 1933. **Mauchline, J.** "The Balaam-Balak Songs and Saga." *Studia Semitica et Orientalia Vol. 2. Presentation Volume to William Barron Stevenson,* ed. C. J. Mullo-Weir. Glasgow: Glasgow University Oriental Society, 1945. **Mowinckel, S.** "Der Ursprung der Bileamsage." *ZAW* 48 (1930) 233–71. **Nestle, E.** "Num 23:19." *ZAW* 28 (1908) 228–29. **Noth, M.** "Israelitische Stämme zwischen Ammon und Moab." *ZAW* 60 (1944) 11–57. **Orlinsky, H. M.** "Rābás for Šākáb in Num 24:9." *JQR* 35 (1944/45) 173–77. **Pakozdy, L. M. von** "Theologische Redaktionsarbeit in der Bileam Perikope." *Von Ugarit nach Qumran.* ed. J. Hempel and L. Rost. BZAW 77. Berlin: Töpelmann, 1958. **Parker, I.** "The Way of God and the Way of Balaam." *ExpTim* 17 (1905) 45. **Perles, F.** "Zu Numeri 24:23." *ZAW* 29 (1909) 73. **Powell, T.,** *The Oracles of Balaam.* Diss. Pasadena, Fuller Theological Seminary, 1981. **Rad, G. von** "Die Geschichte von Bileam." *Gottes Wirken in Israel.* Neukirchen: Steck, 1974. **Rost, L.** "Fragen um Bileam." *Beiträge zur Alttestamentliche Theologie.* ed. H. Donner. Göttingen: Vandenhoeck and Ruprecht, 1977. **Sayce, A. H.** "Who was Balaam?" *ExpTim* 15 (1903/4) 405–6. **Schmidt, L.** "Die alttestamentliche Bileamüberlieferung." *BZ* 23 (1979) 234–61. **Seybold, K.** "Das Herrscherbild des Bileamorakels Num 24:15–19." *TZ* 29 (1973) 1–19. **Smick, E. B.** "A Study of the Structure of the Third Balaam Oracle (Num 24:5–9)." *The Law and the Prophets.* ed. J. H. Skilton. Nutley N.J.: Presbyterian and Reformed Publishing Co., 1974. **Stanley, D. M.** "Balaam's Ass or a Problem in New Testament Hermeneutics." *CBQ* 20 (1958) 50–56. **Sutcliffe, E. F.** "De Unitate Litteraria Num 22." *Bib* 7 (1926) 3–39. ———. "A Note on Num 22." *Bib* 18 (1937) 439–42. **Thom, A.** "Balaam's Prayer." *ExpTim* 16 (1905) 334. **Thomas, D. W.** "The word רָבָע in Numbers 23:10." *ExpTim* 46 (1934/35) 285. ———. "Some Further Remarks on Unusual Ways of Expressing the Superlative in Hebrew." *VT* 18 (1968) 120–24. **Tosato, A.** "The Literary Structure of the First Two Poems of Balaam (Num 23:7–10, 18–24)." *VT* 29 (1979) 98–106. **Vermes, G.** *Scripture and Tradition in Judaism.* Leiden: Brill, 1961. **Vetter, D.** *Seherspruch und Segensschilderung. Ausdruckabsichten und sprachliche Verwirklichungen in den Bileam-Sprüchen von Numeri 23 und 24.* Stuttgart: Calwer Verlag, 1975. **Vosté, J-M.** "Les Oracles de Balaam D'Après Mar Išoʿdad de Merw (c. 850)." *Bib* 29 (1948) 169–94. **Wagner, S.** "Offenbarungsphänomenologische Elemente in der Bileam-Geschichte von Num 22–24." *Theologische Versuche* 5 (1975) 11–31. **Wharton, J. A.** "The Command to Bless: An Exposition of Numbers 22:41–23:25." *Int* 13 (1959) 37–48. **Yahuda, A. S.** "The Name of Balaam's Homeland." *JBL* 64 (1945) 547–51.

Translation

¹ *And the people of Israel set out, and encamped in the plains of Moab on the other side of the Jordan from Jericho.* ² *And Balak the son of Zippor saw all that Israel had done to the Amorites.* ³ *And Moab was terrified of the people, because they were many. Moab was overcome with fear of the people of Israel.* ⁴ *And Moab said to the elders of Midian, "This* ᵃ *assembly will now lick up everything round us, as a bull licks up the grass of the field." And Balak the son of Zippor was king of Moab at that time.* ⁵ *And he sent messengers to Balaam the son of Beor at Pethor, which is near the River* ᵃ *in the land of the Amavites,* ᵇ *to call him, saying, "Behold, a people has come out of Egypt. Behold, they cover the face of the earth, and they have settled opposite me.* ⁶ *Come now, curse this people for me,* ᵃ *since they are too strong for me.* ᵇ *Then perhaps I shall be able to defeat them, and drive them from the land. For I know that he whom you bless is blessed, and he whom you curse is cursed."*

⁷ *And the elders of Moab and the elders of Midian went with the fees for divination in their hands, and they came to Balaam, and reported to him Balak's words.* ⁸ *And he said to them, "Lodge here tonight, and I will bring back word to you, as Yahweh speaks to me." And the leaders of Moab stayed with Balaam.* ⁹ *And God came to Balaam and said, "Who are these men with you?"* ¹⁰ *And Balaam said to God, "Balak the son of Zippor, king of Moab, has sent to me, saying,* ᵃ ¹¹ *'Behold,* ᵃ *a people has come out* ᵃ *of Egypt, and it covers the face of the earth. Come now, curse them for me. Perhaps then I shall be able to fight against them, and drive them*

out.'" ¹² And God said to Balaam, "You shall not go with them. You shall not curse the people, for they are blessed." ¹³ And Balaam arose in the morning, and said to the leaders of Balak, "Go to your own land,ᵃ for Yahweh ᵇ has refused to let me go with you." ¹⁴ And the leaders of Moab arose and went to Balak, and said, "Balaam refuses to come with us."

¹⁵ And Balak yet again sent leaders, more of them and of higher rank than these. ¹⁶ And they came to Balaam and said to him, "Thus says Balak the son of Zippor, 'Let nothing hinder you from coming to me. ¹⁷ For I will confer great honor upon you, and all that you say to me I will do. And come I pray, curse this people for me.'" ¹⁸ But Balaam answered and said to the servants ᵃ of Balak, "Even if Balak were to give me his house full of silver and gold I could not go beyond the commandment of Yahweh my God in anything, small or great.ᵇ ¹⁹ But now, you also stay the night, that I may know what more ᵃ Yahweh may say to me." ²⁰ And God ᵃ came to Balaam in the night and said to him, "If the men have come to call you, then rise, go with them, but do only what I tell you."

²¹ And Balaam rose in the morning, and saddled his ass, and went with the leaders of Moab. ²² But Yahweh's ᵃ anger was stirred because he went. And the angel of Yahweh stood in his way as his adversary. And he was riding on the ass, and there were two servants with him. ²³ And the ass saw the angel of Yahweh standing in the road, with a drawn sword in his hand. And the ass turned off the road and went into the field. And Balaam struck the ass to make her return to the road. ²⁴ And the angel of Yahweh stood in a narrow place between the vineyards, with a wall on either side. ²⁵ And the ass saw the angel of Yahweh, and as she pushed against the wall she pressed Balaam's foot against the wall. And again he struck her. ²⁶ And the angel of Yahweh went ahead, and again he stood in a narrow place, where there was no way to turn, either to right or left. ²⁷ And the ass saw the angel of Yahweh, and she lay down under Balaam. And Balaam's anger was stirred, and he struck the ass with his stick. ²⁸ And Yahweh opened the mouth of the ass, and she said to Balaam, "What have I done to you, that you have struck me these three times?" ²⁹ And Balaam said to the ass, "Because you have made a fool of me. I wish I had a sword in my hand, for then I would kill you." ³⁰ And the ass said to Balaam, "Am I not yours, the one you have ridden all your life long to this day? Have I ever done this to you before?" And he said, "No."

³¹ And Yahweh opened Balaam's eyes, and he saw the angel of Yahweh standing in the way, with his drawn sword in his hand. And he bowed his head, and fell on his face. ³² And the angel of Yahweh said to him, "Why have you struck your ass these three times? Behold, I have come out to oppose you,ᵃ because your way is perverse ᵇ before me. ³³ And the ass saw me and turned aside before me these three times. If she had not turned aside from me, surely just now I would have killed you and let her live." ³⁴ And Balaam said to the angel of Yahweh, "I have sinned, for I did not know that you stood in the road against me. Now therefore if it is evil in your sight, I will go back again." ³⁵ And the angel of Yahweh said to Balaam, "Go with the men, but only the word which I speak to you shall you speak." And Balaam went on with Balak's leaders.

³⁶ And Balak heard that Balaam was coming. And he went out to meet him at Ar ᵃ of Moab by the Arnon on his frontier. ³⁷ And Balak said to Balaam, "Did I not send time and again to call you? Why did you not come to me? Am I not able to honor you?" ³⁸ And Balaam said to Balak, "Behold, I have come to you. But

now what power have I of myself to say anything? The word that God puts in my mouth, that I will speak." ³⁹ And Balaam went with Balak, and they came ᵃ to Kiriath-huzoth. ⁴⁰ And Balak sacrificed cattle and sheep, and sent to Balaam and to the leaders who were with him.

⁴¹ And next morning Balak took Balaam, and brought him up to Bamoth-baal. And he saw from there the nearest of the people.

²³:¹ And Balaam said to Balak, "Build for me here seven altars, and prepare for me here seven bulls and seven rams." ² And Balak did as Balaam had said. And he ᵃ offered on each altar a bull and a ram. ³ And Balaam said to Balak, "Stand beside your whole offering,ᵃ and I will go. Perhaps God ᵇ will come to meet me. And whatever he shows me I will tell you." And he went to a bare height.ᶜ ⁴ And God ᵃ met ᵇ Balaam. And Balaam said to him, "I have prepared the seven altars, and I have offered on each altar a bull and a ram." ⁵ And Yahweh ᵃ put a word in Balaam's mouth, and said, "Return to Balak, and thus shall you speak." ⁶ And he returned to him, and behold, he and all the Moabite leaders were standing beside his whole offering.ᵃ ⁷ And he (Balaam) uttered his oracle,

"From Aram ᵃ Balak has brought me, (4+4)
The king of Moab from the eastern mountains:
'Come curse Jacob for me, (3+3)
And come, denounce Israel!'
⁸ How can I curse one ᵃ whom God has not cursed? (2+3)
How can I denounce one whom Yahweh has not denounced? (2+3)
⁹ For from the top of the mountain I see him,
And from the hills I watch him. (3+2)
Behold, a people living alone,
And that has not reckoned itself among the nations! (3+3)
¹⁰ Who can count the dust of Jacob,
Or number the fourth part ᵃ of Israel? (4+3)
Let me die the death of the righteous,ᵇ
And let my end ᶜ be like his!" (4+3)

¹¹ And Balak said to Balaam, "What have you done to me? I sent for you to curse my enemies, and behold, you have done nothing but bless them." ¹² And he answered, and said, "Must I not keep to the words that Yahweh ᵃ puts into my mouth?"

¹³ And Balak said to him, "Come with me to another place from which you may see them. From there you shall see the nearest of them, but shall not see them all. Then curse them for me from there." ¹⁴ And he took him to the field of Zophim, to the top of Pisgah, and built seven altars, and offered a bull and a ram on each altar. ¹⁵ And Balaam ᵃ said to Balak, "Stand here beside your whole offering,ᵇ and I will meet God ᶜ over there." ¹⁶ And God ᵃ met Balaam, and put a word in his mouth, and said, "Return to Balak, and thus shall you speak." ¹⁷ And he came ᵃ to him, and behold, he was standing beside his whole offering,ᵇ and the Moabite leaders with him. And Balak said to him, "What has Yahweh spoken?" ¹⁸ And Balaam uttered his oracle,

"Rise, Balak, and hear,
Listen to me ᵃ you son ᵇ of Zippor. (3+4)
¹⁹ God is not a man that he should lie,ᵃ
Nor a son of man that he should change his mind. (4+3)

> Has he spoken, and will he not do it?
>> Or has he declared, and will he not fulfill it? (4+3)
> ²⁰ Behold, I received a command ^a to bless.^b
>> He has blessed,^c and I cannot revoke it. (3+3)
> ²¹ He has not discovered ^a iniquity in Jacob,
>> Nor has he seen mischief in Israel. (3+3)
> Yahweh his God is with him,
>> Acclaimed in him as king. (3+3)
> ²² God ^a brings them out of Egypt,
>> He has as it were the horns of a wild ox. ^{bc} (3+3)
> ²³ For there is no enchantment against ^a Jacob,
>> And no divination against ^a Israel. (3+2)
> Now is the time for it to be said of Jacob,
>> And of Israel, 'What has God wrought!' (3+3)
> ²⁴ Behold, a people rearing up like a lioness,
>> And rampant like a lion. (3+2)
> He will not lie down till he devours the prey,
>> And drinks the blood of the slain." (4+3)

²⁵ And Balak said to Balaam, "Do not curse them at all, nor bless them at all." ²⁶ But Balaam answered, and said to Balak, "Did I not tell you, 'All that God ^a says, that I must do'?" ²⁷ And Balak said to Balaam, "Come now, I will take you to another place. Perhaps it will be good in God's eyes for you to curse them for me from there." ²⁸ And Balak took Balaam to the top of Peor, overlooking the desert. ²⁹ And Balaam said to Balak, "Build for me here seven altars, and prepare for me here seven bulls and seven rams." ³⁰ And Balak did as Balaam had said, and offered a bull and a ram on each altar.

^{24:1} And Balaam saw that it was good in Yahweh's eyes to bless Israel, and he did not go, as at the other times, to resort to enchantments, but set his face towards the wilderness. ² And Balaam lifted up his eyes, and saw Israel encamped, tribe by tribe. And the spirit of God came upon him. ³ And he uttered his oracle,

> "The word of Balaam the son of Beor,
>> And the word of the man whose sight is clear.^a (4+4)
> ⁴ The word of him who hears the words of God,^a
>> And who sees the vision of the Almighty,
>> Falling down,^b but having his eyes uncovered. (3+4+3)
> ⁵ How ^a fair are your tents, O Jacob,
>> Your encampments, O Israel! (3+2)
> ⁶ Like rows of palms ^a that stretch afar,
>> Like gardens by a river; (2+3)
> Like aloes ^b that Yahweh has planted,
>> Like cedars ^b beside the waters. (3+2)
> ^{7a} Water shall flow from his buckets,
>> And his seed shall be in many waters.^a (3+3)
> His king shall be taller than Agag,^b
>> And his kingdom shall be lifted high. (3+2)
> ⁸ God guides ^a him out of Egypt,
>> He has as it were the horns of a wild ox.^b (3+3)

He shall eat up the nations his adversaries,
    And shall break their bones in pieces,
        And pierce them with his arrows.   (3+2+2)
9 He couched, he lay down like a lion,
        And like a lioness. Who will rouse him up?   (3+3)
Blessed be they that bless you,
        And they that curse you be accursed!''   (2+2)

10 And Balak's anger was stirred against Balaam, and he struck his hands together. And Balak said to Balaam, "I called you to curse my enemies, and behold, you have persisted in blessing them these three times. 11 Therefore now flee to your place. I said, 'I will certainly honor you,' but behold, Yahweh has kept you back from honor." 12 And Balaam said to Balak, "Did I not tell your messengers whom you sent to me, saying, 13 'If Balak gives to me his house full of silver and gold, I would not be able to go beyond the word of Yahweh, to do either good or bad of my own will. What Yahweh ª speaks, that I speak'? 14 And now, behold, I am going to my people.ª Come, I will let you know what this people will do to your people in the days to come." 15 And he uttered his oracle,

"The word of Balaam the son of Beor,
    And the word of the man whose sight is clear.   (4+4)
16 The word of him who hears the words of God,
    And knows the knowledge of the Most High.   (3+3)
The vision of the Almighty he sees,
    Falling down, but having his eyes uncovered   (3+3)
17 I see him,ª but not now.
    I behold him,ᵇ but not near.   (3+3)
A starᶜ shall come forthᵈ out of Jacob,
    And a scepterᵉ shall rise out of Israel.   (3+3)
It shall crush the headsᶠ of Moab,
    And the skullsᵍ of all the sons of strife.ʰ   (3+3)
18 ª And Edom shall be his by conquest,
    And Seir,ᵇ his enemies, shall be his,
        While Israel does valiant deeds.   (3+4+3)
19 By Jacob shall dominion be exercised,ª
    And he shall destroy the survivors of Ar.ᵇ"   (2+3)
20 And he looked on Amalek, and uttered his oracle,
"Amalek was the first of the nations,
    But his endª shall be utter destruction."   (3+3)
21 And he looked on the Kenite, and uttered his oracle,
"Your dwelling place is secure,ª
    And your nest is set in the rock.   (2+3)
22 Nevertheless Cain shall be devastated.ª
    How longᵇ shall Asshurᶜ take you away captive?" (4+3)
23 And he uttered his oracle,ª
"ᵇ Alas, who shall live when God does this?ᵇ
24 And shipsª shall come from the coast of Kittim,ᵇ
    And shall afflict Asshur,ᶜ and shall afflict Eber.ᵈ (3+3+3)
And he also shall come to utter destruction.''

25 *And Balaam rose, and went, and returned to his place.*
And Balak also went his way.

Notes

22:4.a. The demonstrative occurs in Sam, G, Syr, Vg.

5.a. G and Vg read "near the river of the land."

5.b. MT reads literally "land of the sons of his people." Sam, Syr, and Vg read "Ammon"—probably in an attempt to interpret a difficult text. A. S. Yahuda (*JBL* 64 [1945] 547–51) suggests "land of the children of *ʿĀmu*" which he locates in northern Mesopotamia. A fifteenth century B.C. inscription from Alalakh refers to Amau as territory between Aleppo and Carchemish—hence "Amavites" (NEB).

6.a. On the unusual form of the imperative see GKC § 670. Cf. also Num 22:11, 17; 23:7.

6.b. G has the plural "us."

10.a. The word is lacking in MT and Sam, but is attested in G, S, and Vg and seems to be required.

11.a. Reading עם יצא as in v 5 (supported by Sam, G, Tg).

13.a. G translates אדניכם "to your master."

13.b. "Yahweh" is supported by MT, Sam, S, Vg. G has "God," which may be an attempt to keep the text in line with the use in v 12.

18.a. G has ἄρχουσιν "leaders" (cf. v 14). As in v 13 G appears to provide a smoother text.

18.b. G adds a reference to Balaam's own mind cf. Num 24:13.

19.a. On the use of the jussive here see GKC § 109f.

20.a. Sam has "the angel of God."

22.a. MT reads "God," but there is strong support for "Yahweh" in Sam and some G witnesses. "Yahweh" corresponds with the usage throughout vv 22–35 and seems preferable.

32.a. Sam and the versions add "against you" to לשטן "as an adversary."

32.b. The root ירט occurs only here and in Job 16:11, and appears to mean "precipitate" (transitive). G has οὐκ ἀστεία "not seemly."

36.a. Literally "the city of Moab" (see *Comment* on Num 21:28).

39.a. Sam, S, Tg read a hiphil "and he led him."

23:2.a. The verb is singular, so that the reference to Balaam and Balak (lacking in G), could be a gloss. J. A. Paterson (56) suggests that it was added by a scribe who thought Balaam's statement in v 4 required such an addition.

3.a. Sam and Syr read the plural in order to harmonize with v 1.

3.b. MT has "Yahweh," but Sam and G support "God."

3.c. A difficult word. The meaning "baldness" is suggested by Job 33:21; hence "bare height." As G. B. Gray points out (344) it is not clear that the versions had anything other than MT before them. Though עלה "ascend" rather than הלך "go" would be the verb to expect the presence of the plural "bare heights" in Jer 3:2, 21; 4:11; 7:29; 12:12; 14:6; Isa 41:18; 49:9 makes the traditional rendering preferable to other suggestions.

4.a. G has "the angel of God."

4.b. Sam has the root מצא "to find."

5.a. G reads "God," and Sam "the angel of God."

6.a. Sam, G, and S read the plural (cf. 23:3ᵃ). G adds a comment to the effect that the spirit of God came upon him (cf. 24:2).

7.a. The possibility of emending to "Edom" (a familiar "error" in textual criticism) has been considered (*BHS*), but there is no textual support.

8.a. On the rare suffix see GKC § 58g.

10.a. G reads δήμους "peoples," translating perhaps רב עם "multitude of the people." It is possible to read רבע as רבבת "myriads," and J. de Vaulx (276) prefers "cloud." NEB translates "dust" and "fourth part" as "host" and "hordes" respectively. See also D. W. Thomas, *ExpTim* 46 (1934–35) 285.

10.b. The plural is difficult to justify since כמהו "like him" requires a singular antecedent; see the discussions by W. F. Albright (*JBL* 63 [1944] 207–53) and D. N. Freedman (*ZAW* 72

[1960] 101–7). The versions read כהם "like them," and this is preferred by W. Rudolph (*ZAW* 52 [1934] 113–20).

10.c. G understands this to mean "descendants."

12.a. G reads "God."

15.a. Following Sam and G.

15.b. Sam and Syr have the plural (cf. vv 3, 6).

15.c. "God" seems to be presupposed. G reads "to interrogate God."

16.a. Following G. MT has "Yahweh."

17.a. G and Vg read "returned."

17.b. Sam and Syr have the plural (cf. vv 3, 6, 15).

18.a. Reading עלי or אלי.

18.b. On the form בנו see GKC § 90, 96 (cf. also 24:3, 15).

19.a. Probably a jussive (see GKC § 109i).

20.a. G, S and Vg vocalize לֻקָּחְתִּי "I have been taken."

20.b. Following Sam, G, S, and Vg.

20.c. In Sam and G "I have blessed."

21.a. The subject is probably God, but Syr and Tg assume it to be Balaam.

22.a. For discussion of the textual problems in this verse see W. F. Albright (*JBL* 63 [1944] 215).

22.b. Following Albright rather than MT in suggesting that Israel rather than God is being likened to the wild ox. The versions appear to be strongly interpretative.

22.c. J. A. Paterson (58) thinks the verse to be out of place.

23.a. This seems preferable to "in Jacob/Israel" (Tg).

26.a. MT has "Yahweh," but "God" is supported by Sam, G, and Vg.

24:3.a. G has "who sees truly." The versions generally appear to be interpretative. J. M. Allegro (*VT* 3 [1953] 78–79) links the phrase to a root suggesting that Balaam was irritated at having to bless.

4.a. The first clause is present in MT and some G witnesses, but not in Sam. It is probably best to retain it. J. A. Paterson (58) wishes to insert the clause from v 16 about the knowledge of the Most High at this point on the grounds that the parallelism requires it, and that the first description of the seer ought to be as full as the second. In fact there is parallelism in "the words of God" and "the vision of the Almighty," the irregularity occurring therefore in the third clause of the verse. This third clause may then be a gloss, attempting to describe the way in which Balaam receives his vision.

4.b. G interprets as "in sleep."

5.a. On the use of מה to express admiration or astonishment see GKC § 148a.

6.a. Literally "torrents"—hence "valley" (RSV). The parallelism suggests the name of a tree, and "palm" seems likely (NEB); see J. de Vaulx, 284.

6.b. The view has been expressed that "aloes" and "cedars" be reversed in this couplet since cedars are not found by water (G. B. Gray, 363; W. F. Albright (*JBL* 63 [1944] 207–53); J. de Vaulx, 284).

7.a.a. G gives a messianic interpretation to this couplet, referring to a man who shall emerge from their descendants and rule many peoples (cf. also Syr).

7.b. Sam, G, VL, Aq, and Sym read "Gog" (cf. Ezek. 38:2–3, 14, 16, 21; 39:1, 11). Vg and Tgᴶ interpret in the light of 1 Sam 15:10–23.

8.a. Sam and G read the root נחה "to guide." W. F. Albright (*JBL* 63 [1944] 207–53) accepts this on the text critical principle of *lectio difficilior*, the more difficult reading being in general the more likely. Thus יצא "bring out" (MT) regularly occurs in association with the exodus, but not so נחה.

8.b. See on 23:22.b.

13.a. G has "God."

14.a. G has "to my place," and Syr "to my country."

17.a. G reads this as a Hiphil "I will show him."

17.b. G reads "I bless him" or "I declare him blessed."

17.c. Tg⁰ gives this a precise royal interpretation.

17.d. Reading זרח with G. It is possible that דרך means "to march forth."

17.e. G reads "a man," Syr "a prince," and Tg⁰ "an anointed one"—all interpretative translations.

17.f. Literally "corners" and perhaps the corners of the head are intended. G, Tg⁰ and Vg interpret in terms of the leading men of Moab.

17.g. Following Sam and reading וְקָדְקֹד (cf. Jer 48:45) in place of וְקַרְקַר (MT; see GKC § 55f). MT means "to exterminate" or "to devastate." The emendation gives good parallelism.

17.h. There may be a reference here to a pre-Moabite tribe cited in the Egyptian Execration texts—"the sons of Sutu" (cf. also Jer 48:45).

18.a. W. F. Albright (*JBL* 63 [1944] 207–53) suspects disturbance in the text and rearranges as follows: vv 19b, 18a, 18b, 19a, 18c (n.b. how v 19b links easily with the end of v 17). 1QM 11:7 has v 19 before v 18, and is further evidence of the corrupt state of the text.

18.b. 1QM 11:7 lacks the references to both "Edom" and "Seir," speaking only of "the enemy" as being his by conquest.

19.a. W. F. Albright (*JBL* 63 [1944] 207–53) inserts "his enemies" to make the clause a better length.

19.b. See on 22:36. The versions interpret as "towns" or "cities."

20.a. This could be read as "posterity" (cf. 23:10).

21.a. W. F. Albright (*JBL* 63 [1944] 207–53) inserts "Cain" in this clause.

22.a. G reads "he shall be to Beor a nest of trickery" reading קֵן עָרְמָה.

22.b. W. F. Albright (*JBL* 63 [1944] 207–53) eliminates "he" and translates "while" or "as long as."

22.c. NEB takes the root to be "to dwell" (ישׁב), while Albright (*JBL* 63 [1944] 207–53) reads שׁור "to behold," "while I behold the captives."

23.a. MT, Sam, and Vg give no indication as to whom this oracle is addressed. G reads "Og" (cf. Num 21:33–35). Albright (*JBL* 63 [1944] 207–53) suggests "Gog," the Gagaya of the Amarna tablets.

23.b.b. There is no parallel to this, and it may be that a clause is missing. Following Albright (*JBL* 63 [1944] 207–53) it is possible to read the text as אִים יְחִי מִשְׂמֹאל "the isles shall be gathered (or shall assemble) from/to the north" (cf. J. de Vaulx, 296 and NEB). This offers a good parallel with the first clause of v 24. As all would agree the Hebrew is very obscure. We have chosen to adhere as closely as possible to MT.

24.a. Sam and G connect this with the verb יצא "to go out." This is preferred by GKC § 93y. The reference to "Kittim" (Cyprus) gives "ships" a certain likelihood.

24.b. W. F. Albright (*JBL* 63 [1944] 207–53) emends to מִירְכַת יָם "from the farthest sea." J. de Vaulx (296) thinks "Kittim" a late interpretation. Vg speaks of "Italy" and Tg⁰ of "the Romans."

24.c. W. F. Albright (*JBL* 63 [1944] 207–53) originally proposed an emendation removing all reference to "Asshur," but later returned to a reading closer to MT (*Yahweh and the Gods of Canaan* [London: Athlone Press, 1968] 16n.40).

24.d. G, Syr, and Vg interpret as "the Hebrews."

Form/Structure/Setting

Earlier analysts were agreed that the Balaam stories, whatever their ultimate origin, had an integral place in JE, and that elements within them could be attributed to J and E respectively (cf. e.g. A. Dillmann, 135–67; H. Holzinger, 104–11; B. Baentsch, 589–92; H. Gressmann, 318 n.4; G. B. Gray, 309–13; A. H. McNeile, 123–24; O. Eissfeldt, *Hexateuch*, 183–89). Confidence about the locations of the division between J and E varied, but it was widely agreed that both were present. Apart from 22:1, which has stylistic features that associate it with the P itinerary, the chapters exhibit no traces of P.

Evidence of unevenness in the tradition was not hard to find. The episode of the speaking ass in 22:22–35 stands in tension with the preceding story in 22:1–21. In vv 22–35 Balaam is accompanied, not by the Moabite chiefs, but by two servants (v 22), and more importantly the angel seeks to prevent Balaam's journey (v 32), despite the fact that divine consent had previously been secured (v 20). After his confession (v 34) Balaam receives permission to continue (v 35), but this seems redundant in the light of v 20. The divine name criterion has to cope with difficult textual problems in this section, but in general Elohim seemed to be the norm in vv 2–21 (an indicator of the Elohist), and Yahweh in vv 22–35 (an indicator of the Yahwist). The fact that v 36 makes a natural sequel to v 20 tended to confirm the accuracy of the analysis, with E continuing in vv 36–41. The attempts of E. F. Sutcliffe (*Bib* 18 [1937] 439–42) to harmonize the traditions did not prove generally convincing. Further source indicators were widely accepted. With regard to 22:22–35 the only other example of a talking non-human is the serpent in Gen 3, another text widely attributed to J. Revelation by night, on the other hand, is characteristic of E (vv 8–9, 19). Some (e.g. Gray, 309–13) found further complications—a doublet in v 3a and v 3b, irrelevance in v 4b (the reference to Balak as "king" after v 2), and inconsistency in v 5 about Balaam's home. Gray concluded that the reference to Ammon (as he considered it) in v 5 was J, and the reference to the River was E. In J, then, Balaam is an Ammonite, and in E an Aramaen, and E is inclined to call the messengers "leaders" or "men." Gray therefore found significant J elements in vv 2–21—in vv 5 (minus "Pethor which is by the River") 6–7, 11, 17–18 and also in v 37.

In 23:1–30 it was customary to see E as the fundamental component. The "leaders" of Moab continue to function here (vv 6, 17) just as they had done in the E parts of 22:2–21. The text critical problems regarding the divine name were of course recognized, but it was easy enough to adopt the readings which gave "God" in the narrative parts, leaving a solitary "Yahweh" in the oracles (v 21). A link between 23:20 and 22:12 (E) confirmed the connection. It is in this part that the divine name criterion becomes particularly difficult, and that the danger of adopting readings to suit the theory becomes acute. As a matter of fact the MT narrative in Num 23 has "Yahweh" six times (vv 3, 5, 12, 16, 17, 26), and "Elohim" only once (v 4), with one indeterminate reference (v 15). Even G, which generally prefers "Elohim" has "Yahweh" in v 17.

It was customary to see in 24:1–19 the continuation of the J narrative. The oracles contained here have special reference to Judah (vv 4 [cf. Gen 49:9], 17–19) and are therefore naturally attributable to J. The divine name criterion favors J (vv 1, 11, 13 [twice]) with the possibility that the reference to "God" in v 2 should be rendered "divine spirit." The connection between 24.19 and 22:18 confirmed Gray's conclusion that J was present in 22:2–21. It was also suggested that in 24:1–2 Balaam realizes for the first time that it is Yahweh's purpose to bless Israel, in which event it cannot be the sequel to Num 23. The repetition of 23:23, 24 in 24:8, 9 could be taken as further indication that the two chapters are not from the same source. Gray recognized that there was not much further evidence for J in Num 24, and conceded that v 25 is closer to Gen 32:1–2 (E) than to Gen 18:33b (J).

There was general recognition that the last three oracles (24:20–24) are an interpolation, with the reference to Assyria (Asshur) indicating material that is no earlier than the second half of the seventh century.

Those scholars who did not accept the existence of the Elohist (e.g. W.

Rudolph, *Der "Elohist,"* 97–128) were inclined to recognize the tensions between 22:22–34 and the rest, but to attribute the whole to the Yahwist, who
here combines two separate Balaam stories. Unevenness in Num 23–24 could
be attributed on this basis to redactional activity and glossing.

The independence of the four Balaam oracles was widely recognized, and
the question of their age was regularly considered. Gray's conclusions represent a typical mainstream view. He suggested that the oracles were obviously
composed to fit into some story of Balaam (see 23:7–8, 18, 20; 24:3, 15),
though noted that only with the first two is a close structural connection
with the story to be found. He was critical of those who argued for a post-
exilic date, pointing out the spirit of national confidence which they exhibit,
and which he believed linked them most closely with the blessings of Jacob
(Gen 49) and Moses (Deut 33). He suggested that the reference to Agag in
24:7 was not a reliable indicator of an origin in the time of Saul, and that
though 24:18–19 best fit the time of David, they may not be original. He
argued that the poems envisage Israel as something more than Judah, and
are thus likely to be earlier than 721, the date of the fall of Samaria, and
possibly earlier also than the division of the kingdom. The allusions in 24:7,
17 seemed to presuppose the monarchy, so that a date earlier than David
was improbable.

Many modern analysts have sensed an artificiality in many of the attempts
to distinguish J from E in this section. It arises from a wooden approach to
the content and structure of the early narrative tradition, and the assumption
that anything attributable to that tradition must by definition be traceable
to J, to E, or to the redactor. This perception is not entirely new (see the
reference to Kalisch in Gray, 310), but the view that there is here an independent narrative tradition has gained ground in recent times. W. Rudolph (*Der
"Elohist,"* 127–28) traced it to premonarchic times (22:3–21, 36–41; 23:1–
26; 24:25), and argued that this had been combined with an equally old
but separate tradition, only part of which survives (22:22–34). Rudolph suggested that separate poems had been added—from the time of Saul (24:3b–
9) and David (24:15b–29). In his view the Yahwist, working during the period
of the united monarchy, put this material together, providing connecting
links in 23:27–28, 24:1–3a, 10–15a). A somewhat similar view is held by E.
Lipiński (*VT* 20 [1970] 445–50).

M. Noth (171–75) adopted a fairly traditional literary critical view of the
section, assigning 22:21–35; 23:28–24:19 to J and 22:41–23:26 to E. Secondary
editorial material in 23:27, 29–30 links the two versions together, while 24:20–
24 contains obvious additions. The real difficulties lie for Noth in 22:2–21.
Doublets and variants indicate the presence of J and E, but nothing more
as to their identity. Of more interest to Noth are the roots of the story. Its
setting is apparently in the area to the east of the northern end of the Dead
Sea, and Israel and Moab are evidently living as near neighbors. Noth believed
that Balaam and Balak were probably historical figures, and that the nucleus
of the story goes back to an early period when a man of God called Balaam
came from a distance, and, though not an Israelite, acknowledged Yahweh,
and pronounced words of blessing on Israel.

Doubts about the J/E distinction were stimulated by W. F. Albright (*JBL* 63 [1944] 207–53) who queried the usefulness of the divine name criterion in this section. J. Sturdy (157–58) has further observed that to divide the first two oracles from the second two misses the steadily increasing firmness and confidence of the prophecies of Balaam. It would be impossible, he suggests, to reverse them, and place the prophecies of Num 24 before those of Num 23. The story must therefore be essentially a continuous whole, the only significant exception being the ass material in 22:22–35. Sturdy suggests that this independent folktale was originally told about someone else, and that it has been transferred to Balaam and inserted here to provide added delay and tension. Its use heightens the sense of God's action in the story.

A. W. Jenks (*The Elohist*, 55–57) accepts Albright's view that the divine names are used so inconsistently as to be useless for distinguishing sources. He is convinced, however, of the presence of E—the theme of prophetic revelation in dream or vision being held sufficient to sustain this belief. The E tradition is found by Jenks in 22:2–21, 36–40; 22:41–23:26, the rest being additional. Any inconsistencies in 22:2–21, 36–40 are attributable to the growth of the tradition in E circles. At the very least Jenks has supplied persuasive linguistic reasons for suspecting that this material is essentially a unit of tradition.

In broad outline this is also the stance of L. M. von Pakozdy (*Von Ugarit nach Qumran*), but W. Gross (*Bileam*) offers a radically different kind of analysis which produces a number of originally distinct units which have no particular correspondence with the customary Pentateuchal sources. The main entities identified by Gross are:

1. A story on the theme of prophetic obedience (contained essentially in 22:4–21, 36–41; 23:1–7, 11–18, 25; 24:11, 25).

2. An account of how a Yahwistic prophet resists a foreign king and acts as God's mouthpiece instead (contained essentially in 23:26–30; 24:1–3, 10, 12–15).

3. The story of the ass, which originally was an account of the experience of a blind seer (22:22–35).

A further unit of tradition is recognized in 22:2–4, but the rest can be seen as editorial or other additions.

In the matter of the oracles there have been trends in more recent times favoring earlier datings. S. Mowinckel (*ZAW* 48 [1930] 233–71) had adopted a fairly conventional critical view, linking 24:3–9, 15–17 with the tenth century and 23:7–10, 18–24 with the late seventh century (the story itself he dated to the middle of the ninth century). The trend toward an earlier dating for the oracles begins primarily with W. F. Albright (*JBL* 63 [1944] 207–53), who argued for a twelfth century date, and for Balaam as historical and the originator of the sayings. D. Vetter (*Seherspruch und Segensschilderung*) has offered a new analysis of the oracles, and his linguistic investigations lead him to posit a formal category—the "seer saying," in which a blessing for the group is a key feature. Comparisons with the blessing elements in the patriarchal traditions lead Vetter to conclude that the transition from a family based society to that of the tribe led to the emergence of the seer. He is the one who acts in place of the head of the family as the giver of blessings. The original *Sitz-im-Leben,* Vetter thinks, is the preparation for battle among the tribes before the settlement in Palestine.

J. de Vaulx (256–65) has proposed an overall history of the Balaam tradition along the following lines:

1. Pre-Israelite legend. He thinks that many of the ritual procedures in the text reflect the methods of the Mesopotamian *baru* or Arab *kahin* diviners (see also J. Liver, *Eretz Israel* 3 [1954] 97–100). Balaam is thus a celebrated pre-Israelite figure, probably from the sanctuary at Beth Peor (see also S. Mowinckel, *ZAW* 48 [1930] 233–71), and the earliest legends, de Vaulx thinks, would have depicted him as honest and faithful to his god. The tribe of Gad, for a long time associated with the area, may have transmitted the tradition to Israel.

2. Prophetic oracles—Yahwistic (24:3–9, 15–19) and Elohistic (23:7–10, 18–24). In de Vaulx's opinion the structure of these texts is comparable to that of Sumero-Akkadian mantic texts, though the magical features of such oracles have been modified through their transmission in Israel, and the imprint of the tribal poem (Gen 49; Deut 33; Judg 5) has been left upon them. He thinks that the Yahwistic oracles do not presuppose any familiarity with the Balak story, and that they have obvious points in common with the blessings of Jacob in Gen 49:9–12. The prosperity and peace they reflect is that of the united monarchy. By contrast the Elohistic oracles are found to presuppose the Balak story, and in de Vaulx's opinion are best traced to the eighth century, and to the time of Jeroboam II. He finds particular points of correspondence with the blessing of Moses in Deut 33 (cf. Num 23:9//Deut 33:15; 23:22//Deut 33:17; 23:24//Deut 33:20; 23:9//Deut 33:28; 23:21–22//Deut 33:1–5). These oracles give in de Vaulx's opinion a fair expression of Elohistic theology, dissociating Israel from the magic of other peoples. In this general approach de Vaulx is close to S. Mowinckel (*ZAW* 48 [1930] 233–71) and O. Eissfeldt (*HUCA* 32 [1961] 179–90).

3. The Yahwistic traditions. These include in particular the story of the ass (22:22–34), but also the tendency to localize Balaam among the peoples of the south, and the description of the men as "messengers" rather than "leaders" (E). Balaam emerges in these traditions as a kind of *baru.*

4. The Elohistic story (22:2–21, 35–41; 23:1–30). As with the oracles de Vaulx sees this as an interpretation and amplification of the Yahwistic story. Balaam is now an important personage requiring more important ambassadors. He is less the magician charged to curse, and more the interpreter of the divine will (22:8; 23:3). He is thus much more a prophet of Yahweh (22:38; 23:5, 12, 16–17, 26; 24:13), and thinks of Yahweh as his God (22:18; cf. 22:8, 13, 19; 23:3). De Vaulx is noncommittal about the date, and is uncertain about Mowinckel's wish (*ZAW* 48 [1930] 233–71) to make it Josianic.

5. The redaction. This keeps the main outline and impact which the Elohistic adaptation has given to the ancient tradition, but de Vaulx suspects that the final form has some polemic against false prophecy, particularly in its use of the ass episode.

Uncertainty about the validity of the J/E distinction, and a proper caution about adopting readings to suit preconceived theories, have led to various attempts to make new sense of the divine name variations. P. Heinisch (88) had argued that the author lets Balaam use the name Yahweh, and that only in his first meeting with Balak (22:38) does he use Elohim. Balak by contrast uses Elohim, only using Yahweh after he has heard the name from Balaam (23:17; 24:11). Heinisch also argued that the author preferred Elohim in dream contexts (22:9–10, 12, 20) and moments of revelation (23:4; 24:2). This approach does not seriously engage with the textual problems. W. Rudolph (*Der 'Elohist,'* 127–28) sought to establish a pattern in which Elohim is used by the narrator and Yahweh only in the speeches of Balaam and Balak. This, as with the approach of Heinisch, could be as arbitrary as the classical J/E analyses. L. M. von Pakozdy (*Theologische Redaktionsarbeit*) and A. W. Jenks (*The Elohist*, 55–57) are inclined to attribute the textual confusion to the complex processes of redaction and the various theological interests to which the tradition has been exposed. Countless scribes and storytellers must have puzzled over the story of a foreign seer who is also Yahweh's prophet. Would such a prophet use Yahweh's personal name? The equivocation and uncertainty is reflected in the present state of the text. J. de Vaulx (256–65) sees in the use of Elohim a likely indicator of the pre-Israelite origins of the tradition.

Some Conclusions

It is important, as an initial step, to establish an attitude to the textual problems surrounding the use of the divine names. These must be resolved on their own merits, and not controlled by *a priori* theories of the literary analysis or of the author's intention. The difficulties need not be exaggerated. In poetry and prose together there are in all forty-five occurrences of the divine name. This includes the uncertain clause in 24:4 (see *Notes*) and omits 23:15 where the divine name in MT and Sam appears to be missing (see *Notes*). In twenty-nine of these the text seems secure, with MT, G and Sam in agreement. In 23:8 there is a simple reversal of clauses in G which need not concern us. In a further thirteen cases G witnesses to Elohim where Sam and MT witness to Yahweh, ten of these being found in the ass story. It seems best to regard this feature as an Elohistic tendency in G which is not original. Reluctance to use the personal name in later Judaism makes it unlikely that the Masoretic tradition would alter a previously Elohistic text. This view is supported by the fact that there is no example of Yahweh in G in opposition to an Elohim in MT. G exhibits therefore a marked preference for Elohim. If it is proper to talk of an "Elohising tendency" then the question naturally arises as to why G has failed to carry through the job in a thorough fashion; Yahweh survives in twelve places. It could be that G chooses to retain "Yahweh" in the *speech* of Balak and Balaam where it occurred in the textual tradition. This would explain G's Yahweh in 22:8, 13, 18, 19; 23:17; 24:11, 13. If the same holds good for the oracles then 23:8, 21; 24:6 would also be explained. This leaves only two places (22:34; 24:1) where G retains "Yahweh" in pure narrative. Both may be oversights, particularly the first, and in general there seems sufficient ground for suspecting an Elohising tendency in G, aimed at securing some consistency of usage. The *Translation* reflects this.

On the other hand where G has the powerful support of Sam against MT it deserves to be taken very seriously. This occurs in three places (22:22; 23:3, 26), and the combined witness of G and Sam is accordingly reflected in the *Translation.*

It is obvious that these textual considerations cannot be judged conclusive, but they do constitute a reasoned and consistent attitude to the text, and that is a prerequisite for proper literary analysis.

With respect to the tradition as a whole it seems reasonable to argue that there is a firm and coherent *Elohistic base narrative,* which has been amplified and elaborated by Yahwistic traditions, and perhaps by the Yahwist himself. This Elohistic story is preserved in all essentials in 22:2–7, 9–12, 20, 36, 38–39; 23:1–4, 7–11, 18–30; 24:2–10, 15–19, 25. The key components of the story are as follows:

1. Balak, king of Moab, encourages the Midianites to join him in a deputation to Balaam, the Mesopotamian seer, with a view to securing a curse on the Israelites (22:2–7).

2. God consults with Balaam, and forbids him to go (22:9–12).

3. In the night God resolves to let Balaam go, on condition that he speaks only the word given (22:20).

4. Balak meets Balaam, and is reminded that only the word given can be spoken. They go to Kiriath-huzoth (22:36, 38–39).

5. Balaam and Balak offer sacrifices, and God meets Balaam (23:1–4).

6. Balaam utters the first oracle, to the dismay of Balak (23:7–11).

7. Balaam utters the second oracle, reminding Balak that he must speak God's word (23:18–26).

8. Balak proposes another location, and further sacrifices are offered (23:27–30).

9. Balaam, inspired by God's spirit, utters the third oracle, provoking Balak's anger (23:27–30).

10. Balaam is prompted to deliver the fourth oracle (24:15–19).

11. Balaam and Balak then go their separate ways (24:25).

Essentially this is a coherent and satisfying story, though the effects of the redaction mean that it may not read entirely smoothly in its present form. To treat it as a whole does justice to the development evident in the four oracles, as observed by Sturdy (157–58). It also makes sense of the development in Balak's attitude to the oracles—from astonishment (23:11), to irritation (23:25), to outright anger (24:10). In describing the story as Elohistic (i.e. in its use of "Elohim") there is no particular reason for linking it with a source E. The use of Elohim may indicate, as in Num 21:4–9, some non-Israelite or pre-Israelite roots for the story, and it may have been preserved in prophetic circles (cf. the Moabite material in Judg 3:12–30). There is no substantial reason for supposing that it was at any time part of a continuous E narrative. The age of the tradition at this stage in its development is difficult to judge, but it may perhaps be assigned to the period of the divided monarchy.

Even if this is correct it has to be recognized that there is an earlier tradition of Balaam and Balak (cf. Mic 6:5). As de Vaulx suggests Balaam was probably a familiar figure in Transjordanian tradition—the oracles suggest he was Syrian—and it seems likely that the Elohistic story has made him into a Mesopotamian seer. It could be that the pre-Elohistic form of the tradition still survives in vv 3, 4ab[a]. Here Moab is the subject, and an anti-Israelite alliance is proposed with Midian. The elders of Moab and Midian approach Balaam for help (v 7ab[a]), but God refuses to allow it (v 12). The suggestion made by Baentsch (592–95) and others that Midian is a late interpolation is unlikely; if that were the case there would surely have been a more sustained involvement of Midian in the rest of the story. It is the Elohistic story which introduces Balak, thereby eclipsing but not eliminating the elders who become Balak's messengers. This provided the Elohistic author with a way of incorporating the four pro-Israelite oracles, which were also linked in tradition with the name of Balaam.

The date and provenance of the oracles remains obscure, but they are probably old. As W. F. Albright recognized (*JBL* 63 [1944] 207–53) the orthographic evidence does not demand that they be twelfth or thirteenth century, but makes it unlikely that they are later than the tenth or early ninth century. The view of de Vaulx that the oracles in Num 24 belong to the period of the united monarchy seems likely, and also his opinion, along with Mowinckel, that those in Num 23 are in some way dependent on them, though he may be dating these later oracles too late. The Syrian origin of Balaam is attested in 23:7, and this is a further pointer to the original independence of the oracles. They are of the same genre as the tribal blessings in Gen 49 and Deut 33—cf. also Gen 27:27b–29 (for close comparison Num 23:9//Deut 33:28; 23:22//Deut 33:17; 24:9//Gen 27:29). It may have been the Elohistic author who first linked the oracles with the tradition of the elders of Moab and Midian, building his larger story around them.

The Yahwistic components appear to be an accretion to the Elohistic story. They have sufficient common characteristics to warrant an analysis along Elohistic/Yahwistic lines, and those scholars who attempt radically new analyses are inclined to destroy the essential coherence of the Elohistic base narrative. The Yahwistic material can be set out as follows: 22:8, 13–19, 21–35, 37, 40–41; 23:5–6, 12–17; 24:1, 11–14, 20–24. This material is distinguished primarily by its use of the divine name "Yahweh," and by its description of the messengers as "leaders." In terms of the view we have chosen regarding the early narrative tradition this may very well be the Yahwist's own adaptation of the story. His concern is to:

1. Emphasize that it is *Yahweh* who controls events, and that Balaam is aware of this and sensitive to the divine word (22:8, 13, 19; 23:5–6, 12, 16).

2. Emphasize the importance of the occasion through a second deputation to Balaam involving important personnel (22:14–16).

3. Emphasize the worthiness of Balaam. Not only is he sensitive to Yahweh's word, but he also recognizes Yahweh as *his* God (22:18), and he refuses to be enticed into faithlessness by the promise of wealth and honor (22:16–18, 37; 24:11–14). In 24:1 he reacts properly to the first two oracles.

4. Emphasize that right from the outset Yahweh is against the evil inten-

tions of men, and will not let them prosper. This is achieved by the inclusion of the popular story about the ass. Whether this was traditionally associated with Balaam or whether the Yahwist himself so links it cannot now be determined. The story also helps to show that there is a basic consistency in Yahweh's attitude. It may appear that v 20 as compared with v 12 (both in the Elohistic story) constitutes a change of mind on his part. "Not so," says the Yahwist. At the deepest level he is opposed to the whole enterprise, and the permission to go, repeated in v 35, must be understood in that light. It is fair to add that the ass story does not depict Balaam in a seriously disadvantageous light. The popular story was probably highly satirical, with its account of how an ass perceives the angel while the so-called prophet remains blind. Even the beasts are more perceptive than he! In the Yahwist's hands however Balaam is shown as receiving divine revelation and taking the role of the true penitent (vv 31–34), as well as receiving a true commission (v 35).

5. Multiply the ritual procedures which are intended to secure the curse (22:40), and to associate these with the false worship of Baal (22:41). The procedures are also emphasized by Balak's attempts to secure better success from different places (23:13–15). The Elohistic narrative does this between the second and third oracles (23:27–28), but the Yahwist introduces another move between the first and second.

6. Emphasize that Balaam's prophetic ministry covered other topics relevant to the Yahwist's time, thereby revealing Balaam to be a true prophet (24:20–24). J. de Vaulx (295–97) argues persuasively that originally these oracles referred to peoples settled in the south of Palestine—the Amalekites, the Asshurim of Gen 25:3, 18; Josh 13:2; 2 Sam 2:9; Ps 83:9, and possibly Hos 5:13; 10:6, the Sea Peoples (Philistines), the Kenites, and the Hebrews of 1 Sam 14:21. He also thinks that with the passage of time the oracles have been reinterpreted and adapted to provide new meanings for new situations. This may well explain why some shcolars (e.g. M. Noth, 194) believe parts of the oracles to be very late, traceable perhaps to the Greek period. It does seem likely that the Yahwist had a hand in this process, and it may be he who first associates them with the ministry of Balaam. As an author working in the seventh century he may also have understood the references to Asshur as applicable to Assyria. For further discussion of these oracles see *Comment*.

It would appear therefore that the tendency of the Yahwistic material is to heighten and emphasize elements inherent in the Elohistic base narrative. This supports the view that the Yahwistic material is the accretion rather than the reverse. What the Yahwist here presents is yet more material to give substance to his Transjordanian journey. It may be that he was encouraged in this by Mic 6:5 which juxtaposes Exodus, Balaam traditions, and a journey from Shittim to Gilgal. There is no reason for supposing that this verse necessarily presupposes Num 21–24 in their present form, but the juxtaposition may well have fostered the idea of a Transjordanian journey. In particular the Yahwist has drawn on Elohistic material which derives ultimately from the traditions of the Transjordanian tribes.

The significance of the Aramaic inscriptions found at Tell Deir-ʿAlla in

Jordan is not easy to assess (see J. Hoftijzer, *BA* 39 [1976] 11–17). They tell of a prophet Balaam who is "seer of the gods," and who receives a message from them in the night, apparently urging the godless to repent. There is also a series of curses which is probably to be attributed to him. The text is a sixth century work. The inscription seems to give general support to the impression that the roots of the Balaam tradition are in Transjordan, and that he is probably a figure of the first millenium rather than the second.

The only priestly element in the whole section is the itinerary note in 22:1.

Comment

22:1. בערבות מואב—"in the plains of Moab," i.e. the fertile area to the east of the Jordan, and immediately to the north of the Dead Sea.'

Jericho is the modern Tell es-Sultan. For information about excavations there see G. Foerster and G. Bacchi, "Jericho," *Encyclopedia of Archaeological Excavations in the Holy Land.* ed. M. Avi-Yonah (London: Oxford University Press, 1976).

3. Older commentators were inclined to see a literary doublet in the repetition. As J. Sturdy (160) suggests, the repetition is probably emphatic, as in much Hebrew poetry.

4. The "elders of Midian" are mentioned only here and in v 7. They were probably more prominent in earlier stages of the tradition (see *Form/Structure/Setting*).

5. There is a king of Edom named Bela son of Beor in Gen 36:32, and this has led some to favor an Edomite origin for Balaam (e.g. S. Mowinckel, *ZAW* 48 [1930] 233–71; A. H. Sayce, *ExpTim* 15 [1903/4] 405–6). The grounds for supposing an identification of Bela and Balaam are not strong, and the theory has no further support in the text.

Pethor is probably to be equated with Pitru on the west bank of the Euphrates, some twelve miles south of Carchemish. It is mentioned in Assyrian sources (cf. also Deut 23:5). The "River" is a reference to the Euphrates.

On "the land of the Amavites" see *Notes*, and particularly A. S. Yahuda, *JBL* 64 (1945) 547–51. A short journey is not necessarily implied by any part of the story, and so the reading "Ammon" (favored by H. Holzinger, 104–5; G. B. Gray, 326 and others) is not necessary.

6. The enterprise implies a faith in the automatic power of the spoken word in the mouth of the seer or prophet.

7. קסמים "fees for divination," payment for such services apparently being the norm (cf. e.g. 1 Sam 9:7–8).

15. Balak believes that Balaam's support can be bought—with greater honors and financial rewards.

20. For other appearances by night see Job 4:12–16; Zech 1:8.

22. מלאך יהוה "the angel of Yahweh." According to N. H. Snaith (288–89) the "angel" constitutes a stage in the development of the theory of divine transcendence when it was no longer acceptable to think of God as speaking to man directly. On the other hand, as Snaith himself observes, there are

various narratives where "Yahweh" and the "angel of Yahweh" occur apparently interchangeably (Gen 16:7–12; Judg 6:11–24; Zech 3:1–5). That being so it may be asked why "Yahweh" survives at all in such narratives. It seems likely that Israel's rejection of pictorial representations of deity meant that manifestations of Yahweh could only occur through messengers in human form. Constant interchange in stories (between Yahweh and his angel) may have been thought desirable and pursued deliberately. The privilege of "seeing God" is granted to very few, and on very unusual occasions (Exod 24:9; Ezek 1:26).

22. לשטן לו "as his adversary." In later texts this becomes a personal name for a divine official who tests the faithful (Job 1:6–12; 2:1–7), who acts as prosecutor (Zech 3:1), and who becomes ultimately the enemy of Israel (1 Chr 21:1). It is a short step from this to Satan as the personification of cosmic forces of evil familiar in apocalyptic literature.

22. The two servants are identified in the Palestinian Targum as Jannes and Jambres (cf. 2 Tim 3:8). The lack of reference to Balak's messengers is an indication of the ass story's independence.

24. משעול "a narrow place," with the root meaning "to be deep," and probably implying a narrow place between two walls. G assumes that the ass is in a field in a deep furrow.

28. The only other example of a communicative creature in the OT is the snake in Gen 3:1. It is a common feature of folklore.

32. ירט "perverse," though the Hebrew may mean "precipitate." The enterprise in which Balaam is engaged is a reckless one. It is possible that the original folk tale told of Balaam's return, as this divine remark and Balaam's penitence (v 34) might suggest.

36. On "Ar of Moab" see *Comment* on Num 21:15 (cf. Num 21:28). The Arnon is here depicted as Moab's northern frontier.

39. Kiriath-huzoth means "the town of streets." Its location is unknown.

40. The meaning may be that Balak slaughters the animals in preparation for the forthcoming sacrifice.

41. Bamoth-baal is literally "the high places of Baal," possibly the Bamoth of Num 21:19 (see *Comment* on Num 21:19).

41. קצה "nearest," literally "end." The rendering "nearest" understands "end" to signify one extremity or wing of the Israelite host (RSV). The word might mean the full extremity, hence "the full extent" of NEB (see also 23:13).

23:1. The choice of "seven" is not explained. The number has sacred significance in a wide variety of religious contexts and cultures.

3. שפי "a bare height" (see *Notes*). Balaam's withdrawal is based on the hope that God will meet him. This occurs in v 4, but no hint is given of how the meeting occurs or of what it consists, though there is an allusion to some kind of divination in 24:1. The Yahwist is only interested in the fact that Balaam is a prophet, and that Yahweh puts a word in his mouth.

7. וישא משלו "uttered his oracle" (NEB). The older renderings, "parable" (RV) or "discourse" (RSV), recognize the fact that משל has close links with wisdom; see *Comment* on 21:27. This association stems from the fact that the word can readily be used of pithy sayings constructed in parallel lines, and involving some kind of comparison. The use of the word in association

with Balaam's sayings suggests that it need not be limited to wisdom, and that a wide variety of artistically structured poems might be so called. In the context "oracle" seems appropriate.

7. Aram (see *Notes*) is Syria, and the eastern mountains are the ranges of the Syrian desert (cf. Jer 49:28; Ezek 25:4, 10). The location is vague; it is the Elohistic author who fixes Balaam's place of residence as Pethor (22:5). A. S. Yahuda (*JBL* 64 [1945] 547–51) prefers to translate "mountains of the Qedem land." He points out that the children of Qedem are often mentioned as allies of Midian and Amalek (Judg 6:3, 33; 7:12; 8:10), and he thinks that in Jer 49:28; Ezek 25:4, 10; Job 1:3 they are Bedouin.

9. This part of the poem is reminiscent of the blessing of Moses in Deut 33:28. Israel's solitary (or perhaps "secure" existence; cf. the use of בדד in Jer 49:31; Ps 4:9 [Heb.]) existence is a consequence of her sense of unique commitment to Yahweh. The last clause might be taken to mean that Israel does not conspire against the nations, and therefore poses no threat which calls for a curse (cf. J. H. Hertz, *ExpTim* 45 [1933/4] 524). It may be nevertheless that 23:9b is intended to contrast sharply with 23:10a. Israel's insignificant beginnings are very different from the ultimate divine purpose.

10. עפר "dust," apparently a metaphorical reference to Israel's large numbers. According to S. Gevirtz (*Patterns in the Early Poetry of Israel* [Chicago: Chicago University Press, 1963]64) collecting the dust from the feet of a victim to be cursed or bewitched was a part of Akkadian curse rituals. It still seems likely that the Israelite storytellers understood the allusion to be to Israel's numerical strength (cf. Gen 13:16; 28:14).

In the final couplet Balaam appears to aspire to the blessing that is Israel's (cf. A. Guillaume, *VT* 12 [1962] 335–37). W. F. Albright (*JBL* 63 [1944] 207–53) thinks there is a misunderstood oath here.

13. Balak intends to persist until a favorable oracle is obtained. The meaning is not clear (see *Comment* on 22:41). It may be that Balak fears that a sight of all Israel would lead to an unfavorable oracle.

14. שדה צפים "field of Zophim" or "field of the watchers" (NEB). The site is unknown. For Pisgah see *Comment* on Num 21:20.

18. קום "rise," a literal rendering of a word which here probably means "pay attention." D. Vetter (*Seherspruch*, 19) sees wisdom elements in the verse (see also *Comment* on 23:7).

19. בן־אדם "a son of man"; i.e. "a mere mortal". (cf. Ps 8:5). For the idea that God will not change his mind see 1 Sam 15:29. There are various stories where it is asserted that a divine intention is altered. This tends to occur in strongly anthropomorphic texts (e.g. Gen 6:6) or in response to prophetic intercession (e.g. Exod 32:14; Amos 7:3, 6). In general the larger purpose of God in the OT is unchanged and unchanging.

20. לקחתי "I received a command," literally "I have taken." W. F. Albright (*JBL* 63 [1944]207–53) suggests reading "I have been brought" (see also *Notes*), but this seems unnecessary.

21. The subject of the first clause could be impersonal—"no one has discovered. . . ."

21. עמל/און "iniquity"/"mischief." These renderings conflict with the tradition of disaffection in the wilderness and it might be possible to translate

"misfortune"/"trouble." On the other hand a reference to Israel's faithfulness would fit very well the massively confident spirit of the Balaam oracles. The provenance of the oracles (see *Form/Structure/Setting*) means that a tension with the disaffection tradition is not a difficulty. S. Mowinckel (*ZAW* 48 [1930] 233–71) preferred to translate the words as "sorcery"/"divination," but these ideas emerge in 23:23, and it is not certain that they are intended here.

21. ותרועת מלך בו "acclaimed in him as king." תרועה is used of the sound of the trumpet, or of battle shouts, as well as the acclamation of the king. There is a strong expression here of the conviction that Yahweh alone is Israel's king.

22. תועפת ראם "horns of a wild ox"—an allusion to the ancestors of domestic cattle, now extinct (cf. Deut 33:17). The point of the metaphor may be "strength" (cf. G) or "height" (cf. Tg), but "horns" are also a symbol of royalty (Ps 89:17), and therefore "majesty" may also be in mind.

23. קסם/נחש "enchantment"/"divination." These words apparently indicate two techniques of consulting God. According to N. H. Snaith (295–96) נחש has to do with the observation of the flight of birds or of omens generally, while קסם has to do with the casting of lots (e.g. by arrows; Ezek 21:26).

Given the context "against Israel" seems preferable to "in Israel" (see *Notes*). Such techniques were considered illegal in Israel according to Deut 18:11. Though "against" seems best there may also be some disparagement of the techniques.

24. For this image cf. Mic 5:8.

27. Balak persists, hoping that yet another location will secure the desired result.

28. ראש הפעור "the top of Peor, overlooking the desert"; a site probably close to the sanctuary of Baal of Peor (Num 25:3, 5). "The desert" (or Jeshimon) is probably a general reference to the lower Jordan valley. The word is used of other desert regions in 1 Sam 23:19 (cf. also Num 21:20).

29–30. The same procedures are adopted by Balaam (cf. 23:1–2).

24:1. The Yahwist assumes that Balaam had in fact used divinatory techniques, though there is no hint of this in the Elohistic story. The assumption is based perhaps on 23:23.

The significance of the reference to the wilderness is not clear. It may be that since the worship of Yahweh has its roots in the wilderness Balaam is now looking toward the true source of inspiration.

2. רוח אלהים "the spirit of God." The empowering divine "spirit" has not previously been mentioned in the story. It inspires judges (Judg 14:6) and kings (1 Sam 11:6), as well as prophets (Num 11:17; 1 Sam 10:10). In the earliest OT texts it is generally a temporary endowment for a specific task. In the Elohistic story it provides an insight into the real source and mode of prophetic speech.

3. נאם "the word of," a typical expression of the third and fourth oracles, occurring six times in all (cf. also 2 Sam 23:1; Isa 1:24; Ps 110:1). It is very frequent in prophetic oracles in the phrase "says Yahweh."

3. שתם העין "whose sight is clear" (see *Notes*). The phrase is difficult. According to N. H. Snaith (297) the root is used of boring a hole through the seal of a wine-jar. A tube could be inserted through which the wine

would be drawn. The idea "clear" (NEB) in the sense of unobstructed contact with God seems as appropriate as any.

4. שדי "the Almighty," an ancient divine name (cf. Gen 49:25), adapted later by P (Gen 17:1). The real meaning is unknown. Some associate the word with the Akkadian *šādū* "mountain," in which event Shaddai may originally have been thought of as god of a particular peak or of mountains in general. Others have associated the name with the root "to pour forth," and hence perhaps with the giving of rain. N. Walker ("A New Interpretation of the Divine Name 'Shaddai,'" *ZAW* 72 [1960] 64–66) links the name with *SHAZU*, one of Marduk's names, and suggests that it means "omniscient." The word occurs most commonly in the book of Job. Its presence in the Joseph blessing (Gen 49:25) suggests that it may have been introduced to Israel by the Joseph tribes.

4. נפל "falling down." G interprets this to mean "to fall asleep," and thus into a prophetic trance in which the prophetic eye is "uncovered." The meaning appears to indicate a trance rather than natural sleep. NEB "who with staring eyes sees in a trance."

6. נחלים "rows of palms" or "valleys." The former seems a better parallel to the "gardens" of the next clause. See also *Notes*.

6. אהלים "aloes" (see *Notes*). N. H. Snaith (298) understands this as the eaglewood native to parts of India and Malaya. Like the "cedar" of the next clause it is capable of giving off a pleasant smell. Snaith is right to resist emendations which seek a Palestinian allusion, because the author is deliberately seeking exotic metaphors. Cedars do not in fact grow beside water, a further indication that the allusions are exotic and/or poetic (cf. Ps 45:8; Prov 7:17 for further reference to "aloes").

7. The first two lines are difficult (see *Notes*). There is apparently a reference to irrigation buckets and to a well-watered land. The general meaning that Israel is to be prosperous and fruitful seems clear. This fruitfulness will encompass her crops, her flocks and herds, and her population.

7. אגג "Agag" (see *Notes*). Agag is mentioned in 1 Sam 15:32–33 as the Amalekite king slain by Saul. A reference to this king is probably intended here. He and his kingdom are a symbol of power.

8. See *Comment* on 23:22.

9. For the image of the lion cf. 23:24 in the second oracle. For the conclusion of the oracle cf. Gen 27:29.

10. ויספק את-רפיו "struck his hands together," apparently a sign of contempt or derision (cf. Lam 2:15; Job 27:23).

14. באחרית הימים "in the days to come." For a study of the pre-exilic use of this phrase see E. Lipiński (*VT* 20 [1970] 445–50).

15–16. The opening of the fourth oracle is similar to the opening of the third, but there is an additional clause referring to עליון "the Most High." This deity was evidently associated with Jerusalem (Gen 14:18–22), and may have been the manifestation of El worshiped at the pre-Israelite sanctuary there (cf. Deut 32:8; Pss 18:14; 78:17, 35, 56; 83:19).

17. On the first two clauses see *Notes*. The meaning seems to be that this is a prophecy for the future. Balaam is speaking of Israel not as she is now but as she will be.

17. כוכב "a star" cf. Isa 14:12 where this is a metaphor for a king, as should probably be understood here.

17. שבט "a scepter." NEB renders "comet," so retaining in English an astronomic parallel with "star."

On the final couplet see *Notes*. It is customary to see here a reference to David's Transjordanian expeditions. Among recent commentators K. Seybold (*TZ* 29 [1973] 1–19) argues that a specific purpose of this fourth oracle is to present David as a successful conqueror, like the Pharaohs of Egypt. Whether or not this is a primary purpose it seems likely that a reference to David is intended. Moab and Edom were certainly a part of his empire.

18. Seir (see *Notes*) is the ancient capital of Edom (Judg 5:4) in the opinion of N. H. Snaith (300), but the allusion here may be intended as a simple synonym for Edom. More specifically Seir denotes the chief mountain range in Edom (cf. Deut 33:2).

19. See *Notes*. Ar in Moab is first mentioned in Num 21:28 (see *Comment*).

20. The Amalekites are described by J. Sturdy (180) as a confederacy of nomadic tribes, operating in the deserts to the southeast of Palestine. According to Pentateuchal tradition they fought with Israel at an early stage on the journey from Egypt (Exod 17:8–16), and they remained hated enemies through to Davidic times (cf. e.g. 1 Sam 15:1–3). They are rarely mentioned thereafter, and this suggests that this oracle may be relatively early.

20. ראשית גוים "the first of the nations." In what sense Amalek was "first" is unclear. It could be an allusion to her strength, or more probably to a supposition that she was one of the most ancient.

21. The Kenites occupied the southeastern part of the hill country of Judah, and were closely related to the Israelites (cf. Judg 4:11 and the discussion of Num 10:29–32). There is also Saul's friendly warning in 1 Sam 15:6, and David's good relationship with them in 1 Sam 30:29. W. F. Albright (*Yahweh and the Gods of Canaan* [London: Athlone Press, 1968]41) finds evidence for the supposition that they were metal workers.

21. קנך "your nest," a play on the name "Kenite." This is probably a reference to their place of origin in the mountainous parts of Midian or the Sinai peninsula.

22. Cain (cf. Gen 4:1–17) is assumed to be the ancestor of the Kenites.

22. לבער "shall be devastated." W. F. Albright (*JBL* 63 [1944] 207–53) translated as "for burning" and understood the allusion as a play on the word "kenite" meaning "metal worker" or "smith."

On the second clause see *Notes*, and the suggestions of J. de Vaulx under *Form/Structure/Setting*. An original reference to the local tribe of Gen 25:3 may have been reinterpreted in terms of Assyria, the dominant power in the eighth century.

23. The text is particularly difficult (see *Notes*).

24. Kittim refers originally to Kition, a town in Cyprus, and can be used of Cyprus itself, or of any maritime people to the west of Palestine (cf. e.g. Jer 2:10; Ezek 27:6). In later texts (e.g. Dan 11:30), and often in intertestamental literature, it is used of the Romans.

Asshur is probably a reference to the Assyrians (cf. 24:22), but there is no known event to which the oracle might be alluding.

Eber may be the ancestor of the Hebrews cited in Gen 10:21–25.

It seems best to follow de Vaulx and to see the original perspective of the oracle in terms of the invasions by the Sea Peoples in the thirteenth and twelfth centuries. The passage of time and the ebb and flow of political fortunes yielded new meanings, some of which have affected the present state of the text.

Explanation

This lengthy section tells of a determined attempt on the part of Balak, the Moabite king, to frustrate Israel's triumphant progress. He seeks the assistance of a Mesopotamian diviner, Balaam, with a view to securing a divine curse on the interlopers. Balaam is depicted from the outset as a true prophet of Yahweh who is bound to declare the true word of God. He is reminded of Yahweh's fundamental hostility to the exercise by the intervention of the angel and the perceptive ass. In the event Balak is the frustrated party. On four occasions Balaam prophesies, and each time the divine word is one of blessing on Israel. In brief, Israel is to be countless as the dust, fierce as a lionness, prosperous, and the destroyer of Moabite and Edomite power. Throughout the story there are rich ironies—in the perceptiveness of the ass, and in the way the stratagems of the Moabite king rebound on his own head. The story ends with a few short oracles relating to other peoples, and with the departure of Balak and Balaam from Israel's path.

The story is evidently not a priestly tradition. The author of Numbers works it into his itinerary, locating the incident in the plains of Moab (22:1), but otherwise the story is entirely free of distinctive priestly features. It has been customary to assume that the story formed part of the JE tradition, though this should not be taken for granted. The priestly author himself could have drawn the story in from an independent source as an encouragement to exiles profoundly aware of the apparent power of other political and religious forces. On the other hand there are reasons for thinking the story did form part of what we have called the Yahwistic redaction. We have suggested that the Yahwist needed filler material for his Transjordanian journey, and this story fits his purpose well. The spirit of triumphant advance, foreshadowed in Num 21:1–3, and continued in Num 21:10–35 is maintained here. The story is essentially a celebration of the powerlessness of enemies to hinder Israel, and corresponds well enough with the confident spirit of Josianic times. There are also some thematic links which associate the oracles with the framework of the Yahwistic narrative as it emerges in Gen 12:1–3.

The promise made to Abram includes a land, a great nation, blessing, a great name, well-being for those who bless Abram and misfortune for those who curse, and well-being for all nations in Abram's blessing. There is sufficient correspondence between this and the oracles of Balaam to suggest that the promise to Abram is in some measure a commentary on the oracles. To require an exact correspondence would be to misunderstand the nature of interpretative commentary. The demise of Assyrian power during Josiah's reign created a vacuum which that king was evidently able to exploit, and which allowed a resurgent and aggressive Yahwism to flourish. The Yahwist himself is part of this movement, and the incorporation of the Balaam material into the traditions of a united Israel is entirely natural. His chief concerns are to emphasize that it is indeed Yahweh who controls events, and that Balaam is a true prophet of Yahweh. His major textual contribution to the tradition is apparently the story of the ass. This is probably a popular story, which may not originally have been linked with Balaam, but in its present form and context it serves the Yahwist's purpose well (see *Form/Structure/Setting*).

The bulk of the tradition appears to have been Elohistic, originally independent, and incorporated by the Yahwist. There is no strong reason for supposing that this Elohistic story was part of a parallel wilderness journey to be designated E. All the indications are that the Transjordanian journey in the Yahwist's account is composed of filler material of varied type and origin. It may be that the Elohistic story originated in prophetic circles, among those groups which must have provided material on the deliverers for the book of Judges, and on Elijah and Elisha and other "men of God." Balaam is here depicted as a Mesopotamian seer. He is ultimately allowed by God to go with the messengers, and in the event utters blessings rather than curses on the Israelites. The story is a dramatic vindication of the independence of the prophetic spirit over against kings, and of the invincibility of Israel under God. The roots of the story may lie close to those of the traditions of Ehud and the Moabite oppression (Judg 3:12–30). The reason for making the vague reference to Aram (23:7) into something much more precise— Pethor (22:5) is not entirely clear. It may be that that city, like other parts of Mesopotamia, was renowned for its divinatory expertise, in which event the effect is to make Balak seek the best assistance available.

It is possible that the Elohistic author worked with an earlier form of the tradition in which the elders of Moab and Midian, prompted by Moab, seek Balaam's help against Israel. The god of Balaam is against such an undertaking and forbids it (22:3–4ab,ª 7ab,ª 12). It is perhaps the Elohistic author who names Balak as the king of Moab, and who develops the story so as to work in the four oracles of Balaam of Aram. The early tradition which included Midian and the oracles themselves may be traced perhaps to the period of the united monarchy.

With the passage of time the tradition of Balaam undergoes a number of other remarkable developments. The favorable element in the picture of Balaam, which emerges at its strongest in the Yahwist's story, begins to fade, and the antagonism to all things anti-Israelite is highlighted. In Deuteronomy the tradition is used as a ground for excluding Moabites from the Yahwistic community (Deut 23:3–6). Balaam himself begins to emerge as hostile to Israel, and Yahweh refuses to hear him (Deut 23:5; Josh 24:10). The priestly author of Numbers extends this process in Num 31:16, implicating Balaam in the seduction and apostasy of Num 25:1–18. As one of the enemies of Israel he is killed (Num 31:8; Josh 13:22). From this basis it was open to later Jewish exegesis, from the Targums to the Talmud, to enlarge upon the sins of Balaam. He becomes a man moved by cupidity and vanity, the bad man of history, almost above all other. Early Christian interpretation follows a similar pattern, seeing in Balaam the forefather of the libertines or Nicolaitans who appear to have gained influence in the Christian communities (2 Pet 2:15–16; Jude 11; Rev 2:14). At a later stage Origen (Hom 13:7) was able to find in him the ancestor of the Magi from the east who saw the star which heralded the birth of Jesus (Num 24:17; Matt 2:2). Interpretation was not necessarily forced into a single path. It is true that study of the pre-literary history of a tradition is often speculative in some respects but the subsequent history of the Balaam tradition is an indication that the enterprise and many of its procedures are justified.

In summary the story is a powerful celebration of the certainty of Israel's success. Her triumphant progress to the land of promise cannot be halted or even hindered by the stratagems of adversaries. Yahweh's control is such that the worst they can do turns to a positive good in Israel's favor. This overwhelming confidence in the success of God's good purpose persists in Christian theology. The coming of God's rule to the world he made cannot be hindered or turned aside by the scheming and devices of men.

Apostasy at Shittim (25:1-18)

Bibliography

Henke, O. "Zur Lage von Beth Peor." *ZDPV* 75 (1959) 155–63. **Jaroš, K.** *Die Stellung des Elohisten zur kanaanäischen Religion.* Freiburg: Vandenhoeck and Ruprecht, 1974. **Mendenhall, G. E.** "The Incident at Beth Baal Peor (Nu. 25)." *The Tenth Generation* (Baltimore: Johns Hopkins University Press, 1973) 105–121. **Reif, S. C.** "What enraged Phinehas? A Study of Numbers 25:8." *JBL* 90 (1971) 100–6.

Translation

[1] And Israel stayed at Shittim, and the people began to have sexual relations [a] with the Moabite women. [2] And these invited the people to the sacrifices of their gods. And the people ate, and bowed down to their gods. [3] And Israel yoked himself to Baal of Peor. And the anger of Yahweh was kindled against Israel. [4] And Yahweh said to Moses, "Take all the leaders [a] of the people, and hang them in the sun before Yahweh, [b] that the fierce anger of Yahweh may turn away from Israel." [5] And Moses said to the judges [a] of Israel, "Put to death, each of you, those of his men who have yoked themselves to Baal of Peor."

[6] And behold, one of the people of Israel came and [a] brought a Midianite woman to his family, [a] in the sight of Moses and the whole congregation of the people of Israel, while they were weeping at the door of the Tent of Meeting. [7] And Phinehas son of Eleazar son of Aaron the priest saw it, and he rose up from the middle of the congregation and took a spear in his hand. [8] And he went after the man of Israel into the shrine, and pierced both of them through, the man of Israel and the woman, in her shrine. [a] So the plague was stopped from the people of Israel. [9] And those that died by the plague were twenty-four thousand. [a]

[10] And Yahweh spoke to Moses, saying, [11] "Phinehas son of Eleazar son of Aaron the priest has turned my wrath away from the people of Israel. He was zealous with my zeal among them, so that I did not consume the people of Israel in my zeal. [12] Therefore say, 'Behold, I give to him my covenant of peace. [a] [13] And it shall be to him, and to his descendants after him, the covenant of a perpetual priesthood, because he was zealous for his God, and made atonement [a] for the people of Israel.' "

[14] And the name of the dead man of Israel, who was killed with the Midianite woman, was Zimri son of Salu, a leader of a fathers' house of the Simeonites. [15] And the name of the Midianite woman who was killed was Cozbi daughter of Zur, who was the head of a clan (that is, of a fathers' house) [a] in Midian.

[16] And Yahweh spoke to Moses, saying, [17] "Harass the Midianites, and smite them, [18] for they have harassed you with their wiles, with which they beguiled you in the affair of Peor, and in the affair of Cozbi, the daughter of the Midianite leader, their sister, who was killed at the time of the plague which took place on account of Peor."

Notes

1.a. G has read ויחל (cf. Lev 19:29; 21:9) "profaned themselves."

4.a. *BHS* conjectures that the root רשע "wicked" may be intended rather than ראש "head."

4.b. Sam appears to have a gloss, indicating that it was those who had joined themselves to Baal of Peor.

5.a. שבטי "tribes" is attested in Sam and G.

6.a.-a. G understands this to mean that the man brought his brother to the Midianite woman.

8.a. *BHS* suggests textual corruption here, with קבתה an erroneous repetition of קבה earlier in the verse. For an alternative explanation of the difficulties in this verse see *Comment*.

9.a. According to 1 Cor 10:8 the figure was twenty-three thousand. This may be an error on Paul's part.

12.a. *BHS* wonders whether שלום "requittal," "retribution" should be read here (cf. Mic 7:3).

13.a. There is no need to emend the text to make a future (see *Comment*).

15.a. An explanatory gloss (see J. A. Paterson 60).

Form/Structure/Setting

It is widely recognized that vv 1–5 belong to JE. Israel is presented as העם "the people" (vv 1, 2, 4), there is an interest in specific alien cults, much as in Exod 32, and the role of the שפטים "judges" (v 5) in connection with justice is attested, for example, in Exod 18:21–27. The formulation which tells of the kindling of Yahweh's anger (v 3) is found widely in texts attributable to the JE tradition (e.g. Gen 30:2, 39:19; 44:18; Exod 4:14; 22:24; 32:19, 22; Num 11:1, 10, 33; 12:9; 22:22, 27; 24:10). By contrast it is generally accepted that vv 6–18 belong to P. Israel is העדה "the congregation" (vv 6, 7), and the designation בני ישראל "people of Israel" (vv 6, 8, 11, 13) is common enough in priestly texts. There is an obvious interest in the sons of Aaron as priests, and in the stopping of a plague (cf. Num 17:13, 15 [Heb.]). The concept of atonement (כפר), and the title נשיא "leader" (v 14) are further signs of P. While this division of the material is reasonably easy to establish the further analysis of the text poses many problems.

1. The Yahwistic Tradition (vv 1–5)

Many analysts recognize that this material is not uniform, and there was good support for the view that vv 1–5 contain parallel narrative threads (cf. e.g. A. Dillmann, 167–69; B. W. Bacon, 237–38; H. Holzinger, 126–31; B. Baentsch, 622–24; H. Gressmann, 334 n.2; O. Eissfeldt [*Hexateuch*, 190–91]; C. A. Simpson, 270; G. B. Gray, 380–89). J. de Vaulx (299) also offers some support for this kind of approach. One of the most popular of such analyses set vv 1a, 3a, 5 over against vv 1b, 2, 3b, 4.

There have been some who prefer to see all five verses as essentially a unit (e.g. W. Rudolph, *Der "Elohist,"* 128–31), but an alternative view with some merits is to see the real dichotomy between vv 1b–2 and vv 3–5. The former speaks of apostasy involving Moabite women, and the latter of apostasy to Baal of Peor. The last clause in v 2 brings the expression of disaffection in that verse to a natural conclusion, while the sudden appearance of a covenant with Baal of Peor in v 3 is awkward. The tradition of apostasy with Moabite deities (vv 1b–2) depicts Israel as העם "the people," while that involving Baal Peor (vv 3, 5) presents her as ישראל "Israel." It must be conceded that the connection of v 4 to these traditions is not entirely clear. It speaks of "the people," and has often been supposed to offer an alternative punishment to that of v 5. On the other hand v 4b, in speaking of Yahweh's anger, seems to refer to v 3, while a tension between v 4 and v 5 is not necessarily to be assumed. Moses immediately executes all the leaders to avert the divine anger, and then gives orders to his judges to kill other individuals who had taken part in the alien cult. It seems reasonable to treat vv 3–5 as the Baal Peor tradition.

A number of analysts assign the Baal-Peor material to E, particularly among those who trace parallel threads of narrative through vv 1–5. The "judges" of v 5 (cf. Exod 18:21 [E]) have been a reason for associating vv 1a, 3a, 5 with E, and the links between v 2 and 34:15 (J?) have been a ground for associating vv 1b, 2, 3b, 4 with J (see e.g. G. B. Gray, 380–83; J. de Vaulx, 299). There has also been some preference for E among analysts who are inclined to see vv 1–5 more as a unit (e.g. K. Jaroš, *Die Stellung des Elohisten*). The story's affinities with the tradition of the golden calf in Exod 32 (often considered to be E) would be a point of substance here. On the other hand A. W. Jenks (*The Elohist*, 58–59), who is fully committed to an E presence in the book of Numbers, finds insufficient ground for positing its presence here.

The arguments for an Elohistic presence are in fact not very substantial. The reference to "judges" amounts to very little, and there are grounds for believing that Exod 32 is not part of E. The Baal-Peor tradition may very well be the Yahwist's—a story he has chosen to locate at Shittim (v 1a—cf. Josh 2:1; 3:1). The story is another illustration of his use of filler material for his Transjordanian journey. If this view of the Baal-Peor material is correct, then the Moabite material in vv 1b–2 may very well be a gloss. There are good reasons for associating Exod 34:15–16 with a deuteronomistic redactor (see e.g. M. Noth, *Exodus*, 261–63; J. P. Hyatt, *Exodus*, 323–26), and in view of the connections in v 2 the same may obtain here. Such an analysis is bound to be uncertain, and the possibility that the whole is a Yahwistic unit remains. In that event the Yahwist would be speaking first in general terms of a Moabite apostasy (vv 1b–2), and then more specifically of a particular act (vv 3–5) which led to specific divine judgment.

The background and origin of the tradition taken up by the Yahwist is obscure. M. Noth argues that originally it was not an occupation story (*Pentateuchal Traditions*, 74–75). In his view the Baal-Peor sanctuary was probably visited by central Palestinian tribes. Less likely is his suggestion that the story was originally an etiology based on צמד "yoked" (vv 3, 5), and referring to a place in the vicinity of Shittim (cf. also H. Gressmann, 334–38). The etiological theory is hard to sustain. Where was the place, and what was its name? On the other hand the view that there was or had been a popular Baal-Peor cult in the north is supported by Hos 9:10. For the prophet the Baal-Peor event seems to lie well in the past. He links it closely with the discovery of Israel in the wilderness. The cult may have been at its most popular in the time of the united monarchy when Israel certainly controlled the area in question. V. Fritz (*Israel*, 130–31) thinks that the story was probably transmitted within the tribe of Gad, but there is no good reason for supposing a long process of transmission for the details of the story in their present form. Gadite tradition or recollection may have drawn Hosea's attention to Baal-Peor; mere acquaintance with Hos 9:10 is sufficient basis for the Yahwist to tell his own story of Israel's apostasy there.

G. E. Mendenhall (*The Tenth Generation*, 105–21) argues that the historical root of the tradition is an outbreak of epidemic disease. This may have been brought by tribes migrating south into Transjordan. The rituals instituted to remove the plague, sacrifices to the deity and ritual sexual intercourse with outsiders, constituted a breach of covenant for Israel. The validity of such reconstruction is hard to assess; some such event may underlie the tradition, but there is nothing in the existing story to demand it.

2. *The Priestly Tradition (6–18)*

It seems clear that the Yahwist's story in vv 1–5 has been supplemented by substantial priestly material. The fact that the executions are only commanded and not effected in vv 1–5 suggests that the Yahwist's story has been shortened, and that a priestly author (probably the author of Numbers) has added more material forming a conclusion of greater interest to him (see M. Noth, 195–99). In vv 1–5 there is no reference to "weeping" or "plague," yet these are assumed by the author (vv 6–9). The fact that both occur elsewhere in the wilderness traditions (cf. e.g. Num 11:10; 17:11 [Heb.]) may have justified this assumption. In Num 17:11 "wrath" and "plague" are virtually synonymous, and the "anger" of Num 25:3 may have been naturally understood in terms of plague.

It seems likely that one source of the priestly author's inspiration is Ps 106:28–31. There are sound reasons for supposing that this psalm belongs to the exilic or early post exilic period (W. Beyerlin, "Der *nervus rerum* in Psalm 106" *ZAW* 86 [1974] 50–64), in which case its text was probably familiar enough to the priestly author. The psalm speaks directly of Baal-Peor and a plague, and it is likely that this also contributes to the priestly author's assumptions in Num 25. Moreover for the psalmist the role of Phinehas is to bring the plague to an end—a plague prompted, not by a Midianite woman (as in Num 25:6–18), but by the Baal-Peor event itself. So it would appear that Ps 106:28–31 is the natural bridge between Num 25:1–5 and Num 25:6–18. Not only does it speak of a plague at Baal-Peor, but also of an intervention by Phinehas.

Whether these events occurred in the full form of the Yahwist's story, now apparently shortened by the priestly author, cannot be determined with certainty. If they did not then the psalmist has provided a substantial elaboration of the tradition, presumably in the interests of those represented by Phinehas. As a matter of fact this does not appear to be the psalmist's method elsewhere in the psalm; on the whole his handling of the tradition appears to be restrained. If Phinehas did indeed appear in the Yahwist's tradition then it may well be that he was one of the "judges" cited in v 5. It would appear that he for one acted decisively, executing judgment (Ps 106:31),

and thereby winning to himself a permanent reputation as a righteous man
(Ps 106:31).

It would thus appear that the major adaptation of the tradition is attributable to the priestly author. For him the Phinehas of the psalm, and probably
of the Yahwistic tradition, is a son of Aaron. For the Yahwist he was perhaps
a Levite—hence the need for the author to abandon the original conclusion
to the story. For him the most important part of the action of Phinehas was
that he slew Zimri, an Israelite, and Cozbi, a Midianite woman, whose gross
action had been the real factor in the coming of the plague. In so doing
the permanent reputation which Phinehas had won for himself (Ps 106:30)
is reinterpreted as a covenant of peace, assuring him and his descendants
of a permanent and honored place within the priesthood. The author was
also interested in the introduction of a Midianite element into the story,
partly because of Midianite involvement with Moab in the Balaam story (Num
22:4, 7), and also because it provides a good basis for the Midianite war
which he intends to introduce at a latter stage (Num 31). This latter point
is brought out in vv 16–18 where Midianite influence is also discerned in
the Baal-Poer apostasy, though no such claim had apparently been made
by the Yahwist.

There have been various attempts to understand and explain the motivation
behind the priestly author's adaptation of the story. Why particularly was
there a need to vindicate the priesthood of Phinehas, and why was this particular way chosen? J. de Vaulx (300) discerns some ancient rivalries in the Zadokite priestly line, while M. Noth (195–99) has seen in the story a simple
legitimization of the descendants of Phinehas in the high priestly office.
F. M. Cross (*Canaanite Myth*, 201–3) has seen the rejection of the Elides of
Shiloh (1 Sam 1–4) behind the story, while G. B. Gray (385–86) had also
posited ancient roots for the story, deep in Zadokite tradition. Absence of
evidence tends to make speculation about a long tradition hazardous. In Josh
24:33 there is a note that the burial place of Eleazar was "Gibeah of Phinehas,"
but the possibility that the verse is a priestly gloss of no great age is strong.
It seems unlikely in any case that the priestly family of Phinehas in post-
exilic times was in fact of northern origin. The parenthetical character of
the allusions in Judg 20:27–28 is also reasonably easy to perceive, and there
is no strong reason for supposing that the gloss preserves ancient tradition,
despite suggestions to the contrary. The fact that a son of Eli bore the name
(1 Sam 4:17) is probably irrelevant. Tradition indicated the end of his line,
and attempts to establish links between him and the Phinehas of Num 25
are speculative. The crucial improbability is that the post-exilic priestly orders
would have accepted such a group with such connections. It seems then that
the Phinehas of Num 25 must be associated in the first instance with the
post-exilic group who carried the name, some of whose members returned
to the land with Ezra (Ezra 8:2; 1 Esdr 5:5; 8:29). It seems likely that in the
author's time their credentials as priests were in doubt. The genealogy had
already established them as true sons of Aaron (Exod 6:25); this story justifies
that view. There is no indication here that exclusive rights to some kind of
priesthood are being claimed, or that the high priesthood is at stake. The
issue is essentially the credentials of Phinehas as a priest.

One possibility which would square with the apparent growth and shape of the tradition is the supposition that Phinehas had been a Levitical group promoted to the priesthood, and that this promotion was what prompted the doubt as to its credentials. As already suggested it is possible that Phinehas was a Levite in the Yahwistic tradition, revealing a zeal for Yahweh in the execution of apostates comparable to that shown by the Levites in general in Exod 32:25–29. The grounds for their promotion may have lain partly in their Babylonian connections, and partly in displays of outstanding zeal at the gates of the Temple in excluding those of mixed marriage. This after all is a crucial part of the function of Phinehas in the story as it stands. The chronicler's note that the family of Phinehas superintended the Levitical gatekeepers (1 Chr 9:20) could be based on such a fact, or alternatively, of course, on the story in Num 25 itself. In any event Phinehas is the epitome of watchful zeal at the Temple gate.

Comment

1. Shittim means "acacia trees," and the site is probably the modern Tell Kefrein. This is just to the east of the Jordan, and some ten miles east of Jericho (cf. Josh 2:1; 3:1).

3. ויצמד "yoked himself," an expression occurring only here and in Ps 106:28, which recounts the same incident. G uses a word which suggests initiation into the mysteries (see further N. H. Snaith, 302). In Hos 9:10 the sin is described as "separation to shame," using the root נזר. J. Sturdy (184) suggests that the notion of being "yoked" may imply sexual rites. On the other hand it could be figurative, with the service of these gods being considered a yoke of slavery. The rarity of the phrase may be indicative of some technical cultic term, the meaning of which is now lost. Clearly some formal recognition by the Israelites of the Baal localized at Peor is implied. Baal was widely recognized in Canaan as the fertility god. The myths concerning his death and resurrection, his links with fertility, and many of the rites associated with his worship, were rejected by thorough Yahwists, particularly those influenced by the prophetic tradition.

4. ראשי "leaders" or "captains" (see *Comment* on Num 14:4).

4. והוקע אותם ליהוה נגד השמש "and hang them in the sun before Yahweh." The meaning is obscure. The punishment is probably similar to that described in 2 Sam 21:6, 9 where the Hiphil of יקע is again employed. There have been a variety of suggestions as to what this means. G understands "exposure" (favored by A. Dillmann, 169–70). Aquila believed the victims to have been "impaled." Some form of hanging on a gibbet or cross is supposed in Vg and Tg. W. Robertson Smith (*The Religion of the Semites* [London: A. and C. Black, 1907] 419 n.2) suggested that the victims were thrown from a cliff. This is supported by N. H. Snaith (302), and assumed by NEB. M. Noth (197) notes the use of the Qal in Gen 32:26 with the sense "to be put out of joint," and proposes an exceptionally cruel form of punishment in which bones were put out of joint, and the victims left exposed to the heat of the sun. It is possible that "in the sun" means simply publicly or in broad daylight (cf. 2 Sam 12:12; Jer 8:2).

5. אנשיו "his men." Each judge is thought of as having specific responsibility for this tribe, or for a section of his tribe (cf. Exod 18:25–26).

6. It has been suggested by J. de Vaulx (299–302) (cf. also F. M. Cross, *Canaanite Myth*, 201–3) that the sin was to do with the "shrine" (v 8), and was specifically cultic. It seems more likely that the sin is here in v 6, and that the Israelite has married the Midianite, a view supported by B. Baentsch (624–25); L. E. Binns, 178; J. G. Vink, *Priestly Code*, 123. If the sin were something other than this it would seem reasonable to expect some reference to it in v 6, especially as Phinehas is apparently already responding to it in v 7. The marriage does of course lead on to cultic sin as v 8 implies.

7. The name Phinehas is apparently of Egyptian origin, and seems to mean "the Negro."

8. קבה "shrine"; cf. "pavilion" (*RV*) and "inner room" (rsv, neb). The word occurs only here. There is a similar word in Arabic for a camp sanctuary, and some cultic room is probably intended. A part of the Tabernacle, as suggested by J. Sturdy (184–85) seems less likely. Failure to mention it in the detailed descriptions of the Tent elsewhere in P would be most remarkable. S. C. Reif (*JBL* 90 [1971] 100–6) has evidence to suggest that קבה might be a separate tent shrine, and this seems the best interpretation. To the author the shrine is alien. The familiar pattern of intermarriage/intersexual relationship leading to apostasy (vv 1–2) is here repeated in v 6 and v 8.

8. אל־קבתה "in her shrine," literally "through her belly." S. C. Reif (*JBL* 90 [1971] 100–6) notes the similarity between קבה and קבתה, and his suggestion "in her shrine" makes good sense in the light of his evidence about the meaning of קבה. On the other hand there is no reason to suppose that the crime is essentially about the woman's installation in the קבה for cultic purposes, either for divination regarding the plague or for obtaining an oracle. The theme is rather of an alien interrelationship leading to alien cultic observance.

8. ותעצר המגפה "so the plague was stopped" (see *Comment* on Num 17:13 Heb.).

11. בקנאו את־קנאתי "zealous with my zeal" (cf. Num 11:29; Sir 45:23). The zeal of righteous anger is intended. Because Israel's faith is based on a relationship between God and his people, Yahweh has an absolute claim on Israel's loyalty.

12. בריתי שלום "my covenant of peace" (cf. v 13; Mal 2:5). neb interprets this in terms of "security of tenure," and is probably correct to do so. If "peace" were vocalized as שַׁלֻּם the meaning would be "my covenant as a reward." There is no reason to suppose that the sons of Ithamar or other sons of Eleazar are thereby excluded (see *Form/Structure/Setting*).

13. ויכפר "made atonement" (see *Comment* on Num 17:11 Heb.).

14. It may be that the names of the offenders were added later as an afterthought, since they first appear at this very late stage in the story. J. Sturdy (185) wonders whether there is a sly attack here on contemporaries who claimed descent from Zimri son of Salu.

15. Zur is one of the five Midianite kings cited in Num 31:8.

16–18. These concluding verses foreshadow the Midianite war which is to follow in Num 31.

Explanation

This story tells of Israel's failures—even on the border of the land. At Shittim they become involved with Moabite women, and, inevitably, with Moabite cults, particularly those connected with the Baal of Peor. Moses is instructed to execute the offenders, but the attention of the story turns to the specific offense of an Israelite and a Midianite woman. A marriage appears to have been arranged, but Phinehas son of Eleazar, the priest, takes the initiative and kills them both in the woman's shrine. This secures for all time the place of Phinehas and his descendants in the priestly office. The Midianites are thus implicated in the Peor incident, and the whole affair becomes a pretext for the Midianite war of Num 31.

It would appear that the literary base of the story is a truncated Yahwistic tradition in vv 1–5. The roots of this tradition may be a recollection, also evident in Hos 9:10, of a popular cult at the time of the united monarchy. The Yahwist himself may have had little more than Hos 9:10 to work with. The fact that his story has been shortened is suggested by the lack of any reference to the actual carrying out of the executions. In view of the tradition preserved by the psalmist in Ps 106:28–31 it seems possible that Phinehas was one of those who acted decisively as "judge," and who thereby won for himself a lasting reputation as a righteous man. His action would have been comparable to that of the Levites, described by the Yahwist in Exod 32:25–29, in relation to the apostasy of the golden calf. In view of his subsequent priestly connections it seems possible that the Yahwist himself recognized Phinehas as a Levite.

The Yahwist thus concludes the triumphant Transjordanian journey with a story of Israel's disaffection, and it would be useful at this point to seek an overview of his achievement in piecing together the story of Israel's journey from Egypt to the land of promise, and in particular of his handling of disaffection. Prior to the coming of Yahweh at Sinai he tells four stories with a disaffection component, the deliverance at the sea (Exod 14:11–12), the bitter water at Marah (Exod 15:24), the gift of the manna (Exod 16:4), and the water from the rock at Meribah (Exod 17:2–3). In these stories Israel's survival is at stake, and her doubts and fears receive a gracious response. The disaffection after Sinai is of a different order and is consistently punished. These events in Num 25:1–5 are the culmination of a series which may have been organized by the Yahwist according to a fixed pattern. The second phase in Israel's journey, from Sinai to the borders of the land, can itself be divided into two parts: from Sinai to Kadesh, and from Kadesh to the Jordan. The pattern can be set out as follows:

apostasy (the golden calf—Exod 32)
   discontent (Taberah/quail—Num 11)
      insubordination—individuals (Miriam and Aaron—Num 12)
         insubordination—Israel (Kadesh and Hormah—Num 14)
      insobordination—individuals (Dathan and Abiram—Num 16)
   discontent (snakes—Num 21)
apostasy (Shittim—Num 25)

Israel's sin is the controlling factor in each of these stories, and it may be that the Yahwist's familiarity with the pluralism and subservience of Manasseh's reign adds this darker color to the post-Sinai journey traditions. As for this particular story it had become familiar to the Yahwist through the presence of Hosea's oracles in the south, and some attention to the tradition in the presentation of Israel's history seemed to be required. As filler material for the Transjordanian journey it could be incorporated easily at this point. It was an appropriate tradition in its own right for a generation which still reflected on the fall of Samaria in 721 B.C., and which had increasingly begun to interpret that event in terms of religious apostasy. The new search for an independent religious and national consciousness in Josianic times had no place for those who yoked themselves to Baal.

The priestly author of Numbers takes up this tradition, and as usual he adapts it for his own purposes. The Phinehas of Ps 106 and of Yahwistic tradition becomes a son of Aaron who slew an Israelite man, Zimri, who had entered into a marital relationship with Cozbi, a Midianite woman, and who together were engaged in cultic observances at an alien shrine. It would certainly be possible to see here a fourth major sin in the author's account of the history—following the sins of the community (Num 14), the Levites (Num 16), and Moses and Aaron (Num 20). Each of these stories gives good insight into the priorities of post-exilic Judaism. The attitudes which were held to threaten most the stability and security of the community were a despising of the land (Num 14), false aspirations to the priesthood (Num 16), and arrogant claims which failed to give due honor to God (Num 20). To these may be added intermarriage and apostasy (Num 25). On the other hand it would appear that the author's chief interest in the story is not the sin of Zimri and Cozbi, the precise nature of which is not easy to determine (see *Form/Structure/Setting* and *Comment*), but the vindication of Phinehas in his priesthood, and the Midianite dimension to the Baal-Peor episode. The latter provides an excellent springboard for the Midianite war to be described later in Num 31. It seems possible that Phinehas represented a Levitical group which had been promoted to priesthood. They had links with Babylonian Judaism (see *Form/Structure/Setting*), and may have been particularly zealous against mixed marriage and in the exclusion of foreigners at the temple gates. In that event the story vindicates their promotion. The story may therefore be resolving doubts about their credentials and/or providing grounds for their supervision of the Levitical gatekeepers (1 Chr 9:20).

Within the priestly author's scheme it is possible to suggest another purpose for the narrative. Ever since the deaths of Nadab and Abihu in Lev 10 the priestly account operates with something of a priestly triumvirate with Aaron at its head, and with his sons Eleazar and Ithamar as assistants. As the material in Num 1–4 makes clear there are always functions for the sons. The death of Aaron (Num 20) and the promotion of Eleazar created a gap which Phinehas readily fills, and which the story justifies. Viewed in this light the story can be seen, along with the investiture of Eleazar in Num 20, as evidence of God's continuing commitment to the priestly leadership, despite its failures. This pattern of continuing commitment on God's part, after the great sins, has been noted as a constant feature of the account of the journey given in Numbers.

The author here concludes the second main section of the book—the account of Israel's journey from Sinai to the borders of the land, with particular emphasis on its setbacks and successes. It is a story in which failure is honestly and realistically acknowledged, and in which failure brings dire consequences to those who miss the mark, but also a story in which human failure does not ultimately defeat the good purpose of God. There are always ways in which that good purpose can work its way through the morass of human inadequacy, and this must be judged one of the author's major theological contributions to the OT understanding of God.

The Second Census (25:19–26:56)

Bibliography

Auld, A. G. *Joshua, Moses, and the Land.* Edinburgh: T. and T. Clark, 1980. **Harrelson,** **W.** "Guidance in the Wilderness. The Theology of Numbers." *Int* 13 (1959) 24–36. **Lindblom, J.** "Lot casting in the Old Testament." *VT* 12 (1962) 164–78. See also Num 1:1–47 (*Bibliography*).

Translation

[19a] *And it happened after the plague,* [a] [26:1] *That Yahweh spoke* [a] *to Moses and to Eleazar son of Aaron* [b] *the priest, saying,* [2] *"Take a census of all the congregation of the people of Israel, from the age of twenty and upwards, by fathers' houses, all eligible for military service in Israel."* [3] *And Moses and Eleazar the priest spoke* [a] *with them in the plains of Moab by the Jordan at Jericho, saying,* [4a] *"Take a census of the people* [a] *from twenty years old and upwards, as Yahweh commanded Moses."* *And the people of Israel who came out of Egypt were:*

[5] *Reuben, the firstborn of Israel: the sons of Reuben:* [a] *of Hanoch, the clan of the Hanochites; of Pallu, the clan of the Palluites;* [6] *of Hezron, the clan of the Hezronites; of Carmi, the clan of the Carmites.* [7] *These are the clans of the Reubenites. And their number was 43,730.* [a] [8] *And the sons of Pallu: Eliab.* [9] *And the sons of Eliab: Nemuel,* [a] *Dathan, and Abiram. These are* [b] *the Dathan and Abiram, chosen from the congregation,* [c] *who defied Moses and Aaron in the company of Korah, when they defied Yahweh.* [10] *And the earth opened its mouth and swallowed them, along with Korah, when that company died, when the fire consumed 250 men. And they became a warning sign.* [11] *But the sons of Korah did not die.*

[12] *The sons of Simeon by clans: of Jemuel,* [a] *the clan of the Jemuelites; of Jamin,* [b] *the clan of the Jaminites; of Jachin, the clan of Jachinites;* [13] *of Zohar,* [a] *the clan of the Zoharites; of Shaul, the clan of the Shaulites.* [14] *These are the clans of the Simeonites—22,200.*

[15] *The sons of Gad* [a] *by clans: of Zephon,* [b] *the clan of the Zephonites; of Haggi, the clan of the Haggites; of Shuni, the clan of the Shunites;* [16] *of Ozni,* [a] *the clan of the Oznites; of Eri,* [b] *the clan of the Erites;* [17] *of Arodi,* [a] *the clan of the Arodites; of Areli, the clan of the Arelites.* [18] *These are the clans of the sons of Gad, according to their number—40,500.* [a]

[19] *The sons of Judah were Er and Onan. And Er and Onan died in the land of Canaan.* [20] *And the sons of Judah by clans were: of Shelah, the clan of the Shelanites; of Perez, the clan of the Perezites; of Zerah, the clan of the Zerahites.* [21] *And the sons of Perez were; of Hezron, the clan of the Hezronites; of Hamul,* [a] *the clan of the Hamulites.* [22] *These are the clans of Judah, according to their number—76,500.*

[23] *The sons of Issachar by clans: of Tola, the clan of the Tolaites; of Puah,* [a] *the clan of the Puaites;* [b] [24] *of Jashub, the clan of the Jashubites; of Shimron, the clan of the Shimronites.* [25] *These are the clans of Issachar, according to their number—64,300.*

[26] *The sons of Zebulun by clans: of Sered, the clan of the Seredites; of Elon, the*

clan of the Elonites; of Jahleel, the clan of the Jahleelites. **27** *These are the clans of the Zebulunites, according to their number—60,500.* [a]

28 *The sons of Joseph by clans: Manasseh and Ephraim.* **29** *The sons of Manasseh: of Machir, the clan of the Machirites. And Machir was the father of Gilead; of Gilead, the clan of the Gileadites.* **30** *These are the sons of Gilead: of Iezer, the clan of the Iezerites; of Helek, the clan of the Helekites;* **31** *and of Asriel, the clan of the Asrielites; and of Shechem, the clan of the Shechemites;* **32** *and of Shemida, the clan of the Shemidaites; and of Hepher, the clan of the Hepherites.* **33** *Now Zelophehad son of Hepher had no sons, only daughters; and the names of the daughters of Zelophehad were Mahlah, Noah, Hoglah, Milcah, and Tirzah.* **34** *These are the clans of Manasseh. And their number was 52,700.* [a]

35 *These are the sons of Ephraim by clans: of Shuthelah, the clan of the Shuthelites; of Becher, the clan of the Becherites; of Tahan,* [a] *the clan of the Tahanites.* **36** *And these are the sons of Shuthelah: of Edan,* [a] *the clan of the Edanites.* **37** *These are the clans of the sons of Ephraim, according to their number—32,500. These are the sons of Joseph by clans.*

38 *The sons of Benjamin by clans: of Bela, the clan of the Belaites; of Ashbel,* [a] *the clan of the Ashbelites; of Ahiram, the clan of the Ahiramites;* **39** *of Shephupham, the clan of the Shuphamites; of Hupham, the clan of the Huphamites.* **40** *And the sons of Bela were Ard and Naaman: of Ard, the clan of the Ardites; of Naaman, the clan of the Naamites.* [a] **41** *These are the sons of Benjamin by clans. And their number was 45,600.* [a]

42a *These are the sons of Dan by clans: of Shuham, the clan of the Shuhamites. These are the clans of Dan by clans.* **43** *All the clans of the Shuhamites, according to their number—64,400.* [a]

44a *The sons of Asher by clans: of Imnah, the clan of the Imnaites; of Ishvi,* [b] *the clan of the Ishvites; of Beriah, the clan of the Beriaites.* **45** *Of the sons of Beriah:* [a] *of Heber, the clan of the Heberites; of Malchiel, the clan of the Malchielites.* **46** *And the name of the daughter of Asher was Serah.* **47** *These are the clans of the sons of Asher, according to their number—53,400.*

48 *The sons of Naphtali by clans: of Jahzeel, the clan of the Jahzeelites; of Guni, the clan of the Gunites;* **49** *of Jezer, the clan of the Jezerites; of Shillem, the clan of the Shillemites.* **50** *These are the clans of Naphtali by clans. And their number was 45,400.* [a]

51 *This was the number of the people of Israel—601,730.*

52 *And Yahweh spoke to Moses, saying,* **53** *"To these shall the land be divided for an inheritance, according to the number of names.* **54** *To the larger you shall give a large inheritance, and to the smaller you shall give a small inheritance. Each shall be given his inheritance according to his numbers.* **55** *But the land shall be divided by lot. According to the names of their fathers' tribes they shall inherit.* **56** *Their inheritance shall be divided by lot between the larger and the smaller."*

Notes

19.a. Some see the continuation of this verse in Num 31:1 (see J. A. Paterson 60). It seems reasonable to see it as a transition between 25:18 and 26:1.

1.a. Sam uses the root דבר "to speak."

1.b. The reference to Aaron is lacking in G.

9.a. The verb is singular in MT (cf Num 1:2).

4.a. Some such clause as this has to be assumed, there being an evident gap in MT. It would be possible to omit "saying" at the end of v 3, and to assume a statement that Moses and Eleazar carried out the census (cf. Syr); see further J. A. Paterson, 60.

5.a. *BHS* proposes the addition of "by families" as in vv 12, 15 etc. See also J. A. Paterson, 60; J. de Vaulx, 304.

7.a. G^A reads 43,750.

9.a. *BHS* suspects that Nemuel belongs in v 12.

9.b. The verb is singular in MT.

9.c. *NEB* reads this as "conveners of the congregation."

12.a. Syr reads Jemuel (cf. Gen 46:10; Exod 6:15). MT has Nemuel.

12.b. Gen 46:10 and Exod 6:15 read Ohad. MT reads Jamin. The variation is hard to explain.

13.a. Gen 46:10 and Exod 6:15 read Zohar. MT reads Zerah.

15.a. G places the Gadite material (vv 15–18) after Zebulun (v 27) (cf. also Gen 46:16).

15.b. Gen 46:16 reads Ziphion.

16.a. Gen 46:16 reads Ezbon.

16.b. There is strong support for Adi in Sam, G, and S, but Gen 46:16 reads Eri.

17.a. MT reads Arod, but Gen 46:16, Sam, G, and S favor Arodi.

17.b. Sam reads Aroli, S reads Adil, G and Vg read Ariel.

18.a. Some witnesses read 44,500.

21.a. The form is Hamuel in Sam and G.

23.a. MT reads Puvah, but Puah is supported by Sam, G, S, Vg, and 1 Chr 7:1.

23.b. MT reads Punites.

27.a. G places here the information about Gad (in vv 15–18), and follows Gad with the Asher material (in vv 44–47).

34.a. Some G witnesses read 62,500.

35.a. The reading is Taham in Sam, and Tanak in G.

36.a. MT reads Eran, but Sam, G, and S support Edan.

38.a. Sam reads Ashbeel, and G Ashuber.

40.a. Sam lacks a reference to Naaman.

41.a. Some G witnesses read 35,500.

42.a. J. A. Paterson (60) suggests that the Dan text may be corrupt. Only one family is cited, and only in v 43 does כל-משפחת "all the clans" occur. The single family is remarkable in view of the fact that overall Dan is second in numerical strength.

43.a. There is some G witness to the figure 64,600.

44.a. The Asher material appears after that of Zebulun and Gad at v 27 in G.

44.b. Sam and G support Ishvah. Both Ishvi and Ishvah occur in Gen 46:17.

45.a. This is lacking in Sam and G, but supported by Gen 46:17.

50.a. There is some G witness to 30,300.

Form/Structure/Setting

There is no difficulty in assigning this section, along with Num 1:1–47, to priestly sources. It is evidently a similar kind of census to the one conducted in the opening chapter of the book, and it is intended to reconstitute Israel after the disasters of the plague. Some analysts have seen signs of early P elements in the section, though there has been no general agreement about their extent (cf. e.g. J. Wellhausen, 184–86; H. Holzinger, 132–33; B. Baentsch, 627–35). It has been observed that there is no explicit reference to the former census, and that v 4 speaks explicitly of "the people of Israel who had come out of Egypt," as though the deaths on the journey had not in fact occurred. A. Kuenen (100) was not so persuaded, finding the text of vv 3–4 uncertain, and seeing the linking of Moses and Eleazar as evidently late.

The relationship of the chapter to Gen 46 was also a point of discussion. G. B. Gray (387–89), among others, found Num 26 dependent on Gen 46 for the names of the tribal families. The enumeration of tribes in MT he found to be following the order of Num 1:20–43 (except for the reversal of Ephraim and Manasseh), whereas G keeps the order of Gen 46 (see *Notes*). On the matter of the section's literary history Gray saw two possibilities— either a second census in PG has been annotated and possibly recast by a later priestly author (adding vv 8–11, 30–33), or else the entire section is to be attributed to PS. As with the first census Gray has nothing to suggest about the origin of the figures, his only observation being that in both cases there are exactly six tribes above the 50,000 mark, and exactly six below it.

M. Noth (202–4), in line with his views about the antiquity of the family lists (see *Form/Structure/Setting* on Num 1:1–47) sees this as the oldest element in the section. For him the family list must belong to a time when the division into tribes and families or clans still had some significance in Israel—namely before the appearance of a constitutional organization with different methods of division. By the latter he appears to mean the period of the monarchy. How such an ancient list survived to be incorporated into Num 26 cannot now be explained. Taking this view Noth argues for the dependence of Gen 46:8–27 on the list here; it is seen as a transformation of the material in Num 26 into a pure genealogical scheme. The census figures Noth judges to be an originally independent element within the tradition. He observes that though different from those given in the first census they are in general remarkably similar. The marked drop in Simeon's figures is compensated for by big increases in those of Manasseh and Benjamin. The view that the figures originate in a misunderstanding of the original meaning of אלף "thousand" is obviously applicable here—a view refined by G. E. Mendenhall (*JBL* 77 [1958] 52–66) (see *Form/Structure/Setting* on Num 1:1–47) and strongly supported by N. K. Gottwald, *The Tribes of Yahweh* 270–76. On this view the figures would originally have claimed that Israel consisted of 569 troops or companies, consisting in all of 5,730 men fit for military service. Noth himself is in favor of this hypothesis, and raises the possibility that the figures, so understood, originate in Israel's premonarchical period. He sees the differences in the two sets of figures (Num 1 and Num 26) as indicative of decreases or increases in manpower, and therefore of tribal importance. The specific difficulties in vv 52–56 about the division of the land have long been recognized (see e.g. B. Baentsch, 627–35). Is the land to be divided by lot, or in accordance with the size of the various tribes? Noth sees in this part of the section evidence of very late editorial work, traceable to the period at which the Pentateuchal narrative is joined to the "deuteronomistic historical work." He suggests that there is a very faint attempt to remove the difficulty in vv 55–56, which he judges to mean that the lot will fall in such a way that the inheritance will correspond to the sizes of the tribes. This view may be compared with that of N. H. Snaith (307) who thinks that for P the general locality is decided by lot, but the exact limits by need.

J. Sturdy (189) accepts Noth's view that the list of families and the figures were originally independent, but is of the opinion that is more likely that Num 26 has simply taken them from Gen 46 rather than the reverse, or else that both drew them from a common source. He is inclined to the view that the list is relatively early, but is undecided about the origin of the census figures.

J. de Vaulx (305–11) also sees the names and the figures as originally distinct, and also inclines to Noth's view about the originality of Num 26 over Gen 46. For him a list of families is likely to be more ancient than a list of persons (as in Gen 46). In a number of the names (e.g. Shechem [v 31], Hepher [v 32], Tirzah [v 33], Shimron [v 24]) Noth and de Vaulx see the names of Canaanite towns which entered into alliance with the tribes, and therefore another indication of antiquity. As for the figures de Vaulx thinks it possible to see the influence of history in the various increases and decreases. Some such ebb and flow can be discerned in a comparison of the blessings of Gen 49:1–27 and Deut 33:6–25. As for the origin of the figures de Vaulx notes, but does not commit himself to, the kind of approach suggested by Mendenhall.

A detailed investigation of vv 52–56 has been conducted by A. G. Auld (*Joshua, Moses, and the Land*, 73). Following in general the analysis of M. Wüst, he sees the core of the passage in vv 52–54 which establishes the principle of division by size. To this the principle of division by lot has been added in a rather labored way in v 55, while v 56 attempts to make sense of the two principles.

In evaluating the literary features of the section and the various comments made upon it we can reasonably say that the section as it stands is the work of the priestly author of Numbers. It also seems reasonable to argue that he has worked together some originally independent information about various families and about the sizes of the respective tribes. Into this he has built material from elsewhere in his book—vv 9–11 (cf. Num 16:1–35) and v 33 (cf. Num 27:1). The family lists, the census figures, and the division of the land can be considered in turn.

The Family Lists

It is important to recognize that the antiquity or otherwise of the lists and the priority of Gen 46 or Num 26 are two different questions. It would be perfectly possible for the names to be old, for the families to be transformed into persons (as in Gen 46), and yet for Num 26 to be dependent nevertheless on Gen 46. The two lists have to be examined carefully, side by side, observations have to be made, and likely inferences drawn. A comparison suggests that there is every reason for believing there to be some kind of literary relationship. There are few significant divergencies, and most of these are intelligible as transcriptional errors. Ohad son of Simeon is present in Gen 46, is attested also in Exod 6:15, but is missing in Num 26. Ishvah son of Asher is also missing in Num 26. Becher, Ehi, and Rosh, sons of Benjamin are further absentees from Num 26, though the Benjamin text appears to be particularly corrupt with various other names appearing in divergent forms. Variations of this type are most likely to be the product of transcriptional error and other forms of corruption. As for the direction of dependence it seems best to suppose that Num 26 is building on Gen 46. Overall it contains more information (notably on Manasseh), and it lacks nothing which is not attributable to accidental omission. The disagreement whereby Gen 46 makes Ard and Naaman sons of Benjamin while Num 26 makes them sons of Bela is more intelligible as a clarification on the part of Num 26.

The order and content of the tribal lists is also of interest. The order in Gen 46 is controlled by the mothers of the various tribes (Leah-Zilpah-Rachel-Bilhah) as is customary in the book of Genesis as a whole (cf. Gen 29:32–30:24; 35:21–26). The ordering in Num 26 agrees in the main with that in Num 1. The exception, the reversal of Ephraim and Manasseh, may be explained by the amount of family information available about Manasseh, and by its considerable increase in size. It is in G that there appears to be an attempt to reorganize Num 26 into something of the order given in Gen 46. It seems clear then that Num 1 and Num 26 follow one pattern of ordering and Gen 46 another—one that is typical of Genesis in general, and which is even evident in the Yahwist's work in that book. A reasonable conclusion to draw is that there is no sign in this particular area of a dependence of Gen 46 on Num 26.

An obvious divergence in the two tribal lists is the fact that Levi is one of the twelve in Gen 46, but is excluded in Num 1 and Num 26 in accordance with the principles espoused by the priestly author of Numbers in Num 1:48–54. The number twelve is preserved in Numbers by splitting Joseph into Ephraim and Manasseh. Here too there is no indication that Gen 46 is drawing on Num 26. On the contrary the priestly author of Genesis has patterned his tribal list on the listing of the tribes established in the pre-priestly Yahwistic tradition, and in this Levi has his own place. It is to the priestly author of Numbers that we must look for the separation of Levi from the rest. Had Gen 46 been working with the family lists of Num 26 it would be reasonable to expect his tribal list to reflect that dependence.

Noth's argument for the priority of Num 26 depends partly on a general tendency in Israel to personalize family or group traditions—a process more evident in Gen 46 than in Num 26. That there was such a tendency is likely enough, but there is no reason for supposing that it was uniformly simple, and that once established there would be no tendencies operating in the other direction. We have to remember that personalization has already been achieved in the pre-priestly Yahwistic tradition (Gen 29:32–30:24). The priestly author of Gen 46 may possibly have personalized the family names available to him, but there is no reason for supposing that he has drawn them from Num 26 rather than an independent source. In itself it is just as reasonable to suppose that Num 26 is an expansion of Gen 46, setting out the details at fuller length. In view of the fact that Genesis seems to be an earlier priestly product, it seem better to assume that the Numbers list is dependent upon it. An implication of Noth's which is impossible to sustain is the notion that tribes and families or clans ceased to have significance after the appearance of a constitutional organization with other methods of division. The evidence of P itself is proof that that was not so.

It should also be noted that some of the information also occurs in the book of Joshua (cf. the Manasseh material in Josh 17:1–6). There is good reason for believing that the author of Numbers drew on and elaborated parts of the book of Joshua in the latter part of his own book. In this instance, however, it would appear that the Joshua text is an attempt to work in the information about Manasseh (and particularly Zelophehad and his daughters)—information derived from the book of Numbers. Some alignment of that information with the earlier material about Manasseh's inheritance (Josh 17:7–13) was obviously desirable.

The family names may indeed be old, though it is difficult to say how old. The view that they were already in lists in pre-monarchic times seems unlikely unless convincing explanations can be offered as to how and why such lists would have been preserved over such a period of time, and through the disturbances of the exile. The compilation of such lists may more probably be traced to the need for identity evident in the exilic and early post-exilic periods (see the discussion of the names in Num 1:1–47). That the names themselves represent accurate recollection in the main seems likely. That they are in any sense complete is improbable, the single family for Dan being a likely indication of this.

The Census Figures

It was suggested with respect to the large census returns in Num 1 (see *Form/Structure/Setting*) that the final figure might be the product of priestly reflection on the offerings made for the construction of the tabernacle in the book of Exodus. It was suggested that the breakdown among the tribes was derived from this final figure, and that it was based on an intuitive sense of the size of the individual tribes in relation to one another, or on an intelligent evaluation of their fortunes as described in the blessings in Gen 49 and Deut 33. There are no such bases for interpreting the figures here. This is not necessarily a reason for suspecting the validity of the suggestion regarding Num 1. What lies behind both computations are texts in the Yahwistic tradition such as Exod 12:37 and Num 11:21. These set the overall level in the region of 600,000. This is evidently the guiding principle for the author of Numbers in both texts.

The suggestions of M. Barnouin (*VT* 27 [1977] 280–303) face the same problems as in Num 1 (see *Form/Structure/Setting* on Num 1:1–47) while the suggestion that the final figure there represents the numerical value of certain letters (gematriya) does nothing to solve the problems here in Num 26. To say that the redactor has reduced the overall figure to show that Israel suffered a loss as a result of her sins does not answer the question—why 601,730? The difficulties attaching to G. E. Mendenhall's approach (*JBL* 77 [1958] 52–66) apply more sharply here. There is no real explanation as to why the troop or company size of the tribes should now be different, or why they should diverge so widely. In Num 1 Simeon would have about five men per troop, but about nine in Num 26. Gad would have about fifteen in Num 1 and twelve and a half in Num 26. Reuben would have about eleven in Num 1 and about seventeen in Num 26. Issachar would have about seven and a half in Num 1 and about five in Num 26. One of the largest variations is in Manasseh—an average of six and a quarter men per troop in Num 1, but some thirteen and a half in Num 26. If it is assumed that both lists are early it is hard to explain why troop sizes should vary so much in such a relatively short space of time.

One possible approach to the problem is offered by W. Harrelson (*Int* 13 [1959] 24–36). He suggests that the numerical shifts in Num 26 serve primarily a theological purpose. The greatest loss is suffered by Simeon, and this reduces them to about the number of the Levites. This puts the brothers on an equal footing and provides an effective fulfillment of Gen 49:5–7. Harrelson admits that the prominence given to Issachar, Zebulun, Dan, and Asher has no known connection with historical events, and also that the raising of Manasseh over Ephraim seems to violate Gen 48:13–22. In these cases Harrelson sees simply a concern to vindicate the sovereignty of God who purely of his own will causes some to prosper and others to decline.

There may be something in this approach, particularly with respect to Simeon, but if so, the author's handling of Gen 48:13–22 seems inconsistent. Another possibility is that the author has been influenced by his idea of the size of each tribal inheritance. As vv 52–56 make clear each inheritance is determined in part by lot and in part by the numerical size of the tribe. The possibility that the figures in vv 1–51 are the product of an evaluation of the territory occupied by the various tribes is real. There are reasons for thinking that a good deal of the third part of the book of Numbers (Num 26–36) is an adaptation and development of tradition already present in the books of Deuteronomy and Joshua. In this instance the author's guidelines were perhaps the tribal boundaries delineated in Josh 13–19. It is as difficult to know how the priestly author might have understood these boundaries as it is to know how they were originally drawn, but it remains a possibility that this material provided some sort of guide for determining the strengths of the respective tribes. It must of course be remembered that we are concerned here with the author's perceptions of the boundaries, not the boundaries as intended in Josh 13–19, nor the boundaries as they actually existed in Solomonic or later times. The tradition of an allowance for size is already embedded in Josh 13–19—in 17:14–18 precisely, and the priestly author of Numbers may have held that this was a general principle. In his circumstances it was probably as impossible as it is for us to determine accurately the meaning of the boundary divisions in Josh 13–19, which are in any case incomplete. The tribal calculations may therefore have been based on an estimate of the amount of territory each tribe was thought to have possessed.

As previously shown here and in Num 1 the general figure of 600,000 was already fixed in pre-priestly Yahwistic tradition, and it remains to be asked whether anything can be said about the origins of this very large figure. One possibility is that it arises from reflection on ancient poetry where more than once Israel or individual tribes are depicted as thousands upon thousands (Gen 24:60; Num 10:35–36; Deut 33:17). There are also ancient texts where the divine chariotry seems to be so defined (Deut 33:2; Ps 68:18 [Heb.]). It is therefore not surprising that the Yahwist should think of a number so large, nor that the priestly author should make it precise in the context of two military censuses.

The Division of the Land

The author here appears to have two main purposes. He had probably noted in Josh 17:14–18 how some allowance is made for tribal size, and he wished to establish that as a general principle—hence the stipulations in vv 52–54. Yet he could not ignore the deuteronomic historian's view that the land west of the Jordan was divided by lot (Josh 15:1; 16:1; 18:6, 10)—hence v 55. It may well be that v 56 is an attempt to combine the two ideas, implying perhaps that the lot casting corresponded with tribal size, or that general localities were fixed by lot, and precise limits by need.

The author's second purpose, as elsewhere in this third part of his book, is to make it crystal clear that Moses, not Joshua, was the original recipient of the command to divide the land. This tendency is comparable to the Chronicler's desire to make it clear that all temple details are Davidic rather than Solomonic. According to earlier tradition the Transjordanian tribes were given their land by Moses, and this is supported in the deuteronomic history (Josh 13:15–32). Earlier tradition saw the land to the west of the Jordan as divided by lot under Joshua (Josh 14:13; 15:13; 17:14; 18:10). The priestly author's purpose here in Num 26:52–56 is to make it clear that Joshua was no more than the agent of a revelation about the apportionment of the land previously given to Moses. It is to Moses alone that important divine revelation is given.

Comment

2. The people to be numbered indicate that this, as in Num 1, is a military census. This is an important preparation for the Midianite war (Num 31) and the occupation of the land.

4. Reference to "the people of Israel who came out of Egypt" seems strange in view of the fact that this is the second census, and that the first generation of refugees is supposed to have died. The text is however uncertain (see *Notes*), and it may well be that the allusion is to the tribal and family list rather than the census figures. In that event v 4b belonged originally with the family list (see *Form/Structure/Setting*).

5. The names are also given in Gen 46:9; Exod 6:14; 1 Chr 5:3.

9. Here the priestly and Yahwistic traditions of Num 16 are brought closer together.

10. לנס "a warning sign," elsewhere the priestly author uses אות "sign" (cf. e.g. Num 17:25 Heb.), and it may be that this digression in vv 9–11 is a later addition. It is noteworthy that in Num 17:3 (Heb.) the censers, not the offenders, are the "sign."

11. The author here recognizes that there were sons of Korah in post-exilic times (1 Chr 26:1–19). The superscriptions to Pss 42–49, 84, 85, 87–88 suggest that the sons of Korah were temple singers.

13. Shaul is described in Gen 46:10 as the son of a Canaanite woman.

19. The deaths are described in Gen 38:7, 10.

20. According to Gen 38:5 Shelah is the son of Judah by the daughter of Shua. Perez and Zerah were the twin sons of Judah by Tamar (Gen 38:29–30).

26. There is a Zebulunite named Elon among the judges (Judg 12:11).

29–34. The material here is unusually complicated (see *Form/Structure/Setting*). In Num 32:39 Gilead is given by Moses to Machir. This may be a genealogical representation of that fact. In Josh 17:1–2 Machir is said to be the firstborn of Manasseh, his other male children being Abieżer, Helek, Asriel, Shechem, Hepher, and Shemida. In Josh 17:3, however, Hepher is the son of Gilead (cf. 1 Chr 2:21–23; 7:14–19 for other differences).

31. M. Noth (207) concludes that the reference to Shechem in the clan list must be a reference to the well-known town of that name—an indication that it has been incorporated as a clan into the tribe of Manasseh.

33. The reference to Zelophehad and his daughters may be an addition—included in the light of Num 27:1–11. M. Noth (207) suggests that the "daughters" all have topographical significance. The feminine endings suggest to tradition that they were daughters. Tirzah was certainly a well-known city. Noah and Hoglah occur in the Samaritan ostraca as districts (so too do Iezer [as Abiezer] and Helek [v 30] and Shemida [v 32]). Noth concludes that, as with Shechem, these names are originally places and districts incorporated into Manasseh.

35. In Gen 46:21 and 2 Sam 20:1 Becher belongs to Benjamin, and some have thought that this allusion belongs in v 38. In 1 Chr 7:20 there is however a Bered which belongs to Ephraim.

36. M. Noth (208) takes the verse to be an addition, part of the clan Shuthelah having become independent. Nevertheless he judges the information contained to be old.

38–41. The Benjamin genealogies pose numerous problems. M. Noth (208) thinks that the original clan list occurs in vv 38–39, and that v 40 is an addition naming two more clans. The formula in v 40a is irregular, and v 40b would be the original continuation of vv 38–39.

42. M. Noth (208) sees in the fact that only one Danite clan is mentioned an indicator of the tribe's smallness. The large census figure is held to reflect different historical circumstances. For discussion of the relationship between the family lists and the census figures see *Form/Structure/Setting*.

46. The origin of the name of Asher's daughter cannot be explained, nor the reason for its inclusion. It was probably an element in the list available to the priestly author and he saw no reason to exclude it.

55. The lot is widely attested in the ancient near east as a means of dividing land. It provided an impartial method, the mysterious operation of which could readily be interpreted as the will of God (cf. its use in 1 Sam 10:20–21; Acts 1:24–26).

Explanation

This section marks the beginning of the third major division of the book (see *Introduction*). The author is not going to provide an account of the settlement west of the Jordan. Deuteronomy must in any event come first, and the deuteronomic historian's work in the book of Joshua provided a definitive account of those events. There is certainly some priestly editing in the book of Joshua, but it is far from being a major priestly revision along the lines offered in the books of Exodus, Leviticus, and Numbers. Nevertheless the priestly author of Numbers has a variety of preparatory matters to be resolved before the giving of deuteronomic law and the settlement can be told. Many of these matters in the third part of his book are in fact a reinterpretation of deuteronomic and settlement tradition.

The first concern, however, is to reconstitute the community. The book had begun with the taking of a census whereby the hosts of Israel ready for battle are duly numbered (Num 1:1–47). After the disasters of the second major part of the book the community must be set up once more as a large force under God's providence, ready for battles and the settlement to come. Here we see again, as so often in the second part of the book, the author's concern to. emphasize that sin does not ultimately deflect God from his good purpose for Israel. The people are once again ready to be God's community for the journey to the given land. The slight overall reduction in numbers is probably of no great significance; the 600,000 of tradition are still available to fight God's war and fulfill his purpose.

The author has constructed the section from a family list associated with the various tribes, and from a set of census figures. It seems likely that the family list is drawn in the first instance from information given in Gen 46 (see *Form/Structure/Setting*), but its ultimate origins are obscure. The need for a sense of identity among Jews in the exilic and early post-exilic periods may have prompted the compilation of such lists.

The census figures were probably the author's own construction. To guide him there was the already established tradition of 600,000, which in turn may have been derived from an interpretation of ancient poetic texts (see *Form/Structure/Setting*). He had already used this tradition in Num 1:1–47, and his own reflections on the tabernacle had led him to give it greater precision. His calculations here may have been influenced by texts in Gen 49 and Deut 33, indicating the varying fortunes of the tribes, and also by his own assessment of the territory occupied by each tribe. It seemed to him that there were elements in tradition suggesting that tribal size was a factor in determining the land occupied (Josh 17:14–18), and to give some indication of respective strengths was very appropriate here. In vv 52–54 he therefore goes on to assert that a division according to tribal size was a general principle. This had to be aligned with the deuteronomic historian's tradition of a division of the land by lot (Josh 15:1; 16:1; 18:6, 10), and hence vv 55–56. The author may have supposed the lot casting corresponded remarkably with tribal size, or that general localities were fixed by lot and precise limits by need.

A key feature of the author's handling of deuteronomic tradition in this third part of the book is his determination to make it clear that Moses was the recipient of all divine revelation. This tendency is comparable to that evident in the Chronicler's work, where David is given all the details for the construction of Solomon's temple. In deuteronomic tradition some of the land to the west of Jordan is allotted by Joshua (Josh 14:13; 15:13; 17:14; 18:10). The priestly author of Numbers takes up the tradition of an allotment in Transjordan by Moses (Josh 13:15–32), and makes it clear that the total allotment was a revelation to Moses, to the west of the Jordan as to the east. Joshua merely activates an apportionment of the land already revealed to Moses. It was important to Babylonian Judaism in the exilic and post-exilic periods to establish the feasibility of such revelation being given outside the land. The authenticity of their own vision for the future of the restored community depended upon it.

The Second Levitical Census   (26:57–65)

Bibliography

See Num 3:1–51 (*Bibliography*).

Translation

⁵⁷ *And these are those numbered of Levi* ᵃ *by clans: of Gershon, the clan of the Gershonites; of Kohath, the clan of the Kohathites; of Merari, the clan of the Merarites.* ⁵⁸ *These are the clans of Levi:* ᵃ *the clan of the Libnites, the clan of the Hebronites, the clan of the Mahlites,* ᵇ *the clan of the Mushites, the clan of the Korahites. And Kohath was the father of Amram.* ⁵⁹ *And the name of Amram's wife was Jochebed the daughter of Levi, who was born* ᵃ *to Levi in Egypt. And she bore to Amram Aaron and Moses and Miriam their sister.* ⁶⁰ *And to Aaron were born Nadab, Abihu, Eleazar, and Ithamar.* ⁶¹ *But Nadab and Abihu died when they offered strange fire before Yahweh.* ᵃ ⁶² *And those numbered of them were 23,000, every male from a month old and upwards. For they were not numbered among the people of Israel because there was no inheritance given to them among the people of Israel.*

⁶³ *These were those numbered by Moses and Eleazar the priest, who numbered the people of Israel in the plains of Moab by the Jordan at Jericho.* ⁶⁴ *And among these there was not a man of those numbered by Moses and Aaron the priest, who had numbered the people of Israel in the wilderness of Sinai.* ⁶⁵ *For Yahweh had said of them, "They shall die in the wilderness." There was not a man of them remaining, except Caleb the son of Jephunneh, and Joshua the son of Nun.*

Notes

57.a. The reading is "sons of Levi" in Sam, Syr, and Tg.
58.a. The reading is "sons of Levi" in Sam and G.
58.b. G has Korahites instead of Mahlites.
59.a. MT is obscure, but a passive probably gives the intended sense.
61.a. G adds "in the desert of Sinai" (cf. Num 3:4).

Form/Structure/Setting

Analysts are agreed that this material is priestly, and it is evidently the priestly author's account of the second census—a continuation of the information he has supplied in Num 26:1–56. The difficulties arise in connection with the origin of the Levitical census figure, and the background to the Levitical genealogy provided in these verses.

The number of Levites in the second census is virtually unchanged. The corresponding figure in Num 3:39 was 22,000, and this has increased in the new census to 23,000. There is no breakdown of the figures here, comparable to that supplied in Num 3:22, 28, 34. It was previously suggested (see *Form/ Structure/Setting* on Num 3:1–51) that the relatively few numbers of Levites counted there reflect the balance of accredited post-exilic Levites over against lay people. Reasons for the small increase here are not easy to suggest, except that God's commitment to the Levitical order (an important theme in Num 17) is underlined.

A particular difficulty attaches to the priestly genealogy. According to Num 3:17, and Num 3–4 in general, there were three main Levitical families— Gershon, Kohath, and Merari. This view is sustained here in Num 26:57. According to Num 3:18–20 Gershon has two sons—Libni and Shimei, Kohath has four—Amram, Izhar, Hebron, and Uzziel, while Merari has two—Mahli and Mushi. This picture is supported by Exod 6:16–19, and would appear to be the final definitive priestly view. The new introduction at the beginning of v 58 however gives a strong indication that a different list has been incorporated into the priestly work. The traditional analytical explanation has been to see the influence of priestly redactors and supplementers (see e.g. J. Wellhausen, 184–86; H. Holzinger, 132–33; B. Baentsch, 627–35). More recently there has been a tendency to see rather the incorporation in v 58 of older Levitical tradition (see e.g. M. Noth, 209; J. Sturdy, 192; J. de Vaulx, 315). Five Levitical families are mentioned—Libni, Hebron, Mahli, Mushi, and Korah. The names from the definitive genealogy which do not occur here are Shimei (Gershonite), Amram, Izhar, and Uzziel (Kohathites), while Korah in the definitive version is made a son of Izhar (Exod 6:21). The definitive listing is also reflected in the Chronicler's account (1 Chr 5:27–6:34).

Some modern commentators see the content of v 58 as very old—de Vaulx associates it with the time of the judges. There is some reason for thinking that some at least of these names were originally of geographical significance. Libnah (Josh 15:42) and Hebron were both cities in the south of Judah, and Korah might be linked with the city so named in 1 Chr 2:43. A reference to "sons of Korah" on a pot found at Arad confirms Sturdy's view that all five names are probably southern cities where Levites originally lived along with Simeon their old ally (Gen 34:30). Noth compares the name Mahlites with Mahlah in v 33, while Mushi has often been associated with "Moses," there being a pre-priestly tradition in Exod 2:1 to the effect that Moses was of Levitical origin.

It may well be that v 58 contains a list of Levitical families preserved during the exile among Levites in Palestine. The possibility that the list has its roots in the south is therefore very real; only so would such Levites be acceptable to Babylonian Judaism. A process of adjustment to Levitical claims, and of acceptance of elements of Levitical tradition, is one we have traced at many other points in the book of Numbers. This acceptance of more Levitical families as accredited led to the construction of a formal genealogy, tracing Levitical interconnections and tracing in particular the relationship of these families to the sons of Aaron. This is the contribution of what we have called the definitive genealogy. The author preserves the material intact as a sign of his commitment to the place of Levitical tradition within the purposes of God.

Comment

57. For the Levitical names see *Comment* on Num 3:1–51.

58. For discussion of the origin of these Levitical names see *Form/Structure/Setting*.

59. The Kohathite succession is of particular interest because Moses and Aaron belong to it. The family connections of Moses and Aaron are established in older tradition (cf. Exod 4:14; 15:20).

60–61. The reason for a priestly succession through the younger sons of Aaron is given once again (cf. Lev 10:1–7; Num 3:1–4).

62. There is no point in a military census for Levi (i.e. of those aged twenty and over), and so the same principle is applied as previously (cf. Num 3:39).

64. The author here makes it clear that the reference in v 4 to those who left Egypt must be understood in relation to tribes and families, and not to numbers. The second census covers a new generation.

65. cf. Num 14:29–30.

Explanation

Having reconstituted the community after the disasters of the journey (Num 26:1–56) the author now reconstitutes the Levitical order by means of a second census. Just as vv 1–56 echo Num 1:1–47 so these verses echo and balance the establishment of the Levitical community as outlined in Num 3–4. The author does this by reasserting the definitive basic structure of the Levitical genealogy (v 57), by linking Moses and Aaron with it (v 59), by vindicating the priesthood of Eleazar and Ithamar once again (vv 60–61), and by conducting a second census of Levites (v 62). He also provides an explicit reason for the separation of the Levitical census from that of the community as a whole; the Levites do not have their own inheritance among the rest of the people (v 62). This is older Levitical tradition (cf. e.g. Deut 10:9), incorporated like other such tradition elsewhere in the book of Numbers to facilitate the establishment of the new Levitical order. As Num 35:1–8 will make clear this does not mean for the author of Numbers that the Levites lack places to live. The point is rather that they do not own landed property.

The author has also included ancient Levitical tradition in v 58 (see *Form/Structure/Setting*). This may not have initially been available to the priests of Babylonian Judaism. In the early post-exilic period it became possible to accredit these Levitical families, and they become important components in the full and definitive Levitical genealogy which is eventually constructed.

The author's concluding observations (vv 63–65) make it clear that, Joshua and Caleb apart, this is a new community. All those implicated in the rebellions of the journey are dead, and a new beginning is to be made. The community about to engage in the settlement is a purged and renewed community. This also has its place in the apologetic concerns of Babylonian Judaism.

The Daughters of Zelophehad (27:1-11)

Bibliography

Bamberger, B. J. "Revelations of Torah after Sinai." *HUCA* 16 (1941) 97–113. **Davies, E. W.** "Inheritance Rights and the Hebrew Levirate Marriage." *VT* 31 (1981) 138–44. **Lemaire, A.** "Le 'Pays de Hépher' et les 'Filles de Zelophehad' á la lumière des ostraca de Samarie." *Sem* 22 (1972) 13–20. **Snaith, N. H.** "The Daughters of Zelophehad." *VT* 16 (1966) 124–27. **Valk, Z.** "The Right of Inheritance of a Daughter and Widow in Bible and Talmud." *Tarbiz* 23 (1951/52) 9–15. **Weingreen, J.** "The Case of the Daughters of Zelophehad." *VT* 16 (1966) 518–22.

Translation

[1] *And the daughters of Zelophehad son of Hepher son of Gilead son of Machir* [a] *son of Manasseh* [a] *drew near* [b] *(from the clans of Manasseh* [b] *son of Joseph). And these were the names of his daughters: Mahlah, Noah, Hoglah, Milcah, and Tirzah.* [2] *And they stood before Moses and before Eleazar the priest and before the leaders and all the congregation at the door of the Tent of Meeting, saying,* [3] *"Our father died in the wilderness. But he was not among the congregation of those who gathered together against Yahweh, in the congregation of Korah. He died for his own sin. And he had no sons.* [4] *Why should the name of our father be taken away from his clan because he had no son? Give us a possession* [a] *among our father's brothers."*

[5] *And Moses brought their case before Yahweh.* [6] *And Yahweh spoke to Moses, saying,* [7] *"The daughters of Zelophehad are in the right. You shall give them* [a] *possession of an inheritance among their* [a] *father's brothers, and cause the inheritance of their father to pass to them.* [8] *And you shall say to the people of Israel, 'If a man dies, and has no son, then you shall cause his inheritance to pass to his daughter.* [9] *And if he has no daughter, then you shall give his inheritance to his brothers.* [10] *And if he has no brothers, then you shall give his inheritance to his father's brothers.* [11] *And if his father has no brothers, then you shall give his inheritance to his next nearest kinsman, and he shall possess it. And it shall be to the people of Israel a statute and judgment, as Yahweh commanded Moses.'"*

Notes

1.a.-a. Lacking in G.
1.b.-b. Lacking in Vg.
4.a. Sam has "possession of an inheritance" (cf. v 7).
7.a. Feminines are required here (as in some MT mss and Sam); see J. A. Paterson 61.

Form/Structure/Setting

Analysts have had no difficulty in identifying this section as priestly (cf. e.g. J. Wellhausen, 114–15; A. Kuenen, 98; H. Holzinger, 136–37; B. Baentsch,

635–36; G. B. Gray, 397). The passage speaks of the "leaders" (v 2), the "congregation" (v 2), and the door of the Tent of Meeting (v 2). The names of the daughters link the passage with the census list (Num 26:33), and there are clear references in v 3 to the Korah incident in Num 16. Some of the earlier analysts (e.g. Wellhausen and Baentsch) suspected the presence of the basic P narrative, while others (e.g. Kuenen and Holzinger) thought it supplementary. Kuenen thought for example that the passage rests on the same motive as the year of jubilee—retention of ownership of land with the original proprietor—and that law (Lev 25) is generally considered late.

M. Noth (211–12) was in no doubt that the passage, though dependent on priestly phraseology, was a later addition to the P narrative. In terms of its form the story has obvious affinities with that of other difficult cases embedded within the priestly literature (cf. Lev 24:10–23; Num 9:6–14; 15:32–36). On the other hand Noth argues that the legislation itself (vv 8b–11) goes well beyond the terms of the case in point, and that it could therefore be composed of older traditional legal material. The rest of the section, with its concern to secure the rights of daughters, is deemed by Noth to be relatively late. This general view is supported by J. Sturdy (193–94) and J. de Vaulx (318–20). The section is also used by P. Grelot ("Les dernières étapes de la rédaction sacerdotale," VT 6 [1956] 174–89) in his attempt to fix the date of the final priestly redaction.

The section's formal affinities with Num 9:6–14; 15:32–36 make it reasonable from our point of view to see here a major contribution from the author of Numbers. The form is relatively simple. A problem is put before Moses, who then consults God, who in turn makes a pronouncement leading to a general principle. This seems to be a regular pattern in very late parts of the Pentateuch, when the corpus of Sinaitic law was complete, and also the deuteronomic corpus given on the borders of the land. The story has something of the character of a midrash, aimed at resolving later questions in the light of previously given legal principle. This in turn creates wilderness precedents for application in future cases of difficulty (see further J. Weingreen, VT 16 [1966] 518–22).

The only question remaining is the extent to which the author used traditional material. It is often pointed out that the daughters correspond in name to towns west of the Jordan—Noah in Zebulun (Josh 19:13), Hoglah in Judah (Josh 15:6), and Tirzah in Manasseh (Josh 12:24; 1 Kgs 15:21). It is not unreasonable to suppose that the same applies to Mahlah (cf. 1 Chr 7:18) and Milcah. It is difficult to determine whether there is ancient tradition behind the narrative. The transformation of town names with feminine endings into daughters of Zelophehad could very well be the work of the author of Numbers. The point he wishes to make is simply that women have a right of inheritance. The material in Josh 17:1–6, which tells of how Num 27:1–11 was put into effect, would appear in the main to be a gloss, specifying as it does in v 4 that the origin of the request goes back to Mosaic times.

Whether there is traditional material in vv 8–11 is also difficult to determine. An order of precedence—sons, daughters, brothers, uncles, other relatives—is established. It seems possible that the author of Numbers is offering an adaptation of the situation which seems to have been envisaged in deuteronomic law. There only sons seem to be recognized as heirs, and there is particular stress on the rights of the firstborn (Deut 21:15–17). If a man dies without a son his brother must take the widow as wife, and the first son becomes heir to the deceased (Deut 25:5–10). These principles are also implicit in the story of Gen 38 and in the book of Ruth.

N. H. Snaith (*VT* 16 [1966] 124–27) has difficulty with the fact that viewed in one way the story of the daughters of Zelophehad appears to cut across all we know from elsewhere about Israelite laws of inheritance. He concludes that the story is not really about inheritance in legal terms, but an attempt to explain how the tribe of Manasseh came to occupy territory to the west of the Jordan (cf. Josh 17:1–6). The heir normally receives two portions (Deut 21:17) and so the five daughters receive ten (Josh 17:5). What this suggestion does not fully explain is why the portions should fall to daughters rather than sons. Could not the story about Manasseh's occupation of land to the west of the Jordan be composed in terms of sons? It seems best to face the fact that Num 27:1–11 is about the rights of daughters, and to look for ways of understanding its relationship to the marriage and inheritance principles set out in Deuteronomy. It seems most unlikely that the author wished to abrogate the principle of levirate marriage (Deut 25:5–10); that was firmly entrenched in deuteronomic law, and the author's objective is to fill in legal gaps not to abrogate. Though the point is not stated explicitly it is surely to be assumed that Zelophehad's wife is dead, and that the principle the jubilee law is designed to secure (Lev 25:10)—that land be held by a man and his family in perpetuity—is endangered. The divine ruling given here ensures that this danger is averted. There is therefore no particular reason for seeing traditional material in vv 8–11. These stipulations simply extend the principle, ensuring that even should there not be daughters the inheritance is kept as closely as possible within the family. The stipulations viewed in this light do not conflict with the Deuteronomic levirate principle but rather confirm it, because the surviving brother who marries the widow is in fact producing children for his deceased brother. Such children would inherit the dead man's property, not that of the surviving brother and actual father. The stipulations here in vv 1–11 would also cover situations in which there was no brother to marry the widow.

Comment

3. The reference to Zelophehad's sin seems to mean that he shared the general fate of the whole exodus generation. Rabbi Akiba suggested that he was the sabbath breaker of Num 15:32–36, but this was not general rabbinic opinion (see B. J. Bamberger, *HUCA* 16 [1941] 97–113). The author views Korah's sin in a very serious light, and the daughters are anxious to show that he was in no way implicated.

4. The continued existence of a man's "name" was important to Israelites, and one way in which it could be preserved was in connection with the inheritance of his land by his descendants.

5. The fact that Moses has no immediate reply to the request causes some confusion and embarrassment to the rabbis (see B. J. Bamberger, *HUCA* 16

[1941] 97–113). Some limit Moses' ignorance, others see in it a punishment for his sin, and others a sign of his humility or a good example to future judges on matters of which they are uncertain.

11. משפט לחקת "a statute and judgment," evidently technical legal terminology, and hence NEB's "legal precedent" (cf. Num 35:29).

Explanation

This section tells of how the daughters of Zelophehad seek to secure a right to their father's property. He has died without male heirs, and there is no clear stipulation indicating their position, or the destination of the property. It is reasonable to assume that there is no widow to bear children by her dead husband's brother, in accordance with the requirements of Deut 25:5–10. Moses addresses the question to God, and specific guidelines are given, indicating that the daughters do indeed have the right to inherit, there being no sons, and extending the chain of precedence among other close relatives.

It appears that the section is essentially the work of the priestly author of the book of Numbers. The story is tied in with the Korah incident in Num 16, and with the census list in Num 26 (see *Form/Structure/Setting*). It appears to be his construction. The names of the daughters may have been derived from the names of ancient towns, three of them occurring as such in the deuteronomic history.

The story is possibly intended to resolve a particular issue which had become pressing in the author's time. The circumstances of exile and return made the question of access to land, and the associated rights, a real and very live issue. A particular question, left unanswered in deuteronomic law, concerning the rights of daughters, is here given a clear and definitive answer. Here again, as in Num 26:1–56 and Num 26:57–65, we see the author of Numbers, working on and expanding and interpreting certain elements in the deuteronomic and historical tradition. The section comes naturally enough at this point since persons cited in the census list (Num 26:33) are here the subject of the request.

It also seems likely that the author is motivated by the exilic/post-exilic jubilee principle which receives its fullest exposition in Lev 25. This principle was intended to secure the point that all landed property should be kept within the family of the original owner. This principle was based on the theological premise that ultimately all the land was Yahweh's (Lev 25:23). The system of divine distribution was therefore not to be disturbed by the economic activity of man. Insisting that daughters had the right to inherit where there were no sons, and spelling out a chain of precedence beyond the daughters meant that a man who died without sons and wife would nevertheless keep the land within his family, and thus preserve his name. The further question of what should happen to the property inherited by daughters when they marry is not touched on here. The matter is tackled in the appendix in Num 36.

Theologically the section presses the rights of women to a clear and recognized legal position within the sphere of property law. They are seen as a proper channel through which the threads of possession and inheritance may properly be traced. The section also affirms the fundamental jubilee principle that the unregulated appropriation of landed property is harmful to the well-being of the community. It tends to make some Israelites economically dependent on others, though all are equal in status as members of God's community. Its other defect is its fundamental failure to recognize that the land in the last resort is God's, and must be distributed according to his laws. Man holds the land as steward, not as its owner or ultimate master.

The Commissioning of Joshua   (27:12–23)

Bibliography

Coats, G. W. "Legendary Motifs in the Moses Death Reports." *CBQ* 39 (1977) 34–44. **Lindblom, J.** "Lot Casting in the Old Testament." *VT* 12 (1962) 164–78. **Lipiński, E.** "Urim and Tummim." *VT* 20 (1970) 495–96. **Loewenstamm, S. E.** "The Death of Moses." *Tarbiz* 27 (1957/58) 142–57. **Long, B. O.** "The Effect of Divination upon Israelite Literature." *JBL* 92 (1973) 489–97. **Péter, R.** "L'imposition des mains dans l'Ancien Testament." *VT* 27 (1977) 48–55. **Robertson, E.** "Urim and Thummim: what are they?" *VT* 14 (1964) 67–14.

Translation

[12] *And Yahweh said to Moses, "Go up this mountain Abarim,*[a] *and view the land* [b] *which I have given to the people of Israel.*[c] [13] *And when you have seen it, you also shall be gathered to your people, as your brother Aaron was,*[a] [14] *because you rebelled against my word in the wilderness of Zin, when the congregation contended, and did not* [a] *sanctify me at the waters before their eyes."* [b] *These were the waters of Meribah Kadesh in the wilderness of Zin.* [b] [15] *And Moses spoke to Yahweh, saying,* [16] *"Let Yahweh, the God of the spirits of all flesh, appoint a man over the congregation,* [17] *Who shall go out before them* [a] *and come in before them, who shall lead them out and bring them in, so that the congregation of Yahweh may not be as sheep which have no shepherd."* [18] *And Yahweh said to Moses, "Take Joshua son of Nun, a man in whom is the spirit, and lay your hand upon him.* [19] *Make him stand before Eleazar the priest and all the congregation, and you shall commission him in their sight.* [20] *You shall invest him with some of your authority,*[a] *so that all the congregation of the people of Israel may obey.* [21] *And he shall stand before Eleazar the priest, who shall make consultation for him by the judgment of the Urim before Yahweh. At his word they shall go out, and at his word they shall come in, both he and all the people of Israel with him, the whole congregation."* [22] *And Moses did as Yahweh commanded him. He took Joshua and made him stand before Eleazar the priest and the whole congregation.* [23] *And he laid his hands* [a] *upon him, and commissioned him, as Yahweh had spoken* [b] *by the hand of Moses.*[b]

Notes

12.a. In reading "Nebo" G appears to be bringing the text into line with Deut 32:48.
12.b. "Of Canaan" has been added in G and S (cf. Deut 32:49).
12.c. G has "as an inheritance" (influenced by Deut 32:49).
13.a. G adds "on Mount Hor" (influenced by Deut 32:50).
14.a. The negative has to be assumed (cf. G, Syr, and Deut 32:51).
14.b. Perhaps an explanatory gloss drawn in from Deut 32:51.
17.a. Tg[J] has a long gloss at this point, explaining that the reference is to war.
20.a. "glory" in G, Vg, and Syr.
23.a. The singular occurs in Sam and Syr.
23.b.-b. The phrase is lacking in Vg.

Form/Structure/Setting

There is no problem in recognizing this section as priestly. Israel is depicted as "congregation" (vv 14, 16, 17, 19, 20, 21, 22), and the story refers very clearly to the priestly account of the death of Aaron (v 13; cf. Num 20:22–29). There is also a recollection of the priestly tradition of water from the rock (v 14; cf. Num 20:1–13). The phraseology of Num 16:22 (P) is repeated in the invocation of "the God of the spirits of all flesh" (v 16). Eleazar is functioning as Aaron's successor (vv 19, 20), and is responsible for the priestly Urim, first mentioned in the priestly parts of the book of Exodus (Exod 28:30).

Many problems remain, however, and among them the relation of the passage to the account of the death of Moses in Deut 32. Analysts have also noted that the death of Moses is to occur shortly, judging by v 13. Quite apart from the large corpus of deuteronomic law yet to be given there is the problem of the relationship of v 13 to Num 31:2, an evidently priestly text, where it becomes clear that Moses is to conduct the Midianite war before he dies. A popular solution among the older analysts was to attribute vv 12–14 (or vv 12–13) to later editing, and to see the rest of the section as the basic PG narrative (see e.g. H. Holzinger, 136–37; B. Baentsch, 637–40; G. B. Gray, 399–400). If the insertion of Deuteronomy and much of Num 28–36 is judged a product of the compiler of the Hexateuch then there need not have been much in PG separating the account of the institution of Joshua in vv 15–23 and the account of the death, now preserved in Deut 32. This is feasible, but still fails to offer an explanation for the inclusion of vv 12–14.

M. Noth (213) pays particular attention to the relationship of vv 12–23 and Deut 32:48–52. He concludes that the latter is likely to be more original on the grounds that it alludes only to the death of Moses, and not like vv 15–23 to the question of his successor. This leads him to suppose that only vv 12–14 belonged to the original P narrative, that Deut 32:48–52 repeats and amplifies it, and that vv 15–23 are added later when the Pentateuch is linked to the deuteronomic history. It is, after all, in the deuteronomic tradition that the closest links between the death of Moses and the installation of Joshua are established (Deut 3:23–29; 31:1–8; Josh 1:1–2). J. Sturdy (196) accepts this analysis, and like many others sees Num 28–36 as essentially an addition to P, thereby easing the difficulty of the time lag between this section and the death of Moses. J. de Vaulx (321–25) is more disposed to perceive the unity of the passage, suggesting that an old deuteronomic tradition (E?) (Deut 31:14, 23) has been used to create a priestly tradition modeled on the account of the death of Aaron in Num 20.

De Vaulx's suggestion about the unity and origin of the tradition is useful, and there is no difficulty in attributing it to the priestly author of Numbers. It is natural enough that he should wish to give his own version of the institution of Joshua. The principles are set out in Deut 31:14, 23, and since Joshua is to play such a crucial role in the forthcoming settlement it is entirely proper from the priestly point of view that he should be commissioned in a way comparable to that provided for Eleazar at the time of the death of Aaron.

There is probably also some use of Deut 34, a chapter telling of the death of Moses, and without any necessarily priestly features. In Deut 34:9 there is reference to a laying on of hands, and it is on this theme that Num 27:12–23 appears to build.

It would, of course, have been possible for priestly editors to build in this tradition at some suitably late stage in the book of Deuteronomy. There are clear signs of priestly editing in Deut 32:48–52, and the account of the institution of Joshua could conceivably have been introduced at that point. On the other hand there are also reasons for telling the story here. The themes of possession and inheritance had been raised in vv 1–11, and it was appropriate enough to turn attention at this point to the one through whom possession of the land would be achieved. More important is the parallel which this section offers to Num 20:22–29—the death of Aaron and the commissioning of Eleazar. It was important, after the disasters of the journey, to reassert God's commitment to the enterprise, and in particular, with the sin of Moses very much in mind, to the leadership. We have already seen this kind of concern at many points in the second part of the book, and here it appears again. There is thus no reason for feeling that the long gap between v 13 and Deut 34 requires the assumption that Num 28–36 are necessarily not of a piece with the rest of the book. Deut 34 is in any case essentially deuteronomic; the priestly author of Num 27:13 must have known of it, and also that there was still much work for Moses to do (in Deuteronomy). The author's real interest in v 13 is not to make a precise chronological point about the death of Moses, but to point out that Moses like Aaron sinned in the wilderness and would not therefore enter the land. He does not wish the reader to lose sight of the fact that Moses and Aaron sinned together in Num 20:1–13, and therefore here in v 13 is keeping fresh in the mind the events of Num 20:22–29 (in particular v 24). It is this interest which is further enforced in Num 31:2.

Comment

12. Abarim is a general name for a mountain range. Deuteronomy has the more precise designation "Mount Nebo" (Deut 32:49).

13. Later Jewish interpretation was much exercised by the death of Moses. Why was he not worthy to enter the land, and how could he die like an ordinary mortal? Some approaches accused Moses of further sins; others suggested that he died on account of Adam's sin (for further discussion see S. E. Loewenstamm, *Tarbiz* 27 [1957/58] 142–57).

14. The reference here is to the story in Num 20:1–13. In the words "contended" and "sanctify" there is a play on the place name Meribah Kadesh.

16. אלהי הרוחת לכל-בשר "the God of the spirits of all flesh" (see *Comment* on Num 16:22).

17. אשר יצא . . . ואשר יבא "who shall go out . . . and come in." This is probably technical terminology from the military sphere (cf. e.g. Josh 14:11; 1 Sam 18:13–16; 1 Kgs 3:7; 2 Kgs 11:9). The shepherding imagery can also be military (cf. e.g. 1 Kgs 22:17).

18. איש אשר-רוח בו "a man in whom is the spirit" (cf. Deut 34:9). This

seems to be a permanent endowment for Joshua, rather than a temporary empowering for specific action (see *Comment* on Num 11:18).

The laying on of hands here signifies the transference of leadership from Moses to Joshua (see *Comment* on Num 8:10).

20. מהוד "some of your authority." This word occurs only here in the Pentateuch. Majesty and splendor are often denoted by it (cf. e.g. Ps 96:6). M. Noth (215) sees the transference of something effective, perhaps even visible. "Vitality" is a possible rendering.

21. The author is anxious here to assert that though Joshua is in some sense the successor of Moses he is in no way on a par with him. Unlike Moses he has no direct contact with God, being dependent on the guidance offered through the priestly oracle.

Urim is part of the sacred lot ("Urim" and "Thummim") which in the priestly scheme was kept in the high priest's breastplate (Exod 28:30; Lev 8:8). The usual conclusion is that these were two flat stones capable of giving a positive or negative response to a question on the basis of the way they fell when cast. A mixed response (one positive, one negative) would perhaps be considered indecisive, in the way suggested by 1 Sam 28:6. G understands 1 Sam 14:40–41 in terms of Urim and Thummim. That the handling of this particular oracular device was an ancient Levitical privilege is suggested by the old text in Deut 33:8. It is generally believed that in post-exilic times these objects were merely part of the high priest's vestments and not for regular use, though the meaning of Ezra 2:63=Neh 7:65 is unclear. There is some indication that in pre-exilic times the kind of question which might be addressed to mechanical devices such as Urim and Thummim was increasingly addressed to the prophet (cf. 1 Kgs 22:7; 2 Kgs 3:11).

Explanation

This section tells of a divine command to Moses to view the land from the mountains of Abarim. Because of his sin at Meribah Kadesh he is not to be allowed to enter the land, and so like Aaron he will shortly die. In the light of this Moses makes a request that someone replace him as the leader of the community, specifically, it appears, for the forthcoming campaigns. Joshua is chosen by God and is duly commissioned before Eleazar the priest for his task. Joshua is to be guided by the priestly oracle in all his military undertakings.

The section appears to be essentially the work of the priestly author of Numbers. Moses still has many duties to perform, supremely the giving of his farewell discourses and laws, as preserved in Deuteronomy. The author has two specific objectives in preparing us at this early stage for the death of Moses.

In the first place he wishes to link the death of Moses as closely as possible with that of Aaron (Num 20:22–29). The exclusion of Moses from the land is to be understood primarily as the consequence of his and Aaron's sin at Meribah Kadesh. It is particularly important to make this point before the somewhat different view of the matter enshrined in the book of Deuteronomy occurs (cf. e.g. Deut 3:26).

His second concern is to introduce Joshua at a reasonably early stage as the successor of Moses, specifically in the matter of military leadership. There was already a Mosaic charge to Joshua in Deut 31:23, but this section in Num 27:12-23 gives the charge a distinctly priestly flavor. The particular reason for making the choice of Joshua clear at this point is that this choice signals God's commitment to the leadership, despite the disasters of the wilderness journey. We have seen this to be a persistent concern in the second part of the book of Numbers. Despite the sins of the community and its leaders, along with the merited consequences of those sins, there is nevertheless always a new beginning. Moses and Aaron are not to enter the land with the people, but the need for leadership is fully cared for in Eleazar and Joshua. Even the sin of Moses himself is not a blight on the community's future.

Joshua therefore represents the lay leadership for the settlement, and there is particular stress on his responsibility for conducting the campaigns of occupation. On the other hand he is evidently not a second Moses. The uniqueness of divine revelation to Moses remains. Joshua's subservience to the priestly oracle of Eleazar, even in those matters which are to be his direct concern, the fighting of Yahweh's war, is particularly noteworthy. This stipulation in v 21 underscores the priestly author's view of the community as a priestly theocracy, and doubtless serves the interests and concerns of post-exilic Judaism.

The third part of the book has so far revealed itself to be concerned with preliminary matters relating to the land. This is a theme which unites many of the otherwise varied and disparate elements in Num 26–36. In Num 26 the community is reconstituted through the census, and thereby rendered ready for the settlement. In Num 27:1–11 the question of property rights within the land is raised, and settled in an ordered fashion. Here the question of the lay leadership for settlement of the land is resolved in favor of Joshua the son of Nun. Here, too, as elsewhere in Num 26–36, there is adaptation and expansion of deuteronomic and deuteronomistic tradition (see *Form/Structure/Setting*). It is as though certain priestly points must be made before the great complex of deuteronomic tradition begins.

The List of Offerings   (28:1-30:1)

Bibliography

Auerbach, E. "Die Feste im alten Israel." *VT* 8 (1958) 1–18. **Goudoever, J. van** *Biblical Calendars.* Leiden: Brill, 1959. **Gray, G. B.** *Sacrifice in the Old Testament.* Oxford: Clarendon Press, 1925. **Levine, B. A.** "The Descriptive Tabernacle Tests of the Pentateuch." *JAOS* 85 (1965) 312–13. **MacRae, G. W.** "The Meaning and Evolution of the Feast of Tabernacles." *CBQ* 22 (1960) 251–76. **Martin-Achard, R.** *Essai biblique sur les fêtes d'Israël.* Geneva: Labor et Fides, 1974. **Morgan, D. F.** *The So-Called Cultic Calendars in the Pentateuch* (*Ex 23:10–19, 34:18–26, Lev 23, Nu 28–29, Deut 16:1–17*). *A Morphological and Typological Study.* Dissertation, Claremont, 1974. **Morgenstern, J.** "The Three Calendars of Ancient Israel." *HUCA* 1 (1924) 13–78; *HUCA* 3 (1926) 77–107; *HUCA* 10 (1935) 1–148. **Orlinsky, H. M.** "Numbers XXVIII 9, 12, 13." *VT* 20 (1970) 500. **Rainey, A. F.** "The Order of Sacrifices in Old Testament Ritual Texts." *Bib* 51 (1970) 485–98. **Rost, L.** "Zu den Festopfervorschriften von Numeri 28 u. 29." *TLZ* 83 (1958) 329–34. **Segal, J. B.** "Intercalation and the Hebrew Calendar." *VT* 7 (1957) 250–307. ———. "The Hebrew Festivals and the Calender." *JSS* 6 (1961) 74–94. **Snaith, N. H.** *The Jewish New Year Festival.* London: SPCK, 1947. ———. "Numbers XXVIII 9, 11, 13." *VT* 19 (1969) 374. **Thompson, R. J.** *Penitence and Sacrifice in Early Israel.* Leiden: Brill, 1960.

Translation

²⁸:¹ *And Yahweh spoke to Moses, saying,* ² *"Command the people of Israel, and say to them, 'My offering, my food* ᵃ *for my fire offerings, my soothing odor, you shall take care to offer to me at its appointed time.'* ³ *And you shall say to them, 'This is the fire offering which you shall offer to Yahweh: two unblemished male lambs a year old, every day, as a regular offering.* ⁴ *The one lamb you shall offer in the morning, and the other lamb you shall offer in the evening.* ⁵ *Also a tenth of an ephah of fine flour for a cereal offering, mixed with a quarter of a hin of beaten* ᵃ *oil.* ⁶ *It is a regular whole offering, ordained at Mount Sinai for a soothing odor, a fire offering to Yahweh.* ⁷ *Its drink offering shall be a quarter of a hin for each lamb. In the holy place you shall pour out a drink offering of strong drink to Yahweh.* ⁸ *The other lamb you shall offer in the evening. Like the cereal offering of the morning, and like its drink offering, you shall offer it as a fire offering, a soothing odor to Yahweh.*

⁹ *On the sabbath day* ᵃ *two unblemished male lambs a year old, and two tenths of an ephah of fine flour for a cereal offering, mixed with oil, and its drink offering.* ¹⁰ *This is the whole offering of every sabbath, in addition to the regular whole offering and its drink offering.*

¹¹ *On the first day of every month you shall offer a whole offering to Yahweh: two young bulls, one ram, seven unblemished male lambs a year old.* ¹² *Also three*

tenths of an ephah of fine flour for a cereal offering, mixed with oil, for each bull;
and two tenths of fine flour for a cereal offering, mixed with oil, for the one ram.
¹³ And a tenth of fine flour mixed with oil as a cereal offering for every lamb, for a
whole offering of soothing odor, a fire offering to Yahweh. ¹⁴ Their drink offerings
shall be half a hin of wine ᵃ for each ᵇ bull, a third of a hin for a ram, and a
quarter of a hin for a lamb. This is the whole offering for each month throughout
the months of the year. ¹⁵ Also one male goat for a purification offering to Yahweh.
It shall be offered in addition to the regular whole offering and its drink offering.

¹⁶ On the fourteenth day of the first month is Yahweh's passover. ¹⁷ And on the
fifteenth day of this month is a feast.ᵃ For seven days shall unleavened bread be
eaten.ᵇ ¹⁸ On the first day there shall be ᵃ a sacred assembly. You shall do no laborious
work. ¹⁹ And you shall offer a fire offering, a whole offering to Yahweh: two young
bulls, one ram, and seven male lambs a year old. Ensure that they are unblemished.
²⁰ Also their cereal offering of fine flour mixed with oil; three tenths of an ephah you
shall offer for a bull, and two tenths for a ram. ²¹ A tenth you shall offer for each
of the seven lambs. ²² Also one male goat for a purification offering, to make atonement
for you. ²³ You shall offer these in addition to the whole offering of the morning,
which is a regular whole offering. ²⁴ In the same way you shall offer daily, for seven
days, the food of a fire offering, a soothing odor to Yahweh. It shall be offered in
addition to the regular whole offering and its drink offering. ²⁵ And on the seventh
day you shall have a sacred assembly. You shall do no laborious work.

²⁶ On the day of firstfruits, when you offer a cereal offering of new grain to Yahweh
at your feast of weeks, you shall have a sacred assembly. You shall do no laborious
work. ²⁷ And you shall offer a whole offering,ᵃ a soothing odor to Yahweh: two
young bulls, one ram, seven male lambs a year old.ᵇ ²⁸ Also their cereal offering of
fine flour, mixed with oil, three tenths of an ephah for each bull, two tenths for one
ram, ²⁹ a tenth for each of the seven lambs, ³⁰ with one male goat, to make atonement
for you. ³¹ You shall offer them and their drink offering in addition to the regular
whole offering and its cereal offering. Ensure that they are unblemished.

²⁹:¹ On the first day of the seventh month you shall have a sacred assembly. You
shall do no laborious work. It is a day for you to blow trumpets. ² And you shall
offer a whole offering, a soothing odor to Yahweh: one young bull, one ram, seven
unblemished male lambs a year old. ³ Also their cereal offering of fine flour, mixed
with oil, three tenths of an ephah for the bull, two tenths for the ram, ⁴ and one
tenth for each of the seven lambs, ⁵ with one male goat for a purification offering,
to make atonement for you, ⁶ in addition to the whole offering of the new moon,
and its cereal offering, and their drink offering, as prescribed, a soothing odor, a fire
offering ᵃ to Yahweh.

⁷ On the tenth day of the seventh month you shall have a sacred assembly, and
you shall mortify yourselves. You shall do no work.ᵃ ⁸ You shall offer a whole offering
to Yahweh, a soothing odor: one young bull, one ram, seven male lambs a year old.
They shall be to you without blemish.ᵃ ⁹ And their cereal offering of fine flour, mixed
with oil, three tenths of an ephah for the ᵃ bull, two tenths for the one ᵇ ram, ¹⁰ a
tenth for each of the seven lambs, ¹¹ and one male goat for a purification offering,
in addition to the purification offering of atonement, and the regular whole offering
and its cereal offering, and their drink offerings.

¹² On the fifteenth day of the ᵃ seventh month you shall have a sacred assembly.
You shall do no laborious work, and you shall keep a seven day feast to Yahweh.

[13] *And you shall offer a whole offering, a fire offering, a soothing odor to Yahweh. On the first day* ª *thirteen young bulls, two rams, fourteen male lambs a year old. They shall be unblemished,* ᵇ [14] *and their cereal offering of fine flour, mixed with oil, three tenths of an ephah for each of the thirteen bulls, two tenths for each of the two rams,* [15] *and a tenth for each of the fourteen lambs,* [16] *and one male goat for a purification offering, in addition to the regular whole offering, its* ª *cereal offering and its* ª *drink offering.*

[17] *On the second day twelve young bulls, two rams, fourteen unblemished male lambs a year old,* [18] *with the cereal offering and the drink offerings for the bulls, for the rams, and for the lambs, by number, as prescribed,* [19] *and one male goat for a purification offering, in addition to the regular whole offering and its cereal offering, and their drink offerings.*

[20] *On the third day eleven young bulls, two rams, fourteen unblemished male lambs a year old,* [21] *with the cereal offering and the drink offerings for the bulls, for the rams, and for the lambs, by number, as prescribed,* [22] *and one male goat for a purification offering, in addition to the regular whole offering and its cereal offering, and its drink offering.*

[23] *On the fourth day ten young bulls, two rams, fourteen unblemished male lambs a year old,* [24] *with the cereal offering and the drink offerings for the bulls, for the rams, and for the lambs, by number, as prescribed,* [25] *and one male goat for a purification offering, in addition to the regular whole offering and its cereal offering, and its drink offering.*

[26] *On the fifth day nine young bulls, two rams, fourteen unblemished male lambs a year old,* [27] *with the cereal offering and the drink offerings for the bulls, for the rams, and for the lambs, by number, as prescribed,* [28] *and one male goat for a purification offering, in addition to the regular whole offering and its cereal offering, and its drink offering.*

[29] *On the sixth day eight young bulls, two rams, fourteen unblemished male lambs a year old,* [30] *with the cereal offering and the drink offerings for the bulls, for the rams, and for the lambs, by number, as prescribed,* [31] *and one male goat for a purification offering, in addition to the regular whole offering and its cereal offering, and its drink offering.*

[32] *On the seventh day seven young bulls, two rams, fourteen unblemished male lambs a year old,* [33] *with the cereal offering and the drink offerings for the bulls, for the rams, and for the lambs, by number, as prescribed,* [34] *and one male goat for a purification offering, in addition to the regular whole offering and its cereal offering, and its drink offering.*

[35] *On the eighth day you shall have a closing assembly. You shall do no laborious work* [36] *And you shall offer a whole offering, a fire offering, a soothing odor to Yahweh:* ª *one bull, one ram, seven unblemished male lambs a year old,* [37] *and the cereal offering and the drink offerings for the bull, for the ram, and for the lambs, by number, as prescribed,* [38] *and one male goat for a purification offering, in addition to the regular whole offering and its cereal offering, and its drink offering.*

[39] *These you shall offer to Yahweh at your appointed feasts, in addition to your votive offerings and your freewill offerings, for your whole offerings, and for your cereal offerings, and for your drink offerings, and for your shared offerings.'* ''

[30:1] (Eng.40) *And Moses told the people of Israel everything, just as Yahweh had commanded Moses.*

Notes

28.2.a. *BHS* suggests לֶחֶם֙ "the food of . . ." (cf. 28:24).
5.a. "beaten" is lacking in Sam and G.
9.a. G, Vg, and Tgᴺ add "you shall offer."
14.a. A reference to "wine" occurs in Sam, Syr, Vg, and Tgᵒ, and is obviously intended. Its absence in MT is probably accidental. It occurs later in the verse in MT, and should perhaps be deleted there.
14.b. Following Sam and G.
17.a. "Of unleavened bread" is meant (cf. Lev 23:6).
17.b. Sam and G read "you shall eat"; but cf. Ezek 45:21. Sam and G may be harmonizing the text with v 18.
18.a. G reads "you shall have" as in v 25.
27.a. Sam adds "a fire offering" (cf. v 24).
27.b. Sam has "they shall be to you without blemish" (cf. 28:19; 29:8).
6.a. Lacking in G.
7.a. In G, Syr, and Vg "laborious" (cf. 29:12, 35).
8.a. Syr lacks "they shall be to you."
9.a. The indefinite article occurs in G and Syr.
9.b. Lacking in Syr.
12.a. "This" in Sam, G, and Syr.
13.a. The first day is obviously intended, and occurs in G.
13.b. Sam adds "to you."
16.a. The plural occurs in G.
36.a. G has the formulae of 29:6b here.

Form/Structure/Setting

Analysts have been in no doubt that this long and detailed description of the sacrifices for the main festivals belongs to the priestly level. There has also been fairly general agreement that this is late priestly material (see A. Dillmann, 180–85; J. Wellhausen, 184; A. Kuenen, 99; H. Holzinger, 140–41; B. Baentsch, 640–41; G. B. Gray, 402–7). Kuenen argued that the chapters are out of place here and should really follow Lev 23. An indicator of the lateness of the section was the fact that quantities left to the freewill of the people in Lev 23 are here fixed. Kuenen also thought that 28:3–8 had been taken over from Exod 29:38–42, and that the section as a whole here is an attempt to deal exhaustively with the subject in hand—an obvious sign of later exposition. Dillmann had pointed out that the feast of the new moon, ignored in Lev 23 (but see Num 10:10), is here placed on a level with the other feasts. Moreover in Num 29:12–34 the Feast of Tabernacles seems to be more important than Passover—it has more sacrifices assigned to it—but there is no hint of such pre-eminence in Lev 23:34. These phenomena were all held to be best understood in terms of the lateness of Num 28–29. Certain phrases were also held to be generally untypical of earlier P tradition—"food for my fire offerings" (28:2), "ordained at Mount Sinai" (28:6), "in the holy place" (28:7), and "strong drink to Yahweh" (28:8).

Gray suggested that the section is "not improbably post-Ezran in origin." He points out among other things that this is the only place in the Pentateuch where a systematic table of quantities to be used at regular public offerings is to be found. He also examined what was required of the prince in Ezek

45:18–46:15, and the scattered allusions to quantities in Num 15:1–16; Exod 29:38–42 and Lev 23:13, 18–20. He can find no verbal dependence of Num 28–29 on Lev 23, and concludes that the two sections are probably based on a festal calendar now lost. Clear indicators of lateness for Gray are the fixing of the Day of Atonement on the tenth day of the seventh month, which may not have been determined even as late as Ezra (cf. Neh 9:1), and the quantities required, which in all respects appear to be later and more systematized than any in Ezek 45–46 and Lev 23. Gray also thought it likely that Neh 10:34 implies only one whole offering, and that therefore Num 28–29 is to be dated sometime between Ezra and the Chronicler (who recognizes the Pentateuchal scheme of things).

For reasons such as these it has become customary in criticism to see in these two chapters some of the latest OT developments with regard to sacrifice. Earlier practice fixed the festivals in line with agricultural operations, which would naturally have varied, according to the weather, from year to year (Exod 23:16; 34:22; Deut 16:9). The quantities offered were left to individual discretion, with the reminder that giving should be in accordance with the measure of Yahweh's blessing (Deut 16:10, 17). It should also be noted that the sacrifices here required throughout the year are exclusively whole offerings and purification offerings. There is certainly scope for votive offerings and freewill offerings (29:39), but those with which the section is concerned are the sacrifices made over entirely to God, in which laymen had no share. The prominent place given to shared offerings in the earlier laws is absent here.

M. Noth (219–20) and J. Sturdy (200–1) also see the section as supplementary. For Noth it is an appendix, not so much to P as to a completed form of the Pentateuchal tradition. It finds its place here after the intimation of the death of Moses (Num 27:12–14) as the definitive and most systematic treatment of the subject in hand. It presupposes Lev 17–26 (H), Lev 1–7, and is also in Noth's view later than Num 15:1–16, because what is demanded there as something new—the addition of cereal offerings and drink offerings— is here presupposed. For the most part Noth finds the section to be a literary unit, though he suspects the various references to the goat as a purification offering for atonement to be later additions. Also secondary in his opinion are the stereotyped pedantic references to the fact that all sacrifices are to be offered *in addition to* the regular whole offerings. Other minor additions are discerned in 29:6a[a] and 29:11b[a], both tending to disrupt material which originally probably belonged together. Noth also recognizes in the passage some ancient and archaic forms of expression: the description of the sacrifices as God's "food" (28:24; cf. Lev 21:6, 8, 17), the "soothing odor" (e.g. 28:2 and elsewhere), and the term "sacred assembly" (28:18, 25, 26; 29:1, 7, 12).

J. de Vaulx (326–45) lays a good deal of stress on the role of the author of Numbers in this section, collecting and systematizing the somewhat diverse material available to him in other parts of the Pentateuch and in Ezekiel. In earlier festal law de Vaulx argues for a strong influence from Canaan, aligning the festivals to agricultural operations, but after the death of Josiah he suggests an influence from the Babylonian calendar (2 Kgs 24:1). This is the influence which survives in Judaism throughout the exilic and post-exilic period, and which emerges here in Num 28–29. In de Vaulx's opinon the table probably dates to the Persian period; it is unlikely to be later since important later festivals receive no mention (cf. Esth 9:21; 1 Macc 4:59; 7:49).

There is nothing in these discussions which precludes the possibility that this section is compiled by the priestly author of Numbers. Signs that the author has built on existing priestly material—in Exod 29 and Lev 23—is in line with this view. Arguments that Num 28–29 are out of place here only hold good on the assumption that P is to be understood in terms of PG/PS sort of relationship. There may well be supplementary elements within P but much of the seeming dislocation makes sense if it is assumed that each of the books of the Tetrateuch was edited as a whole, and carries with it a priestly identity and integrity of its own. This section in Num 28–29 constitutes the definitive view of the author of Numbers on the matter of the calendar, and on the fixed quantities to be offered on each occasion. The incorporation of the new moon feast—reckoned with also in Num 10:10— is a further distinctive contribution from this author. Those minor words and phrases, held to be untypical of P, can also make sense in the light of our hypothesis; what may be untypical of P as a whole need not be so within the narrower confines of the book of Numbers. Whether or not Gray is correct in placing the material later than Ezra depends on an uncertain interpretation of Neh 10:34; our view that the work of Ezra and the author of Numbers are to be closely associated remains a very plausible one.

The achievement of the author of Numbers here in relation to previously existing law is essentially one of addition rather than alteration. It may be true that there are no necessary signs of literary dependence on Lev 23, but it remains likely nevertheless that this H material was familiar to the author, and that he used its framework as a basis for the construction of his own calendar. It seems likely that the author was also familiar with the texts in Ezekiel. Since the quantities given there were evidently not of Mosaic origin, and were in any case the responsibility of the prince, it was not difficult for him to make adjustments. The result of these adjustments is to make some offerings more costly. The daily whole offering is two lambs not one, to be offered morning and evening, one on each occasion. The celebration on the first of the month is seven lambs (not six) and two bulls (not one), with the goat as a further addition. The offerings for the feast of Tabernacles are more substantial overall—fourteen lambs, two rams, thirteen bulls decreasing progressively to seven over the seven days of the feast (seven rams and seven bulls in Ezekiel). At other points the offerings are less—for sabbath only two lambs (not six and one ram), and for unleavened bread only two bulls (not seven).

With respect to these differences it seems likely that the author of Numbers thinks of his list as additional rather than an alternative. The texts in Ezekiel speak consistently of the sacrificial responsibilities of the "prince," who for the author of Numbers would have been the governor. His concern here in Num 28–29 is to outline the responsibilities of the people. It may be that responsibility for providing the materials still lay with the civil leadership, as Ezek 45:22 suggests, but the laws of Num 28–29 are clearly addressed to the community and are for the community.

The author's other concern is to fix the quantities for the whole and purification offerings—those sacrifices which are entirely Yahweh's. It is no concern of his to underplay the shared offerings mentioned in earlier laws, but he does attach particular importance to the total dedication and cleansing of the community implicit in these particular offerings. There is no particular reason for accepting Noth's view that the goat of the purification offerings is a later addition. It has an integral place in Ezekiel's offerings for the Feast of Unleavened Bread, and its use is here extended by the author of Numbers.

With respect to deuteronomic tradition it seems likely that the author wished to give a fuller calendar and more detailed sacrificial information than that contained in Deut 16:1–20. There was for him—as also for the other priestly contributors to the Pentateuch—a substantial Mosaic tradition in this area which needed to be asserted before the giving of Deuteronomic law itself.

Comment

28.2. קרבני-את "my offering," a word emphasizing that these are to be the sacrifices which are wholly Yahweh's.

2. לחמי "my food," see in particular L. Rost (*TLZ* 83 [1958] 329–34). This, along with the phrase "soothing odor" (see *Comment* on Num 15:3), is probably to be understood figuratively in its present context. The language may nevertheless reflect ancient belief about the nature and purpose of sacrifice which should be understood more literally.

3. The NEB translation omits any reference to "fire," though this seems to be required by the Hebrew. The regular offering was made daily, and according to N. H. Snaith (312) was the basis of the whole sacrificial system. It was certainly a feature of the pre-exilic temple (2 Kgs 16:15), where it appears that an animal was offered in the morning and grain in the evening. In Ezek 46:13–15 there is a morning offering of one lamb. Here, as in Exod 29:38–42, two lambs are offered, one in the morning and one in the evening. The author builds on the Ezekiel text, specifying the amount of fine flour to be used (one tenth of an ephah), and the amount of oil (a quarter of a hin), and adding a drink offering. According to Lev 6:13–16 the fine flour was divided into two—one portion for the morning, and one for the evening.

4. הערבים בין "in the evening," literally "between the two evenings" (cf. Exod 16:6; Lev 23:53; Exod 12:6; 29:39, 41; Num 9:3, 5, 11). A narrow period of time seems to be required in Exod 16:6, and "between dusk and darkness" seems the most likely meaning. Other suggestions included "between noon and sunset," and "between sunset and dark."

5. The rules for the cereal offering of Num 15 are here presupposed. On the "ephah" and the "hin" see *Comment* on Num 15:4.

6. The author seems anxious to assert that these laws have the full force of Sinaitic law. He may also be making a direct reference to Exod 29:38–42.

7. בקרש "in the holy place." According to Sir 50:15 the drink offering is poured out at the foot of the altar. If that is so, and if there was a real continuity of practice then "holy place" here must refer to the inner court

where the altar of whole offering stood, and where priests ate the purification offering. In Num 18:10 this area is called "the most holy place," a name which elsewhere is used of the innermost sanctum where only the high priest went. These confusions may perhaps be explained, as N. H. Snaith (313–14) suggests, in terms of the differences in ground-plan between Solomon's temple, and the post-exilic temple.

In pre-exilic texts the drink offering occurs only in Gen 35:14 (E?), and this has to do with the setting up of an altar. The origin of the custom is unknown, and it is unclear how common a feature it was in pre-exilic times. It may have been so well established as to need little mention, or it may to all intents and purposes have been a post-exilic innovation in the Israelite cult.

7. שכר "strong drink," an unusual description of the wine used for the drink offering. A related Akkadian word occurs in Babylonian sacrificial terminology, and it may well have been drawn from there in exilic times (see J. Sturdy 201).

8. כמנחת "like the cereal offering" the reference being to the whole of the offering (grain and animal). Both together constitute the author's "fire offering." Only part of the grain went to the altar; priests received the rest (Lev 7:9–10).

9. The sabbath offering is twice the normal daily quantity. In Ezek 46:4–5 the quantities required as an offering by the prince are larger—six lambs and a ram, in addition to cereals and oil. It is the flour which is mixed with oil, not the cereal offering—see further N. H. Snaith (VT 19 [1969] 374) and H. M. Orlinsky (VT 20 [1970] 500).

11. There is early evidence of celebrations on the first day of the month in 1 Sam 20:5; 2 Kgs 4:23; Isa 1:13; Amos 8:5; Hos 13. The offerings required here in Numbers are considerable, and make this a significant festival. According to N. H. Snaith (315) the association of the goat of the purification offering with this celebration goes back to times when protection was sought against demons who were supposed to be operative in the dark days of the new moon. G. B. Gray (410) suggests that it may have been developed by priestly legislators because of the importance of the new moon in fixing the calendar, and also because they often sought to preserve but transform customs that had a great hold on the people at large. The rules for the prince on this occasion (Ezek 46:6, 7) envisage only six lambs and one bull, and no goat.

16. The Passover is mentioned to give a complete picture of the calendar, but since it is considered a home festival (contrast Deut 16:2) by priestly legislators, no temple sacrifices are required (cf. Comment on Num 9:1–14). In Ezek 45:21–22 Passover seems to be understood as the first of the seven days of the Feast of Unleavened Bread, but a clear distinction is made here in Numbers.

17. The proposals in Ezek 45:23–24 envisage more bulls and rams, but omit the lambs.

18. מלאכת עבדה "laborious work" (cf. Lev 23:8) meaning all occupations and forms of business which require labor.

26. וביום הבכורים "on the day of firstfruits," an unusual title for the Feast of Weeks. In earlier texts (Exod 23:16; 34:22; Deut 16:10) this seems

to have been a movable feast, determined by agricultural requirements. Some differences emerge in Lev 18 where only one bull is required (here two), but two rams (here one). In Lev 23:19 there is also a reference to shared offerings. These are deliberately omitted here (see *Form/Structure/Setting*). The earliest requirements for this feast are not known, though some have suggested two lambs and two loaves of new bread.

29.1. This celebration on the first day of the seventh month is not mentioned in Ezekiel, and is probably quite a late innovation. It is mentioned in H (Lev 23:23–25). It was probably singled out as a special day because it stood at the beginning of the seventh month, which under the influence of the Day of Atonement had become the most sacred of all. It is possible that if, as some argue, Israel did indeed have a new year festival, then this day is a reflection of it. The pre-exilic year is generally believed to have begun in the autumn. Here in Num 28–29 the festival is fixed in the light of the Babylonian calendar where the seventh month is autumnal.

1. יום תרועה "a day to blow trumpets," "acclamation" (NEB). In Num 10:10 trumpet blowing is associated with the beginning of every month. The special mention they receive here is probably explained in terms of influence from Lev 23:24.

2–5. At the Feast of Tabernacles there were two bulls, but the total offered on this first day of the seventh month is nevertheless very substantial—exceeding that of Unleavened Bread, for example.

7. This day is *Yom Kippur,* the Day of Atonement, so named in Lev 23:27, and a special day of penitence and fasting. This could have been old pre-exilic new year's day (see on 29:1) (cf. Ezek 40:1). There is no trace however of a pre-exilic Day of Atonement.

7. ועניתם את-נפשתיכם "and you shall mortify yourselves," literally "you shall humiliate yourselves." Penitence and fasting are central to the observance (cf. Num 30:13; Isa 58:3, 5; Ps 35:13; Heb 9:7–12, 23–28).

8–11. The offerings for the Day of Atonement are the same as those required on the first day of the seventh month.

11. The purification offering of atonement is a reference to the goat for Azazel, the use of which on the Day of Atonement is described in detail in Lev 16.

12. This is the Feast of Tabernacles, an ancient and important celebration in Israel. The celebration of harvest had apparently become linked with remembrance of the deliverance from Egypt and the sojourn in the wilderness, and living in tents was apparently part of the festival. All of these elements are present in the H text (Lev 23:39–43). Tent dwelling is not mentioned here in Numbers, and in literal terms this may have become a thing of the past. In earlier texts the feast is described in Exod 23:16; 34:22; Deut 16:13–15.

13–38. In Ezek 45:25 the offerings for the Feast of Tabernacles are the same as those proposed for the Feast of Unleavened Bread. The total sacrifice would amount to forty-nine bulls, forty-nine rams, and seven goats. The total required here in Numbers for the community is seventy bulls, fourteen rams, ninety-eight lambs, and seven goats—an altogether larger sacrifice than that required of the prince in Ezekiel.

17. The reason for the daily decline in the number of bulls used is un-known—from thirteen to eight as the festival proceeds. J. Sturdy (207) suggests that it may indicate that the intensity of joy declines as the feast goes on, but it is not clear why this should be so. L. E. Binns (198–99) suggested that it may symbolize the waning moon, though he also thought it possible that a gradual decline to the ordinary day's quantity is intended.

35. עצרת "a closing assembly" (NEB). In pre-exilic times an עצרת was held on the seventh day of the Feast of Unleavened Bread (Deut 16:8; cf. Isa 1:13; Amos 5:21). The day after the Feast of Tabernacles is so described in Lev 23:36 and Neh 8:18. The word can also be used of a special fast day (Joel 1:14; 2:15). According to the Chronicler the climax of rejoicing on the eighth day of the dedication of Solomon's temple was עצרת (2 Chr 7:9, cf. 1 Kgs 8:66).

Explanation

This section tells of the offerings required on eight distinct occasions:
1. The daily sacrifice—morning and evening.
2. The sabbath sacrifice.
3. The sacrifice of the first day of the month.
4. The sacrifice of the Feast of Unleavened Bread.
5. The sacrifice of the Feast of Firstfruits (Weeks).
6. The sacrifice of the first day of the seventh month (Trumpets).
7. The sacrifice of the tenth day of the seventh month (the Day of Atonement).
8. The sacrifice of the eight days of the Feast of Tabernacles.
A passing reference to Passover completes the calendar, but no public sacrifices are required on this occasion because of its domestic character.

Four kinds of offering are envisaged for these occasions—whole offerings (the burnt flesh of animals), cereal offerings (grain and oil), drink offerings or libations (wine), and purification offerings (one goat). The section provides a complete and systematic account, and appears to be based on similar material in Exod 29, Lev 23, and Ezek 45–46 (see *Form/Structure/Setting*). Quantities for cereal offerings and drink offerings have already been given in Num 15:1–16; here a particular concern is to give specific quantities for the whole offering and the purification offering. This and the fixing of the dates for the various celebrations are the main contributions made by the section.

There is good reason for thinking that the section is to all intents and purposes the work of the overall author of the book of Numbers. Earlier laws in relation to the major festivals had given considerable stress to the shared offering. The author's purpose is not to underplay these; they were traditional elements in the feasts, and it was no concern of his to remove them. His interest rather is to regulate and systematize the offering which was wholly Yahweh's—the whole offering—and the offering which rendered the community acceptable and fit to worship—the purification offering. It seems likely that divergent customs had obtained hitherto, and that the author here brings to bear a definitive judgment for the worship of the second temple.

It is not particularly difficult to see why the material should come at this particular point in the book. Those who make the section supplementary, on the grounds of its being "out of place" in relation to Num 27 and subsequent material, beg the question as to why editors should insert the material at this point. Reasons adduced for an insertion may just as well hold good as reasons for originality. It seems likely that the regulation of these matters was a pressing question in relation to the return and restoration; they may even have been integral to Ezra's mission itself. Their inclusion at a point when the people are on the verge of entry into the land seems appropriate therefore. There is in any case an excellent precedent for the giving of law on the borders of the land in Deuteronomy; it seems appropriate then that the author's definitive account of these public sacrifices should be given here. The somewhat fragmentary impression created by other Pentateuchal law on the subject of festivals is here dispersed—particularly in the matter of dates and quantities. As we have seen (*Form/Structure/Setting*) particular stress is laid on the whole offering, denoting the dedication of the community, and the purification offering. Both dedication and purification may be seen as key elements in the author's vision of the reconstituted community, a theme begun in Num 26. Another unifying factor in the material in this third part of the book is the theme—the land. Just as 27:1–11 dealt with problems of possession in the land, and 27:12–23 with leadership for the land, so 28–29 present a pattern for worship in the land. The concern to interpret deuteronomic tradition applies again here—as in many parts of Num 26–36. The festal law of Deut 16:1–17 is not the last Mosaic word on the subject; the priestly author sees in Num 28–29 the essential framework in which that law must be understood.

An obvious effect of this calendar is to give a new status and importance to the festivals of the first day of the month, particularly to the first of the seventh, and also to the Day of Atonement. The importance of the Day of Atonement had already been established in Lev 16. In Num 28–29 its importance in relation to the other feasts and observances can be better appreciated.

The overall theological emphasis focuses on the costliness of worship, through the whole offering, and on the acceptability of the community, through the purification offering. The principles of dedication and acceptability remain fundamental to the activity of worship. Before true worship can be offered the community as a whole, not merely individuals, must be forgiven and restored (i.e. purified and rendered acceptable). The community in turn must recognize that worship and the cult are no substitute for a costly commitment; they are in themselves a costly dedication of resources.

A Woman's Vows   (30:2–17)

Bibliography

Davies, G. H. "Vows." *IDB* r-z 792–3. **Pedersen, J.** *Israel: Its Life and Culture III–IV* London: Oxford University Press, 1940, 324–30. **Vaux, R. de** *Ancient Israel: Its Life and Institutions.* London: Darton, Longman, and Todd, 1961, 39–40, 465–66.

Translation

²⁽¹⁾ *And Moses spoke to the heads of the tribes of the people of Israel, saying, "This is what Yahweh has commanded.* ³⁽²⁾ *When a man vows a vow to Yahweh, or swears an oath, putting himself under a binding obligation, he must not break his word.*ᵃ *He shall do everything that he has said.* ⁴⁽³⁾ *And if a woman vows a vow to Yahweh, putting herself under a binding obligation, while young and still living in her father's house,* ⁵⁽⁴⁾ *and if her father hears of her vow,*ᵃ *and the binding obligation*ᵃ *under which she has put herself, and if he says nothing to her, then all her vows shall stand, and every binding obligation*ᵇ *under which she has put herself shall stand.* ⁶⁽⁵⁾ *But if her father disallows her on the day that he hears of it, no vow of hers, no binding obligation of hers, shall stand. And Yahweh will absolve her, because her father disallowed it.* ⁷⁽⁶⁾ *And if she is married to a husband, while under her vows or a binding obligation rashly uttered,* ⁸⁽⁷⁾ *and if her husband hears of it, and says nothing to her on the day that he hears, then her vows shall stand, and her binding obligations under which she has put herself shall stand.* ⁹⁽⁸⁾ *But if on the day that her husband comes to hear of it he disallows it, then he shall render her vow*ᵃ *which was upon her invalid, and the rash utterance by which she put herself under a binding obligation.*ᵇ *And Yahweh will absolve her.* ¹⁰⁽⁹⁾ *But any vow of a widow, or of a divorced woman, any binding obligation under which she has put herself, shall stand against her.* ¹¹⁽¹⁰⁾ *And if she vowed in her husband's house, or put herself under a binding obligation with an oath,* ¹²⁽¹¹⁾ *and if her husband heard of it, and said nothing to her, and did not disallow it, then all her vows shall stand, and every binding obligation*ᵃ *under which she has put herself shall stand.* ¹³⁽¹²⁾ *But if her husband makes them null and void on the day that he hears them, then whatever she says, by way of vows or of binding obligations, shall not stand. Her husband has made them void. And Yahweh will absolve her.* ¹⁴⁽¹³⁾ *Any vow and any binding obligation to morify herself her husband may confirm or make void.* ¹⁵⁽¹⁴⁾ *But if her husband says nothing to her from day to day, then he confirms all her vows, and all her obligations, that are upon her. He has confirmed them, because he said nothing to her on the day that he heard them.* ¹⁶⁽¹⁵⁾ *But if he makes them null and void some time after he has heard of them, then he shall bear her*ᵃ *iniquity."*

¹⁷⁽¹⁶⁾ *These are the statutes which Yahweh commanded Moses, concerning a man and his wife, and concerning a father and daughter who is young, and still living in her father's house*

Notes

3.a. Sam has "words."
5.a. Plural in Sam, G, and Syr.
5.b. Plural in Sam and Syr.
9.a. G, Sam, and Syr read plurals, bringing v 9 into line with v 8.
9.b. G explains that this is because her husband had made them invalid.
12.a. Sam, G, Syr, and Tg have the plural.
16.a. The suffix is feminine in MT, but masculine in Sam, G, and Syr.

Form/Structure/Setting

Analysts have had no difficulty in recognizing this section as priestly. The framework in vv 2, 17 contains obviously priestly terminology, while the idea of "bearing iniquity" is likewise characteristic (v 16). It has also been widely argued that the section is supplementary (e.g. J. Wellhausen, 114–15; A. Kuenen, 99; H. Holzinger, 146; B. Baentsch, 648; A. Dillman, 185–87; G. B. Gray, 413). Along with Num 28–29 the section appears to break up the flow from Num 27, where Joshua is instituted as military leader, to the war against the Midianites in Num 31. Kuenen saw here a legislative attempt to fill a gap in the laws concerning vows (Lev 27; Num 6:1–21), the kind of omission which is only discovered by experience, and which points therefore to the lateness of the text. Analysts in general found it difficult to discover any significant contact with the wider context, and this in itself was judged a likely indicator of supplementary material. Gray's attention to textual detail drew out some typical priestly phraseology—כִּי אִישׁ "when a man" (v 3; cf. Num 5:6), מַטּוֹת "tribes" (v 2; cf. Num 1:4), and לְעַנֹּת נֶפֶשׁ "to mortify" (v 14; cf. Num 29:7). On the other hand he saw peculiar features in the root אָסַר "binding obligation" (vv 3, 4, 5, 6, 7, 8, 9, 10, 11, 12, 13, 14, 15), in the use of דָּבָר for "his word" (v 3), and in מִבְטָא "rash utterance" (vv 7, 9). Gray saw in these features and in the approximation of style and treatment to later Rabbinic discussion evidence for lateness and for attributing the section to PS.

M. Noth (224–25) also argues for the section's looseness in its present context. He draws attention to the two categories of commitment in the section: the "vow" (נֶדֶר), and the "binding obligation" (אָסַר). He notes that the latter is mentioned only here in the OT, and concludes that it is unlikely to be early in any way. J. Sturdy (209) supports this assessment of the age of the section, but perceives a thin thread linking it with Num 28–29, namely the fact that vows are often made in connection with sacrifices (Lev 7:16; Num 15:3; 29:39). Sturdy suspects that the principles contained in the chapter are old, but recognizes that there is no way of demonstrating this. J. de Vaulx (326–30) also perceives the links between sacrifice and vows, made explicit in the immediate context (Num 29:39), and therefore is quite happy to treat Num 28–30 as a whole.

It seems best to accept the connections established by Sturdy and de Vaulx, and to see here a further contribution by the priestly author of Numbers. There are sufficient linguistic connections with P to justify such an assumption, while the peculiarities noted by Gray are not really substantial enough to warrant the view that the chapter is not integral to the book. The matter of vows and freewill offerings has just been raised in Num 29:39, and this reference provides the stimulus for the inclusion of more material on vows at this point. The general principle that vows must be kept is asserted firmly in v 3; the exceptional circumstances created by vows made by women are treated at length in the following verses. The principle that vows must be kept was already integral to deuteronomic law (Deut 23:22–24). Here once again is evidence of the priestly author's concern to build on such law. That he should do so here on the borders of land where deuteronomic law was promulgated is entirely appropriate. That he should wish to make his points prior to the promulgation of this law is also understandable. There was also a need to clarify and fill out existing priestly tradition on the subject. Rash commitments, which in some way were unwitting, are touched on in Lev 5:4–5, while Lev 27 looks at the question of the redemption of persons and property vowed to Yahweh. The author here examines the way in which vows made by a woman may in some circumstances be rendered void by the father or husband responsible for her. The interest in the rights of women, evident also in Num 27:1–11, gives a further degree of cohesion in this third part of the book.

Comment

2. This address to the "heads of the tribes" is unusual (cf. 1 Kgs 8:1–2; 2 Chr 5:2). Elsewhere in the Hexateuch the phrase "heads of the fathers' (houses) of the tribes" occurs (Num 32:28; Josh 14:1; 21:1).

3. נדר "a vow." This is perhaps a positive commitment to give something, such as the sacrifice of a freewill offering. It occurs elsewhere in situations of danger or special need (Gen 28:20–22; Judg 11:30–31).

3. אסר "a binding obligation." In contrast to the "vow" this is perhaps a negative commitment, to some kind of abstention (M. Noth, 224–25) (cf. 1 Sam 14:24; Ps 132:3–4; Acts 23:21). Thus Jephthah's vow is an illustration of נדר and the Nazirite commitment to abstinence an example of אסר (Judg 11:30; Num 6:1–21) (N. H. Snaith, 321). Snaith recognizes that אסר is a late word, and that originally נדר covered both types of commitment.

3. לא יחל דברו "he must not break his word"; to do so would be profanation (cf. Eccl 5:4–5; Deut 23:21–23).

4. בנעריה "while young," a term applied widely for a youthful woman (cf. Judg 19:3; Amos 2:7; Job 31:18), but in this context evidently meaning an unmarried but marriageable girl.

Older unmarried women are the only group not taken into account in this section; in Israelite society there were probably few of them.

5. It seems clear that the father does not have to hear the vow itself, only that it has been made. Once he has heard about it he must register any objection immediately. For the use of the root קום denoting "validity" see Gen 23:17, 20; Deut 19:5.

6. הניא "disallows," a root meaning "to frustrate" or "to forbid." It appears to have a technical legal sense here; cf. Num 32:7, 9 where Gad and Reuben are charged with seeking to frustrate the settlement (cf. also Ps 33:10).

6. יסלח "will absolve," a root which often carries the sense of "forgiveness." There may be something of this idea here, though the more strictly legal sense of release from a commitment and its consequences may be central.

7–9. In view of the fact that these stipulations appear to be repeated in vv 11–13 it may be that this part of the section deals with the situation of a woman who is engaged but not yet living in her husband's house. This view is supported by N. H. Snaith (322) and J. Sturdy (210), and is best accepted. The alternative is to suppose that vv 11–13 are a repetition, for the sake of emphasis, made in the light of the fact that the vows of widows and divorcees (v 10) do in fact stand.

7. On the subject of rash speech cf. Lev 5:4; Pss 15:4; 106:33; Prov 20:25; Eccl 5:2; Sir 18:23.

10. This makes it clear that women can in fact make vows which are not subject to alteration. The existence of a man with authority over her makes the difference between this and the other cases under consideration.

11. This verse suggests that vv 11–13 are handling a situation different from that described in vv 7–9. There the situation is that of a woman who is engaged but not yet living in her husband's house. Here it is the case of the married woman who is now living with her husband in his house.

14. לענת נפש "to mortify herself" (cf. Num 29:7); any kind of act of self-denial seems to be in mind. The phrase is often used of fasting (Lev 16:29; 23:27–29, 32; Num 29:7; Ps 35:13; Isa 58:3, 5).

15. מיום אל-יום "from day to day," evidently a different way of emphasizing the need for immediate action on the part of the husband if he is to disallow the vow. J. Sturdy (210) points out that the man cannot meditate on a vow, and thereby any use of prohibition as a weapon in married strife is precluded.

Explanation

This section deals with the binding character of vows. Any such commitment by a man must be observed to the letter. The same holds good for widowed and divorced women. A commitment made by a young unmarried woman, still living in her father's house, can be disallowed by the father. So too can the commitment of a betrothed woman, provided the husband acts immediately when he hears of it, and likewise any commitment made by a married woman living with her husband. In all of these exceptional cases the father or husband must act at once if the commitment is to be disallowed. The kinds of commitment in mind appear to cover freewill offerings and also promises of abstention.

There is good reason for suspecting that this is essentially the work of the priestly author of the book of Numbers. It offers, like many other parts of this third major part of the book, an extension of principles of deuteronomic law—in particular Deut 23:22–24. The principle there enunciated about the binding character of vows is here enforced, but significant qualifications are made in the matter of commitments made by those women who are under the authority of fathers or husbands. The author wishes to make these qualifications prior to the promulgation of deuteronomic law itself, but at the same basic location on the borders of the land. It follows appropriately enough the cultic material in Num 28–29, and in particular Num 29:39, where the matter of vows and freewill offerings is raised. The question may well have been of topical importance in the author's time; judging by this section and Num 27:1–11 the status of women and its implications in different areas was of particular interest.

It is hard to know how old are the principles here set out. It is quite clear that the making of special commitments to Yahweh was an old and well established practice (cf. Gen 28:20–22; Judg 11:30–31; 1 Sam 1:11; 14:24). The vow of Hannah (1 Sam 1:11) is of particular interest, because there is some indication that Elkanah may have had the power to prevent it. He gives her permission to do as she wishes (1 Sam 1:23), and it is arguable that this is the first time he has heard of the vow. Given the patriarchal character of Israelite society, and the economic dependence of women upon men, it seems likely that from an early stage it was felt necessary to control the religious freedom of women. Whether there was legislation for this at an early stage is difficult to determine. It is also difficult to suggest how old the principle of immediate action by father or husband might have been. The author of Numbers is obviously anxious to draw clear and unambiguous guidelines in a situation which he judged to be excessively lax. There is no obvious sign of a concern to create radically new social structures to control the way in which women and men relate to one another. On the other hand he is anxious to secure protection for both men and women. The husband and father must be protected from any excessive commitments made by women who are not ultimately responsible for finding the resources by which those commitments can be honored. But equally the woman deserves protection, and a clear and immediate response must be made if the vow is to be disallowed. There is to be no delay or equivocation which might leave an ambiguous situation, nor is there room for an inconsistent attitude to the vows the woman wishes to make. She has no reason to fear that her vows which are allowed may be unfulfilled, leaving her vulnerable to the judgment of God.

The Midianite War   (31:1–54)

Bibliography

Binns, L. E. "Midianite Elements in Hebrew Religion." *JTS* 31 (1930) 337–54. **Coats, G. W.** "Moses in Midian." *JBL* 92 (1973) 3–10. **Dumbrell, W. J.** "Midian—a land or a league?" *VT* 25 (1975) 323–37. **Eissfeldt, O.** "Protektorat der Midianiter über ihre Nachbarm im letzten Viertel des 2 Jahrtausends v. Chr." *JBL* 87 (1968) 383–93. **Gunneweg, A. H. J.** "Mose in Midian." *ZTK* 61 (1964) 1–9.

Translation

[1] *And Yahweh spoke to Moses, saying,* [2] *"Exact vengeance for the people of Israel on the Midianites. Afterwards you shall be gathered to your people."* [3] *And Moses spoke to the people, saying, "Arm [a] men from among you for the war, that they may [b] go against Midian, to carry out Yahweh's vengeance on Midian.* [4] *You shall send 1000 from each of the tribes of Israel to the war."* [5] *So there were provided, from the thousands of Israel, a thousand from each tribe, 12,000 armed for war.* [6] *And Moses sent them, a thousand from each tribe, [a] to the war, along with Phinehas son of Eleazar [b] the priest to the war, [c] with the vessels of the sanctuary, [d] and the trumpets for the alarm in his hand.* [7] *And they made war on Midian, as Yahweh had commanded Moses. And they killed every male.* [8] *And they killed the kings of Midian, along with the rest of their dead—Evi, Rekem, Zur, Hur, and Reba, the five kings of Midian. And they also killed Balaam son of Beor with the sword.* [9] *And the people of Israel took captive the women of Midian, and their children—along with all their cattle, their flocks, and their property, as the spoils of war.* [10] *All their cities in the places where they lived, and all their encampments [a] they burned with fire.* [11] *And they took all the spoil and all the booty, both of man and of beast.* [12] *And they brought the captives, and the booty, and spoil to Moses and to Eleazar the priest, and to the congregation of the people of Israel, to the camp in the plains of Moab by the Jordan at Jericho.* [13] *And Moses and Eleazar the priest and all the leaders of the congregation went [a] to meet them outside the camp.* [14] *And Moses was angry with the officers of the army, the commanders of the thousands and the commanders of hundreds, who had come from service in the war.* [15] *And Moses said to them, [a] "Have you let all the women live? [a]* [16] *Behold, these caused the people of Israel, [a] through the counsel of Balaam, [a] to act treacherously against Yahweh in the affair at Peor, and so there was the plague among the congregation of Yahweh.* [17] *Now therefore kill every male among the children, and kill every woman who has had intercourse with a man.* [18] *But all the young women who have not had intercourse with a man keep alive for yourselves.* [19] *And encamp outside the camp for seven days. [a] Whoever of you has killed any person, and whoever has touched any corpse, [a] purify yourselves and your captives on the third day and on the seventh day.* [20] *You shall purify every garment, every article made of skin, everything made of goat's hair, and every article of wood."* [21] *And Eleazar [a] the priest said to the men of war who had gone to the battle,*

"This is the statute of the law which Yahweh has commanded Moses, 22 *only the gold, the silver, the bronze, the iron, the tin, and the lead,* 23 *everything that can stand the fire,* ᵃ *shall you pass through the fire,* ᵃ *and it shall be clean. But it shall also be purified with the water for purification. And whatever cannot stand the fire you shall pass through the water.* 24 *And you shall wash your clothes on the seventh day, and you shall be clean. And afterwards you shall come into the camp."* ᵃ

25 *And Yahweh spoke to Moses, saying,* 26 *"Count all the booty that was taken, both of man and beast, you and Eleazar the priest, and the heads of the fathers' houses of the congregation.* 27 *And divide the booty into two parts—between the warriors who went out to battle, and all the congregation.* 28 *And levy tax for Yahweh from the men of war who went out to battle. It shall be one out of every 500, of persons,* ᵃ *oxen, asses, and flocks.* ᵇ 29 *Take* ᵃ *it from their half, and give it to Eleazar the priest, as a contribution to Yahweh.* 30 *And from the people of Israel's half you shall take one drawn out of every fifty, of persons, oxen, asses, flocks, and all the cattle, and give them to the Levites who are in charge of the Tabernacle of Yahweh."* 31 *And Moses and Eleazar did as Yahweh had commanded Moses.*

32 *Now the booty remaining of the spoils which the men of war took was 675,000 sheep,* 33 *72,000 cattle,* 34 *61,000 asses,* 35 *and 32,000 persons—all women who had not had intercourse with a man.* 36 *And so one half, the share of those who had gone out to war, was in number 337,500 sheep.* 37 *And the tax for Yahweh of sheep was 675.* ᵃ 38 *The cattle were 36,000, of which the tax for Yahweh was seventy-two.* 39 *The asses were 30,500, of which the tax for Yahweh was sixty-one.* 40 *The persons were 16,000, of which the tax for Yahweh was thirty-two persons.* 41 *And Moses gave the tax, which was the contribution, to Yahweh, to Eleazar the priest, as Yahweh had commanded Moses.*

42 *And from the people of Israel's half, which Moses had separated from that of the men who had gone to war,* 43 *(now the congregation's half was 337,500 sheep,* 44 *36,000 cattle,* 45 *and 30,500 asses,* 46 *and 16,000 persons)* 47 *from the people of Israel's half Moses took one of every fifty, both of persons and of beasts, and gave them to the Levites who were in charge of the Tabernacle of Yahweh, as Yahweh had commanded Moses.*

48 *And the officers in charge of the thousands of the army, the commanders of thousands and the commanders of hundreds, came near to Moses,* 49 *and they said to Moses, "Your servants have counted the men of war who are under our command, and there is not a man missing from us.* 50 *And we have brought Yahweh's offering, what each man found, articles of gold, armlets and bracelets, signet rings, earrings, and beads, to make atonement for ourselves before Yahweh."* 51 *And Moses and Eleazar the priest received from them the gold, all wrought articles,* 52 *and all the gold of the contribution that they offered to Yahweh, by the commanders of thousands and the commanders of hundreds, was 16,750 shekels.* 53 *(For the men of war had taken spoils, every man for himself.)* 54 *And Moses and Eleazar the priest received the gold from the commanders of thousands and of hundreds, and brought it into the Tent of Meeting, as a memorial for the people of Israel before Yahweh.*

Notes

3.a. MT has the Niphal. The Hiphil seems preferable, as in Sam, G, Syr, and Vg, since a passive or reflexive is difficult to make sense of.

3.b. *BHS* wonders whether "Yahweh" (יהוה) should be read in place of ויהיו "they may be/go" (cf. G).
6.a. G has added "with their power."
6.b. G has added "son of Aaron."
6.c. This second reference to the war is superfluous, and is omitted by G.
6.d. Tgʲ adds a reference to Urim and Thummin (cf. Num 27:21).
10.a. Vg adds a reference to towns and villages, while Tg stresses attacks on religious centers.
13.a. The singular occurs in Sam, G, and in one MT ms.
15.a.-a. Sam, G, Syr, and Vg all read "why have you let all the women live?"
16.a.-a. J. de Vaulx (354) understands this to be a gloss in MT, deriving from a tradition hostile to Balaam (cf. Vg). This is not certain. Syr has a substantial explanatory gloss, defining the event as a revolt against Yahweh. G contrasts the counsel of Balaam with that of Yahweh. The text is difficult, but it seems best to accept MT.
19.a.-a. J. de Vaulx (356) treats this as a gloss, interrupting the rhythm of the verse.
21.a. According to Sam Moses tells Eleazar to make the speech. The reference to Moses later in the verse is absent in Sam.
23.a.-a. G lacks this clause, perhaps through homeoteleuton (*BHS*).
24.a. In Sam Eleazar conveys the message, in the terms of vv 21–24 (MT).
28.a. G adds "and cattle" (cf. v 30).
28.b. Sam adds "and cattle" (cf. v 30).
29.a. The singular occurs in Sam.
37.a. Syr has 6,750 here, and also multiplies the other figures in vv 36–40 by ten.
53. This verse is understood as a gloss by J. A. Paterson (64), who suggests that it indicates that though the officers made an offering the common soldiers kept all that they could lay their hands on (see *Comment*).

Form/Structure/Setting

There is general agreement that this section cannot be earlier than the priestly parts of the Pentateuch. It has some very obvious points of priestly interest, its general subject matter being the offerings which are the outcome of the war. Eleazar is alongside Moses, much as Aaron is in P, and Israel is presented as a "congregation" (vv 12–13, 27). The allusions in v 2 link up with P elements in Num 25:16; 27:12, as do those of v 6 with Num 10:9, those of v 16 with Num 25:6, and those of v 19 with Num 19:16.

There has also been general agreement that the chapter is a very late addition to the priestly document (see e.g. A. Dillman, 187–92; J. Wellhausen, 115; A. Kuenen, 99; H. Holzinger, 148–50; B. Baentsch, 650–51; G. B. Gray, 418–19). A number of peculiar and allegedly non-priestly features have been noted—the description of the people as העם in v 3, the use of טף "child" (v 9), עם הצבא "the men of war" (v 32), the use of מסר "to deliver" (v 5) in the sense of "to provide." המחצה "the half" in vv 36, 43, מכס "tax" in v 28, and the deterential "your servants" instead of "we" in v 49. The improbabilities of the figures (no Israelite losses and huge spoils) and the appearance of Eleazar as an independent expounder of the Mosaic law were also seen by some as indicators of very late material. Gray stressed the midrashic character of the narrative as something untypical of PG, and pointed out that Num 27:12–23 (PG in his view) does not anticipate a war with Midian before the death of Moses, and still less a war in which Joshua would have nothing to do. Further support for such a view came from A. H. McNeile (163–64), and L. E. Binns (xxxvi).

M. Noth (228–33) shows some perplexity about the real subject matter of the section and its literary history. It seems clear to him that vv 48–54 (the independent offering of the commanders) is dependent on the preceding material, and he also observes that vv 13–47 are generally thin in content and exhibit some signs of not being a literary unit. He suspects, for example, that vv 13, 19–20 are a later addition, interrupting the original sequence of thought, and that vv 21–24 constitute a further addition. He can see little in the section as a whole (vv 13–47) which might form the nucleus of the present text. The report of the Midianite war in vv 1–12 is considered by Noth for this role, but it seems to him to be too colorless and schematized to have served such a function. This makes it difficult for Noth to see here any independent element of tradition to which the rest of the section has been added at later stages. He is convinced however that the section is very late, and that it ought to be considered a supplement to a completed form of the Pentateuch, and not to P alone. The fact that it presupposes Num 25 in its complete form, itself with late elements, is taken as an indicator of this. Noth does not think it likely that an old variant of the Baal-Peor story told of Midianite rather than Moabite women, since there is no indication anywhere in Num 31 of old elements. Dependence on Num 25 is an adequate explanation of all the features that Num 31 has to offer.

The midrashic character of the story, and the fact that it belongs to the P traditions are the points emphasized by N. H. Snaith, 324. J. Sturdy (214–26) also points to midrashic features, but is content to describe the section as P. He also makes the substantial point that priests and Levites are here given a share of the spoils of war, and that this reflects the great concern evident elsewhere in P for the proper support of the priests and Levites. This, as we have previously noted, is a feature of the book of Numbers, and calls in question the view that the chapter is unrelated to the overall context, and is necessarily a very late addition.

J. de Vaulx (353–61) does attempt a search for older literary features within the chapter. He notes the use of "Israel" (v 4) rather than "people of Israel," a feature we have perceived as characteristic of the Yahwist's Transjordanian traditions. He also draws attention to the names of the five Midianite kings (v 8) (Gray was not certain that they were Midianite names), and to the reference to the ancient ban (חרם) and division of the spoils. On the other hand the presence of Eleazar is seen as an evident addition (the verbs are singular in vv 27–28, 51, 54 [and v 13 in Sam]). De Vaulx goes on to cite Cazelles who found a core narrative in vv 1–20, 22–23a, 26–30, with the later additions to be found essentially in vv 21, 23b–25, 31–54.

De Vaulx himself finds a unity and coherence in the chapter in the sustained use of a wide range of biblical texts. The story of Balaam is interpreted in terms of the sin of Baal-Peor (vv 8, 16). The announcement of the death of Moses (v 2) recalls what has already been foreshadowed in Num 27:12–23. An army of twelve thousand going out to slay all the men and married women recalls the battle of Jabesh in Judg 21:10–12. De Vaulx also discerns recollections of Gideon's exploits against the Midianites in Judg 6–8. It is worth noting that Tgᴶ on Num 31:7 divides the army into three companies (as in Judg 7:16). Points of contact between MT and Judg 6–8 are the trumpets (Num 31:6/Judg 7:16), and the total destruction of the enemy (Num 31:10,

17/Judg 8:12). The offering of the spoils of war in Num 31:50–54 is reminiscent of Judg 8:24–27. The account of the purification of the warriors and the booty is inspired by legislation in Lev 11:32 and Num 19:18–19. The procedures regarding the division of the booty are reminiscent of the principles laid down by David (1 Sam 30:24–25), albeit with some alterations. The offering of the leaders in vv 48–50 recalls the earlier offering of Num 7:2. It is this handling of such a wide range of biblical texts which helps to justify the description of the section as midrash. History is not to be found here; the section is rather a theological reflection on "the day of Midian" (Isa 9:3; Ps 83:10).

It seems best to conclude that here again we see the work of the priestly author of Numbers. Arguments for a non-priestly element in the chapter do not amount to much. The description of Israel as "the people" (v 3) is certainly ususual, but is not unique in priestly texts (cf. Exod 36:5–6; Num 17:6), and there is no good ground for supposing that the other peculiarities listed could *not* be priestly. The argument about the improbabilities of the figures is curious, because this would appear to remove such chapters as Num 1:26 from the priestly corpus. The relationship of the section to Num 27:12–23 is more of a difficulty, but there are no insuperable problems if the wider context of the book is taken into account. It may be true that Num 27:12–23 does not in itself anticipate war with Midian, but it is clear that the section Num 25:16–18 does. There is no particular reason why the Midianite theme should be taken up again in Num 27:12–23. Joshua is there commissioned to take over one of Moses' roles when Moses himself is dead. He is not yet dead in Num 31, and there is therefore no reason why Joshua should be directly involved. The war can therefore be fought in priestly style, with Moses in overall charge, and Phinehas responsible for the sanctuary objects (v 6). These items presumably take the place occupied by the ark in older traditions.

As a matter of fact the chapter functions in a cohesive way within the book of Numbers as a whole. The book begins in Num 1 with a military census, depicting Israel as an army; here in vv 1–12 the priestly author gives his illustration of how a war may be fought. In Num 10:1–10 he had described the use of the trumpets in war; here in vv 1–12 those principles are put into effect. In Num 19 he had described purification procedures to be followed after contact with death; here in vv 13–24 is an opportunity to apply those principles, and to illustrate how they may operate in practice. In Num 18 and elsewhere he has paid particular attention to the maintenance of the clergy; here in vv 25–47 is a narrative illustration of the application of the tithing principles previously explained. In Num 7 and Num 28–29 he has stressed the importance of a dedication symbolized by costly offering; here in vv 48–54 is another illustration of that kind of commitment. To appreciate that this war for the priestly author is primarily a cultic occasion is to understand why it occurs at this point, after the extended treatment of cultic matters in Num 28–30. He evidently wishes to establish a priestly orientation to the Yahweh war to be advocated in Deuteronomy and fought in Joshua. It seemed good to fix this perspective before any division of the land (Num 32) takes place.

As most commentators recognize there is unlikely to be much by way of ancient tradition in the section. The sole purpose of the narrative seems to be to provide a setting for the purification, division of the spoils, and the offering which follow the battle. Even if Cazelles is correct in identifying a core text with additions, the original is not likely to be very old. The five kings of v 8 may constitute the oldest elements of tradition here, but they in turn, like so much in the chapter, may have been drawn from other biblical texts—in this instance from Josh 13:21. As a matter of fact it is distinctly possible that Josh 13:21 is the basis for the whole tradition. It shows no sign of priestly revision, and was arguably part of the deuteronomistic history. This verse links these Midianite "kings" with the campaign against Sihon, and it is quite possible that this prompted the idea of an independent Midianite war, described here in Num 31:1–12.

If there is any sort of historical kernel (as suggested by W. J. Dumbrell (*VT* 25 [(1975) 323–27] following W. F. Albright) it must be sought through Josh 13:21; Num 31, as de Vaulx argues, is midrash, the product of sophisticated theological reflection.

Comment

2. תֵּאָסֵף אֶל־עַמֶּיךָ—"you will be gathered to your people"; cf. Num 20:24; 27:13.

3 הֶחָלְצוּ "arm." N. H. Snaith (324–25) suggests that the root means "to withdraw"; in the context of a campaign such as this the idea must be to extract men for the army, and thus release them for the campaign.

4. אֶלֶף לַמַּטֶּה אֶלֶף לַמַּטֶּה "1000 from each of the tribes"; cf. Judg 20:8–11. J. Sturdy (216) points out that with tribes of very different sizes (Num 26) this round figure is a sign of the unrealistic character of the account.

6. This Yahweh war is a holy war—hence the presence of the sanctuary vessels and the trumpets (cf. Num 10:1–10). Neither Moses nor Joshua (cf. Num 27:12–23) are required to lead the campaign. Eleazar would perhaps be rendered unclean by contact with death if he were to engage in the battle; he is required rather to conduct the purification ceremonies which follow. Hence Phinehas is sent out in charge of the sacred objects, and perhaps of the battle as a whole—cf. Eleazar's handling of the unclean censers in Num 17:2 (Heb.) in preference to his father Aaron. The special sanctity required of the high priest is indicated in Lev 21:10–15, and the special zeal of Phinehas, justifying his selection for this task, in Num 25:6–15.

6. וּכְלֵי הַקֹּדֶשׁ—"the vessels of the sanctuary" (cf. Num 3:31; 4:15; 18:3; 1 Kgs 8:4; 1 Chr 9:29; 2 Chr 5:5). These objects appear to take the place of the ark (cf. Num 10:35–36; 14:44; 1 Sam 4:4). The view of the conduct of the war revealed here is not unlike that of the Chronicler (cf e.g. 2 Chr 20:20–23).

6. וַחֲצֹצְרוֹת "and the trumpets" (cf. Num 10:3–10; 2 Chr 13:12).

7. The unreality of the narrative emerges again—the death of every male must mean the end of the Midianites—contrast Judg 6:1–6.

8. The names also occur in Josh 13:21, and Zur is mentioned in Num

25:15 as the head of a Midianite family. In Josephus and in Nabataean inscriptions Rekem is the early name of the city of Petra.

The close association of the Balaam stories in Num 22–24 with the Baal Peor story in Num 25:1–5 suggests the idea that Balaam had led Israel astray, and hence his death here (cf. Josh 13:22) (cf. Jude 11 for Balaam's reputation in early Christianity).

10. The first clause is awkward; it may be wishing to specify the places in which they *now* lived, in contrast to those they had occupied originally.

10. טירתם "their encampments" (cf. Gen 25:16; Ezek 25:4; Ps 69:26; 1 Chr 6:29).

11. השלל "the spoil" . . . המלקוח "the booty." According to N. H. Snaith (326) the first is strictly to do with the flocks, and the second with "that which is seized." The author appears to use both words without any obvious difference of meaning.

14. The anger of Moses may be compared with that of Samuel in 1 Sam 15:17–19. The principle of the "ban" in holy war required the dedication of booty to Yahweh through destruction—whether of men, beasts or objects. A failure to act in this way constituted a serious infringement of the ban (cf. Josh 7:1 cf. also *Comment* on Num 21:2).

14. פקודי "officers" (cf. 2 Kgs 11:15). The root is used elsewhere by the author of the "numbering" that takes place in the census (cf. Num 1:45). Since the census is a military matter it is not so divergent a usage as G. B. Gray (422) suggests.

16. בדבר בלעם "the counsel of Balaam" or perhaps "on Balaam's departure" (NEB). The phrase could be rendered "the Balaam affair." Against NEB is the killing of Balaam in v 8, which makes likely a translation which thoroughly implicates him.

19. The principles followed here are those set out in Num 19:12, 16–19. The rites which follow go well beyond anything prescribed there, but their application to the booty is thoroughly consistent with the purification principles of Num 19.

21. There is some textual support in Sam for a Mosaic command to Eleazar here (see *Notes*), and this would certainly be more consistent with the usual pattern in P. On the other hand the book of Numbers does envisage a priestly theocracy under Mosaic law, and it is not entirely surprising to find Eleazar the priest taking the initiative here (cf. Num 27:21). The Mosaic origin of the statute is of course acknowledged.

23. As N. H. Snaith notes (327) a purification procedure involving fire is not found elsewhere in Israelite tradition. It is found in other ancient near eastern cultures, and may have been drawn in by the author from Babylonian custom.

25–27. The division into halves—for warriors and for people—is in accordance with 1 Sam 30:24–25.

28. The tax levied here is not attested in earlier tradition. N. H. Snaith (327) suspects that it is ancient, but there is no solid support for this supposition. A desire to secure means of maintenance for the priests and Levites (or simply to affirm again and again that they must be systematically supported) is central to the author's objective. The tax may well originate with him.

29. One out of every 500 captives belonging to the warriors goes to Eleazar and the priests. One out of every fifty of those belonging to the people goes to the Levites.

32. יתר "remaining of." It is hard to be certain what is meant here. NEB reads "over and above," but what this would mean in practice is obscure. RSV's "remaining of" seems preferable. The author's intention is perhaps to indicate the quantities of spoil that "remained" after the battle was over, and which could therefore be taken as spoil. N. H. Snaith (329) conjectures that the army would need to be fed on the way home, but does this cover the women of v 35 (cf. also A. H. McNeile, 168)? The story is not "realistic" enough to suggest that the need of the army was in the author's mind. Snaith also suggests that the stripping of the slain involved spoils not covered by the half and half allocation (cf. v 53), but the point is not clearly made here, and its relevance is uncertain.

49. The safe return of every man is an obvious indication of the unrealistic character of the story.

50. This tradition may be based on the story of the ornaments taken from Midian in Judg 8:24–26.

50. קרבן "offering," probably a gift for the temple, and not specifically for the personal use of the priests.

50. איש "each man." This could mean the officers (v 48), or each man in the whole army (perhaps the latter in view of v 53).

50. לכפר על־נפשתינו "to make atonement for ourselves" (see *Comment* on Num 17:11). See also Exod 30:12 where each man is to give a "ransom" for his life. J. Sturdy (217) understands the idea to be one of payment in thanksgiving. The idea of a life having been spared and of a return made is integral. This does not preclude the notion which seems to obtain elsewhere in Numbers that "atonement" provides protection from the wrath of God. There had after all been errors in the taking of spoil (vv 14–16).

On the various objects described in this verse see G. B. Gray, 424.

53. The point of this note is not entirely clear. It has been supposed to mean that the offering was made by the officers only, and that the men of war kept their spoils. If that were the case the point would probably have been made more clearly—v 52 is by no means necessarily claiming that the offering came from the commanders alone. It was rather through them that the offering was made. It seems best to take v 53 as a note indicating that the offering was from the spoils taken by every man in the army.

54. זכרון—"as a memorial" (cf Num 17:5 [Heb.]). According to N. H. Snaith (329–30) the purpose was to remind Israel of the event. J. Sturdy (217) points out that many scholars prefer to understand it as a reminder to Yahweh to remember Israel (as in NEB). In a technical sense the offering probably is a reminder to Yahweh, but the author probably intends the whole incident to be an encouragement to Israel's continuing generosity.

Explanation

In an idealized way this section tells of a battle against the Midianites, and of its consequences. The Israelites send out one thousand warriors from each tribe, and conduct a devastating campaign against the five Midianite kings and their armies. Moses is angry that all the women have been taken captive, on the grounds that they, along with Balaam, had led Israel to sin at Baal Peor. All male children are to be killed, and only the virgin women are to be kept. Strict purification procedures are to be observed covering all the persons and objects involved in the war. The spoils of war, both captives and beasts, are to be divided into two equal parts, one for the warriors and the other for the people, and a tax is to be levied on each half, in the interests of priests and Levites respectively. The quantities of spoil taken are carefully enumerated, and a concluding offering involving the gold and jewelry captured is presented as a memorial before Yahweh. The quantities taken are enormous, and the success of the venture is total.

The story has little "realism," and is best understood as a midrashic construction, celebrating the power of Yahweh to defeat enemies, emphasizing the need in all circumstances to support the priests and Levites, and pressing the importance of giving generously from resources in support of the sanctuary. There is no pressing reason for supposing that this is not the work of the priestly author of Numbers. Here is his opportunity to show aspects of his legislation in operation—the trumpets of Num 10 are in use, the purification principles of Num 19 are applied, and support for priests and Levites (Num 18) is shown in operation. Right from the outset (Num 1) Israel is depicted as an army ready to march—the census is for military purposes—and here is the opportunity to show the army successfully at work, fighting Yahweh's sacred war.

There are various reasons why it is appropriate for the priestly author to posit a Midianite war. Above all there was the tradition in the deuteronomistic history (Josh 13:21) which associated the defeat of Sihon with the defeat of the five Midianite kings mentioned here in v 8. It is probably this which gives the author his traditional base from which to posit an independent Midianite campaign. There were also the Balaam traditions, and some of those preserved by the Yahwist (as we have suggested) implicated Midian in the Balaam affair (e.g. Num 22:7). There was ground then for seeing the Midianites as a cause of Israel's difficulties at this point, for associating the tradition about Phinehas with a Midianite apostasy (Num 25:6–15), and for preparing the ground for a major Midianite war (Num 25:16–18). It is this war which the author here recounts.

Another reason for positing a Midianite war may have been the fact that older Yahwistic tradition presents Midianites in close and friendly association with Israel. There are even family connections between Moses and the Midianites (cf. e.g. Num 10:29). Deuteronomic law in Deut 23:3–8 is silent about relationships with them. The author of Numbers, like Ezra, has no sympathy for foreign marriages (cf. Num 25:6–15), and is anxious perhaps to close any loopholes in which the example of Moses is cited. The truth of the matter so far as the author is concerned is that the Midianites are eliminated. How he understood the Midianite conflict of Judg 6–8 is not clear, but the models that matter for all future practice are the Mosaic models, and these here in Num 31 exclude the possibility of future relationships with Midianites. This is one reason why the Midianite war must be fought while Moses is still alive. Israel's attitude must be one of sustained and ruthless hostility. Here again are evidences of the author's concern, in this final part of his book to expand, elaborate, or enforce the deuteronomic law which is shortly to follow. Deut 23:3–8 helps to define attitudes to other peoples; Num 31 makes matters plain with regard to the Midianites.

The war itself, described fairly briefly and in stylized form in vv 1–12, becomes the basis for further priestly teaching. It becomes possible to show how the purification laws in Num 19 may work out in practice, and how ways should constantly be sought of supporting the priests and Levites. It is also important to see here the author taking up another position in relation to Deuteronomy and the deuteronomistic tradition. The Yahweh war shortly to be advocated in Deuteronomy and fought in Joshua is here given a priestly perspective. In general terms that perspective underlines the deuteronomic commitment to the extermination of all alien influences. More specifically it seems likely that an interpretation of deuteronomic war law is evident here. In Deut 20:14 permission is given, apparently on any campaign, to take all the women, children, and cattle, as spoil, and these are freely available for Israel's use. This law is framed in the second person singular, and is arguably one of the earlier laws in the book. A qualification is made in Deut 20:15 that this only obtains for the cities which are "very far off," namely those which are not part of the land given by Yahweh. In the cities in the land all aliens who live there must die. In Deut 21:10–14, a text of apparently similar age, instructions are given about how a woman from a "far off" city who is beautiful and desired as a wife, is to be treated. It seems likely that the author of Numbers has precisely these stipulations in mind, and that he wishes to interpret and expand them. Any such woman, he is saying, must be a virgin, and furthermore the spoils in general are not for the free use of Israel. A tax must be levied for the support of priests and Levites, and it is also fitting that a generous gift should be made for the support of the sanctuary itself (vv 48–54)—that Yahweh may continue to remember Israel.

It may also be that the spoils of war here symbolize the wealth of Judaism in the diaspora. Money which the exiles had secured during their sojourns outside the land is indeed to be offered in support of the priests and Levites, and in support of the sanctuary. Some Jews may have been dubious about this, but the author of Numbers, in and through this story, makes it clear that such resources are necessarily and fittingly offered in support of the restored sanctuary in Jerusalem. As such they will function as a memorial before Yahweh. It is clear enough that Israel in the post-exilic era lacked all opportunity to fight a war of the kind envisaged here—hence the "unrealism" of the chapter, and its essentially cultic character. To understand the function of the story along cultic lines in the post-exilic context is therefore appropriate. The returning exiles had the same basic problems as the first settlers—to secure a footing, and to establish an identity, in the land. The generous support of all Jews was essential to the success of the enterprise. The section's major theological contribution is the principle that the identity of the people of God as a group can only be secured by the full-hearted and generous participation of all.

The Settlement of Reuben and Gad
(32:1–42)

Bibliography

Auld, A. G. *Joshua, Moses, and the Land.* Edinburgh: T. and T. Clark, 1980. **Bergmann, A.** "The Israelite Tribe of Half Manasseh." *JPOS* 16 (1936) 224–54. **Loewenstamm, S. E.** "The Relation of the Settlement of Gad and Reuben in Nu. 32:1–38. Its Background and Its Composition." *Tarbiz* 42 (1972) 12–26. **Mauchline, J.** "Gilead and Gilgal; some Reflections on the Israelite Occupation of Palestine." *VT* 6 (1956) 19–33. **Mittmann, S.** *Deuteronomium 1:1–6:3 literarkritisch und traditionsgeschichtlich untersucht.* BZAW 139. Berlin: De Gruyter, 1975. **Mowinckel, S.** *Tetrateuch-Pentateuch-Hexateuch. Die Berichte über die Landnahme in den drei altisraelitischen Geschichts-werken.* BZAW 90. Berlin: A. Töpelmann, 1964. **Olávarri, E.** "Sondages à ʿArôʿer sur l'Arnon." *RB* 72 (1965) 77–94; *RB* 76 (1969) 230–59. **Segal, M. H.** "The Settlement of Manasseh East of the Jordan." *PEFQS* 50 (1918) 124–31. **Weippert, H.** "Das geographische System der Stämme Israels." *VT* 23 (1973) 76–89. **Wüst, M.** *Untersuchungen zu den siedlungsgeographischen Texten des Alten Testaments. I. Ostjordanland.* Wiesbaden: Reichert Verlag, 1975. See also Num 34:1–15 (*Bibliography*).

Translation

¹ *Now the sons of Reuben and the sons of Gad* [a] *had very large herds of cattle. And they saw the land of Jazer and the land of Gilead, and behold, the place was a place for cattle.* ² *And the sons of Gad and the sons of Reuben* [a] *came and spoke to Moses and to Eleazar the priest, and to the leaders of the congregation, saying,* ³ *"Ataroth, Dibon, Jazer, Nimrah, Heshbon, Elealeh, Sibmah,* [a] *Nebo, and Baal-Meon,* [b] ⁴ *the land which Yahweh smote* [a] *before the congregation of Israel,* [b] *is a land for cattle, and your servants have cattle."* ⁵ *And they said, "If we have found favor in your sight, let this land be given to your servants for a possession. Do not take us across the Jordan."*

⁶ *But Moses said to the sons of Gad and to the sons of Reuben, "Shall your brothers go to war while you sit here?* ⁷ *Why do you discourage the heart of the people of Israel from going over into the land which Yahweh has given them?* ⁸ *This is what your fathers did when I sent them from Kadesh-barnea to see the land.* ⁹ *For when they went up to the valley of Eshcol, and saw the land, they discouraged the heart of the people of Israel from going into the land which Yahweh had given them.* ¹⁰ *And Yahweh's anger blazed hotly on that day, and he swore, saying,* ¹¹ *'Surely none of the men who came up out of Egypt, from the age of twenty and upwards,* [a] *shall see the land which I swore to give to Abraham, to Isaac, and to Jacob, because they have not followed me wholeheartedly.* ¹² *None but Caleb, son of Jephunneh the Kenizzite,* [a] *and Joshua son of Nun, because they have followed Yahweh wholeheartedly.'* ¹³ *And Yahweh's anger blazed hotly against Israel, and he made them wander in the wilderness for forty years, until all the generation that had done evil in Yahweh's sight was consumed.* ¹⁴ *And behold, you have risen up in your father's place, a brood of sinful men, to provoke again the fierce anger of Yahweh against* [a] *Israel.* ¹⁵ *For if you turn away from following him, he will again abandon them* [a] *in the wilderness. And you will destroy all this people."*

16 *And they came near to him, and said, "We will build folds here for our cattle, and cities for our dependents,* 17 *but we ourselves will take up arms, ready to go* ᵃ *before the people of Israel, until we have brought them to their place. And our dependents shall live in the fortified cities because of the inhabitants of the land.* 18 *We will not return to our homes until the people of Israel have inherited, each man his inheritance.* 19 *For we will not inherit with them on the other side of the Jordan and beyond, because our inheritance has come to us on this side of the Jordan, to the east."* 20 *And Moses said to them, "If you will do this, if you will indeed take up arms to go before Yahweh for the war,* 21 *and every armed man of you will indeed pass over the Jordan before Yahweh, until he has driven out his enemies from before him,* 22 *and the land is subdued before Yahweh, then, after that, you shall indeed return, and be free of obligation to Yahweh and to Israel. And this land shall be your possession before Yahweh.* 23 *But if you will not do so, then behold,* ᵃ *you have sinned against Yahweh. And be sure your sin* ᵇ *will find you out.* 24 *Build cities for your dependents, and folds for your sheep, and do what you have promised."* 25 *And the sons of Gad and the sons of Reuben said* ᵃ *to Moses, "Your servants will do as my lord commands.* 26 *Our dependents, our wives, our flocks, and all our cattle, shall remain there in the cities of Gilead.* 27 *But your servants will pass over, every man who is armed for war, before Yahweh to battle, as my lord says."*

28 *So Moses gave command concerning them to Eleazar the priest, and to Joshua the son of Nun, and to the heads of the fathers' houses of the tribes of the people of Israel.* 29 *And Moses said to them, "If the sons of Gad and the sons of Reuben, every man who is armed for battle before Yahweh, will indeed pass with you over the Jordan, and the land is subdued before you, then you shall give them the land of Gilead for a possession.* 30 *But if they will not pass over with you armed,* ᵃ *they shall have possessions among you in the land of Canaan."* 31 *And the sons of Gad and the sons of Reuben answered, saying, "As Yahweh has said to your servants, so will we do.* 32 *We will pass over armed before Yahweh into the land of Canaan, and the possession of our inheritance shall remain with us* ᵃ *beyond the Jordan."*

33 *And Moses gave to them, to the sons of Gad and to the sons of Reuben, and to the half tribe of Manasseh, the son* ᵃ *of Joseph, the kingdom of Sihon, king of the Amorites, and the kingdom of Og, king of Bashan, the land and its cities with their surrounding territories, the cities of the land throughout the country.* 34 *And the sons of Gad built Dibon, Ataroth, Aroer,* 35 *Atroth-shophan,* ᵃ *Jazer, Jogbehah,* ᵇ 36 *Bethnimrah* ᵃ *and Bethharan, fortified cities, and folds for sheep.* 37 *And the sons of Reuben built Heshbon, Elealeh, Kiriathaim,* 38 *Nebo,* ᵃ *and Baalmeon* ᵇ *(their names being changed),* ᶜ *and Sibmah. And they gave other names to the cities which they built.* 39 *And the sons of Machir, the son of Manasseh, went to Gilead, and took it, and dispossessed* ᵃ *the Amorites who were in it.* 40 *And Moses gave Gilead to Machir the son of Manasseh, and he settled in it.* 41 *And Jair the son of Manasseh went and took their tent villages, and called them Havvothjair.* ᵃ 42 *And Nobah* ᵃ *went and took Kenath and its villages, and he called it Nobah,* ᵃ *after his own name.*

Notes

1.a. Sam has "and the half tribe of Manasseh" here (probably an addition in the light of v 33). Sam has the same addition in vv 2, 6, 25, 29, 31.

2.a. G and Syr have Reuben before Gad, as in v 1. The same holds good for G in vv 25, 29, 31, and for Sam and Syr in vv 6, 25, 29, 31, 33.

3.a. Following Sam and G (cf. v 38). MT has Sebam, Syr has Sebah, and T⁰ has Simah.

3.b. MT has Beon. *BHS* suggests that Baalmeon (v 38) is intended.

4.a. G reads "handed over."

4.b. G, Syr, and Vg read "people of Israel."

11.a. G has added "those able to distinguish between evil and good."

12.a. G has added "the separated" or "consecrated" (ὁ διακεχωρισμένος). G appears to be generally interpretative and expansionist in this section.

14.a. Following Sam which reads עַל. MT has אַל "to" or "towards."

15.a. Syr reads "you."

17.a. *BHS* suggests חמשים (also GKC § 72p) "in groups of fifty" or "in five divisions" (cf. Josh 1:14; 4:12; Judg 7:11)—see also R. de Vaux, *Ancient Israel*, 216–17; J. Paterson, 64.

23.a. Lacking in G and Syr.

23.b. Sam and Syr read "sins."

25.a. The plural is required here Sam, G, Syr, Vg, and some MT mss.

30.a. G has additions again, though without substantial alteration of the sense. The general effect is to make the meaning plainer.

32.a. G reads "and you will give."

33.a. G has "the sons of Joseph."

35.a. G lacks Atroth and reads "Shophar." Sam has "Shaphim," S has "Shopham," and Vg has "Etroth and Shophan."

35.b. Sam reads "Jagbohah."

36.a. G has "Nimrah."

38.a. G omits Nebo.

38.b. Sam and Syr have "Baalmon."

38.c. Apparently a gloss. Tgᴶ provides a long gloss about Nebo as the place of Moses' death, and other information.

39.a. The plural is required (with Sam, Syr, Tgᴶ). MT has the singular.

41.a. Syr adds "to this day."

42.a. G reads "Nabau . . . Naboth" in this verse.

Form/Structure/Setting

It has been customary among analysts to see in this section a complex literary compilation, comprising elements from P and from JE, and perhaps also from deuteronomistic sources. The question was discussed in detail by J. Wellhausen (115–17, 351–52), who concluded that vv 1–15, 20–27, 39, 41–42 provide the base narrative from JE, the remainder being redactional material from priestly and other sources (cf. also A. Dillmann, 192–202). A. Kuenen (101–2) discerned an altogether stronger priestly influence, seeing in vv 1–5, 16–32 some strong links with his source P2. There are undoubtedly strong priestly features in these verses—the references to Eleazar and the leaders (vv 2, 28), the use of the root נחל "to inherit" (vv 18, 19; cf. Lev 25:46; Num 34:13), the idea of being "armed for war" (v 27; cf. Num 31:5; Josh 4:13), and the use of the root אחז for "having possessions" (v 30; cf. Josh 11:9, 19; Gen 34:10; 47:27). Kuenen was unwilling to call the material P2 because in Num 26:29–34 (his P2) Machir is Manasseh's only son, and cannot therefore refer only to the eastern half of the tribe, as is required in vv 33, 39, 40. His solution was to suppose that the original P2 narrative dealt separately with Gad and Reuben on the one hand, and the half tribe of Manasseh on the other, with the account of the latter omitted by the later redactor.

H. Holzinger's analysis (152–55) was particularly complex—with elements of J in vv 5, 20–21, 22a, 23a, 25–26, 27, of J1 in vv 39, 41, 42, of E in vv

16–17, 24, 34–38, and with evidences of the JE redactor in vv 1, 2a, 3, 4, 5, 16, 17, 20–27, 33a, 40. Supplementation of a deuteronomistic kind was discerned in v 17. Fragments of PG were found in vv 2b, 4a, 18, 19, and possibly 28a. Supplementary priestly elements were discovered in vv 5, 22a, 22b, 23b, 27, 33b, and more substantially in vv 6–15 and 28–32. This analysis is clearly closer to Wellhausen than Kuenen in tracing a firm early narrative tradition in vv 1–32 as well as vv 33–42. The same is true of B. Baentsch (659–62) who assigned vv 1b, 4b, 5–6, 20–23, 25–27, 33, 39, 41–42 in the main to J, and who found E in vv 3, 16–17, 24, 34–38. Baentsch found P elements in vv 1a, 2b, 4a, 18–19, and priestly redactional texts in vv 7–15 and vv 28–32. Deuteronomistic redaction could be traced in vv 33a, 40. A commitment to a heavy J and E presence is also evident in H. Gressmann's analysis (310 n.2), while W. Rudolph (*Der "Elohist"* 131–38), though eschewing E, also finds a firm J base in the chapter at large. O. Eissfeldt (*Hexateuch*, 192–95) pursued a division of the text based on a distinction between J (vv 2–15, 20b–23, 25–32) and E (vv 1, 16–20a, 24, 33–38), with the traditions of vv 39–42 assigned to L. In all three parts Eissfeldt saw strong evidence of redactional activity. Despite differences of opinion on matters of analytical detail it seems that many of the older analysts were agreed about there being a substantial JE presence. Quite apart from the material in vv 33–42 which is devoid of obviously priestly marks there were obvious signs of tension in vv 1–32. The new beginning in v 28 appeared to be priestly, and for many this was good enough ground for dividing the preceding material into J and E. A good illustration of the conclusions reached is offered by Baentsch. For him P has "Reuben and Gad" asking for land east of the Jordan and offering to help to the west. In E "Gad and Reuben" make the same suggestion, and there is more emphasis on city building. In J "Gad and Reuben" ask not to be led over the Jordan, and receive the Mosaic rebuke.

An early movement away from this type of analysis is apparent in G. B. Gray's approach (425–27). He thought it wise to distinguish sharply between vv 1–38 and vv 39–42, and saw no need to assign the latter to any of the major sources. He took them to be fragments from an ancient source, while in vv 1–38 he saw a free composition by a later writer, working on materials derived from both JE and P, and having the present composite form of the story of the spies in Num 13–14 before him. He concluded that the chapter in its present form does presuppose Num 27:15–23 (P), but is itself presupposed by Num 34:14–25. Gray recognized obviously priestly elements, and also some deuteronomistic phrases in vv 7–13. He also pointed out certain words and phrases which he considered to be more characteristic of JE: טף for "dependents" or "little ones," references to the blazing of Yahweh's anger, and מקנה for "cattle." On the other hand he concluded that a strict analysis of the chapter could not satisfactorily be carried through. He thought it most likely that the whole narrative had been recast, and that it is not a simple compilation from JE and P, as is usually found elsewhere.

More recent analysts feel less obliged to assign everything to one of four main sources, and are inclined to push Gray's approach further. M. Noth (234–36) points out various features which make it clear that the chapter is not a literary unit. The desired territory is referred to in v 1 as "the land of Jazer and the land of Gilead," while in vv 26, 29 only "Gilead" is mentioned. The tribes requesting it are Reuben and Gad in v 1, but elsewhere Gad and Reuben. The appearance of the half tribe of Manasseh in v 33 is unexpected and unexplained. Deuteronomistic phrases appear, in v 33 for example, while elsewhere (in vv 2b, 28) the priestly style is unmistakable. The earlier analysts were of course aware of these phenomena; the difference is that Noth does not feel bound to press them into a source analytical mold. He believes that the basic form of the chapter is neither deuteronomistic nor priestly. He argues that it differs from the deuteronomic view of the conquest east of the Jordan, as found in Deut 2:26–3:22, and he further maintains that the priestly writer was not at all interested in the detailed proceedings of the conquest. In his opinion neither P circles nor D circles would have given any weight to the wishes of individual tribes in the allocation of possessions. For Noth the basic tradition must therefore belong to the older Pentateuchal sources, here making their final appearance in the book of Numbers, but the succession of revisions and additions which give the section its present form do not lend themselves to traditional source critical identification. The "priestly" elements, for example, are not a coherent narrative, and stem from the fact that this is the predominant style in Numbers as a whole.

It has to be admitted that subsequent discussion has tended to dissipate rather than confirm any sort of consensus with respect to the section. J. Sturdy (221–22) argues that the chapter is "basically by J," and that it contains a story he has developed himself to explain the fact that Reuben, Gad, and part of Manasseh were to be found east of the Jordan. This called for special explanation since the main movement, as he envisaged it, was an invasion from east to west. The J story in Sturdy's view is found in vv 2, 4–6, 16a, 17, 20–23, 25–27, 32a, 34–38. The enlargements of the narrative, according to Sturdy, come mainly from the priestly school. The most substantial are vv 7–15, which take for granted Num 13–14 in their final form, and vv 18–19, 28–31, 32b, added by an editor who cannot see the promise of Reuben and Gad as a sufficient guarantee to serve as a basis for giving them the land they seek. He therefore provides Eleazar and Joshua to make sure that they keep their word. In vv 39–42 Sturdy sees another group of old and independent traditions which tell of the occupation of Gilead by elements of Manasseh—essentially a separate story, but also worked in, he thinks, by P.

J. de Vaulx (362–71) begins by comparing the view of the Transjordanian settlement given in vv 34–42 with that offered by Josh 13:8–32. Following S. Mowinckel (*Tetrateuch, Pentateuch, Hexateuch*, 16, 77–78) he concludes that the Joshua text is certainly the later, offering a schematic view of the more ancient traditions. Taking into account Num 21:21–35, which tells of a conquest of Transjordan by all Israel, he suggests a literary history for the section along the following lines:

1. Ancient traditions of the tribes of Reuben and Gad (vv 34–38). This is a list of the cities built by the two tribes, and is comparable to the traditions in Judg 1 where each tribe conquers certain territory in Canaan. The difference is that this tradition speaks not of conquest, but of construction and naming. The towns indicated in v 37 must have been within the sphere of influence

of Sihon king of Heshbon (cf. Num 21:25). These, according to de Vaulx are pre-monarchic, and the unwarlike character and declining numbers of Gad and Reuben are well attested in ancient texts such as Judg 5:15–16; Gen 49:4; Deut 33:6.

2. An "Elohistic" story (the essential content of vv 1–32 and either E or JE). The Blessing of Moses had already celebrated the supremacy of Gad (Deut 33:20–21), and this explains those verses (vv 2, 6, 25, 29, 31, 33) which cite Gad first. De Vaulx notes in particular the modes of address in vv 25–27 which in effect characterize Moses as a king—the one who assures the unity of the tribes—and this suggests a monarchic background for the story.

3. The definitive redaction (vv 1–42), which includes vv 6–15, reflecting the fusion of Num 13–14, vv 28–32, reflecting Num 27:12–23 (P), and using Gilead as a general term for Transjordan, and finally v 33 and vv 39–42 which are the redactor's complete picture of the division of Transjordan, taking in the half tribe of Manasseh, as well as Gad and Reuben—a view which reflects the schematic sacerdotal vision of the division of the land in Transjordan.

S. E. Loewenstamm (*Tarbiz* 42 [1972] 12–26), conducts a wide-ranging analysis, taking in Deut 3:16–20, Josh 13:8–28; 21:43–22:6, and suggesting that an old tribal tradition told how Moses let Gad and Reuben settle in Transjordan for economic reasons, and to rebuild the towns. This narrative has been transformed by later theory which considered Joshua as leader of an army containing all the tribes, and which conquered the whole of Canaan. This theory required that only the participants in this common war could be recognized as legitimate members of Israel. This adaptation of the tradition is later enlarged by Moses' homiletic speech, based on the story of the spies, and which reflects the latest version of the originally Calebite tradition. The reference to Eleazar the priest and to the leaders of the congregation are also drawn in at this stage of the tradition's history, while the sequence Reuben-Gad (v 1) may be later still.

S. Mittmann (*Deuteronomium 1:1–6:3*, 95–107) has also analyzed Num 32, and he concludes that the oldest literary core (either J or E) is in vv 1, 16–17b, 34–39, 41–42. This tells of the resolve of Gad and Reuben to settle in the east, but also of their willingness to campaign in the west; it also tells of their city building, and of the military activities of certain Manassites in Transjordan.

M. Wüst (*Untersuchungen zu den siedlungsgeographischen Texten*, 59–118) has explored the section in the light of his theory about the literary character of the Transjordanian tradition. His fundamental contention is that important parts of the Transjordanian story are essentially the product of redactional activity in the form of additions to P. So the reference to Machir (v 39) arises, not from ancient tradition, but from a false identification of the Gilead of Num 26:29 with the Gilead in Transjordan. Jair and Nobah (vv 41–42) (drawn in from Judg 10:3 and Judg 8:11 respectively) were given links with Manasseh, and so the notion of "half Manasseh" developed. In the rest of the section the only basic elements from tradition appear to be the association of Reuben with Jazer and Heshbon (vv 1, 16, 37–38) and of Gad with Dibon (v 34). A. G. Auld (*Joshua, Moses, and the Land* 15, 32, 83) offers some observations on the complexities of the chapter, and is agreed that "half Manasseh" is a late element in both Numbers and Joshua.

In the light of these varying approaches any reconstruction of the text's literary history is bound to be tentative, but it seems fair to say that there are no overwhelmingly persuasive reasons for treating this text in a radically different way from others in the book of Numbers. We have argued that there was a Yahwistic Transjordanian tradition (Num 21:1–25:5), and there is good reason for supposing that it continues here. The "priestly" elements are scattered, and as the older analysts showed, it is not difficult to isolate substantial sections of non-priestly material. Our reconstruction of the Yahwist's work and purpose suggests the need for some account of Transjordanian settlement. The Yahwist's revision of tradition aimed to bring a united Israel into the land from the east, across the Jordan, yet there was evidence enough of Israelite settlement on the other side of the river. There may even have been traditions, preserved in Judg 12:1–16 and Josh 17:14–18, of a Transjordanian settlement *from the west*. In any event, explanations, and a degree of standardization, were necessary.

The difficulty is to fix the limits of the Yahwist's work. Is it slight, as with Mittmann, or more extensive, as with Sturdy and many of the older analysts? It seems likely that there were two main pieces of traditional material available to him. There was the list of cities in vv 34–38, cities reputedly reconstructed by Gad and Reuben. Such a list is likely to derive from archives, and ultimately from Gadite and Reubenite sources. But there were also traditions of the tribe of Manasseh relating to the area, and preserved by the Yahwist in vv 39, 41–42. Though Nobah is not called a Manassite (v 42) his exploits are framed in the same form as vv 39, 41, and the information probably derives from the same source. These traditions speak of dispossession by separate groups in much the same way as do the traditions of Judg 1, and it is not unreasonable to suppose that they are of similar vintage. It is worth noting that Gideon belonged to Manasseh (Judg 6:15), and that his campaigns take him into Transjordan (Judg 8:4) and close to the cities of Nobah and Jogbehah (Judg 8:11). The likelihood of ancient Manassite activity and settlement in the region is real, and Wüst's attempts to explain all this material in terms of late redaction are not necessarily persuasive. He has certainly pointed to texts which probably influenced the creation of the tradition (e.g. Judg 8:11), but has not shown that this must necessarily be very late and not the work of the Yahwist. It seems reasonable to suppose that the Yahwist was aware of Gadite, Reubenite, and Manassite tradition about Transjordan, and that he felt obliged to do some justice to it. He does not imply, however, a major settlement by Manasseh. It would seem that the circumstances of his time did not require him to explain a presence of Manasseh in Transjordan—hence only Gad and Reuben figure in the main narrative.

It is on the basis of the Gadite and Reubenite building operations that the Yahwist constructs his own story of the request made by Gad and Reuben to settle east of the Jordan. The precise limits of the story cannot be fixed with certainty, but a coherent and well-rounded Yahwistic story can be found in vv 1, 16–27. It seems sensible not to build too much on the order Reuben-Gad in v 1; it may be from the author of Numbers for whom Reuben regularly appears at the head of lists, but the textual witness for the usage in Num 32 as a whole is not always secure (see *Notes*). The Yahwist's story would include the proposal of Gad and Reuben to occupy the land of Jazer and Gilead, but with a recognition of their responsibility to the other tribes (vv 1, 16–19). Moses agrees with the proposal (vv 20–24), and the people of Gad and Reuben respond to the official Mosaic pronouncement (vv 25–27). The royal role adopted by Moses in these verses corresponds with the Yahwist's presentation of him in other contexts. The Yahwist then includes the city list from tradition (vv 34–38), which he is able to present as cities which the soldiers of Gad and Reuben built for their dependents. This in turn prompts him to include a reference to Manassite activity in the region (vv 39, 41–42).

The rest of the section can be viewed as an accumulation of tradition around the Yahwistic core—in two main stages. The first has some affinities with deuteronomistic style and concern. It recognizes that land ought in fact to be allocated by Moses, and makes the proposal by Gad and Reuben a deferential request (v 5). It then goes on to provide the Mosaic rebuke (vv 6–15), recalling Israel's failure at the time of the initial reconnaissance of the land. This was an important theme in deuteronomistic interpretation of the wilderness period (cf. Num 14:11–23; Deut 1:19–46). There are a few signs of priestly editing in these verses, but it seems unlikely that an editor working with the completed form of Num 13–14 would have failed to mention the reconnaissance of the whole land (v 9). The bulk of the material in vv 6–15 appears to be working with the Yahwistic reconnaissance tradition alone. It seems likely that v 40 also belongs to this level in the tradition, recognizing as it does the importance of an allocation of land by Moses.

The second major accumulation of tradition is priestly, and this is attributable to the priestly author of Numbers. He introduces v 2 which brings in Eleazar and the leaders of the congregation, and also v 4. In v 3 he adds a selection of the cities from the list in vv 34–38, perhaps omitting those which were no longer familiar. Minor editing in vv 6–15 is the phrase "from twenty years old and upwards" (v 11), and the involvement of Joshua, as well as Caleb, in the role of faithful spy (v 12). The purpose of vv 28–33, which are also priestly, is to enforce the Mosaic pronouncement from the Yahwist's story (vv 20–24), to ensure that Eleazar and Joshua are charged with supervising the arrangement, and to interpret the old Manasseh traditions of vv 39, 41–42 in terms of a Mosaic allocation to the "half tribe" of Manasseh (v 33).

In summary, the picture is as follows:

Pre-Yahwistic tradition	vv 34–38; vv 39, 41–42
Yahwistic story	vv 1, 16–27
Deuteronomistic adaptation	vv 5–15, 40
Priestly adaptation	vv 2–4, 28–33 (minor editing in vv 11, 12)

Comment

1. The ordering Reuben-Gad is the priestly order of seniority (cf. the census list in Num 1). The order Gad-Reuben which is usually found in the section appears to be the Yahwist's. In his time Gad was much the more important (cf. Gen 49:3 and the reference to Gad on the Mesha inscription). See *Notes* for some textual variants in the section.

1. Jazer is usually a town (see *Comment* on Num 21:24), but here it is evidently an area. The Yahwist appears to use it for the northern half of the land between the Rivers Jabbok and Arnon.

The land of Gilead must mean the southern half of the land between the Jabbok and Arnon (contrast P in v 29 where it is used of the whole area). All the places cited in vv 3, 34–37, except Jazer, are in the southern half of the area. In vv 39–42 (the pre-Yahwistic tradition) Gilead appears to be different again—perhaps the land to the north of the Jabbok, or else, more narrowly, a city or mountain (see M. Noth, 237).

3. Ataroth is believed to be the modern Khirbet ʿAṭṭarûs, about eight miles northwest of Dibon, and eight miles east of the Dead Sea. The Mesha inscription says that "the men of Gad dwelt in Ataroth from of old." This inscription, otherwise known as the Moabite Stone, was inscribed in about 830 B.C. by Mesha, king of Moab, and celebrates successes against Israel. Mesha also claims that Ataroth was built by an Israelite king, but was captured by himself, and that a massacre ensued.

3. Dibon is Dibân, about four miles north of the Arnon, and twelve miles east of the Dead Sea. This was apparently Mesha's capital.

3. Nimrah is close to the modern Tell Nimrin, and excepting Jazer is the most northerly of the sites mentioned here.

3. On Jazer see *Comment* on Num 21:24.

3. Heshbon is Ḥesbân, and was Sihon's capital (see *Comment* on Num 21:26).

3. Elealeh is el-ʿÂl, a village close to Heshbon, and to the northeast. It is often mentioned in close association with Heshbon (cf. Isa 15:4; 16:9; Jer 48:34).

3. The whereabouts of Sebam are unknown.

3. Nebo is mentioned on the Mesha inscription, but its location is not known. Mesha claims to have captured it from Israel, and to rule the population of some seven thousand people. He also claims to have taken "the vessels of Yahweh and dragged them before Chemosh," the Moabite God.

3. Daalmeon is Maʿîn, ten miles south-southwest of Heshbon, and some ten miles to the east of the Dead Sea. Mesha claims to have built it, but reconstruction must be meant.

6. Cf. the accusations made against Gad and Reuben in Judg 5:17.

7. את-לב תנואון "discourage the heart," a unique way of referring to Israel's disaffection in the wilderness. The same root is used in Num 30:6 (Heb.) for the disallowing of a woman's vows.

8. On Kadesh-barnea cf. *Comment* on Num 13:26; 20:13, and cf. also Deut 1:19; 2:14; 9:23; Josh 10:41; 14:6–7.

12. Caleb is a Kenizzite in Josh 14:6, 14; Judg 1:13 (cf. Gen 36:11, 15, 42; 1 Chr 1:36, 52).

14. תרבות "a brood of," a word which occurs only here.

15. Cf. Josh 22:18 for a further example of action by the Transjordanian tribes which may be judged prejudicial to Israel as a whole.

16. גדרת "folds," literally "sheep walls," made of stone. The reference to "cattle" in this context is strange, and is perhaps an error.

17. נחלץ חשים "will take up arms, ready to go." MT appears to say "will equip ourselves hastening before. . . ." An emendation of חשים to חמשים would suggest numbered groups of soldiers (see *Notes*). NEB reads ". . . as a fighting force."

22. והייתם נקיים "you shall be free of obligation." J. Sturdy (223) suggests that this means the obligation to be called up for military service, along with the rest of Israel. There is some support for this in Deut 24:5 where the idea occurs in relation both to the army and other public affairs.

23. The personalized view of sin suggested here may be compared with that in Gen 4:7.

25–27. The formal courtly style adopted in these verses has often been noted—"your servants," "my lord," and "commands." Moses exercises the authority of a king.

29. On the priestly view of Gilead see *Comment* on v 1.

30. No indication is given here of how possessions might be assigned to Gad and Reuben in the land to the west of the Jordan. This in any case is of no consequence to the author. J. Sturdy (223) argues that vv 28–32 are introduced by P to give tautness and precision to the story; an eventuality which will not occur does not need further attention.

33. J. Sturdy (223) thinks the reference to Og a later addition. There is no necessary contradiction between the statements here and the traditions of conquest in Num 21:21–31. This is the formal Mosaic allotment to specific tribes of land previously conquered by Israel as a whole.

The priestly author would probably have understood the division of Transjordan in the light of Josh 13:15–33 where Reuben is evidently the most southern, with Gad to the north as far as the Jabbok, and with Manasseh occupying land further to the north in Bashan.

34. On Dibon and Ataroth, see *Comment* on v 3. Dibon belongs to Reuben in Josh 13:17 (cf. Num 21:30; Isa 15:2; Jer 48:18, 22 for indications of Moabite occupation).

34. Aroer is the modern ʿArâʿir, situated on the southern edge of the Arnon gorge, and about three miles southwest of Dibon. In Josh 13:9 it functions as a southern boundary town in the land to the east of the Jordan. Mesha claims to have rebuilt the city. There appears to have been a small fortress there in the early bronze age, which was apparently restored in the iron age.

35. The location of Atrothshophan is not known.

35. On Jazer see *Comment* on Num 21:24.

35. Jogbehah is probably the modern Jubeihât, five miles to the northwest of Rabbath-Ammon, the modern ʿAmmân.

36. On Bethnimrah see *Comment* on v 3.

36. Bethharan is south of Bethnimrah, both being situated on the eastern edge of the Jordan valley.

37. For Heshbon and Elealeh see *Comment* on v 3. Heshbon belongs to Gad in Josh 21:39 (cf. Isa 15:4; 16:9; Jer 48:2 for indications of Moabite occupation).

37. Kiriathaim is Khirbet el-Qureiyât, about three miles northwest of Dibon. Mesha claims to have rebuilt it when he rebuilt Baalmeon.

38. For Nebo, Baalmeon, and Sibmah see *Comment* on v 3.

38. Commentators have often suspected that the parenthetical note, "their names being changed," is indicative of the fact that both names Nebo and Baalmeon contained the names of deities rejected by Israel (Baal, and for Nebo cf. Isa 46:1). The meaning may be that the names should be read in a different form, so that the offensive deities are not cited. The form "Beon" (v 3) is probably precisely such an alteration.

39. For early testimony to the importance of Machir see Judg 5:14.

40. Cf. Deut 3:15. The verse interrupts the context (see *Form/Structure/ Setting*).

41. Jair is mentioned in Judg 10:3 as "Jair the Gileadite." There he is one of Israel's judges.

41. חותיהם "their tent villages," NEB reads "tent villages of Ham," also N. H. Snaith, 334. There is no obvious antecedent for "their," and this could be correct. Ham is mentioned in Gen 14:5—the site being twenty-five miles to the east of the Jordan, and to the northwest of Ramoth Gilead. Sixty such villages are mentioned in Josh 13:30; 1 Kgs 4:13, thirty in Judg 10:3–4, and twenty-three in 1 Chr 2:22 (sixty in v 23).

42. If Judg 8:11 is accurate Nobah was situated near the Jogbehah of v 35. It may be the modern Qanawât, but this may be too far east for a close association with Jogbehah. Nobah is not known elsewhere as a personal or tribal name. J. Sturdy (224–25) suggests that the man is a creation, designed to explain the name of the place.

Explanation

This section tells of a request made by the people of Gad and Reuben to occupy the land of Jazer and Gilead in Transjordan. They justify the request in terms of the land's suitability for their cattle and flocks. Moses at first interprets their request in terms of the unwillingness to enter the land evident in Num 13–14, arguing that once again certain elements in the community are discouraging the rest from taking possession of the land which Yahweh has given. The Gadites and Reubenites return with a counterproposal which involves settling their dependents in Transjordan while their soldiers go with the rest of Israel to help in the occupation of the land to the west of the Jordan. Moses agrees to this, and charges Eleazar and Joshua with the responsibility of seeing that the promise is indeed kept. The allocation of land to Gad, Reuben, and also half Manasseh is then recorded, along with a note of the cities Gad and Reuben built, and the successful military operations of certain members of the tribe of Manasseh.

It seems highly probable that there is a significant Yahwistic contribution here, specifically in vv 1, 16–27. The Yahwist had available a list of cities which had been built by Gad and Reuben (vv 34–38), drawn perhaps from archives. To this he adds certain settlement traditions (vv 39, 41–42) relating to the same area, and which came from the tribe of Manasseh. These cease to be settlement stories as such, and become accounts of successful military operations which cleared the territory of Amorites. The fact that Gad and Reuben had indeed settled in Transjordan was something requiring explanation, and it is this that the Yahwist provides in his story in vv 16–27. The explanation was necessary because of the Yahwist's commitment to an all Israel invasion of the land from the east. How is it then that there were significant Israelite settlements in Transjordan? The story provides the answer. With this the Yahwist's account in the book of Numbers comes to an end. It is possible to argue that his story continues in parts of the book of Joshua, and culminates in the covenant-making at Shechem—in the base narrative of Josh 24. The story here in Num 32 has some relevance to the circumstances of Josiah's time. The covenant-making in which Josiah involved his people (2 Kgs 23:2) must include those settled in Transjordan. They retain their basic privileges and responsibilities as an integral part of the people of God. The "royalty" of Moses in the story (see *Form/Structure/Setting*) foreshadows the rule of Josiah, the Davidic king.

The deuteronomistic editing of the exilic period took overall a more pessimistic view of Israel, and took a particular interest in the rejection of the land in Num 13–14 (cf. Num 14:11–24; Deut 1:19–46; 9:23–29). Here in Num 32:5–15 these editors saw in the request of Gad and Reuben the seeds of the old unwillingness to take possession of the land God had given. Investigation of the factors which had led to the loss of land were always uppermost in the minds of deuteronomistic editors, and a lack of a serious commitment to Yahweh and his gift was often a major feature of their analysis. The fact that Moses was responsible for the allocation of land is made to emerge in vv 5, 40, corresponding with the view of the deuteronomic historian in Josh 13–19.

The priestly author of Numbers needed to bring this tradition into line with the overall priestly perspective. The involvement of Eleazar, Joshua, and the leaders of the congregation in vv 2–4, 12, 28–33 reflects this concern. The reference to the age of those who died in v 11 is another reflection of the priestly perspective (cf. Num 14:29). The author's main contribution to the tradition is therefore in vv 28–33. The point that the agreement must be meticulously observed is enforced. Eleazar and Joshua, the priestly settlement leaders, are given the weighty responsibility of ensuring that it is so observed. His final contribution is to make it clear that the Manasseh traditions of vv 39, 41–42 do indeed indicate settlement there, and that this can be squared with Manassite settlement to the west in terms of the "half Manasseh" idea (v 33). For the priestly author too there was the need to make the point that all Jews should demonstrate a real commitment to the land—even those whose dwelling is far removed from the land itself. In the time of Ezra and Nehemiah that commitment could be exercised in terms of financial and moral support, and that must entail a respect for the fact that Jerusalem and its temple are still God's city, and therefore the natural center of Judaism world-wide. Such support was not to be regarded as merely voluntary. It was to be viewed as a necessary part of belonging to the people of God, a divinely given responsibility as well as a privilege. Through the figures of Eleazar and Joshua steps are taken to ensure that that responsibility is indeed recognized and acted upon.

The theology of the people of God always involves a sense of united purpose and common commitment. The encouragement of a sense of mutual responsibility and interdependence among widely scattered Christian communities is a regular feature in Paul's letters. Without this perception of a common identity and a single goal the activity of the agents of God's rule is liable to become diffuse and ineffective.

The Wilderness Itinerary (33:1–49)

Bibliography

Coats, G. W. "The Wilderness Itinerary." *CBQ* 34 (1972) 135–52. Davies, G. I. "The Wilderness Itineraries." *TB* 25 (1974) 46–81. ———. *The Way of the Wilderness*. Cambridge: Cambridge University Press, 1979. Lagrange, M. J. "L'Itinéraire des Israélites." *RB* 9 (1900) 63–86. Simons, J. *Geographical and Topographical Texts of the Old Testament.* Leiden: Brill, 1959. Walsh, J. T. "From Egypt to Moab: A Source Critical Analysis of the Wilderness Itinerary." *CBQ* 39 (1977) 20–33.

Translation

¹ *These are the stages in the journey of the people of Israel, when they went forth out of the land of Egypt, company by company, by the hand of Moses and Aaron.* ² *And Moses wrote down their starting points, stage by stage, by command of Yahweh. And these are their stages according to their starting points.* ³ *They set out from Rameses in the first month, on the fifteenth day of the first month. On the day after the passover the people of Israel went out defiantly in the sight of all the Egyptians,* ⁴ *while the Egyptians were burying all their firstborn, whom Yahweh had struck down among them. On their gods also Yahweh executed judgments.*

⁵ *And the people of Israel set out from Rameses, and encamped at Succoth.* ⁶ *And they set out from Succoth, and encamped at Etham, which is on the edge of the wilderness.* ⁷ *And they set out from Etham, and turned back* [a] *to Pi-hahiroth, which is east of Baal-Zephon, and they encamped before Migdol.* ⁸ *And they set out from Pi-hahiroth,* [a] *and passed through the middle of the sea into the wilderness, and they went a three days' journey in the wilderness of Etham, and encamped at Marah.* ⁹ *And they set out from Marah, and came to Elim. At Elim there were twelve springs of water and seventy palm trees, and they encamped there.* [a] ¹⁰ *And they set out from Elim, and encamped by the Sea of Reeds.* ¹¹ *And they set out from the Sea of Reeds, and encamped in the wilderness of Sin.* ¹² *And they set out from the wilderness of Sin, and encamped at Dophkah.* [a] ¹³ *And they set out from Dophkah, and encamped at Alush.* [a] ¹⁴ *And they set out from Alush, and encamped at Rephidim, where there was no water for the people to drink.* ¹⁵ *And they set out from Rephidim, and encamped in the wilderness of Sinai.* ¹⁶ *And they set out from the wilderness of Sinai, and encamped at Kibroth-hattaavah.* [a] ¹⁷ *And they set out from Kibroth-hattaavah, and encamped at Hazeroth.* ¹⁸ *And they set out from Hazeroth, and encamped at Rithmah.* ¹⁹ *And they set out from Rithmah, and encamped at Rimmon-perez.* ²⁰ *And they set out from Rimmon-perez, and encamped at Libnah.* [a] ²¹ *And they set out from Libnah, and encamped at Rissah.* [a] ²² *And they set out from Rissah, and encamped at Kehelathah.* [a] ²³ *And they set out from Kehelathah, and encamped at Mount* [a] *Shepher.* ²⁴ *And they set out from Mount Shepher, and encamped at Haradah.* [a] ²⁵ *And they set out from Haradah, and encamped at Makheloth.* ²⁶ *And they set out from Makheloth, and encamped at Tahath.* [a] ²⁷ *And they set out from Tahath, and encamped at Terah.* [a] ²⁸ *And they set out from Terah, and encamped at Mithkah.* [a] ²⁹ *And they*

set out from Mithkah, and encamped at Hashmonah. [a] [30] *And they set out from Hashmonah,* [a] *and encamped at Moseroth.* [31] *And they set out from Moseroth, and encamped at Bene-jaakan.* [a] [32] *And they set out from Bene-jaakan, and encamped at Hor-haggidgad.* [a] [33] *And they set out from Hor-haggidgad, and encamped at Jotbathah.* [a] [34] *And they set out from Jotbathah, and encamped at Abronah.* [35] *And they set out from Abronah, and encamped at Ezion-geber.* [36] *And they set out from Ezion-geber, and encamped in the wilderness of Zin* [a] *(that is Kadesh).* [37] *And they set out from Kadesh, and encamped at Mount Hor, on the edge of the land of Edom.*

[38] *And Aaron the priest went up Mount Hor* [a] *at the command of Yahweh, and died there, in the fortieth year after the people of Israel had come out of the land of Egypt, on the first day of the fifth month.* [39] *And Aaron was one hundred and twenty-three years old when he died on Mount Hor.*

[40] *And the Canaanite, the king of Arad, who lived in the Negeb in the land of Canaan, heard of the coming of the people of Israel.*

[41] *And they set out from mount Hor, and encamped at Zalmonah.* [42] *And they set out from Zalmonah, and encamped at Punon.* [a] [43] *And they set out from Punon, and encamped at Oboth.* [44] *And they set out from Oboth, and encamped at Iye-abarim,* [a] *in the territory of Moab.* [45] *And they set out from Iyim, and encamped at Dibongad.* [46] *And they set out from Dibon-gad, and encamped at Almon-diblathaim.* [a] [47] *And they set out from Almon-diblathaim, and encamped in the mountains of Abarim, before Nebo.* [48] *And they set out from the mountains of Abarim, and encamped in the plains of Moab by the Jordan at Jericho.* [49] *They encamped by the Jordan from Beth-jeshimoth* [a] *as far as Abel-shittim* [b] *in the plains of Moab.*

Notes

7.a. Sam and Tg[J] read the required plural here. G and Syr refer to an encampment at Pi-hahiroth at this point (cf. Exod 14:2). J. Paterson (64–65) emends the text to agree with Exod 14:2.

8.a. Following Sam, Syr, Vg. MT has "before Hahiroth"—probably an error.

9.a. G adds "by the waters," influenced perhaps by Exod 15:27.

12.a. G has "Raphaka" here, and in v 13.

13.a. Sam reads "Alish" here, and in v 14.

16.a. G offers an interpretative translation "graves of craving."

20.a. Sam reads "Lebonah" here, and in v 21.

21.a. G reads "Dessa" here, and in v 22. Tg[J] has "Beth-Rissah."

22.a. G reads "Makelath" here, and in v 23 (cf. MT's "Makheloth" in vv 25–26).

23.a. "Mount" is lacking in G here, and in v 24.

24.a. G reads "Charadath" here, and in v 25.

26.a. G reads "Kataath" here, and in v 27.

27.a. G reads "Taphath" here, and in v 28.

28.a. Sam reads "Mithikah" here, and in v 29. G reads "Matckka."

29.a. G reads "Zelmonah" here, and in v 30 (cf. MT's "Zalmonah" in vv 41–42).

30.a. Some think vv 36b–41a should be incorporated at this point (see *Form/Structure/Setting* and *Comment*).

31.a. G reads "Banaia" here, and in v 32.

32.a. Some MT mss, G, and Vg read "Mount Gidgad."

33.a. G reads "Etebatha" or "Zetebatha."

36.a. G adds "they set out from the wilderness of Zin, and encamped in the wilderness of Paran," perhaps under the influence of Num 10:12.

38.a. G lacks the reference to Mount Hor.

42.a. Sam and Syr have "Phinon" (G has Phino) here, and in v 43.

44.a. G has "Gai" here, and in v 45.

46.a. G has "Gelmon Deblathaim" here, and in v 47.
49.a. G has "in the middle of Asimoth."
49.b. G reads "Belsa" or "Belsattim."

Form/Structure/Setting

There was general agreement among older analysts that this section is relatively late (see A. Dillmann, 202–8; J. Wellhausen, 184; A. Kuenen, 102; H. Holzinger, 160–61; B. Baentsch, 672; G. B. Gray, 443–44). Some attributed it to PS; others saw in it a late compilation drawing on a variety of Pentateuchal traditions. Among the affinities with P is the fact that all P's stations and geographical references (with the exception of the wilderness of Paran) are included here. The age of Aaron noted in v 39 corresponds with texts peculiar to P (cf. Exod 7:7). The reference to the execution of judgments on the Egyptian gods (v 4b; cf. Exod 12:12), the locations near the Sea of Reeds (v 7b; cf. Exod 14:2), and the account of the death of Aaron (v 38; cf. Num 20:22–29) all betray a familiarity with P tradition. Stylistic features linking the material with P are ויחנו "and they encamped at," and ויסעו מן "and they set out from" (see on Num 21:4). Equally characteristic of P are the superscription (v 1), the dates (vv 3, 38), and the reference to the companies (v 1).

It was also clear that a number of places listed here do not occur in P. Among these Marah (cf. Exod 15:22), Kibroth-hattaavah (cf. Num 11:34), Hazeroth (cf. Num 12:16), and Shittim (cf. Num 25:1) were found in texts generally attributed to J. Four others (Moseroth, Bene-jaakan, Hor-haggidgad, and Jotbathah) occur only in Deut 10:6–7. A number of places to be found in JE are omitted here—Shur, Massah/Meribah, Taberah, Hormah, and the six places cited in Num 21:12–13, 16–19 (the valley of Zered, Arnon, Beer, Mattanah, Nahaliel, and Bamoth). Furthermore in JE Hazeroth and Kadesh appear to be next to one another, whereas the itinerary here has eighteen stations between them. Some indicators of a familiarity with the JE tradition are the three days' journey leading to Marah (v 8b; cf. Exod 15:22), the springs and trees at Elim (v 9; cf. Exod 15:27), and the allusion to the king of Arad (v 40; cf. Num 21:1–3).

There are also a number of places which are peculiar to this itinerary— Dophkah, Alush, Rithmah, Rimmon-Perez, Libnah, Rissah, Kehelathah, Mount Shepher, Haradah, Makheloth, Tahath, Terah, Mithkah, Hashmonah, Abronah, Ezion-geber, and Zalmonah. Other features which give this section something of a flavor of its own are the claim that Moses wrote down this itinerary (v 2), the reference to the burial of the firstborn (v 4a), and the dating of Aaron's death (v 38b). Gray among others concluded that these phenomena are best explained by the view that the itinerary is a late compilation which uses P and JE, and also some other source(s), oral or written, no longer extant (cf. also A. H. McNeile, 176).

M. Noth (242–46) took a view which in practice is little different. He sees here an attempt to present a comprehensive route, using a form of Pentateuchal narrative in which the collation of sources (JEP) has already taken place. He infers from the numerous names not found elsewhere in the Pentateuch that the author has included a proper independent itinerary; we are not confronted here with isolated additions. In the second part of the itinerary he discerns a route leading from the north end of the Gulf of Aqaba (from Ezion-geber in v 36) to the Transjordanian mountains on the plateau north of the Arnon. According to Noth sufficient of the stations are identifiable to warrant such an assumption. This moreover is not the route of Num 20:14–21, and Noth's tentative suggestion is that the list of names is an Israelite "pilgrim route" to and from a Sinai situated in northwest Arabia. J. Sturdy (227–28) sees the compiler as a late writer within the priestly school, and recognizes in the list of stations not mentioned elsewhere an older itinerary.

J. de Vaulx (372–79) prefers to examine each of the major elements in the list successively. In vv 5–8 he notes close connection with the priestly texts in Exodus (Exod 12:37; 13:20; 14:2). This route, he thinks, could well be "the way of the Philistines," explicitly rejected as Israel's route in the Elohistic material of Exod 13:17–18. He also notes in vv 9–16 a strong influence from the Yahwistic itinerary, and suggests, following M. J. Lagrange (*RB* 9 [1900] 63–86), that another part of the itinerary was a route to the Egyptian mines of Serbal. He is not so confident as Noth that many of the sites not otherwise mentioned are easily identified, and therefore reserves judgment on Noth's theory of a pilgrimage route to Sinai. Some allowance must be made for the possibility that the lists of names reflect the journeyings of different tribes in the area in question. In general de Vaulx thinks that the priestly author has used here a variety of ancient traditions containing fragments of itineraries, and edited them accordingly. Adjustments had probably already taken place, and it was not difficult for him to provide the simplified view of the journey that now survives in this section. A broadly similar approach is suggested by G. W. Coats (*CBQ* 34 [1972] 135–52).

J. T. Walsh (*CBQ* 39 [1977] 21–33) conducts a detailed analysis of the Pentateuchal itineraries, and concludes, on stylistic grounds, that there are two distinct lists which must have been independent and concurrent versions of the journey. The first is found in Exod 12:37; 13:20; 17:1; 19:2a; Num 10:12; 21:10–11; 22:1, and the second in Exod 13:17–18a; 15:22, 27; 16:1; 19:1, 2b; Num 10:33, and possibly Num 20:1, 22; 21:4, 33. The remaining material is stylistically diverse, but may constitute notes and fragments from a third list, relating to Transjordan. The only agreement with respect to stations in the two main lists is the Wilderness of Sinai.

G. I. Davies (*TB* 25 [1974] 46–81) distinguishes between forward and backward looking itineraries in the ancient world. The former would be for planning purposes, and the latter for recording past journeys, often in relation to royal military campaigns. The material in Numbers would be backward looking, and the *Sitz-im-Leben* of both would be administrative circles at the courts. In *The Way of the Wilderness* Davies makes a number of other important observations. He suggests that the itinerary notes in the main narrative are derived from the list in Num 33:1–49, and that the incorporation of these notes into the main narrative is probably traceable to a deuteronomistic redactor. This means that the places named cannot be identified with the assistance of elements in the stories with which they are associated; the association of name and story is secondary. On the basis of literary form Davies is persuaded that the itineraries in Num 33 do describe routes; they are no haphazard lists of places. They probably stem in his opinion from "descriptions of routes, oral and written, which were already employed by travellers" (p 76). Within vv 1–49 Davies distinguishes four likely routes—from Rameses to Yam Suf (The Sea of Reeds—though Davies prefers "Red Sea" as the closest modern designation), from *Yam Suf* to the Wilderness of Sinai, from the Wilderness of Sinai to Kadesh, and from Kadesh to "Beth-Jeshimoth as far as Abel Shittim."

Within the terms of our own approach it seems reasonable to conclude that the list of place names given here in its present form is the work of the priestly author of Numbers. There are good grounds for seeing a priestly influence in the content and style of the itinerary, as shown in classical analysis. Some of the priestly material—such as the reference to the death of Aaron—could be regarded as a gloss, but as has been shown the priestly style—as evidenced in the reference to "encampment" and "setting out"—is arguably integral. The question then arises as to whether this is a very late compilation, tabulating the sites mentioned in the completed stories (as is often supposed), or whether, as Davies suggests, the list is independent of the stories, providing locations at which the stories could be fixed. There is something to be said for the latter view. The absence from the list of the wilderness of Paran is easier to explain. It was not originally part of the list, but since the priestly author knew of it he cites it in his story at the appropriate points (Num 10:12; 12:16; 13:3, 26).

The inclusion in the list of many place names not used in the stories is readily intelligible if the list already existed and was incorporated wholesale by the priestly author—albeit in his own style, and with priestly elaboration at specific points. It would have been impossible to tell stories about all the places, but their names existed in tradition, and deserved to be retained. The most serious difficulty for the view that the list is a late compilation is the fact that many of the Yahwist's place names are not in fact compiled in this list—among them Taberah (Num 11:1–3), Hormah (Num 14:39–45; 21:1–3), and such places as Beer, Mattaneh, Nahaliel, Bamoth, Pisgah from Num 21:16–21. It seems likely therefore that the list of place names here in Num 33 is the skeleton on which the flesh of the wilderness stories has been built.

The further question arises as to whether this list or one like it provided a skeleton in the same way for the Yahwist's account of the journey. It seems likely that it did not—at least in its present form. The Yahwist has as many as ten place names in his story which do not occur in this list. It seems likely nevertheless that the Yahwist would have constructed his account of the journey in a similar way. Lists of place names were available to him, and he attached his wilderness stories to some of these.

The overall argument can be summarized as follows:

1. The Yahwist was aware of a route from Egypt to Sinai, including such places as the wilderness of Shur, Marah, and Massah/Meribah (Exod 15:22–25; 17:1–7). There is a strong etiological element in the Marah and Massah/Meribah stories, and it is difficult to determine whether the stories are

prompted by the place names, or whether the place names are a fictional product of the stories.

2. The Yahwist was also aware of a Transjordanian route (see on Num 21:16–20), derived perhaps from commercial archives or sources rather than pilgrim itineraries.

3. The Yahwist connected these routes with stories located at other sites in the general area—at Hazeroth and Kadesh, and at other places where the etiological element is strong (Taberah, Kibroth-hattaavah, and Hormah).

4. It seems probable that the Yahwist did not include an overall summary of the itinerary at this point in his story. Had he done so it seems likely that it would have survived in some form in Num 33, and the absence of many of the Yahwist's stations makes this improbable.

5. An exhaustive list was compiled subsequently, and this survives in Num 33. It was appended to the Yahwist's account, but is earlier than the priestly revision of the Pentateuch, and stems perhaps from deuteronomistic sources. This compilation was made from archives derived from commercial sources, but was made independently of the Yahwist's account. It is not surprising that some names occur in both, but the absence of some of the Yahwist's names, and the presence of a rather different Transjordanian route suggests essential independence.

6. The priestly authors of Exodus and Numbers took up this list and used it as the skeleton on which to fit their own priestly stories of the wilderness period. The author of Numbers presents the list in his own style, and with some elaborative detail from his own traditions.

The question remains as to whether the various components of the list in Num 33 can now be traced. Walsh's literary critical conclusions are reached on the basis of very limited criteria, and it seems best to follow through the view that the list is compiled from commercial sources. In that event there would appear to be four routes—from Egypt to Sinai (vv 5–15), from Sinai to Ezion-geber (vv 16–35), from Ezion-geber to Kadesh (v 36), and from Kadesh through Transjordan (vv 37–49). The lack of stations between Ezion-geber and Kadesh, a distance comparable to that between Sinai and Ezion-geber, is remarkable. The compiler evidently lacked information about such a route, and could only assume that Israel took it; the same holds for the journey from Kadesh to southern Transjordan.

Another remarkable feature is the placing of the Sea of Reeds after Elim (v 10). This is either an error, as Noth suggests, or perhaps a false inference from the fact that there was water at Elim. Another possibility is that the list envisages a different site for the Sea of Reeds. For the Yahwist it is evidently close to Egypt, whereas in the list it appears to be further to the east. If this is correct then the compiler has simply incorporated the list of stations as he finds it in his sources without assessing it critically in the light of Yahwistic tradition (see *Comment* on v 10).

The sites in vv 30b–34a also occur in Deut 10:6–7, though in a somewhat different order. This confirms our view that the deuteronomists had indeed been working on the itinerary, and both texts agree in placing these sites after Sinai.

Comment

2. This is one of the few references to writing activity on the part of Moses (cf. Exod 24:4).

3. Rameses is mentioned in Gen 47:11 and Exod 12:37. In Exod 1:11 it is cited as one of the two cities which Hebrew slaves built for the Egyptians. It was probably situated at Qantir or may have been the ancient Tanis nearby.

3. ביד רמה "defiantly," literally "with a high hand" (cf. Exod 14:8; Num 15:30).

4. On the burying of the firstborn cf. Exod 12:28–30.

5. Succoth is cited in Exod 12:37. This may be an area in Wadi Tumilat, but a specific city has not been identified.

6. Etham (cf. Exod 13:20) is an Egyptian name meaning "wall" or "fortification." Shur (Exod 15:22) carries the same meaning in Hebrew. There appear to have been defensive fortifications along the line of the present Suez Canal. A specific city with the name Etham has not been identified.

7. Pi-hahiroth (cf. Exod 14:2) must have been to the west of the Bitter Lakes; only so could the Israelites have been trapped by water. Baal-zephon may be Mount Casios on the Mediterranean coast. Migdol (cf. Exod 14:2) may be the place mentioned in Jer 44:1; 46:14; Ezek 29:10; 30:6 and situated at the northern extremities of Egypt. G. I. Davies (*The Way of the Wilderness*, 81) thinks there was a "Migdol of Seti-Merneptah" to the south of Wady Tumilat.

8. בתון|-הים "through the middle of the sea." In this itinerary the Israelites do not reach the Sea of Reeds (v 10) until they have passed Elim. The old song (Exod 15:4) locates the deliverance from the Egyptians at the Sea of Reeds, but neither the Yahwist nor the priestly author specifically say that the deliverance took place there. The Yahwist evidently understood the Sea of Reeds to be close to Egypt; the priestly authors, in the light of Num 33:8, may have taken it to be the Gulf of Suez—see v 10. From the point of view of this itinerary the "sea" here may be one of the lakes to the east of Egypt.

8. דרך שלשת ימים "three days' journey," a familiar feature of the Yahwist's account (Exod 3:18; Exod 15:22; Num 10:33).

9. Marah means "bitter," and is usually identified as the modern ʿAin Ḥawâra, situated some twenty-five miles down the east coast of the Gulf of Suez (cf. Exod 15:23).

Elim (cf. Exod 15:27), despite its trees and springs cannot be located with certainty. It may be the oasis of Wadi Garandel, some seventy-five miles from the Bitter Lakes.

10. The Sea of Reeds in this itinerary is probably the Gulf of Suez itself. What was originally envisaged in the old song in Exod 15:4 cannot now be determined (see *Comment* on v 8).

11. The wilderness of Sin (cf. Exod 16:1) cannot be fixed with any precision.

12. Dophkah does not occur in the Exodus account. The attempt to associate it with Serābîṭ el-Khâdim must be judged very uncertain (see G. I. Davies, *The Way of the Wilderness*, 84).

13. Alush (also not in Exodus) is unknown. It has sometimes been associ-

ated with Wady el-ʿEsh, but this is philologically dubious. For this site, as for Dophkah (v 12), much depends on the whereabouts of Sinai.

14. Rephidim (cf. Exod 17:1) is possibly Wady Refâyid, some thirty miles north-northwest of the southern tip of the Peninsula. If this identification is accurate it gives support to the view that for this itinerary at least Sinai is at the southern end of the Peninsula. The priestly author in Exod 17:1 links the Yahwist's Massah/Meribah (Exod 17:2–7) with Rephidim.

15. The wilderness of Sinai (cf. Exod 19:1–2) cannot be located with precision. It was probably in the general vicinity of Jebel Musa, the traditional site of Sinai itself.

16. Kibroth-hattaavah is unknown (see *Comment* on Num 11:34).

17. The site of Hazeroth is not known for certain (see *Comment* on Num 11:35). It has sometimes been associated with Wady Ḥuḍeirat about forty miles northeast of Jebel Musa.

18b–30a. These twelve sites are unknown. Assuming that Sinai in this itinerary is the traditional site (Jebel Musa) near the southern end of the Peninsula, then these twelve places must be a list of stations on the way to Ezion-geber. The same would be true of Abronah in vv 34–35.

30. Moseroth (cf. Deut 10:6) was the place where according to the deuteronomists Aaron died—but contrast the priestly tradition in v 38 and Num 20:22–29.

31–33. The four sites mentioned here also occur in Deut 10:6–7—albeit in a slightly different order. The arrangement here is probably a correction. The sites are unknown, but must be situated between Sinai and Ezion-geber.

36. Ezion-geber (cf. Deut 2:8; 1 Kgs 9:26; 22:49; 2 Chr 8:17; 20:36) is probably the modern Tell el Kheleifah, near Elath, and situated at the head of the Gulf of ʿAqaba. An alternative in the same vicinity is Jezirat Faraun.

There are about fifty miles between Ezion-geber and Kadesh, but no stations are given. On the wilderness of Zin cf. Num 13:1; 20:1; 27:14; Deut 32:51; Josh 15:1.

J. Koenig has propounded a theory about the itinerary from the wilderness of Sinai to Kadesh which sees in it a pilgrimage route involving Noth's more northerly location for Sinai. For a fair presentation and critique of this theory see G. I. Davies, *The Way of the Wilderness*, 87–89.

37. On Mount Hor, see *Comment* on Num 20:22.

38–39. The details about the date of Aaron's death and his age are found only here, apparently an addition by the priestly author.

40. The material here is quoted by the priestly author from Num 21:1.

41. Zalmonah is unknown, and occurs only here. The references in Judg 9:48; Ps 68:15 appear to refer to a different place.

42. The location of Punon/Pinon (cf. Gen 36:41; 1 Chr 1:52) is not certainly known, but is often traced to Khirbet Feinan.

43. On Oboth see *Comment* on Num 21:10. G. I. Davies (*The Way of the Wilderness*, 90) objects to Noth's identification of Oboth as Ain el-Weibeh on the grounds that it produces an inexplicable detour to the west. He prefers a location to the north of Khirbet Feinan on the way to Khirbet Ay.

44. On Iye-abarim see *Comment* on Num 21:11. The name appears to mean

"the ruins of Abarim," and the place must have been situated in the Zered gorge. G. I. Davies (*The Way of the Wilderness*, 90) suggests that the name survives in Khirbet Ay.

45. Dibon-gad is Dhiban, the Moabite capital. The name Gad is here associated with it because of Gadite occupation at some stage (see *Comment* on Num 32:34–38).

46. Almon-diblathaim is probably the Beth-diblathaim of Jer 48:22, and the Mesha Inscription (see *Comment* on Num 32:38; cf. also Josh 21:18 for Almon).

47. The mountains of Abarim are mentioned in Num 27:12—where they involve Moses alone rather than Israel as a whole.

49. Bethjeshimoth (cf. Josh 12:3; 13:20; Ezek 25:9) is in the Jordan valley, some twelve miles southeast of Jericho and on the eastern side of the river, the modern Tell el-ʿAzeimeh.

Abel-shittim (cf. Num 25:1) is the modern Tell Kefrain—in the highlands east of the Jordan, and about five miles from the river.

Explanation

This section purports to be the list which Moses compiled of stations on the route from Egypt to the borders of the land. It seems probable that the list envisaged a site for Mount Sinai at the traditional location of Jebel Musa, near the southern tip of the Sinai Peninsula. The journey thus described would involve four major changes of direction, thereby giving the itinerary as a whole four essential components—from Egypt to Sinai, from Sinai to Ezion-geber, from Ezion-geber to Kadesh in the wilderness of Zin, and from Kadesh through Transjordan to the borders of the land. Despite its length the third component from Ezion-geber to Kadesh has no stations, and it seems likely that the compiler of the list lacked information about such a journey. Many of the sites occur in the preceding Pentateuchal narratives, and some have specific stories attaching to them—at both the Yahwistic and priestly levels of the tradition. Many of the sites cannot be identified with certainty (see *Comment*), and sixteen occur only in this list.

It is difficult to be confident about the origins and background of this compilation. The Yahwist himself must have had some notion of a route from Egypt to the land, and we have sought to argue that the construction of a Transjordanian journey for Israel is specifically his. It seems possible that parts of the route could have been drawn from sacral sources (routes for pilgrims) or more probably from court archives which recorded routes for travelers in general, and perhaps for trade and commerce in particular. It seems likely that material of this kind provides the original skeleton on which stories of the wilderness period could be built.

It seems difficult to argue however that the list here in vv 1–49 is in any real sense the Yahwist's, though many places would naturally have occurred both in his idea of the journey and in this list. This conclusion is suggested primarily by the absence from the list of such key places in the Yahwist's story as the wilderness of Shur, Massah/Meribah, Taberah, and Hormah. It is also possible that he sited Sinai rather nearer to Kadesh. Furthermore the Transjordanian routes are different (see the Yahwist's sites in Num 21, lacking here), though geographically the two routes cannot have been far removed.

On the other hand there are grounds for thinking that the list is not essentially a priestly compilation or a very late redaction. It is clear that at certain points, as for example in the remarks about the death of Aaron, there is priestly elaboration, but there is no way in which this material can be considered integral to the itinerary itself. The failure to include the wilderness of Paran (important to the priestly story), and some of the Yahwistic sites, suggests that the itinerary as such is not priestly, and is not a very late compilation. It seems more probable that priestly authors (in both Exodus and Numbers) had the itinerary at hand, and that they used it as the skeleton or frame on which to build the traditions which were important to them, and thereby to construct the story of the wilderness period familiar to us. We have no reason for supposing that the authors were familiar enough with the geography of this area to construct an itinerary for their stories from scratch. They probably needed assistance from official sources, and these would probably be the commercial archives already mentioned.

It seems best to conclude that the route contained here in vv 1–49 was added to the Yahwist's story subsequently, but before the priestly authors began work on the tradition, and that it therefore provided the frame on which they could build. There is some evidence from Deut 10:6–7 that deuteronomists were working on the details of Israel's route, the sites mentioned there occurring here in vv 1–49, but not in the Yahwist's work. The order of these sites is slightly different, but there seems to be clear indication that they were working on the Sinai/Ezion-geber component in the itinerary. Perhaps the essentials of the list in vv 1–49 are to be traced to deuteronomistic sources. It was natural enough that the priestly author should add an introduction in vv 1–4, and certain other notes from the earlier stories in vv 9, 38–40, as well as recasting the list in his own style (the departures, and encampments). The itinerary comes appropriately enough at this point of the story, with the journey now complete, and the process of occupation about to begin.

The list itself is a testimony to the faith that God led Israel in a progressive and ordered fashion from Egypt to the borders of the land. Within the limits of the time it reveals the exercise of scholarly skills and resources in relation to the faith held. The precise journeys taken by the groups who later constituted Israel can now be shown to be both complex and uncertain. The importance of this enterprise in vv 1–49 is the application of the knowledge then available to the fundamental faith that it was Yahweh who brought Israel safely from the miseries of slavery in Egypt to independence and well-being in a fruitful land.

General Guidance about the Occupation
(33:50–56)

Bibliography

Auld, A. G. *Joshua, Moses, and the Land.* Edinburgh: T. & T. Clark, 1980.

Translation

50 And Yahweh spoke to Moses in the plains of Moab by the Jordan at Jericho, saying, 51 "Speak to the people of Israel, When you pass over the Jordan into the land of Canaan, 52 then you shall drive out all the inhabitants of the land before you, and destroy all their carved figures, and destroy all their molten images, and demolish all their high places. 53 And you shall take possession of the land ᵃ and settle in it, for I have given the land to you to possess it. 54 You shall inherit the land by lot according to your families. To a large tribe you shall give a large inheritance, and to a small tribe you shall give a small inheritance. Wherever the lot falls to any man, that shall be his. ᵃ According to the tribes of your fathers you shall inherit. 55 But if you do not drive out the inhabitants of the land before you, then those of them whom you allow to remain will become like hooks in your eyes and thorns in your sides, and they shall cause you trouble in the land where you live. 56 And I will do to you as I thought to do to them."

Notes

53.a. G adds a reference to the expulsion of the inhabitants of the land. Vg includes a reference to the "purification" of the land.
54.a. G adds a reference to his name being there.

Form/Structure/Setting

These verses have provided some difficulty to analysts. Elements which are evidently priestly (vv 50–51, 54) are mixed with material which seems foreign to P, some of which has affinities with the conclusion of the Holiness Code in Lev 26 (cf. vv 52–53, 55–56 and Lev 26:1, 30) (see J. Wellhausen, 117–18; A. Kuenen, 98). In particular the motivation given seems very much in accord with that given in Lev 26. It remains true on the other hand that some of H's favorite phrases are lacking—such as "I am Yahweh," and references to the need for holiness—and so there was no general agreement among earlier analysts as to whether these verses are a genuine fragment of H, or else a recollection of H from the pen of a priestly author. H. Holzinger (165–66) linked vv 50–51, 54 with PG and the rest with PS, a view taken also by B. Baentsch (683–84). G. B. Gray (449–50) took a contrary view, drawing attention to the peculiarity of משכית "carved figures," and במת "high places" which occur nowhere else in the Pentateuch except Lev 26:1,

30. He suggests that two laws are here combined—one from H itself, and one from PS.

Affinities between the Holiness Code and Deuteronomy have long been noticed, and A. H. McNeile (179) was inclined to ascribe the whole of vv 50–56 to D, with the exception of v 54 (P). The destruction of Canaanite objects of worship, as required here, is particularly characteristic of texts often assigned to deuteronomistic sources (e.g. Exod 23:24, 31–33; 34:11–16; Deut 7:1–6; 12:2–3). The use of הוריש (v 52) for "dispossession" is frequent in D, while "high places" (v 52) are common in deuteronomistic literature (e.g. Jer 7:31; 2 Kgs 23:8). The stumbling block which survivors will become, as described in v 55, has some affinity with deuteronomistic texts in Josh 23:13 and perhaps Judg 2:3. L. E. Binns (xxxvii) was content to talk of a combination of elements from D (or H) and P.

Among more recent analysts M. Noth (248) describes the section as strongly deuteronomistic in content and form, while noting of course the influence of Num 26 in v 54. For him this is an indicator that the whole section of Num 33:50–34:29 presupposes an edited Pentateuchal narrative at a comparatively late stage, and also the formation of the deuteronomic history. For him therefore the section must be very late, and be part of the editorial unification of these two major narrative complexes—the Pentateuchal and deuteronomistic.

J. Sturdy (231) takes a more traditional view, seeing here the work of the priestly writer drawing together older traditions. One part of this (vv 52–53) keeps its deuteronomic style, and v 55 may also stem, according to Sturdy, from the common stock of phrases used by that school of writers.

J. de Vaulx (382–83) sees the section as the beginning of the final major part of the book, running through to the end in Num 36:13, and a code for the division of Canaan among the tribes. He takes the section to be primarily the work of the priestly redactor, reaffirming the kind of legislative requirement found in such texts as Exod 34:10–16 (J); Exod 23:20–32 (E), and Deut 7:2–6 (D).

A. G. Auld (*Joshua, Moses, and the Land*, 74–75) conducts a detailed linguistic analysis of the passage, and concludes that it must have been drafted by someone familiar with both deuteronomic and priestly terminology, though not, he thinks, in one piece. He is persuaded of the lateness of the section, that in its first edition it is of a piece with 34:1–29, and that the whole is secondary to the book of Joshua.

From our perspective it is reasonable enough to conclude that the section is essentially the work of the priestly author of Numbers. We can agree with de Vaulx that it marks the beginning of the end of the book. We have argued that the third major section of the book is concerned with issues relating to settlement, and in these closing stages this issue comes into sharp focus. The author is therefore anxious to elucidate what he considers a necessary precondition for the division and ultimate occupation of the land to the west of the Jordan. There must be a total elimination of all alien peoples along with all their religious influences. The author's method is thus to summarize, by the deliberate use of ideas and language from D and H, the main impact of traditional teaching from these sources about relationships between Israel and others in the land. If Exod 34:10-16 may be considered Yahwistic and not deuteronomistic then there is Yahwistic influence too. On the whole we may agree that the main influence is deuteronomistic. Ideas from H, itself building on D, have been drawn in specifically from Lev 26:1, 30. The author reaffirms these traditional convictions, with the addition of his own conception from Num 26:52-56 that the land is to be divided by lot. This overall view of the section fits in with our view that what unites much of this third major part of the book (Num 26-36) is a concern to enforce, build on, and to some degree adapt Deuteronomy prior to its forthcoming promulgation on the borders of the land.

Comment

52. משכית "carved figures" (cf. Lev 26:1). Tg interprets this as "places of worship." These figures would probably be made from stone, in contrast to the "molten images" of metal, also referred to here.

52. צלמי מסכת "molten images" (cf. Exod 34:17; Lev 19:4; 1 Sam 6:5, 11; Ezek 16:17; 23:14)

52. במת "high places" (cf. Lev 26:30). These are Canaanite hill shrines. These sites are explicitly rejected by the deuteronomic historians, and a Judaean king's attitude toward them determines the historian's evaluation of the king and his reign (cf. e.g. 1 Kgs 14:23).

52. The piel of אבד "destroy" occurs twice in this verse. Elsewhere in the Pentateuch it occurs only in Deut 11:4; 12:2.

54. This verse repeats the essential content of Num 26:52-56.

55. This kind of warning, in a much more elaborate form, is found in Deut 28:15-68 (cf. also Exod 23:33; 34:11-13; Deut 7:16). For the imagery found here cf. also Josh 23:12-13; Ezek 28:24.

Explanation

This short section introduces the last major part of the book's third section. In particular it is an important preliminary to the delineation of the land and the description of how it is to be divided in Num 34:1-29. With Israel about to enter the land Moses gives what is, for the book of Numbers, his final exhortation to faithfulness. The command to expel all alien influences, human and religious, comes naturally at this point—with the description of the boundaries and the procedures of division to follow immediately. The division of the land is referred to explicitly in v 54, as previously in Num 26:52-56. All the inhabitants are to be driven out, and the religious centers, along with all representations of deity, are to be destroyed. If this is not done then the inhabitants of the land will be a constant snare and hindrance to Israel, as well as a serious threat to her well being.

The likelihood is that this section is essentially the work of the priestly author of Numbers. His influence is clearest in v 54, with its reference to the division of the land by lot, but there is no good reason for seeing the rest as fragment(s) from other sources. The message and imagery are essentially deuteronomistic, with embellishments from Lev 26:1, 30, and the priestly author wishes to enforce this message in his own way. It is as applicable to his day as it was to the circumstances of Josianic and exilic times, in which the deuteronomistic literature appears to have its essential rootage. It is true that there was no possibility of conducting a holy war along the old lines, but the priestly author was anxious to recapture the old uncompromising spirit, which would resist all alien influences in the interests of discovering a new national identity and self-consciousness, thereby making the people a suitable vehicle for the fulfillment of the divine purpose. The activity of Ezra in the realm of foreign marriage (Ezra 9:1–10:44) indicates the kind of action which was possible, and which for the priestly author would have embodied the old uncompromising spirit.

The NT vision eschews all narrow nationalisms, but it is not unaware of the need for senses of identity and consciousness of self if groups are to discover themselves and their roles in the wider world. In the NT that group is the church, which must attain a self-understanding and self-awareness if it is to discover and be true to God's purpose for it in the world.

The Boundaries of the Land (34:1–29)

Bibliography

Aharoni, Y. "The Province List of Judah." *VT* 9 (1959) 225–46. **Alt, A.** "Das System der Stammesgrenzen im Buche Josua." *Kleine Schriften zur Geschichte des Volkes Israel Vol 1.* Munich: C. H. Beck, 1953. **Auld, A. G.** *Joshua, Moses, and the Land.* Edinburgh: T. & T. Clark, 1980. **Cross, F. M. & Wright, G. E.** "The Boundary and Province Lists of the Kingdom of Judah." *JBL* 75 (1956) 202–26. **Gorg, M.** "Zum 'Skorpionenpass' (Num 34:4: Josh 15:3)." *VT* 24 (1974) 508–9. **Kallai-Kleinmann, Z.** "The Town Lists of Judah, Simeon, Benjamin, and Dan." *VT* 8 (1958) 134–60. **Kallai, Z.** "The Boundaries of Canaan (Nu. 34 cf. Ez. 47:13–20) and the Land of Israel (Jos. 13–19) in the Bible." *Eretz-Israel* 12 (1975) 27–34. **Mackay, C.** "The North Boundary of Palestine." *JTS* 35 (1934) 22–40. **Noth, M.** *Die israelitischen Personennamen im Rahmen der gemein-semitischen Namengebung.* BWANT 3/10. Stuttgart: W. Kohlhammer, 1928. ———. *Das System der Zwölf Stämme Israels.* BWANT 4/1. Stuttgart: W. Kohlhammer, 1930. **Schunk, K. D.** *Benjamin.* BZAW 86. Berlin: A Töpelmann, 1963. **Weippert, H.** "Das geographische System der Stämme Israels." *VT* 23 (1973) 76–89.

Translation

[1] *And Yahweh spoke to Moses, saying,* [2] *"Command the people of Israel, and say to them, When you enter the land of Canaan* a*—this is the land that shall fall to you for an inheritance, the land of Canaan according to its borders—* [3] *then your south side shall be from the wilderness of Zin along the side of Edom, and your southern boundary shall be from the end of the Dead Sea on the east,* [4] *and your boundary shall turn south up the ascent of Akrabbim, and pass by Zin, and its southern limit shall be Kadesh-barnea. It shall go on to Hazar-addar,* a *and pass along to Azmon,* [5] *and the boundary shall turn from Azmon to the Brook of Egypt, and its termination shall be at the sea.*

[6] *"And for the western boundary, you shall have the Great Sea and its coast. This shall be your western boundary.*

[7] *"This shall be your northern boundary. From the Great Sea you shall mark out a line to Mount Hor.* [8] *From Mount Hor you shall mark it out to Lebo-Hamath, and the termination of the boundary shall be at Zedad.* [9] *Then the boundary shall extend to Ziphron,* a *and its termination shall be at Hazar-enan.* b *This shall be your northern boundary.*

[10] *"And you shall mark out your eastern boundary from Hazar-enan to Shepham.* a [11] *And the boundary shall go down from Shepham to Hariblah,* a *on the east side of Ain. And the boundary shall go down, and reach to the ridge east of the sea of Chinnereth.* [12] *And the boundary shall go down to the Jordan, and its termination shall be at the Dead Sea. This shall be your land with its boundaries all round."*

[13] *And Moses commanded the people of Israel, saying, "This is the land which you shall inherit by lot, which Yahweh has commanded to give to the nine tribes and to the half tribe.* [14] *For the tribe of the sons of Reuben by fathers' houses, and the tribe of the sons of Gad by their fathers' houses, have received their inheritance,*

and also the half tribe of Manasseh. ¹⁵ *The two tribes and the half tribe have received their inheritance beyond the Jordan at Jericho to the east, toward the sunrise."*

¹⁶ *And Yahweh spoke to Moses, saying,* ¹⁷ *"These are the names of the men who shall divide the land to you for inheritance—Eleazar the priest, and Joshua son of Nun.* ¹⁸ *You shall take one leader from every tribe, to divide the land for inheritance.* ¹⁹ *These are the names of the men—from the tribe of Judah, Caleb son of Jephunneh.* ²⁰ *From the tribe of the sons* ^a *of Simeon, Shemuel* ^b *son of Ammihud.* ²¹ *From the tribe of Benjamin, Elidad* ^a *son of Chislon.* ²² *From the tribe of the sons of Dan a leader,* ^a *Bukki* ^b *son of Jogli.* ²³ *From the sons of Joseph: from the tribe of the sons of Manasseh a leader,* ^a *Hanniel son of Ephod.* ^b ²⁴ *From the tribe of the sons of Ephraim a leader,* ^a *Kemuel son of Shiphtan.* ²⁵ *From the tribe of the sons of Zebulun a leader,* ^a *Elizaphan son of Parnach.* ²⁶ *From the tribe of the sons of Issachar a leader,* ^a *Paltiel son of Azzan.* ^b ²⁷ *From the tribe of the sons of Asher a leader,* ^a *Ahihud* ^b *son of Shelomi.* ²⁸ *From the tribe of the sons of Naphtali a leader,* ^a *Pedahel son of Ammihud."* ^b ²⁹ *These are the men whom Yahweh commanded to divide the inheritance for the people of Israel in the land of Canaan.*

Notes

2.a. *BHS* suggests the deletion of "Canaan," making v 2 as a whole more intelligible (cf. also J. Paterson, 65).
4.a. Josh 15:3 reads "Hezron and Addar." G reads Arad.
9.a. G reads "Dephrona," with other variants.
9.b. G reads "Asernain," with other variants.
10.a. G reads "Sheppham," with other variants.
11.a. Following MT. Sam and G read ארבלה "Arbela."
20.a. Lacking in G, Syr, and Vg.
20.b. G reads "Shalamiel" (cf. Num 1:6).
21.a. Sam, G, and Syr read "Eldad" (cf. Num 11:26).
22.a. The reference to "leader" is lacking in one MT ms, Syr and Vg.
22.b. G reads "Bakchir."
23.a. The reference to "leader" is lacking in two MT mss, S, and Vg.
23.b. G reads "Ouphi."
24.a. The reference to "leader" is lacking in Syr and Vg.
25.a. The reference to "leader" is lacking in Syr and Vg.
26.a. The reference to "leader" is lacking in Syr.
26.b. G reads "Oza," and S "Azor" (עזור).
27.a. The reference to "leader" is lacking in Syr and Vg.
27.b. G reads "Achior," with other variants.
28.a. The reference to "leader" is lacking in two MT mss, Syr, and Vg.
28.b. G reads "Benamioud," apparently reading "son of" twice.

Form/Structure/Setting

Earlier analysts had little hesitation in assigning this material to P (see A. Dillmann, 208–14; J. Wellhausen, 117; A. Kuenen, 98; H. Holzinger, 165–66 [PG/PS]; B. Baentsch, 684–89 [P/PS/RP]; G. B. Gray, 449). There is the obvious presence of Eleazar and Joshua in v 17 (cf. P in Num 20:22–29; 27:12–23), while in v 19 Caleb is "leader" of Judah (cf. P in Num 13:6). There are the usual priestly introductory formulae, and vv 16–29 with their list of names have obvious affinities with the priestly material in Num 1:5–

15; 13:4–15. Gray was more inclined to link the material with PS than with PG, but was not insistent about it.

The priestliness of the section is clear; the more difficult questions concern the relationship of the section to comparable material in the book of Joshua, and this has been taken up in more detail by more recent analysts. M. Noth (248–51) notes that the description in vv 1–12 is orientated toward specific details given in the book of Joshua concerning the division of the inheritance in Canaan. He also points out in vv 13–15 a use of the deuteronomistic presentation of the conquest east of the Jordan. On the other hand the list of names in vv 17–28 follows comparable lists in Num 1:5–15; 13:4–15, and this gives Noth further grounds for his assumption that this part of the book of Numbers presupposes the deuteronomic history and also the Pentateuchal narrative at an edited and late stage. This section for Noth, like Num 33:50–56, is part of the editorial unification of those two great literary complexes. As for the boundaries Noth has no doubt that the details here have been drawn directly from Josh 15:1–4. Only one frontier point (on the south) is missing in Num 34, and this Noth takes to be a mistake. In another case two frontier points in Josh 15 are combined to make one in Num 34.

The northern and northeastern frontiers pose more problems for Noth, and for scholars in general. They are notoriously difficult to fix (see *Comment*). Noth points out that the style of presentation agrees throughout with that in Joshua, though as a matter of fact no comparable frontier is described there. The same basic list of frontier posts is found in Ezek 47:15–18, though with some variants and additions. Its reappearance in Ezek 48:1–2 as the boundary of Dan (though with further variants) suggests to Noth that vv 7–11 here in Num 34 have been drawn from a Danite boundary list—Dan being the most northerly of the tribes.

In Noth's opinion the list of names given in vv 19–28 can scarcely be dependent on old tradition, although some of the names give an archaic impression. They must have been borrowed therefore from an older stock of names. The fact that there are only ten names in the list indicates for Noth that the Transjordanian settlement is presupposed. Some of the names are of ancient type (e.g. Ahihud, v 27), and others are attested in older texts (e.g. Shemuel, v 20 [cf. 1 Sam 1:20]; Elidad, v 21 [cf. Eldad in G and Num 11:26]; Kemuel, v 24 [cf. Gen 22:21]; Paltiel, v 26 [cf. 2 Sam 3:15]). The ordering of the tribes follows in general the geographical position of the future tribal territories, moving from south to north (as also in Josh 18–19). Exceptions to this are Judah's precedence over Simeon, perhaps on account of Judah's post-exilic importance, and Manasseh's over Ephraim (as in Num 26:28–37).

J. de Vaulx (385–87) argues that Noth's account of the northern frontiers does not really do justice to the style and content of vv 7–8, which in his view diverge from that of Josh 15–19. He finds traces of two different boundary lines, a theory which is inclined to depend on site identifications which remain uncertain (see *Comment*).

A. G. Auld (*Joshua, Moses, and the Land*, 74–79) finds in vv 1–2 a mix of deuteronomistic and priestly language (as in 33:50–51), while in the structure and details of the boundary list he finds closer connections with the border information in Joshua and Ezekiel than the present form of the texts might suggest. He also argues in detail for the secondary nature of vv 13–15, and vv 17b–19a. His inclination throughout is to argue for the priority of the information in Joshua over that in Numbers, including the material in Numbers which is arguably the first draft.

From our perspective it seems reasonable to conclude that the whole section is essentially the work of the priestly author of Numbers. The indicators noted in the work of the classical analysts are sufficient to justify this assumption. It also seems reasonable to assume that in doing his work he has made use of the deuteronomic history in the book of Joshua, and also elements from the book of Ezekiel. His source for the southern frontier is probably the southern boundary of Judah, as given in Josh 15:1–14. Karkar is omitted, perhaps as Noth suggests by mistake, or perhaps because it was no longer familiar to the author's contemporaries. The working together of Hezron and Addar into Hazar-addar may also be explained in terms of contemporary realities. Resort to the book of Ezekiel was necessary because Joshua lacks boundaries for the tribe of Dan which eventually took up position in the far north (cf. Josh 19:47). The northern boundary given in Ezek 47:15–17 is:

The Great Sea—Hethlon—Zedad—Hamath—Berothah—Sibraim—Hazer-hatticon—Hazar-enon.

That given here in Num 34 is:

The Great Sea—Mount Hor—Hamath—Zedad—Ziphron—Hazar-enan.

There is enough similarity here to suggest dependence or a common source; variations may again be explained in terms of what the author of Num 34 was able to trace in his own time. That this was indeed Danite territory was made clear to him by Ezek 48:1. For the eastern border (vv 10–12) the author appears to be working from a different tradition or on his own initiative, there being little obvious correspondence between v 11 and Ezek 47:18. Here too the author may be locating boundaries on the basis of places familiar to him and his contemporaries.

It is hard to say what earlier tradition if any these boundaries may reflect. The area held by David and Solomon was probably similar in general terms— Berothah and Hamath occur in 2 Sam 8:8–9. On the other hand David's empire also included Edom and Damascus, but not the land of the Philistines. The boundaries given here are probably in some measure idealistic. The clause "from Dan to Beersheba" (cf. e.g. Judg 20:1) is probably an indicator of the usual north-south limits of the land. The more expansive "from Lebo-hamath to the brook of Egypt" (cf. e.g. 1 Kgs 8:65) corresponds more closely with the view presented in Joshua and Ezekiel, and reflected here in Num 34. The most expansive and idealistic vision of all is found in the Yahwist's promise in Gen 15:18 where the land will stretch from the brook of Egypt to the Euphrates.

The list of leaders given in vv 16–29 is essentially the work of the priestly author of Numbers. Some of the names may indeed be ancient, but many are well attested in late texts (e.g. Shemuel v 20 [cf. 1 Chr 7:2]; Ammihud, v 20 [cf. Num 1:10]; Bukki, v 22 [cf. 1 Chr 5:31; Ezra 7:4, Bukkiah, in 1 Chr 25:4, 13]; Hanniel, v 23 [cf. 2 Chr 7:39]; Kemuel, v 24 [cf. 1 Chr 27:17];

Elizaphan, v 25 [cf. Num 3:30]; Paltiel, v 26 [cf. Palti, Num 13:9, Piltai, Neh 12:17, Phaltiel; 4 Ezra 5:16]; Pedahel, v 28 [cf. Padahzur, Num 1:10]). It was clear that the same names from earlier lists in the book of Numbers could not be used; this was a new generation, and, Judah apart, each tribe needed a new leader. As with the other lists of names this may have been constructed on the basis of tribal record and recollection, put together by the Babylonian exiles. In preparing the list the priestly author reveals once again one of his chief purposes in this part of his book—to prepare for the forthcoming occupation of the land as recorded in the book of Joshua.

It was also necessary to align this material with the settlement of Gad, Reuben, and half Manasseh to the east of the Jordan—hence the explanations recorded in vv 13–15.

Comment

4. עקרבים למעלה "the ascent of Akrabbim," or "scorpions"—(see M. Gorg, *VT* 24 [1974] 508–9; cf. Josh 15:3; Judg 1:36). This is probably the modern Naqb eṣ-Ṣafā. According to Ezek 47:19 Hazazon-tamar (the modern ʿAin el-ʿArûs) was also part of the boundary in this region.

The site of Zin is unknown—presumably it gives its name to the wilderness of Zin (v 3 cf. Num 13:21; 33:36).

Kadesh-barnea is Kadesh (see on Num 13:26 cf. Num 33:36), the modern ʿAin Qadeis. This is the most southerly point of the boundary.

The site of Hazar-addar is unknown.

Azmon might be the modern Quṣeimeh—about sixty miles south of Gaza.

5. The brook of Egypt is the modern Wady el-ʿArîsh (cf. Josh 15:4, 47; 1 Kgs 8:65; 2 Kgs 24:7; 2 Chr 7:8; Isa 27:12, and perhaps Amos 6:14).

The sea mentioned here is the Mediterranean.

6. It appears that Israel never in fact occupied the whole area designated here—namely all the coastal plains down to the Mediterranean. The Philistines ceased to be the threat they had been in pre-monarchic and early monarchic times, but they continued to hold their position in the southwest. N. H. Snaith (340) cites as an exception a very short period when Hezekiah revolted and imprisoned Padi of Ekron in Jerusalem. It is doubtful whether this really constitutes an occupation. For witness to much later Hasmonean influences in the area see 1 Macc 10:76; 12:33–34; 14:5.

7. Mount Hor is obviously not the site of Aaron's death (Num 20:22; 33:38), and cannot be identified with certainty. The boundary intended to start between Tyre and Sidon, and run eastward to the foot of the Lebanon range (see N. H. Snaith, 340).

8. For Lebo-hamath see *Comment* on Num 13:21. It was situated at the head of the Orontes river.

The site of Zedad is unknown, but for detailed topographical discussion of this and other sites on the northern frontier see J. Simons, *The Geographical and Topographical Texts of the Old Testament* (Leiden: E. J. Brill, 1959).

9. Ziphron and Hazar-enan are both unknown.

10. והתאויתם "you shall mark out," taking this to be the hiphil of the verb in vv 7–8. MT as it stands means "you shall desire for yourselves."

The site of Shepham is unknown. In Ezek 47:18 the eastern boundary is defined by the Jordan and the Dead Sea alone.

11. This cannot be the Riblah on the Orontes (cited in 2 Kgs 25:6). Sam and G call the site Arbela (see *Notes*), but as J. Sturdy points out (235) this cannot be the Arbela of 1 Macc 9:2.

The whereabouts of Ain is not known. The word means "spring," and it may be that a further word is missing. G. B. Gray (461–62) suggests that it may be ʿIyyon mispronounced (1 Kgs 15:20; 2 Kgs 15:29).

11. כתף "the ridge," following NEB. RSV renders "the shoulder of the sea of Chinnereth" (cf. Josh 15:10).

Chinnereth means "harp-shaped," and is another name for the Sea of Galilee or Lake of Gennesareth (cf. Josh 19:35; Deut 3:17).

12. The lower part of the eastern frontier follows the line of the Jordan down to the Dead Sea.

13–15. Cf. Num 32:33.

19. Caleb is the only leader who figures elsewhere in the book (Num 13:6, 30; 14:6, 24, 38; 26:65). As one of the two faithful spies it is not surprising that he is Judah's representative.

22. The ordering of the tribes corresponds in general with that found in Josh 18–19. Dan is probably thought of as still occupying its more southerly position.

Explanation

This section tells of a command by Yahweh to Moses to explain to the Israelites what the borders of the land are to be. The description is in some measure idealized, indicating a wide stretch of territory which Israel did not ever entirely occupy. Some of the sites are difficult to identify, particularly those on the northern and northeastern frontiers. It is clear nevertheless that the land is intended to stretch as far south as Kadesh, as far west as the Mediterranean, and to include the Jordan as part of its eastern frontier. The fact that Reuben, Gad, and part of Manasseh occupy land to the east of the Jordan is duly noted. The section goes on to tell of the appointment of a leader from each of the remaining ten tribes to assist in the division of the land by lot. These are evidently under the supervision of Joshua and Eleazar.

There is good reason for thinking that the section, in both of its major parts, is in all essentials the work of the priestly author of Numbers. He is anxious to make the point that the directions about the extent of the land were in fact given to Moses himself, and that the arrangements to follow in the book of Joshua were all part of the true Mosaic revelation. It also seems likely that he wished to clarify the position about the true borders of the land, particularly in the north and east. The book of Joshua, representing the viewpoint of deuteronomic historians, depicts a land which can scarcely have extended much further north than a line from Tyre to Leshem (the later city of Dan)—hence the familiar, and probably earlier, description of the land as "from Dan to Beersheba." Deuteronomistic editors however had already provided a more expansive view in which the northern extremity was Lebo-hamath, and the southern the Brook of Egypt (1 Kgs 8:65). It is this tradition which the author of Numbers develops, with the assistance of information about a similarly far-flung northern border in Ezek 47:15–17.

This extension of the northern boundary also made necessary some adjustments on the east, and here the author provides a list of sites in vv 10–11 which takes the border back down to the Sea of Chinnereth (the Sea of Galilee). Such a list was lacking in Ezek 47:18. Another difficulty facing the author was the fact that deuteronomic tradition recognized a significant Transjordanian settlement of Gad and Reuben, whereas the tradition in Ezek 47:18 seemed to fix the Jordan as the true eastern frontier of the land proper. The author can only reaffirm in v 12 the tradition from Ezekiel, and the traditional view in vv 13–15 that Gad and Reuben had received an inheritance in Transjordan. To this he is bound to add his own conviction (see on Num 32:33) that half Manasseh had also settled in Transjordan.

The southern and eastern boundaries present no problem. The author takes up the southern boundary of Judah, as delineated in Josh 15:1–4, and with minor modifications makes it the southern border of the land as a whole. That the Mediterranean was the western border was clear to him from Josh 15:12; 16:3, 8; 17:10; 19:29. In this part of the section it is easy to see once again the dependence of Numbers on the book of Joshua, and the author's interest in preparing for and clarifying the process of occupation as described in Joshua.

The idea of a division of the land had already been established by the author in Num 26:52–56. It was appropriate from his point of view that further details about the arrangements for this should be seen as part of the true revelation to Moses. Accordingly he deputes his two settlement leaders, Eleazar and Joshua, along with ten specified leaders, one from each of the tribes involved in the settlement west of Jordan, to be responsible for the division of the land. Details of how this is carried out are to follow in Josh 13–19; the important point for the author is that the initial arrangements were revealed to Moses. There is further illustration here of how the author of Numbers handles tradition in a way comparable to the Chronicler. Just as the Chronicler is anxious to establish that though Solomon built the temple the details and preparations for its construction had all been revealed to David, so the author of Numbers is concerned to show that though Joshua and Eleazar are the leaders through whom the division of the land takes effect the original revelation was to Moses himself—the man who in fact remains outside the land, and does not enter it. Here, as in other parts of the book of Numbers, Babylonian Judaism finds in Moses, the man who remains outside the land, an authority figure to justify the leading role it sought to play in the affairs of the returned exiles in Palestine.

There is no clear indication that the author is handling very early tradition in the list of names and in the ordering of the tribes. The list presupposes the deuteronomic view that there was a significant Transjordanian settlement—there being only ten tribal leaders named. Some of the names may be ancient in form, but many are readily attested in late literature, and as with the earlier lists of names recorded in the book it seems likely that the author himself has compiled them from exilic records, based on the recollections of exiles. The ordering of the tribes is essentially geographical in this instance—with the four most southerly tribes coming first (vv 19–22; Judah, Simeon, Benjamin, Dan), followed by the two central tribes (vv 23–24; Manasseh, Ephraim), and finally the four in the far north (vv 25–28; Zebulun, Issachar, Asher, Naphtali). In Josh 13–19 the deuteronomic historian preferred to focus first on Judah, Ephraim, and Manasseh, before turning at the beginning of Josh 18 to the seven other tribes. These are headed by Benjamin and Simeon from the south, followed by the four from the far north in the order given here in Num 34, and finally by Dan. It is natural enough that the priestly author, who is wishing to give an overall and definitive view of the geography of the land in this section, should abandon the order of the deuteronomic historian, and also the order which for varying reasons he has adopted elsewhere—as for example in Num 1–4. His aim is to begin in the south and to move progressively northward, giving Dan its original and more southerly location.

The section is obviously appropriate at this point in the story. The author has nearly reached the end of the material he wishes to include prior to the promulgation of Deuteronomy. Having given instructions that the land must be cleared of all alien influences (Num 33:50–56) it is natural that he should go on and give what for him at least must have been a very clear delineation of the land and its frontiers. From this it is equally appropriate that he should proceed to indicate something of the means (the personnel) through which the division of the land among the various tribes is to be effected.

The section thus confirms the author's overall theological conviction that the land is the gift of Yahweh. The gift moreover is not a nebulous conception in the mind of God, but a carefully delineated area of territory. The inheritance God gives to Israel is real and substantial, not detached or other-worldly. It is in addition an extensive territory; God does not stint in his giving. Just as God has planned the journey from Sinai to the borders of the land, so the processes of occupation and settlement are planned by him. Israel's right response is to accept the truth of this, and to obey.

The Levitical Cities (35:1-8)

Bibliography

Albright, W. F. "The List of Levitic Cities." *L. Ginzberg Jubilee Volume.* New York: American Academy for Jewish Research, 1945. **Alt, A.** "Festungen und Levitenorte im Lande Juda." *Kleine Schriften zur Geschichte des Volkes Israel Vol 2.* Munich: C. H. Beck, 1953. **Auld, A. G.** *Joshua, Moses, and the Land.* Edinburgh: T. & T. Clark, 1980. **Buit, M. du** "Quelques contacts bibliques dans les archives royales de Mari." *RB* 66 (1959) 576–81. **Cazelles, H.** "David's Monarchy and the Gibeonite Claim." *PEQ* 87 (1955) 165–75. **Frick, F. S.** *The City in Ancient Israel.* Missoula MT: Scholars Press, 1977. **Gunneweg, A. H. J.** *Leviten und Priester.* Göttingen: Vandenhoeck & Ruprecht, 1965. **Haran, M.** "The Levitical Cities: Utopia and Historical Reality." *Tarbiz* 27 (1957/ 58) 421–38. ———. "Studies in the Account of the Levitical Cities." *JBL* 80 (1961) 45–54, 156–65. **Mazar, B.** "The Cities of the Priests and Levites." *Congress Volume SVT* 7. Leiden: E. J. Brill, 193–205.

Translation

[1] *And Yahweh spoke to Moses in the plains of Moab by the Jordan at Jericho, saying,* [2] *"Command the people of Israel that they give to the Levites, from the inheritance of their possession, cities to live in. And you* [a] *shall give to the Levites pasture lands round about the cities.* [3] *And the cities shall be theirs to live in, and their* [a] *pasture lands shall be for their cattle, and for their livestock, and for all their beasts.* [4] *The pasture lands of the cities, which you give to the Levites, shall extend from the wall of the city outwards for 1000* [a] *cubits all round.* [5] *And you shall measure, outside the city, 2000 cubits for the east side, and 2000 cubits for the south side, and 2000 cubits for the west side, and 2000 cubits for the north side, the city being in the middle. This shall belong to them* [a] *as pastureland for their cities.* [6] *The cities which you give* [a] *to the Levites shall be the six cities of refuge, to which you shall allow the homicide to flee.* [b] *And in addition to these you shall give them forty-two other cities.* [7] *All the cities which you give to the Levites shall be forty-eight, with their pasture lands.* [8] *And for the cities which you shall give from the possession of the people of Israel, from the larger tribes you shall take many, and from the smaller tribes you shall take few—each in proportion to the inheritance which it inherits* [a] *shall give of its cities to the Levites."*

Notes

2.a. G and Syr read the third person plural.
3.a. MT has a masculine suffix; the pasture lands of the Levites. Sam has a feminine suffix; the pasture lands of the cities.
4.a. G reads "two thousand," harmonizing with v 5.
5.a. "To you" in Sam, G, Syr, and Tg [J]: "to them" in MT.
6.a. G reads "you shall give the cities to the Levites . . ." (cf. also v 7).
6.b. Syr explains that the cities are for the homicide who has killed by accident.

The construction of v 6 is difficult. J. Paterson (66) suggests that the last clause is a gloss, explaining "forty-eight" in the next verse.

8.a. The singular occurs in Sam, Syr, and one MT ms.

Form/Structure/Setting

Analysts have been in general agreement that this section belongs to the priestly material in the book of Numbers (see e.g. A. Dillman, 214–27; J. Wellhausen, 183–84; A. Kuenen, 97–98; H. Holzinger, 169; B. Baentsch, 691–92; G. B. Gray, 464–67; A. H. McNeile, 183). The section bears obvious witness to the priestly view of the Levites, and makes further provision for their support. An obvious difference between this and deuteronomic tradition can be appreciated by a comparison with Deut 18:1. In D the Levites have no territorial possession in Israel, and Deut 18:6 makes it clear that they were scattered among various Israelite tribes. It was equally obvious that Ezekiel knew nothing of Levitical cities as described here in Num 35. In Ezek 48:13–22 the Levites have a slice of land apportioned to them, and are to live there together, not as here in cities scattered throughout the land. This idea of Levitical cities occurs only in what are arguably late texts (e.g. Lev 25:32–34; Josh 14:4; 21:1–42; 1 Chr 13:2; 2 Chr 11:14; 31:15–19; Ezra 2:70=Neh 7:73; Neh 11:3, 20, 36). Much earlier texts (e.g. Gen 49:7; Judg 17:7; 19:1) seemed to suggest a situation in which Levites were scattered all over the land. In general therefore scholars were of the opinion that the picture of Levitical cities described here was highly idealized. Many of the cities cited as Levitical in these late texts were thought not to have come into Israel's hands till centuries later (Dillmann), while the locations of some (e.g. Hebron and Holon, Anathoth and Almon; see Josh 21 for the names) seemed to be so close to one another that the surrounding pasture lands would have overlapped. In the case of Hammoth-dor they would have covered part of the Sea of Galilee.

This degree of idealization led many (e.g. Holzinger, Baentsch, Gray) to designate the section to PS. Gray also pointed to certain peculiarities atypical of P as a whole—the combination of בהמה and רכש in v 3 for livestock and beasts, and the use of קיר with the meaning "wall" in v 4. Interpretations of Num 18:20, 24; 26:62 suggested that the priests and Levites receive tithes and dues *instead of* landed property, and the natural conclusion for these analysts was that the earlier passages in the book represent the position of PG, while Num 35:1–8 and Lev 25:32–34 belong to PS. Gray himself was of the opinion that despite its idealizations this section is more realistic than Ezekiel's, and that the prophet's ideals have been adapted with modifications from P. The amount of land required for the priests and Levites by Ezekiel is about forty square miles—considerably in excess of the fifteen and a half square miles suggested here. Ezekiel's scheme is shaped entirely by the need to maintain a holy cordon round the Temple, positioned as it is at the center of the land. The picture here in Num 35:1–8 is governed at least to some degree by the actualities of the situation.

In summary it would be fair to say that what most inclined earlier analysts to speak of "idealization" in this passage was the difficulty of squaring the

whole notion of "Levitical city" with indicators from pre-exilic times of historical realities. The naming of the cities in Josh 21 did nothing to alleviate
the difficulty. There the sons of Aaron receive thirteen from Judah, Simeon,
and Benjamin, while the Kohathites receive ten from Ephraim, Dan, and west
Manasseh, the Gershonites thirteen from Issachar, Asher, Naphtali, and east
Manasseh, and the Merarites twelve from Reuben, Gad, and Zebulun. This
seemed to presuppose the late organization of the Levitical families, and
was difficult to square with pre-exilic indications that priests lived in a variety
of places, some of which occur in Josh 21, but others not (cf. e.g. 1 Sam
1:3; 21:1; 22:19; Amos 7:10; Jer 1:1). Nothing is known about whether these
priests owned land in and about the city. It does appear that priests could
own land (1 Kgs 2:26; Jer 32:6–15), but in neither case does it seem that
the land belonged to the tribe of Levi, or to the individuals concerned by
virtue of their being priests. In Deuteronomy Levites are evidently scattered
throughout the cities of the land, and many lived without property (Deut
12:18; 18:6). It may be that Deut 18:8 implies that individual Levites owned
land, but the position is far from clear. As a whole the Levites in D are
commended to the charity of other Israelites on the specific ground that
they have no landed property (Deut 12:12, 18–19; 14:19, 27; 16:11, 14; 26:11–
13). For these reasons earlier analysts are generally agreed that the Levitical
city is an idealization, with little or nothing by way of rootage in historical
realities, and certainly of no great age.

A. Alt ("Festungen und Levitenorte") was among the first to offer some
kind of challenge to this consensus. He showed that all the cities listed in
Josh 21 were on the peripheries of the two kingdoms, a long way from Jerusalem and Bethel, and he went on to suggest that the list was of Josianic origin.
The king brought all the priests in Judah to Jerusalem (2 Kgs 23:8), and
apparently put to death the priests of the high places in the towns of Samaria
(2 Kgs 23:19–20). This raises the possibility that the idea of Levitical cities
is a response to the needs of Levites without livings and/or an attempt to
place men sympathetic to centralization of worship in the outlying parts of
the kingdom. M. Noth (252–53) also argued that the idea of cities of residence
for Levites goes back to deuteronomic ideology, and that the original form
of Josh 21 was indeed deuteronomistic. He pointed out that the notion of
Israelite tribes handing over cities in proportion to their size must be a development of the tradition in Josh 21, since there can be no question of any
correspondence between the size of tribal territory and the number of cities
to be handed over. He also argued that this section (vv 1–8) along with the
next, vv 9–34, is dependent on the final form of Josh 20:1–21:42, the point
being that vv 1–8 and vv 9–34 have little to do with one another excepting
the observation in v 6 that six of the Levitical cities are to be the cities of
refuge. In Noth's view this means that this section belongs to the redactional
unification of Pentateuchal Narrative with that of the deuteronomic history.
What Joshua carried out had in fact been commanded by God through Moses.

Recent investigation has tended to concentrate on the question of the
age and background of the list, and to cast doubt on the notion that the
Levitical city is a very late idealization. W. F. Albright ("The List of Levitic
Cities") followed through Alt's suggestion that the list is not utopian but

based on concrete facts. Using Josh 21:1–40 and 1 Chr 6:54–81 he constructed a list he judged to be almost complete, and maintained, in opposition to Alt, that it dates to the period of the united monarchy. The fact that some (e.g. Gezer, Aijalon, and Taanach) were not taken by Israel until this period means that it cannot be earlier; on the other hand such information about northern cities would not be available or applicable in the south after the division of the kingdom, and the list would therefore not have been compiled after that event.

M. du Buit (*RB* 66 [1959] 576–81) compares the "towns of the Levites" with the "towns of the Benjaminites," attested in the royal archives of Mari. The kings of Mari assigned their turbulent nomads to specific cities, where controlling them would be less difficult. The independent and aggressive spirit of the Levites is well attested in earlier texts (e.g. Gen 49:5–7; Exod 32:25–29; Deut 33:8–9), and the comparison with Mari suggests possibilities for the background of the Levitical cities.

An influential recent study is that of B. Mazar ("The Cities of the Priests and Levites"). He dates the institution of the Levitical cities to the end of David's reign, when Solomon was co-regent. He leans heavily on 1 Chr 26:30–32 with its reference to the installation of Levites of Hebron in some kind of supervisory office; this reference to service of the king he thinks is unlikely to be a post-exilic construction. Hebron was the place where David was first acclaimed as king, and these Levites, Mazar suggests, were among his most loyal supporters. The text of Josh 21 suggests further Levitical settlements, taking in land to the west of the Shephelah and in the coastal and central plains, as well as in Transjordan. Mazar suggests that their function was defensive, but also fiscal—collecting revenues and administering royal interests. A number of the settlements (e.g. Elteke, Gibbethon, Gath-rimmon, and those in Moab and northern Transjordan) could only have been made, Mazar argues, during the united monarchy. Later they were lost to Israel, never to be retrieved. The reason for such a settlement policy would be in part to control areas of doubtful loyalty—and hence the absence of settlements around Jerusalem, and also in Ephraim and Manasseh where there was a stronger sense of Israelite solidarity. J. Gray (*Joshua, Judges, and Ruth* [London: Nelson, 1967] 27–28) who follows Mazar closely suggests that Shechem was exceptional because of the need to safeguard Davidic interests at this old Yahwistic shrine. The settlements in Benjamin may have been necessary to counteract the influence of the sanctuary at Gibeon and any continuing support for the house of Saul. This approach to the problem has won a good deal of support— e.g. from J. Sturdy (237–38) who speaks of colonies of Levites being planted at weak points in the state's defenses, and F. S. Frick (*The City in Ancient Israel*, 140–42) who thinks Mazar's thesis "the most satisfactory one yet set forth."

M. Haran (*JBL* 80 [1961] 45–54, 156–65) wishes to contest both the utopian and the realistic extremes, arguing that elements of both are present in the tradition. His main aim is to identify and distinguish these elements. The utopian is evident in the measurements (an exact square for each city), in the jubilee legislation of Lev 25, in the claim that the cities are exclusively Levitical, and in the differentiation between cities for priests and those for

Levites. The realistic is evident in the location of the cities (contrast Ezekiel's highly utopian picture), in the fact that the forty-eight cities are not notable shrines and cannot be fitted in the ideal boundaries of the land as envisaged in Num 34:1–12, and in the fact that P's numerical calculations would suggest the allocation of only two or three cities to the Levites, and not thirteen. It may be added that Haran's conclusions do not seriously affect most modern realistic interpretations, Mazar's included.

Among other proposals R. de Vaux (*Ancient Israel*, 366–67) suggests that the list of cities represents the dispersal of the Levite population after the foundation of the temple and after the organization of the official cult at Bethel in the north. This explains, in de Vaux's view, why there are no Levitical cities in the immediate environs of Jerusalem or in the center of Israel. Alt's view still has its supporters. See e.g. A. H. J. Gunneweg (*Leviten und Priester* [Göttingen: Vandehoeck & Ruprecht, 1965] 64–65) while J. A. Soggin (*Joshua* [London: SCM; 1972] 204) argues for both Solomonic and Josianic influences. Josiah, he suggests, wished to restore an ancient institution, and to provide an income for the Levites whose means of support had been removed by centralization of the cult.

J. de Vaulx (391–96) also argues for a realistic view of the city list. The real idealization is in Ezekiel, while the list in Josh 21 offers a practical distribution of Levitical cities and shows no awareness of the later priest/Levite distinction. Following the suggestions of du Buit, de Vaulx supposes that the tribe of Levi, faithful to the nomadic ideal and the purity of primitive Yahwism, was slow to settle. In due course its members were authorized to settle in certain cities in the territory of other tribes; they were not the only inhabitants, nor were they in charge. The authorization stems primarily from David and Solomon, who note their loyalty and zeal, and choose cities on the frontiers of the land. Some become cult specialists, and begin to take up residence at the sanctuaries, but the rest face increasing difficulty in the old Levitical cities. Their lack of resources is something which Deuteronomy seeks to remedy by commending them to the care of the Israelites. The priestly author in Num 35:1–8 was thus faced with a variety of traditions about the Levites. According to de Vaulx he preserves the notion of Levitical dispersion among the tribes (v 2), and also the obligation to make provision for the Levites (v 8). At the same time he avoids anything that would undermine the conception of the uniqueness of the one sanctuary at Jerusalem. He also avoids words like "heritage" or "possession," contenting himself with vaguer terminology such as "to give" and "residence." In this way, de Vaulx suggests, he avoids any contradiction of the principle that Yahweh alone is the sole heritage of the Levites. Installed on the frontiers of the land they protect the people against the enemies of Yahweh. Dispersed among the people they exercise their mission of making the Torah known to the people (cf. Deut 33:9–10; Hos 4:4–6).

This survey of opinion makes it clear that final and definitive conclusions are not yet attainable. The following is a tenable view of the history of the tradition which corresponds well enough with our overall view of the book.

1. There are reasons for supposing that Num 35:1–8 is dependent on parts at least of Josh 21 (see further A. G. Auld, *Joshua, Moses, and the Land,*

79–80). In its present form however Josh 21 in undoubtedly priestly. It has Joshua and Eleazar as leaders (v 1), and it also divides the clergy into sons of Aaron and the three Levitical families in precisely the way favored by the book of Numbers. The idea that this provision was a revelation to Moses is present in v 2. It seems best to assume that the final form of Josh 21 and Num 35:1–8 belong to the same level of priestly tradition. The author of Numbers may well have elaborated the deuteronomic history itself, as well as providing in Num 26–35 something of a prologue to it.

2. The idealization or utopianism stressed by earlier analysts, and identified precisely by Haran, must be recognized as such, and assigned to relatively late priestly sources—in this instance perhaps to the priestly author of Numbers.

3. It seems likely nevertheless that the list of Levitical cities existed in some other form in the deuteronomic history (Josh 21). The historian may well have seen in such a list a way of providing for the Levites. The arguments adduced for "realism" have some force, at least to the extent that they suggest the presence of earlier traditional material. It is worth adding that the principle of allotment required in v 8 (more from the larger tribes and less from the smaller) is not accurately observed in Josh 21. There Naphtali gives only three cities, though at the second census (Num 26) the tribe was larger than Ephraim or Gad, each of which gives four. Furthermore although Issachar and Dan are both twice as large as Ephraim, all three tribes give the same number of cities. This suggests that in the list of Levitical cities the priestly author of Numbers is indeed handling older tradition which does not readily correspond with his adaptations.

4. The list of cities is probably derived from Levitical tradition. As we have suggested elsewhere the author of Numbers is interested in such tradition and its use, quite apart from its presence in the deuteronomic history. The tradition is traceable to Josianic, or perhaps to Solomonic times. The former is perhaps preferable. A policy of centralization necessarily raised acute difficulty for provincial Levites, and that some provision should be made by central authority is probable. That this provision should include the right to live in certain towns some distance from the central sanctuary is likely. A right to some of the land for grazing purposes would be natural. Solomonic solutions tend to lean heavily on late texts from the Chronicler (e.g. Mazar), or else on tenuous reconstructions of Levi's early history (e.g. de Vaulx). The argument that the list could only have operated at the time of the united monarchy is not conclusive. Despite the "realisms" of the tradition there are evident utopian and idealistic elements present, and an ideal may well be envisaged even if the land is not actually controlled. Nevertheless Solomonic roots cannot be precluded, and de Vaux's proposal in relation to the foundation of the sanctuaries at Jerusalem and Bethel is as persuasive as any.

5. The author of Numbers is evidently anxious to point out that this institution is a Mosaic provision. This may not have been clear in the deuteronomic history, and it would be thoroughly in keeping with one of his major concerns in this third part of his book—to provide a prologue for the forthcoming deuteronomic laws and accounts of the settlement. There were also two particular elements in Levitical tradition to which he wished to do justice. The

first was that the Levites who function as priests have the right to be supported by the community. He was able to incorporate this principle into his new hierarchical arrangements in Num 18:20–24. The second was that those Levites who do not function as priests have the right to live in specified cities with grazing rights for their livestock. There is therefore no necessary contradiction between Num 18:20–24 and Num 35:1–8. As de Vaulx shows, the author uses vaguer terminology which precludes the notion that the cities are the "possession" or "heritage" of the Levites. The real tensions arise between the provision made in the book of Numbers, and the attempt made in Lev 25:32–34 (probably at a later stage) to apply the principles of redemption and jubilee to the Levitical city.

Comment

2. ומגרש "pasture lands," better than "common land" (NEB); literally "places of cattle driving."

4. According to J. Sturdy (238) this requirement envisages a circular city, whereas v 5 depicts a square of pasture land around the city. These inconsistent pictures are worked together, and Sturdy suggests the author would have thought it pedantic to dwell on the inconsistency. G. B. Gray (467–68) surveys a number of attempts to harmonize the two texts. If it is judged unlikely that the priestly author would allow such a tension to stand unresolved then one solution would be to assume that G does in fact preserve the earlier text (see *Notes*). NEB suggests that the one thousand cubits are to be measured from the *center* of the town (v 4). It may be best to assume that the cubits of the Levitical pasture lands are cubit frontages of land—in other words on each side of the city there was a block of land with a frontage of two thousand cubits (v 5), and a depth of 1000 cubits (v 4).

6. ערי המקלט "cities of refuge." This verse provides the link with the next section (Num 35:9–34), where the function of the cities is discussed in detail.

8. This principle of allotment (more from the larger tribes and less from the smaller) operates also in Num 26:54 and 33:54. It is part of the priestly author's adaptation of the deuteronomist's principle of division by lot.

Explanation

This section tells of the provision of cities for the Levites, and the guarantee of grazing rights to them in the surrounding pasture land. The section speaks not of Levitical rights of ownership, inheritance, or possession, but of the right to live in the cities and to pasture livestock there (contrast Lev 25:32–34). Measurements controlling the amount of land available for such purposes are given. There are forty-eight cities in all, and these are named in Josh 21. They include the six cities of refuge (to be discussed further in vv 9–34) and are to be given to the Levites on the basis of the strengths of the various tribes, the larger providing more such cities than the smaller.

That the priestly author should turn to this question at this point is entirely appropriate. He has just dealt with the arrangements for the division of the land among the various tribes in Num 34. Now is the moment to introduce his arrangements for the Levites. There is every likelihood that in including this material he is incorporating Levitical tradition (see *Form/Structure/Setting*). There was of course another Levitical tradition, preserved and adapted in Num 3–4, 18, which stressed that the Levites have no inheritance among the tribes. This tradition was strongly supported in Deuteronomy, and the author of Numbers was able to work it into his conception of the clerical hierarchy. What we have here is a subsequent provision, a later piece of Levitical tradition. Deuteronomy commended Levites to the care of the community, and the provision of cities to live in and land for their livestock is a natural solution. This latter Levitical tradition may have been a response to the problems posed by dispossessed Levites when the cult was centralized by Josiah. The possibility that Solomon was the first to initiate a policy of Levitical settlements cannot be precluded (see *Form/Structure/Setting*), but Deuteronomy itself remains silent on the subject, and it is only in the work of the exilic deuteronomists (Josh 21) that the city list actually appears.

For the priestly author of Numbers the deuteronomic list in its original form in Josh 21 was the basis for his contribution here in Num 35:1–8. It gave him opportunity to fulfill two of his interests—the incorporation and adaptation of Levitical tradition, and the reinterpretation of deuteronomic material. The assigning of cities in Joshua's lifetime is shown to be the product of a specific revelation to Moses. Moreover this traditional list of Levitical cities must be worked into his clerical hierarchy—with some cities granted to the sons of Aaron, and others to the three Levitical families which he has identified as the essential components of Levitical genealogy. The bulk of this reinterpretation comes in Josh 21 itself; here in Num 35:1–8 the author is content to suggest, in an idealized way, the extent of the pasture land and above all to make it clear that the essential arrangements were fixed within the lifetime of Moses.

In the circumstances of his own time it was useful to the author to establish the principle of a significant Levitical presence in the provinces. This would have assisted their developing role as teachers in the post-exilic period (cf. 2 Chr 17:9). In general terms the section also helps to support a point made previously—that the clergy in general and the Levites in particular have a right to community support and to resources.

The Cities of Refuge   (35:9-34)

Bibliography

Auld, A. G. "Cities of Refuge in Israelite Tradition." *JSOT* 10 (1978) 26–39. ———. *Joshua, Moses, and the Land.* Edinburgh: T. & T. Clark, 1980. **David, M.** "Die Bestimmungen über die Asylstädte in Jos. 20." *OTS* 9 (1951) 30–48. **Dinur, B.** "The Religious Character of the Cities of Refuge and the Ceremony of Admission into them." *Eretz-Israel* 3 (1954) 135–46. **Driver, W.** "The Release of Homicides from the Cities of Refuge. A Critical Monograph on Nu. 35:25. Abridged by the Author." *Grace Journal* (Grace Theological Seminary, Indiana) 1, 2 (1960) 7–22. **Frick, F. S.** *The City in Ancient Israel.* Missoula: Scholars Press, 1977. **Greenberg, M.** "The Biblical Conception of Asylum." *JBL* 78 (1959) 125–32. **Horst, F.** "Recht und Religion im Bereich des A.T." *EvT* 16 (1956) 49–75. **McKeating, H.** "The development of the law on homicide in Ancient Israel." *VT* 25 (1975) 46–68. **Nicolsky, N. M.** "Das Asylrecht in Israel." *ZAW* 48 (1930) 146–75. **Ramsey, G. W.** "Speech Forms in Hebrew Law and Prophetic Oracles." *JBL* 96 (1977) 45–58. **Schulz, H.** *Das Todesrecht im Alten Testament.* BZAW 114. Berlin: A. Töpelmann, 1969. **Schunk, K. D.** "Ophra, Ephron und Ephraim." *VT* 11 (1961) 188–200.

Translation

⁹ *And Yahweh spoke to Moses, saying,* ¹⁰ *"Speak to the people of Israel, and say to them, When* ᵃ *you cross the Jordan into the land of Canaan,* ¹¹ *then you shall select cities to be cities of refuge for you, that the homicide who kills any person by accident may flee there.* ¹² *And the cities shall be for you a refuge from the avenger,* ᵃ *so that the homicide shall not be put to death before standing trial before the congregation.* ¹³ *And the cities which you give for cities of refuge shall be six.* ¹⁴ *You shall give three cities beyond the Jordan, and three cities in the land of Canaan to be cities of refuge.* ¹⁵ *These six cities shall be for refuge for the people of Israel, and for the resident alien, and for the temporary settler, so that any one who kills any person by accident may flee there.*

¹⁶ *"But if he struck him down with an iron instrument, so that he died, he is a murderer. The murderer shall be put to death.* ¹⁷ *And if he struck him down with a stone in the hand, capable of killing a man, and he died, he is a murderer. The murderer shall be put to death.* ᵃ ¹⁸ *Or if* ᵃ *he struck him down with a wooden weapon in the hand, capable of killing a man, and he died, he is a murderer. The murderer shall be put to death.* ¹⁹ *The avenger of blood shall himself put the murderer to death. When he meets him he shall put him to death.* ²⁰ *And if (the homicide) stabbed* ᵃ *him out of malice, or threw a missile* ᵇ *while lying in wait, so that he died,* ²¹ *or if in enmity he struck him down with his hand, so that he died, then he who struck the blow shall be put to death. He is a murderer. The avenger of blood shall put the murderer to death when he meets him.*

²² *"But if he stabbed him on the spur of the moment without enmity, or threw a missile at him without lying in wait,* ²³ *or used a stone, capable of killing a man, but without seeing him, so that he died, and if he was not his enemy, and did not*

seek his harm, ²⁴ then the congregation shall judge between the homicide and the avenger of blood, in accordance with these ordinances. ²⁵ And the congregation shall protect the homicide ᵃ from the hand of the avenger of blood, and the congregation shall restore him to his city of refuge, to which he had fled, and he shall live in it until the death of the high priest who was anointed with the holy oil. ²⁶ But if the homicide shall at any time go beyond the bounds of his city of refuge to which he had fled, ²⁷ and the avenger of blood finds him outside the bounds of his city of refuge, and if the avenger of blood kills the homicide, he shall not be guilty of blood, ²⁸ because the man must remain in his city of refuge until the death of the high priest. But after the death of the high priest the homicide may return to the land of his possession.

²⁹ "And these things shall be for a statute and judgment to you throughout your generations in all your dwellings. ³⁰ If any one kills a person, the murderer shall be put to death only on the evidence of witnesses, and no person shall be put to death on the testimony of one witness. ³¹ Moreover you shall not accept payment for the life of a murderer who is guilty of death. He shall indeed be put to death. ³² And you shall not accept payment from him who has fled to his city of refuge, that he may return to live in the land before the death of the priest. ᵃ ³³ You shall not thus defile the land in which you live, ᵃ for blood defiles the land, and no expiation can be made for the blood shed in it, except by the blood of him who shed it. ³⁴ You ᵃ shall not make the land in which you live unclean, the land in which I dwell, for I Yahweh dwell in the midst of the people of Israel."

Notes

10.a. G reads "you shall cross. . . ."
12.a. G, S, and Tg have "of blood," as is customary in this section.
17.a. Sam has a Qal future, "the murderer shall die."
18.a. Perhaps "and if . . ." (Sam, G, Syr, Vg).
20.a. Syr reads "struck."
20.b. "Missile" has to be understood (cf. G and v 22 where it is explicit).
25.a. Sam reads המכה "the striker."
32.a. Sam, G, and Syr have "the high priest" (cf. vv 25, 28).
33.a. Sam, G, Syr, Vg, and Tgᴺ have "you live." MT has "you are."
34.a. This is singular in MT, but plural in Sam, G, Syr, Tg, and a few MT mss.

Form/Structure/Setting

Analysts have had no difficulty in recognizing evidence of the priestly levels of the Pentateuch in this section (see e.g. A. Dillmann, 917–21; J. Wellhausen, 183–84; A. Kuenen, 97–98; H. Holzinger, 169; B. Baentsch, 692–96; G. B. Gray, 469). Just as Deut 19 offers a substantial advance in the law on claiming sanctuary (as compared with that in the Book of the Covenant—Exod 21:12–24) so this law offers a development of that preserved in Deut 19. There (cf. also Deut 4:41–43) three cities are assigned, to which three more are to be added if Israel's territory does indeed reach to the full extent promised. Here in Num 35:9–34 six cities are assigned at once, and unconditionally. The rules given here are altogether more detailed, and for the first time, the technical term "cities of refuge" occurs. An obvious indicator of lateness

is the references to the death of the high priest (vv 25, 28). The description
of Israel as the "congregation" (vv 12, 24–25), and the introduction to the
section in vv 9–10 are characteristically and obviously priestly. The notions
of "defilement" and "uncleanness" (vv 33, 34) point in the same direction.
There is also a close relationship with Josh 20, which in its final form is
also priestly. Note the references to law by the hand of Moses (Josh 20:2),
and the high priest and congregation in Josh 20:6.

Gray pointed out three respects in which this law can be seen as a relatively
late modification of ancient custom. In the first place, he suggests, ancient
law made no distinction between accidental and deliberate homicide. Second,
ancient law permitted compensation by the death of *any* member of the homicide's family, whereas here stress is laid tacitly on the fact that only the murderer can lose his life. Third, the present law forbids the redemption of
the life of the murderer by any sort of money payment. On the other hand
it still puts the responsibility on the avenger of blood—the representative
of the injured family—not on a representative of the community.

Both Holzinger and Baentsch were prepared to find substantial elements
of PG in the section—for Baentsch the whole of vv 9–29 may be so assigned—
with the rest attributable to PS. Gray was content to label the material as P.

M. Noth (254–56) has argued strongly that these instructions stem ultimately from Josiah's centralization of the cult, and that Josh 20 (part of the
deuteronomic history in its original form) was the author's foundation text.
He is also inclined to the view that Josh 20 in its final literary form has
been utilized for the construction of this section. Noth detects a more original
version of the law of refuge in vv 4–5. Here quite clearly the elders of the
city of refuge have to decide the right of the homicide to asylum. Noth also
asks whether the question of "intention," as raised in v 16 and onward, was
always of a piece with vv 9–15. In favor of the view that it is an addition is
the fact that the word for "homicide" designates a killer without evil intent
in vv 11–12, whereas in vv 16–21 it has become something of a technical
term for a conscious and deliberate murderer. Nevertheless Noth remains
uncertain about how much can be based on observations such as this; he is
aware also of irregularities within vv 16–21. Among Noth's other ideas is
the suggestion that the role of the high priest here would have been formerly
played by the king. The possibility of earlier tradition in the section is recognized by J. Sturdy (241), but without further comment.

We noted with regard to vv 1–8 how some of the older critical orthodoxies
have more recently been called in question, and the same obtains here in
vv 9–34. The view that the cities of refuge were a logical and necessary result
of the centralization of the cult was given its classical formulation by Wellhausen, and has received further support by F. Horst (*EvT* 16 [1956] 49–75)
and N. M. Nicolsky (*ZAW* 48 [1930] 146–75). Among the challenges to this
view is M. David's suggestion (*OTS* 9 [1951] 30–48) that the cities are a
post-exilic fabrication. In the other direction M. Greenberg (*JBL* 78 [1959]
125–32), supported by F. S. Frick (*The City in Ancient Israel*, 137–40), has
suggested that the city of refuge was not intended to replace the older custom
of seeking refuge at an altar, but to supplement it. In Greenberg's view the
cities would have been necessary before the elimination of the local shrines

by Josiah. The shrines themselves could never have been permanent places of refuge. Evidence about blood guilt and asylum in other near eastern cultures suggests to Greenberg that the prolonged period in a city of refuge also had a punitive function. For him the institution of the cities of refuge is more likely to date to the period of the united monarchy.

H. McKeating (*VT* 25 [1975] 46–68) is also of the opinion that the Josianic reform did not intend to eliminate the ancient system of refuge. For him the authorities are seeking to regulate it (see Deut 19:1–13) by putting more emphasis on the role of the city, and less on that of the tribe.

J. de Vaulx (396–403) identifies five general stages in the development of the laws on asylum:

(1) The fugitive had to take refuge in the sanctuary, and grasp the horns of the altar (1 Kgs 1:50–53; 2:28–31; cf. Pss 27:2–5; 31:2–4). This may have been the normal procedure in Canaan prior to the settlement.

(2) The Book of the Covenant recognizes the importance of a place of refuge in cases of unpremeditated homicide (Exod 21:13), but does not allow asylum to be a permanent protection in cases of murder (Exod 21:14).

(3) The centralization of worship (reflected in Deut 4:41–43; 19:1–13) and the suppression of the local sanctuaries meant that cities in the provinces lost their sacred character, but some were preserved as places of asylum for cases of accidental homicide. A special role is now given to the elders of these cities (Deut 19:12) of delivering a murderer into the hands of the avenger of blood.

(4) In the deuteronomic history (Josh 20:4–5) this picture is changed slightly. Here the elders have a role at the outset, in the requirement that they question the fugitive before granting him admission to the city—presumably with a view to satisfying themselves that death was indeed accidental (v 5).

(5) The post-exilic legislation found in Josh 20:1–3, 6, 9, and here in Num 35:9–34, reveals further important developments. A technical term "city of refuge" is presented (vv 11, 13–14, 25–28, 32; Josh 20:2; 1 Chr 6:42, 52), and the law is said to be applicable also to aliens and temporary residents (Josh 20:9). Supreme authority has passed from the elders to the congregation (vv 12, 24–25; cf. Josh 20:6) (cf. the role of the congregation in Lev 24:14–16; Num 15:32–36). The homicide must remain in the city till the death of the high priest (vv 25, 28; Josh 20:6), and failure to observe this makes him liable to death at the hands of the avenger of blood (vv 26–28). No money payment can be received as recompense for any case of homicide, accidental or deliberate (vv 31–32).

A. G. Auld's investigations (*JSOT* 10 [1978] 26–39; *Joshua, Moses, and the Land,* 79–85) point to the lateness of the text in vv 9–34. Among other things he argues for the dependence of vv 9–15 on the tradition of Levitical cities in vv 1–5, 7–8, and for the general priority of tradition in the book of Joshua over that contained in these later chapters of the book of Numbers.

Solutions to the problems and uncertainties which these discussions raise are bound to be tentative, but it is certainly not difficult to suggest an approach which fits our overall view of this third major part of the book (Num 26:1–35:34). In general terms de Vaulx's observations are acceptable. The texts in Exod 21:13–14 make it clear that refuge was an ancient institution, and also that inadvertence was recognized as a legitimate defense. At the outset the sanctuary, not the city, was the focal point of asylum; laying hold of the horns of the altar was essential. It is probably true therefore that from the time of the united monarchy every city with a sanctuary was in a sense a city of refuge, though the technical term "city of refuge" may not as yet have been coined.

Josiah's program of centralization necessarily called for adjustments in asylum procedure, and certain cities are specified to which fugitives may go. Initial legislation (the second person singular prescriptions of Deut 19:1–13) cited only three cities, all situated to the west of the Jordan (v 2), but apparently left open the possibility of three others (vv 8–9). A role for the elders is envisaged—the handing over of a murderer (v 12). In the construction of the deuteronomic history this legislation is incorporated in the book of Joshua (Josh 20:4–5, 7–8). The selection of the cities is associated with Joshua himself, and all six are named—those to the west of the Jordan being Kedesh, Shechem, and Kiriath-arba, and those to the east being Bezer, Ramoth, and Golan. A further role for the elders is also suggested—the interrogation of the fugitive before he is granted admittance (Josh 20:4). It is possible that the deuteronomistic editing in Deut 4:41–43 is a little later, making it clear that the selection of cities in Transjordan was indeed the work of Moses.

The priestly author of Numbers recognizes that the six cities were an arrangement revealed to Moses, and may have coined the term "city of refuge." It may also be his adaptation of the deuteronomic history that we find in Josh 20:1–3, 6, 9. It is true enough that this entails a remarkably spacious view of the land for one familiar with the relatively narrow boundaries of the post-exilic community. The priestly presentation is shaped primarily by the spacious view of deuteronomic tradition, and a large land is found elsewhere in priestly writing (see e.g. the reconnaissance of the land undertaken in Num 13). The involvement of the high priest is natural enough in post-exilic regulations. It is possible that in this the author is here adapting pre-exilic custom in which the death of the king marks an amnesty for the fugitives.

The refusal of money payments (vv 31–34) could be priestly innovation, or at least an attempt to check what was considered an undesirable tendency. The basic principle that it must be life for life is reaffirmed, and linked with priestly concepts of uncleanness, defilement, and expiation. It is a little surprising that no account is taken here of blood shed accidentally, and of how that may properly be expiated. It is possible that the death of the high priest is understood as the means by which expiation is secured.

In v 30 the priestly author brings basic deuteronomic principles about witnesses into direct association with the law of blood vengeance and asylum (Deut 17:6; 19:15). Here is a further development, revealing the law of Num 35:9–34 as the most advanced available in the OT. The absence of a role for the elders is not intended to preclude the view of their importance in deuteronomic texts. The priestly author is simply concerned to stress that in reality it is the holy community which acts in judgment. This is essentially a theological comment rather than a prescription of procedure, no indication being given as to how the whole congregation could so act. The point is that individuals who officiate in such situations do so as representatives of the sacred congregation of God.

Comment

11. The principle of asylum is an ancient one found in many and varied cultures. N. H. Snaith (343) cites evidence to the effect that it is still operative among the Marsh Arabs of Mesopotamia. The custom of blood vengeance enshrined the duty of the next of kin of a murdered man to shed blood for blood. This was a deeply rooted principle, and a time of respite would obviously be required if distinctions between murder and manslaughter were to be made effective.

On unwitting or accidental sin see Num 15:24.

12. מגאל "from the avenger"; i.e. the next of kin (so rendered in NEB). The recovery of money owing was another duty of the next of kin (see *Comment* on Num 5:8). Other responsibilities were the contracting of a levirate marriage (Ruth 3:13), the redemption of a kinsman from slavery (Lev 25:47–49), and duties in relation to property (Lev 25:25; Ruth 4:1–6; Jer 32:8–12). The role of "avenger" is thought of as a duty in the interests of justice, not as a manifestation of anger or blood lust.

12. עמדו לפני . . . . למשפט "standing trial," literally "standing before . . . for judgment"; cf. Num 27:2; Deut 19:17; Josh 20:6; Zech 3:1 for "standing before" in a forensic sense.

13. The six cities are listed in Josh 20:7–8. Three were widely spaced in Transjordan—Bezer (possibly Umm el-ʿAmad—fifteen miles east of the mouth of the Jordan), Ramoth-Gilead (about twenty miles east of the Jordan and to the southeast of the Sea of Galilee), and Golan (the modern Saḥem el-Jōlân—eighteen miles east of the Sea of Galilee).

To the west of the Jordan were Kedesh (Tell Qades) in Galilee, Shechem (Tell Balâṭa) occupying a central position, and Hebron (el-Khalîl) in the south.

15. For the non-Israelites mentioned here see *Comment* on Num 9:14.

16. For a briefer account of possible eventualities see Exod 21:12–14. Iron instruments do not seem to have the qualification "liable to cause death" which applies to the implements of wood and stone cited in vv 17–18 (cf. also Exod 21:18–19) perhaps because iron would necessarily be so considered. Deut 19:5 makes it clear that the metal head of an axe might cause accidental death.

19. This verse stresses the traditional duty of the "avenger."

20. יהדפנו "he stabbed him" (RSV), or possibly "pushed him" (over a cliff or off a parapet). NEB translates "sets upon a man openly."

22–23. Cf. Deut 19:4–5.

24. על המשפטים האלה "in accordance with these ordinances"; i.e. those just cited.

25. This implies that the examination of the case takes place elsewhere. J. Sturdy (242) conjectures that it would be the man's own city or else Jerusalem. It could also be the place nearest the scene of the death; cf. the stipula-

tions in Deut 21:1–9 which indicate the responsibility of elders and judges in the nearest city in those cases of homicide where there is nobody to put on trial.

The reference to the death of the high priest probably implies an understanding of the death as expiating any blood guilt. The high priest is the representative sacred figure. The phrase "high priest" is a late usage (Lev 21:10; 2 Kgs 12:10; 22:4, 8; Hag 1:1; Zech 3:1; Neh 3:1).

27. אֵין לוֹ דָם "he shall not be guilty of blood" (cf. Lev 20:9; Ezek 18:13).

29. לְחֻקַּת מִשְׁפָּט "a statute and judgment," "legal precedents" (NEB) (cf. Num 27:11). These are common words for legal requirements, but the phrase occurs only in these two places.

30. This requirement regarding witnesses occurs in Deut 17:6 (a second person singular text) in relation to a charge of idolatry, and also in Deut 19:15 (a second person plural text) in relation to any charge.

31. וְלֹא תִקְחוּ כֹפֶר "and you shall not accept payment." Other cultures allowed the practice (see also 2 Sam 21:4). The Koran (2:173–74) permits it even for willful murder. The priestly author rejects it on the ancient principle of life for life.

32. This makes it clear that the principle of v 31 applies to accidental as well as willful murder. Only the death of the high priest is a satisfactory expiation. The shedding of human blood defiles the land (v 33), and can only be compensated for by human death (cf. Gen 4:10–11).

The reference to "the priest," not as the "high priest" may be an indication that the author of Numbers is using older Israelite tradition in these references to the sacred representative of the community.

34. The idea of God's presence at the center of the community's life is important to the priestly author of Numbers (cf. Num 5:3; 23:21, and the position of the Tent of Meeting in Num 1–4) (cf. also Exod 29:45–46; Zech 2:10). It is fitting that he should conclude his work on this note.

Explanation

This section gives more information about the six cities of refuge cited in Num 35:6. It makes clear that they are to be places of sanctuary for those who kill accidentally. The next of kin of the dead person may act on the principle "life for life" before the intention and motivation of the killer has been properly ascertained. Three of the six cities of refuge are to be situated in Transjordan. The law goes on to cite various examples of what would constitute deliberate murder, and what should be construed as accidental homicide. The role of the congregation is to resolve such questions, and in the case of the latter to protect the killer from blood vengeance. Any person granted sanctuary must remain in the city of refuge until the death of the high priest; if he fails to observe this rule his life may be forfeit at the hands of the next of kin. The high priest is representative of the community at large, and his death expiates the blood shed accidentally. The law also requires more than one witness to establish a case of deliberate murder, and the penalty for this is always death. The custom of money payment in restitution for killings is absolutely precluded, both for deliberate and accidental deaths.

The section is in all essentials the work of the priestly author of Numbers. As elsewhere his method is to build on and to develop received tradition. The principle of sanctuary, and the need to distinguish between deliberate and inadvertent killings had long been established in the Book of the Covenant (see *Form/Structure/Setting*).Originally refuge would have been sought at the local sanctuary. The deuteronomic reforms, with their abolition of the local sanctuaries and the centralization of worship, called for some adaptation of earlier custom. In earlier deuteronomic law three cities west of the Jordan are suggested as places of refuge for the accidental case of homicide (Deut 19:1–13). Later legislation takes up the earlier tentative view about the possibility of three other cities in Transjordan, and names them (Deut 4:41–43). All six are named in the deuteronomic history (Josh 20:7–8).

The priestly author of Numbers has contributed his editorial observations in Josh 20:1–3, 6, 9, making it absolutely clear that the arrangements made were a revelation by God to Moses before he died. Another of the priestly contributions is to work into the tradition an indirect role for the high priest. The death of the king may have functioned similarly in pre-exilic tradition, in which event the author is making a relatively minor adaptation. His concern is evidently to secure the priestly principle that there must be an appropriate death to expiate killing. Since human death can only be expiated by human death the high priest is able to meet this requirement. The author is also anxious to ensure that the principle of restitution by money payment, which he himself has done much to establish and secure in other connections, should not apply in relation to killing. His other main contribution is to bring the deuteronomic principle of more than one witness into direct association with laws concerning homicide.

The law thus bears witness to the development of important legal principles. The importance of motive and intention is clearly recognized, and steps are taken to ensure that justice be understood in those terms, and duly safeguarded. All of this was of course fundamental to deuteronomic law. What the priestly author achieves is a synthesis of these essentially ethical insights with traditional sacral principles about death and its effects on both the community and the land. A way is shown by which both the sacral and ethical principles can be safeguarded and made effective.

It is not surprising that the author should wish to discuss this question at this particular point. There is of course his desire to establish these legal principles as a fundamental revelation to Moses, and it is appropriate and necessary that this should be made clear prior to the giving of deuteronomic law. The concern which unites many of the elements in this third major part of the book of Numbers emerges again here. Furthermore, within these latter chapters, a discussion of the question is natural and coherent at this point. Provision for the division of the land (Num 34:16–29) led naturally to a discussion of the Levitical cities (Num 35:1–8), and since six of these were to be cities of refuge it was natural that discussion of their function should follow here in Num 35:9–34. Moreover, as vv 33–34 make clear, these laws about homicide and asylum have to do directly with the land and its protection. Here too a dominant theme in Num 26:1–35:34 emerges. For the priestly author the land must not only be secured and properly assigned, but it must also be properly protected from all possible defilements. The taking of human life constitutes the greatest risk of defilement, and deserves this particular attention and concern. Proper steps must therefore be taken to ensure that the holiness of the land is secured. This is after all entirely constant with the priestly author's overall theological view. The holy God lives at the center of the community in the middle of the land, and Israel's response must be an appropriate recognition of the fact.

The Case of the Daughters of Zelophehad Resumed   (36:1–13)

Bibliography

See Num 27:1–11 (*Bibliography*).

Translation

¹ *And the heads of the fathers' (houses) of the family of the sons of Gilead, the son of Machir, son of Manasseh, of the families* ᵃ *of the sons of Joseph, came near and spoke before Moses* ᵇ *and before the leaders, the heads of the fathers' houses of the people of Israel,* ² *and they said, "Yahweh commanded my lord to give the land for inheritance by lot to the people of Israel.* ᵃ *And my lord was commanded by Yahweh* ᵃ *to give the inheritance of Zelophehad our brother to his daughters.* ³ *But if they become married to any of the sons* ᵃ *of the other tribes of the people of Israel then their inheritance will be taken from the inheritance of our* ᵇ *fathers, and added to the inheritance of the tribe to which they belong. So it will be taken away from the lot of our inheritance.* ᶜ ⁴ *And when the jubilee of the people of Israel comes, then their inheritance will be added to the inheritance of the tribe to which they belong. And their inheritance will be taken from the inheritance of the tribe of our fathers."*

⁵ *And Moses commanded the people of Israel according to the word of Yahweh, saying, "The tribe of the sons of Joseph is right.* ⁶ *This is what Yahweh commands concerning the daughters of Zelophehad, 'Let them marry whom they think best, except that they shall marry with the family of the tribe of their father.* ᵃ ⁷ *The inheritance of the people of Israel shall not be transferred from one tribe to another. For every one of the people of Israel shall cleave to the inheritance of the tribe of his fathers.* ᵃ ⁸ *And every daughter who possesses an inheritance in any tribe of the people of Israel* ᵃ *shall be wife to one of the family of the tribe of her father, so that every one of the people of Israel may possess the inheritance of his fathers.* ⁹ *So no inheritance shall be transferred from one tribe to another, for each of the tribes of the people of Israel shall retain its own inheritance.' "*

¹⁰ *Just as Yahweh commanded Moses so the daughters of Zelophehad did.* ¹¹ *For Mahlah, Tirzah, Hoglah, Milcah, and Noah,* ᵃ *the daughters of Zelophehad were married to sons of their father's brothers.* ¹² *They were married into the families* ᵃ *of the sons of Manasseh, the son of Joseph, and their inheritance remained in the tribe of the family of their father.*

¹³ *These are the commandments and the ordinances which Yahweh commanded by Moses to the people of Israel in the plains of Moab by the Jordan at Jericho.*

Notes

1.a. G, Vg, and Syr have the singular "family."
1.b. G has here "and before Eleazar the priest." J. A. Paterson (66) thinks it an accidental omission from MT, but it may more probably be an addition in G.

2.a.-a. The clause is awkward. The Pual is strange, especially with the Piel in the preceding clause. J. A. Paterson (66) suggests an accidental omission of את before אדני, and the removal of ב from יהוה—thus "and Yahweh commanded my lord. . . ." He also suggests that "Yahweh" may be an intrusion. *BHS* suggests either "and Yahweh commanded us . . ." (reading ואתנו for אדני, and the Piel צוה) or "and my lord commanded in the name of Yahweh. . . ." (inserting בשם and also reading the Piel). G. B. Gray (477–78) offers reasons for accepting the passive.

3.a. Lacking in G and Syr.

3.b. Syr reads "of their father" here, and in v 4.

3.c. Many mss read a plural.

6.a. A feminine ending is correct, as in many mss and Sam.

7.a. 1Q3:9 adds that all the men must also marry within their tribe, which is not necessarily implied in MT (cf. also Vg).

8.a. Vg is more strict, insisting that every daughter must be married within her tribe.

11.a. The order is not the usual one. Sam, and G (some mss) have the order of Num 26:33; 27:1; Josh 17:3.

12.a. The singular occurs in one MT ms, G, Syr, and Vg.

Form/Structure/Setting

The connection between this passage and Num 27:1–11 is obvious, and analysts have had no difficulty in assigning it to P (see e.g. A. Dillmann, 221–23; J. Wellhausen, 114–15; A. Kuenen, 97–98; H. Holzinger, 172–73; B. Baentsch, 696–99; G. B. Gray, 476–78). Holzinger, Baentsch, and Gray assign it to PS, with only v 13 as a concluding formulation from PG. The section appears to be a supplement to Num 27:1–11. The aim of the earlier section was to prevent property from passing away from a man's descendants; the aim of this section is to enforce and sustain the basic motivation by forbidding women who inherit from marrying into another tribe. Gray also pointed to minor variations in style and expression which he judged to be indications of another hand—e.g. the expression "families of the sons of Joseph" (v 1) (contrast "families of Manasseh son of Joseph" in Num 27:1). These stylistic observations seem to amount to very little. Gray also noted a difference of approach. Here it is made to Moses and the leaders, the heads of the fathers' houses, but there to Moses, Eleazar, the leaders, and all the congregation. The textual variants (see *Notes*) do not remove these contrasts. Other differences were shown in the introduction of the law in v 5 (contrast Num 27:6–8). The supplementer was evidently influenced by PG, but not exclusively so, with the use of אדני—"my lord" (v 2) and מטה for "tribe" (v 8) being more characteristic of the early narrative tradition.

M. Noth (257–58) describes the section as an appendix to Num 27:1–11. He also suggests that the reference to the jubilee in v 4 is out of place, from both a literary and factual point of view. It seems to suggest that in the year of jubilee everything remained as it was, whereas we would expect, in the light of Lev 25, that the original conditions of possession would be reinstated. Noth is inclined to take v 4 as an irrelevant addition. He also sees the concluding formula (v 13) as not belonging specifically to the present chapter, but generally to the final sections of the book.

N. H. Snaith (345–46; also *VT* 16 [1966] 124–27) is perplexed by the chapter. He points out that ancient Israelite custom fixes inheritance through the male line, and hence the custom of levirate marriage (Deut 25:8–10). Even if this section is an attempt to put right the situation created by the abandonment of that ancient principle in Num 27:1–11 there is still a difficulty, since in Snaith's view v 4 assumes that the reversion of property at the jubilee is concerned with inherited land. He argues that this is wrong, and that the reversion applies only to property that had been sold. J. Sturdy (244) sees the section as a coda to the whole book, and is apparently less worried by the problems perceived by Noth and Snaith. His explanation of v 4 is simple— that there was a jubilee custom, not cited in Lev 25:8–34, whereby a transfer of ownership through marriage is confirmed in the jubilee year. It is this rule which is here rescinded in this section (cf. also J. de Vaulx, 405). N. Gottwald (*The Tribes of Yahweh*, 265–67) has addressed himself to the difficulties, and concludes that there are some signs of earlier tradition in vv 5, 8. In this the inheriting daughters must marry into the same *family* (משפחה) as that to which their father belonged. The expansion of the ruling into an intertribal affair, he suggests, is the work of the P traditionist as he envisages the disruption in the year of jubilee when the inherited land of the daughters would pass into the control of their husband's tribes.

It seems best to assume that the section is indeed a supplement or appendix to the completed book of Numbers (with the exception of v 13 which may have been the priestly author's own conclusion). Had the priestly author himself been responsible for vv 1–12 it is hard to see why he should have added it at the end of his book. Had the problem raised by the section been in his mind he would simply have worked the content of vv 1–12 into Num 27:1–11. Some of the more significant stylistic features noted by Gray—those more typical of the Yahwist—bear out this conclusion. It is true that v 4 raises problems, but they are not insuperable. It seems very likely that jubilee thinking did not cover property gained through marriage, and that the regulations in Lev 25:8–34 cover only purchased land. The compiler of the appendix was anxious that the principle established in Num 27:1–11 should be sustained. Daughters without brothers do have the right to inherit. He was anxious nevertheless that this should not lead, in the event of their marriage, to the gradual redrawing of tribal boundaries. These were sacrosanct. For further discussion of Snaith's difficulties with these laws see *Comment* on Num 27:1–11. It is far from obvious that there is any earlier tradition within the section; it is explicable in all respects as an extended gloss on Num 27:1–11.

Comment

1. For the tribal divisions mentioned here see *Comment* on Num 1:9; (cf. also Num 17:18; 31:26).

4. היבל "the jubilee" (see Lev 25:8–34). The word means "a ram's horn." The fiftieth year was ushered in with the blowing of ram's horns. The extent, if any, to which jubilee principles were applied is unknown; many believe them to be purely idealistic.

11. In 1 Chr 23:22 the sons of Kish marry the daughters of their uncle Eleazar, who died without male offspring.

13. This summary covers the material from Num 1:1–35:34; cf. Lev 27:34 where the author of Leviticus concludes his book with a similar statement.

Explanation

This section is a supplement or appendix to the property regulations given in Num 27:1–11, and it functions as an appendix to the book as a whole. The earlier laws in Num 27:1–11 allowed for daughters to inherit where there were no sons, but did not consider the question of what would happen were those daughters to marry. Was there not a risk that if they married outside their ancestral tribe the tribal boundary lines would have to be redrawn, and that some tribes would suffer serious loss of land? This section remedies the deficiency, and requires that daughters who do inherit property under the terms of Num 27:1–11 (and many would not) must marry within their own tribe. As in Num 27:1–11 the question is raised in relation to the five daughters of Zelophehad, a member of the tribe of Manasseh. The section concludes with the report that they did as Moses had directed.

The position of this material within the book of Numbers, and certain formal and stylistic features (see *Form/Structure/Setting*) suggest strongly that this is compiled by an author willing to use both the priestly and Yahwistic elements in tradition. The new provisions in Num 27:1–11 seemed to be deficient, and the loophole is duly closed. The integrity of the tribes as distinct entities within the people of God must be preserved. This concern arises naturally from the principle enunciated in Num 26:52–56 that the land is to be divided among the tribes and an inheritance for each to be received. The section is a witness to the need for a continuing interpretative attention to the tradition received, and for a concern that the basic motives and intentions of that tradition be perceived and rendered effective.

Index of Authors Cited
Ancient

Index of Principal Subjects

Index of Biblical Texts
Old Testament

Apocrypha

New Testament

Extra-Biblical Literature